The Fourth Lad

The Post-War memoirs of a Geordie Lad's

Growing pains

Sydney Carr

To Beth, the love of my life.

CONTENTS

Author's Note

This is a personal narrative of my memories of my first twenty years. Memories of my earliest days are obviously not as strong as those in the later part of the book; I have therefore embellished my scantest memories to ensure the story is complete. 90% of the events happened as I have described them

The dialogue of many of the characters is written, where appropriate, in Geordie dialect with the words spelt phonetically. These are not spelling mistakes or typing errors. For those readers not familiar with the Geordie dialect, I have listed the Geordie words I have used along with their meanings at the end of the book. I have not included words that should be easily understood. The pronunciation of these Geordie words I leave entirely to the reader.

Part 1

Pont Street

1

A Painful Beginning

Completely unaware that I was doing my utmost to drown out his voice, Winston Churchill growled triumphantly from within the wooden boxed radio standing on the sideboard in the kitchen of our gloomy miners' terraced house. 'Yesterday morning at 2.41 am, at General Eisenhower's Headquarters, General Jodl, the representative of the German High Command, and Grand Admiral Doentiz, the designated head of the German State, signed the act of unconditional surrender.'

'JESUS CHRIST BETTY!' squawked Mam at my diminutive twelve-year-old sister who was nursing me on her knee, 'Can ye not stop that blidy, bubbly-bugger crying for a minute while we listen to Chorchill? His blidy crying is enough to drive any bugger to suicide man.'

'He's hungry man Mam!' Betty spat back, joggling me in her arms as she tried in vain to comfort me.

'He'll have te blidy well wait ontil Chorchill's finished,' said Mam angrily before taking a long drag from her Woodbine and blowing a cloud of foul smelling smoke contemptuously toward Betty.

It was May the 8th 1945; I was seven weeks old when Mam and five of her brood listened to the Prime Minister's VE Day speech. Hitler had committed suicide and Germany's armed forces had surrendered; something I couldn't be blamed for but I am sure that given enough time, Mam would find a reason to blame it on me as she seemed to do for everything else that went wrong in her life.

Not that I have any memories of my first two years; my earliest recollection is when I had just turned two; the ferocious, never-ending winter of 1947 had blanketed the drab streets of Ashington with cleansing white snow. Fed up with my constant wailing, heavily pregnant with twins and with my one-year-old sister in her arms, Mam led me from the warmth of the kitchen to the back door of our miners' cottage. Holding my tiny hand, she opened the door wide, allowing in a freezing blast of ice-cold air and a light that was so white and bright that after the gloom of the kitchen, it forced me to squint and turn my head away.

Turning my head back slowly, I squinted through half-closed eyelids at the snow piled high above my head. It was smooth and flat where the door had been, its height intimidating and bewildering. Torn between reaching out to touch the strange, icy white bank and hiding behind Mam's pinny, I chose the latter.

1

Looking down at me already shivering from the freezing wind, Mam muttered, 'By yor a Soft Shite,' and closed the door - instantly shutting out the bitter cold and blinding light.

Mam called me a 'Soft Shite,' so often that I responded to that just as much as I did to 'Syd.'

She led me back into the security of the kitchen warmed from the heat and the glow of the coal fire burning fiercely in the black-leaded, cast iron, cottage range. This room was the heart of our three up and two down house, the room where my family spent most of its time when at home.

Pont Street, one of the toughest but friendliest streets in one of the toughest mining towns of the North East, consisted of a long dreary row of yellow-bricked, grey-slated, colliery houses, one of many such rows formed up in long serried ranks like a vast Napoleonic army. The rows were interspersed with schools, churches, parks and a few shops that together, made up the area called 'The Hirst' or, as the local folk pronounce it, 'The Horst.' In the 1940s, this and a similar area of terraced cottages on the other side of town formed the bulk of the residential areas of Ashington in Northumberland; the largest mining 'village' in the world, a town with no real history, being the product of the booming coal industry of the late 19th century. A tough, drab and at times, a bleak place to grow up, post-war rationing made it even more austere. As with other mining towns and villages, the miners and their families provided warmth, humour and a strong community spirit that was borne out of shared adversity.

At two-years-old, I was the sixth born, the fourth lad of seven kids with the distinct possibility of more to follow! Betty, my diminutive 14-year-old sister and the oldest of the bunch, had assumed responsibility for looking after me during those early years. Mam, like so many other wives of her generation, was almost perpetually pregnant and with a large brood to look after and a house to run, she had little time to devote to an individual child, let alone her constantly whingeing, snotty-nosed two-year-old.

Consequently, I had more affection for Betty than my mother who was far too busy and hard-hearted to provide the love and indulgences lavished on children today. Being one of many in a home of meagre comforts and sibling rivalries, I sought comfort and solace from whoever could best provide it; for me, my oldest sister did just that.

It was shortly after the visit to the back door, that I found myself, along with four of my brothers and sisters confined to bed with measles. Poorly nourished, we were pray to all childhood ailments and successfully succumbed to them all at one time or another.

Mam had bedded all five of us in two double beds in the large sparsely furnished bedroom that overlooked the back lane. Ron, a ten-year-old lad with learning difficulties who lived next door had called in to see how we were and sat on the end of one of the beds annoying Eric.

At two years old, I was the second youngest and had not yet taken on the emaciated appearance of my older brothers as I still carried a fair amount of puppy fat; padding that would disappear as soon as Mam stopped feeding me National Health baby food.

Grim-faced and annoyed at having to cope with sick kids and a demanding husband, Mam swept into the bedroom, stirred the embers of the fire, checked that we were all in bed and then hurried downstairs and out across the back lane to the coalhouse where she loaded a shovel of coal to get the fire going again. The coal-house on the other side of the lane lined up with other coalhouses, outside toilets, and air-raid shelters to form a row of outhouses that ran in parallel with the houses, making the lane appear narrower than it actually was.

Bored with our confinement and inactivity, I slid off the end of the bed and after regaining my balance on unsteady feet, I found myself drawn toward the glow from the embers of the freshly stirred fire and tottered toward the small fire-place. A warning yell from my sister Pat went unheeded as I stepped onto the hearth where my overlong, hand-me-down nightgown, wrapped itself around my chubby feet and propelled me face first into the fireplace and onto the glowing embers, searing and scorching my unprotected left cheek and chin. I let out a heart-wrenching, piercing scream of pain and shock that filled the bedroom and echoed down the stairs to where Mam was returning with a shovel of coal.

Eric, my scrawny seven-year-old brother ran over and grabbing me with his right hand, tried to pull me out of the fire but let go when he burnt his left hand, which he had foolishly placed on the grate to steady himself.

Screaming, 'Bugger, bugger,' he began hoping around the room as though he had burnt his foot and not his hand.

Fortunately, for me, Ron also reacted and dashing across he grabbed my nightgown and pulled me out, throwing me onto the carpet where I rolled around screaming in agony. Ron had also burnt his hand in the process and retreated to the corner of the room where he crouched down and blew pathetically on his singed skin. His national health glasses slipped to the end of his nose, forcing him to hold his head back in order to see the damage that to him was obviously far worse than my burns, certainly more than enough for him to jump up and run cry-ing for the door in his lopsided, lame way.

My screams had stopped Mam at the foot of the stairs, the shrillness of it causing her to drop the shovel scattering coal across the passageway. The continu-ing sounds of screaming and shouting propelled her upwards, where she collided with Ron who was frantically trying to escape the pandemonium in the room be-hind him and reach the safety of his home next door and the solace of his Nana. Unfortunately, for him he was in Mam's way; she threw him aside as if he were a rag doll to bump and roll to the foot of the stairs before she burst into the bedroom, where she quickly took stock of the scene in front of her.

3

Eric was still hopping around, waving his right hand in the air and cursing loudly. Nine-year-old Pat was kneeling over me with her hands in the air, screaming as loud as I was; four-year-old George was sitting up in bed with a look of detached bewilderment and Baby Vivian had started to scream in sympathy.

Mam went to the source of the loudest screaming, where she thought Pat was trying to kill me, and yelled, 'Eee my God what the bloody hell's happened?'

Traumatised by what she had seen, Pat was unable to answer coherently and between sobs only managed to gasp, 'He's….fire ….burnt….fell in.'

Grasping the situation immediately, Mam scooped me up and grabbing a blanket from one of the beds, she wrapped me up in it and barked orders, 'Pat look after this lot till Aa get back, the rest of ye stay in yor bloody beds.'

As I screamed and struggled in the blanket in her arms, Mam grabbed Eric as he hopped around the room and demanded, 'What's up with ye?'

Looking for sympathy, Eric answered pathetically, 'Aa've burnt me hand trying to pull him oot the fire Mam.'

Quickly examining his hand, she then brushed him aside muttered, 'Soft Shite,' and raced for the door with me in her arms.

Ron's gargantuan Nana was waiting at the foot of the stairs, 'What the bloody hell hev ye done to wor Ron?' she demanded as Mam, raced down the stairs, barging into her.

'Bugger off back te yor sackless bairn before Aa put a cut in yor heed, this bloody Soft Shite has fallen in the frigging fire,' Mam spat as, despite the size difference, she swept Nana Brown aside.

Despite the deep, wet snow that covered the pavements and ankle-deep slush on the roads, she ran the half a mile to Ashington Hospital where, almost collapsing from exhaustion, she staggered into casualty demanding help. Doctors and nurses were quickly on the scene and whisked me away for treatment as Mam looked on - annoyed at having her routine disrupted. 'As though I don't have enough to contend with withoot this bloody happening!' she cursed aloud.

Over the next few days, I underwent a series of operations in an attempt to mend the damage to my face. A surgeon grafted skin from my thighs and backside onto the worst of the burns so you could say that they made an arse of it! I was lucky that the embers had been so low and managed to get away with just two of the burns being severe enough to require consideration for plastic surgery.

Before my discharge from hospital a week later, a doctor discussed my injuries with Mam and advised her to take me back to the hospital when I reached eleven in order to have the scars assessed by a specialist, for consideration for remedial plastic surgery. However, when the time came, she did not, her motherly skills at that time were somewhat eroded and she probably could not be bothered. Besides, when I was eleven, I managed to cut the tip off my left index finger and she had to contend with that, as well as ensuring I did not pass my eleven plus examination!

4

Ashington hospital was used to dealing with minor emergencies to children and at one stage had a separate page for recording accidents and emergencies to kids from Pont Street. You did not live in Pont Street you survived it! There was also something of a stigma attached to living there; it was one of the toughest and poorest streets in Ashington where some of the largest of the hard-working families lived. Large families with great Border names, Turnbull, Armstrong, Johnstone and us, the Carrs, survived the hardships of the street, arguing, fighting, and playing our rough and ready games together.

It was during one of these games that my next visit to Ashington Hospital became necessary.

At age five I had a younger sister Viv, who was to cause so much mischief for me later, and I had watched my twin sisters June and Julia arrive and remember being held up to look into their cot to see them. I then remember that there was only Julia and shortly after, she too was gone. As a five-year-old, my priorities did not include mourning and I do not recall any family grief at the time but I am sure there must have been ample. Dennis had been born after the twins, and finally, there was Mary but unfortunately, she did not survive childbirth.

It was with two-year-old Dennis toddling behind that I ventured out to play with the older lads. Cowboys and Indians were the then current favourite game thanks to the Western showing at the 'Piv' – 'The Pavilion,' one of 5 picture houses in Ashington and a place of magic for two pennies on a Saturday morning.

Being the youngest and smallest, Dennis and I had no say in deciding who were to be Cowboys and who were to be Indians; as the older lads had made bows and arrows from bamboo rods and Indian headdress from strips of cloths and feathers torn from a tatty feather boa, we were to be the Cowboys. In addition, we were the only two small enough to fit inside the fort disguised as a battered, empty metal dustbin the lads had placed in the middle of the street!

Dennis was safe, he was so small the Indians could not see him to fire their arrows at as he squatted in the bottom of the bin where he quickly became smothered in grey coal ash as he shouted, 'Bang, bang' while waving his little metal pistol about, causing a fair amount of damage to my painfully skinny shins. It was left to me to put my head over the parapet, point and fire my not so trusty, cork firing, third generation hand me down rifle at the Indians who were in no great danger as the spring in the rifle was long past its best and could not even manage a proper 'pop.' When fired the cork 'plopped,' pathetically toward the circling savages, travelling only a few inches before the string attaching it to the rifle jerked it back.

The Indians on the other hand; magnificent in their various feathered headdresses and warpaint of black soot, were capable of inflicting terror, which they did, and actual bodily harm with their bamboo arrows, which they also did. Cowering back below the top of the bin, I reloaded while listening to the whoops and yells of the circling savages. Not wanting to brave the storm of arrows I knew would greet me if I lifted my head too high; I hunkered down as low as I could as arrows pinged of the metal bin.

Eric, the Chief of the Redskins, shouted, 'Haway you bloody sissy, put yor heed up, and shoot back man.'

Not wishing to be a 'bloody sissy,' I swallowed hard and pushed my pop gun over the top, and timidly followed it with my head in order to take aim. As expected, I met a hail of bamboo arrows, a particularly well-aimed one fired by my brother George or his pal Matty Storey hit my left ear with such sublime accuracy that it actually lodged in my ear hole. I'm sure it must have looked bizarre - a be-wildered, wide-eyed five-year-old's face poking out of a dustbin with an arrow sticking out of his ear! I was lucky that the arrow was not one of the ones the lads used to fire at targets as they had large nails tied to their end! Nonetheless, there I was in a bin with an arrow sticking out my ear.

The realisation of what had happened sank home and on touching the shaft of the slender piece of bamboo protruding from my right ear, I began a long and accurate impersonation of an American police car siren I had heard at one of the matinees at the Piv. My Wailing allied with the sight of the arrow in my ear and the fear of Mam's retribution was too much for the Indians, they cleared off quick-er than if John Wayne and the whole of the US 7th Cavalry had just galloped round the corner to come to my rescue.

My screams brought my Mam out the house and running over to the bin where she lifted me out and yelled, 'Stop screaming ye soft shite, yor scaring the poor bairn.'

Dennis was also screaming at this stage, not because of the arrow in my ear but because I had stepped on him several times, as I had leapt about inside the bin trying desperately in my terror and pain to climb out.

Mam tried to move the arrow from my ear with a surprising gentleness but it was firmly wedged, filling me with even more fear. I wanted to cry in terror but being more afraid of Mam than the arrow, I swallowed my sobs and struggled to keep quiet.

'Aa cannit get the bugger oot,' she muttered.

That prompted me to ask between sobs, 'Will me brains fall oot, if ye pull the arrow oot Mam?'

'Nur ye soft shite they winnit, anyway ye hevn't got any bloody brains or ye wouldn't have a frigging arrow sticking oot ye lug hole would ye?'

'No brains!' I was mortified; mind you, it probably explained why I could not do sums like my older brothers and sisters but how was I going to cope without any brains? I would be unable to learn anything when I went to school, not that that was my chief concern at that precise moment.

Mam had another gentle tug at the arrow but it only made me cry in fright as I moved my head with the arrow - I did not want any brains I might have to spill out through my damaged ear-hole.

6

Nana Brown had waddled out to her front gate to see what the commotion was and seeing Mam tugging at the arrow and not knowing how deeply embedded it was, she said, 'Ye best be careful Etty, it might be holding back blood!'

'Holding back blood,' I thought, 'what blood?' and shouted, 'Leave it in man Mam, or Aa'll lose all me brains and blood and die.'

'Shut up ye simple bugger, the bloody things jammed in tight,' she spat, 'Aa suppose Am gannin te hev te tek ye to the bloody hospital te hev it taken oot.'

Lifting Dennis from the dustbin with one hand, she deposited him at the back door, yelling, 'Betty look efter the bairn while I tek this sackless sod te the bloody hospital.'

Taking me by the arm, she marched me to the hospital being careful to ensure that I did not bump the arrow that protruded two foot from my ear into any curious passers-by. I limped along beside her, my left leg that was not hurt, had developed a sympathy limp as I worried about having to go through life with an arrow in my ear, or worse, with no brains!

Ashington Hospital had a new entry for Pont Street that probably read something like, 'Child with arrow in ear!' We were really living up to our reputation as the Wild West of Ashington!

Incredibly, the arrow had only wedged in my ear without damaging the eardrum and only required a firm and steady pull by the Doctor to extract it before he applied TCP to the scratches'. The TCP started my impersonation of an American police car siren again!

It was not until the arrival of my uncle Alex a year later that I would dare to play cowboys and Indians again.

On a cool grey afternoon in late autumn, a large black taxi drove slowly into Pont Street and up to our house where it stopped! A taxi in Pont Street was a rare event and more than enough to start curtains twitching. Certainly enough for a fair smattering of the nosier housewives who, wearing turbaned headscarves, floral pinnies and with arms crossed defensively over bulging bosoms, to come out of their houses and stand at their low back gates to stare brazenly at the taxi and its occupant.

Cars of any type in the back lanes were a rarity but a taxi; well who on Earth would waste good money on a taxi? The figure that appeared from the vehicle could not be more out of place; he slowly straightened himself up to a thin and gaunt six foot and stood silently taking in his surroundings. He looked ancient but was probably only in his early sixties. Immaculately dressed, he was wearing highly polished, black Oxford shoes, pinstriped trousers, a smart black jacket with below, a grey waistcoat complete with watch and gold fob. A spotlessly white, perfectly starched shirt collar with a beautifully knotted tie complementing it and on his head, a pristine bowler but the most impressive item of his ensemble was the huge handlebar moustache that spread across his face like the wings of a soaring seagull. He reminded me of a tall and elegant version of 'Pa Broon' who appeared in the Scottish Post.

This was my Uncle Alex; he walked to the door and waited whilst the taxi driver took a large metal trunk from the boot of the taxi and placed it on the ground next to him. After paying the driver, he knocked solemnly on the door and waited as we snotty nosed kids gathered around him, curious in an impertinent way as to who this strange man was.

When Mam opened the door, he said in a quiet voice, 'Hello Etty, I've come to stay,' and so he did until he passed away many years later. A bachelor all of his life, he had lived with his sister who had recently died and as Dad was his nearest relative, he had decided Mam should look after him. A six-foot bairn in his sixties joined our family of Mam, Dad and eight other bairns.

He made his arrival more acceptable to us kids by placing half a crown in each of our grubby hands, a small fortune to us that required careful and hasty consideration on how and when to spend it. Hasty, because if we hung onto it, Mam would take it from us for safekeeping and that would be the last we would see of it.

I knew exactly what I wanted to spend my money on; I had spent many long minutes with my nose pressed against the glass window of the local corner toy shop staring at a beautiful, camouflage painted, clockwork model Spitfire that was on display and dreamed of owning it. I had often imaged what it would be like to be the pilot of that beauty and now I could be, except, confined to barracks as I was with cold, flu or measles or some such other ailment, I was unable to go to the shop.

I worried that some other fortunate kid might have money to spend and would snap up the Spitfire but I surely worried needlessly; after all what other kid in Pont Street would have half a crown to spend.

The next morning my friend Billy, wandered into the sitting room and hitched up his over large shorts that had obviously upset his stockings as they had slid away from them forming untidy circles around his chubby ankles as he stood looking down at me.

Mam had bedded me down on the sofa and as I looked pathetically up at him from below an old blanket he asked, 'Aa divvint suppose you can come oot, can ye?'

'Nah,' I replied holding up my shiny money, 'but can ye gan to the Toy Shop and get me the Spitfire in the window?'

'Aalreet, nee bother,' he said.

'Mind ye bring it straight back here and Aa'll let ye have a play wiv it,' I said, desperate to get my hands on the toy aeroplane.

I reluctantly handed over the large and beautiful shiny half-crown and off he went, leaving me to wait with my heart racing in anticipation of the thrills and delights to come. I imagined myself as a diminutive Battle of Britain Fighter Pilot blasting Nazis out of the sky as I soared high above Pont Street in my beautiful Spitfire.

I should have mentioned that my pal - my so-called pal, was a bit on the chubby side and had a love of sweeties.

He returned and stood before me with a sheepish smile on his face, his hands behind his back holding what I took to be 'My' Spitfire.

'Gis it, Gis it,' I yelled, trying to get up off the sofa in order to rest the prize from him.

'It's been sold, so I got you some sweeties and toy soldiers instead,' he said while picking at a large piece of half-chewed fruit gum from the gap where one of his front teeth had been.

I was devastated, the soldiers were grand, and we would fight some fine battles together, and the sweeties that Billy had not already devoured were okay, but I would never be able to take to the air to shoot down Nazis. Brother George, on the other hand, was racing up and down the street with a beautiful, camouflaged Spitfire held high above his head, doing just that!

It was the following week when I was back on my feet that I decided it was time to play Cowboys again. Not wanting another arrow shot into an unprotected orifice, I had decided against including Indians in my game! Mam had declared I was not fit enough to go to school but wanted me to play outside as Dennis had replaced me on the sofa, bedded down with whatever ailment I had endured.

Dennis being out of action left his toys ripe for plunder! Being the youngest meant he had the best toys, the rest of us making do with hand me downs and the odd item skilfully made by Dad, my favourite at that time was a fort with an entrance ramp so steep that my little band of toy soldiers had to become paratroopers just to gain entry.

Uncle Alex watched from his now semi-permanent position in the chair by the kitchen fire as I strapped on Dennis's six-guns and then struggled in vain to pull on his tiny, imitation leather waistcoat. From his vantage point, Uncle Alex could warm his bony frame and keep an eye on the availability of whatever food Mam was preparing. It was also handy for spitting into the back of the fire whilst he was puffing on his pipe, producing clouds of evil-smelling smoke that fought to overpower the equally foul smoke from Mam's Woodbines.

After chuckling at my antics for a couple of minutes, he rose stiffly from his chair and disappeared into the front room that had become his bedroom at night. He reappeared a few minutes later carrying an immaculate fedora and grey waistcoat.

Handing them to me, he said, 'Here Bonny Lad put these on and ye'll look like a proper cowboy,' a real compliment coming from someone who was alive when cowboys still rode the range.

In an effort to prevent it from swallowing me completely, he balanced the Fedora at an angle on the back of my head and then helped me on with the waistcoat. This was quite difficult as it kept sliding off my almost non-existent shoulders and when he eventually balanced it in position, it hung over my six-guns pre-

9

venting a quick draw. He solved the problem by pulling the waistcoat tight around me and fastened it with a large safety pin before buckling my six-gun's holster around the waistcoat that now hung over my knees.

Convinced I made Roy Rogers look drab, I hitched up my stockings, which being made of wool and more than a little well worn, retained no shape and immediately slid down my skinny legs again. Finally, I adjusted my silver six-guns and swaggered toward the great outdoors, ready to take on any gunslinger that might be loitering in the Bad Lands of Pont Street.

'Be careful Bonny Lad,' Uncle Alex shouted after me as I tottered outside, not that he was in the least bit interested in my welfare, he was worried that I might damage his precious Fedora and waistcoat that he had only allowed me to wear in order to ingratiate himself with Mam. She had watched the proceedings whilst nonchalantly skinning a rabbit on the kitchen table ready for that night's potpie. Having been brought up on a farm, a bit of blood and animal viscera were nothing to Etty as with a flourish she flung the guts onto the kitchen fire, creating an instant sizzling and spitting and an awful smell that helped propel me through the back door.

Strolling menacingly up and down the Street, I tried to look steely hard and mean, not easy with an angelic face and a hat that kept swallowing my head whole. Mimicking John Wayne, I narrowed my eyes and squinting as though I had sties, I searched in vain for baddies.

My reputation as the fastest gun in Pont Street must have been widespread as not one of the baddies was brave enough to show his face; I had not considered the fact that they were all at school! Mind you, it was just as well there were none, I couldn't afford any caps for my pistols, the only ammunition I had were my shouts of 'Bang Bang,' and those would probably not have scared anyone.

Bored with a desolate Pont Street, I decided I might have better luck if I rode out onto the range and headed for my imaginary horse tied up outside our house. When I reached the backyard, I looked around the small wooden fence that came to the top of my head and saw Dennis's piebald horse standing quietly below the long galvanised metal bathtub that hung on outside of the pantry wall. This was a real horse – albeit made of tin with little wheels attached to each hoof. Built for two to four-year-old kids to sit upon and ride, I reckoned, as I was just a skinny five-year-old, it should be able to carry me off at a gallop.

I dragged the hobbyhorse out into the Street, placed my left foot in the stirrup, and hauled myself onto its back, clutching the reins tightly to prevent it galloping off.

Firmly in the saddle, I yelled 'Yahoo,' and began to jump madly up and down on the stirrups; this was how the horse galloped - in theory anyway. Pressing up and down on the stirrups caused rods concealed inside the body of the metal horse to move back and forth. Connected to the top of the pivoted legs, the rods moved the legs back and forth on their wheels.

10

This was supposed to propel you forward, only it did not, not very much anyway. The result was that after two minutes of frantic jumping, I was knackered and I had barely left the back gate. The ripples in the concrete surface of the back lane did not help, preventing as they did the wheels moving very far in any direction. However, determined to gallop off, I renewed my efforts with frantic speed causing the Fedora to fall from my head and under the metal wheels of the erratically jerking hobbyhorse. Oblivious to the damage I was doing to the precious Fedora, I continued my manic pounding until, with a frightening screech of metal, the horse collapsed to the ground, legs stretched out front and back in total surrender.

Standing straddled over the lifeless wreck that had been Dennis's galloper, its reins still in my hands, I uttered my first profanity, 'BUGGER!' Terror replaced the initial shock I felt at the collapse of the dapper painted hobbyhorse as I realised the enormity of what I had done.

I thought, 'If Mam sees this she'll have to spend the rest of her life in jail for killing the 'Fastest Gun' in Pont Street.' I knew I would have to try to hide the evidence and I took my first step in developing the art of subterfuge, a skill I needed to master if I was to survive Pont Street and Mam.

Lifting the lifeless metal hobbyhorse, I steadied it prior to dragging it back into the yard, hoping to lean it in an upright position against the wall of the pantry. That was my plan but it was then that I saw the Fedora! Having had the metal wheels of the hobbyhorse gallop back and forth over it, it was in a truly sorry state.

I uttered my second and third profanities; standing holding the dead hobbyhorse with the squashed and battered Fedora at my feet, I looked up to the heavens and shouted, 'BUGGER BUGGER,' with the desperation only someone caught red-handed committing the worst crime known to man could feel. The hat was a shapeless mess with black streaks across the brim where the wheels had had churned over it. It looked completely ruined.

My mind in turmoil, I thought of the awful retribution that would be served upon me if I were caught as I dragged the hobbyhorse back into the yard. I then spent some time positioning it against the wall, desperately trying to make it look as normal as a metal horse could. After some anguished minutes of trying to stop the legs from shooting forward or backwards from under its metal body, which they did several times, I eventually managed to stop them from moving by placing small stones in front of the wheels and felt as satisfied as I could be that it looked undamaged.

With my little heart beating madly, I left the yard to retrieve the Fedora to see if I could carry out any repairs to lessen the damage, not to the hat, but to me should I return it in its current sorry state.

As I left the yard, the black cross-Labrador that lived further down the street confronted me. It was a large dog, especially to a five-year-old; however, it was very friendly and loved to play with the kids in the Street. It stood in front of me, tail wagging madly, its face almost level with mine, its eyes bright with antici-pation and excitement at the thought of the coming chase.

In its mouth was the battered mess that was Uncle Alex's Fedora!

The next five minutes felt as though they added fifty years to my fragile five.

My cry of 'Howay Blackie, gis the hat,' only acted as a signal for him to plant his feet firmly, readying to spring away should I make a move to grab his new found toy, which he did when I reached forlornly forward to try and grasp the hat. At first, he let me chase him around in circles as he bounded gleefully round and round, allowing me to get close but not close enough. After a few minutes, he realised that he had exhausted that part of the game as I sat down in the middle of the street with tears of fear and frustration running down my cheeks. Walking up behind me, he playfully nudged the back of my head with the hat, then trotted in front of me with it still firmly grasped in his teeth.

Cruelly, he allowed me to grab the hat so that he could start the second part of his game – tug of war! I desperately held onto the hat with both hands as he began to back up, growling with delight, giving the occasional shake of his head, which threw me from side to side.

He eventually had me stretched flat out and was slowly dragging me down the street to certain doom. Strength borne out of fear had enabled me to hang on for that long but that strength was leaving me. Just when I thought I would have to let go, I found myself saved.

Blackie's owner had come out into the street to see where his dog was and seeing what was happening, he yelled, 'Stop teasing me dog, ye little bugger or ye'll get a kick up yor arse.' On hearing his master's voice, Blackie let go the Fedora and bounded off down the street, tail wagging madly at having enjoyed a great game.

I lay exhausted and tearful, glad that Blackie had gone but very worried about my immediate future. I stood up slowly and brushed my skinned knees, fear masking any pain as I looked at the hat or should I say the dirty, soggy mess that had been a hat. Using the sleeve of my threadbare jersey, I wiped away tears and snot from my face and began trying desperately to brush off the black marks and dog slaver from the battered hat.

That was when I witnessed my first miracle.

Uncle Alex's small wardrobe of clothes was of excellent quality, the Fedo-ra being no exception and as I brushed, I saw that the marks were coming off. I wiped the dog slaver off with my sleeve and the more I brushed and pulled at the hat the more it began to resemble its old self. Eventually and to my astonishment and almost unbearable relief, it took on its original shape and appearance, if just a tad grubby. I gingerly placed it on the back of my head and walked self-consciously back into the house.

'Back already Bonnie lad,' Uncle Alex asked, relieved to see his precious clothes returned in one piece.

12

'Aye, thanks a lot, I'll just put them on yor trunk,' I said sheepishly and walked quickly into the sitting room, placing the waistcoat and Fedora as neatly as possible on the top of his metal trunk. Luckily, for me, Uncle Alex's sight was not what it used to be and he did not notice any change in his precious hat or if he did, he never mentioned it.

Later that afternoon, sitting at the kitchen table with the rest of the younger kids, we were enjoying some of Mam's rabbit potpie, thankfully without any rabbit meat on my plate. There was not too much conversation as we were all intent on devouring as much pie and bread as we could before Mam chased us off the table to make way for the older children, it was survival of the fittest, and we were all keen to survive.

Mam was hovering above us making sure we ate as fast as we could when our relative peace and tranquillity was disturbed by an almighty metallic crash followed by screams and blaspheming, the like we had only heard from Dad. Mam rushed to the back door followed by the five youngest members of her brood to see what or who was causing the commotion.

'Bugger my eyes,' she exclaimed, 'what the bloody hell hev ye done lad?'

We craned our necks to peer round Mam to see whom she was talking to; it was Ian Brown from next door, Ron's nine-year-old diminutive and bonny brother. He was sitting in the middle of the tiny backyard clutching his left foot whilst rocking back and forth in agony, muttering words that I was sure were so rude that they would make his teeth fall out. Next to him, Dennis's hobbyhorse lay on its belly, legs stretched fore and aft in a position I recognised from earlier!

Feelings of guilt began to flood my mind but changed quickly to turmoil. I was certain that Mam was about to dish out swift and terrible punishment on poor Ian, whom I liked and admired, but if I spoke up I knew that punishment would surely come my way.

On seeing his beloved horse lying spread-eagled and knackered, Dennis began to howl, something he had down to a fine art!

Mam put her hand round his skinny shoulder, pulling him into her leg as she said to Ian, 'Eeee laddie, look what ye've done to wore Bairn's horse.' Ian was in too much pain to care about the Bairn's horse or his howling; he was more concerned that the metal underbelly of the horse had cut his big toe off; at least, that was how it felt.

'George, gan and get Nana Broon,' screeched Mam over the noise of Dennis' wailing and Ian's swearing. As George rushed off, Mam stepped forward and picked the blaspheming heap that was Ian up by his shoulder with her right hand while still holding onto Dennis with her left. Ian hung there like a rag doll, still in agony, still clutching his foot and still crying obscenities, wondering what the bloody hell had happened.

He came round most afternoons to play with George and Eric and often had a furtive sit on Dennis's hobbyhorse, as even at that early age, he wanted to be

13

a jockey. The metal horse was the nearest thing to a real horse he was going to find in Pont Street - apart from the milkman's and Rington's tea delivery horse and cart and those were far too big. That afternoon he had put his foot in the stirrup and had begun to swing himself up when its legs splayed open, crashing the metal body down on his plimsoll-clad foot.

Mam was shaking the poor lad so hard; I thought his head would fall off.

'Eee Etty, what are ye deeing to wore Ian?' a perplexed Nana Brown asked as she heaved her enormous bulk into view.

'Whey man the little Bugger's broken wor Bairn's horse,' Mam yelled over Ian's shouts of pain and Dennis's even louder screams that he had raised, realising that he could milk the situation for a replacement horse or perhaps something better as he could never get the useless thing to move anyway.

Nana rescued Ian and clutched the now whimpering lad to her huge bosom in a vain attempt to console him, just as Mam raised her hand as if to strike him. It was at this point that guilt got the better of me and I tugged Mam's pinny, ready to confess.

'Mam, Mam,' I said dejectedly, pulling on her pinny to grab her attention, desperate to prevent Ian from suffering Mam's vengeance. I wish I had not.

'And ye can shut up ye little bugger or Aa'll put a cut in yor heed like a navies bait tin,' she growled, bringing down the hand intended for Ian onto my unprotected head. The sudden unexpected attack drove away all thoughts of confession and feelings of guilt and I retreated inside rubbing my head in anger at the injustice of the blow – after all, I hadn't even told her that I had knackered the horse!

Nana Brown took Ian to Ashington Hospital; 'Child with fractured toe caused by fall from horse (hobby).'

Dennis's expert wailing gained him a smart tricycle from Bob Orwell's shop, on tick of course.

14

2

Skating and Bleeding

That year was also my first winter at school, a wooden two-roomed hut for infants in the yard of the South Junior School. A few hundred yards from Pont Street, the school was a solidly built, late Victorian, red-bricked building surrounded by a high red brick wall.

Going to school on cold winter mornings was a miserable affair; forget climbing out of a warm bed to an equally warm house, having a hot breakfast, pulling on warm coats, before a loving mother walked you to school.

We were woken by Mam screaming, 'You little buggers better be up oot of them beds and off to school or Aa'll give ye such a bloody hiding,' which she shouted from the comfort of her own bed and probably with a fag in her hand.

Dad would not be home from work as he had recently got the job of 'Fore-Overman' a sort of Head Foreman at the colliery and worked from 1 am until 9 am. He would be lucky if she was up for him when he got home.

It was left to my older brothers and sisters to get us younger ones out of bed, light the fire, make cups of tea and jam or sugar sandwiches and then make sure we pulled on whatever hand me downs had reached us at that time before we dragged our reluctant bodies to school.

It was on a freezing misty morning that I learned how to ice skate!

Having wrapped ourselves up against the cold as best we could, I walked to school with Eric, who at ten was our leader and seven-year-old easily led George. Eric and George wore thick grey serge shorts and blousons that bulged at the front where large grey buttons held the thick material closed. I was very envious of these and looked forward to wearing George's next year - if they survived a year in Pont Street.

My attire consisted of long baggy, black serge shorts that hung to my knees and a thick, slightly small even for my skinny frame, black jacket tightly buttoned over a thick wool jersey. A bright red, knitted wool balaclava cocooned my head, fitting so tightly that it only left a small hole at the front, causing my mouth to pucker and my eyes to squint. A pair of large matching mittens that came almost to my elbows completed my outfit.

A smattering of wind-driven snow blew down the long streets, settling in nooks and crannies, some sticking to the edges of small sheets of ice that dotted the paths and roads. We wore wellies for protection, mine in the best tradition of 'hand me downs,' were, at least a couple of sizes too big, covering my knees and constantly catching on the bottom of my shorts. This meant that walking was not a straightforward task - if I lifted my feet too high, the wellies fell off. As it was, they flopped clumsily on the pavement as my skinny legs propelled them forward,

15

causing my socks to wrinkle hopelessly around my soles and heels and all the while the wellies made a strange sound that we called, 'Fallumping' as I shuffled gamely on.

Before we reached school, Eric came up with a brilliant idea, 'Let's gan skating on the pond ower at the Three Fields.' The pond was almost a mile distant, lying half way between Ashington and the neighbouring town of Newbiggin-by-the-Sea. 'It's boond to be frozen,' he said, convincing George that it would be much better to go skating than spending the morning sitting in a cold classroom for sums and history, besides the nit nurse was due that day and lately, George had been scratching his head rather a lot.

I obviously had no say in the matter but felt quite excited at the idea of 'skating' although I was not sure what that entailed. I followed them along, having to run clumsily every few yards in order to keep up as my wellies were determined to stop any normal forward movement. More than once they succeeded in stopping progress altogether by smacking into each other as I tried to get one past the other, resulting in me falling onto the cold, frosty ground.

'Haway man or we'll leave you behind,' from Eric, was sufficient for me to pick myself up and struggle on.

On reaching the field where the pond lay, we found it clad in a beautiful, pristine coat of white frost, with tendrils of mist and wind-blown snow drifting across the frozen grass. Completely frozen over, the pond looked black and foreboding, the blackness accentuated around the edges where spikes of white-frosted grass sprang up from below the ice.

Panting heavily from the effort of dragging my heavy wellies across the field I arrived at the pond a minute behind Eric and George who were in animated discussion. I stopped and innocently watched my breath burst from my mouth to condense into tiny white clouds in the cold air, oblivious to my two older, more mature brothers' discussion on the best method of testing the ice's suitability for skating.

I should have paid attention!

Eric, who was quite bright as well as being the heaviest, decided that the sensible thing to do was for the lightest of us to try the ice first to make sure it was strong enough for skating. Obviously, I was not keen on this decision and protested but the two of them pushed me toward the ice with words of encouragement.

'Gan on man, it'll be great,' said Eric.

'You'd better get on or Aa'll bray ye,' said George - nicknamed the 'Bull' by the family; I took his threats seriously!

With some trepidation and just a little excitement at the thought of gliding across the ice, I ventured gingerly forth. The first couple of steps were fine, I felt the wellies beginning to slide over the ice and tried to keep my feet up with them. It was on the third or fourth step that I heard the first crack; more of a small crackling noise but it was too late, my progress on the slippery ice had suddenly gathered speed as my wellies decided to start skating with me inside them!

16

They shot off across the ice toward the middle of the frozen pond as flailing my arms madly; I desperately tried to stay upright while Eric and George screamed, 'GAN ON.'

I must have travelled ten or so yards when the cracking sound became louder and the progress of my wellies halted abruptly when, after a particularly loud crack, my left wellie disappeared below the broken ice followed almost immediately by right. My forward momentum propelled me onwards, albeit without my wellies that luckily for me, being the over-large hand me downs that they were, had slipped effortlessly from my feet.

The pond had not finished with me; I was in the middle and tried to run across to the safety of other side but with each step I broke through the ice plunging my numbed feet into the frozen water below. Fortunately, the pond was, in reality, nothing more than a very large puddle created from rainwater, no more than eighteen inches at its deepest, and not some deep, dark, permanent pond that might have swallowed both my wellies and me.

I reached the other side too terrified to cry, shaking uncontrollably and suffering from shock, I was sure I had been on the brink of falling through the ice to disappear forever. My stockings had not survived the crossing either, they too were somewhere beneath the ice.

I looked back across the pond to where my two brothers were, expecting to see pity or consternation on their faces or the pair of them racing frantically around the pond to help me. Instead, they were laughing hysterically, George with his hands clenched between his legs to stop him from peeing himself. So much for brotherly love - in their defence, it must have looked funny and Eric knew the pond was not deep.

However, I was barefoot in a frozen field in the depth of winter and a mile from home! How I managed to run home without developing frostbite I will never know, my red woollen mittens that Eric had me pull on my feet and required pulling back on every hundred yards or so, probably prevented disaster.

I arrived back at Pont Street, cold, wet, miserable and exhausted, only to be left shivering on the doorstep by Eric and George who decided that sums, history and the nit nurse were preferable to Mam's wrath, and ran off to school.

I, on the other hand, could not escape and went inside to feel the cosy warmth of the kitchen fire surround me just before Mam's inquisition began.

'What the buggery are ye deein hyem?' - Slap.

'Why aren't ye at school?' - Slap.

'Where's ye bloody good wellies?' - Slap.

'Where the bloody hell are yor stockings ye sackless little bugger ye?' - Slap, slap.

She did not give me the opportunity to answer, nor could I have as I was crying loudly both at the pain from the slaps and the feeling of despair that her lack of thought for my well-being gave me. She continued her ranting seemingly unconcerned that one of her fragile offspring had at best, narrowly escaped frostbite, and at worst, drowning. Her methods of questioning tended to be quite physical and I had not yet developed the essential survival skill of lying to Mam successfully. Instead of being comforted after my ordeal, I received a good hiding to end a less than perfect morning.

Dad shouting down stairs, 'Shut that little bugger up, I'm trying to sleep,' only increased her wrath and produced another well-aimed slap.

Opposite Nana Brown's, and squashed between brick built toilets and coalhouses, a sturdy, lean-to wooden shed had been built by some previous occupant of her house. Painted green and with a net curtained window, the shed provided sanctuary on wet days when Mam would not allow the younger element of her brood to play indoors. It had a substantial workbench in front of the window, a few tools on the rack below and various other boxes and paraphernalia stacked at the back. The bench provided a surface big enough for us to play board games on, our then current favourite being Monopoly.

Much to his and our delight, Ian Brown had received the game a few days earlier for his birthday and the day before we had spent a happy hour or more learning its intricacies. On this particular afternoon, Ian was the Car, George the Boot, ginger-haired Matty the Top Hat and me, well I wasn't considered old enough to play with them. To appease me they made me the banker and I delighted in carefully stacking and counting the exotic paper money.

Ian who had played the game most was doing very well; he had houses on some of the yellow and green streets and was about to place a hotel on a very expensive bit of real estate close to the Start.

George and Matty were not doing so well; they had both spent some time in jail and had suffered some tough 'Chance' cards. George had a couple of railway stations and the waterworks while Matty, who had only managed to build a house on the Old Kent Road, had just spent the majority of his cash on Bond Street when his dice decided he was going to spend a short break in Ian's newly acquired hotel in Mayfair.

Matty stared in horror as he moved his top hat along the board, 'Five, six, seven frigging hell!' he said with menace, 'how much is that gannin te cost me?'

'A lot more than ye've got,' Ian replied with some delight, 'yor oot.'

This only served to infuriate Matty even more.

He glared at me and demanded, 'Give me some mair money – noo.'

Flinching and swallowing a large lump that had just formed in my throat and with a bravado I was not feeling, I yelled back, 'Ye canna have owt, ye oot man.'

An enraged Matty rewarded me with a sharp cuff to the right ear, knocking me off the wooden box I had been perched on.

George immediately came to my defence, pushing Matty hard on the shoulder he shouted, 'Leave wor Young'un alen man, yor oot.'

18

This was too much for Matty, taking George by surprise, he leaped on him and being bigger and heavier, forced him onto the cramped floor of the shed and landed a swinging right hook on George's nose, causing blood to splatter across his face and the floor.

Satisfied at the pain he had caused, Matty jumped up and with a swipe sent the monopoly board, its cards, houses, hotels and playing pieces flying across the bench. Opening the door to the shed he shouted, 'It's a bloody sissy's game anyway,' and ran off down the back lane to his home before George could retaliate.

'Bastard,' said George as he rose from the floor and was about to give chase when he noticed the blood streaming down his face and instead ran across the lane to our house to have the flow stemmed. I ran after him worried that he might die or have to have a skin graft on his nose from his arse as I had had for my burns- there was an awful lot of blood.

This left Ian to rescue the scattered game cursing to himself and vowing never to play with that mad-bugger Matty again.

Reaching the house, George ran inside seeking help from Mam, but she immediately dragged him out shouting, 'Get oot, ye'll get blood all ower the kitchen floor man.' Pulling his head back none to gently, she shoved the cloth she had been using to clean pastry tins with, firmly onto his tender nose, squeezing hard as she did so.

'Who did this?' she demanded of George.

'It wath tha bathdard Mathy Story,' he gasped from below the now blood-soaked pastry cloth.

Mam spent some time alternating between squeezing and releasing George's nose to see if the bleeding had stopped and all the while plotting revenge against Matty for daring to attack one of hers. The bleeding eventually stopped and Mam sent George inside with his head held back so far that he could not see where he was going with the inevitable result; he crashed into the kitchen door banging his already painful nose and making him cry, something George rarely, if ever did.

It also made Eric who had just come through from the sitting room, laugh - a big mistake.

George launched himself Kamikaze like at Eric but Mam intervened, knocking George to the floor in mid-flight before she grabbed Eric by the shoulder and pushing him out the back door, ordered, 'Get yorsell doon the street and sort that bugger Matty Story oot.'

This was the law of the jungle - the law of Pont Street, attack one and you attack all. Mam had decided that Eric should reclaim the Carr family honour, he had to 'bash up' Matty Story.

Eleven-year-old Eric was three years older than Matty and therefore in my Mam's eyes, he should have been capable of bashing him up, however, Eric was not exactly big; in fact he was puny compared to his adversary to be, the solidly built Matty.

With some trepidation, Eric walked down the street, worrying about the prospective fight, frightened more at the thought of Mam's retribution should he lose, rather than actually fighting.

Having wound himself up and steeling himself for the fray, he reached the Storey's door and yelled bravely, 'Come oot Matty 'n' try and hit me and Aa'll give ye a right hammering.' Hearing no response, he shouted once more and waited.

Again, there was no reply, so it was with some relief that he turned and started back down the lane rehearsing what he would say to Mam. 'The coward wouldn't cum oot,' sounded most feasible.

Unfortunately, for Eric, Matty had been in; he had watched from behind net curtains while Eric shouted and offered violence. Not sure whether or not he would win a straight fight with Eric, he had waited until Eric had turned to walk away before he headed quietly to the open back door. Picking up one of his dad's steel toe capped pit boots as he left his house, he ran toward an unsuspecting Eric, who was still deep in thought, concocting his alibi for not fighting.

Matty ran stealthily up the lane, pit boot held high above his head and at the last moment brought it crashing down on the back of Eric's head. The result was spectacular. Eric dropped as though felled, which he was, and for the second time that day, Carr blood flew everywhere.

Seeing his handiwork, Matty ran home terrified, certain that he had just murdered Eric and that he would probably have to spend the rest of his life in a Borstal.

Eric staggered to his feet, not at all sure what had just happened but he knew he was in trouble and wobbled home, his tee shirt turning red from the flow of blood from the gash to his head. Mam, who still had the towel clamped to George's nose that refused to stop bleeding after its collision with the door, stared in horror when a blood-soaked Eric staggered into the house.

'Jesus Bloody Christ,' she blasphemed, abandoning George to wrap the already blood-soaked towel around Eric's wound, 'Whaat the bloody hell's happened te ye?'

Eric did not have a clue what had happened to him, except his head hurt like hell and he felt very sick, so he muttered under the towel, 'Aa divvint knaa Mam, Aa think some bugger's twatted me on the back of the heed!'

Mam lifted the towel from the back of his head and warned, 'Divvint ye bloody swear at me ye frigging little bugger ye,' and jammed the towel back down, splattering more blood over her piny that was already covered in George's blood.

Abandoned by Mam, George sat on the bottom of the stairs by the back door watching blood dribble from his nose onto the lino while singing, 'Put another nickel in the nickelodeon, all Aa want is a towel, a towel, a towel!'

Mam looked angrily at George as she dragged Eric to the back door where George's puddle of blood was getting larger by the second and snarled, 'Shut up ye bloody little Waster or Aa'll murder ye.'

20

George looked up and spat back, 'Ye'll hev te hurry up if ye want te murder me cos am nearly frigging deed from loss of blood!'

I had been standing by the window watching with opened mouth horror as my two big brothers bled to death when Mam spun round and started to shout at me, 'Get a towel for George from the....' but didn't finish, as she turned she stepped into George's lovely red puddle, causing both feet to shoot from under her. She flew backwards, propelling a half conscious Eric back into the kitchen where he collided with the table, his nose and left eye taking the full force of the blow. As she fell, Mam's left arm swung out for support and met with George's nose, a nose that had almost stopped dripping blood. The blow knocked him backwards onto the stair splattering the walls with a revitalised flow of his bright red blood.

'Frigging Hell!' George screamed as he grasped his battered nose to try to stem the flow.

Mam's fall ended with the back of her head smacking horribly into the back door as her right elbow crashed into the doorframe. She sat still for a moment, covered in blood from two of her offspring; dazed and not completely with it, her eyes glazed as she slowly raised her left hand to the back of her head before bringing it forward to look at the sticky blood that covered it.

This was too much for me; I began crying at the sight of my Mam, and brothers bleeding to death on the kitchen floor, a floor that was beginning to look as though it belonged in a slaughterhouse.

Mam hauled herself up, looked at her elbow that was also bleeding and shouted at me, 'Stop yor bloody wailing ye soft shite ye and get some frigging toowels oot of the cupboard and gan and get Pat to clean this bloody mess up.'

A few minutes later as I helped Pat to wash the blood from the lino, Mam hurried off to Ashington Hospital, bloody towels wrapped around her own head and those of her two wounded offspring.

The hospital register might have read:
1. Child with laceration to head caused by pit boot (empty)?
2. Child with severe nosebleed caused by kitchen door?
3. Woman with lacerations to head and elbow? – Pont Street – police informed!

A Grand day at the Seaside

Summer eventually arrived and was soon in full swing as the long school holiday began with glorious weather that made Pont Street almost pleasant; almost. Housewives escaped their daily grind to gossip with neighbours at back doors and men tired after a day's hard graft at the pit sat on doorsteps sipping a reflective cup of tea or if they were very lucky, a bottle of stout while enjoying the early evening sun. Kids played imaginative street games and got up to all sorts of innocent mischief.

After a few days of holiday and on a particularly hot summer's morning, Eric, George, and I were running wild in the kitchen. Standing at the kitchen table in the centre of the room, Mam was busy making dough while throwing the odd slap at us when we were in range. Uncle Alex sat by the fire, on the old leather cottage chair, smoking his pipe and counting his coins prior to his midday sojourn to the local Working Mans' Club.

The fire that blazed away even on this hot day had an oven either side and in front, a metal and brass fender with a shovel and fire tongs leaning against it. The pantry was in the corner between the fire and the window and contained a small Belfast sink with a cold-water tap that provided the only source of water in the house. In this tiny room, we carried out dishwashing and family ablutions and stored pots, pans, and our meagre supply of rations.

Under the window in the kitchen, our newly rented Rediffusion radiogram stood between two chairs. A low sideboard filled the wall opposite the fire and to the left of this was the door to the stairs and back door, while to the right was the door to the back passage leading to the sitting room and seldom-used front door. The cluttered kitchen was not a large room for three kids to be running around in, especially when Mam was trying to cook.

Fed up with the racket in the cramped space and kids permanently under her feet, Mam planned a picnic in order to have her three feral lads out of the house and give herself a bit of peace from our rampaging.

'Eric,' she said holding him tightly by the arm to stop him from chasing George round the kitchen table, 'Aa'll mek some jam sandwiches for ye and George and ye can tek a bottle of weter and gan off to Newbiggin for the day; and take that simple bugger with ye,' she said pointing to me. I had just knelt down in front of the chair next to the radiogram and had begun drawing on a scrap of paper on top of the chair.

George had his favourite record playing - our only record.

'Put another nickel in, in the nickelodeon, all I want is music, music, music,' it sang loudly for the umpteenth time before Mam switched the power off at the wall causing it to wind pitifully down in mid-song.

Having made sure that we had pulled on our woollen swimming trunks under our khaki shorts, she thrust sandwiches, a bottle of water, and one towel at us, her planning and preparation finished, she ushered us out the back door with, 'Mind be back for tea.'

We headed off toward the 'Three Fields' that led the way to Newbiggin-by-the-Sea and what we were sure would be a grand day out. Eric had the water, George the sandwiches and I the large towel that proved to be quite a bundle for a six year old. It kept unwrapping and tripping me, causing me to pick myself up and shuffle quickly along behind the other two in order to keep up.

It was about 10 o'clock when we reached the second of the 'Three Fields' that had a broad track running through it toward the coast. A field of turnips grew on the right of the track, with a field of wheat on the left that had a heat haze shimmering over the top of its ripening heads as they swayed almost imperceptibly in the gentlest of breezes.

We stopped to take a drink of water, both to quench our thirst on this red-hot day and to wash down the remains of the jam sandwiches. These had only lasted as far as the first field before we devoured them, the remains of the filling evident on my cheeks.

Still hungry, George suggested, 'We can eat a couple of snaggys (turnips).'

We took up his suggestion and pulled up several before we found one that we considered worth eating in that it did not have as much soil clinging to its fat body as the others. Without any form of an implement, eating the snaggy involved biting chunks of the thick skin off, spitting them out and biting more chunks off until we revealed sufficient flesh below to bite into and chew. Never good sharers, we each had to have one but only took a few bites from the heavy snaggys to satisfy any remaining hunger we had before we dumped them along with the many others we had pulled up.

Our attention then went to the wheat field that was quietly minding its own business enjoying the hot mid-morning sun!

'That wheat's as tall as ye Syd, let's play hide, and seek,' said Eric.

We chased each other around the field, disappearing in the sun-ripened wheat that bowed to our mad charging, leaving flattened trails in our wake until thirsty from our game, we flattened a large area of wheat into a den that hid us from view and sat down to have another drink of water. Lying down on the trampled crops staring up at the clear blue sky, my breathing still heavy from our exertions and Eric and George lying laughing close by, I felt euphoria and contentment. It had been a good day so far and the thought of the beautiful sandy beach at Newbiggin filled me with even more excitement.

After a few minutes, we stood up without a saying a word and made our way back to the track, leaving behind us the damaged wheat in the shape of a very strange crop circle. It was about another mile and a half to Newbiggin and by the time we got there, we were tired and thirsty again and needed to refill our empty bottle with water.

Newbiggin was then, a delightful seaside village with a crescent shaped bay lined with large Victorian terraced houses, each with a lovely garden sloping to a promenade that stretched the length of the bay. Shelters punctuated the promenade and a ramp split it in the middle, where a rack of 'Shuggy' or swing boats full of children, sat next to brightly painted Northumbrian fishing cobles waiting to go to sea. Above the ramp was a small square with 'Bertorelli's' 'Riveria' Ice Cream Parlour on one side with the Coble Inn on the opposite.

An ancient sandstone church stood above rocks at the north end of the bay with caravans and a golf course on the links behind. At the south end, the bay ended with an outcrop of rocks known, as the 'Needles Eye' due to a natural arch formed by sea erosion. Newbiggin was also a mining town but as the mine was inland from the beach, it did not spoil the town's charm.

On reaching the outskirts, we stood for a short while in front of a small grocer's shop, drooling at the bottles of pop, cakes, biscuits, and crisps on display. Not having a penny between us, we reluctantly left the shop window and made our way to the promenade and saw that the beach was busy with families and small groups of children enjoying the sun and sea.

'Where are we gannin to get some weter Eric?' I asked a little desperately.

Thirsty himself, he replied, 'Howay, we'll gan up to the back of the big hooses and knock on a door and ask somebody.

The rear of the Victorian terraced houses had large walls hiding back yards that contained coalhouses, toilets and brick sheds, or outhouses. We tried the door to the yard of the first house but it appeared bolted on the inside so we moved onto the next. It opened and we entered nervously closing the door behind us. It was a large yard with bikes, a dustbin and the obligatory large galvanised bath hanging on an outhouse wall.

Shyly, I hid behind George as we followed Eric, advancing timidly across the yard to the open back door when the ferocious barking of what sounded like a very large dog from within the house stopped us in our tracks. We turned to flee but were too slow, a large Alsatian came bounding and barking from inside the house.

Terrified that the dog might eat me alive, I dived through the open door of the outside toilet, followed quickly by George and then Eric who slammed the door behind him. The toilet was an appropriate place to hide as the sound of the Alsatian barking and scratching at the door was enough to terrify the poo out of three of us. We pressed against the door with strength borne out of fear, not having uttered a sound, all three of us far too scared to speak.

'Quiet lass, come on quiet doon,' a voice said in the yard.

Immediately the dog stopped and a stern woman's voice, continued, 'Who's in there? ye can come oot, she winnit hurt ye.'

25

'We're not coming oot we that big monster oot there missus,' George said defensively.

'Will yor dog eat us?' I squeaked.

There was a relieved laugh from the yard as the woman realised her intruders were children. 'Hang on and I'll put her inside,' she said and we heard the sounds of a door being opened then closed.

'Come on then, come oot and let's see you,' she said reassuringly.

Eric opened the toilet door and the three of us nervously walked out; I making sure I was behind the other two.

'Ee, mind I divvint think I need fear ye three,' said the woman, a handsome 40 something wearing a bright red floral dress with a white apron. She stood looking us up and down - three scruffy, thin boys with tousled hair, wearing grubby tee shirts, khaki shorts and well-worn plimsolls, Eric still clutching the empty pop bottle and me with a dishevelled towel hanging from underneath my arm.

'Can we have some weter please missus?' blurted Eric, looking at her pleadingly.

'Ye look as though ye need mair than weter pet,' she replied, reaching behind George to take my arm.

She gently pulled me forward and said, 'Yor a bonny little bairn noo aren't ye, a bet you'd like a cake and a nice cup of tea?' I was too in awe to speak and stood there grinning shyly.

'Where are you from boys?' she inquired as she led me toward the house with Eric and George following.

'Ashington missus,' Eric replied, 'we've come to gan on the beach, but we drank wor weter waalking here.'

'Eee ye haven't walked all the way here from Ashington have ye pet,' she asked in wide mouthed astonishment.

'Whey aye man, it's not far,' George responded in his gruff direct manner.

'Where's the dog missus,' I asked nervously as she opened the door to her kitchen.

'Divvint fret bonny lad, she's locked up in the wash hoose and anyway she wouldn't harm you,' she replied.

The next half hour or so was wonderful.

She sat us down at a table in her bright spacious kitchen, plied us with delicious, homemade sponge and rock cakes, and poured cups of freshly made tea to quench our thirsts.

'Am sorry Aa haven't got any pop for you bairns but we divvint drink it here,' she said rubbing my already tousled hair.

'Ta very much, this is smashing,' Eric spluttered through a mouthful of rock cake as we stuffed as much of this unexpected bounty down our throats as we could. We left shortly after with a full bottle of water and an apple and rock cake each and promised to call in and see her again the next time we were in Newbiggin.

26

'Tell yor mam she can send the little one to live with me if she wants to get rid of him,' she shouted after us as we made our way to the corner of the back lane. Her offer terrified me, although she was the loveliest, kindest woman I had ever met, the thought of leaving my Mam and the rest of the family was enough to have me running toward the beach.

Eric led us to an empty spot on the beach near the water's edge and took the bedraggled towel from me; he stretched it out on the warm, soft sand. He and George then carefully laid our water and newly acquired rations onto the towel pulling a corner over them to protect them from the hot midday sun.

Stripping our shorts and tee shirts off, we stood proudly in all our under-nourished glory, ready for the sea. To say there wasn't an ounce of fat between the three of us would have been an understatement; thin arms and legs dangling from skinny, rib protruding torsos made our round faces seem over large for our bodies, but it was our swimming costumes that made the spectacle comical. These were navy-blue, close-knitted woollen trunks held above our belly buttons by brightly striped, elastic belts, fastened with metal snake shaped buckles. The trunks were quite close fitting, unless, like mine, they were hand-me-downs and, therefore, did not fit quite so snugly, in fact, there was quite a bit of space around my skinny thighs causing me to display my dangly bits a little too often.

Worse, when wet the wool reacted as wool does to water; they absorbed a large amount, stretched and lost the close fit they had. This caused the crutch to hang several inches lower than intended. To compensate, we pulled the trunks up until the crutch was where it should be in order to protect our modesty. This meant that the belt was now chest high and looked even more ridiculous. Our answer to this problem was to roll the belt and waistband down to an acceptable level leaving us looking as though we had small tyres around our waists.

None of this really mattered to me; sartorial elegance was not high on my list of priorities when I was six. I ran around with the trunks generally flapping around my thighs and in doing so, left red marks in the tenderest of places.

Actually getting into the sea was something of a spectacle. The hot sun had warmed our thin bodies and having no fat protection against anything cold, we did not take gladly to the coldness of the North Sea. The three of us tiptoed into the cold water squeezing our elbows into our sides, our hands waving frantically, faces grimacing against the shock. Standing at the water's edge, we let the small waves lap over our feet as we tried to pick up the courage to go further in, daring each other to go first. As expected, George was first; running in he turned and began gleefully and with great gusto kicking water up at Eric and me, the cold water felt like an electric shock to our sun-warmed bodies and created instant panic.

I ran from the water while Eric who was trying desperately to protect himself from the splashes screamed at George, 'Give ower or Aa'll daad ye in a minute.'

Eventually, we were all cavorting in the water, constantly adjusting swimming trunks and generally having a great time. We had also found a stretch

27

of calm warmer water, formed and protected at low tide by a sand bank about twenty yards off shore.

Several other kids were also playing in the pool and we joined in with them until George jumped on a lad who had just splashed him, holding his head under water just a tad too long. The lad ran screaming back to his mother who chased us off while screaming obscenities and death threats.

Wading through the warm water to the sandbank, the three of us began to construct a series of canals and fortifications that Brunel would have been proud of. As we built and dredged, we were unaware that the tide was creeping in until it began devouring our outermost fortifications.

George spotted the danger first, 'Shit, the bloody tides coming in roond behind us,' he yelled.

Of the three of us, he was the only good swimmer; I had not yet learnt and Eric could barely swim, but worse he had a terrible fear of deep water. Without looking for escape routes, we panicked and ran into the sea heading straight for the shore.

I was soon in difficulties. We had only gone a few yards before the water was up to my neck and I yelled in fear for the other two to save me.

Eric was having to deal with his own fears and waded on desperate to get to the safety of the shore but George turned, grabbed my arm and pulling me to safety shouted, 'Howay ye soft shite, it's not that deep.'

I certainly would not have made it without him as at the deepest point it was well over my nose and mouth, it was only his dragging that kept me going. Because he was holding me, I stopped panicking and we both made the shore safely. My swimming trunks, however, had not made the crossing and had slid off somewhere in the middle. I had been too intent on reaching safety to retrieve them, besides George had been dragging me too quickly for me to grab them. I ran to the towel and carefully sat on it pulling a free end over my skinny thighs to hide my embarrassment.

Eric who had been a little traumatized by his self-induced panic to get back to shore, was beginning to regain his composure and yelled at me, 'Ye better not be sitting on them rock cakes or ye'll get a daading.'

It was then that we noticed the family next to us were in fits of laughter at our antics.

'Not very kind,' I thought to myself, 'after all I nearly drowned.'

The father of the group came over to us still chuckling and said mockingly, 'I divvint knaa what all the panic was aboot lads if ye'd gone off to the left ye would have seen that the sandbank is still attached to the shore and ye could've walked off alang there.'

This did not help my embarrassment as one of the man's daughters who must have been about my age, was still giggling while playfully putting her tongue out at me; this only made me blush even more - if that was possible. Eric sat down next to me and started to eat a rock cake, ignoring the giggling family while trying

28

to look cool in his baggy trunks. George meanwhile waded into the sea and rescued mine from the water's edge where the small waves were playing with them.

He threw the sodden trunks at me and yelled, 'Here ye are Young'un, put these on before you scare every bugger with that weapon of yours.'

I spat back, 'Bugger off' and swiftly pulled them on, stretching them all the way up to my armpits before rolling them back down to my waist.

Desperate to get away from our mockers, Eric stood up and said, 'Aa've had enough of the beach, haway, get dried off and we'll gan alang to Church Point and get some willicks.'

George added, 'We'd better hurry cos the tides coming in.'

We hastily dried; Eric and George carrying out various contortions while stripping off wet trunks and pulling on shorts behind the towel while I, having stripped off my trunks that I had just pulled on, had to stand naked, trying unsuccessfully to protect my modesty while holding the remaining rock cakes and apples, waiting for my turn with the towel.

When he was dressed, George wrapped our goodies in the towel whilst I pulled on my shorts and tee shirt. We then headed for the promenade carrying our wet trunks in hand, George with the towel of Goodies slung over his shoulder.

As we made our way up the beach, we passed three girls making a large meal of sand pies and sand cakes, using large flat pebbles as plates. From their similar looks, they had to be sisters. I stopped to look at their layout of various sandy dishes and noticed that the girl in the middle was staring at me with big blue eyes and a smile that neither mocked nor teased; a smile of warmth and tenderness of the like I had never seen before. I noticed that her hair was in small plaits, plaited into two larger ones that hung down either side of her face.

I was suddenly aware that her two companions were giggling and whispering to each other.

The girl in the middle with the beautiful blue eyes and gentle smile said, 'Do you want some cake?' Feeling a growing blush burn my neck and devour my face, I was too shy and embarrassed to move or speak and stood there with a gormless smile on my red face.

George rescued me with a gruff shout of, 'How man, get a move on, or the tide'll be in before we get there.' His voice broke my immobility and I quickly hurried after them but took several furtive looks back at the blue-eyed girl who watched us as we ran off.

We left our goodies on a dry ledge whilst we scrambled hurriedly over the rocks collecting willicks from amongst the abundant seaweed at Church Point. George had fashioned the towel into a bag shape and we rapidly filled it as we harvested the large black shells. It was then that I took an unplanned swimming lesson.

In amongst the rocks slippery with seaweed, there were numerous pools of various depths as well as channels of deeper water leading to the open sea. Slipping on a weed-covered rock, near a large cluster of willicks I was trying to reach,

I plunged head first into one of the deep channels. The cold water stole my breath and I gasped desperately, inadvertently swallowing a large mouthful of salty water before I came up spluttering, doggy paddling wildly as I tried to reach the side.

Eric and George who were twenty or so yards away began clambering toward me as I struggled in the deep water but before they could reach me, a passing fisherman reached in and hauled me to safety.

He stood holding me at arm's length as the seawater ran of me, 'Whey you're not much of a catch,' he laughed before putting me gently down.

A few yards away, his mate asked mockingly, 'Are ye gannin to keep that one Bob, or are ye gana throw it back?'

I stood penguin-like, with my upper arms held close to my body while I spat out the remnants of the seawater I had swallowed and felt very sorry for myself.

'Yor supposed to put yor cossie on forst ye daft bugger,' George said as he came up beside me.

'Gis the towel,' I said to him desperately trying to reach for it.

He held the shell filled towel behind him and said, 'Ye can sod of, it's full of willicks man.'

'A canna gan hyem like this,' I cried, 'me Mam'll kill is man,' and pleaded desperately for the towel, as Eric and George looked at me with frustration born of having to put up with a younger, weaker brother.

My rescuer stepped forward and said, 'Haway lads, come up to wor hoose and the missus'll dry him off.' A sturdy, ruddy-faced man of about forty, he took my hand in his and led me a short distance past drawn up cobles to the Fishermen's cottages on the edge of the town. A neat terrace of bungalows overlooking the bay, they had small gardens at the front enclosed with low brick walls.

We walked along the path next to the gardens, past gates with boxes of crabs on display on chairs with hand-drawn signs advertising their price. He led me into a bungalow near the middle of the terrace while Eric and George remained outside, George still holding the towel bulging with the willicks we had collected.

'Here ye are lass,' the Fisherman said to his wife who had been busy at the kitchen sink. 'Can you clean this one up, Aa've just caught him off Church Point,' he chuckled.

'Eee whatever's happened to the poor bairn?' she inquired, rinsing her hands and drying them on her pinny.

'The silly buggers only falling in collecting willicks,' he replied and wandered back outside to speak to his friend.

The woman led me into a small neat bathroom and began to fill the bath.

'Get yorsell into there pet and Aa'll ring yor wet clothes oot,' she said to me whilst testing the water.

She did not put much water into the bath as her man would be needing hot water later but it was sufficient for me. She left the bathroom as I took off my wet pumps and stripped of my equally sodden tee shirt and shorts. Self-consciously, I climbed into the bath, the first real bath I had seen let alone sat in.

The woman reached around the door and took my wet clothes saying, 'Use the green towel to dry yorsell off properly pet,' and disappeared back into the kitchen.

I sat in the bath taking in my surroundings; clean white tiles with a black border that ran around the room, and below the window, a washbasin with a hot and cold tap. This was luxury I had not seen before and being unaccustomed to it, I felt strangely uncomfortable. Feeling very vulnerable, I quickly washed then pulled the plug, enjoying the novel experience of watching the water disappear down the hole before reaching for the towel to dry myself. Once dried, I wrapped the towel around me and shyly walked back into the kitchen where I found Eric and George eating crab sandwiches and drinking tea.

'Haway pet, there's some for ye as well,' the woman said ushering me to an empty chair.

Eric looked across at me and feigning sadness, said, 'I went back to get our cakes and cosies but the seagulls had got wor cakes.'

'Never mind bonny lad, these are better than cakes,' the woman interjected handing one to me. They were absolutely, delicious and with a cup of strong sweet tea, they made me feel ready to take on the world again.

My Tee shirt and shorts were steaming away on the Rayburn in the corner of the kitchen, the Fisherman's wife constantly checking them and turning them to speed the drying process. As I finished my second sandwich, she handed my now steaming clothes to me and ushered me to the bathroom to get dressed.

I re-joined Eric and George who were thanking the woman just as Eric re-trieved our pop bottle from amongst our swimming trunks and asked if she would fill it for us. She did, and then took us to the garden gate, and waved goodbye, probably glad that she did not have to feed us every day.

Enjoying the afternoon sun and feeling very content, we strolled along Newbiggin High Street making our way back toward the three fields, George still had the towel full of winkles, Eric was carrying the bottle of water and as we walked, we ate the three apples we had kept from our first benefactor.

Walking past the Memorial Garden opposite the tiny railway station where the trains from Ashington and beyond terminated, Eric asked, 'Syd do ye knaa that's where the Ashington train comes in?'

Is it,' I replied.

'Aye, it's the Ashington, Newbiggin train.'

'Oh,' I said in response.

'Go on ye say it - fast.'

'Say Whaat?'

'Ashington – Newbiggin Train.'

I did.

Eric urged me on saying, 'Come on man ye've got to keep on saying it fast.'

'Ashington Newbiggin train - Ashington Newbiggin train,' I kept on innocently repeating as fast as I could, until on the fourth repeat, it came out as 'Aa shitinthe Newbiggin train!'

This brought howls of laughter from the other two and a puzzled look on my face, not having fully grasped what I had said.

It was not until George said, 'Ye dorty little bugger, fancy shitting in the Newbiggin train,' that I realised what was going on.

I repeated slowly, 'Aa shit in the Newbiggin train,' and began to giggle as we continued on our way, shouting the phrase at each other and laughing even more when we received a frown of disapproval from three elderly ladies sitting on a bench by the Garden.

It was about four o'clock when we got to the first of the three fields and saw in the next field a very large man stomping around the track between the turnips and cornfield.

'It's the bloody farmer,' hissed Eric out the side of his mouth as a feeling of dread crept over us. It was too late to turn and run as he had seen us, besides he would soon catch me and even if we did escape, it would mean a long detour home that we were far too tired to undertake.

The farmer watched us approach and stood in the centre of the track, an uprooted turnip in each hand and an angry expression adorning his weather-beaten face.

'Divvint say owt,' Eric whispered, as we walked toward the giant who blocked our way home.

I was terrified at the sight of him, well over six foot and burly with it, I wondered if he had climbed down a beanstalk, although I could not see any and anyway there were no clouds for it to disappear into as the sky was still clear and blue. We halted in front of him, staring up at his irate face, wondering what terrible punishment he was about to heap on us.

'Div ye lads knaa oot aboot this bloody mess?' he growled angrily, waving the uprooted turnips first at the small pile on his right and then at the trodden wheat on his left.

As warned, I kept my mouth shut and stared up at him in fear, imagining him eating us alive while he sang, 'Fi fo fi fum I smell the blood of an Englishman.'

Eric and George also remained silent while the farmer continued to glare at us menacingly.

'Well,' he said, 'do you?'

Eric swallowed and replied sheepishly, 'We divvint want to get anybody into trouble mister.'

'TROUBLE,' roared the farmer, causing me to move further behind George, 'Trouble, Aa'll ge ye trouble if ye divvint tell me what ye knaa.'

Feigning innocence, Eric looked up at him and said, 'We were walking across here this morning Mister and we saw Matty Story and his brother running roond yor wheat, we told him he shouldn't be doing it, but he said he'd bash us up if we said owt.'

My mouth dropped open at this; I could not remember seeing Matty Story that morning! Realisation slowly dawned on my naive brain and I had to fight to stop myself smiling.

'Matty Story Ye say,' said the farmer, 'and where does he live eh?'

Eric continued his subterfuge, 'Aa divvint want to get him into trouble Mister,' he replied, rubbing the almost healed scar on the back of his head.

Stooping toward Eric, the farmer growled, 'Ye'll be in trouble if ye divvint tell me!'

Eric gave him the address and asked the farmer to promise not to say who had told him. The farmer promised and stormed off toward his car, a green Ford parked beyond the third field. As we stood watching him go our fear slowly changed to glee as we thought of this enraged bull charging into Pont Street looking for the Story's' house.

We continued on our way, trying to imagine the scene at the Story's' with the Farmer storming in on our unsuspecting neighbours when George spotted something lying in a large discoloured patch of grass in the last of the three fields.

'Aren't them your wellies?' he said to me, pointing to two black smudges lying close together in the lower part of the field where the sun had finished drying out the large rain pond.

I ran over and found that sure enough, they were my wellies, looking unaffected after having spent several months underwater.

I reached down, picked them up emptying a trickle of water from each of the sun-warmed wellingtons and shouted back to the other two, 'It's them, and they're aalreet.' I ran back to join them waving my wellies madly in the air with delight.

It was not long before I found the wellies very heavy and awkward to carry, so just before teatime, with the sun still high in the sky, three young scallywags walked into Pont Street. The tallest carrying a bottle of water and three woollen swimming trunks, one of which he wore on his head, the middle-sized one with a towel full of winkles slung over his shoulder and the smallest fallumping along in wellies while wearing a pair of plimsolls like gloves.

As we entered Pont Street, we saw the green Ford car parked outside the Story's house.

Eric said, 'Howay ye two, be quick and get past before the farmer comes oot.' As we scurried past the house, our heads ducked below the back fence, we heard angry shouting coming through the open door. This increased our glee, spurring us on to the safety of our house, giggling as we went.

33

Wearily and happily, we walked into the sanctuary of the kitchen where the smell of food cooking on the open fire greeted us; a clootie dumpling was boiling away in a large black pan, steam rising in clouds that disappeared up the chimney.

Mam, busy with her proggy tool, thrusting short strips of cloth cut from an old overcoat into the canvas base of the 'clippie mat' she was making, asked, 'I suppose ye'll be wanting yor tea noo?'

'Aye please,' we answered in unison with the feigned desperation of kids who had only had a jam sandwich each all day!

Later on, while we were waiting for the willicks to finish boiling, Betty sat next to me and asked what we had been up to and as I told her in excited bursts, I noticed that she smelt very nice and saw that she was wearing her best frock.

'Where ye gannin?' I asked looking up at her.

'She's got her boyfriend coming and they're gannin oot,' piped up Viv who at four and a half was beginning to hone her skills as a stirrer.

Rubbing my shoulders, Betty smiled at me and said, 'Ye'll see him later when he comes to pick me up.' I winced as she rubbed and with a look of concern, she pulled back the already stretched neck of my tee shirt to look at my skinny shoulders.

'Eee Mam, look at the poor bairn's shoulders, they're all sunburnt,' she said with some concern.

Looking across from where she had returned to her clippie mat making, Mam said, 'That simple bugger hasn't got enough sense to knaa to keep his shoulders covered when it's hot.'

Still at the table and not wishing to be branded simple as well, Eric and George did not think it wise to mention their sunburn.

Betty's new boyfriend turned up and stood self-consciously in a smart suit by the fire as Mam with her proggy tool held menacingly in her hand, scrutinised him before giving him a withering look of contempt and blowing cigarette smoke in his direction.

We, the four smaller members of her brood, who were sitting around the table plucking the snotty looking bodies from the freshly boiled willicks with bent hair clips before stuffing them into our mouths, stared at him, weighing him up.

Fourteen-year-old Jim came in and joined us at the table to help devour the willicks and looking straight at Betty's boyfriend asked, 'Whaat's that?'

'Wor Betty's fancy pants bloody boyfriend,' George spluttered through a mouthful of willick slime.

The smell of boiled willicks and the smoke from Uncle Alex's pipe and the woodbine sticking out of the corner of Mam's mouth, combined to stop the bewildered lad from speaking. He composed himself and was just about to speak, when without taking his eyes of the poor lad, Uncle Alex sat forward and spat into

34

the back of the fire, causing a short but loud hissing sound; this was too much for the him, certainly enough to drive any thought of polite conversation from his mind.

Betty came to his rescue and taking his hand ushered him to the door and safety. I felt happy seeing the look of delight on her beaming face as she and her boyfriend escaped the confines of our madhouse but also sad, realising that I would not be receiving her full attention in the future.

Later, lying in bed between George and Dennis, I thought what a grand day out it had been and when I closed my eyes, I saw a little girl with plaits in her hair, bright blue eyes and a warm smile; I drifted off feeling full, contented and happy.

4

Goodbye Granddad

Sundays followed a long-established routine; Mam and Dad would lie in bed until ten before dragging themselves downstairs with their first fags of the day hanging from their lips. Barking through their smokers' coughs, they would chase their unruly throng outside to play, providing Dad with the space he needed to carry out his ablutions - shaving at the kitchen table before disappearing upstairs to put his suit on. He would then stroll to a Workmen's Social Club, one of more than twenty in Ashington; meet his cronies and partake of three or four pints of beer and perhaps, a couple of whiskies.

In the meantime, Mam along with Betty and Pat prepared Sunday dinner. This was the best meal of the week and Mam's was the best there was. Several pans, full of vegetables fresh from Dad's allotment would be boiling on the open fire while a small joint of meat slowly roasted in the oven along with potatoes and giant Yorkshire puddings. The smells coming from the kitchen would have us drooling in anticipation as we played outside.

Mam did not allow us to sit down to eat until Dad got back from his Club, usually about two o clock. The youngest bairns would go to meet him on his way back in the hope that the booze had mellowed him sufficiently enough for him to demonstrate his generous side to his cronies by slipping each of us a few pennies.

Over the years, Mam had begun to resent this chauvinistic routine and had begun to hatch a plan. After all, brought up to expect better, she had not thought she would have to lead this sort of life. One of five sisters and one brother, Henrietta (Etty) was a Waterford and had been used to living in relative comfort on a farm. By the time, she was eighteen she had been groomed for marriage to the lad who lived on the large farm next door and her life was moving along very nicely – until George Carr saw her at a dance.

The Carrs and Waterfords got along very well, just so long as they stayed well away from each other. An old-fashioned feud existed between the two Northumbrian farming families, probably dating back to cattle rustling days, when families often took it upon themselves to beef up their stock by taking cattle from the Scots or if they were too strong, a family closer to home, often with a bit of rape and pillage thrown in for good measure.

You can imagine the turmoil created when a few months after meeting my father, Mam told her parents she was pregnant! It must have gone down like the proverbial lead balloon. However, it would have been nothing compared to what must have occurred when she told them the father was not the boy from the neighbouring farm – 'It was George Carr, one of them "Carrs."'

A hasty marriage arranged; the two guilty parties marched to the church while their respective families glared at each other from opposite sides of the aisle. Immediately after the ceremony, Mam's mother handed her a suitcase of belongings and bade her, 'Goodbye,' the last word she said to Mam for eight long years.

Dad received similar treatment from his family but expecting it; he had spent some time visiting local coal mines to find a job with a cottage in order to provide for his newly acquired pregnant wife. The years that followed had been a real struggle for them but now, working for the newly nationalised mining industry and newly promoted, life should have been getting better. It would have, except they kept producing offspring every year or so, that meant with so many mouths to feed and bodies to clothe, as well as cronies to drink with, finances would always be tight.

Mam finally built up enough courage to bring her plan into action, her resolve to do lay down a marker strengthened by the knowledge that she could not bear any more children, not after Mary. 'Enough was enough, what was good for the goose was good for the gander.'

On the second Sunday of the school holidays, the family routine had begun as normal; Dad was at the Working Mans' Club and Mam cooking dinner. We kids were playing in the street, not wanting to wander too far when Sunday dinner was only an hour away.

At about twelve o clock, Mam went to the pantry, washed her hands and wiped her face with the flannel then said to Betty, 'Keep an eye on dinner lassie,' and then disappeared upstairs. Ten minutes later, she came down wearing her best frock, hair brushed, face lightly powdered and applying bright red lipstick as she re-entered the kitchen.

She looked flushed but her face was set with purpose.

'Ee where ye gannin Mam?' asked Betty, looking at her in wonder.

'What's good for that waster is good for me. I'll see you later lass, ye and Patsy look after dinner,' she replied and strode purposely out the door.

We were in mid game, trying to haul Dennis onto the roof of the coal-house currently substituting for a temple in India, where Gunga Din and his English soldier friends were preparing to fight off marauding Indian tribes.

The sight of Mam looking very handsome in her striped frock with her handbag over her arm and a steely look in her eyes stopped us dead. She breezed past us with her head held high, staring straight ahead as we stared in open-mouthed astonishment as she disappeared into the avenue at the end of our terrace.

Dennis began to wail for his Mam who appeared to have left us all; I worried who was going to cook dinner and Eric and George looked at each other in amazement. After all, she should be in the house making sure there was enough food to go round. I wondered if, and hoped that she was going off to buy some more meat as we rarely got more than a slither of the delicious luxury.

'Bloody hell,' exclaimed Eric, and we all scrambled to the kitchen door to find out what was going on.

'Where's me Mam gannin Betty?' Eric asked breathlessly.

'Aa divvint knaa' she replied, ferociously beating the Yorkshire pudding batter, 'bugger off ontil dinner's ready,' she ordered.

She might have only been five foot tall but we did not dare challenge her, so we went back outside to our game wondering if that was the last we would see of our Mam. We could not blame her if she was running off, who in their right mind would put up with us lot, especially during school holidays.

The sun shone down on Mam as she marched the half-mile or so to the Social Club behind Woolworths where she paused outside to summon up all her courage before stepping forward and with a huge sigh, entered the lions' den.

It was the first time she had been inside a Club or even a pub for that matter, the unfamiliar sights, sounds and especially smells unnerved her. She stopped in the doorway to the bar, allowing her eyes to become accustomed to the cool gloom of the room after the brightness and glare of the midday sun. The club was busy but not full and she noticed that the group of men at the far end of the bar who had been in animated conversation were staring at her in open-mouthed silence. The few other members scattered around the bar also stopped talking or drinking and stared in disbelief at this woman who had just come into *their* bar.

You would have heard a pin drop as Mam, having got her bearings, walked across to an empty table in a corner just opposite the group of drinkers by the bar. She sat down behind one of the low tables, settling back into the imitation leather upholstery of the bench that ran around that corner of the room and fixed her eyes defiantly on a spot over the far window, a set and very determined expression on her face.

Rubbing his hands anxiously, the barman walked over to her, not quite knowing what to do, this was the first woman he had ever seen in the bar and he was not sure whether to throw her out or ignore her. 'What do you want lass?' he asked, meaning, 'What the bloody hell are you doing in here, there're no women allowed?'

'Aa'll hev whatever the baldy headed bugger over there is having,' she replied, pointing at my bewildered and acutely embarrassed Dad who was wishing the ground would swallow him up.

The Barman looked at Mam in astonishment and said, 'He's drinking whisky Missus.'

'Right, I'll have one of them.'

Aa suppose you want a double as well?' said the barman sarcastically.

'Aye, if that's what he's drinking,' she replied defiantly.

One of the men standing next to Dad broke the silence that had gripped the group, turning to Dad he said, 'Isn't that yor Etty Geordie?'

Dad nodded, too dumbfounded to speak, wishing he were somewhere else.

With a quizzical expression on his face, the Barman looked over to Dad for help. Dad swallowed and nodded his head confirming Mam's order to the perplexed man.

A few minutes later, Mam sipped her first whisky, the amber liquid burning its way down her throat and into her chest forcing her to stifle a rising, gagging-cough, just managing to control it. She found the afterglow pleasant and enjoyed the warm feeling spreading through her. It was her first drink of alcohol but it was not to be her last.

Later, the pair of them walked back into Pont Street, Mam with a victorious smile on her face was linking Dad, holding him close to her as though she had just won him in a man catching competition. Dad, on the other hand, looked as though he had just lost his liberty - which he had!

The atmosphere at dinner was just a little strained but Mam had won, that was the last time Dad went out on a Sunday without her.

The following Sunday heralded a new Routine: Mam and Dad got up after their usual lie in but there was something strange; Mam was wearing shorts and a white blouse with whitened sandshoes while Dad was wearing lightweight trousers with his shirt unbuttoned at the neck and sleeves rolled up. It was the first time I had seen Dad dressed without a tie!

Mam started to prepare Sunday dinner with Betty and Pat but left them to it at about eleven when her and Dad, who had been reading the Sunday Sun, got up and went outside.

We stood and watched as Dad walked across the lane, opened the wooden door to one of the air raid shelters built between the toilets and disappeared inside the building. There was a bit of banging and cursing before he emerged a couple of minutes later holding the handlebars of a bike that as he emerged, grew into a tandem. Not having seen one before I stood in awe as it came into view and I wondered what it was.

He eventually got the machine into the lane and lined it up facing south.

Holding it steady, he looked at Mam and said, 'Howay then Etty, let's be gannin.'

Mam walked over and mounted the bike, adjusting her shorts, which had revealed more leg than she had intended.

'Right-o George, am ready,' she said with one foot on the ground the other on a pedal ready to push off.

Dad mounted the bike and after a couple of false starts that brought hoots off laughter from us, they wobbled off down the street and disappeared into the avenue.

Dinner was a little later than usual and Sundays would never be the same again.

A couple of days later, Mam gathered George, me, Viv and Dennis together in the kitchen and gave each of our faces a good flannelling, leaving them tingling and just a tiny bit sore.

'Yor gannin to see ye Granddad Carr today bairns so you'd better behave yorsells or ye'll feel the back of my hand,' she warned us with a look that could scare a grown man and often did.

I had been wondering why Mam had given us freshly washed tee shirts and shorts to wear that morning. There was nothing out of the ordinary about the regulation, multi-striped tee shirts and khaki shorts we boys wore or the checked gingham frock that Vivian had been given to wear, what marked the day out as different were four pairs of shiny, new brown sandals Mam brought out of the sitting room. The 'Ticky Man' must have been.

She lined us up one by one and solemnly put the new sandals on our feet.

I received the obligatory, 'Bah yor a soft shite laddie, stand still or Aa'll give you something to mither aboot,' when I winced as she pulled the leather through the buckle of my sandal far too tightly, nipping the skin on my foot. This made me hop about trying to get the sandal off before I finally fell onto the floor. She grabbed my leg and pulled me to her, trapping my still twitching leg between her knees in order to get to my foot. Thankfully, she slackened the buckle allowing blood to flow back to my pinched foot and roughly pushed me to one side before gently lifting Dennis onto her knees and fitting his sandals.

George said, 'Aa'll put me an on,' and grabbing his sandals he ran to the foot of the stairs to do so.

Granddad and Granny Carr lived down a quiet country road in a terraced cottage in the tiny hamlet of Chevington, about seven miles north of Ashington. I had been there before and looked forward to seeing them and tasting some of Granny's delicious homemade cakes as well as playing in the fields that surrounded their cottage.

Sitting next to the window, I found the bus trip to Chevington as exciting as usual, as I looked at the unspoilt Northumbrian countryside. Viv sat between George and me and we tried desperately not to touch her, she being a girl! Mam and Dad sat in front of us; Dennis on Mam's knee; Dad, looking even more morose than normal was wearing a black suit and tie, the significance of which was lost on us kids!

It was another glorious day when Mam hurried us off the bus at Chevington Road Ends and fussily gathered us together until the bus had departed before herding us toward the cottage a mile or more down the quiet road. Once the noise of the bus had disappeared, the only sound that remained was that of birds singing in the high hedgerows and our shouts and giggles as we ran down the road chasing each other or stopped to look through gates making 'Mooing' sounds at the huge black and white cows in their fields.

41

My thoughts turned to my huge Granddad and the way he had to duck his head to pass through the doors in his cottage, 'Dad,' I asked tentatively, 'why's Granddad so big?

Dad smiled and answered, 'Aye he was a big bugger wasn't he.'

His use of the past tense escaped me and I said, 'He's the biggest man Aa've ivvor seen.'

Dad looked down at me and said, 'Whey he's that big because his Great, Great, Great, Great Granddad was Willie Carr.'

'Who's Willie Carr?' I asked.

Dad smiled and said, 'Whey man he was the "Giant of Blyth."'

'A giant!' I almost shouted, 'did he live up a beanstalk?'

Mam interrupted and said, 'Gan on George tell the bairns aboot Willie Carr.'

George, Vivian and I jostled for places as we walked along, waiting for Dad to tell us about the giant, Mam picking up Dennis so he could hear.

With a wry smile, Dad said, 'Aboot two hundred years ago my ancestor was a blacksmith in Blyth.'

'Did he shoe horses?' asked George.

'Nur,' Dad continued, 'he made things for the ships, like anchors and chains but I suppose he might have shoed horses as weel. He was famous for carrying anchor chains and drinking gin and used to show off his massive strength for a drink, oh and he did some prize fighting as weel.'

I imagined a giant walking along with an anchor in each hand, chains dragging along behind and asked, 'Hoo big was he Dad?'

'Six foot four but that made him a giant in them days.'

I tried to picture six foot four and not sure how tall that was, asked, 'Hoo big is six foot four?'

Dad thought for a moment and answered, 'Just a couple of inches smaller than yor Granddad.'

I thought for a second and asked, 'Whey does that make Granddad a giant as weel?'

'Just aboot,' Dad answered.

Then he said, 'He's fettled a few buggers in his time mind.'

Mam interrupted saying, 'Aye he knocked the landlord oot at the Widdrington Inn cos he wouldn't sell him a drink after last orders.'

'What happened to him?' asked George.

Dad took up the story, 'The landlord phoned the Bobby who came to throw Granddad oot and yor Granddad knocked him doon as weel.'

'Heck,' I said, 'what happened to him, did he gan te prison?'

'When the Bobby cum roond he phoned Morpeth Police Station and they sent a Black Maria full of policemen.'

'Did they lock him up?' Viv asked.

'Whey nur,' Dad went on, 'he knocked most of them buggers doon as weel and the rest backed off and let him gan hyem. They went te the cottage the next day and arrested him when he was sober.'

Mam said, 'He was boond ower te keep the peace but was back in the pub the same night as though nowt had happened.'

'There was only one bugger that yor Granddad was feared off,' Dad said smiling.

'Who's that Dad?' I asked, wondering if it was another Giant.

'Yor Grandmother.'

'Me Granny, but she's just little!' I said incredulously.

George added, 'That's stupid, Granddad's two times bigger than Granny man.

'Aye yor right,' Dad said, 'but when he was drunk or swore she took a bamboo rod to him and always gave him a good walloping.'

'Did he not try to stop her from hurting him?' I asked, picturing my tiny Granny beating my giant Granddad.

'Nur yor Granddad might have bashed a few men in his time but he would never raise his hand to a woman, especially not your Granny,' Dad said.

'Not like ye,' Mam hissed at Dad.

We were approaching the cottages and Mam gathered us together again.

'Right A want ye's all to be on yor best behaviour,' and glaring at Viv, she said menacingly, 'and Aa divvint want te hear a cheep from ye when yor in yor Granny's hoose, got that?'

I was foolish enough to ask, 'Can we play in Granddad's field Mam?'

I just managed to duck sufficiently to take the power out of my Mams swinging hand as she snarled, 'What have Aa just towld ye, there'll be nee running around today, de ye understand that ye simple bugger?'

I had received her message but could not understand why we could not play in the field, after all, this was where the grownups had sent us to run wild on our last visit. Granddad had a smallholding that included the small field where he kept goats. He had taken on the smallholding when he was too old to manage his farm and none of his three sons wanted to take it on, not that he had offered it to Dad!

We turned off the road and around the corner of the end red brick cottages and onto the cobbled back lane that led to Granddad's back door, easily recognisable by the large green water butt outside.

As we approached the door, Mam again warned, 'Noo be quiet all of ye.'

Jim, Dad's younger brother who still lived at home came out to greet us and walked straight up to Dad, solemnly shaking hands with him before they whispered a few words to each other. He then greeted Mam with a hug and a few more whispered words.

43

I was wishing they would hurry up, I wanted to get in and see Granny and have some of her cakes but my Mam's warnings prevented George, Vivian or I from entering.

Mam eventually ushered us into the cottage sitting room where my tiny Granny, who had been sitting tearfully by the fire, rose and went to my Dad saying, 'Hello bonny lad,' and reached up to hug him. Diminutive and very neat, Granny barely gave Mam the time of day - Mam being a Waterford and the descendant of a Gypsy Queen to boot.

Granny then gave each of us kids a kiss on the cheek, not being used to such overt signs of affection we all wiped our cheeks while smiling embarrassingly, still it was better than being beaten with a bamboo rod!

I still had no idea why everyone was so solemn and stood by the table that was dressed in a white linen tablecloth and laden with cakes and sandwiches. I was desperate to reach out and take one but a stern glance from my Mam was enough for me to retreat empty-handed to join the others in the shadows.

Granny took Dad's arm and said, 'Come on George pet, I'll tek ye up to see him,' the two of them disappearing through the door to the stairs.

Mam followed them, while black suited Uncle Jim, a bachelor all his life and a man of few words stood silently looking into the fire, ignoring the four of us standing quietly, looking covetously at the bounty on the table. With Mam gone the temptation of the cakes and sandwiches proved too much for us, we advanced cautiously toward the table and stared at them for a while, until George, being the bravest lifted his hand up toward some cream topped buns.

'Ye'd best leave them until your Granny says to have them,' Uncle Jim said without turning his head, and in a voice so deep and sad that all four of us retreated to behind the sofa to stand in nervous silence.

I could not understand why my Granddad was upstairs; ever since being told we were coming, I had been looking forward to seeing him. The huge man had a full head of white hair, matching beard and gentle eyes that filled you with warmth when he smiled at you. He obviously loved children and had made us welcome on our last visit, showing us around his small holding, pointing out to us all the different types of vegetables he was busy growing.

Eventually, looking even sadder than before, Mam, Dad, and Granny came back into the room and stood beside our morose Uncle.

Granny looked up at my Mam and said, 'Come on Etty we'll make the tea,' and led her into the tiny kitchen.

Dad came across to where we were still half hiding behind the sofa and said, 'George, Syd, haway, come with me and say good bye to your Granddad.' We reluctantly left our spot by the table and followed him in silence up the stairs as I wondered where Granddad was going.

A long narrow passage with two doors off to bedrooms ran from the top of the stairs to a small window at the far-end. The net-curtained window provided very little light at my level, especially as a wooden trellis with a huge and very long ornate box standing on it blocked most of it. The box was backlit from the window casting it into shadow and making it appear dark and very foreboding.

Dad bent down and picked me up, slowly revealing the contents of the box in all their Gothic horror! What I saw made me cling to Dad with all my strength. Stretched out before me was the figure of a man, a very tall man. I was by his feet and he seemed to stretch on forever as my eyes followed the body slowly up and up, past his huge crossed hands until they eventually reached the face, a large face covered in white hair with eyelids closed tight. With a gasp, I realised that I would never see the warmth of his eyes again as with horror, I recognised my dead Granddad.

'Is he Deed Dad,' I whispered, finding it hard to breathe and desperate to get away from this awful sight.

'Of course he is stupid,' said George, peering at Granddads boots over the bottom of the coffin.

'Sssh,' Dad whispered as he squeezed along between the coffin and the wall of the passage toward my Granddad's head with me still in his arms. I was terrified and wondered why he was taking me along there and clung to him for dear life. When he got to the top of the coffin, to my horror he said, 'Gan on kiss yor Granddad goodbye,' and lowered me toward that huge, dead, white-haired face.

I tried in vain to climb up my Dads arms as he lowered me closer, holding me so that my face was an inch above the lifeless face, 'Gan on,' he urged. I tried to hold myself clear but he lowered me until my face was resting on the soft white hair of his beard and I was gasping for breath, tears running down my cheeks and falling onto my dead Granddad. He held me there for a second before he took me back to the end of the coffin, and swapped me with George, putting him through the same ordeal.

I was still trembling in shock, tears blurring my vision when dad lowered George down next to me. He furiously wiped his mouth with the back of his hand and spat, the spittle spaying all over my tee shirt.

'Settle doon noo,' Dad said and ushered us down stairs. Because of their age, Viv and Dennis escaped the horrors of the farewell kiss.

Back downstairs, Mam gave us a cake each and ushered us outside while the adults sat inside drinking tea.

'Who killed Granddad?' I asked George through a mouthful of cake as I began to feel a little better.

'Nee bugger you daft sod,' he replied, 'he died of auld age man.'

Dennis who was still unaware of why we were there asked 'Whose been killed? Has Syd killed somebody?'

This infuriated George, and he said, 'Nebody's been killed man, Granddads deed that's all, Syd didn't kill him.' He was angry at having to explain everything to his ignorant younger brothers and sister.

45

Viv who had been half listening to the conversation saw a chance to create some mischief and not having fully understood what had been said or what was happening, skipped into the cottage yelling with a cheeky grin, 'Mam wor Syd's kilt Granddad!'

Mam leapt to her feet and with a fearsome look on her face, dragged Viv out by the arm, the grin wiped from her face.

Looking at them approaching, I thought, 'Oh no here it comes and I haven't done anything.' In a bid to save my skin I ran forward shouting, 'Aa didn't kill him Mam,' desperate to avoid punishment for someone else's crime.

Mam pushed Viv toward us, and much to my relief said, 'Aa knaa bonny lad, it's this wicked little bugger here opening her mooth withoot bloody thinking,' and turned and stormed back into the cottage.

A little later and much to my dismay, our older siblings turned up to pay their respects and we watched as they were ushered into the cottage.

As they quietly filed into the cottage, I thought, 'There's not going to be many cakes left after all them have had some.'

The following day, Eric, George, Ian Brown and I were playing cricket in the back lane, Eric batting, George bowling with an old tennis ball, Ian keeping wicket while I fielded, running back and forward a headless chicken, chasing the ball in whatever direction Eric hit it. George was about to bowl again when a large, dark grey car turned from the avenue into the lane and slowly headed towards us. The car was very curvy almost round, with a rounded roof, rounded wheel arches, rounded bonnet, and rounded boot; it was a grey and very shiny Austin A45 and we watched in awed silence as it drove slowly toward us.

Eric and Ian dragged the dustbin that we had been using for stumps to one side as the car pulled up alongside George.

The driver's window was down and a round face peered out of the round car and asked in a deep voice with an unusual accent, 'Can you tell me where George Carr lives son?'

George froze, unsure whether to answer as he frantically tried to remember what mischief he might have been up to that warranted a visit from someone in a car, 'He might be a detective,' he thought to himself.

Eventually, he said, 'Aye, I live ower there,' and pointed to our house.

The driver chuckled and said, 'It's not you I've come to see lad, it's your Dad.'

He got out of his round car and stood for a moment taking in his surroundings. He was a very round man. He had a round balding head with round shiny cheeks, several round chins, and a large round body, looking to me as if he was trying to burst out of his skin! We stood gawping at this smartly dressed, round man, wondering who he was, and what he wanted from our Dad.

'I'm your Uncle Alec,' he said smiling.

'Yor not coming to live with us an all?' ventured a worried George.

46

'No son, I've just come for your Granddads funeral.' he replied as he walked to the back door, leaving us to stare in envy at his new, big, round, and shiny car.

Having arrived the night before and staying at my Auntie Jen's house in Highmarket on the other side of town, he had driven over to see my Dad, his younger brother. Mam had told us that Uncle Alec lived in Norwich where he owned a couple of bicycle shops but this was the first time any of us younger ones had seen him.

A little later, Eric, George and I were enviously peering through the front window of the car when Uncle Alec came outside and obviously happy to show off his pride and joy, asked, 'Do you boys want a ride in my car?'

We nodded furiously, excited at the thought of travelling in this beautiful machine, we had never ridden in a car before let alone an almost brand new one. He opened the back door warning us to be careful with the leather seats and we climbed in perching ourselves carefully on the rear bench seat. Once we were in, he climbed into the front and drove off around the streets, his arm leaning on the open window with a self-satisfied, vain smirk on his round face.

The trouble with being small and sitting in the centre of the rear bench seat of a car is that it is difficult to see out of the windows; it spoilt my journey by having such a limited view. To better my vantage point I turned and climbed on my knees onto the seat to look out of the small back window and in doing so pushed my new sandals on the top of the leather seat to lever myself up. To my horror, I heard a ripping sound and quickly turned and slid back to my original position and looked to see if the other two had heard the rip. I was lucky, they both had their faces pressed against the windows and the noise of the wind through the open window had masked the sound from my Uncle.

I looked down at the seat, my heart pounding and saw where the point of the buckle of one of my sandals had punctured the pristine leather, leaving a neat one-inch rip. My mind was in turmoil, I could not begin to think what punishment I would receive for spoiling my Uncle Alec's new car so I put my hand over the rip to hide it from view and sat there like a condemned man for the rest of the trip.

Back at Pont Street, I continued to sit with my hand over the rip until Eric and George had climbed out of the car and then quickly scurried out after them closing the door behind me, not daring to look at my round Uncle. He left later in the day as I stood with the others watching him go, wondering when he would find the rip and when he would send for me to receive punishment for my disgraceful act of vandalism, even though it had been unintentional.

As it was, he did not find it until the following day and my Auntie Jen's son, Cousin Alec, found himself blamed for something he had not done. I had almost forgotten about the incident but still felt a little guilty when I heard a few days later that Alec had taken the blame for my misdemeanour - for a few seconds anyway.

Granddads funeral took place a few days later; little ones not included. I watched in awe as my oldest brother Jim put on his very smart ATC uniform and marched out the door with the Mam, Dad and Betty. Left in charge of looking after the four youngest ones, Pat ensured there would be no mischief that day.

Shortly afterwards Granny Carr and Uncle Jim moved to a new council house in Hadston, a small village a few miles from Chevington, where Granny's sister and other daughters lived.

During the following months, members of the family meticulously dug over Granddad's smallholding many times - not to remove weeds or to plant vegetables. Some years earlier, not trusting greedy bankers, he had taken the proceeds from the sale of his farm and did not tell anyone what he intended to do with the cash. Believing he had hidden the money somewhere in his Chevington smallholding, the Family attacked it with picks and shovels but to no avail, the cash remains unfound.

Toward the end of the summer holidays, Jim returned from having spent his summer wild camping at the Chine with his mates Chris, and Bob. Their tent had been an old whitewashed sheet tied between two poles and then pegged down. They whitewashed the sheet in order to give it some waterproofing and it had proved to be quite effective keeping them dry during a light shower of rain.

The Chine was the estuary of the river Wansbeck, a mile South of Newbiggin where sand dunes rolled down to the river mouth and local Fishermen moored a handful of small fishing boats and dinghies. It was a lovely spot to camp and a great place for adventure, especially for fourteen-year-old lads, as there would have been many other lads and lasses of their age camping there.

When he got back, he told us in graphic detail of having seen a Spitfire crash into Newbiggin Bay; his description was so vivid that I believed for most of my life that I had actually witnessed it myself. The fishermen of Newbiggin had taken part in the salvage of the fighter, the crew of the boat finding the body of the unfortunate pilot having the sad task of returning him to shore.

A day or so later, on a wet and miserable overcast morning, Mam had banished Eric, George and me to the back yard as Dad had just gone to bed after his long shift at work. We were damp, miserable, and hungry - nothing new as we were always hungry; just the level of hunger varied.

Jim, who had been to Dad's allotment, came into the yard and stopped to look at the three of us, huddled in the corner and as he did so, a look of anger and resentment spread over his face.

'Right ye three hang on there a minute, Aa'll be back,' he said before disappearing into the house. He returned a few minutes later looking slightly red faced but with a set and determined look on his face.

He ordered, 'Haway then,' and walked off down the street with the three of us trotting on behind. We did not dare ask where we were going or why, not the way he was looking, so we hurried along behind him, almost running to keep up with his brisk pace.

As we turned onto Milburn Road I thought we must be going to the Pictures at the Piv but wondered who was going to pay, so asked, 'Are we gannin te the pictures Jim?'

He looked back over his shoulder as he marched on and smiling he answered, 'Aye we might be Young'un but forst Am gannin te get ye three summick te eat.' Eric and George looked at each other and smiled in anticipation while I wondered if he was going to buy some crisps or sweets and almost drooled in anticipation but before we reached the Piv, Jim marched into the café a few doors before the Piv and turned to beckon us in.

I'd never been in a café before and I don't think the other two had either; this one had a counter down the right side and seating cubicles down the left but what struck me was the wonderful smell. The smell of hot food and drinks swam over me and I stopped to swallow them eagerly.

George said, 'Bloody hell summick smells bloody smashing,' and like me, raised his head slightly to sniff in the warm comforting smells.

The three of us, all wearing baggy shorts, drizzle-damp threadbare pullovers, socks wrinkled around our ankles and our feet stuffed into battered plimsolls, stood by the door feeling very self-conscious.

'Sit yorsells doon lads,' Jim ordered before turning to the woman behind the counter, 'Can Aa hev three pies, mash, peas and gravy please Missus and four teas as weel?'

The woman took down Jim's order and after some mental arithmetic said, 'That'll be four and sixpence pet.'

Much to our astonishment, Jim pulled out a crumbled, ten-shilling note, handing it to the woman who took the money and after rummaging in the cash register handed over his change. As Jim joined us at the table, we sat excitedly and eagerly waiting for this unexpected bounty.

George asked, 'Where did ye get ten bob from?'

'Oot of yor father's wallet that's where,' he answered defiantly.

'De ye mean ye stole it from him?' Eric guessed, amazed that he had dared to sneak into Dad's bedroom and take the money while he slept.

Jim answered, 'Aye that's right, if that owld bugger can afford te gan drinking with his cronies every night, he can afford to buy ye lot some food.'

We did not ask any more questions as the meal had arrived and we were too busy stuffing hot food into our mouths to waste effort in talking.

It was then that Les, a thirty-year-old distant cousin who was currently lodging alongside Uncle Alex in our front room, came in looking very flustered.

He stormed up to where we were eating and said to Jim, 'By bloody hell lad yor in bloody big trouble, yor dad's gannin mad at hyem, he reckoned ye'd tak-

49

ing his ten bob and he says he'll swing for ye if ye divvint get the money back right noo!'

I stopped eating and looked at Jim to see if he was frightened of been murdered by Dad and asked, 'What are ye gannin te de Jim?'

Jim smiled defiantly and said to Les, 'Whey it doesn't look as if he's gannin te get his money back does it, cos these hev eaten it.'

George was quickly finishing off his pie, determined not to lose any to mad dads or worried cousins and spluttered through a mouthful of pie and mash, 'Aye yor too frigging late.'

Jim said, 'Divvint rush, finish yor food and Aa'll gan and sort this oot with the miserable owld Bugger,' and rose from his seat, placing two shillings from the ten bob on the table.

'Here Eric,' he said, 'tek this money and the three of yor gan te the matinee,' then turned and left, followed by a perplexed Les who was sure he was going to be witness to murder.

There was no murder and we never found out exactly what happened but Jim apparently stood up to Dad, arguing that he should feed his kids before he spent money on his cronies and booze. Whatever did happen, my big brother became even more of a hero to me.

The Sunday night ritual of bath and haircuts signalled the end of the summer holidays and the start of a new term at school. Mam hauled the tin bath into the kitchen and placed it in front of the fire where the kettle and a couple of large pans were boiling water. She bathed Dennis first, followed by the rest of us in order of age, Eric being the last. It was also his last ritual bath as he was approaching eleven.

The process was not pleasant; Mam scrubbing and gouging skinny unprotected bodies with a coarse soapy flannel was quite painful, especially when she was mining deep inside your ear with a corner of the flannel.

While Mam dried us off, Dad organised his hand operated hair clippers, comb and scissors in preparation for butchering our unruly mops. He was not what you would call gentle and his clippers were far from sharp but he thought he was a dab hand at it and enjoyed the task. He did not cut our hair in order to improve our appearance; he just wanted to ensure that our hair did not provide a suitable refuge for nits!

Mam, emptying the bath and taking it outside where she hung it on the outside of the pantry wall was the signal for Dad to begin butchering. He pulled out one of the kitchen chairs and ordered Eric to come forward and be tortured first.

His method of cutting hair was simple; using his scissors, he cut a line around our heads to mark where he was to use the clippers too. Above that line, he used the scissors to shorten the hair, occasionally snagging and pulling out the odd hair or two that brought winces from us. He then used the clippers to cut our hair

50

below the scissor mark. This was a relatively straightforward procedure but also a quite painful one due to his lack of finesse and his none too sharp instruments.

Eric and George had both suffered the procedure and were rubbing sore patches on their heads when Dad lifted me into place. It went as normal, Dad snipping and clipping with relish until, trying to get my hair as short as possible, he dug the clippers just a bit too deep, causing the corner of the clippers to cut into my neck just behind the ear, leaving a small but very painful wound.

I had already winced a few times as he had unintentionally pulled out a few hairs but when I let out a louder cry as the clippers cut me, Mam, back at her clippie mat said, 'Trust that soft shite to cry.'

Pushing his thumb over the cut to hide it from Mam and to stem the trickle of blood, Dad said, 'Keep still, or ye'll mck it worse.' I sat motionless wondering just how much worse it could get.

Eric, who had been stupid enough to pass his eleven plus the year before, was anxiously trying to get his uniform ready for the following day when he was due to start at Bedlington Grammar School. Starting a new school can be traumatic enough but Mam and Dad's inability to appreciate the commitment required to ensure he was ready made his stress a lot worse than it needed to be.

His uniform was not of the correct school pattern; it was a green, non-standard blazer with a poorly sewn on badge and, his first long trousers, a grey pair, had a patch on the back. Through their neglect, they had ensured that he would be a target for bullies as soon as he got to school. What makes the whole episode sad is that grants were available for uniforms but our parents were not prepared to make the little effort required to process applications. Consequently, Eric was to suffer almost unbearable humiliation.

We were ready for school.

5

Penny A Pee

Betty was working at a small local factory that made cake decorations, Jim was in his last year at school, Pat, who was coming to terms with her damaged eyesight, was in her second year at senior school. Eric was making his first trip to Bedlington Grammar and George and I had the task of taking Viv to school for the first time. Mam did not bother to get out of bed to see any of us off to work or school, not when she could stay in bed until the early morning pandemonium had ended.

For me, the start of the new term meant a move from the wooden infants' first year classroom to the second year classroom in the main building. The atmosphere in the main building was very different to the bright well-lit hut where I had spent the first year. The main building consisted of a large gloomy main hall with classrooms grouped the outside that were accessed by large half-glazed doors. The classrooms were typical Victorian with large windows set high in the wall to prevent schoolchildren from looking out and being distracted from their lessons.

The new term also marked our new teacher's savings scheme, designed to help us save our pennies for Christmas or some other grand occasion in the future, if we had any pennies! She explained the scheme to us on the first day and asked everyone to join the scheme and bring in sixpence a week commencing the following day.

Arriving home that evening, I excitedly explained the scheme to Mam who was half listening as she prepared the evening meal.

'Aye,' she said 'gan on and start, it'll save me having to buy ye presents.' That was not the response I had hoped for, I had wanted to buy presents for the others; I had not expected to have to pay for my own.

She gave me a threepenny bit to add to the three large pennies she knew I had collected from returning pop bottles to the corner shop and said, 'Here ye are, Aa'll give you sixpence every week.' Naively, I believed her.

The boys' toilets at the South School were in the playground up against the perimeter wall and were quite basic consisting of a row of cubicles at the back with a long urinal in front. The urinal was simply an area of the five and a half foot surrounding wall, rendered and treated with some sort of black waterproof coating, it had an open drain at the foot of the wall that carried the urine away. During the first break of the day, I hurried to the toilet where I found George, Matty and a couple of other lads in animated discussion.

'Bet ye that we can piddle higher up the wall than ye two,' Matty said to the two other lads as he stood nonchalantly with his elbow on George's shoulder, his ginger hair glowing in the morning sun. The lads just wanted to use the urinal and get back to play but like most of the other kids; they were intimidated by Matty and afraid to refuse the challenge.

'It's a penny a piddle, the winner keeps the money,' George said holding his hand out for the coppers.

One of the lads, a blonde well-scrubbed boy in George's class, nervously said, 'I've only got a thrupenny bit,' and held it out to show George.

Matty grabbed the coin saying, 'You can have three goes then,' knowing that the lad might just about manage one pee.

I stood watching with two or three other boys who had come in and who were now keen to see the outcome of the challenge.

'Right you gan forst,' Matty ordered and stepped back to let them have a go.

The first lad stepped up to the mark, prepared himself, took aim, and squirted a stream of pee onto the wall. He rose onto his tiptoes, desperately trying to get his pee as high as possible. It was a good effort and he left a wet mark just above his head and two-thirds up the wall while the audience murmured words of appreciation.

'Not bad, now you,' Matty said as he pushed the blonde lad forward.

The lad was clearly unhappy and nervously prepared himself. Obviously intimidated by Matty and embarrassed by having to perform with an audience, the blonde lad struggled valiantly to pee. His face contorted with the effort but the more he tried the less likely it seemed he was going to succeed. Finally, he man-aged to squeeze out a trickle of pee that wet his shoes and splashed the bottom of the wall. The mocking laughter from the other boys embarrassed the poor lad even more and blushing scarlet; he raced out of the toilets to distance himself from the two bullies.

I felt desperately sorry for him but could not say or do anything in that company.

'Reet, we'll show you how it's done,' Matty bragged as George stepped forward and sent a stream of pee almost to the top of the wall, then with a flourish waved it about leaving a large wet arc across the wall. This drew gasps of admira-tion and several 'wows' from the onlookers.

Matty stepped up, and preparing himself said, 'Not bad Geordie but watch this.' He sent forth a torrent of urine that splashed the wall in front of him, then leaning back; he nonchalantly began to lift his aiming point higher up the wall. Higher and higher, he peed, closer and closer to the top it splashed until with a lit-tle thrust of his hips, he peed straight over the top of the wall.

The lads who had been watching started to shout and cheer but at the same time a roar came from the other side of the wall.

'WHAT THE BLOODY HELL…?' bellowed someone from the other side of the wall, directly below where Mattie's pee must have fallen.

The male teacher on playground duty, who had been standing next to the wall smoking a cigarette, came rushing into the toilet yard. His face was puce with anger; evidence of Mattie's success staining the shoulders of his tweed jacket. He was beside himself with rage knowing exactly what the unexpected shower was.

'Who did this?' he demanded, pointing at his shoulder. 'Come on who did it?'

By this stage, I was desperate for the pee I had gone in for and this shouting was making my need to pee even more so that I stood cross-legged trying not to wet myself.

Matty and George were not going to own up and none of the other lads were brave enough or foolish enough to point the finger at them. This silence enraged the teacher even more.

'Right,' he demanded 'you lot, let's see how high you can pee?' I was delighted at this order and ran forward to relive myself but the teacher stopped me in my tracks.

'Not you, it's the big lads am talking to,' he said holding me back while he pushed Matty, George and two of the onlookers forward to the urinal. 'Go on show me how high you can piss up the wall,' the Teacher ordered.

The two onlookers did their best peeing half-heartedly halfway up the wall while Matty and George just stood there, their bladders already empty.

Comprehension spread across the angry teacher's face, 'Storey, Carr,' he shouted, 'it was one of you two, wasn't it?' a look of triumph on his angry face.

They kept quiet.

'Come with me you two, I know how to find out which one of you did it,' the teacher growled and led them off to vent his fury upon them.

I just about made the urinal when the school bell rang, signalling the end of the break, and I had to pee and pee I did for what seemed like ages. Desperate to finish and join the line to get back into class I desperately squeezed as hard as I could to finish peeing and ran out of the toilets trying to tuck myself away as I did so.

I found myself greeted by titters and sniggers from my classmates who were still in line waiting to go in while our teacher looked for me.

'Miss, Miss, he's here Miss,' they yelled pointing and laughing at me while I tried in vain to hide at the end of the line. My embarrassment was short lived and we returned to class to enjoy a double lesson of art.

Matty and George, on the other hand, were not going to enjoy the rest of the morning. The Teacher took them to the kitchen and made them wait outside while he went inside, filled a glass pitcher with water, picked up a glass, and rejoined them outside. He made them drink several glasses of water each; refilling the pitcher in order to make sure they both drank until he was satisfied, they had had enough. He then made them stand in the corner of his classroom for the next two periods, at the end of which Matty and George both looked in agony, desperate to rid themselves of the painful weight in their bladders.

As I left my class to go home at lunchtime, I saw the Teacher frog marching Matty and George to the toilet, and along with several others, I followed to see what was happening but not daring to go in, we stood outside and listened.

'Right you two let's see how high you can piss now,' bellowed the teacher from inside. As we stood outside listening, one of the lads pointed to the top of the wall where a stream of urine was splashing over. To our amazement, as we watched, a second stream of urine joined the first.

'Bloody hell Geordie, that's the first time ye've managed that,' Matty shouted, not realising he had just incriminated himself.

'Got ye,' yelled the Teacher triumphantly. We then heard him angrily talking to the two champion pee-ers and wondered what punishment they would receive. The Teacher emerged dragging a struggling Matty with him and marched off to the head's office. George came out smiling and we walked off together heading home for lunch.

'What did he giv ye?' I asked.

'Oh just some lines, but did ye not see? Aa pissed ower the top of the wall man,' George said with pride. Although he was pleased, he could pee as high as Matty Story, I am sure it would be a long time before he drank so much water again!

The first weekend of the new school term was interesting.

Dad had gone off very early on Saturday morning without having had his normal sleep after finishing his shift at the pit. Later on, while we younger ones were playing outside a horse and cart turned into the street from the avenue, the horse, clip-clopping toward us. We watched with little interest as it approached; a large black horse with a white star on its forehead and white feathers above its hooves, pulling a neat flatbed wagon mounted on four lorry wheels. However, our interest did pick up when we recognised the driver; it was Dad.

As soon as we realised who it was, we ran forward waving and cheering and walked back alongside the horse our minds racing with possible reasons for him having a horse and cart.

Dad stopped the wagon next to our coal house where oldest brother Jim was leaning on a large shovel. All miners, including Dad, received concessionary coal from the NCB and even with two fires burning almost constantly, we had accrued a large surplus that filled the coal house almost to the roof. Dad had muttered something about having to get rid of it before next year but this comment went over our heads.

Jim and Dad spent 20 minutes shovelling coal onto the back of the wagon, being careful to ensure it would not roll off once the wagon was moving. They loaded over half of the contents of the coal house before Dad stopped, mopping sweat from his forehead, he turned to Eric who had been admiring the horse with the rest of us and ordered, 'Gan and get our bait (packed lunch) from yor Mam lad, yor coming as weel.'

A few minutes later, Dad set of with Eric and Jim sitting next to him on the front of the wagon and headed for Granny Carr's new council house, nine miles away at Hadston. George and I sat on the back and had a ride as far as Station Road in the centre of Ashington before jumping off and walking home.

The round trip took them all day and when they arrived back just before tea, Dad was fast asleep on the back leaving Jim to proudly drive the rig home.

Once home, Dad made Jim and Eric brush and wash the back of the wagon for ages warning them, 'Mek sure it's spotless, we'll want it again next year.'

Eric asked, 'Are we taking some more coal to Granny's next year?'

'No' was the only reply he got, giving us no idea what he wanted it for next year.

Over tea Eric told us of the long trip to Granny's and back, the lunch she had given them and of the inside toilet upstairs next to a bathroom! We were envious and kept interrupting him, asking for more details on what they had seen and done and he was more than happy to oblige.

On Sunday morning, Mam and Dad got up after their lie in and came into the kitchen where the majority of the brood were eating sandwiches and drinking tea. I noticed that Mam did not have her cycling shorts on; instead, she was wearing trousers and a large jumper that I recognised as one of Dad's.

Confused I asked, 'Why are ye wearing me Dad's jumper Mam?'

She smiled uncharacteristically at me and replied, 'Ye'll all find oot soon enough,' and poured herself a cup of tea before starting to prepare Sunday lunch.

Later, while all the lads were playing football in the back street with me in goal to ensure goal scoring was easy, Mam and Dad came out of the house in very strange attire. We stopped playing and stared in amazement; Mam was wearing a large overcoat, trousers, and a headscarf, Dad a large, waxed overcoat with 4 patch pockets and a large belt with a brass buckle. What made it strange was that it was early September and it was a lovely warm, late summer's day.

Dad crossed the street to our converted air-raid shelter, unlocked the padlock on the door, and went inside.

I asked George, who was looking as puzzled as I felt, 'There gannin to be hot on the tandem wearing all them clothes, why are the dressed like that?'

'Buggered if Aa knaa Young'un,' he answered while staring at the shelter door.

To our amazement, Dad came out wearing a crash helmet with goggles strapped to the top and on his hands huge leather gauntlets. He was pushing a motorbike! A motorbike, we had no idea he had one and ran forward to inspect it. We were on the up if Dad had bought a motorbike!

That was not all; Mam took us into the air-raid shelter and proudly showed us her brand new washing machine. It was almost state of the art for 1951; it consisted of a large round zinc tub on legs, a mangle attached to the side and a lid with a handle in the centre that connected to revolving paddles on the inside.

57

Mam demonstrated how her life was to be revolutionised as she stood over the machine turning the handle with gusto, explaining how the paddles would beat clothes clean. I was confused as to how it was going to make her life easier as it looked like hard work to me!

Back outside Dad kicked the motorbike into life and gave the throttle a couple of twists so that we could hear the engine. The noise was terrific; a deep throaty roar that subsided to a steady rhythmic thumping when he eased back the throttle. Tightening the strap on his helmet, he pulled the goggles over his eyes, mounted the bike and motioned for Mam to climb on. She did so eagerly, a little too eagerly and almost toppled the whole thing over before she settled down behind him, wrapping her arms tightly around him as Dad cursed her clumsiness.

Dad had several attempts at finding first gear before he was successful, then sitting straddling the bike and with a look of immense concentration on his face, he slowly let out the clutch. The bike moved forward very slowly, Dad sliding his feet along the ground until he had sufficient speed to cautiously lift them and attempt to engage second gear.

This was obviously quite difficult as the motorbike veered perilously close to the toilets and coalhouses but he managed to avoid them and keep upright before he veered toward the curb on the other side, just managing to avoid it with an unsteady swerve.

The bike with the two of them on wove its way spluttering down the street before it eventually disappeared into the avenue. Probably not the way Dad had intended, but at least he was out of sight of our critical gazes. He probably had wanted to roar of into the distance, leaving us watching in admiration but his abilities somewhat prevented this.

'When did Dad learn to ride a motorbike?' I asked Jim.

He laughed and replied, 'He hasn't Young'un, not yet anyway,' and chuckling to himself, he walked back into the house.

Sundays continued to evolve.

The second Tuesday back at school was difficult. I had spent the evening before pleading with Mam for the sixpence to hand into the teacher the following day for the class savings scheme.

At first, she ignored me as though I was not there but after a while, my constant pleading obviously began to irritate her as she resolved the matter with a swift slap and screeched, 'Stop bloody mithering me, I'll give you the money in the morning when ye Dad gets hyem.'

Lying in bed that night I realised that Mam had suckered me - dad did not get home until after we had left for school. I spent a restless night worrying about having to face the teacher without sixpence. The ordeal was just as bad as I imagined.

At roll call, the teacher read out the first name on the register, waited while the lad replied, 'Yes Miss,' took his sixpence forward to her desk, and duly handed it over.

She continued with the register, receiving the sixpences from each boy as she went until she called out 'Sydney Carr.'

'Yes Miss,' I replied and stayed in my seat blushing madly.

'Well have you got your sixpence?'

'No Miss, av'e forgot it, but Aa'll bring it in the sefternoon Miss.' I could feel everyone's eyes upon me and knew that no one, especially Miss believed me.

'Okay; Roger Carter,' saying the next name on the register she continued while I sat crestfallen hoping that I would get the money from Dad at lunchtime and regain my credibility that afternoon. I did not get the money and during the rest of the term, only managed to save sixpence once myself. Consequently, every Tuesday roll call I sat and watched as the other boys answered their names and walked up to the teacher to hand over their money while I answered my name and sat in burning embarrassment waiting for the lesson to start.

What made the matter worse was that I knew that several of the boys' fathers worked under my Dad at the colliery and they always had their money.

Wondering what Dad spent his money on, I had asked Mam about it. She replied sarcastically, 'Whore mongering with his cronies at Blyth.' This went straight over my innocent head, where it stayed until I was older, wiser, and knew more about life.

My Tuesday ritual embarrassment was nothing compared to what Eric had to put up with at Grammar school. He rarely had the money that he needed weekly for school dinners and spent many a lonely and miserable hour, waiting at the bus stop for Betty to bring him money that Mam had promised to send. Mam obviously never intended to send Betty with any money but continued to promise Eric that she would.

With a little effort, Mam could have arranged free meals for Eric but she never did. His embarrassment would get a whole lot worse before he left grammar school!

It was about this time that Betty got married. I have no recollection of the wedding only that she married John, the lad from Newbiggin she had been courting for twelve months. I remember being sad and happy at the same time when she left to live in a flat overlooking the golf course at Newbiggin Moor; she did look happy and excited, however.

6

Bonfires and Christmas

As autumn advanced, gangs of lads from each street were on the prowl, not looking for trouble just looking for wood to scavenge which, unfortunately, often meant trouble. Bonfire night was approaching.

Eric, George, Ian Brown, and I were in lower Pont Street breaking up large pieces of wood from an old door. We were in a space between toilets and coalhouses and had been attacking the door for some time without success.

Frustrated at our lack of progress, Eric said, 'Hang on, Aa'll gan and get me Dad's axe,' and ran off to fetch it.

Bonfire night generated great excitement and competition between the streets to see who would have the best show. Lack of funds ensured the street firework displays would not amount to much more than a few basic rockets; perhaps a couple of Catherine Wheels and a few Roman candles but they were still magic nights to us pre-tele children.

We stored all the wood and other burning material we collected, in an old air-raid shelter in order to keep it dry but more importantly to prevent anyone of the other street gangs from stealing it in a raid. The bonfires could not for safety reasons be too large as we built them on the other side of the backstreet to our houses, generally in the spaces between outhouses that had been used for dumping ashes in the days before regular rubbish collections began.

Eric returned a few minutes later with a large, long-handled axe and set about lining up the doorframe for a good chopping. With the doorframe in position, he planted his feet firmly, spat into his hands and grasped the axe determined to show the doorframe that he was the boss and us younger kids how to do things properly. We stepped back to give him plenty of room and stood to watch in admiration as our big brother prepared to destroy the stubborn door.

Lifting the axe up, he placed the blade on the doorframe where he intended to strike, adjusted his aim and taking a deep breath, swung the axe up and back high over his head where, unfortunately, it came into collision with the brick wall of the coal house behind him. The axe hit the wall with a dull thud and bounced off causing Eric to lose control of it.

It seemed to me as if the action in front of us suddenly turned to slow motion. The trajectory of the axe changed and we watched in transfixed horror, as the axe, with predictable inevitably, struck Eric on the back of his unprotected head.

It hit him in almost the same spot that Matty Story had clobbered him last summer!

We were horrified and shocked as he staggered forward dropping the bloodied axe as he just managed to stay upright.

'Frigging hell Eric look at ye shirt,' George yelled.

Eric did not cry out, he just stood there looking dazed as blood ran down his neck, changing the colour of his shirt to crimson. After a couple of seconds his eyes cleared and realising what he had done he raced off home with us running behind, wondering how he was still alive.

By the time he reached home, the back of his shirt was completely red as the wound continued to bleed profusely, but remembering the last time he ran into the house bleeding, he stopped in the yard and shouted, 'Mam, Mam.'

From the urgent tone of his shouts, Mam knew instinctively something serious had happened and rushed to the door. Eric was standing drenched in blood clasping both hands to the back of his head, desperately trying to stem the flow.

She took one look and blasphemed, 'Jesus Christ! Not again,' and rushed inside to get a towel.

She was back in seconds and wrapped a large towel around Eric's head, clamping one hand over the wound and the other over his face in order to apply pressure.

'I bet it was that bloody Matty Storey again wasn't it,' she growled.

Eric tried to tell her it was not but with a towel and Mam's hand clamped over his face, he could only manage a muffled, 'No,' besides he did not care, the pain from the wound was beginning to hurt like hell, and he would dearly like Mam to ease her grip and allow him to breathe!

Mam shouted at George 'Gan and get Jim, he can sort the ginger-heeded bugger oot once 'n' for all.'

George thought about it for a moment, it was very tempting but Matty was a mate of sorts, even if he was a bit of a bully.

'It wasn't him Mam,' he said.

'Divvint ye stick up for that bugger, gan and get Jim,' she screamed back.

George stood his ground and repeated 'It wasn't him man.'

Ian joined in and added, 'It wasn't Matty Mrs Carr.'

Mam prepared to set off to walk toward Ashington Hospital with Eric, holding him in the same grip while he was still trying to breathe and beginning to feel faint from loss of blood or air.

'Who the bloody hell did it if wasn't that worm-eaten, ginger haired bugger?' Mam screamed at us in anger, not just because of the damage to Eric's head but also because she had to walk to the hospital in her piny and slippers again, and dinner still not made.

'He hit hessell with the axe Mam,' I said jogging alongside her.

'Trust ye to say something stupid,' she growled, 'how the bloody hell could he hit himself on the back of his heed with an axe ye simple bugger, eh?'

That was enough for me, I backed off; let Matty be battered, what did I care, rather him getting into trouble than me getting a slap from Mam.

At dinnertime, we managed to convince Mam of the truth, then much to Eric's annoyance, she immediately branded him a, 'Simple Bugger.'

62

Ashington Hospital A&E register had a new entry for Pont Street that probably read; Youth with axe wound to back of head (Pont Street – Tomahawk?).

A few nights later Jim and his mate Bob were sorting out bundles of paper inside the air-raid shelter that contained our store of bonfire material when a raiding party from Sycamore Street struck.

Hoping to go unnoticed, six of them quietly climbed over the alley wall next to the gap between the coalhouse and air-raid shelter. Jim and Bob heard them and hunkered down in the far corner, waiting for their chance to pounce.

George, who was in the back lane, also saw them and yelled, 'We'll get you buggers,' and ran off to get help; even he was not prepared to take on six lads.

Realising they would not have time to carry away any wood worth bothering about, one of the Sycamore Gang lit some paper with a match and threw it spitefully into the shelter and pulled the door closed behind him, slipping the clasp over the latch. They all quickly climbed back over the wall to safety, not being prepared to take on all of the Pont Street lads.

Jim and Bob watched in horror as the burning paper landed on an old sofa that ignited and immediately began to smoulder. Smoke billowed from the sofa, quickly filling the inside of the dark shelter as they clambered over piles of wood to reach the door.

Coughing and spluttering they jumped past the smouldering sofa and made the door only to find they could not open it from the inside. The smoke was now incredibly thick making it almost impossible to breathe forcing them to fall instinctively to their knees in search of air as they battered on the door.

Meanwhile, George who was returning with Eric, Matty, Ian, the Johnson lads and with me running behind, saw the smoke pouring out of the gaps around the door and shouted, 'The bloody swine's hev set fire to wore wood, gan and get some weter.'

As the others raced off to fetch buckets of water, George and I went up to the door, unfastened the hasp, and tried to push it open. We only managed to push it a few inches before something inside stopped us from opening it and then clouds of foul smelling, black smoke engulfed us, driving us back from the door, making us gag from the acrid stench.

George turned and ran off to get water as I stood transfixed watching the smoke pour from the shelter when to my amazement and horror, two smoke blackened figures crawled from the shelter toward me and collapsed on the ground, coughing while desperately trying to suck in air.

At first, I did not recognise the two figures suffering in front of me and was about to run off when Jim looked up at me from his soot blackened face and pleaded, 'Get help Young'un.'

I recognised his voice and turned and ran down the street toward home screaming 'Wor Jim's been burnt.'

Luckily, the others had roused most of the Street and men, women and children were hurrying out of their houses with buckets of water to put out the fire. Mr Turnbull was the first adult there and seeing the plight of the two lads dropped to his knees beside them and began rinsing their faces from the bucket of water he had brought. Regaining their senses, Jim and Bob knelt up and began scooping handfuls of water from the bucket, glad to be washing soot from their stinging eyes. They might not have been so glad had they known that the bucket was the one the Turnbulls used as a piss-pot at night!

In the meantime, I burst into the house yelling at Mam, who was sitting drinking tea, 'Haway man, Jim's been burnt up in the air-raid shelter!' I was convinced that he been badly burnt and would have to have skin grafts on his face like mine.

Stirred from her complacency, Mam ran from the house to see what had happened to her eldest boy but she still had time to shout at me, 'Ye better not be telling lies ye little bugger.'

I ran after her and saw her suddenly sprint ahead as she saw the smoke in the street and realised I had been telling the truth, especially when she saw the two smoke-blackened figures being attended too by several woman while the men and other lads tackled the fire.

The men and lads quickly extinguished the fire, the sofa having produced more smoke than flames and Jim and Bob escaped without any burns but suffered badly from smoke inhalation.

Ashington Hospital A&E register probably read; Youths suffering smoke inhalation (Pont Street, Guy Fawkes Celebrations?)

That night Sycamore Street's pile of bonfire material disappeared!

During the afternoon of 'Bonfire Night,' we were busy dragging wood and kindling from the shelter to erect the bonfire just across the street from our house. Looking like a war hero with his head wrapped in a large white bandage, Eric dragged out the guy Mam had made and stuffed a couple of bangers in its pockets before sitting it in pride of place on the top of the bonfire, ready for nightfall.

Walking into the house for a drink of water, I saw that Mam was busy at the table. Unusually, she was feeling sorry for her battered offspring and was making toffee apples as a treat for us.

'What ye meking Mam?' I asked, the smell of the hot toffee dragging me toward the table.

'Am meking toffee apples to sell,' she said jokingly.

'How much are they Mam?' I asked nervously.

'Tupence each, the same price as the Toffee Apple Man when he comes roond,' she continued to joke.

Not spotting the joke, I was crestfallen and looked up at her and said, 'But Aa've got nee money Mam.'

64

She looked down at me and answered, 'Divvint worry ye can have what's left and there's plenty.'

I ran outside and shouted to the gang of lads working on the bonfire, 'Me Mam's selling toffee apples for tuppence each.'

The response was instantaneous; the thought of crunchy toffee apples was enough to have the lads stop the construction of the bonfire and rush off for money. A couple of them lucky enough to have a few pennies in their pockets ran straight to our house to be the first to buy one.

George, Viv, and I ran into the house and I said to Mam, 'The lads are here to buy some toffee apples Mam.'

She looked at me and said, ' Whey ye silly sod, I was only jo...,' and stopped in mid-sentence when she saw a lad standing in the door holding two pennies out as others began to queue up behind him. You could almost hear her brain working as she looked at us for a second then looked at the lad, paused, then stepped forward, grabbed the money and went back for the toffee apples.

She sold six in quick succession.

Standing next to George, I looked worriedly at the dwindling tray of toffee apples.

'Hev ye got any money George?' I asked forlornly.

'Divvint be stupid man,' he replied, his eyes not leaving the apples.

'What aboot us Mam?' pleaded George for the three of us, 'we've not got any money.'

'There's plenty left,' she said, rearranging the last six on the tray before handing one over to Dennis.

George and I put our hands out for one as a voice from the door said, 'Two toffee apples please Missus Carr.'

Mam brushed past us and sold the apples.

'That just leaves three,' I thought to myself, 'just enough, surely she would give us one now.'

George had seen some more lads approaching the yard and ran outside to confront them, determined to stop them from buying the last of the toffee apples.

'There's nen left, so you can bugger off,' he shouted at the lads who stopped at the gate and began muttering their disappointment.

Just as they turned to leave, Mam came out with the tray and said to them, 'How many div ye bairns want?' and then to our utter disbelief; she sold the last three toffee apples.

She looked at us without sympathy and handed George the empty tray saying, 'Here ye are ye can pick the bits of toffee of the tray, Aa'll mek some more another day when I save up some more sugar coupons.'

She walked off to count her money leaving the three of us squabbling over the few scraps of toffee left on the tray while our friends watched as they crunched crisp, delicious, toffee apples.

George was not happy and stormed into the house and up to Dennis who not being able to get his teeth into the toffee was busy giving his a serious licking.

'Gis that,' George snarled and snatched the apple from Dennis's hand and ran outside to devour his booty. Dennis began to howl and Mam flung her teacup at the retreating George, missing him narrowly, as she also threw a torrent of abuse after him.

Give George his due, he called me after him and shared the toffee apple with me, whether or not this was brotherly love or an attempt to spread the blame for his crime I don't know, I prefer to think it was the former. Nonetheless, there were ructions later that afternoon when George went in to join the family for tea.

He stood his ground under Mam's onslaught and pointing at Dennis he yelled, 'If ye can give that little bugger treats then ye can give us all treats.' That just served to fuel Mam's anger and prolong his beating.

Pat asked me what had happened and when I explained the sorry episode to her, she and Jim who was listening, were both outraged but not the least bit surprised at what Mam had done, the two of them going to George's rescue telling Mam it had not been fair. Etty was defiant and threatened George with all manner of torture if he ever took anything from the poor bairn again but she had stopped her attack on a battered but equally defiant George.

Bonfire Night went off as planned, and luckily for a change, with no disasters or injuries; quite remarkable given how close the bonfire was to our houses.

The night ended with the ritual roasting of tetties. We thrust potatoes into the glowing embers to burn whilst we watched the last of the Catherine wheels perform and finally chased each other with spent rockets. The roast tetties never lived up to their promise; charred black on the outside, hardly cooked on the inside, they were barely edible but we still consumed them with gusto.

Christmas began to draw closer.

A couple of weeks before the big day, Mam and the older ones put up decorations. These went up in a standard format; cheap but brightly coloured, expanding paper streamers were pinned to the ceiling, radiating from the centre light bulb to the outer walls like the spokes of a wheel. She finished the Christmas décor off by hanging concertina paper bells or stars from the middle of each run of streamers.

Next, she reverently placed a scrawny imitation Christmas tree on top of the radiogram in front of the kitchen window and solemnly festooned it with glass baubles, shiny streamers, and large bright lights. The whole effect was tawdry but absolute magic for us kids, signalling as it did, Christmas was only a few days away.

The anticipation of going downstairs to a house full of toys filled us with almost unbearable excitement and hours of speculation as to what presents we would be receiving. However, the joy and happiness that receiving gifts brings, rarely occurred as Father Christmas did not always stop at our house!

On what was to be our last Christmas Eve at Pont Street, we younger children reluctantly went to bed at 8 o'clock but lay awake for hours unable to sleep. We listened to every movement downstairs to see if we could make out what Mam and Dad and our older siblings were saying in the hope that we might get a clue as to what delights, if any, would be laid out for us.

Risking punishment, George and I took turns at sneaking to the top of the stairs in an effort to try to hear what was occurring below. More than once, Jim or Pat feigned anger and chased us back to bed but always ended laughing at our excitement.

There was no pretence of Father Christmas coming, although we may have secretly hoped and believed in him, we knew who provided the toys; if there were any. Beliefs like that were similar to the use of the word 'love,' often thought of, dreamt of and wished for but never openly said for fear of being branded soft.

George was the first to wake, he nudged me and I immediately sat bolt upright in bed, dragging the blankets off Dennis who initially started to complain, then remembering the day asked, 'Is it Christmas now?'

I whispered, 'Yes,' and he climbed out of bed before me.

The three of us pulled on our short pants and excitedly made our way downstairs to the kitchen and stood at the door looking in. The Christmas tree lights were still on and the fire that Jim had banked up before he went to bed provided a welcoming red glow

George switched the light on, causing us to squint desperately as we adjusted our eyes to the brightness as we rushed in to find our presents.

Unwrapped gifts lay in small piles throughout the kitchen, each with a a scrap of paper with a name written on it to identify the recipient. We scrambled from pile to pile eager to find our own, George lingering briefly at each before he moved on to his own that he found on a corner of the table

I found mine on the opposite corner and was delighted at what I saw there; a box with Ludo written on the side, a Boy's Own Adventure book on the top of this and on top of them a small group of metal figures of road labourers. There were a couple of men digging, another with a drill and one with a 'Stop – Go' sign. There were also a tiny set of barriers and a little shelter. In addition, someone had parked a toy dustbin wagon next to the barriers. I was thrilled and immediately began to organise my workforce, the book and game could wait until later.

I looked enviously across at George, who, in deep concentration with his tongue sticking out the corner of his mouth, was busy setting up a clockwork train set. I noticed that he appeared to have more toys than anyone else did!

Dennis was busy trying to put on yet another cowboy outfit but was struggling with the trousers and ended up lying on his back on the floor trying to pull them on.

Eric was next to join us followed closely by Viv, the two of them searching for their presents.

Eric found his next to the radiogram and immediately said, 'Where's me train set?'

George ignored him, having connected the oval of track; he was busy placing the coaches on the line before winding up the tin locomotive.

I was too engrossed in my toys to take notice of the vicious fight that ensued at the other side of the table as Eric tried to claim his train set from a defiant George. The language was not appropriate for Christmas Day and the violence hardly in keeping with Christmas Spirit, but not unusual in our house.

The noise brought Jim downstairs, who, after a brief struggle, dragged the two battlers apart.

'What are ye two fighting ower?' he demanded.

'He's got me train set, Aa knew Aa was getting one and he's got it,' Eric answered angrily.

Jim looked at George. 'What are ye deeing with the train George, I put that on Eric's pile?'

'It was on mine,' George lied, wiping a trickle of blood from his nose, determined not to give up the train set.

Jim held onto George who struggled in vain, as Eric moved the train set onto the floor by his small pile of presents.

When he finished he turned to a still struggling George and warned 'Divvint ye gan near it again or Aa'll give ye another daading.'

'Bugger off,' George spat and held two fingers in the air in a gesture of defiance.

Jim let go of him and went to help Dennis finish putting his cowboy outfit on. Strapping the gun belt around Dennis, he put the little silver pistol into the holster and asked, 'Where's your Winchester rifle?'

Dennis looked at him with a puzzled expression. 'What rifle? Aa didn't get a rifle.'

Jim turned and looked at George who was leaning over the table trying to cover something with his arms. 'Gis it here,' warned Jim.

'What?' George replied, trying to look innocent but failing miserably.

Sitting in Uncle Alex's chair by the fire nursing her new dolly, Viv pointed at George and said with a smug look, 'He's got the rifle.'

Jim went back to George and tried to prise his arms from the table, but George had clamped his hands onto the corners and was not about to give up his booty.

Gritting his teeth he snarled, 'Bugger off ye big bastard.'

Jim responded by slapping the back of George's head; but George did not budge, he just gritted his teeth more and tightened his grip on the table.

'Right ye little sod, Aa'll gan and get me Mam and she'll sort ye oot!' Jim warned and headed for the stairs.

68

Not wishing to suffer a good hiding from Mam that would undoubtedly come his way if she found out he had taken something from the bairn, George let go of the table and picking up the toy rifle he flung it at Dennis shouting, 'Here ye are ye little twat,' using a word he had recently acquired from Mam.

The rifle hit Dennis on the side of the head, stunning him; the shocked expression on his face changing to pain as he let out an almighty scream and began howling at the top of his voice - knowing his cries would bring his Mam to him.

Realising what he had done and the hell that was about to be played when Mam came down stairs, George calmly walked across to Dennis, who was not hurt badly, and with some force punched him on his shoulder knocking him to the floor saying, 'Bloody cry baby.'

He then turned and looked at the foot of the stairs waiting for Mam to arrive and the inevitable punishment that would follow.

Coughing and spluttering while trying to shove her false teeth in, Mam resplendent in her huge flannelette nightgown, squinted under the harsh lights and angry as hell at having been disturbed from her desperately needed beauty sleep, staggered into the kitchen and demanded, 'Whatever's the matter with the poor bairn?' Waiting for an answer, she picked Dennis up and cast an angry look around the room that spelt certain doom for someone.

Jim lied, 'He was running roond in his cowboy suit and fell ower and hurt himself, didn't he Eric!'

Eric looked at Jim, then George and then Mam. 'Aye, he's just fallen ower,' and turned back to his train set. No matter what George had done, he did not want to see him beaten up by Mam, not on Christmas day.

Dennis was trying to speak between huge sobs but was unable to do so as Mam kept on wiping his snots and tears away every time he almost had breath to get it out, so was unable to report George's misdemeanour. George moved sheepishly away from the fireplace to his presents on the table and began playing with them, winking at me as he did so.

Just when we thought it was over, a voice from Uncle Alex's chair said, 'Mam wor George pinched Dennis's gun and bashed him with it, that's why he's crying.'

As Mam turned to George, her face beginning to contort with anger, Jim, Eric and I all shouted, 'No he didn't.'

Jim and Eric quickly positioned themselves between George and Mam.

'Yes he did,' shouted Viv, determined to keep things stirred but instead she received a slap from Mam for her troubles.

Clutching a still sobbing Dennis, she headed back to bed warning, 'There better not be any more noise, or tha'll be bloody trouble.'

Jim walked over to Viv, leaned close to her face and said, 'Your card's marked, bonny lass.'

Viv not fully understanding what he meant said, 'Am telling,' but the look on Jim's face was enough to keep her silent and rooted to the seat.

Christmas day continued with Christmas dinner, our last one in Pont Street. Overall, it had been a good celebration of 'Christ's Birthday; we had all received presents, and we had devoured a turkey that had enjoyed life in Granddad Waterford's back garden until a few days before Christmas.

If there were any celebrations on New Year's Eve, the younger members of the family, including me, missed them as we were all in bed by nine o'clock but we had survived another year at Pont Street.

7

Gala Day

The 'Ticky Man' must have been during the first week in June; Mam proudly showed Eric, George, Dennis and I, brand new and almost uniform Tee shirts, khaki shorts and plimsolls she had bought on HP for us to wear at the Gala.

The Miners' Gala was an annual celebration organised by the miners for all the junior school children in Ashington Assembling outside of their schools, they then marched behind Brass Bands to the Welfare Recreational Fields at the east side of the Hirst where they would compete in sports and if they were lucky, spend a few bob at the fair. The Gala alternated between the Welfare and the Peoples Park on the other side of Ashington.

In the Carr household, only George marched this year while Mam took Dennis, Viv and me to meet him there. Eric was at Grammar school and the rest were too old. George went off to join the march from the South School at about nine o'clock while Mam made sure the rest of us were dressed in our new clothes before she scrubbed our faces with the rough flannel until they shone. Taking off her pinny, she brushed her hair, applied some bright red lipstick and hurried us out the door.

Mam carried Dennis while Viv and I trotted alongside as she led us through the avenues, across Woodhorn Road, past more rows, across Alexander Road, and into the Miners' Welfare, a large area of playing fields with a running track and other sporting facilities. In addition to the Welfare, Ashington also boasted a football stadium, an excellent cricket pitch, a flower park, two large open play parks and the Miners' Recreation Centre or 'Rec'. The Rec at the West side of town had a cricket pitch, football and rugby pitches, several tennis courts, and athletic facilities as well as a large old Gym complete with two sets of changing rooms.

On Gala Day, the Welfare was buzzing with activity; children's' marching bands, two brass bands and a pipe band all battled to be heard above each other and against the noise from a fairground or 'Shows' as we called them. The colours of the band uniforms, especially the Morpeth Pipe Band in their bright red tartan, and the garish colours from the fair produced a treat for our eyes after the drabness of Ashington's smoke filled colliery streets.

Mam looked as excited as we were as she led us past the Shows to the sports field where marshals were desperately trying to organise the children into age groups and sporting events.

A track had been marked out for the junior races such as the sack, egg and spoon, and wheelbarrow races, further into the field the seniors were competing in traditional track and field events on the main athletics track.

Unusually, Mam was keen to see nine-year-old George perform in the junior events and pushed us forward to the edge of the track just as a dozen boys raced past with eggs balanced upon spoons.

'What the deeing Mam?' a confused Dennis asked, watching as eggs were dropped and retrieved and the boys fought for first place, all being cheered on frantically by screaming parents. Mam shushed Dennis as she read the programme handed to her at the gate.

After a couple of minutes of trying to decipher the programme she thrust it at me and said, 'See what time the sack race is on,' and then turned to look for George amongst the many groups of children being lined up for individual events beyond the starting line.

Quickly scanning the programme, I said, 'Aa think it says eleven ten Mam.'

'What bloody good's that to me, a hevn't got a watch?'

'They're on after the three legged race Mam,' I responded hoping that would clear that up but it did not.

'And when the bloody hell is that on?' she countered angrily.

I looked at the programme again and said triumphantly, 'Noo, efter, the egg and spoon race.'

We stood and watched four heats of the three-legged race, laughing uncontrollably at the misfortunes of the less well coordinated of the runners as they collapsed in tangled heaps or shuffled along screaming at each other to get in step. Dennis, Viv and I were hoping the races would end soon so that we could go to the shows but we knew better than to ask Mam when she was intent on seeing George run.

Finally, we saw George lining up with a sack for the third heat of the sack race, the starter ordering them up to the start line and into their sacks. There were ten boys including George, who was near the middle with a fixed determined look on his face. I noticed he had bared his gritted teeth in a way I had seen him bare them many times before; it was not a good omen.

'ON YER MARKS – SET – GO,' yelled the starter and off they bounced. George clutched the front of his sack to his chest with both hands while leaping as far as he could, his teeth still gritted; he was doing quite well, in fact, he was in front as several of the boys had already fallen.

The sacks were quite large and progress was far from easy; eventually, George stumbled but did not fall, however, it was sufficient for the boys on either side of him to catch up and the three of them bounced along almost in unison. The cheering and screams of encouragement from the crowd grew louder with each bounce; Mam in particular was screaming as though George's life depended on the outcome of the race.

Not happy that the other two lads had caught up with him, George released his right-hand from the sack and swung it into the face of his right-hand rival and then changed hands and swung his left fist onto the unsuspecting nose of his left-

72

hand rival. Both boys dropped like stones, clutching their faces, the left-hand one's nose splattering blood as he fell.

George bounced on, oblivious to the angry shouts from the crowd and one of the marshal's shouts of protest. He could see the finishing line and he was going for it, sod the rest.

Nearing the end, he slowly replaced his gritted-teeth grimace with a maniacal grin, but then out of the corner of his eye, he spotted another lad off to his right starting to gain ground on him. George tried frantically to increase his speed but it was to no avail the lad was starting to pull away.

This was too much for George, he stopped bouncing and began running within his sack at an angle toward the other boy.

The crowd realised what was happening and began shouting warnings to the poor lad who, intent as George on winning, was oblivious to the dreadful apparition that was bearing down on him. By this stage, George had abandoned the inside of his sack and was dragging it along behind him as he ran flat out and shoulder charged the poor lad sending him flying.

George leapt over the finish line and then in front of the enraged crowd, tried impossibly, to surreptitiously step back into his sack while grinning inanely as he enjoyed what he believed was his victory. He had lived up to his nickname, 'The Bull,' even if he was just a skinny little nine-year-old.

The track was in chaos, parents were rescuing their battered offspring, others were shouting at the marshals to sort things out and ominously a couple of men were walking toward George, obviously intending to sort him out.

Foolishly, they had not considered Etty!

Mam had watched the carnage with pride; her lad had won and she had cheered him on with gusto but now she realised that not everybody took the same attitude to winning, George was in imminent danger. She took off across the track as though she were competing in the 100 yards dash and arrived at George's side just before the two angry men.

Mam wrapped her arm protectively around George, praising him with, 'Well done Bonny Lad, ye showed them soft buggers hoo to win,' and turned to face the men who were shouting obscenities as they approached.

Mam stopped them in their tracks with both the look on her face and the tirade of abuse she hurled back at them as they approached. Her cursing made their ranting seem like pleasantries.

She lifted her handbag club like in the air, daring them to touch her lad. Sensibly, they stopped and stood open-mouthed, taken aback like scolded schoo children, not sure what to do next, wondering and worrying what this raging harridan was going to do.

With a look of triumphant disdain, she marched defiantly off the track with her arm still around George who, not used to displays of affection, was trying to wriggle free, besides he wanted his winner's certificate and he could see that much to his chagrin, it was been given to the lad he had bowled over.

Ignoring the complaints from other onlookers, Mam brought George safely back to us and gathering us together, she steered us toward the shows, her head held high and a look on her face that defied anyone to challenge her or hers.

'But Mam, am in the obstacle race next man,' George pleaded as she dragged him off.

'I think ye've done enough racing today pet,' she said as she tightened her grip on him, force-marching him on.

Pulling Dennis after me, I ran alongside George and said, 'That was great Geordie, why didn't ye get a certificate for winning?'

Before he could answer, Vivian piped in, 'Cos he's a cheater.'

She managed to duck George's swinging hand but could not avoid Mam's; it caught her on the back of the head. Viv stopped in her tracks and started to scream in outrage but Mam just ignored her and marched on toward the shows still clutching George who now wore a very satisfied smile, as I did, having been on the receiving end of Viv's mischievous tale telling on many occasions. She soon realised no one was interested in her theatricals and ran to catch up.

The day just got better and better.

We walked into the shows, past the candyfloss and toffee apple stalls at the entrance and around the madly whirling Waltzer toward the gaily decorated stalls grouped around the outside.

Packed with families and children enjoying the rides and sideshows, the fairground had a real carnival atmosphere that made me say aloud, 'Cor, this is smashing.'

The sound of Frankie Lane singing, 'Ghosts Riders in the Sky,' from the loudspeakers on the Waltzer and the rattle of the cars as they raced around the switchboard track, flinging their screaming occupants from side to side, felt as exciting as being in a stampede of cattle I had seen at a Matinee Western. The smell from the Candy Floss and Toffee Apple stalls added to the atmosphere, increasing our excitement even more. These were my first shows and I drank in every sound and smell.

As a reward for winning his race, Mam took George to the Coconut Shy to try his skill. We stood and watched while George hurled the wooden balls wildly at the coconuts missing with everyone, cursing as he did so.

'Gis another go Mam,' he pleaded determined to knock the coconuts flying.

Mam gave him a scathing look and replied, you got given half a croon at the gate, spend yer an money,' It was then that the actions of a lad on the next stall caught my eye - it was an air rifle shooting stall.

As George reluctantly spent some of his money and began his second assault on the coconuts, I wandered over to the other stall and watched as a teenager fired, loaded, took aim, and fired again at small metal, man-shaped targets, grouped in rows of six in metal boxes at the back of the stall. Mam, Dennis, Viv and a frustrated George, who had failed to win a coconut, joined me at the stall.

'Can we hev a go on this Mam?' I asked hoping that the generous mood she was in had not yet worn off.

'Aye, go on then, ye and George can both hev ago,' she said handing over sixpence to the stall keeper.

'He's too little Missus,' he said pointing to me.

I was devastated I had never seen anything so exciting; I had never seen a real rifle before, even if they were just air rifles.

'He can hev ago with the ones that fire corks at the other end though,' he continued while beginning to load a rifle for George.

'No - he'll hev one of these like his brother,' Mam said, defying the man to refuse her.

The stall keeper wisely capitulatcd and brought a wooden crate around to the front for me to stand on. We had six shots each, the man loading each one for me as the springs in the rifles were too strong for me to reload.

Leaning the rifle on the counter, I took aim, instinctively lining up the foresight over the target with the centre of the notch of the rear sight. Squeezing the trigger, I felt the tension in the spring release and shoot the pellet to the centre of the target knocking it over with a satisfactory metallic twang.

I was delighted and waited excitedly as the stallholder reloaded the rifle. George had missed and was berating his rifle for making him miss.

Dennis cheered and Viv said, 'Fluke.'

Five shots later and with all six targets knocked over, I stood back beaming with triumph as George continued to complain about the uselessness of his rifle and its sights.

The stall keeper said, 'Well done son, just like Buffalo Bill,' and handed over a bright red prize token, pointing out the prizes available for one token.

George had managed to knock over three.

'Can we hev another go Mam?' asked George, determined to show me who was the better shot.

'Am not wasting money on ye, yor bloody hopeless, but wor Syd can hev another go, I want one of them ashtrays for two tokens,' she said pointing to the cheap fluted glass ashtrays under the two tokens sign.

Feeling like a big game hunter out to bag a meal for his family, I took aim, determined to win the ashtray and praying I would not miss, I squeezed the trigger gently. A few minutes later, my Mam stood clutching the ashtray proudly, proud for herself that one of her off-spring had turned out to be a good shot, not proud of me for having done so.

Nonetheless, I was elated and delighted when the man said jokingly to Mam, 'Tek him away Missus, or he'll win all my prizes.'

We wandered around the shows enjoying the sights and sounds, taking advantage of Mam's benevolent mood.

Dennis asked, 'Can Aa hev a ride on the roond aboot Mam?'

'Aye gan on then, the four of ye can,' she replied, placing Dennis on the driving seat of a brightly, painted tractor.

'Am not gannin on that bloody sissy thing,' George grunted disgustedly before wandering off toward the Waltzer in the centre of the shows.

Viv got into a small car and I climbed onto a motorbike while Mam paid for the rides and stood back waving at Dennis who was spinning the steering wheel of the tractor.

Once the ride began, I was lost in my own little world, crouched over the handlebars of the bolted down motorbike, my imagination took me roaring along city streets, chasing huge American cars full of gangsters who were firing bursts from their Tommy guns at me forcing me to lean frantically from side to side to avoid their bullets.

The ride was soon over and I was brought back to reality when my Mam, who had just lifted Dennis from the tractor said to me, 'Howay ye soft shite,' get off that and gan on the Waltzer with George.' An over developed imagination was not a quality Mam appreciated.

I raced off to join George who was watching other youngsters climbing into the cars of the Waltzer.

'Me Mam's gannin to pay for us to hev a ride,' I shouted trying to make myself heard above the noise.

George was onto the running boards and into a car just as it started, shouting, 'Haway Young'un before she changes her mind.' I climbed onboard just in time.

The ride was exhilarating; as speed picked up, we were spun first one way then the other, rising and falling over the humps, the outside world becoming a kaleidoscope of blurred colours and sounds as we hurtled round the track whooping and screaming with delight. Out of the corner of my eye, I could see that George had adopted his gritted teeth grin and I knew instantly that he was not satisfied with just holding his arms in the air.

As Johnny Ray started to sing, 'Walking my Baby Back Home,' through the loudspeakers, George grabbed the safety barrier in front of us and stood on the seat as though he was about to go water-skiing, the grin growing bigger.

I looked on horrified, certain he would be flung to his death, but one of the teenage attendants nonchalantly walked across the speeding floor, jumped onto the back of our wildly spinning car and reaching forward with one hand, yanked George back into his seat and held him there until the ride finished.

When we climbed out of the car the teenager said to George, 'We'll not let you on again if yor not gannin te behave yorsell,' and held his hand out for money.

George responded with a two fingered salute saying 'Me Mam's already paid ye, ye cheater,' and we ran off laughing to find my Mam and the other two.

Dennis was eating candyfloss and Viv a toffee apple when we caught up with them, Mam not offering George or me either.

'That was great Mam,' I said excitedly. 'Thanks for paying for the ride.'

She gave me one of her sideways looks and said, 'I didn't pay for yor ride, Aa spent the money on the candyfloss and toffee apple for these two.'

George looked at me and we both burst out laughing as we headed for the gate and home.

The following Tuesday evening after tea, Mam kept me indoors while the rest of the lads were playing outside.

'Can a gan oot noo Mam?' I asked every few minutes.

'Not yet just bide yor time til a tell ye.' She obviously had a reason for keeping me in but I could not think why.

Eventually, there was a loud knock on the back door and Mam peered through the net curtain before scurrying toward the front room saying, 'Gan and tell the Ticky Man am not in.' She stood behind the door to the front room waving her hand, motioning me to go to the back door.

Opening the back door, I looked up at the imposing and distinguished figure of the Ticky Man - a six-foot tall, turbaned, grey-bearded Sikh, wearing a dark suit and in his hands, he held a small hard-backed notebook and fountain pen.

In almost a whisper he said, 'Hello sonny is your mother in?'

'No, she's not in,' I lied, feeling guilty and blushing madly.

He smiled at me with his deep brown eyes and said, 'Ok, tell her I'll see her next week will you?'

I nodded, turned my head and shouted, 'Mam, he says he'll see ye next week!'

Chuckling to himself, the Ticky Man closed his little book and turned away as I closed the door, not understanding why Mam was shouting at me for doing as I she told me.

'It's all yor fault anyway, spending me money at the shows; that big, bearded bugger'll be lucky if gets oot next week an' all,' she said adopting the fixed impassive 'Etty', look I knew meant, 'adopt a low profile and escape outside while you can.'

Sitting at the kitchen table a little later I watched as Jim, who just arrived from work, ate his dinner. He had started work at the end of the last mid-term holidays and not knowing where he was working, I decided to ask him after he had finished eating as I did not want to disturb him until he was ready to talk, he was my oldest brother and I lived a little in awe of him.

'What work are ye deeing Jim?' I asked as he pushed his cleared plate to one side and took a sip of tea from the large white mug Mam had just filled.

He smiled at me and replied with a glint in his eye, 'I'm an MP.'

My mind raced trying to fathom out what that meant; I remembered posters of someone called Wilf Owen being in lots of windows a while back and that the poster read something like; 'Vote Wilf Owen your local MP.' However, I also knew that MP could mean Military Police; after all, he was in the Air Training Corps so he could be either.

'What sort of MP are ye?' I asked hoping to hear him say, 'Military Policeman.'

'I'm an MP, that's all ye need to knaa Young'un.'

'I bet yore a Military Policeman?' I said hopefully.

'Na I'm not a Military Policeman.'

'Then do we hev to vote for ye?'

'No ye divvint hev to vote for me,' he said as he went upstairs to change.

Perplexed, I turned to Mam and asked, 'What sort of MP is he Mam?'

She looked at me and said, 'A Mucky Pitmen bonny lad, the same as you'll be when ye leave school.' Ominously, she made it sound like a punishment.

8

Pig, Pram, Horse and Cart

The following Saturday morning, the house was a hive of activity; Mam and Dad helped by Jim and Pat were busy trying to pack ornaments and pictures into boxes.

Dennis asked, 'What's happening Mam?'

'Whey pet, we're gannin to move to a new hoose next week,' she answered, ruffling the top of his hair gently before turning back to her packing.

This news hit me like a bombshell, I was stunned, a little upset and worried, why were we moving? Pont Street might not have been the most desirable of areas to live, but for me at seven years old; it was home and provided me with security, warmth, and family.

'Where are we gannin te Mam?' I asked, perplexed and excited at the same time.

Eric piped up, 'The Fifth Ra (Row) at Highmarket Young'un, right ower the other side of Ashington.'

Apparently, it was just the three younger members of the family that did not know about the move.

Ever since the arrival of my Uncle Alex, Dad had been looking for a larger colliery house, and when offered one earlier that year, he accepted it quickly. It was a three bedroomed end of terrace with a large scullery, kitchen/living room, sitting room and a further downstairs room for Uncle Alex. It had been used as the Pit Doctor's Surgery in the old days, hence the extra rooms.

Dad was entitled to one of the large four bed-roomed 'Gaffers' houses in First Row but much to the Chagrin of the rest of the family, he did not want to live there. His reluctance in moving to the First Row was in the main due to them having small front gardens, whereas the Fifth Row, in common with all the other Highmarket 'Rows,' had a sixty or seventy-foot long garden. Dad was also losing his beloved allotment to a new council estate development, and as our current house only had a handkerchief sized front garden, it appeared as though the Fifth Row would also meet his need to produce vegetables for the family.

The crowded house was obviously getting on Dad's nerves as he suddenly shouted, 'Jesus fucking wept, Etty will ye get them bloody kids oot the hoose noo.'

Mam looked at him with disdain and answered, 'They're your bloody kids an all, ye baldy headed git, give them some money and they can gan to the baths.'

Dad hated anyone mentioning his lack of hair, which to him, blighted his chiselled good looks.

He swore back at her, 'Yor mealy-faced swine ye, Aa'll swing for ye and them one of these days.'

Mam ignored him and he did as ordered. He fished into his pocket, pulled out a two bob piece, and thrusting it at Eric, said angrily, 'Here tek them little buggers with ye and bugger off to the baths for the day.'

Eric took the money and pointing to Viv said, 'Am not taking her,' and stormed upstairs to grab his swimming costume, closely followed by George and me.

Mam picked Dennis up and said, 'Ye'll hev to stay here pet, ye cannit be getting swimming pool chemicals in yor ears noo.'

Dennis was not bothered; he preferred to stay close by Mam where he knew he was best off. None of us was jealous of the special attention that Dennis received, he was the youngest, and we all spoilt him due to him being partially deaf and very frail; he really was the runt of the litter.

The three of us set off for the swimming baths about a mile or more away on the southern edge of town and very near the 'Rows'. It was another glorious summer's day and as we walked along, I constantly bombarded Eric with questions about the Fifth Row.

He dropped another bombshell when he told me I would be changing schools and going to Wansbeck School the week after next.

'What's Wansbeck like?' I asked, feeling even more insecure.

'It's a lot better than the Sooth School,' he replied, 'I might show ye it later.'

We were taking the shortcut through the allotments when George said 'Haway, let's gan to me Dad's allotment and see the pig.'

'Pig!' - this was news to me.

'When did Dad get a pig?' I asked puzzled as to why he would want a pig.

'He's had it a few weeks noo,' Eric answered.

'He's letting it clear the allotment and then he's gannin to take it to the Fifth Ra to clear the garden.'

I was puzzled; I didn't know pigs could clear gardens and an image of a pig wearing wellingtons and using a spade to dig over the garden came to me.

'Yor just kidding,' I said, 'how can a pig clear a garden? That's stupid.'

'It's not stupid, they eat everything and turn the grund ower with their snoots,' said Eric with a superior smile. I still did not believe him but was not prepared to challenge him further so I kept quiet, looking forward to seeing the pig. I was amazed and surprised when we reached the allotment that had always been full of thriving plants and immaculately kept; Dad's pride and joy was a muddy mess and there in the centre was the perpetrator of the carnage, a pink pig, its snout rooting in the soil as it grunted contentedly.

'Isn't it big?' I said excitedly as I hauled myself onto the railings of the allotment for a better look.

'Na it's not even half grown yet, it'll get right big and fat in a few more weeks,' Eric said knowingly.

'Where does it sleep at night?' I asked worried about the animal having to sleep in the mess it was creating.

'In there,' he answered pointing at the shed. 'Me or Jim come and lock her up at night and let her oot in the morning.'

'Has she got a name?' I asked, admiring the pig's ability to shift soil like a bulldozer.

'No, but we can give her one,' said Eric.

'Etty,' George said, laughing at his own joke.

'Nah, Mam'd kill us,' said Eric. 'What aboot Bacon?'

'That's not a lasses' name,' I said. 'What aboot Vivian?'

Eric laughed and said, 'Nah, we'll call her Porky.'

We stood admiring Porky for a while, imitating the grunts and calling for it to come over but the pig wisely chose to ignore us.

'What'll happen when it's stopped growing?' I asked naively.

'We'll eat the fat bugger,' George said, laughing at his own statement.

I immediately had visions of a whole roast pig placed on the kitchen table just as we had seen in a Robin Hood film.

'Cor,' was all I could think of saying as we left the pig and headed for the swimming baths.

On arriving home from school on the following Wednesday, I found Dad securing wire mesh fencing around stout metal stakes he had driven into the four corners of our tiny front garden and there in the centre of the little enclosure he was building was Porky, already rooting the ground. The council bulldozers had arrived at the allotments on Monday forcing Dad to move her. Much to the amusement of 'most' of the locals, for the next three nights Porky lived at Pont Street. We did not see much of Mam that week as she spent each day at our new house, wall papering and painting in preparation for the impending move.

Dad had persuaded the NCB to carry out some alterations to the house including a new tiled fireplace with ovens installed in the kitchen to replace the old black-leaded range, as well as a new smaller tiled fireplace in the sitting room. He also had the stairs moved from the back of the house (facing the back street) to the front of the house (overlooking the garden) in order to give us a larger kitchen, cum dining, cum living room.

By Friday night, excitement had built to a crescendo, making it very difficult to sleep. This was not helped by having to sleep five to a bed on the last night due to the other beds having already being taken to the new house. The morning sun streaming through our curtain-less window at four o'clock ended any hope of sleep and the whole family was out of bed by five.

It was chaos. Dad had left to fetch the borrowed horse and cart while the rest of us fought over cups of tea and toast while Mam was upstairs folding bedding and our meagre supply of clothes.

She eventually came down stairs and stood in the kitchen doorway surveying her unruly brood for a few minutes before wading into the centre and ending the chaos with a few well aimed clips to ears followed by, 'Shut up the lot of ye or Aa'll put a cut in yor heeds like a navvies bait tin.'

None of us knew what a 'cut like a navvies bait tin' actually was but knew that she meant a clout round the head, so we shut up.

She continued to bellow orders like a sergeant major and soon had us organised, packing and carrying. By the time, Dad arrived with the horse and cart we were waiting to start loading the remains of our belongings.

Dad, Mam, Jim and Eric did the heavy lifting while the rest of us kept out the way.

Dennis was looking pathetic, suffering from a lack of sleep he first curled up on an armchair to have a sleep until he was shooed away when that was loaded and then he tried the sofa with the same result. He ended up standing crying forlornly at the foot of the stairs until Mam picked him up and took him outside to show him the horse and cart.

Dad meanwhile was doing the final tying down and organising the move of personnel, while Jim was balancing the long zinc bath on the top of the load. Mam put Dennis down by the horse and cart and walked round to where Dad was now standing by the huge old pram in the back yard.

'Eeeh a think we're ready George,' she said desperate, to be off.

'Aye,' he answered. 'There's just the pig.'

Gathering us all together for final instructions, he said, 'Right, Pat tek Uncle Alex and Viv to the bus, here's the keys for the new hoose, ye'll get there afore us,' and passed her the keys.

'Jim ye come with me and yer Mam on the wagon,' and then he turned to glare and the rest of us.

'Noo,' he said to Eric. 'Tek this pram and rope roond to the front garden and ye, George and Syd, load the pig into the pram and tie her doon and put this old blanket ower her back to stop her getting sunburnt.'

George interrupted, 'Pigs divvint get sunburnt Dad, that's stupid.'

Eric winced knowing what was coming next and I backed off.

Dad grabbed George by the front of his jumper and pulled him to him before lowering his face and growling, 'Divvint argue with me ye bloody little waster or Aa'll throttle ye, of course they get bloody sunburnt, tha pink aren't they,' and pushed him back.

George yelled, 'Ye big bully ye,' and ran off toward the front of the house.

'What happens when we've fastened her into the pram Dad?' Eric asked.

'What do ye fucking think; are ye as brainless as that other bugger? Push her to the new hoose.'

A look of horror spread across Eric's face at the thought of pushing a pram across Ashington, especially with a pig in it; he would be the laughing stock if any

82

of his mates saw him. He started to protest but the look on Dad's face stopped him.

Eric grabbed me by the arm and said, 'Haway Young'un we've a pig to load,' and grabbing the pram stormed off with me trotting behind.

Standing staring at Porky lying contentedly on the dusty patch that had been our front garden, the three of us slowly realised the enormity of the task ahead of us.

George looked at the pig and then the pram and said to Eric, 'Hoo the fuck are we gannin to get that fat pig into the pram,' then burst out laughing when he realised his derogatory name for Porky was not as insulting as he had intended.

'She *is* a fat pig, that's exactly what she is,' he laughed.

Eric studied the problem for a while knowing that we would struggle to lift her into the pram, that is if she would let us lift her.

He said, 'Right, Young'un hold the pram steady and George and me'll lift her in.'

George was already over the wire mesh fence and was kicking Porky to her feet laughing and shouting, 'Haway ye fat pig get yorsell up, we're teking ye for a nice pram ride.'

Porky got to her feet protesting noisily at having been disturbed so rudely and began rubbing her back against the sun-warmed bricks of the house.

Eric was not too keen to get in with her and said to George, 'See if ye can lift her?'

George grabbed her back legs and heaved them off the ground and Porky waddled forward squealing noisily as George held her rear end as though he were in a wheelbarrow race.

Eric and I burst out laughing and began cheering, as George yelled, 'Gee up ye fat pig,' as he and Porky staggered round and round the tiny enclosure.

'Put her doon ye sackless sod,' Dad boomed as he came up behind us. 'Can ye buggers not de oot right? She's only a little un and docile at that,'he growled as he stepped over the fence and effortlessly scooped Porky up, placing her in the pram. With a few quick moves, he had her feet folded beneath her and she was lying contentedly on her belly, her head to the front of the pram below the hood.

'Okay,' he said as he put the blanket over her back. 'Tie her doon so she canna get up and bring her ower.' He held her while Eric passed the rope around pig and pram several times before tying it off.

Dad checked that the pig was secure and said, 'Aa'll see ye at the Fifth Ra,' then turned and walked back to the horse and loaded cart standing at the end of the street. Jim was laughing at us as he held the horse steady, while Mam for a change, looked happy sitting on a chair at the front of the big four-wheeled cart.

Dad climbed up on the front of the wagon and wound the brake free as Jim urged the horse forward, leaving us to make our way to Highmarket with Porky.

83

Eric pulled the hood of the pram up and looked at George and me and said 'Haway then let's push the bloody pig to Highmarket, George ye can push forst.'

George reluctantly grabbed the handle of the pram and leaning into it to get it moving, said, 'This little piggy went to Highmarket - and got bloody eaten,' and we started for our new home, a mile and a half away!

Crossing the avenue into the second Pont Street terrace, big, buxom, Mrs Armstrong who was hanging out washing, stopped to watch our progress down the street.

Obviously keen to glean some new gossip, she stopped us as we approached and said, 'Eeee yor Mam's not gone and had another bairn has she lads?'

George stopped pushing and looked at her with a wry smile, and said, 'Aye missus she has, and we've no room for this one, so we're gannin to eat her.'

'Eee what an aaful thing to say,' Mrs Armstrong replied. 'Come on let me have a look at her.'

Eric added, 'Ye divvint want to Missus Armstrong 'cos she's a bit of a pig to look at.'

Mrs Armstrong looked at Eric as though he was the Devil himself but her curiosity moved her forward to the pram where she pushed the hood forward slightly and pulled back the old blanket revealing Porky's large pink ears.

Porky snorted and Mrs Armstrong screamed and ran into the house yelling, 'You wicked boys, you'll all go to Hell.'

I looked at Eric and asked, 'Will we gan te Hell?'

He looked at me and smiled and said, 'Nur, we're just leaving Hell,' and we headed for the end of Pont Street.

Pont Street, however, was not quite finished with us - just as we were approaching the avenue at the end of the Street, Matty Storey came around the corner! Whistling nonchalantly with his hands thrust deep in his pockets, he stopped in his tracks with a silent whistle on his lips as he took in the sight of the three of us with the pram.

'Fuck,' said George at the handle of the pram.

'Shit,' said Eric at the thought of the coming loss of credibility.

'Bugger,' said I, expecting trouble.

The three of us stood motionless as Matty, hands still in pockets, circled us before stopping at the front of the pram and said with a smirk on his face, 'What are ye three soft shites deeing with the pram?'

'Teking yor sister for a waalk,' George replied as his mouth started to take on that familiar grimace, his teeth beginning to grind.

'Bugger Off,' Matty spat back.

Eric looked at the sneering, ginger-headed Matty, 'Gan on then tek a look, she's bonnier than ye.'

Mattie's curiosity got the better of him; he moved warily forward and peered into the pram to see Porky's ears sticking up over the blanket.

'Fucking hell it's a pig,' he shouted, jumping back with surprise.

84

'Whey that's nee way to talk aboot yor sister man,' Eric said laughing.

You could almost hear Matty's brain working as he tried to think of something clever to say back but he failed and yelled, 'Aa fuck off the lot of ye, yor all pigs,' and turned to walk away.

George stopped him saying, 'Haad on Matty, Aa've summick for ye,' and stepped toward him.

'Aye, and what's that Carrsy?' Matty replied, turning to look at George.

'This,' replied George as he swung a beautifully timed right hook crashing into Matty's face, the blow almost snapping his head off his shoulder, knocking him to the ground, just about conscious.

Kneeling on Matty's chest, George said, 'There's only one pig here Matty and its frigging Ginger.' Placing the palm of his hand on Mattie's nose, he levered himself upright putting all his weight onto to his hand, making Matty's body jerk at the pain from his injured nose. Without a word, George went back to the pram, grabbed the handle, and began pushing it the last few steps out of Pont Street. I jogged alongside looking at George with brotherly admiration.

Eric caught up with George and said, 'Good one wor kid,' and we left Pont Street behind.

The walk to the Fifth Row was long, hot and tiring but thankfully, uneventful. I still had not seen our new house or even the area it was in and despite my fatigue, I was very excited when we turned off Highmarket Main Street, into the cuts between the rows of terraced houses.

As we crossed the back street of the Third Row, Eric pointed at a house three doors down and said, 'That's where Auntie Jen lives.'

I had only met her once, she was an enormous woman of about twenty stone, and I had been terrified that she would sit on one of us and we would disappear forever. On the other hand, her Husband - Uncle Joe, was a diminutive, dapper, five-foot-four and could not have weighed more than seven stone, I always thought of him as Jack Spratt!

We reached the back alley of the Fifth Row and I saw for the first time the long garden or, at least, the new, five-foot high, brown stained picket fence that enclosed the garden. The picket fences were taller than I was, creating a tunnel effect in the narrow cuts that felt intimidating. Eric opened the gate that joined the fence to the house and we pushed the pram through and into the overgrown garden.

Eric said, 'Ye've got some work to de here Porky,' and we left her there as we went round to the back lane to the back door of the house. The horse and cart stood outside the backyard and fifty yards beyond, I could see shunting yards with Ashington Colliery beyond

Jim, who was on the back of the cart sorting out chairs ready to be taken inside, stopped momentarily and said, 'It's aboot time ye buggers got here.'

George replied, 'Ye should try pushing a big fat pig right across Ashington, Aa'll ye had te de was ride ower on a frigging wagon.'

We went in through the back door, through the scullery and into the large kitchen cum dining room where Mam was busy taking crockery out of a cardboard box on the table before carrying it into the pantry to stack on the shelves. Dad, who was in the sitting room putting cushions onto the armchair that he had just placed by the fire, was sweating and breathing hard from his exertions. Uncle Alec had already taken up station on a cottage chair by the fire in the kitchen and had already begun to pollute the air with his pipe smoke.

Mam stopped what she was doing and said, 'Hev yor sells a cup of tea and Eric ye can give yor Dad and Jim a hand to carry in the sofa.'

Looking at me she asked, 'Where's the bairn? He must be parched after that walk?'

I looked at her with some confusion and said, 'Aa divvint knaa where he is, Aa've just got here.'

A puzzled frown furrowed her face, quickly replaced by anger then fright before she snarled, 'What de ye mean? You were told to bring him ower here, divvint tell me that ye've lost the bairn ye simple sod.'

Worried that something had happened to her precious bairn and wearing a look that indicated her intent to vent her anger on me, she advanced toward me with fists clenched, snarling a tirade of abuse.

Eric stepped forward just in time and said, 'Nebody told us owt aboot bringing the bairn, just the pig, we thought the bairn was wiv ye.'

Mam went puce and shouted, 'Oh my bloody god we've left the poor bairn at Pont Street,' and began doing a little jig of fright, frustration and anger, not knowing what to do.

Dad who had heard the exchange was standing in the doorway between the sitting room and kitchen and shouted over the commotion Mam was making, 'Etty for god's sake shut up and let's think.'

None of us, including Dad, was used to seeing her panic. Angry and violent occasionally, but panic, this was unusual and showed how much she cared for Dennis.

Dad grabbed Eric by the arm and said, 'Gan doon the doors to number 35 and ask Geordie Little for a lend of his bike and get yorsell doon to Pont Street and find Dennis.'

Mam was still ranting blue murder, her efforts aided by Pat and Viv who had been upstairs unpacking and had come down to see what the cause of the commotion was.

They joined Mam in wailing 'Eeee we've lost the bairn.'

I was wondering where I could hide, certain the blame would eventually fall on me and I would receive a good battering.

In the middle of all the pandemonium, Jim walked in with a kitchen chair in his arms and stopped to take in the scene before saying, 'What the hell's the matter noo?'

Walking past him to find a bike, Eric said, 'Some buggers left Dennis at Pont Street and Aa've got te gan and find him.'

Jim put the chair down, grabbed Eric's arm to stop him leaving, and said in a loud voice, 'Who's lost?'

Mam replied, 'Eee wore bairns been left in Pont Street and that simple bugger,' pointing to me, 'was towld to bring him.'

Jim smiled at Mam and pulled me behind him before saying, 'No he wasn't told to bring him Mam; you had the bairn last.'

Mam went even redder and snapped back, 'Ye wicked bugger, yor as bad as the rest of these simple buggers.'

Still smiling, Jim said in a quiet voice, 'Aa think ye should all come oot side,' and turning, he walked back out into the yard. We all followed, Mam reluctantly, not sure, what was going on.

Outside, Jim climbed onto the cart and as the rest of us gathered round, he lifted a pile of coats from the sofa and there beneath was Dennis, lying sucking his left-thumb and twiddling his hair with his right-hand murmuring, 'Gola, gola, gola,' totally oblivious to the chaos his absence had created.

Jim picked Dennis up and handed him down to Mam who grabbed him to her breast and began rocking him as though he were a baby.

Looking down at Mam, he said, 'Ye left the bairn by the horse to talk te me Dad so I put him on the sofa, he was nearly asleep and he's been asleep on there ivvor since.'

Panic over, the move in resumed, the cart soon emptied; Porky released to start her mammoth task of clearing the garden and Dad left to take the horse and cart back and ride his motorbike back over from Pont Street.

George and I wandered around the house exploring and found the room with a sloping roof and tiny attic window that had a double and two single beds crammed into it.

This was the bedroom for five growing lads, not very impressive.

Mam had wallpapered and painted throughout and even though the house was one of the oldest colliery houses in Ashington, it smelt fresh and new but that would obviously not last long. She had used a dark brown, mock wood wallpaper to simulate panelling to dado rail height in the kitchen-dining room and although it was very dark, it added warmth to the room.

The highlight of the day came later that evening when we all sat down together at the kitchen table to plates of mince and dumplings followed by a huge rice pudding that Mam had cooked in her new oven. We were in.

Part 2

The Fifth Row

9

Settling Pains

That night, lying in bed next to Dennis and George, I stared at the fading light coming through the small attic window that had been pushed wide open to catch the evening breeze and listened to the unfamiliar sounds of steam engines shunting coal trucks in the near distance. The unfamiliar noises did not keep me awake long; it had been a long day and I soon fell asleep wondering what we would find tomorrow.

A very hot and sunny Sunday morning had the whole family out of bed by nine, each with their own agenda for the day. Dad was in the garden trying to mark out where he was going to lay a path and where the lawn and flower gardens were going but Porky was determined to offer up some ideas of her own whilst rooting around Dad's feet, receiving a kick or two for doing so. Mam was hanging curtains as Betty and Pat prepared vegetables for dinner.

After a cup of tea and some jam and bread, Eric George and I ran out of the house, keen to explore our new surroundings and get out of the house before we were given something to do.

Like Pont Street, the Rows consisted of terraced miner's cottages with outhouses on the other side of the back lane but differed in that they all had very long gardens, ours benefited from being double width as it was an end of terrace with a single story extension to the side. There were eleven Rows laid out in two blocks, First to Sixth and Seventh to Eleventh. Each of the Rows was made up of a number of terraces, the Fifth being the largest with four terraces. In front of ours, there was an open space called, for some unfathomable reason, the 'Boolly,' beyond which was the colliery railway yards where saddleback steam engines shunted coal wagons into trains ready for collection by larger engines. A six-foot high, black painted close-boarded fence separated the railway yard from the Fifth and Sixth Rows.

On the other side of the back lane, a path led past a large Scout Hut and onto a red, metal-sided footbridge and into the Miners' Recreation Sports Grounds and Gymnasium or 'Rec.' To the right of the Fifth Row, the Eleventh Row faced directly onto the colliery baths, canteen, medical centre, and offices, with the main area of sprawling colliery buildings and winding wheels behind.

The red bridge over the shunting lines beckoned us and we were soon standing in the centre, staring at the coal trucks below through the narrow gaps in the planking of the bridge's footway. The sides of the bridge consisted of sheets of red-painted, riveted steel surmounted by a narrow steel parapet. The sides were five foot high and desperate to see what was over the other side, we jumped and clambered up until the three of us were leaning over the parapet taking in the view.

'Look at all that frigging coal,' George said unnecessarily as we looked at six lines of coal trucks stretching off to the colliery some two hundred yards away. George grunted as he hauled himself up until he was standing upright on the top of the narrow parapet, looking down into the top of the full open coal truck about eight foot below his feet.

'Ye can jump inte them wagons from here,' yelled George holding his hands high in the air. Eric and I both dropped back down into the safety of the bridge neither of us as reckless as George.

Eric looked up at George nervously and said, 'Haway man, get doon or ye'll fall off and hurt yorsell and Aa'll get the blame of me Mam.'

'Frig Off,' George yelled and disappeared!

'Bloody hell, Aa knew it,' Eric shouted as he scrambled back up onto the parapet expecting to see George lying in a mangled heap on the ground, twenty or so feet below.

I desperately tried to get back up but needed help to reach the parapet and stopped when Eric shouted down at George, 'Ye stupid git ye might 'av'e missed and killed yorsell.'

I shouted up to Eric, 'Is he aalreet?'

'Aye, he's in the frigging coal wagon messing aboot,' he replied, relieved that he would not have to tell Mam that George was plastered across the railway lines.

Eric dropped down beside me and said, 'Haway Young'un, we'll gan to the other side,' and we made our way to the far end of the bridge.

We stopped at the top of the steps to take in the view; at the foot of the steps, a rough path stretched off into the distance, to the right of which was the 'Rec', the immaculate Miners' Recreation sports grounds. The colliery sprawled out to the east of the Rec and to the north-east, we saw the three huge colliery slag-heaps and another massive area of slag that was increasing in size by the minute as mighty steel buckets borne by a steel ropeway deposited more and more slag in testament to the miners' toiling below.

To the left of the path was an area of ground covered in compacted, grey, pit-slag on which a myriad of supplies for the colliery was stacked. Chocks, gird-ers parts for conveyor belts and numerous other items fought for space. A cana-lised stream trickled through the area to ponds further along the path. In the dis-tance at the north end of the Rec, we could see that the path crossed the main Ash-ington to Ellington road. Beyond this open countryside stretched off as far as the eye could see to where the Simonside hills created three giant steps above the hid-den village of Rothbury.

As we stood looking, George emerged from underneath a coal truck below us and climbed up and over the fence and stood trying to brush off the coal dust and grime that he had collected on his trousers on his first visit to the coal yard.

Eric and I ran down the steps of the bridge to join our grubby and dishevelled brother who was beaming madly, pleased with his adventure.

The three of us ran into the Rec, past a tall hedge enclosing hard tennis court where four youths were smacking a battered tennis ball with equally battered tennis rackets. We watched them for a couple of minutes before walking up to the shabby but imposing Edwardian Gymnasium and changing rooms where we stopped by a rosy-cheeked groundsman wearing navy blue dungarees, who had been fiddling with a huge motor mower.

'Is there any matches on te day Mister?' Eric ventured.

He turned and smiled at the three of us and replied, 'Aye lads, cricket starts at twelve o'clock.'

'Am not watching that sissy game,' George spat, 'is there nee football on man?'

'Not this time of year lad, the pitches are recovering for next season,' the man responded.

'Can we use the gym and changing rooms' mister?' Eric asked.

'My name's Joe and if yor Dad's a pitman ye can.'

'Aye he is, he's called Geordie Carr, and we've just moved into the Fifth Ra,' George replied for Eric.

'I knaa Geordie Carr, so that's alreet, ye can use the showers in the changing room when ye like as well lads but divvint upset the Head Green Keeper as he's got a wicked temper.'

'So's wor Geordie,' said I, smiling.

George spat at me, 'Aa hevn't got a temper man.'

'Yes ye hev,' I answered naively.

George went puce and shouted, 'Am telling ye, Aa divvint hev a frigging temper and ye say Aa hev, one more time and Aa'll frigging bash ye.'

I knew when to shut up and stood there in silence, smiling at him.

Eric smiled at George and said to Joe, 'Thanks mister, Aa'll tek me brother withoot a temper, away to calm doon and we'll hev a look roond.'

We explored the Gym and its two sets of changing rooms, then climbed to the top of the wall bars and hung from the top making monkey noises until a man who was playing Badminton stopped and turned to us shouting, 'Ye three little sods better bugger off before ye get a kick up the arse.'

Duly chastened we clambered down the bars and ran to the Gym door, where George stopped and turned to look back at the badminton players and shouted, 'Hey mister, yor a big frigging ape,' and ran out the door quickly followed by Eric who had suspected some sort of response from George. It took me just a second longer to react before I too ran out as a badminton racket bounced off the wall behind me.

Laughing, we ran off to the top end of the Rec and through the gate to rejoin the rough path that ran between the Rec and the storage area.

'Haway let's gan back to the bridge,' George said, and we turned down the path toward the now distant bridge.

The path had the sports fields on one side with bushes and undergrowth on the other and after a hundred yards or so; we came to the first of two ponds. It was about 30 feet across, surrounded on two sides by reeds and rushes, a perfect wild-life habitat. The pond was full of minnows and sticklebacks while above, dragon-flies zoomed in to hover for a few seconds before they shot off on what seemed like an erratic and random flight path above the reeds. We were soon to discover that frogs, newts and lizards also thrived in and around the pond.

Overhead we could hear and see birds whose names were unknown to us then but would eventually come to recognise by both sight and sound. Curlews, lapwings, swifts, swallows and wagtails flew overhead while coots and moorhens hid in the marshes further north, all thriving here along with thrushes, sparrows, blackbirds and various tits and finches.

We quickly spotted tiny fish swimming close to the edge and squatting, tried in vain to catch them.

Eric said, 'Let's gan and get wor wellies and a bottle to see if we can catch some.' Racing down the path past the second smaller pond, we ran over the bridge and the hundred yards to our new home where we quickly found and pulled on our wellingtons. Eric and George each grabbed a milk bottle from the back yard and sent me to snatch another from next door before we headed back to the pond.

We were soon wading carefully into the pond trying to catch the tiny fish and explore the edge of the reeds. The sun was shining high overhead, reflecting on the ripples of the pond while birds sang happily in the bushes; the smell and sounds of the pond enveloped us; we were in a new world and it was magic.

After some time, George surprisingly demonstrated that he had patience! He stood silent and motionless with his open hand submerged below the water for some minutes.

Suddenly he snatched his hand closed thrusting his closed fist into the air, shouting, 'Got the fugger,' followed quickly by, 'Ouch the bastards stung me.'

He opened his hand to show a small stickleback with its spines embedded in his palm. Eric and I waded over to look at the fish, George holding his hand out proudly, ignoring the sharp pain it was causing him.

'That's a stickleback,' Eric said knowledgeably, 'tha top fins hev got spikes in them to stop other fish from eating it and stupid gits like ye picking them up.'

'Frig off,' George replied and with disdain, flicked the fish from his hand.

'Let's see if we can find some frogs,' he shouted before wading into the reeds. It was hot in the reeds and difficult to wade through so I stuck to the edge while the other two thrashed around inside the small reed bed.

We did not find any frogs but Eric, casting about at the far edge of the pond, did catch a newt, dropping it into his milk bottle and holding it up shouted triumphantly, 'Look at this beauty.'

92

George and I were making our way over to have a look when I got into a little difficulty. My wellies were not as high as theirs were and as I waded over to Eric, the cold pond water flooded into them.

'Bloody bugger,' I shouted but kept on wading; it was pointless not too, not now that my feet were soaking.

Eric and George were laughing at my plight, as my forward motion looked comical due to my efforts not to lose my wellies again. I was holding the bottom of my shorts up with one hand trying to keep them dry; this restricted my leg movement making my steps shorter and all the while, I was waving my free arm frantically in an effort to retain my balance.

We examined the newt in detail before Eric said, 'It must be nearly dinner time we better gan hyem bcfore we're late,' and he led the way back to the path.

On the path I lifted my heels up and back one at a time to let the water pour out of my wellies before we headed for home, Eric carrying his milk bottle with his brightly coloured newt inside. It had been a grand morning and we ran over the bridge laughing and joking, happy with our new surroundings and looking forward to dinner.

We could smell it as we went through the back door into the scullery and into the kitchen where Mam and Pat were busy laying the table while various pans sat bubbling on the fire or kept warm next to it. A tray full of Yorkshire Puddings rested on the open oven door, and behind them, a small roast was waiting.

Mam wiped the moisture from her brow and smiling, asked, 'Where hev ye buggers been then?'

'Catching newts and fish in the ponds,' Eric replied as he kicked his Wellingtons off in the scullery.

She stopped to look at us, just as I kicked off the first off my Wellingtons. As it came free, the boot did a cartwheel spraying water across the floor into the kitchen and over the newly decorated kitchen wall.

Mam's mood changed instantly and I knew with dread what was to come.

She charged toward me snatching up my Wellington on the way and screamed at me, 'Ye bloody simple little bugger ye, ye hevn't got the sense ye wor born with?'

The sight of her rushing toward me made me drop to the floor and huddle up in preparation for the onslaught. I had expected and instantly prepared myself for a good slapping, what I had not expected was her use of the Wellington! She used it like a club, battering me with the heel of the boot while yelling obscenities. I tried desperately to get away and scurried across the floor, half on hands and knees and half on my backside as I tried to use my arms to ward off the blows. I ended up in the corner by the pantry door unable to go any further, my hands and arms squeezed around my head trying in vain to protect myself as she continued the beating.

I was lost in my own little world of pain and grief and was way past crying as sobs racked my body.

I heard Pat and Eric trying to stop Mam and heard her turn on Eric shouting, 'Ye are just as blidy stupid, ye might all have been droond,' and clouted him with my Wellington.

It might have only been a child's' Wellington but in her hands, it was a club.

Eric cried out in pain and quickly backed off as I waited for more punishment but I heard my Uncle Alex's voice rasp, 'Etty Aa thinks that's enough divvint ye?'

He had been in his normal spot in the cottage chair by the fire and witnessing the beating he had risen creakily and hobbled across to Mam, grabbing her arm with his bony hand with a strength that surprised her. His words and grip brought her out of her rage and twisting her hand free she flung the Wellington at me and returned to putting out dinner as if nothing had happened.

Pat, George, Viv, and Dennis who had been standing in shocked silence suddenly began to move again as though coming out of a trance and finished putting chairs around the table for lunch in stunned silence. I was still sobbing in the corner a few minutes later when Dad came in from the garden to cut the meat.

'What's that bugger crying for?' he asked as he sharpened the carver.

'The simple sod nearly droond hessell,' Mam said glaring at the others, defying further comment.

Dad turned to me and said, 'Get yorsell up here for yor dinner noo, before Aa daad ye.'

Still sobbing I climbed onto a chair and sat with my chin on my chest, the pain from my bruises driving any thoughts of food from my mind.

The others ate Sunday dinner in morose silence, apart from Dennis who kept asking, 'Are ye better noo Syd?' until my Mam hushed him by shoving a spoonful of mash into his mouth.

It had been a good day up until then.

Later, after we had cleared the kitchen table and Mam and Dad had gone off on the motorbike, I collected my Wellingtons from pantry door, took them across the back lane, and thrust them into the dustbin.

George, who had been in the lane, witnessed the disposal of my 'wellies' and asked, 'What hev ye done that for?'

I looked at him and replied, 'Every time I wear them I get a good hiding so Aa divvint want the frigging things anymore.' It would be a long time before I wore Wellingtons again.

I do not know whether Mam felt remorse for the beating, or whether or not the venom and rage of the attack had frightened her, or whether or not the sight of the bruises on my thin body she saw as she gave me the ritual Sunday night bath scared her but it marked a turning point. She never again beat any of us. We younger ones continued to receive the occasional well-aimed slap but there were no more savage beatings.

94

The next morning, my arms and back tender from my Mam's punishment, I climbed out of bed and pulled on my shorts and tee shirt, and went downstairs to join the others preparing for school.

Eric had already left in order to catch the bus to Bedlington; Pat was making tea; Viv was whinging about having to go to a new school while George stomped around the sitting room blaming everyone for him not being able to find his sandshoes. Mam was as usual, still in bed; as far as she was concerned, her offspring starting a new school did not warrant disturbing her morning routine as she coughed on her first fag of the day.

Pat, who was due to attend Bothal School at the end of the Third Row, would leave after us. Before we left, she grabbed George by the arm and pointing to Viv and I said, 'Make sure you take these two into the school with you.'

Glaring back at her, he reluctantly muttered, 'They better keep up with me cos am not waiting for them.'

He knew better than to argue with Pat, she matched him when it came to temper and did not take lip from us kids, she was thirteen and having to contend with an unfair world as well as her miserable siblings made her just a tad shirty.

Heading for the door, and without looking at Viv or me, George said, 'Haway de as Black Hannah says,' and we left for our new school.

Wansbeck School was about half a mile away; through the cuts between the Rows to Highmarket; down this street with its eclectic mix of small shops; past the Gaffers' houses in First Row facing a row of smart Edwardian semi-detached houses that ended with the White House Working Men's Club.' Then on through a small plantation to a junction where a sandstone church protected the huge graveyard beyond. From this junction, Wansbeck Road ran south toward a collection of terraced, semi-detached, and large detached houses, regarded as the best housing in Ashington.

The School was a hundred yards down this road, just past a vicarage that hid behind a tall wooden fence. As we walked past the fence, the School came into view and I stopped in my tracks to take it in.

Having been used to the austere Victorian edifice that was the South Junior School; Wansbeck Junior was a revelation. Built in the thirties it consisted of three parallel wings of classrooms running from a large block that contained the hall, toilets, cloakrooms, and offices. There was a playground used for Forms 3 and 4 next to their classroom wing, an area of lawn before the next classroom wing that was for Forms 1 and 2 and beyond that, their playground and finally, the Infants' Wing and their playground.

However, what surprised and delighted me were the classroom wings, these were all single story with Dutch style brick gable ends facing the road and bright red tiles covering the roof. They had completely glazed sidewalls with small panes of glass and matching doors and covered verandas running the full length of the wings. It looked bright and friendly, a wonderful contrast to our last school.

George shouting angrily, 'Haway man or we'll be late,' jerked me from my wonderment and we entered the playground that was already full of kids running around enjoying the morning sun and the start of a new school day. Viv and I timidly followed George into the middle playground where he stood arms crossed, eyes staring defiantly around him; jaw thrust forward, his whole demeanour daring anyone to approach him.

A tousled-haired lad with a huge grin and wearing a polo shirt and shorts that were obviously several generations old, walked boldly up to George and asked, 'Are ye just starting?'

George looked him up and down with contempt and replied in his normal monosyllabic way, 'Why?'

The lad shook his head and walked around George to me and asked, 'How old are ye then?'

I looked at his infectious grin, and smiling back, I replied, 'Seven, how old are you?'

'Am seven as weel, so ye'll be in my class, haway and Aa'll show ye where it is.'

I followed the lad who led me to the Infants' veranda and pointed to the classroom beneath saying, 'That's wore classroom, ye'll be able to sit next te me as nebody else sits there.'

Wondering why he sat on his own, I asked, 'Why does nebody sit next te ye then?'

'Aa divvint knaa, the teacher keeps moving them cos they keep getting me inte trouble,' he said, grinning even more.

'Am Jack Moody from the Sixth Ra, what's your name?

'Am Syd Carr, we've just moved to the Fifth Ra, and that's wor George and Viv ower there,' I answered.

Someone began ringing a bell that had the children racing into lines in front of teachers who had appeared from the main hall.

Jack said, 'Come on that's wor line ower there,' and raced off with me in pursuit, I didn't want to be left on my own in the yard as I could no longer see George or Viv.

The teachers waited until all the kids were standing quietly in line with their hands flat against their thighs. I stood behind Jack copying his stance, hoping it was correct.

The pretty, female teacher in front of our line said, 'Right children in you go,' and the line started to move into the main hall with Jack and me at the back. The teacher patted or touched each of the children for assurance or confirmation that they were hers as they filed past, silently counting until Jack and I reached her.

She grabbed Jack's arm as he went to pass her and said, 'And who is this you've brought along Jack?'

'Syd Carr Miss, he's gannin te sit next to me,' he replied, the grin still firmly on his face.

'Oh is he now,' the teacher said before turning to me saying, 'Have you registered yet Sydney?'

Unsure of what she meant, but certain that whatever it was, I had not, I replied, 'No Miss, Aav'e just got here with me brother and sister.'

'And where are they, might I ask?' she asked.

I looked at her in my baby faced innocence and answered, 'Ye can ask Miss but they've disappeared and Aa divvint knaa where te so Aa canna tell ye,'

Looking just a little vexed, she turned to Jack and said, 'Jack take him to Mrs Joseph's Office and wait to see if he's joining our class,'

I followed Jack into the main building and down a side corridor and found George and Viv sitting in chairs outside a door marked, 'Headmistress.'

George said, 'We've got to wait here until after assembly and see the Headmistress.'

Fifteen minutes later Jack was busy excavating something from his right nostril while George was grilling him for information on the teachers. Viv was sitting swinging her feet back and forwards as hard as she could and I was trying to avoid her feet while wondering if Jack's head was going to cave in as he dug his finger further up his nose.

The sound of heels clipping along the corridor silenced us and we looked toward the sound to see Mrs Joseph heading toward us. A middle-aged woman, attractive in a pleasant, slightly plump way, she was wearing a tweed skirt with a light blue cardigan buttoned to the neck.

'Aa the Carrs and Moody?' she said with a pleasant smile.

'Moody wait here, you three in you come.' She gave us a welcoming chat about the school, and as the South School had informed her that we would be arriving, she had already assigned us to classes.

George, you are in Junior Form 2 at the end of the middle wing; Sydney, Jack will take you back to your class in Infants; Vivian, come along with me to the First Infants.

Jack said to me, 'Haway then,' as the others went off to their classrooms. I followed him back along the corridor and through the cloakroom where a milkman was stacking crates of small bottles of milk provided for all the kids in the school.

'Haad on a minute,' Jack said as he knelt to refasten his sandshoe lace. He did not appear to be very adept at it as it took him quite some time and certainly long enough for the milkman to finish stcking crates and lead his horse and cart to the school gates.

Jack ran across to the crates and lifted two bottles of orange juice from the top crate; each crate contained twenty-two small bottles filled with milk and two with orange.

'Here ye are,' he said, passing a bottle to me. We quickly drank the orange juice followed by a bottle of milk each before running to the classroom, Jack punctuating his running with enormous belches that left me quite envious of this brilliant ability.

I did not get to sit next to Jack; the teacher took one look at the two of us standing together with moustaches of milk and smiled before she rearranged the classroom seating, I was on the opposite side of the room to Jack. I had to go to the toilet twice during the first lesson as did Jack, the teacher making us go individually, suspecting we would get up to mischief had we gone together.

At lunchtime, I collected Viv from her class and along with Jack; we headed for the gate where there was some sort of commotion. A large group of kids had gathered in a circle, shouting and cheering at something in the middle.

Curiosity drove us into the circle to see what or who was causing the commotion - it was George. He was lying on top of another boy with an arm lock around the poor lads head, squeezing as hard as he could while wearing that familiar gritted-teeth grin, his lower jaw pushed forward as he sought to part the lad's head from his body.

The poor lad started to cry and splutter with some difficulty as he begged for release. Satisfied that he had won, George let go of the boy and stood up to a mix of cheers and boos. He brushed himself off, pushed his way through the throng, and headed for home, with us running after him.

When we caught up with him, I asked, 'Who was that ye were fighting George?'

Stomping along, he replied, 'Aa divvint frigging knaa, Aa sit next to him and he said me writing was precise - the cheeky bugger, so Aa had te sort him oot.'

'What does precise mean Geordie?' I asked suspecting it was not derogatory.

'Aa divvint knaa man but it must be summick cheeky mustn't it,' he replied.

Grinning madly, Jack said, 'Aa think we're gannin te have a great time eh?'

We only had two weeks at school before we broke up for the summer holidays but it was long enough for us to get to know our classmates and the surrounding area. The school was a hundred yards from the 'Peoples Park' a large square park with a children's' playground in one corner. The Miner's Institute with snooker hall, table tennis, darts, and a reading room stood next to the park and next to this was the small, indoor municipal swimming pool that we were to use regularly in the holidays.

We spent the holidays making new friends and exploring Highmarket, the open countryside on the other side of the Rec Bridge and 'Sheepwash', a scenic area of open woodland and paths alongside the river Wansbeck a half-mile or so south of home.

It was during this holiday that the dynamics of our play grouping changed. Eric made new friends of his age and at twelve decided, he no longer had time for George or me. George made new friends too so I rarely saw either of them apart from meal times. I became responsible for looking after Dennis that entailed me having my four-year-old brother tagging along whenever I could not sneak out without him.

We said good-bye to Porky, enjoying parts of her for the next two Sunday lunches, friends and relations devouring the rest of her.

Dad planted winter crops in the top part of the garden and turned the area in front of the sitting room window into a small flower garden with a central lawn.

I also made new friends and along with my cousin Alec, we ran wild for six weeks until the new term started. Luckily, no serious accidents prevented us from going back to school; however, Eric had contracted scarlet fever and did not start the new term.

I moved into juniors' Form 1A and was upset when I found out Jack had gone into Form 1B. His friendship was to come in handy during schoolyard clashes between A and B stream boys, a couple of years later.

Eric recovered from scarlet fever but Mam continued to keep him at home telling him and us that he was not ready to go back.

It was almost December before the man from the School-Board called to find out why Eric was not at school. Mam gave him a torrent of abuse for his troubles and sent him packing, as she could not believe the cheek of the man, fancy telling her what to do with her kids.

Poor Eric went back to school in time for the end of term tests and obviously failed them miserably. His embarrassment made worse by still having to wear a non-standard, ill-fitting green jacket with a badly sewn on school badge. Despite having failed his end of term tests, his teachers wanted to remain at grammar school and said that with some extra tuition, he should be able to catch up.

However, Mam had achieved her aim, she used his failed test results to take him out of grammar school and send him to Bothal Secondary, an old Victorian complex at the end of the Third Row. This is what she had wanted all along, no more uniforms, bus fares, or school meals to worry about, let alone sports strips and footwear, she had won at the expense of Eric's education.

She vowed never to put herself through the same bother again and began watching mine and George's progress at school, determined not to have to bother with grammar schools again.

10

Coronation, Trips and Cubs

Three very important events occurred in 1953: the Coronation of Princess Elizabeth, crowned Queen of Great Britain, the Empire and Commonwealth; a television was installed in our sitting room and Dad traded in his motorbike for a motorbike and sidecar. The last of the three had the greatest impact on my life. Things were definitely on the up or so we thought.

Back at school on the run up to and immediately after the Coronation, we kept a class 'Coronation Scrap Book.' Scouring papers and magazines for pictures of our new Queen and her Coronation, we discussed them in class before selecting the best pictures for our book.

It was during one of the early sessions that our teacher told us that we would be going to Whitley Bay to see the new Queen when she carried out her State Tour of Great Britain. Our teacher briefed us carefully on the event and it promised to be a great day out. The outline for the day was to walk to the railway station, catch a special train to Monkseaton and then march to our place amongst lines of schoolchildren from all over Mid-Northumberland; wait for Her Majesty to drive by; wave, cheer, and then march back to Monkseaton for the return rail journey.

I was truly excited until she spoilt it by saying, 'Make sure you all wear Mackintoshes and bring some barely sugar sweets to help you through the morning.' I did not have a Mackintosh and began worrying immediately as to how and where I could obtain one.

Arriving home that afternoon I approached Mam and said with little hope of a positive response, 'Mam, Aa need a Mac to wear when we gan te see the Queen.'

She ignored me and continued peeling a large bowl of potatoes as though I was not there.

'Mam Aa need a Mac,' I repeated while keeping out of slapping range.

'Bugger off ootside and play, I hurd you the forst time and Aa divvint knaa where ye think am gannin to get a frigging Mac from.'

It was the sort of response I had come to expect and resolved myself to going to school, the only one without a Mac. I had thought about missing the big event to save myself the embarrassment but dismissed that idea; I wanted to see the Queen.

In an effort to raise money to buy barley sugar sweets, I started to collect pop bottles that I could return to shops for pennies, certain that if I asked for money for sweets I would receive the same negative response.

Our new television; a small wooden box with a tiny twelve-inch screen, arrived two days before the coronation and was placed with reverence on a small, square occasional table in the corner of the sitting room by the window whilst we sat in excited anticipation waiting for the man to finish connecting it to the newly fitted aerial. When he finally switched it on, we jostled each other for the best vantage point and watched as the screen came to snowy life before the picture of the test card came into focus.

This brought gasps of admiration from everyone - everyone except George who said with some disappointment, 'That's nee good, it's not moving, Aa thought it was gannin to be like the pictures?'

Laughing, the TV man looked at him and said, 'It's just the test card, programmes don't start until five o'clock and then you'll see everybody moving.'

George blushed and said, 'Aa knew that man, Aa was just kidding.' This brought hoots of derisive laughter from the rest of us as George stormed out, threatening to smash the television over our heads.

At five o'clock, we had a new and demanding member in the family. On a glorious early summer's evening when all the younger members of the family would normally be galloping around outside, we were instead sat in the sitting room watching the 'Box'. Luckily, those early television programmes were not that brilliant and after a few days the novelty wore off and we only watched the TV when it rained or just before we went to bed.

The Coronation was the main topic of conversation for days, the papers adding to it by filling their pages with articles and photographs of our beautiful young Queen to be. Mam had told our friends of our new TV and invited them to watch the Coronation with us. We were not the only ones in the Row to have gained a television for the big event but on the day, our sitting room floor was full of kids sitting with necks craned to view the small screen.

Older siblings and neighbours keen to watch the spectacle occupied the sofa, armchairs, and several extra chairs brought in from the kitchen. It was a long event and did not fully occupy the minds of us kids sitting uncomfortably on the floor, resulting in a fair amount of fidgeting, talking, and the occasional squabble that invariably led to chastisement from the adults. However, Dad made the occasion more enjoyable by producing beer for the adults, as well as pop and crisps for the kids.

The afternoon ended with a magnificent argument between Dad and Geordie Little, the later had been foolish enough to comment, 'Aa divvint knaa what all the fuss is aboot, she's only a frigging short arsed box heed, tha aall probably Kraut, Nazis anyway,' he said as the Royal Party stood on the balcony of the Palace waving to the crowd.

Dad, who none of us thought to be any sort of Royalist, turned puce and aided by the three of four bottles of beer he had consumed, unleashed a torrent of abuse on Geordie Little. Dad's language was foul, resulting in the Carr kids, who

102

had heard it before sniggering into our hands while the other kids who had no; looked on in stunned, and shocked silence.

Geordie left immediately followed by his wife but their two younger children, Alan and Jennifer, stayed behind, not wanting to leave while crisps and pop were on the go.

Two days before the school trip to see the Queen, I was still worrying about not having a Mac to wear and had resigned myself to going without, kidding myself that I would not be the only one without a raincoat. Therefore, it was much to my surprise, when after dinner that evening, Mam produced a battered, and rather grubby, navy-blue Burberry Mackintosh she had acquired from somewhere.

I was incredulous; I had not thought that my pleas had even registered with her let alone roused her into action.

'Here, try this on.' she said brusquely.

I pulled on the slightly large Mac and she tugged it into place, fastening the buttons and belt before pulling at the bottom of the hem trying to make it fit my skinny frame and in doing so jerking me roughly back and forth.

'Stand still ye soft shite while Aa look.' she said leaning back to admire her work.

The Mac had seen better days and was a tad grubby but was complete and serviceable. It was far from a perfect fit, the sleeves hanging down over my hands so that only my fingertips showed, but it was a Mac.

'There that's champion,' she said pleased with herself.

'But it's dorty Mam,' I said, foolishly.

'Aa knaa that ye simple bugger, am gannin to wash it for ye.' she replied, unfastening the Mac before roughly dragging it off me.

Relieved, I pictured myself walking to school in a newly washed, ironed, and very smart Mac. Of course, I had not considered the 'Mam Factor!' She could not be bothered to wash it that night; after all, why do anything today that you could put off until the last possible moment, and then only do it if someone pesters you enough. I knew by now that unless I kept at her, she would not wash or iron it, so resolved to remind her throughout the following day, even if it meant a slap or two.

My pestering paid off, at six o'clock in the evening, after another begging plea from me, she snatched the coat from my hands and saying, 'Stop yor bloody whining,' and stormed into the scullery to wash the coat.

Relieved, my hopes soared but then I thought of the effort that was going to be required to get it ironed and my relief faded.

A little while later, she brought the washed and rung out mac into the kitchen and placing the fireguard in front of the fire, hung the coat over it to dry. It was soon steaming nicely so I withdrew to the sitting room to wait a wee while before I asked her to iron it.

103

A little later, watching tele with the rest of the family, I was suddenly aware of a burning smell coming from the kitchen. It could only be one thing and I raced into the kitchen and dragged the now smoking Mac from the fireguard.

Mam, Eric, George, Viv, and Dennis came in to see what had happened as I desperately patted the singed coat, trying to establish the extent of the damage. My worst fears were realised when I found a large hole burnt in the bottom front of the coat on the left-hand side. I was devastated and matters made worse by comments from my loving siblings.

'That's a real hot coat,' said Eric flippantly.

'Mam wore Syd's bornt his coat,' said Viv, needlessly.

'That's knackered it Young'un,' George said, grinning.

Only Dennis showed any concern, he looked at me before saying, 'Ye can wear my coat Syd,' and ran into the sitting room to fetch his small blue overcoat.

Mam grabbed the Mac from me and pulled the frayed and burnt ends from around the hole before saying, 'Here put it on and let's see what we can dee.'

My spirits lifted as I pictured her carrying out a perfect repair with a needle, cotton and a spare piece of Burberry material.

She fastened the coat around me again and we all surveyed the damage at the front of the coat. Any hopes I had of having it repaired disappeared when she took the corner of the damaged part of the coat and folded it back revealing the checked lining that was intact if a little scorched.

Mam grabbed my arm and said, 'Put yor hand in yor pocket te keep the coat folded back ower it and nee bugger'll see the hole.'

I did as instructed and stood there crestfallen, realising I would spend tomorrow trying to hide the prominent hole in the coat as Mam obviously had no intentions of carrying out any repairs, nor was she prepared to do any ironing, especially of a coat with a hole in it.

Early the following morning I walked to school in my clean but creased Mac; the corner nonchalantly held back by my left hand that I had thrust into the pocket of my shorts. It was drizzling lightly and I could feel the cool, refreshing dampness on my face and knees and knew that because I was wearing sandals my socks would soon be wet. The lack of Wellingtons did not bother me; I knew the dangers involved in wearing them and preferred wet feet.

The day might have been dull and damp and my coat a disaster but my spirits were high, I was looking forward to my first train ride and more importantly, to seeing the Queen.

I managed to get through school assembly and walk to the station and board the train without taking my left hand out of my pocket but continued to worry as to how I was going to eat my barley sugar sweets without using both hands and wished I'd put them in my right-hand pocket.

The train ride was short but enjoyable and added to the excitement of the day. At Monkseaton, we paraded by schools and marched off in a huge procession to the coast road at Whitley Bay where we took up our positions. Schoolchildren of junior school age lined the road on both sides as far as you could see and they were all wearing Macs!

The initial excitement faded when our Teacher told us that it would be at least an hour before the Queen's arrival, so she and the other teachers bustled around trying to keep spirits high and handed out small Union Jack flags for us all to wave.

When she came to me, she said, 'For goodness sake Sydney, take your hand out of your pocket,' and thrust a flag at me.

With a dejected look, I took my left hand out of my pocket as I grabbed the flag with my right. The Mac unfurled revealing the burnt hole to the teacher.

Looking at the scorch ringed hole, she smiled and said quietly, 'Perhaps you better keep your hand in your pocket,' and moved quickly on. Relieved, I quickly transferred my barley sugar to my right pocket and returned my Mac to its cover up position.

Just before the Queen was due to arrive, I jostled my way to the kerbside and was sucking madly on a sweet while waving my flag in practice for the arrival of the Royal procession and noticed the children on the opposite side of the road. They were from Newbiggin and mostly girls of about nine or ten, faces shining with damp from drizzle as they talked excitedly to each other.

As I looked across, I found my eyes drawn to a girl, smaller than the rest she was looking directly at me and as I looked back, I recognised the plaited hair and warm smile I had seen two years earlier on the beach at Newbiggin. We stared at each other for what seemed ages before I had the courage to wave. Realising that I had already been waving my flag, I dropped my right hand to my side and bringing my left hand out of my pocket, I raised it to wave gently at her.

Her smile increased and she waved back.

The noise of cheering and screaming children from the direction the Queen was due interrupted our long look and we, along with everyone else turned to watch the approaching procession. The sound of cheering grew louder as it rippled toward us, and we started to cheer as Police Outriders approached. The large black Rolls Royce with vast windows glided past and we caught a glimpse of the Queen waving her gloved hand. She was wearing a sparkling tiara and a beaming smile, and next to her, I saw the larger figure of the Prince resplendent in naval uniform.

It was over in a second. Was I disappointed? Not a bit, fleeting as it was, it did not matter, I had seen the Queen and she was as beautiful as I had imagined. Waiting while the rest of the entourage passed, I could see between vehicles, the blue-eyed girl waving her flag and cheering.

I realised I had left my coat open and began worrying if the Queen had seen it and perhaps said to the Prince, 'Phillip, did you see the little boy with the hole in his Mackintosh?'

I lost sight of the blue-eyed girl and within minutes, we were on our way back to the train station talking breathlessly about what we had just seen, each of us trying to claim he or her had seen more than the others.

On the way, I wondered about the blue-eyed girl, she must be older than I was but she did not look it, perhaps she was there with an older sister.

Shortly after the Coronation, on an overcast Saturday morning, Dad wheeled his motor bike out of the backyard and roared off down the back lane before most of us were out of bed.

A little later, Uncle Alex was slurping a mug of tea in his normal position in front of the kitchen fire, carefully wiping his grand but tea and tobacco-stained moustache after each slurp, ensuring the handlebars were just right. He had not yet lit up his foul smelling pipe to pollute the air but Mam was doing her best with her Woodbines - succeeding quite well in filling the kitchen with smoke while sitting at the table with Dennis on her knee.

I was sitting opposite eating cornflakes heaped with sugar and drenched in milk; I enjoyed this rare treat as I wondered where Dad had gone so early.

Through a mouthful of cornflakes, I asked tentatively, 'Where's Dad gone Mam?'

My question received one of her unfathomable answers; 'He's gone to Blyth to see the sowldgers,' she replied as she buttered Dennis some toast.

'What sowldgers?' I asked, curious as to why he would be going to see soldiers.

'That's for me to knaa and ye te wonder,' she replied half-smiling.

I gave up and concentrated on my cornflakes with images in my head of Dad watching soldiers marching at Blyth.

About an hour later, wearing a homemade Zorro mask and hat, I was on the roof of the air raid shelter, fighting off Mexican soldiers who had disguised themselves as my new mates Percy and Alan, I had just killed Alan for the umpteenth time when I heard a motorbike growling down the lane.

Curious to see if it was Dad back from seeing soldiers, I quickly killed the Mexicans again and leant over the edge of the roof to look down the street. A motorbike was coming toward us with Dad riding it but it was different; the noise of the motor was deeper but what made me quickly drop down from the roof, was the sight of the sidecar attached to it.

Dad brought the outfit to a smooth halt outside our back yard, dismounted, and stood there surveying his latest acquisition with pride. Mam joined us with Dennis still in her arms and Viv hanging on to her piny.

We all stood gawping at the machine as Dad took his helmet, goggles and gauntlets off.

'Did ye get it off the sowldgers Dad?' I asked excitedly.

Dad looked at me as though I was simple and replied, 'What the buggery are ye talking aboot I got it from H&H man.'

Mam stepped forward and demanded, 'Haway man George let's see inside.'

The sidecar was quite long; the lower half was black with a streamlined nose and a small door just in front of the wheel. The top half was white with a black canvas roof and aft of the tiny windscreen there was a window in the door with another behind, and behind that a tiny rear window. There were two matching side windows on the other side next to the bike.

Dad opened the door to the sidecar revealing tandem seats, the front one of which he tilted forward.

Mam opened the door wider and pushed me toward it saying, 'Gan on ye and Viv get in the back.'

The thought of having to share a seat with Viv disgusted me and I stupidly said 'Am not sitting next to hor,' but a quick slap to the back of my head from Mam was enough for me to change my mind, and I climbed in.

There was just enough room for the two of us in the back as I pressed myself as close to the side as possible, trying desperately not to make contact with Viv. Mam climbed into the front with Dennis on her knee and Dad closed the door behind her. Not being able to see past my Mams head, it initially felt a little claustrophobic but at least, I had a view out of the side window.

Dad disappeared into the house and came out a few minutes later with George who, wearing a thick overcoat was pulling on a battered helmet. Grabbing the handlebars, Dad kicked the motorbike into life and climbed on followed by George who settled onto the pillion. Dad then put the bike into gear and slipped the clutch, we were off.

Being cocooned in the tiny back seat was a far from comfortable, especially with Viv but the excitement I felt, made it enjoyable.

Still getting used to the feel of the outfit on the road, Dad drove the bike at a leisurely pace, giving us plenty of time to admire the view and as we rode along Mam recited a popular but crude Geordie nursery rhyme to Dennis:

'Harry Black Barry shit in the quarry,
The quarry was deep so he shit on the heap,
The heap was high so he shit in the sky,
The sky was blue so he shit in the shoe,
The shoe was black so he shit on the cat,
And the cat ran away with shit on its back.'

Viv and I giggled in the back while Dennis repeated each 'shit' with a squeaky laugh.

Mam was obviously happy as she then began singing her favorite song in her not unpleasant voice;

'Over the mountain over the sea,
That's where my heart is longing to be,
Please let the light that shines on me, shine on the one I love.'

Not knowing all the words to the song, she sang the same lines over and over again. Her voice was unusually warm and helped keep us in high spirits despite our cramped seating.

We drove north through Ellington, a remarkably lovely village given its closeness to the drab mining towns, and villages near it. We continued on to Red Row near where my Dad had spent his youth and onto the new council houses at Hadston where Granny Carr had moved too and where some of Dad's sisters lived.

Accompanied by a loud backfire, Dad pulled the bike up outside Granny's red-bricked council semi and we climbed out of our hutch on wheels to spend a pleasant hour or so having tea and cakes with Granny, Uncle Jim and Aunties Mamie, Nellie and Aggie. Still not fully accepted by the Carr Coven, Mam sat for most of the time with a frosty grimace on her face.

A large imposing bureau made of solid mahogany stood against one wall of Granny's sitting room; it had four deep draws, the top one having a drop down front that revealed a beautifully constructed desk. Above this, two glass doors protected four or five shelves that were laden with books. Looking up at them, I read the titles; most of the classics were there; including the complete works of Dickens and Shakespeare; volumes on the First and second World Wars and many others plus a large collection of National Geographic magazines. I was in awe of them and longed to explore their pages but had already been told that the bureau and books were Uncle Jim's pride and joy and not to be touched.

After tea, Dad ushered his relatives outside to show them around his new outfit.

Keen to know about the bike's performance, Aunt Aggie's husband Uncle Vic discussed the motorcycle's engine with Dad. He had been a Sergeant, Typhoon fighter-bomber pilot during the war, flying tank-busting missions over France and Germany and still wore his RAF handlebar moustache and spoke with a soft, southern accent. He had married Aggie during the war when he was stationed at RAF Acklington and had settled there when he was demobbed. With jobs scarce for fighter-bomber pilots in post-war England, he had ended up working in the coal mines but would always be an RAF hero to us.

Eventually, Dad marshalled us back into the sidecar before he walked round to the bike. Granny, Aunties and Uncles stood watching as he grasped the handlebars and kicked the starting motor, the engine spluttered into life only to die immediately.

Dad smiled and kicked again - nothing; kicked again - nothing. His smile disappeared, replaced by a gritted-teeth grimace with jaw pushed forward. I had seen that look worn by my brother George on many occasions and wondered it if it meant the same, after all, Dad's name was also George.

It did mean the same, Dad stepped back from the bike and said to the silent machine, 'You bloody, fucking useless bastard, ye better fucking start or Aa'll tek a sledgehammer te ye, ye fucking twating thing ye.'

There was a collective, shocked tut-tutting from the assembled audience and my four-foot-ten Granny Carr said, 'What did you say George Carr?'

Dad's rage, made worse by the motorbikes refusal to answer him or start up, had clouded his judgement. He Shook the handlebars of the motorbike and kicked the starter several times in quick succession but to no avail, the engine still refused to start. He stepped back panting from his efforts and let rip another stream of foul language.

This was too much for my diminutive Granny, she walked briskly around the sidecar to my Dad and slapping his arm said, 'You wicked, wicked man, swearing like that in front of these canny bairns and your sisters, you ought to be ashamed of yourself,' and continued to slap his arm, forcing Dad to move backwards to escape her wrath.

I was shocked, not by my Dad's swearing, I was used to that but by the sight of him walking briskly backwards to escape his tiny mother's punishment; he looked very much the chastised child. It was then that I noticed that my Mam was laughing, well more of a satisfied guttural chuckle. Dad stood like a naughty child, trying desperately to placate his irate mother while Uncle Vic walked over to the motorbike, unscrewed the petrol filler cap on the top of the tank, and looked inside.

'You're out of petrol George,' he said helpfully.

It did not help; the second loss of face was not what Dad needed.

'Fucking Hell that's all Aa need,' he swore, just when he had almost succeeded in calming Granny down. This latest profanity started her off again, slapping and berating Dad who was at a total loss as to what to do.

Mam's chuckles changed into fits of laughter that made her and Dennis, who was sitting in bewildered silence on her knee, shake violently, a result of which, Dennis also started to laugh nervously. I was not sure whether it was wise to laugh in case Dad saw us but I could not help it, and soon the sidecar was rocking from our combined laughter.

Mam said, 'It's a pity yor Grannie hasn't got her bamboo rod with her, she could hev given him a right walloping!'

She started to laugh crazily until almost in hysterics, she screamed 'Eeee, stop it or Aa'll pee mesell.'

This only served to make us laugh even more, so much so that my sides were hurting.

Seeing the sidecar shake, George walked around and stared in at us as though we were mad, but our laughter was infectious and much to Dad's chagrin,

he also started to laugh. Escaping Granny's slapping he walked around her and up to George and slapped him around the head, not that it did much good as George was wearing his battered helmet. George glared back at Dad but seeing his face red with embarrassment, he started laughing again.

This was too much for Dad, now scarlet with rage he grabbed George by the collar and spat at him, 'Ye better stop fucking laughing ye bloody little waster

109

or Aa'll frigging take that helmet off ye and shove it up yor arse.' All things considered; this was probably not the wisest thing for him to have said.

Like a flock of demented hens, my Aunties began clucking even louder, shaking their heads in shocked disbelief at their brother's behaviour and Granny - well she launched into him again. I began to worry that my Mam was going to have a fit, she was laughing that hard, so hard that she had frightened Dennis and he had started to cry. Viv was staring in open mouth bewilderment and I had managed to stifle my laughter but was thoroughly enjoying the spectacle.

George, who had broken free of my Dad's grip, watched as Granny attacked Dad again and said, 'Ye frigging deserve that ye frigging bully,' and stepped back quickly to avoid my Dad's backhander but not quick enough to escape a swift nip on the arm from Granny.

This started me off again and Mam's laughing became mixed with cries of pain as her body reacted to her laughed fuelled spasms.

Eventually, Granny's anger subsided and things calmed down.

Dad was standing by the motorbike fuming silently, while Mam, who had just managed to control her laughing; wheezed, 'Oh my God my ribs are so bloody sore, what a bunch of sackless buggas they are.'

Aunt Aggie said, 'Vic's gone on his bike to get ye some petrol George.'

Dad was too angry to answer coherently and muttered something while nodding his head.

Later, back on the road, Dad drove out of Hadston and on a few more miles north to Amble, a fishing port and mining village that was in parts very picturesque and in others, drab.

Mam's parents, Granddad and Granny Waterford lived there in a Gothic style, ex-vicarage on the links at the South end of town. Several of my Mam's sisters and her only brother also lived in Amble in houses that Granddad had bought them from the proceeds of the sale of his farm and from a haulage contract for the resurfacing of the Great North Road. Mam had not received a penny, as her family had not been speaking to her at that time.

Apparently, when he finished the road contract, Granddad had gone off on his own for five years; philandering around the world until his money ran out and eventually returned to Amble and Granny as though he had just been to the pub for a pint. Mam had re-established relationships with her family but it was too late for any money from Granddad.

Dad did not turn off the main road to head for any of our relatives; instead, he headed straight out of Amble toward Warkworth.

As soon as my Mam realised this she started to bang on the window of the sidecar and shouted, 'George ye've missed the turn for me Mam's.'

Dad neither heard nor saw her; he could not, what with the roar of the motorbike, the crash helmet and goggles he was wearing and having his eyes fixed firmly on the road ahead. This made Mam very angry.

110

She continued banging on the window and shouted, 'That mealy-faced miserable bugger drags us te see his frigging witchy sisters but winnit stop te see my family.' 'How ye bloody swine, ye,' she yelled, 'stop this frigging bike and Aa'll put a cut in yor frigging head like a navvies bait tin, ye baldy headed miserable get ye.'

Dad rode on oblivious of the maelstrom raging in the sidecar and was completely taken by surprise by the ranting banshee who attacked him when he stopped to admire the view at Alnmouth.

Standing for the first time at one of the most scenic spots on the beautiful Northumberland coast, I was unable to admire the view as my parent's toe-to-toe slanging match completely stole my attention. I smiled to myself and looked at George, and was shocked to see him staring malevolently at Dad. Resentment was growing between the two, Dad because he realised he had lost George's respect and was finding him more difficult to control and George at Dad's heavy-handed discipline.

Having finally run out of insults, Mam and Dad subsided into icy silence before we climbed back into the sidecar and headed for Ashington, passing back across the ancient toll bridge at Warkworth and up the steep hill of the quaint high street to do a left turn in front of the magnificent castle. It had been a great day out.

A few days later, I was walking home from school with Jack when he asked, 'Are ye gannin te come camping with the Cubs te Rothbury?'

I was not in the Cubs and had not known about the camping trip but like his grin, Jack's enthusiasm was infectious, so I asked, 'When are ye gannin?'

'Two weeks' time, ye can join the Cubs tonight and then ye'll be able to come.' Later that afternoon I walked the fifty yards to the Scout Hut with Jack and joined the Cubs

A fortnight later, on a lovely summer's afternoon, twelve Cubs including myself, waited outside the Scout Hut for our transport to arrive. We were all wearing uniforms of navy blue jerseys, caps, and neckerchiefs with woggles, my jersey was a hand me on from Larry three doors down. We all carried camping kit, mine consisted of an enamel mug and plate, knife, fork and spoon, a small towel with a well-used bar of soap, a pair of khaki shorts and a tee shirt; all stuffed into a brown paper bag with string handle.

We waited outside the hut with mounting excitement until our transport, a large dark blue removals van, rattled past the corner at our house and onto the grass in front of us. We helped load the bell tent, blankets, and other paraphernalia into the cavernous rear of the van before climbing on board with our own kit and watched as the Cub leader lifted the tailboard into place, locking us in.

It was probably a very unsafe form of transport for twelve unruly Cubs but it was great fun. As we trundled down the back lane and onto the main road, Jack,

111

in a mock German accent with strong Geordie overtones, led us in a rousing chorus of, 'I love to go a-wandering.'

The tailboard was about five foot high and prevented us from looking out unless we pulled ourselves up and leant our arms over the top. Jack and I were both in that position when a car came up behind, waiting for a chance to overtake. Without a word, we both began making faces at the woman passenger who smiled back and stuck her tongue out at us as she drove past.

Jack's leadership skills then came into play and he lined us up behind the tailboard as he looked through a gap, waiting for cars to approach.

As the first car came up behind us, he shouted, 'Now,' and one after another, we pulled our heads above the tailboard, stuck out our tongue or made a face and dropped down again.

It was great fun and we varied the rate and number of heads that appeared before collapsing back, laughing hysterically. Our antics brought a mixed reception from passing cars, some waved and laughed, others waved their fists or tooted their horns but whatever the response, we enjoyed it and it set the pace for the rest of the camp.

We camped in the grounds of Rothbury Scout Hut overlooking the lovely Northumbrian, sandstone village, nestled as it was in the upper Coquet Valley surrounded by the Simonside hills.

We had a whale of a time - my first time away from home; dressed as Red Indians we ran wild in the woods and spent several hours learning skills such as camp craft and other Cubby things. We also ate loads of beans – we had them in one form or the other with all our meals. At night, we slept in a large bell tent, our feet toward the centre pole, each lying on a rough blanket on top of a groundsheet, with another blanket pulled on top.

Sleep never came early as we talked, sang, and played games until the Cub Master threatened us with violent deaths if we did not shut up. We pulled blankets over our heads trying desperately to stifle our sniggers and waited until he had left before we started all over again.

On the second night, we were lying in our blankets singing at the top of our not very tuneful voices:

'An old cowpoke went riding one dark and windy day,
Up on a ridge he rested as he went on his way,
When all at once a mighty herd of red-eyed cows he saw,
A-plowing through ragged skies and up a cloudy draw.'

And then shouting the chorus as loud as we could

'YIPPEEE-YI YAaaa, YIPPEEE-YI YOoooo
GHOST RIDERS IN THE SKY-E-AY-E-AY,'

112

'Their brands were still on fire and their hooves were made of steel,
Their horns were black and shiny and their hot breath he could feel,
A bolt of fear shot through him as he looked up in the sky,
For he saw the riders comin' and he heard their mournful cry.

'YIPPEEE-YI YAaaa, YIPPEEE-YI YOoooo
GHOST RIDERS IN THE SKY-E-AY-E-AY.'

We did not have the chance to sing the final verse - just as we sucked in our breaths to start, an enormous fart exploded from someone in the tent. It really was quite magnificent and so loud that we all stopped singing and burst out laughing. The perpetrator, Norman a slightly chubby lad who stood out like a sore thumb amongst the rest of the skinny pack, giggled embarrassingly.

I was the first to congratulate him and said, 'Bloody heck Norman, that was the loudest fart Aa've ever hurd.'

Other voices piped up:

'A bet they hurd that in Rothbury!'

'A bet they hurd it in Ashington!'

'A bet they hurd that in Timbuktu!'

'Hang on I can fart louder than that,' someone said, and the farting contest began. I have to admit failure; although I did manage to squeeze one out it was a pathetic affair, especially as Norman had let rip another couple of nuclear bombs.

Jack had not said much and had not farted until he shouted, 'Hang on, shut up.'

He let rip a long and rumbling fart that brought gasps of admiration followed by gasps for breath and curses as the air in the tent became foul and disgusting.

Norman was obviously upset at Jack stealing his thunder!

As the cursing died down he shouted, 'Right beat this,' and started to squeeze; we watched him going bright red with effort as he squeezed out what he thought would be another enormous fart.

It was not that loud and did not sound quite right and we wondered what had happened when Norman suddenly screamed in a high-pitched voice, 'Shit!'

'Ye smell like shit,' someone shouted.

'No man Aa've shit mesell,' he said pathetically and began crying.

He received little sympathy from us and screams of, 'Dorty Shitter,' and 'Smelly Arse,' did not help the poor lad.

Eventually, the Akela came in to see what all the commotion was and dragged the poor lad out to the showers. He suffered some 'Mickey-Taking' for a long time afterwards.

Dad had given me half a crown for pocket money and not having had the chance to spend it, I still had it just before we packed up to go home. Along with the rest of the Pack, I walked into Rothbury to look at what the shops had to offer.

Most of the lads were buying sweets and comics but I spotted a garish brooch with a large green, imitation emerald on display in the window of the gift shop. The label read '2s 5d.' That would leave me a penny but I went in and bought it for Mam. I was still trying to find some love and affection and had not yet realised how self-obsessed, vindictive and selfish she was. To give her, her due she did wear it so she could brag to the neighbours that her kids thought the world off her. She never mentioned my name and never actually thanked me - I was a slow learner.

11

Picnic and Camping

At five o'clock on a spring evening of the following year, the family were all sitting around the kitchen table having dinner. Jim, who had just finished his shift at the pit, was unusually quiet until placing his fork carefully on his plate, he looked across at Dad and said quietly, 'I'm joining up!'

Dad exploded and snatching up the teapot of freshly brewed tea, he spat, 'Nur yor fucking not you bloody waster, ye'll stay in the pit, or Aa'll scald ye with this fucking tea!'

Glaring back at Dad, Jim picked up the gully from the bread plate, and growled, 'Try it and Aa'll stick this in ye.'

We sat in stunned disbelief as Dad swore a couple more times before he calmed down and finished eating his dinner as we realised that Jim had just set new boundaries!

True to his word, he joined up and left us to become Gunner Carr in the Royal Artillery. It also meant that George moved into his bed, leaving Dennis and me to share the big double bed.

Pat finished school and started work at a granary just beyond the end of the Fifth Row and much to Mams annoyance and worry, she started to date boyfriends.

Mam had told George the year before that he was in no way to pass his 11+ exam and he grudgingly obeyed her. Despite his gruff voice and rough mannerisms, he was very bright and his teachers had expected him to pass the exam. As George moved to Bothal County Secondary School and into trousers, Dennis started school; this meant I had the task of making sure he got out of bed and dressed and ready, as well as taking him there and back each day.

Dad did another one of his early Saturday morning disappearing acts but this time, he came back with a car! It may have only been a tiny, black, flat backed Austin 7 but to me, it looked like a limousine. The boot was very small and although built in the Thirties, it was still a car, no more squeezed up next to Viv in the back of the sidecar.

A couple of months later, Dad took the family for a day out to 'Duridge Bay', a huge sweeping bay of pristine, golden sand backed by a deep belt of sand dunes, a favourite weekend spot for the folks of the mining villages of Northumberland.

He parked just behind the dunes in a field next to a small plantation of pine trees. Driving a large old Rover, Cousin Nick Savic, brought my huge Auntie Jen, diminutive Uncle Joe, Janet their daughter who was Nick's wife and Cousin Alec who was a year younger than I was. Uncle Nick had been a guerrilla fighter in the Balkans during the war and having escaped to England at war's end, he had been living in a refugee camp near Morpeth when he met Cousin Janet.

The 'Littles' also came in their old Ford, Mr and Mrs Little, Jennifer and Alan. Jennifer was Vivian's age and unbeknown to me then, had a schoolgirl's crush on me that was to last until long after school.

The men parked the cars in a hollow square with blankets and rugs laid out in between. On the lowered boot lid of the Austin, Dad had strapped a sturdy wooden box that he had filled with a primus stove, fuel, kettle, teapot and all the other bits and bobs needed for picnicking. He unloaded the box and soon had the kettle on the boil while we kids changed into our woollen swimming trunks and made for the beach. We had this stretch of beach to ourselves but could see other groups of people in the distance, some of whom were swimming.

A deep azure sea mirrored the clear blue sky, contrasting with the golden beach that stretched in both directions as far as the eye could see. Although the day was red hot, the North Sea was still very cold, causing us to scream and shriek as we splashed about in the shallows trying to get accustomed to the cold water. Alec, who carried more fat than anyone else, was first to swim but it took a little while longer before the rest of us joined him. Once totally wet the battle with our swimming costumes began, as we tried to protect our modesty in front of Jennifer and Viv but it was an uphill struggle.

While we were playing in the sea, Dad stuck L-plates onto his car and left to drive the dozen or more miles to Alnwick where he had a driving test booked for eleven o'clock.

Mam had told us to be back at the cars for lunch at one 'clock but hunger and hard exercise had us hovering around the cars at twelve thirty. We found Mam busy preparing sandwiches of limp lettuce and tomatoes and could see several plate pies in the box. Dennis picked up a Jammy Dodger and started to eat it while trying to sniff up sea-induced snot that was dribbling from his nose onto his lips, while he used his free hand to hold up his sagging swimming costume; not a pretty sight.

Sensing that Mam might be in a benevolent mood, especially as the Lowries and Littles were there, Viv asked, 'Canna hev a sandwich Mam?'

Mam stopped buttering bread and cast us all a withering look before saying, 'Ye can aall hev a bloody good hiding if ye divvint bugger off and wait till one o' clock, yor Dad's not back yet either, so wait.'

Reluctantly, we wandered back into the sand dunes until one o clock before we all sheepishly walked back to the picnic, our empty bellies growling angrily. Dad drove back into the field as we approached and I noticed that the L-plates were no longer on the car.

As he climbed out Geordie Little asked, 'Did ye pass then Geordie?'

116

'Aye, nee problem with the driving but the bloody brakes failed gannin doon a bank in Alnwick and Aa had to use the gears to slow doon,' he replied non-chalantly.

Gathering like circling vultures, we waited our chance to pounce on the now quite large spread of sandwiches, pies, cakes, biscuits, and pop. The kettle had just boiled and Mam poured the steaming water into the teapot as we inched a little closer, elbowing each other for the best spot for snatching food!

Not wanting the kids to beat her to the food that she had been eyeing up and certainly not wanting to share, Auntie Jen decided now was the time to join the picnic. Having sat quietly melting in the front of Uncle Nick's car since we arrived, she had the front opening door, wide open and all the windows down in an effort to catch some of the gentle breeze but there was not much and as a result, she was sweating heavily, all twenty or more stone of her.

Grabbing the front of the windscreen pillar with her huge fleshy right hand, she wheezed, 'Joe come 'n' help me oot of this bloody car.'

Looking like a neat Steptoe Senior, Uncle Joe scampered over, held his hand out and had it immediately swallowed by Auntie Jen's mighty pudding of a fist.

'Haway then pull,' she squeaked as all seven stone of Joe heaved.

Dad nudged Geordie Little and the two sniggered at the struggle in front of them while all the kids stood gawping at the sight, all that is except Alec, he had seen it many times before and besides he knew that if his mother got there first she would grab a significant portion of the picnic.

With Uncle Joe heaving and a lot of grunting effort, Auntie Jen finally rose from the seat, the car lifting several inches with a sigh as her weight left it. Her eyes fixed firmly on the food she wobbled forward to take her place on the rug, her left hand still gripping Uncle Joe who she was dragging along in her wake.

Turning slowly, she backed herself up to the rug, and ordered, 'Lower me gently Joe.'

At hearing that my dad and Geordie Little both had to turn away as their sniggering was fast turning to laughter and neither wanted to incur Jen's wrath. Mam and Mrs Little both moved quickly to one side, not wanting Jen to sit on them as the huge figure backed up.

The laws of physics were against Uncle Joe complying successfully with his enormous wife's order, but he tried valiantly. He had taken hold of her left hand with both of his and with trembling knees, was trying to lower her as she stretched out her right hand behind her, waiting to take her weight when she was low enough.

The inevitable happened; Uncle Joe was unable to take her weight and she plopped the last foot or so to the ground with her hand still gripping him – she yanked him off his feet and over her left shoulder like a doll! Professional wrestlers would have been pleased with the throw - Uncle Joe flew through the air, cart-wheeling over Auntie Jen and landed with a thud on his knees in the middle of the picnic. His left knee destroyed a corned beef plate pie and his right crushed a pile of sandwiches. His right hand went up Mrs Little's skirt and his left knocked the teapot flying, scalding him as it went.

Mrs Little kicked out at this sudden intrusion and sent Uncle Joe, who was screaming in pain, reeling straight on top of Mam. His momentum knocked her spread-eagle and he ended up lying with his face between her breasts, her legs around his tiny waste.

My Dad was beside himself with fits of laughter at this stage and said to Geordie Little, 'That little buggers had more luck with wor lass than Aa hev for the past five years.' This brought the two of them to their knees, both helpless from laughter.

We kids who had all been in an initial state of shock had also burst out laughing, all that is except Alec who was hopping around shouting, 'They've squashed aall the bloody food man!'

Mam had thrown Uncle Joe as though he was a rag doll, contemptuously to one side and was trying to help Auntie Jen up into a sitting position as she had ended up on her back with her fat legs in the air showing massive pink bloomers, a sight that haunts me still.

As Uncle Joe staggered to his feet and ran around waving his scalded hand in the air squeaking like an injured sparrow, Dad regained his composure and ran after Joe to ascertain the extent of the damage. The scald was not too bad but Dad bundled Uncle Joe into the car and drove off to the Colliery Medical Centre at Ashington to have it tended too.

Before he left, he warned, 'Tha better be something left to eat when I get back.'

The picnic didn't last long; squashed sandwiches were soon devoured as well as the remaining pies and crisps and it was not long before we kids were rampaging around the small plantation while the women cleared away the debris of the picnic. Mam had carefully put aside two plates of food for Dad and Uncle Joe.

To find shade from the full glare of the sun, we had gone to play inside the small plantation where we found it pleasantly cool beneath the trees with the sun filtering through the canopy of upper branches coating the floor of pine needles in dappled sunshine. It was about then that George decided he was going to climb a pine tree! He had an audience to show off too and as he was the oldest kid there, he was going to show us how well he could climb.

Wearing only his woollen swimming costume and 'Jelly' sandals, he was not best equipped for climbing a tall thin pine tree with a trunk covered with spiky stumps of branches sticking out for the first twenty foot to where the top branches were. The rest of us stood cheering him on as he wrapped his arms and leg around the trunk before he wriggled his way upward.

As George climbed upward, Dad arrived back tooting his horn several times as he pulled up. We all turned to look, including George who was about ten feet up the tree. He lost concentration just as the spike of the branch his foot rested on snapped, causing him to slide down the tree, his unprotected arms and legs still wrapped around the rough trunk, holding his torso against it.

His screams grabbed our attention as he slid down, making me wince as I realised what was happening. He fell on his back at the foot of the tree, arms and legs held in the air, his face contorted in pain as we rushed forward. His descent had scratched, sliced, and scraped the inside of his unprotected arms, legs, chest, and stomach leaving him in a bloodied, agonised mess, moaning pitifully on the ground.

I ran over to Dad and shouted, 'Dad George's fallen doon the tree and he's bleeding aall ower.'

Dad, who had been heading hungrily toward the remains of the picnic, cursed and said, 'Bring him ower te the car and Aa'll tek a look at him,' then picking up a sandwich, he thrust it into his mouth while Mam, who was standing looking across at the plantation wondered what had happened but did not move.

I sprinted back to the plantation where Alan and Cousin Alec had helped George to his feet. The three of us helped him back to the cars as he hobbled bow legged with his bloody arms held out from his equally bloody body.

Dennis ran a head, crying for George and straight to Mam where he sobbed, 'George's cut all ower and Aa think he's gannin te die.'

Spurred into action, Mam ran toward us but stopped when she saw the state of George and muttered, 'Jesus frigging Christ, whatever's happened?'

George was in too much pain to speak and hobbled up to her as Viv said, 'He was showing off and slid doon a big tree Mam.' Her reward was a quick slap as Mam picked up George and ran back to the car with him.

Laying him gently on a rug, Mam tried to mop his cuts and scrapes with a tea towel but George stopped her complaining, 'That frigging horts man.'

Turning to Dad who was still eating, Mam screamed, 'Whey, are ye gannin te de something ye baldy heeded waster or are ye gannin te let the poor bairn suffer?'

Stuffing another sandwich into his mouth, Dad walked over and knelt down next to George to look at his wounds and after a second or two said, 'He's lucky there are nee deep cuts, just scratches and scrapes, he'll be alright.'

Grabbing Dad's arm, Mam yelled at him, 'Ye took that skinny little waster ower there te the Medical Centre, ye can de the same for yor bairn, get him inte the bloody car, noo.'

I travelled with George in the back seat of the car as Dad drove to the Medical Centre where the nurse cleaned his wounds and dressed a few deeper ones. Finally, she gave him an anti-tetanus jab and told him to come back in a day or so.

Later that night as we lay in bed suffering from sunburn, George obviously suffering a lot more than everyone else, I felt real anger at my Dad's indifference to George's accident and lay awake for a long while wondering if he would have been that way if it had been anyone but George?

That summer Mam and Dad took their four youngest on their first ever holiday. George, Viv, Dennis, and I squeezed onto the back seat of the tiny Austin that already had several blankets and some change of clothes piled upon it. Dad had filled the box on the boot lid with camping paraphernalia and strapped a hired ridge tent on top and when we were all aboard, it was with some excitement that we drove out of the smoky Fifth Row and onto the road north, heading for Scotland.

Within half an hour, I was carsick and forced to sit in misery for the rest of the trip to Preston Pans, southeast of Edinburgh.

Eventually, we pulled up outside a large and quite dreary looking campsite just opposite the beach while Dad and Mam discussed whether to stay or go on. I do not know if me throwing open the back door and retching violently had anything to do with their decision-making process but much to my relief, we pulled in and set up camp.

The next day after a breakfast of bacon sandwiches cooked on the primus, we drove out of the large, characterless campsite and into Edinburgh. I was spellbound; not only was it the first city I had visited which was exciting in itself but what magnificent city it was. Walking down Princess Street with the castle standing huge and foreboding against an overcast sky left me in awe. Mam was in her element pointing out the various monuments, buildings, and gardens, I was enthralled but George did not appear that interested and walked sullenly behind.

We visited the castle and George's spirits lifted as we sword fenced our way round the battlements until Dad, fed up with our antics, warned 'If ye two buggers divvint stop messing aboot, Aa'll skelp the pair of ye.'

We calmed down as George muttered, 'Miserable owld git.'

We had an even bigger treat in the afternoon when they took us to the zoo; the skies had cleared and we spent a wonderful three or four hours running from cage to compound to see animals we had only seen in magazines or on TV. Standing in front of the Chimpanzee cage, George and I were mimicking them while Dennis stood holding Mam's hand, laughing uncontrollably.

Even Dad managed a chortle and said, 'We'll leave ye two here with yor friends,' and said to my Mam while nodding at George, 'Aa divvint knaa who's the ugliest, him or the bloody monkeys?'

Mam gave Dad a sideways look and said, 'He must tek after ye pet!'

George had also heard what Dad had said and shouted, 'Ye are the biggest frigging ape here,' and ran off down the bank toward the sea lions.

The next day the weather had changed for the worst; under a heavily laden sky, a cool Northeast wind blew drizzle and sand across the beaches. Dad had taken Dennis and me with him in the car to get some milk and bread from a local shop

120

and on the way back, he decided to drive onto the vast, featureless, and almost empty beach.

One or two brave souls were walking on the beach, leaning into the wind and drizzle as if in a Jack Vettriano painting. Dad stopped and we sat watching wave's crash onto the shore, the crests whipped away by the wind to join the rain on its journey across the sand.

After a while, Dad said, 'Right, enough of that, lets gan and hev a cup of tea,' and we drove for about half a mile along the beach and back onto the road a couple of hundred yards from the campsite.

As we drove onto the road, I noticed a Policeman on a bike riding frantically toward us and noticed that Dad had also seen him but chose to ignore him and drove to the campsite gate where he had to stop while a car and caravan negotiated the narrow entrance. This allowed the Policeman to catch up, obviously intending to stop next to Dad's window; he braked so hard he nearly went over the handlebars of his bike.

Still straddling his bike he knocked on Dad's window but Dad purposely looked the other way, ignoring the knocks until the Policeman, who was breathing hard and looking angrier by the second, knocked so hard I thought the window would smash. Without looking at the Policeman, Dad wound his window slowly down, very slowly, annoying the already angry Policeman even more.

He was huge and bent down to look around the inside of the car before saying to Dad, 'I saw you driving on the beach!'

'Aye,' Dad answered in a matter of fact way.

'De ye not know there're no cars allowed on the beach?'

'Obviously not or I wouldn't have been on it.'

'Did ye no see the sign?' the Policeman said, becoming irater and frustrated by the second.

'What sign?' Dad asked, sounding terribly bored.

'That one back there,' answered the Policeman, pointing back to the place we had driven of the beach.

Dad turned awkwardly around and looked back at the sign for a few seconds that seemed ages before saying with some disdain, 'Which way is that sign pointing?'

'What?' spluttered the now very angry Policeman?

Dad looked up at the tall figure and talking to him as though he was a small child said, 'Ye'll notice that the sign is facing the road?'

'Aye, ye canna miss it.'

Dad put the car into gear and said, 'Ye can if ye drive up from the beach, it's facing the opposite way.'

He let out the clutch and began driving toward the now clear gateway.

The Policeman shouted, 'Come back I haven't finished with ye yet.'

Dad shouted back over his shoulder, 'Aye, but Aa've finished with you,' and drove on into the campsite.

121

It was then that I realised my mouth was wide open and I had been staring and listening in disbelief, I had not realised that you could speak to a Policeman like that and felt sure that he would follow us into the campsite and arrest Dad. He did not; he obviously had had enough of the obnoxious little Geordie who wore a very unnerving and sarcastic smile that made him look rather like a miserable Bob Hope.

I do not know whether the Policeman had put Dad off Preston Pans or not but we left the next day and headed for the ferry over the Firth of Forth, next to the magnificent and awe-inspiring Rail Bridge.

Our holiday continued for another ten days and I fell in love with the Highlands. The long walk behind the car as it chugged its way up the Devil's Elbow to the pass at the top was exhilarating, almost as exciting as the ride down the winding road on the other side and on into Braemar, one of a hundred magical moments as we explored this wonderful country.

The Saturday after we got back from holiday, Dad and Mam drove off to Newcastle and came back with a dog from the Animal Shelter. 'Fly,' a small, scruffy, stub-tailed, ginger mongrel walked into the house with his stump wagging furiously. He came over to me and licked my outstretched hand and we became inseparable.

Wherever I sat in the house he would flop down next to me and in the early hours of the morning, he would trot up the stairs and jump up onto my bed and lie across my feet. Every day at four o'clock, he stood in the cut next to the house waiting for me to come home from school, his little tail wagging his body.

However, he would never venture further down the cut than the end of the garden as a large Alsatian lived on the corner of the Fourth Row and it guarded its territory fiercely, Fly was rightly afraid of it. I, like most of the other kids in the area, was also terrified of the big Alsatian that would growl at anyone and everything that ventured too close.

I looked forward to seeing Fly trotting down the cut to greet me, when on most days, we would run off across the Rec Bridge for a mad half hour gallop. Fly was my dog; he returned love unconditionally and was a forgiving companion.

12

Finger Trouble

That summer, Eric finished school and started work at the colliery; we had all expected him to become an apprentice electrician or fitter but for some reason unknown to us at the time, he failed the selection process. Mam was happy, his pay as a pit lad was far more than an apprentice received! He was also spending some considerable time in front of the mirror making sure that his brylcreamed hair was just so as he spent his evenings chasing girls and being chased back.

Back at school, play times during a lovely warm September were great fun, especially in the boys' playground where we had split into two gangs; the Morganites who were the lads in the 'B' classes led by Jack and the Greniites, the lads from the 'A; classes led by Peter Grenfell, the local undertaker's son.

British Bulldog was my favourite and involved one team trying to race across the playground while the other team, operating in twos and threes, tried to capture the runners by lifting them off the ground and tapping the top of their heads three times. Once captured, you joined the other side and became a catcher. Being pretty swift and agile, I always managed to be in the last few runners.

On the first Friday back at school, we had double art in the afternoon during which I painted a picture of the family camping in Scotland, a ridge tent in the centre of the picture next to Loch Lomond with kids playing at the Lochs edge.

I had been showing a talent for art and the teacher was delighted with my work and asked, 'What is your painting depicting Sydney?'

'It's me and my brothers and sister camping at Loch Lomond Miss,'

"Excellent, you'll have to take it home and show your parents, I'm sure they'd love to see it,' she said with a smile.

After collecting Dennis, I rushed home, carefully carrying my painting to show Mam and Dad, sure they would be pleased to see it. Fly was waiting for me in the cuts and he followed me as I ran into the house where Mam was sitting at the kitchen table, deep in thought, fag in hand and a cup of tea in front of her.

'Look Mam, Aa've painted a picture of us camping at Loch Lomond,' I said and handed her the painting.

She took the painting, blew out a cloud of Woodbine smoke over the picture and said without interest, 'Aye champion,' and handed the picture back.

I was about to walk away when she said, 'How are ye getting on at school?'

'Aalreet,' I replied carelessly.

She spat, 'What de ye mean aalreet? Are ye deeing weel or not?'

She surprised me, this was the first time she had shown any interest in how I was doing at school.

'Am aalreet, I'm in the top group in me class,' I replied wondering why she was asking but delighted that she was.

'When's yor eleven plus exam?'

'Am not sure, before Christmas, I think.'

'This was why she was interested,' I naively thought, 'she wants to make sure I have what I need for Grammar School.' I learnt later that that was the last thing she wanted to do.

Fly distracted me, obviously upset at not having our mad half hour gallop, he kept nudging me with his cold nose until I finally shouted, 'Howay lad,' and raced out the door ahead of him.

The following day Mam took Eric to one side and told him to take George and me to visit Betty at her flat in Newbiggin. I was excited when Eric grabbed George and me and told us where we were going, we had not seen much of Betty since her marriage to Jacky and I missed her, often wondering how she was. Before we left Mam took Eric to one side and whispered instructions in his ear while he nodded in confirmation of her orders.

We caught the bus from Highmarket, enjoying the ride through Ashington and the couple of miles to the top end of Newbiggin where we jumped off and ran along the lane to her flat on the upper floor of a Victorian mid terrace overlooking the Golf Links. She had not been expecting us but was delighted to see the three of us when she opened the door to Eric's knock.

'Eee, Aa didn't knaa ye were coming, come on in,' she said ushering us into the Spartan flat that was not much more than a bed-sit. She hurriedly put the kettle on and fussed about preparing tea and sandwiches while for some strange reason, she looked embarrassed!

'Where's Jacky?' Eric asked as we drank the freshly brewed tea.

'He's ower at his Mam's,' she replied sounding relieved and smiled with a faraway look in her eye.

Something was plainly wrong, her bubbling happiness and warmth were missing and there was sadness in her eyes that confused me. She had been so happy when she got married but here she was looking a little lost. I was too young to understand what was happening; the bruise on her arm and the red mark on her cheek were clues that escaped me.

Eric and Betty stood by the sink looking out the window, talking quietly while George and I sat eating sandwiches, oblivious to the situation between Betty and Jacky. We left shortly afterwards, Eric, not saying a word all the way back but I noticed the little muscle at the corner of his jaw twitching as he ground his teeth, he was obviously extremely angry about something. He spent a long time talking to Mam when we got home, she making tutting sounds throughout their quiet talk.

A few weeks later, Dad rushed off to Newcastle Infirmary to see his brother Jim who had been admitted after an accident at work. Uncle Jim had bumped

124

his head in the mine, a common enough occurrence, but Uncle Jim's bump caused a blood clot! He died quietly with my Dad and their tiny mother by his bedside.

A couple of weeks later Uncle Jim's lovely mahogany bureau and books moved into the Fifth Row and a day or so later Betty also moved back in! I do not know which pleased me most, having Betty back or having all those wonderful books in the house. I immediately began reading Treasure Island, the first of many wonderful stories that for me were far more interesting and exciting than TV.

On a dull Saturday morning, a few days after Betty came home, Jacky came to see her. Mam's face was set and quite terrifying to behold as she said, 'The two of ye can gan upstairs and taalk for a bit but then ye can bugger off cos she's staying here.'

Jacky nodded, and Betty led him upstairs leaving me sitting on the sofa reading with Fly next to me, his head on my lap. Dennis was lying on the floor in front of the fire drawing; Eric was in the kitchen drinking a cup of tea; Uncle Alec in his seat by the fire puffing out clouds of blue-grey smoke while Mam Stood near the door to the stairs listening intently.

A scream of pain and anguish suddenly pierced the silence, startling everyone; shouts followed the scream and then heavy footsteps as someone ran down the stairs. On hearing the scream, Mam flung open the door at the foot of the stairs as Jacky burst into the room, brushing her aside as he ran out through the kitchen and scullery into the back lane.

Fly leapt off the sofa and raced after Jacky, snapping at his feet, knowing instinctively that he should attack the fleeing man.

Mam regained her composure and screamed at Eric, 'Get efter that frigging waster and sort him oot.' Eric obeyed without thinking and raced out the house after Jacky, but hurried along by Fly, he was too far ahead for Eric to catch up with him. We followed them out the door to the back gate, Mam beside herself with rage, screamed obscenities at the disappearing figure as Dennis and I watched, totally bewildered as to what we were witnessing.

Uncle Alec came out of the house, grabbed Mam's arm, and said, 'Etty Aa think ye better gan back in and see to yor lassie.'

Mam stopped screaming and looked at him with a startled expression on her face and said, 'Eee, aye the poor little bugger,' and raced back indoors.

I am not sure what Eric would have done had he caught Jacky; Eric was just a skinny fifteen-year-old while Jacky was a taller mature twenty but Eric tried and returned relieved that he hadn't caught him just as Pat came around the corner from the cut to see him returning red-faced and puffing.

Now sixteen, Pat had been to the shops for some hair spray for her evening's preparation before she went to the Red Row dance where lads from RAF Acklington chased the local girls.

She looked at Eric and asked, 'What's going on?'

'That bastard Jacky has just hit wor Betty again and Aa've chased him doon the lane.'

Realisation hit me like a brick, it all became clear, now I knew why Betty had been so unhappy, I wished Fly had been an Alsatian and had torn the bastard apart. He came trotting back up the lane to me and lifted his paws onto my thighs, looking up at me as if to say, 'I saw him off didn't I.'

It was the last time I saw Jacky, Betty stayed with us a while longer and was then sent down South to digs in order to escape further bother.

The following Sunday after lunch we drove across to Hadston to my Auntie Mamie's; I was not aware of it but Granny Carr was poorly, apparently, she had taken Uncle Jim's death very badly and her health was going downhill rapidly. Dad went over to Grannies leaving Mam with Aunty Mamie while Dennis, Viv, Cousin Alec and myself ran around outside.

Having been to the upstairs toilet, I ran downstairs and out the back door to look for the rest of them. They had gone through the heavy, green wooden side door that I struggled to open against a strong wind that was trying to force it shut. As I stepped through, the wind slammed the door shut with brutal force, nipping off the top of my left index finger! The pain was intense causing me to cry out at the shock of it. I gripped my left hand with my right, leaving my shortened finger free and looking down saw that the very top of my finger had disappeared; leaving the bone just exposed and my nail pushed forward as blood flowed out of the wound at an alarming rate.

My cry of pain brought Alec running over to see what had happened, finding me leaning against the wall gasping with pain, he looked at my injured finger and said, 'Bloody hell,' before running into the house to get help.

Mam came out and took one look at my finger before blaspheming, 'Jesus Christ, that's all we frigging need, by you're a sackless bugger - Vivian gan and get yor Dad.'

She led me to the back door, fighting the green side-door as we went and left me outside, dripping blood as she disappeared inside, reappearing almost instantly with a small tea towel that she wrapped around my finger.

Auntie Mamie came out and gave me a hot cup of sweet tea, 'For the shock,' she said as we waited for Dad.

Stomping up the front garden path with a thunderous look on his face, he snarled, 'What's the stupid sod done noo? Viv says he's cut his finger off!'

Mam showed him the wound and after a discussion with Auntie Mamie, Dad drove Mam and me to a house in the village where the District Nurse lived.

A woman in her fifties, she was very kind and gentle and after examining the wound said, 'He needs to go to hospital.'

'Can ye not just stitch it closed?' Dad asked exasperatedly.

The Nurse gave him a sharp sideways look, 'No I can't, he'll probably need a skin graft, so he must go to hospital.'

126

Despite the pain I immediately thought, 'There canna be much more skin left on me bum and thighs for another skin graft, most of it went on my face.'

The Nurse opened a first-aid box and said, 'I'll put a bandage on it till you get him there, but you must get him to hospital as soon as possible.'

Taking a large piece of cotton wool, she placed it directly on top of the open wound where it immediately turned red, so she placed a further piece of cotton wool on top and then wrapped a bandage around the whole thing, including my other fingers.

Dad thanked her and we returned to Aunt Mamie's and picked up the others before driving home. I spent the journey curled up in the corner of the back seat, clasping my hand to my chest, the pain from my finger screaming at me.

Arriving home, I expected Dad to drop the rest of the family off and take me to hospital but instead, Mam took me indoors and told me to lie down on the sofa.

She said, 'Yor Dad's gannin te tek ye to hospital the morn's morning when he gets hyem from work.'

They left me on the sofa with no painkillers or sympathy, the throbbing pain making my hand and arm ache. I was on my own apart from Fly who climbed up next to me on the sofa, knowing instinctively that I was hurt.

The following morning after a very painful and uncomfortable night and desperate to get to the hospital where I hoped to get some relief from the pain, I sat on the sofa waiting until Dad got home.

As usual, he arrived from work at about nine, had a cup of tea and a cigarette, then grudgingly said, 'Haway then let's get ye to hospital so I can get back and get some sleep.'

He looked at Mam and continued, 'Ye better come as weel in case its gannin te take some time.'

Mam had not expected to have to go as well and complained to herself as she took off her pinny before powdering her face. I was just relieved to be going to Ashington Hospital, the small Edwardian cottage hospital 100 yards or so from the town centre and only a short drive from home.

We only had to wait twenty minutes before a young Doctor took me into a room to examine my finger, Dad explaining what had happened.

He slowly and carefully undid the bandage until he exposed the congealed blood-soaked lump of cotton wool, which he examined before asking Dad, 'Did the District Nurse put any Vaseline or other cream dressing on under the cotton wool?'

'No,' Dad answered, immediately realising the implications as he himself was an excellent First-Aider.

'Oh dear,' the Doctor mumbled.

I was not prepared for what happened next; already in a lot of pain that I hoped the Doctor was going to take away, I had not expected him to add to it! He opened up as much of the sticky cotton-wool as he could but it was soon obvious that a large piece of it was stuck to the open wound where the blood that had soaked into it, had congealed.

Despite him pulling at it gently, it sent red-hot needles of pain shooting through my finger as the cotton wool tugged at the bloody flesh below. Tears streamed down my cheeks but I would not let myself cry in front of Dad who was now sitting behind me holding my shoulders.

In an effort to soften and loosen the cotton wool, the Doctor poured some liquid onto it then grasping my hand tightly, pulled firmly until the cotton wool came clear. I nearly passed out with the pain and let out a large groan, as it pulled free.

Looking at the wound, he shook his head, saying to Dad, 'There are still bits inside the wound; I'll have to use tweezers to get them out.'

The next few minutes were a blur of pain and tears as he plucked tiny shreds of sticky wool from the open wound. Eventually satisfied that it was clean, he applied a soft Vaseline soaked dressing and re-bandaged the finger before telling Dad to bring me in the following day when they would carry out a skin graft to close the wound.

Hearing this I said with some concern, 'Where are ye gannin te tek the skin from?' The Doctor smiled and said, 'From your forearm,' and tapped the inside of my arm to show me where.

I had the skin graft under general anaesthetic the following morning and was lying in the recovery room trying to regain my senses. Mam had brought me to the Hospital on the bus, Dad not wanting to have another day's sleep interrupted.

The first thing I noticed as I came too was the foul smell of Woodbine smoke and as I moved, Mam who had been on a chair smoking rushed over and said, 'Good yor awake, hurry up and pull yorsell together and we'll get home.'

Barely able to lift my head, I was trying to work out where I was, and could not understand why I was not in my own bed. Mam went out and came back with a nurse who looked at me and asked a few questions before saying, 'Give him another hour and a cup of tea, and then ye can take him home.'

I did not get a cup of tea until I got home, but I did not have to wait too long as shortly after the nurse left, Mam had me on my feet, dressed and half carried me out of the hospital and along to the bus stop, a couple of hundred yards around the corner.

The following morning I was in the kitchens getting ready for school when George who had been just about to put his shoe on yelled, 'Bastard,' and started to beat the floor.

Curious, I went over to see what he was doing and asked, 'What's the matter Geordie?'

'Frigging "blacklock" in me shoe,' he said while beating the already dead cockroach. We had had these unwelcome visitors for a few months and Dad had spread a white powder around the skirting of the house to kill them. It was working but in the process, the cockroaches became more evident as they came out to die.

Mam shouted from her bed, 'What's aall the noise aboot?'

Walking to the foot of the stairs, I shouted up, 'Wor Geordie has just killed a blacklock Mam.'

There was a moments silence and she shouted down, 'What are ye deeing up?'

'Am gannin to school?'

'Nur yor not, the Doctor said ye canna gan for a fortnight'

'But Aa've a bandage on me finger and me arm, and Aa've got painkillers, I'll be aalreet.'

'No you winnit, you're not gannin.'

That was that, she kept me off school for a lot longer than two weeks, threatening me with all sorts of violence if I went. Naïve as ever, I thought she was actually worried about my finger but long after the bandages had been removed and the scab fallen off the wound, I was still not at school. My accident had provided Mam with the excuse she had been looking for; she could keep me from school so that I missed the 11+ exam.

About four weeks later, still at home, I was sitting reading Ivanhoe from Uncle Jim's collection while Mam sat at the kitchen table smoking when there was a loud knock at the door!

'See who that is,' she said to me.

Opening the back door, I found a large man in a dark blue suit and carrying a briefcase, blocking the light.

'Are you Sydney Carr?' he said consulting a piece of paper he was holding.

I gulped and fearing the worst, answered, 'Aye, why?'

'Is your mother or father in?' he asked, sternly.

'Me Mam's in.'

'Then can I see her?'

'Aye come on in,' I said leading him into the kitchen.

The conversation that followed between them began quietly and amicably but after three or four minutes degenerated into an all-out argument. The School Board Man had obviously come to see why I had not been to school, Mam told him about my accident and he responded by saying it should not have kept me from school, especially just before the 11+ exam for which I was a strong candidate for passing. That was enough for Mam; she flew into a rage and told him she knew what was best for her kids, and the argument raged on and on. He left after extracting a promise from Mam that I would be back at school tomorrow - I was chuffed.

After he left, Mam tore into me as though it was my fault and warned, 'If ye pass that bloody exam ye'll not be gannin to grammar school, ye winnit like it, look at what happened to Eric, he hated it there, and beside we cannit afford it so ye winnit be gannin and that's that.'

I finally grasped what had been going on and resigned myself to ensuring I did not pass my 11+, the embarrassment of failing would be less than that of passing and then having to tell people that I could not afford to go to grammar school.

The following day I found that I had a lot of catching up to do and was struggling, especially in arithmetic. Mrs Towart our teacher, an elderly five-foot spinster who never smiled and gave an excellent impression of a child hater, was demanding and uncompromising, and we were all terrified of her, most of us hating her.

The class was standing to attention reciting the times-tables parrot fashion as she tapped out the rhythm with her ruler; I was okay up to the seventh table but had missed learning the next two. Seeing that I was not reciting the table Mrs Towart stopped the class and called me out to the front.

Grabbing my arm, she said, 'You idle stupid boy, why were you not saying your tables?'

'Cos I haven't learnt them yet Miss,' I said feeling my face begin to burn with embarrassment. She shook my arm and berated me some more before sending me back to my seat. I felt everyone in the class staring at me and thought wrongly, that they were laughing at me.

For the next few days during each arithmetic lesson, she asked me a question that she knew I would not know the answer too and each time I failed to answer, she dragged me to the front of the class to ridicule me again.

During the weekend, I resolved that I would not stand for any more of her ritual humiliation, especially as some of the lads in the class had said that it looked as though she enjoyed doing it. Sure enough, ten minutes into the lesson, she asked me a question but I was confused, I knew the answer, if I gave her the correct answer, there would be no confrontation!

I paused for a second and said, 'I don't know the answer Miss.'

A look of triumph came over her face and she spat, 'Get out here you stupid boy.'

I walked quickly toward her knowing what was coming next as she grabbed my arm and began shaking me, before saying, 'You really are an idle....'

That was as far as I let her rant, I jerked my arm free from her grasp and stepping back yelled at her, 'Get off me, don't ye ever touch me again, do you hear me, you owld witch?'

She stepped back as though scalded, a look of shock and horror spreading across her face. There were gasps and titters from the class - then silence.

Speechless, she stood looking at me, trying to regain her composure as I marched back to my desk and sat down and stared defiantly back at her.

130

She continued the lesson without giving me a second look but when playtime came, she looked at me with menace and said, 'Carr you stay behind.'

After my classmates had all left the room she said, 'Follow me we are going to see Mrs Joseph.'

Fearing the worst, I followed her and waited nervously outside the Headmistresses Office while Mrs Towart disappeared inside and briefed her on the outrage I had committed.

The door opened and Mrs Towart glowered at me and said, 'Come in Sydney.'

I walked into the office and up to Mrs Joseph who was standing by her desk and looked up at her wondering how many wallops I was about to receive.

Trying to look stern, Mrs Joseph said, 'Now Sydney, Mrs Towart tells me that you were very rude to her in her class and called her a name?'

All the resentment, frustration and anger of the past few days erupted and I spluttered angrily, 'She's been picking on me every day since I got back te school. She keeps asking me questions she knaa's I divvint knaa tha answer te, just so she can show me up and knock me aboot, whey am not heving it anymore, am fed up with her picking on me.' I stood with tears of frustration and anger filling my eyes.

Taken aback by my outburst, she said, 'Calm down now, we cannot have this behaviour in school now can we? Mrs Towart you can go back to your class now and I will deal with Sydney.'

Mrs Towart began to object, keen to witness any punishment metered out but Mrs Joseph waved her out and I prepared myself for the strap.

Mrs Joseph turned and looked at me with some concern in her eyes, 'What are we going to do with you?' she said gently.

I opened my mouth to begin again but she held up her hand to silence me and said, 'Sit down and I'll get you a cup of tea.' I was flabbergasted; this was the last thing I had expected. I sat on a wooden chair and waited while she went off to her Secretary's office returning a few minutes later with a cup of tea. She had succeeded in calming me down while I waited and the tea totally disarmed me. I felt awkward and very embarrassed as I tried to balance the cup and saucer and drink the hot tea without scalding myself.

Mrs Joseph talked to me for ten minutes asking about my injury, home and class work in general before she mentioned Mrs Towart.

'She can be a wee bit tense at times Sydney and we must all forgive her for that, I'm sure she did not intend to pick on you and I'm sure she won't do it again but you must learn to control your temper, okay?' I nodded acquiescence and she continued, 'Go back to your class and you must apologise to her at lunch time for calling her a rude name.'

I did apologise and an uneasy truce sprang up between Mrs Towart and me for the rest of the year. In fact, she did not drag anyone out for humiliation during the rest of the term.

131

On the way home at lunchtime, I received a fair bit of stick from some of the lads in the class, 'Fancy picking on a poor owld woman,' they teased but they were all chuffed that someone had finally stood up to her.

On the morning of the 11+, I walked to school feeling miserable but clear on what I had to do. It was a drab, late autumn morning as we stood shivering on the veranda waiting to for the teachers to call us into one of the two cold and uninviting classrooms where we were to sit the exam. When we began, I quickly scanned the paper and answered some of the more obvious questions but for most of the IQ type questions, I wrote down answers I knew to be wrong, apart from one or two. I thought that if I answered them all incorrectly the examiners would know I failed on purpose. I was successful and much to Mam's relief I failed my 11+.

13

Dogs

The weekend after I found out that I had successfully failed my 11+, Dad surprised us all when he walked into the house with a little bundle under his arm. He sat down in the armchair in front of the fire in the sitting room and released a little black and white pup onto the floor.

'This is Rebel,' he said in his monosyllabic way. The pup was wagging his tail so hard he nearly fell over as he trotted around the room excitedly greeting us one after the other before cautiously approaching Fly who rose from the floor while they carried out the compulsory ritual sniffing of each other's back ends.

Fly gave a low growl to establish a pecking order and wisely, Rebel acknowledged his seniority and backed off with his tail down bumping into George who had just walked into the room.

Looking down at the new arrival, George asked, 'Whose is this then?' Rebel was trying to wrap himself around George's legs but his tail wagged so much he had lost control of his rear legs and he fell over in a heap and lay there looking up at George.

Dad replied, 'I've just been given him, he's an Alsatian and Border-Collie Cross.'

Picking Rebel up, George held him to his face, which the pup licked furiously. They bonded instantaneously, I might have Fly for a pet, but there was no mistaking whose dog Rebel was going to be.

A week later we heard the terrible news that little Granny Carr had died. We were all upset but more so the older ones who had known her kindness longer than I had but I still felt bereft as I pictured her at the door of her little cottage at Chevington with tea and cakes waiting on the table in her front parlour. Dad spent a lot of time at Hadston with his older brother, Uncle Alec, arranging the funeral for the following week.

Back at school, myself and about twelve other lads and lasses who had shown some artistic ability were in the school hall where Mrs Joseph had briefed us on a forthcoming art competition. We were to paint a picture using poster colours on any subject we wanted.

I had just seen an adventure movie at the Regal in which John Wayne starred as a deep-sea diver and although I had found the film a bit boring - too many love scenes; I had enjoyed the diving scenes and thus inspired, I painted a deep-sea diver. The figure, complete with brass diving helmet and heavy boots dominated the centre of my picture. I painted seaweed swirling round his legs, exotic fish swimming around his head and in the background a prowling shark.

While I painted I noticed that the art teacher, who was showing Mrs Joseph and another woman around, brought them to look at my painting several times.

We handed the finished paintings in at the end of the session and Mrs Joseph said that she was entering my painting along with three others into a competition open to the children of miners. Not thinking that it was of any significance I quickly forgot about it.

Spring was upon us and on a late afternoon just after tea, we were enjoying some early, warm weather with the back door open for fresh air, Dad was busy building units into the scullery in order to turn it into a kitchen. He was an excellent carpenter and had just built a substantial and very impressive garage come workshop at the bottom of the garden; materials courtesy of the NCB, just that they did not know they had provided them.

George, Dennis and I were playing with Rebel and Fly in the sitting room. The dogs having a whale of a time play fighting until George stood up and said, 'Am gannin for a slash,' and walked out to the back door and across the road to go to the outside loo.

Fly was on top of Rebel pretending he was chewing the pup's neck when Rebel suddenly realised that George was not there. Despite me screaming at him to stay, he scrambled from below Fly and bolted for the back door and my worst fears were realised. An awful screeching of brakes, followed by a terrible yowl and yelping shattered the late afternoon peace and quiet. Racing outside, I was just in time to see Rebel stagger into the back yard as he tried in vain to reach the safety of the house but he collapsed before he could reach the door. Dad was already there and bent over Rebel to see how bad his injuries were when George ran across from the toilet.

'What the frigs happened?' he said looking down at the poor pup.

'He's been run ower Geordie,' I said unnecessarily as Fly pushed his head through and began to whimper.

Dad said to me, 'Put your dog inside noo,' so I pushed Fly back into the house and closed the door just as the unfortunate driver of the car came into the yard.

Looking shocked, he mumbled, 'Am sorry, he just ran oot in front of me, Aa couldn't miss him.'

'Fuck off ye bastard ye've killed me dog,' George screamed at the man.

In his forties and with less hair than my Dad, the poor man did not know George and unfortunately, tried to console him.

Placing his hand on George's shoulder, he said, 'Am very sorry son, Aa'll get ye another pup if ye want?'

George knocked the man's hand from his shoulder and snarled at him, "Aa've towld ye to fuck off ye baldy heeded bastard, noo fuck of before a batter ye,' and picking up the coal shovel, he held it threateningly above his head. The man sensibly retreated as Dad wrested the shovel from George.

134

'Calm doon and look after yor dog,' he ordered, 'I divvint think he's gannin te last long.'

As the stunned man retreated to his car, George knelt down next to me as I stroked Rebel's head as he lay there gasping for breath, blood seeping from his mouth.

I said, 'His side's aall caved in Geordie, a think he's had it.'

George looked at me in disbelief and took over comforting the stricken pup that tried to lift its head when he heard George's voice. Rebel settled his head back and died while George stroked him harder not wanting to believe his dog had gone.

Dad leant over and put his fingers around Rebel's neck, checking for a pulse before straightening up and saying, 'Gan and bury him in the garden doon by the garage and mind me bloody vegetables while ye de it.'

George gave him a withering look before turning to me saying, 'Fetch the spade Young'un,' and gently lifted the lifeless pup, carrying him out the yard and around the side of the house and into the garden.

We dug a deep square hole; George taking his time, stopping every few minutes to shake Rebel in order to reassure himself his pup was dead. I was intrigued, I had never seen George show this sort of emotion before, I knew he was obviously deeply upset at the death but I was just beginning to realise how much. George very rarely showed any soft emotions but here he was showing a side of him I had not known existed.

Satisfied with the depth of the hole George picked Rebel up and gently lowered him into the bottom and knelt at the side looking down at his dead pup.

Picking up the spade, I dug into the soil preparing to throw it into the hole but before I could George held up his hand and said, 'Had on man, he might not be deed,' and then gently shook the lifeless figure repeating his name, 'Rebel, Rebel, Rebel.'

I said quietly, 'Haway Geordie, he's deed man.'

George stood up and leaning over the hole, said, 'The forst fucking thing a get that Aa like and the fucking thing commits suicide.' The tears in his eyes stopped me laughing at his outburst and I quietly filled the hole as George stood silently watching. At that moment, I felt closer to him than I had ever felt before.

He never spoke of Rebel again.

A week later I was enjoying morning assembly at school; we had just sung my favourite hymn, 'All things bright and beautiful,' at the top of our voices. I had not yet learned that I was tone deaf so always sang with great gusto, often to the dismay of those standing close to me.

Smiling, Mrs Joseph walked into the centre of the stage and waited until the children stopped fidgeting, coughing, and sniffing before she spoke.

'School,' she said in her pleasant but firm voice, instantly gaining silence, 'School,' she continued, 'some of you will be aware that four paintings by children

135

in forms Three and Four were selected for entry into a National Art Competition for Children of Miners.' She paused looking over the top of her glasses at the schoolchildren below. 'I have the results in my hand and I am delighted to announce that the winner of the competition is from this school.'

There was a ripple of murmurs across the hall and one or two of my classmates turned to look at me.

Big Howard whispered, 'That might be ye Syd.' It had not occurred to me that I might have won; I had been trying to think who it could have been until Howard had suggested it could be me.

Mrs Joseph said, 'School,' again to silence the whispers and went on, 'The winner of the competition is Sydney Carr! – I am sure you will all join me in giving him a huge round of applause for doing so well and bringing great honour to himself and our school,' she beamed.

The hall erupted into thunderous clapping and cheering, those nearest me patted me hard on the back. I was thrilled and embarrassed at the same time, not used to receiving so much attention let alone praise, I could feel myself blushing violently. After assembly, the art teacher spoke to me congratulating me on winning and told me I had to go to see Mrs Joseph at twelve o'clock when she would explain the prize.

'A prize, what prize?' It was the first I had heard of a prize! My mind raced wondering what I could have won - a cup, a certificate, a set of paints; the possibilities were endless. The rest of the morning was a blur, most of my pals congratulated me and Mrs Towart even told the class how delighted she was that one of her pupils had done so well.

At playtime, after a game of British Bulldog, I wandered off to the toilet and stood at the urinals deep in thought, wondering what my prize was.

A voice rang out behind me, 'How Carrsy! I turned to see a large ginger headed lad from Form 3B, standing legs apart, arms crossed, eyes fixed menacingly on me. 'A bet ye think yor frigging clever, am not frightened of ye just cos yor in 4A.'

I stared back at him wondering what he meant by his threatening statement.

A lad standing behind him said, 'Just cos ye won an art competition doesn't mean ye can de want ye want in the yard.'

'Eh?' was all I could say as I tried to weigh up the situation - the ginger haired lad had obviously come looking for a fight; bigger than me, I guessed he must want to build a reputation by beating up an older lad, but why me?

'Ye knocked me ower at British Bulldog so we're gannin to bash ye up,' he spat.

'Ye mean yer gannin te try,' a voice behind him said.

It was Jack Moody, he walked in and pushed the other lad to one side and held him by the jumper before saying to me, 'Gan on Syd fettle the ginger-heeded twat.'

Knowing that if I stood back and traded blows with the lad his weight would be hard to overcome so I ran at him catching him off guard, and wrapped my left arm around his neck in a chokehold, then using my weight pulled him down.

He thrashed around trying to throw me off but I managed to use my hip to throw him to the toilet floor and squeezed harder with my left arm, applying even more pressure by pulling my left wrist with my right hand.

'Punch him,' a voice shouted so I did. I let go with my right hand and punched him in the face three or four times in quick succession, but without any real force and without causing any damage.

By this time, the small crowd that had gathered inside and outside the toilet were shouting and screaming until they suddenly went quiet. I found myself hauled to my feet my arm still wrapped firmly around Ginger's neck.

'Let go of him now!' a deep voice rang out and I instinctively released my grip, Ginger sank to his knees holding his neck making more of his injuries than they warranted. Mr Foreman the teacher who had been on playground duty had heard the commotion and had pushed through the gaggle of lads to break up the fight.

'Right, you lot back to the yard,' he said pointing to the small crowd.

Making for the door, Jack said to the Teacher, 'That ginger lad there started the fight Sir.'

Mr Foreman looked at Jack and pushed him toward the door saying, 'When I need your advice I'll ask for it Moody, now get back into the yard.'

The teacher took Ginger and me by an arm each and said, 'You know what the penalty is for fighting, come with me to the Headmistress.'

The ginger-headed lad said pitifully, 'I hevn't done oot Sir, he picked on me,' and then he started to cry. I knew better than to protest and stood in silence still shaking from the fight; I knew as well he did that fighting in the schoolyard automatically meant the strap, regardless of who started it.

Standing next to Ginger outside Mrs Joseph's office, my adrenalin was still pumping and I felt an overwhelming desire to lash out at the potential bully. He must have sensed my hostility and not wanting a repeat of the fight he sheepishly backed off into the corner.

The door to the office opened and Mr Foreman ushered us into Mrs Joseph who was standing in front of her desk with the dreaded leather strop in her hand. I knew the routine for fighting; George had briefed me after one of his trips to the Headmistress. She never asked who started it or why; she was there to administer punishment and issue a deterrent.

'Hands,' was all she said, and we obliged, holding our right hands in front of us. She walked to the side of Ginger and lifting the strap up, brought it smartly down on his open hand causing him to wince and snatch his hand closed, pulling it to his chest.

Mrs Joseph looked at him without emotion and said, 'I'm waiting.' Ginger put his hand back and received two more stinging strikes of the strap.

He shook his hand and then held it by his side pressing the open palm against his thigh in an effort to lessen the stinging.

'Out you go,' she said to him and advanced on me.

I pushed my hand out as far as I could and gritted my teeth as the headmistress raised the strap. Expecting a stinging blow, I was surprised when she brought the strap down on my hand but without her normal force - almost gently. I still felt it but it hardly hurt.

She gave me another two of the same, then turned to Mr Foreman, and dismissed him with, 'Thank you John, I'll speak to Sydney on another matter now,'

'Sydney I'm thrilled as you must be at your success in the art competition, I have a letter here for your parents that you must give them today as I need a reply by the end of the week.'

'Yes Miss,' was all I could manage; I was still surprised at the non-punishment.

'It is all very exciting, and I hope they grasp this wonderful opportunity, it will be marvellous for you.'

'Yes Miss,' I answered wondering what she was talking about, what exciting opportunities! I was too embarrassed to ask as she obviously thought I knew and I did not want to look foolish for not knowing something.

A little late leaving school at lunchtime, Viv and Dennis had already left for home leaving me to walk slowly along, trying to figure out what Mrs Joseph had said. It was almost one o'clock when I reached the cut between the gardens of the Fourth Row.

As I approached the gap between the terraces I saw Fly running toward me, he must have been waiting for at least twenty minutes and was rushing forward stump wagging madly.

Just as he crossed the back street of the Fourth Row, a huge dark shape shot out from the right and caught him in full gallop. With abject horror I realised the Alsatian had my pet and raced the ten yards to the corner, listening to the terrible and savage sounds of a one-sided dogfight. Turning the corner, I saw that the Alsatian had Fly by the back of the neck, shaking him like a rag doll as Fly screeched painfully.

The Alsatian had its back to me, rear legs apart bracing itself, intent on killing my dog. Without thinking, I ran up and kicked it between its legs as hard as I could; my foot sank home, lifting the dog off its back feet and spinning it to one side. It dropped Fly and let out a howl of pain, and tried to run back to its house but the pain between its legs caused it to fall over several times.

The noise brought the dog's owner out of her house, as well as Mrs Robertson from two doors down the other way. The Robertsons, like ours, were a large family and I was friendly with Alan, their son of my age.

Bending over Fly, who was holding his head at weird angle and whimpering pathetically, I tried to calm him until I felt a hand grip my shoulder; it was the dog's owner, a severe-looking woman in her thirties.

'What hev ye done te me dog?' she demanded trying to drag me to my feet.

Mrs Robertson shouted over, 'I think ye better leave him alen Pet, his dogs been hurt by your big, black bastard of a thing,' and turning to Alan who had left his dinner to see what was going on, she said, 'Gan and get Etty Carr, quick.'

Alan dashed off as I and the dog's owner exchanged angry words.

'Your bloody dog chases everybody, he should be put doon,' I shouted at the woman trying to break free from her grip and tend to my injured pet.

She screamed back, 'Divvint ye speak to me like that ye cheeky little bugger or Aa'll give ye a good hiding,' The argument raged on until something in the cut next to our house caught her eye, causing her to let go of me and scurry back to her house.

I looked up the cut and saw Mam with a thunderous look on her face, half running down the cut, she was a magnificent sight, like a battleship under full steam, no wonder the woman fled.

She came steaming up to me, looked down at Fly, and said, 'Was it that big black bugger of a dog?'

Before I could answer, Mrs Robertson said, 'Aye Etty it was and that wicked bugger in there was picking on your laddie.'

You could see Mam's hackles rise, she could knock us around but woe betides any bugger else who tried, she looked at me and said, 'Get Fly home bonnie lad, am gannin to hev some words we that bloody young witch.'

I picked a whimpering fly up and staggered back to the cut, catching a glimpse of Mam storming into the unfortunate woman's house with Mrs Robertson and a few other nosey neighbours gathering outside to enjoy the one-sided argument.

George, Viv, and Dennis were standing in the cut next to Dad's garage waiting to find out what had happened.

'What's wrang we Fly?' George asked.

'That frigging Alsatian got him,' I spluttered holding back tears and struggling with the weight of my pet.

Reaching for Fly, George said, 'Here man, let me carry him.'

I turned my shoulder on him and said, 'No man, Aa've got him,' and struggled up the cut to reach our house.

Viv had gone on to see whom my Mam was sorting out but Dennis walked alongside me stroking Fly's head. I laid him down on the carpet in front of the fire in the sitting room and had a close look at his injuries. There were two deep puncture wounds on the back of his neck and another underneath where the dog had gripped him. Surprisingly, they were not bleeding heavily and I was quickly able to clean them with a small towel that George brought me.

139

Poor Fly was in shock and trembled violently while I stroked him as George leant over us and said, 'We divvint hev a lot of luck with frigging dogs do we Young'un?'

Muttering obscenities under her breath, Mam came into the sitting room and said, 'Ye buggers let me knaa if that bloody dog ever chases ye again?'

I did not go back to school that afternoon, spending it tending Fly, who, all though he sat up, he kept whimpering and his trembling continued.

Mam was angry when I had refused to eat the plate of beans she had put out for lunch, calling me a 'Soft Bugger.'

I was still with Fly when the others arrived back from school later in the afternoon and Viv chose to ask Mam, 'What prize has wor Syd got Mam?'

'What are ye taalking aboot?' asked mam, her eyes lighting up.

'He's won a painting competition and everybody says he's got a big prize.'

I had forgotten all about it and remembering the letter Mrs Joseph had given me, I reached into my pocket and pulled out the now crumpled envelope.

Mam demanded, 'What prize hev ye got?'

I looked at the letter and said, 'I divvint knaa, it's in this letter, Mrs Joseph towld me to give it te ye and Dad and she wants a reply by Friday.'

'Does she now?' Mam said, as she snatched the letter from me to rip it open. Putting on her reading glasses, she spent some time reading and re-reading it.

'What is it Mam?' Vivian asked trying peer over her shoulder.

Never ye mind,' hissed Mam, before folding the letter up and stuffing it into the pocket of her pinny.

Fly had continued to whimper quietly throughout the afternoon but had responded to my stroking, twice licking my hand. Worried that he was going to die in front of me the way Rebel had, I walked into the kitchen where Mam was laying pastry over a large pan of mince and onions.

'What are we going te de aboot Fly Mam?' I asked. Having seen her come to our rescue in the Fourth Row I had naively thought that she would be concerned about Fly's condition.

'What de ye expect me te de?' she asked looking at me angrily.

'He might die if we divvint tek him te a vets,' I said forlornly realising she wasn't in the slightest bothered.

'Who the bloody hell's gannin te pay for a vet ye simpleton, Aa'll give ye two bob and ye can tek him te the slaughterhoose and hev him put oot his misery.' Shocked and unable to reply, I went back to Fly and dabbed his wounds again.

When Dad got up for his tea, he had a look at Fly's wounds and said without compassion, 'The best thing ye can de for the dog is te hev him put doon, the poor animals in pain.' I was devastated, I had hoped against all the odds that he might have taken Fly to the vets but I should have known better.

Before Dad ate his tea, Mam showed him the letter I had brought and as he read it, I heard her say, 'There's no bloody way he can gan.'

140

That was all I heard as they went into the scullery where I could just about hear their angry voices but not what they were saying.

I spent the night on the sofa lying next to Fly trying to comfort him but his trembling hardly stopped. I lay awake my mind in turmoil, trying to decide what best to do for my pet. I knew that a vet was out of the question and I hated to see him suffering, besides, both Mam and Dad had said that I should have him put out of his misery and I still believed that they knew best.

Come morning I had resolved to do what I thought was best for my dog, I would have him put to sleep even though he had sat up and lapped some water.

I stayed away from school again and when Mam came downstairs, I asked her for the two shillings she said it would cost to have him put to sleep. When she gave me the money without argument, I knew it was final; I was going to lose my pet.

I carried Fly outside and across to the Rec Bridge where I gently put him down on the top step and with tear filled eyes, I sat stroking him as I quietly talked to him for half an hour, trying to tell him it would end his pain, trying to convince myself I was doing the best thing for him.

Carrying him back to our yard, I put him in the old pram we had moved Porky in and set off for the abattoir. Not wishing to go through the cuts, I walked to the end of the Row before turning towards town. The abattoir was past Wansbeck School, behind a terrace of private houses next to the park. In my grief, I made no effort to avoid walking past the school and as I approached, I could hear children's' voices in the playground.

Half way along the railings, my friend Frank shouted from the schoolyard, 'Where ye gannin with the pram Syd, are ye taking yor dollies for a walk?'

Without stopping, I looked him in the eyes and said angrily, 'Fuck Off.'

A robust but sensitive lad, Frank realised immediately something serious had happened so he shut up but some of the other lads could not resist shouting what they thought were funny comments. I ignored them and walked on. I found out later that Dennis told Frank what had happened and he told the rest of my school pals.

The smell and noise from the Abattoir hit me before I reached it, the noise of machinery mingled with that of cattle in the small pen next to the building and an unpleasant unrecognisable smell mixed with what smelt like TCP hit me as I approached. It was a single-story, red-bricked building with open garage-style doors leading to a large bay with another set of closed doors beyond. To the right there was a small office and as I stood nervously gripping the pram handle, a large heavily built man in bloodstained white overalls and Wellingtons came out of the office.

'Hello son, what are ye efter?' he asked.

I looked up at him and with some difficulty said, 'Me dogs badly hurt Mister and Aa've brought two bob to have him put doon, me Mam and Dad said it's the best for him.'

141

The man asked incredulously, 'What?

My emotions had the better of me and I could not speak, I stood there lost in grief unable to repeat myself.

His demeanour and tone changed instantly as he bent over to look down at me, 'Come on let's have a look at yor dog' he said sympathetically.

Fly, who had started to shake almost uncontrollably as we had approached the Abattoir, gave a low growl as the man pulled back the blanket. I reached in and settled him by stroking his head, then showed the man the wounds on Fly's neck.

The gentle giant studied the wounds for a while then stood upright and asked, 'De ye think a lot of yor dog son?'

'Aye Mister Aa de, he's a great dog.'

'What's his name?'

'Fly.'

The man chuckled and said, 'It suits him, I tell ye what son, the bites are hardly life threatening and am sure he'll be champion if ye look after him for a few days.'

I suddenly felt elated, here was a man whom I thought obviously knows about animals, telling me Fly will be champion, he must right, 'Fly will be okay.'

'I'll tell ye something else,' the man said, 'when ye get home tell yor Mam and Dad te come here and I'll put them both doon for nowt.' I stood there imagining this huge Mam putting a gun to my Mam's head, but quickly dispelled the frightening image.

Him saying, 'Gan on son tek yor dog home, am sure he'll be fine,' was enough for me to turn the pram and walk home with almost a spring in my step, I felt a heavy weight lifted off my shoulders. Back home I carried Fly back into the sitting room and laid him down in front of the fire and stroked him, noticing that his trembling had stopped.

Woodbine in hand, Mam walked in and asked, 'Why hev ye brought him back?'

'The man said he'll be all right in a few days and he doesn't need putting doon,' I replied hurriedly.

'Did he noo,' she said' 'whey am not looking efter the bloody thing, give me the two bob back.'

Handing her the money, I said with some satisfaction, 'Ye should gan and see the man Mam; he said he'll put ye doon for nowt.'

Glaring at me with one of her set, tight-lipped looks, she snarled, 'Divvint ye be cheeky with me or ye'll get a good hiding and ye can get yorsell back te school.' I stared back at her without fear and shook my head, I was euphoric; my dog was going to be all right.

At lunchtime, I took some aspirins out of the sideboard drawer, crushed four up, mixing them with a half-tin of dog food, and placed it in front of Fly. He ate most of it before settling back onto the blanket on the carpet.

142

After some toast and a cup of tea, I left for school happy that Fly was going to live and that the aspirins would take away his pain. When I got home in the afternoon, Fly had not moved but he managed a little wag of his tail when I bent to stroke him and I knew then that he was going to recover.

In a buoyant mood, I walked back into the kitchen and asked Mam, 'What prize did I win Mam?' Now that Fly was going to be okay I had begun to wonder what was in the letter.

'Nowt important just a trip, that's all.'

'Where te?'

'Nee where important,' she answered and turned away.

Knowing I was not going to get any more information from her, I instead asked, 'Will ye give me a letter to tek back to Mrs Joseph in the morning?'

'Aye likely as not,' she said without looking at me. I knew that I would have to keep on at her if she was to write a letter.

I was successful and despite the fear of a good hiding for bothering her, she did write a few lines when I put a pen and paper in front of her later that evening.

I asked, 'What hev ye written, Mam?'

'Never ye mind, it's for yor headmistress, not ye,' she said as she sealed the envelope and handed it to me.

The following morning in Mrs Joseph's office, I handed her the letter and waited while she opened it. As she read it, I watched her smile disappear to be replaced by a frown.

'Well that is very short and not so very sweet,' she said looking at me over her glasses from the other side of the desk.

'Do you know what your mother has written Sydney?'

'No Miss.'

'Well she has said - that you, unfortunately, will not be able to go; that's very sad as I'm sure you must have been terribly excited?'

'Not really Miss, I don't know where the trip was too.'

She stared at me with a puzzled expression on her face and asked, 'Did your parents show you the letter I gave you?'

'No Miss.'

'So you think you have won a trip?'

'Yes Miss.'

She shook her head and sat looking out of her window deep in thought. I felt embarrassed at this silence and stood there feeling very self-conscious.

Eventually, she turned to me and smiled, 'Sydney, you have won an art scholarship to a top-class art school in Yugoslavia, courtesy of the Miners' of that country.'

Stunned, my mind was racing as Mrs Joseph went on to explain who had organised the competition and that the scholarship included all costs and it was obviously an opportunity of a lifetime.

143

'It is such a pity that your parents will not let you go,' will you ask them to come and talk to me or ask if I can come and talk to them?'

'Yes Miss,' I muttered, images of learning to draw and paint in an art school filling my mind.

I was angry, very angry - why had my parents not told me what the prize was? Why would they not let me go? Mrs Joseph had said 'all costs paid,' it would not be like grammar school, I could not understand why not.

Running home at lunchtime, I confronted Mam, 'Why didn't ye tell me I could gan te Art School?'

Smoking at the kitchen table she looked at me with disdain and said, 'Ye cannit gan and that's aall there is te say.'

Realising it was pointless arguing with her, I said, 'Aa'll speak te me Dad when he gets up,' and walked inot the sitting room to see o Fly.

'Please yorsell but yor not gannin,' she shouted after me.

I could not concentrate on my lessons that afternoon; I sat at my desk formulating the argument I was going to put to Dad when he got up for his tea. I had to convince him to let me go to art school; it would be so exciting. I had no qualms what so ever about leaving home - positive it would be a great adventure.

Walking home with Dennis, who at seven was also beginning to show a talent for drawing, we talked about what art school might be like and where Yugoslavia was. I had some idea as Cousin Janet's husband Nick, came from there; I would be able to ask him all about it.

Unusually, Dad was already up when I got home, he was at the kitchen table opposite Mam, both smoking and drinking tea and had been in an animated discussion when I walked in. As normal, Uncle Alex was sitting in his chair in front of the kitchen fire and must have heard their conversation.

I decided to check on Fly before I tackled Dad and walked into the sitting room to tend to my pet that had been well enough to go into the garden the night before. He was not there!

Walking over to the window, I looked out to see if he was in the garden but I could not see him so I rushed into the kitchen and asked, 'Where's Fly Mam?'

Turning her face to the window, she took a long drag on her fag before blowing it out slowly but it was Dad who answered, 'He went oot earlier and hasn't come back in yet.

I looked at him and he nervously averted my stare before saying, 'I've looked for him but canna see him oot there,' he muttered pointing to the boolly. I turned and went out to look for my dog, art school and everything else could wait.

As I headed for the door I heard my Uncle Alex say, 'May God forgive the pair of ye.'

Running over to the boolly, I shouted 'Fly' but could not see him, so I ran over the Rec Bridge into the Rec and back over again, shouting his name all the while. Up and down the Fifth Row and finally to the Fourth Row cut, just in case

144

Fly had wandered down there. Unable to find him I raced home, hoping that he had returned and ran into the kitchen where George, Viv, and Dennis were having their tea.

'Is he back?' I asked hopefully.

George turned and through a mouthful of food said, 'Na, he's not come back, Dad says he's probably been knocked doon like Rebel,' and turned back to his tea.

'Sit doon and have yor tea,' Mam ordered, 'ye can look for him efter.' I reluctantly sat and ate some food but wanted to go out to look for Fly.

Dennis looked across at me and said with sympathy, 'Aa'll help ye look after tea Syd.' I nodded and quickly finished eating.

Dennis and I spent a couple of hours wandering the streets shouting 'Fly' and asking everybody we met if they'd seen a little ginger dog. We did not find him and returned home tired and dejected. The rest of the family were watching television when we walked in, most of them ignoring us.

'Have ye fund Fly then?' George asked showing some concern, especially after having lost his own dog so recently.

Shaking my head, I answered, 'No, we've looked aall ower and canna find him.'

'The poor bugger'll be lying deed by some roadside,' George volunteered. This was too much for me and I walked into the kitchen to sit at the table, head in hands, desperately worried for my pet.

Despite searching for days, I obviously never found Fly, and no one mentioned Art College again.

14

Gala Day and Bikes

As the end of my last term at Wansbeck Juniors' approached, Mam bought me my last pair of khaki shorts for the annual Children's Gala. Looking forward to wearing my first pair of long pants, I was bitterly disappointed when she thrust the shorts and new tee shirt at me.

'Ye'll wear these till ye start Bothal School,' she said in response to my plea for long trousers.

The Saturday morning of the Gala was bright and warm with a gentle June breeze blowing down the street as our school lined up at the Store Corner ready to march to the Welfare. We had the furthest of all the schools to march, so led by a colliery band with a number of NUM marshals and teachers shepherding us along we were the first to set off. Viv, Dennis, and I were marching and before we left, Mam had told me to look after them, as she was not going.

Unlike my older brothers who had all played football for their school teams, I had never really enjoyed the game and had often demonstrated that I was less than adequate at it. Mind you they had been brought up 'Doon the Horst" where all the lads played football and where brilliant footballers like the 'Charltons' grew up.

I had, however discovered that I could run faster than average and when I did play football, I was always out on the wing, generally racing around like a headless chicken, achieving very little other than tiring myself out. Because I could run, our teacher had entered me in the 50 yards Dash and Obstacle Race in the Junior Sports events and I felt disappointed that Mam would not see me perform.

The first highlight of the day was being handed a half-a-crown and apple by the NUM Officials at the entrance to the Welfare where organised chaos was as normal, in full swing as hundreds of kids tested the Marshals' abilities to the full. Several bands continued playing after arriving and the fairground was in full swing, once again giving the Welfare a carnival atmosphere that attracted young and old from all over town.

I gathered Viv and Dennis and went to confirm which of the three running tracks I was competing on and at what time.

Viv complained 'Aa divvint want te watch ye running, Aa want te gan te the shows.'

Looking angrily at her, I said, 'Me Mam said Aa hev te look after ye so yor frigging weel gannin te watch.'

We each had the half a crown we received from the NUM Officials, plus another shilling Dad had given me to spend at the shows and I had another shilling that I had secretly collected from returning pop bottles to the shops. Just before my heat of the 50 yards Dash and not wishing to lose the money, I handed it over to Dennis and said, 'Haad on te this till am finished running and divvint let her have owt yet.'

A few minutes later, I lined up for the race with nine other lads, some of them wearing running shorts and vests but most of us in shorts and tee shirts. Like most of the other lads, I wore sandshoes but one lad had a smart pair of running shoes on and he looked very professional.

Worrying about Dennis holding our money, I was looking over to where he and Vivian were standing when the Starter shouted, 'ON YER MARKS - SET - GO,' this caught me off guard and I raced off in last place.

Desperate to catch up after my bad start, I concentrated on sprinting to the finish, oblivious of the other lads until I felt the tape pull on my chest and arms and slowing down; I turned to see that I had won easily. I was flabbergasted; I had hoped to do quite well but had not expected to win.

As I walked back smiling, one of the marshals grabbed me and thrust a winners' certificate in my hand, and asked, 'Name?'

'Sydney Carr mister, what de ye want me name for?'

He wrote my name down on the list he was holding and said, 'Be back here at two o'clock for the final,' and walked off.

When I reached the other two, Dennis said, 'Ye won that really fast Syd are ye getting a prize?'

'Nur, just a certificate, but am in the final at two o'clock.'

Viv looked at me and said, 'Whey am not watching ye then cos Aa'll be at the shows.'

'Ye'll be in bloody hospital if ye divvint stay with us,' I threatened, realising it was a mistake, as soon as I had said it.

My warning was like a red rag to a bull – Viv shouted, 'Bugger off, am not scared of ye,' and ran off to the shows.

'Shit,' I said angrily, and then remembering the money said, 'she'll come back, she hasn't got any money.'

'She has, she took it off me,' Dennis said sheepishly.

'Frigging hell,' I said wanting to chase after her but could not as I was due for the obstacle race in five minutes. I couldn't be angry with Dennis; knowing that Viv would have tricked him into handing over the money.

Lining up next to Jack Moody for the Obstacle race, we began baiting each other.

'Am gannin to beat ye,' Jack said.

'Nur Aa'll beat ye easy,'

'Aa bet ye, Aa win.'

'Nur Aa'll win.'

The course consisted of obstacles made from benches, hurdles and wooden horses but the last obstacle was a large, thin roped net laid loosely on the ground.

148

When the race began, Jack and I were soon in the lead, totally disinterested in the rest of the runners, we were racing each other. Clearing the other obstacles, we reached the net neck and neck and scrambled underneath it. It was loose and awkward to negotiate, constantly snagging our hands, feet and heads, slowing us down as we fought to crawl through to the other side.

We reached the far side together, still ahead of the rest of the field but as I stood up Jack yelled, 'Bloody hell, me frigging foots caught.' Stopping, I turned to see him struggling to loosen his foot and felt torn between finishing and helping him.

I shouted at him, 'Aa thought ye were gannin to beat me?'

Looking up at me and laughing, he shouted, 'Bugger off.'

Running back, I helped him free before the two of us ran to the line pushing and shoving each other all the way, laughing madly as we did so. We didn't win but were surprised to receive a big cheer from the onlookers, so ran around in a little circle with our arms in the air as though we had just won Gold at the Olympics.

We trotted over to Dennis and said, 'Haway let's gan and find Viv,' and the three of us went to the fairground to find her and our money.

'I knaa where she'll be,' I said and headed straight for the Waltzer where 'Singing the Blues,' was blaring out of the loudspeakers. Sure enough, she was standing next to the railings watching the cars rattle around the track, and did not see us coming.

Knowing how slippery she could be, I pointed to the steps at the far side and said to Jack, 'Gan aroond that way in case she runs away.'

It was just as well I did; despite the noise from the blaring music and rattling machinery, she turned at the last moment and saw Dennis and me approaching. She was off like a startled rabbit – straight into Jack's arms and struggled to break free as we reached her but Jack held her tight.

'Give me the money back noo,' I demanded.

'Bugger off,' she said defiantly.

Dennis looked at her and warned, 'If ye divvint give is the money back Aa'll tell me Mam.'

She knew when she was beaten, Mam would listen to Dennis and as a result, she would get a good hiding.

Reluctantly, she said, 'Aalreet, here it is but Aa've spent some of it.' I took the money and counted it, she had spent her half-a-crown and another sixpence!

'I looked at her with disgust and said, 'Whey that's your share spent, yor getting nowt more.'

She spat, 'A hate ye, ye git ye.' and ran off again.

Looking at Dennis, I asked him, 'Bugger her Den what de ye want te gan on?'

I paid for the three of us to ride the Waltzer and we whooped and screamed as the spinning car threw us from side to side, as it hurtled around the track.

After the ride Jack said, 'Aa'll see ye later Aa've got te find me Mam,' and went off to look for her.

Realising, I only had four shilling and sixpence left, I said to Dennis, 'Ye can have two-bob but am gannin on the rifle range.'

Dennis bought himself some Candy Floss and joined me at the Shooting Gallery where I had handed over my shilling for three goes, I wanted to win a cut glass vase that was three vouchers; sure my Mam would be proud of me when I handed it over.

Winning the first two vouchers easily, I started to load the first of the last six pellets when I heard the voice's of young girls, talking and giggling behind me. Curious, I turned to see a group of six or seven girls of about thirteen year's old standing watching me. Instantly drawn to the smallest girl in the group I saw that she had her hair in a ponytail now but I still recognised those smiling blue eyes and immediately blushed. Wearing a blue dress with puff sleeves, white socks, and black shoes, she looked lovely.

I was devastated; here I was eleven years old and still wearing shorts, I thought I must have looked like a real bairn but she still smiled at me. I tried to hide my embarrassment and turned to busy myself with the task of winning the vase and fired my six pellets, winning my third voucher, exchanging that and the other two I had won for the vase. Turning round, I hoped to be able to show the Blue-Eyed Girl my trophy but she and the other girls had gone.

Dennis said, 'Ye can shoot like…' but I cut him off.

'Did ye see where them lasses went?'

He looked puzzled and asked, 'What lasses?'

Disappointed, I replied, 'Never mind, haway we'll have a walk roond and see if we can find Viv.' I was not the least bit interested in finding Viv; I wanted to see if I could find the blue-eyed girl again. We wandered around the fair for ages before I spotted her watching one of her friends throwing hoops at the Hoopla Stall.

Stopping twenty or so yards away, I said to Dennis, 'Haad on,' and stood there trying to look inconspicuous without taking my eyes off her.

Dennis looked at me and asked, 'Whaat we deeing?'

I snapped back, 'Haad on man,' my mind racing, I wanted to talk to her but knew I would be laughed at; she must be older than me and I was in shorts, besides, I couldn't understand why I wanted to talk to her, so I just stood there like a dummy.

Her friend threw her last hoop unsuccessfully and they turned to walk toward where we were standing, she spotted me and began to smile. I could not move and just wanted the ground to swallow me and hide my embarrassment until Dennis saved me.

'What time are ye running again Syd?'

I had forgotten all about the final; suddenly able to move again I said, 'Bloody hell, haway man,' and raced off leaving the Blue-Eyed Girl looking with amusement at my rapidly disappearing back.

I arrived at the starting area, breathing heavily and asked a marshal what the time was.

'It's five te two, why? Are ye running?' he asked.

'Aye I'm in the final of the 50 yards dash.'

'Ye must be Carr?' he replied, 'We've been shouting for ye.'

Handing the vase and my certificate over to Dennis, I followed the man to the start where nine other lads had already lined up, several wearing proper running gear. I had had a long day; first the two-mile march here, my run in the heats and the obstacle race but I did not feel tired, on the contrary, I felt exhilarated and was excited at running in the final. Seeing the blue-eyed girl again had also made me feel strangely happy.

'Another bloody certificate,' I said to Dennis a few minutes later, showing him my winner's prize. 'Aa thought I might have got a cup or summick - we better try and find Viv before we gan hyem,' and I led him back to the fair again, secretly hoping to see the blue-eyed girl but there was no sign of her or her friends when we got there.

We found Viv leaning against the rail of the Waltzer talking to Jack who blushed and looked very sheepish when we joined them.

'Aa've just been making sure she doesn't bugger off Syd,' he said looking very embarrassed.

I looked at him and thought, 'Does he like wor Viv,' then quickly thought 'Knaa ne bugger could like hor.'

Grinning, I said, 'Haway then let's gan hyem,' and the four of us walked back through Ashington to the Fifth Row. It was a long walk after a long hot day and we were glad to walk into the cool of the house where we found Mam sitting with a cup of tea and a small glass of a dark brown liquid.

'Here ye are Mam,' I said proudly handing over the cheap cut glass vase to her, 'I won it on the air rifles.'

She took it and examined it through the cigarette smoke she had just blown out and said, 'Champion,' before taking a sip from the little glass.

'Wor Syd wouldn't let me hev any money Mam,' Viv said jealous of Mam having been pleased by the vase.

Mam looked at her, then me but before she could speak Dennis said, 'She spent her money Mam and kept on running away and wor Syd's got certificates for running.'

Mam took another sip, said, 'Aye champion,' and turned to look out the window.

School term ended and the long summer holidays began and to my immense relief and satisfaction, I finally got my first pair of long trousers, a pair of George's old ones, I was chuffed.

A few days later, a bunch of us were playing cricket in the street in front of the Scout Hut when Frank appeared on a bike! Bikes were prized possessions and we were all very envious.

He nonchalantly dropped his bike on the grass, walked over to us and asked, 'Can I join the game?'

George said, 'Nur, we've got even sides.'

As Frank turned to walk away, I spotted an opportunity and shouted after him, 'Ye can hev my place if a can hev a ride on yor bike?'

He agreed so I ran over to the bike, picked it up, and saw that it was not new and far too big for either him or me but it looked perfectly serviceable. I lifted my leg over and felt the cross bar dig into my crutch. 'This is going to be painful,' I thought.

I pushed off, pressed down on the pedal, and immediately fell in a heap on the concrete road.

'Bugger,' I said and picked the bike up again.

Frank shouted, 'It's too big for ye man.'

Perched ready for another go, I looked back at him and shouted, 'It's not that it's too big, Am faalling off becos I've nivvor ridden one before,' and pushed off, immediately falling over again.

I spent a painful thirty minutes trying to master the brute of a bike and had only managed a few feet but had succeeded in skinning my shins and knocking my testicles twice, leaving me writhing on the floor on both occasions but I was not ready to give up.

Then, almost as if by magic, it happened, I was riding the beast, I could not reach the saddle so had to contend with standing on the pedals rising and falling with each rotation, my testicles brushing the crossbar on every fall. It was brilliant, I felt as though I was flying. As I headed for the Sixth Row, I heard a cheer go up from the lads, who had been following my progress with some amusement and had provided a constant barrage of advice and heckling.

Riding the bike round and round the Sixth Row, my legs trembled with the effort until I finally dismounted by falling in a heap next to the Scout Hut. Lying on my back looking up at cotton wool clouds drifting across the sky I felt elated; I just had to get a bike.

The next day I started to collect bike parts in the hope I could build my own but found it difficult to obtain a frame and, therefore, had to put the project on the back burner during the rest of the holidays.

Mam and Dad took the younger part of their tribe, along with the Lowry's, Little's and Page's on a camping holiday to Ingelton in Yorkshire. It was a great

152

spot by the river next to the village and we had a brilliant time exploring the waterfalls and caves in the area.

My woollen swimming costume had its last outing in the river when I was attempting to cover my modesty as I tried to catch eels.

I didn't succeed and when Jennifer Little ran giggling back to their tent shouting 'Aa've seen Syd's willie,' Dad took me off to a gift shop and I came back with a close fitting blue costume with white stripes on the side. I felt like 'Superman' but looked more like 'Stickman' as my body still carried less fat than a greasy chip. Dennis was very envious of my new swimming costume, as he still had to contend with his sagging down to his knees. Having been there, I knew how it felt but now in my new bather, I felt very superior.

Jennifer followed me around for a large part of the holiday and even travelled in our car a couple of times so that she could sit next to me; I wasn't sure that I minded and began to find her attentions quite pleasurable.

After the summer holidays, I walked to Bothal school for the first time, excited at having at last reached senior school age. It was only three hundred yards away at the end of the third terrace of the Third Row and meant I left home after Viv and Dennis who still had to walk to Wansbeck School.

Meeting up with Tom Payne who had been in my class at Wansbeck, we explored the single storey, Victorian red-bricked buildings together before going into the classroom and finding seats next to each other, marking the start of a close and long friendship. Whereas I was slightly Mediterranean looking, Tom was taller with blonde hair and high cheekbones; he had to be of Viking descent, a complete contrast to me. He lived in the Eleventh Row with his father, a stable hand at Coneygarth Drift Mine where Dad ran the fore-shift.

After our first day, we were walking home together when a commotion in the alleyway at the bottom of the long gardens of the Fourth Row drew us toward the noise coming from a circle of lads baying like dogs at two others in the middle.

Tom said, 'It's a fight; bloody awful school this if there's fights every night.'

Looking into the melee, I said, 'It's wor Geordie and his mate Ray!'

Standing at the back of the little crowd, we watched the two combatants battle, and it was a battle. There was no posturing as they stood toe to toe and slugged it out, each punch landing home with brutal force and a sickening thud. This was the first time I had heard punches land with such force and such noise, it was sickening and intimidating but strangely exhilarating.

Urged on by the crowd, George and Ray battled on until both of them were almost on their knees, neither one wanting to give up. I wanted to stop it, worried at the brutality of the fight and the damage they were doing to each other but knew I stood no chance of getting close to them; it, therefore, came as a great relief when eventually the older lads stepped in and parted them.

153

Blowing hard and with blood-streaked faces, they stood glaring at each other, as they leant into the restraining arms of the older lads, both still prepared to continue the fight, both totally exhausted but unbowed.

I don't know who started first but suddenly George and Ray were laughing an exhausted laugh, brushing aside the other lads, they staggered off together laughing and joking with each other as though nothing had happened. No one ever tried it on with George or Ray after that fight.

As Christmas approached, I still had not succeeded in making a bike and had begun asking - almost pleading with Mam for a bike for Christmas. I knew I risked a slapping but also knew if I was to get a bike I had to drive the idea home.

On a cold grey day, the week before Christmas, Mam sat down at the kitchen table and wrote a letter, sealed it in an envelope then handed it to me and said, 'Tek this to Bob Orwell's and get a bike and bring it back here.' Tremendously excited, I happily snatched the note and headed off for Orwell's shop in Milburn Road close to where we had lived in Pont Street. I knew that Mam usually did her Christmas shopping by sending a begging letter for toys to Bob Orwell, promising that she would pay for them by instalment. Eric had always had the task of taking the letter but as he was now past the age where he was interested in toys, the task fell to me. I suspect George had not been given the job as if Bob Orwell refused, as he had done on occasion in the past, George would have probably taken some toys anyway.

It was about a mile and a half to Orwell's and I walked briskly along imaging what it would be like to ride my own bike back, I hoped it would be blue. When I reached the shop, I stopped outside and looked in at the many bikes on display in the window and at the toys further back in the shop. I wondered if I would be able to manage to ride a bike and carry toys at the same time or if I would have to push the bike and carry the toys.

Pushing open the shop door, the bell rang on its spring above as I entered and I saw Bob Orwell at the counter at the far end of the shop.

I think he probably recognised me as one of the Carr brood and asked, 'What are ye efter lad?'

I walked across the bare wooden floor and thrust my Mam's letter at him saying, 'Aa've come for a bike for Christmas Mr Orwell.'

He took the letter and glared down at me trying to look angry but not succeeding before saying, 'Hev ye, lets hev a look.'

He read the letter carefully and then disappeared through the back door into his storeroom as I waited with rising excitement and a stomach full of butterflies; I could hardly contain myself. I looked at the bikes in the window and spotted a blue one with touring handlebars, it was exactly what I dreamed of owning and hoped he would bring its twin from the rear of the shop.

154

Hearing him returning, I turned and looked to see which bike he was pushing - my Jaw dropped, the butterflies immediately replaced by a hollow and empty feeling when I saw the silver girls' bike he wheeled in.

'Yor Mam says yor sister is a couple of inches smaller than ye so this should be just right.'

I had to fight back tears of anger as I realised what Mam had done, how could she I thought? She knew I wanted a bike so much.

Mr Orwell adjusted the saddle and checked the brakes as I watched in stunned disbelief.

'Right-oh son, here ye are, take care riding home noo.'

Taking the handlebars, I pushed the bike toward the door, and then remembered toys; stopping, I turned and asked, 'Is there any toys to collect Mr Orwell?'

'TOYS!' he shouted, 'Toys! Bloody hell Aa'll be bloody lucky if a get paid for that, noo bugger off before Aa tek it back.'

I felt like giving him it back but instead opened the door and pushed the bike through and onto the pavement.

The overcast gloomy day matched my mood as I rode the bike home the back way along Green Lane, not wanting to be seen riding a girls' bike that was too small for me. Feeling cheated and sick, I could picture Viv gloating over her new bike, especially as she knew I was trying to get parts to build one. I was so angry I had to stop myself from getting off the bike and throwing it in the ditch.

Arriving home, I left the bike in the yard and walked into the house where Mam, busy preparing dinner looked up at me and said, 'Divvint tell me ye didn't get the bike?'

I looked at her and said angrily, 'Aa did, it's in the yard.'

Wiping her hands on a tea towel, she snapped, 'Fancy leaving it in the yard where she'll see it ye simple bugger, gan and bring it in here.'

Walking to the back door, I spat, 'Fetch it yorsell,' and stormed out the house and off across the Rec Bridge.

All trust I had for my Mam should have disappeared that day but it didn't, I would be caught by her devious ways on several more occasions but what really rubbed salt into the wound, was that Viv hardly ever used her new bike.

15

Lakeland Adventure

The first weekend of the school summer holidays of '57', arrived in the middle of a mini heat wave so Dad decided that the 'Clan' would embark on a trip to the Lakes in his latest car, an Austin A10. Mam, as normal, filled the travelling box with bread, butter, limp lettuce, cheese slices, tomatoes, biscuits and other goodies, in addition to lots of brew kit.

Dad had told Aunty Jen about the outing and she ordered the Lowries to prepare for a long day trip. Dad had also told the Littles and Pages and by ten o'clock, they were in their cars parked behind the Lowry's and ours as we prepared for the off.

Dad gathered the other three drivers together to discuss the best route and after much discussion, he climbed into the car muttering, 'It'll be a miracle if all them simple buggers mek the end of the street let alone Ulswater!'

Dennis travelled on Mam's knee in the front and I shared the back seat with George, Viv, and Jennifer Lawson who had asked to come with Viv but spent most of the journey leaning on me. It was a lovely journey across rural Northumberland, through Alston and on into Cumberland, the scenery was fantastic and Mam was in a good mood, pointing out landmarks on the way.

At Twelve o'clock Dad pulled off the A66 onto a large grass verge just before Penrith and said, 'We'll have a cup of tea while we wait for the rest to catch up.' The Lowries were right behind us and the Littles a few hundred yards behind them but we had lost the Pages.

Told that it was going to take a good half hour to organise a quick lunch of cheese sandwiches and tea, George, Alan Little, Alec and myself ran across a field to look at Brougham Castle at the other side of the river. It was a beautiful spot with the river flowing swiftly through the tree-lined banks that framed the sandstone castle, standing sentinel on the far side. With the sun high in the sky, the river looked deep, cool and inviting below the nettle-covered bank on the near side.

George considered he was too old to join in our game of knights and instead searched the riverbank for access to the water while we galloped around. I was in the middle of a joust with Alec when we heard George yelling obscenities from below the bank.

Galloping our chargers over to the sound of his voice, and sword fighting all the way, we reached the steep crumbling bank where we dismounted and looked over the edge. The bank was about six feet high with a nettle covered, rough, sandy slope that fell down to the river, a trail of squashed nettles marked George's path down the bank and into the water. Waist deep in the river, he had grasped hold of the nettles to prevent the flow from washing him away but appeared to unable to haul himself out.

When he saw us peering down at him, he yelled, 'Haway ye sackless buggers, get me oot, am frigging stuck.'

'Where were ye gannin Geordie?' I asked trying hard not to laugh.

He looked up and angrily spat, 'Aa was just trying to see if we could plodge across the river, noo help me oot.'

Alec, unfortunately, began laughing and said 'Yor supposed to tek yor shoes and socks off before ye gan plodging man.'

Alan joined in, 'A bet yor having a piss in the river ye dirty bugger.'

I knew this was a mistake and did not join in especially as I saw George's lower jaw push forward as he gritted his teeth.

'Shut up man or he'll murder ye,' I warned the other two but they kept on laughing as I looked for a branch or something similar for George to grasp onto; I need not have bothered. Stung by the lads' taunts and oblivious to the stings he had from the nettles, he used them to haul himself up the bank, before dragging himself over the edge and chased after the other two.

Fleet of foot, Alan raced off like a scalded cat but chubby Alec was no match for George's speed. George chased him for a few yards, grabbed him in a headlock and then wearing the set grimace that warned of danger, he dragged the now screaming Alec back to the river.

When he reached the bank, he threw Alec over the edge, straight into the nettle patch, which he rolled through before disappearing into the deep water below. He was completely submerged and out of site for a second or two before exploding out of the water like an enraged hippopotamus.

Water streaming from him he screamed, 'Aa'll fugging kill ye, ye bastard,' and tried to scramble back up the bank.

The steepness of the bank, the nettles, and the water were all too much for Alec, his angry exertions soon slowed as his energy disappeared. He eventually flopped onto the nettles too exhausted to bother about their stings and lay there like a beached mini-whale. Alan re-joined us at the bank and the three of us looked down at the pathetic sight below us and burst out laughing.

Dejectedly, Alec lifted his head and shouted in a pathetic voice, 'Bastards.'

We scrambled down the bank and dragged him sodden and exhausted back to the top before the four of us collapsed in a heap. Streaked with mud, our hands covered in nettle stings, and in Alec's case, much of his face as well, we all burst out laughing again. Walking back to the cars, we gathered Dock Leaves and rubbed them on our stings to lessen the irritation but we were muddy, wet and dishevelled when we climbed over the fence next to the cars where Mam was making tea with water from the freshly boiled kettle.

She looked up at us, shook her head and muttered, 'Sackless buggers,' and turned back to making tea.

158

Auntie Jen, who had not moved from the front seat of her car yelled at Alec, 'Eeee my God what hev ye been up to? Come here and let's hev a look at ye.'

Squelching across to his mother, he said pathetically, 'Aa fell in the river and they had to pull me oot.'

George smiled and bending down, snatched a cheese sandwich, shoving the majority of it into his mouth in his not so genteel way.

Walking across to George, Dad glared at him and warned, 'Ye better not hev had out te de with him falling in!' George glared back at Dad and without saying a word, shoved the rest of the sandwich into his mouth, and walked away. The hostility between the two was still growing.

I was still rubbing dock leaves on my hand when Jennifer came up and said, 'Do ye want a sandwich, Syd?' Embarrassed by her attention, I did not look at her or answer her question and brushing past her; I took a sandwich and walked to the front of the car to look back at the castle.

In the meantime, Auntie Jen had grabbed Alec and had started to take the sodden clothes of the bedraggled lad, tut-tutting as she did so. She dragged his pants from around his legs while Alec tried desperately to stop her from exposing him to the rest of us. Viv and Jennifer began sniggering and pointing at the podgy white body with a beetroot-red face atop just as George stepped forward and looked Alec slowly up and down.

'How, Alec, did you leave summick in the river or is that all ye've got?' George mocked.

Crossing his hands over his diminutive member, Alec spat, 'Bugger off.'

Auntie Jen grabbed him protectively to her massive bosoms and said, 'Niver mind that bugger Pet, he's all cock and nee brains.

Having almost disappeared between his Mam's breasts, Alec shouted over his shoulder, 'Aa didn't fall in the river, that rotten bugger pushed me in.'

George was busy wringing out the wet tee shirt he had just stripped off and ignored the shout but Dad walked up to him and snarled, 'Whey! Did you push him in?'

Glaring back at Dad, George said quietly, 'Aye Aa did, so what?' Dad lifted his hand as if to slap him but George stood his ground and stared defiantly at him.

Dad stood with his hand raised for a second or two, then turned and walked to the front of the car muttering, 'Aa'll swing for that little bastard one of these days.'

With a look of satisfaction spreading across his face, George watched Dad walk away before grabbing another sandwich, biting viciously into it.

Shortly afterward, Dad had a quick discussion with Uncle Nick and Geordie Little before saying to the rest of us, 'Reet, it doesn't look as though Percy is coming this way, he's probably gone alang the A69 and doon through Carlisle so we'll get on before we lose the whole day.'

Back in the car, Jennifer was leaning heavily against me, making me feel a

159

tad claustrophobic and I desperately wanted to be out in the fresh air while at the same time I was enjoying the feel of her next to me. I was very confused.

Half an hour or so later, we were driving along the banks of Ullswater admiring the breath-taking scenery when Mam said, 'Ee isn't that them up aheed?' Sure enough, Percy Page and his wife Marti were standing at the entrance to a rough lay-by next to the lake; both frantically waving at us.

Dad drew alongside them while Mam wound down her window to talk to the pair but before she could, Dad shouted across the front seat, 'Where the buggery hev ye been, we waited at Brough an hour for ye?'

Marti, an attractive, dark-haired woman in her thirties, stared in wide-eyed bewilderment and screeched, 'Eeeeeeeee George we went through Carlisle man, Eeeeeeee.' Marti said Eeeeeee a lot, especially when she was confused, bewildered or excited, which seemed to be pretty much all the time.

Percy drawled, 'Well George, I lost you north of Nuucastle so I came along the A69 and then down the A6 and...'

Dad cut him off, a queue of cars was beginning to build up behind us. 'Nivvor mind that noo,' he said, 'follow on and this time, keep up - we're gannin te stop at Glenridding.'

A little while later, our convoy of cars pulled into the car park of the imposing grey stone Hotel on the banks of Ullswater in the pretty village of Glenridding. Immediately the doors of the cars swung open as we kids burst out as though newly released from some dreadful prison and George headed for the lake, the rest of us following on behind like sheep.

Dad shouted after us, 'Divvint wander off, we're just gannin in for a quick drink.'

The quick drink was anything but quick, it was an hour or so later before they emerged in high spirits, Mam saying, 'Bide here while we pop ower to the shop, we're gannin te stop here for the night.'

They walked off leaving us talking excitedly about staying in this very posh hotel, wondering what we would have to eat and how big the bedrooms were.

Alec said, 'There's boond te be lots of food and there'll be waiters running and fetching more, it'll be great.'

'That's all ye think of ye fat bugger,' George spat, 'we'll be lucky if them miserable old gits get us owt, they'll just get drunk!'

It wasn't long before the grownups walked back across the car park, the women carrying bulging brown paper carrier bags while Dad and Geordie Little carried a crate of ale between them and Nick and Percy carried more bottles of ale in their arms.

Puzzled as to why they wanted the shopping if we were staying in the hotel, I asked, 'Mam why hev ye got all that stuff if we're staying here?'

She gave me a sideways glance and shook her head and said, 'We're not staying here ye simple bugger, we cannit afford their prices, we're gannin te camp in the fields ower the other side of the lake.'

160

George mocked, 'A towld ye didn't Aa ye daft sod.'

'Na ye didn't,' I said, 'and anyway we've got nee tents or owt.'

Obviously more relaxed with several beers inside him, Dad said, 'We div-vint need tents on a day like this man, Nick used to sleep in trees when he was a partisan, didn't ye Nick?'

Smiling knowingly, Nick answered in his thick accent, 'Yes George, ve sleep in them bloody trees so bloody Nazis don't find us.'

Looking very worried, Alec ran to his huge mother and cried, 'Mam Aa divvint hev to sleep in a tree tonight div Aa?'

Out of breath from the effort of waddling to and from the shop, she re-plied, 'Nee buggers gannin te mek ye sleep in a tree bonny lad, ye'll sleep in the car with me.'

I could not resist it, my mind was working overtime at the thought of the two of them sleeping in the back of their car and I said, 'Mind yor Mam doesn't roll on top of ye Alec or we'll niver find ye again.'

The campsite, if you could call it that was a field at the southeast corner of the lake, a hundred yards or so from a substantial Lakeland farm where Dad had sought permission to camp. It was a splendid spot; the field was large, slightly undulating and sloped down to the lakeshore with dry-stone walls enclosing the three other sides. A track ran behind the wall opposite the lake and beyond that, the steep side of a fell climbed up to the east.

The cars stopped in single file, a few feet apart, near the centre of the field and we all spilled out to take stock of our surroundings. The women began organ-ising cooking arrangements while the men opened bottles of ale and stood admir-ing the view. We kids ran whooping and yelling down to the lake where we tried with varying degrees of success, to skim pebbles across the placid lake, disturbing its mirror-like surface.

Young Percy turned around to look up at the bracken-covered slopes of the fell, and said, 'A bet ye can see for miles from the top of there.'

Looking up at the fell top, I followed the skyline around, taking in the mountains, until I was looking west across the lake toward the high peak of Hel-vellyn above Patterdale.

In awe of the majesty of the view, I turned back to look at the fell behind us and said, 'Am ganging up there,' and began walking toward the dry-stone wall.

Dennis as normal fell in behind me, followed by Alan, young Percy, and Alec; George continued throwing pebbles into the lake. The first obstacle was the huge dry-stone wall, which we stormed as if it were the ramparts of an ancient cas-tle, all of us that is, except Alec who was finding it difficult to heave his podgy bulk up the wall. We were shouting encouragement from the other side when there was a dull thud followed by a howl of pain and cursing. The cursing grew fainter as Alec, who had obviously fallen off the wall ran back to his mother for solace.

161

Alan laughed, 'Sir Alec de Plump couldn't get ower the castle wall.'

'Onward withoot him, men,' I cried, 'The big bugger wouldn't get up the hill anyway.' We began running up the slope but after a few yards, we had to stop to get our breath back as the steepness of the slope bit into our skinny thighs and stole the air from our lungs.

'Bugger this,' Percy gasped, 'Am gannin back,' and turned back down the hill followed quickly by Alan.

'Are we gannin back?' Dennis asked hopefully.

I looked up the steep slope and replied, 'Whey Am not, Am gannin up there,' and began climbing the slope at an angle to lessen the steepness as Dennis followed on.

We climbed up through the bracken, which finally gave way to open fell that was interspersed with crags that provided us with wonderful views along the length of Ullswater. Feeling hot and sweaty in the late afternoon sun, our legs ached with the effort but we continued on traversing to the south and onto a shoulder that led up to the summit ridge.

Jeans and tee shirts were not best suited to the climb but our plimsolls were comfortable enough going up if a little slippery in places. Finally, after 40 minutes or so, we collapsed on the summit ridge, our legs shaking from this new form of exercise. We lay there for some time before I sat up to take in our position on the fell and noticed that compared to the giants around us, it was very modest but to us it seemed like Everest and provided us with breath-taking views across the lake and surrounding hills.

Dennis croaked, 'Am thirsty, Aa want a drink and summick te eat.'

Amazed that my emaciated little brother had managed to make the top of the hill and feeling thirsty and hungry myself, as well as beginning to chill in the fell-top breeze I said, 'Haway then let's gan doon and get a drink.'

Going up had been strenuous for me at twelve years old and even tougher for eight-year-old Dennis but going down was a nightmare. Our toes crushed painfully into the front of our plimsolls as we walked and slithered down, our knees and thighs aching with the effort, Dennis began crying when we were nearly down and we had to sit and rest until he calmed down.

Sobbing pathetically, he cried, 'This is your fault, Am gannin to tell Mam on ye. This was his normal cry when things did not go his way and often resulted in me receiving a clip from Mam for failing to look after 'The Bairn,' but despite sore feet and aching limbs, I was enjoying myself far too much to worry about Mam.

We were too tired to climb the wall when we finally got down and had to walk round to the gate to enter the campsite. The smell of cooking drifted over the open field as we walked wearily to the cars and I could see everyone was sitting on the grass around our car where they were eating from enamel plates that Dad kept in the boot.

Dennis collapsed on to Mam nearly spilling the all-in stew she had been

162

eating. She was about to chastise him when she saw how red his face was.

'Eee where the bloody hell have ye been?' She asked worriedly.

He began to wail, 'Syd made me waalk up the hill and me feet, and legs are aall broken and sore,' he spluttered.

Mam looked at Dennis then spat at me, 'Ye bloody simpleton ye, fancy dragging the poor Bairn up the bloody hills, ye could have killed him ye bloody waster ye.'

Looking at them both, I muttered, 'Aa wish Aa had,' obviously not meaning it.

I grabbed an enamel cup, filled it with water from the Jerry can, and quaffed the cool liquid and felt as though steam was coming from my head.

Mam was busy tending to Dennis and I asked, 'Is there any dinner?'

'Not for ye,' she spat.

Feeling hungry and angry, I cast my eyes around for the pot that the stew must be in until Jennifer said, 'Ye can share mine, Syd.'

Noticing her plate was nearly empty I said, 'Nur Thanks, it's aalreet,' but, of course, it wasn't alright.

'Sorry Young'un,' George said, 'But Aav'e finished mine.'

Beginning to feel desperate, I looked around and saw that Alec had turned his back on me and was eating as fast as possible, just in case I attempted to steal his precious stew.

'Here!' a voice behind me said and I turned to see Dad holding a spoon and an enamel soup plate full of stew with two slices of bread on the top. I grabbed the plate and spoon as I finally saw the large pot the stew was in, still on the primus behind the car.

'Hoo far did ye gan up the hill?' Dad asked looking up toward the summit.

'Right to the top of this one,' I replied pointing with the spoon to the fell, we had climbed. 'Ye cannit see the top from here, it's further on.'

Dad looked at me and smiled, actually smiled! He walked to the back of the car, reached into the boot and pulled out a bottle of ale, knocking the top off on the lip of the boot.

'Here,' he said, 'Ye've earned that,' and thrust the bottle toward me.

Grasping the bottle, I took a large mouthful of the brown liquid, and swallowed; then realising how awful it tasted, I tried hard not to embarrass myself by pulling a face of disgust.

'Can Aa hev a bottle faather?' George asked, already knowing the answer.

Dad looked at him and said, 'Aye if ye run up to the top of the hill and back ye can,' then took a sip from the bottle he had just picked up and turned his back on George.

Standing up, George walked down to the lake in disgust.

The all-in stew of potatoes, tinned carrots and tinned stewing steak was delicious and I devoured it greedily, mopping up the watery gravy with bread. Finished, I picked up the bottle of ale and walked down to the lakeside where all the

163

kids, less Dennis, had gathered again.

'Gis a drink Young'un,' George asked.

I took a small sip and gladly handed over the bottle to him and watched as he took a large swig, belched, and pulled a face saying, 'By that tastes like shite!'

The rest of the lads asked for a taste and we passed the bottle around taking small sips of the bitter liquid, all of us trying to be nonchalant as we swallowed the ale.

Vivian came over and said, 'Can Aa hev a drink, Syd?'

'No,' I replied, 'it's just for lads.'

'Aa'll tell me Mam,'

'Bugger off,' I shouted at her and immediately the other lads took up the call, 'Bugger off, Bugger off.'

Enraged, Vivian ran off up the hill, presumably to tell Mam but I didn't care and sat down on a fallen tree to admire the view as Jennifer joined me.

'Syd, while you were up the hill your George tried to kiss me but I wouldn't let him but you can kiss me if you want.' She paused, and then said quietly, 'but not in the dark cos I don't want a baby!'

I was shocked; I didn't know that kissing in the dark made babies!

Not wanting to risk giving her a baby, I kissed her quickly on the cheek and walked off to where the lads were, 'Better safe than sorry,' I thought.

We found a Tarzan rope tied to the branch of one of the trees and were having a great time grabbing the rope as high up as we could before swinging out over the lake and back. As we swung on the rope, the five men with bottles of ale in their hands wandered down to watch us. Initially, they shouted encouragement urging us to swing out higher and further until the ale and excitement got too much for Mr Little.

Shouting, 'Here man, let me show ye buggers how it's done,' he ran and dived for the rope, grasping it with both hands, his speed and momentum carrying him out over the lake until the rope snapped taught but his body kept going until he was horizontal, forcing him to let go of the rope. His feet continued upwards as his head swung downwards, straight into the icy waters of the lake. There was an almighty splash as he hit the water and disappeared under before coming up arms flailing as he thrashed around madly.

Dad and the other men were laughing almost hysterically as we kids jumped up and down, cheering at him splashing wildly in his panic.

Mrs Little, who had witnessed her husband's mishap, came rushing down to the lake screaming, 'He can't swim, he can't swim!'

Hitching up her dress, she began wading into the cold lake until Dad managed to stop laughing and shouted, 'Haad on man Missus - Geordie, stop splashing aboot and stand up.'

Geordie Little managed to get to his feet and to his embarrassment found he was in just three-feet of water. He splashed his way back to his wife who grabbed him and pulled him to the bank as though he had narrowly missed drown-

164

ing.

Mr Page said to Dad, 'I don't think I'll be having one of them Baths tonight George.'

'Aye Aa divvint think Johnny Weissmuller need worry aboot his job as Tarzan just yet,' Dad replied sarcastically.

Later, as the sun began to dip behind the fells, turning the sky and lake crimson and gold, the men stood by the lake bank peeing the contents of several bottles of ale into the water while discussing the Toons chances in the new season while the women busied themselves around the cars organising places for us to sleep.

Mam laid a blanket on the ground next to the car onto which George, Dennis and I climbed before she threw another blanket on top of us. Mam and Dad were going to sleep on the ground in front of the car with another two blankets; Vivian had gone to sleep in the back of the Little's car with Jennifer.

Lying on the blankets talking, we watched the men down by the Lake and saw that Uncle Nick had climbed a tree, presumably looking for somewhere to sleep. Tired from the day's excitement and our bellies still full of stew, we were all soon asleep.

I woke up feeling cold and sore, my thighs aching from climbing the fell and my hip sore from the hard ground. Looking around, I realised I had slid off the blanket and was lying in the open, several feet from a huddled shape wrapped in the two blankets above me. Wearily, I stood up, walked to the blankets, and tried unsuccessfully to rest one from George who grunted and pulled them closer.

Unable to wrestle a blanket from George, I turned as a movement caught my eye and I saw a shadowy figure walking from the lakeside in the direction of the farm. I was too tired to find out whom it was and climbed into the front of the car noticing that Dennis was already asleep in the back and lying down, I quickly nodded off on the front bench seat.

The sound of Mam's voice woke me and I peered out of the steamed up window to see what was happening. Rubbing the sleep from my eyes I opened the car door and drank in the cool fresh mountain air as it replaced the stale air inside. Mam was busy making tea and buttering bread while George stood next to her waiting for a sandwich as he sipped scalding tea gingerly from a battered enamel mug.

As I sat on the edge of the front seat pulling on my tattered plimsolls, Dad with fag in hand, said, 'Hurry up and get yor shoes on, ye and George are gannin doon te the farm for some eggs.' Not trusting George, Dad handed me two shillings, a sixpenny piece and a brown paper carrier bag and said, 'Ask for twenty, te mek sure every bugger gets one.'

George and I headed off across the field to the farm as the morning sun began to chase the shadows of the fells from the field whilst a gentle breeze stirred the surface of the water of the huge lake making it sparkle like a field of diamonds

165

in the bright sunlight.

Approaching the farm, we slowed when a Border Collie made a crouching run toward us and gave a half-hearted bark before trying to shepherd us into the impressively large farmyard that had several outbuildings forming two open squares on either side of the main dwelling.

George said, 'Ye gan roond te the front door and ask for the eggs and Aa'll hev a look roond the back.'

I did as he directed and rattled the doorknocker as hard as I could and stood back. After a few seconds, the door opened and a smiling, ruddy-faced woman, wearing a very large navy blue sweater and corduroy trousers tucked into Wellingtons, confronted me.

'And what can A do for you, eh?' she said bending down to look me in the eyes.

Holding up the money Dad had given me, I blurted, 'Can Aa hev twenty eggs please missus?

'Whey I hevn't got the eggs in out the barns yet lad but Aa'll see what Aa've got in the kitchen.'

She disappeared into the house while the Collie crouched a few feet away, glaring at me, presumably waiting to herd me into a pen. The woman returned a few minutes later clutching eggs that she counted into my open carrier bag.

'There's nine there lad, that's all I've got at the moment.' Crestfallen, I imagined that I was unlikely to get an egg and would most definitely get a harsh mouthful from my mother for failing to carry out a simple task.

The woman took sixpence and said that she would have some more in 30 minutes or so if I wanted to come back. That lifted my spirits and as I walked back toward the campsite, I thought, I certainly wouldn't mind having to walk back to buy more eggs.

George, who had his jumper rolled up at the front, cradling the bulging contents in his arms, came up behind me as I went through the big five bar gate that closed off the track to the field.

'Hoo many eggs did ye get Young'un?' he asked as I swung the gate closed.

'The woman only had nine but we can gan back and get some more later.'

'Hoo much did ye spend?' he asked grinning,

'Just sixpence,' I replied, wondering what he had in his arms.

'Reet,' he said, 'here take these off me one at a time and coont them inte yor bag.' George opened his arms slightly to reveal a nest of eggs.

'Where did ye get them from?' I asked as I started to count the eggs into the carrier bag

'I was just looking roond the barns and I foond them just lying in these hay racks waiting te be picked up man; hoo many is tha?'

'There's fowerteen,' I said grinning,

'Right with the nine ye got, that meks twenty-three, noo give me a shilling and ye keep a shilling and tell me Dad ye gave the farmer all the money,' he said as he took the bag of eggs from me.

'But we'll get inte trouble for stealing the eggs and money,' I said feeling very worried.

George just grinned back and said 'Nur we winnit, nee bugger'll knaa if ye divvint tell them.

Later, as we all sat at the edge of the lake eating egg and bacon butties, washed down with strong, hot tea while enjoying the glorious view before us, Dad said to Mam, 'Twenty three eggs for two 'nd six is good, we should buy some more before we leave.'

I nearly choked on my tea at the thought of Dad asking for another twenty-three eggs for two and sixpence and the repercussions that would ensue!

George looked calmly at me, winked, and said, 'We got her last ones Dad, she winnit hev anymore till the morn.'

'Aa whey niver mind, they were champion,' Dad replied and walked back up to the car.

It was just after midday before Dad began organising the packing of our kit and preparations for leaving. Once the cars were loaded, the men began to reverse them down the field before driving forward toward the gate, all going well until Mr Page reversed! The other three cars were loaded and lined up facing the gate as Marti Page rolled up a blanket and stuffed into the boot of the car closing the lid with a thump, before turning the raised handle to lock it.

Percy had had the bonnet up to check his oil and water and was just closing it as my Dad shouted over, 'Haway man Percy get a bloody move on.'

Marti began to panic and shouted, 'Eeeeeeeh come on Percy or they'll leave us again.'

Climbing into his car muttering to himself, Percy started the engine and grimaced when he crunched the gear into reverse just as Marti ran to the back waving her hand madly shouting 'Eeeeeeeh, come on, come on,' as if Percy was paying attention to her instructions – which he obviously was not.

Annoyed at Dad shouting at him, and by Marti's wild gesturing, Percy released the handbrake and let out the clutch turning the steering wheel sharply to the left.

The car lurched backwards, narrowly missing Marti who was forced to jumped aside screaming, 'Eeeeeeh.'

Percy frantically straightened the steering wheel as he lifted his foot off the accelerator and slammed it down onto the brake pedal. He then sat with a bemused look on his face as the front wheels locked and the car slid gracefully backwards down the hill to toward the small ledge that dropped onto the tiny shingle beach at the lake's edge.

All eyes were on the car as it slid backward with a helpless Percy inside and a panicking Marti running madly after it. The car slowed but not enough, the

167

rear wheels dropped over the ledge with a thud, stopping the car instantly. Marti's mad dash did not stop as quickly, with hands flailing madly, the speed of her run and the downhill slope propelled her past the car and straight into the cold waters of the lake where the water conspired to trip her and she flew head first into the lake.

The shock of the cold water had Marti leaping around like a cat on a hot tin roof as she let out an almighty 'Eeeeeeeeeeeeeeeeeeeh!'

The rest of us were in hysterics as she sloshed her way out of the water to the car and pulled open the door to confront a startled looking Percy. Marti was trying unsuccessfully to compose herself in order to berate Percy but could only manage even more 'Eeeeeeehs'.

We kids ran over with young Percy to watch the fun close up but it was too much for him, he was clearly shocked at the sight of their ditched car and his sodden mother shaking his bewildered Dad while screaming 'Eeeeeeeee' at the top of her voice.

Wearing his sarcastic smile, Dad was the first adult to arrive and looked at the two of them before mimicking Oliver Hardy; 'That's another fine mess you've got us into Stanley.'

Recognising the Oliver Hardy line, we began laughing at the poor Pages even more until my Dad shouted, 'Reet shut up ye bloody lot and let's get this bugger oot of the weter.'

Mam took Marti by the arm and led her off to where the other cars were, presumably to dry her off, while Dad organised the rest of us to push the car up the hill.

'Right Percy,' he shouted once he had the men and lads arranged around the car. 'Put her in second gear and divvint ower rev the bloody thing and wait until Aa say noo.'

Dad went to the rear of the car and shouted, 'Reet every bugger push – Noo Percy, Noo.'

We were all pushing like mad, as Percy let out the clutch sharply, causing the car to jerk violently and stall.

Dad shouted, 'Haad on everybody,' and we stopped pushing as he walked up to the driver's door and looked in at Percy and said through clenched teeth, 'Tek – the – fucking - handbrake – off - you sackless sod ye.'

With the handbrake off, four men and five lads heaving and Percy using the accelerator and clutch properly, the car juddered and slid but slowly began to climb over the little ledge and up the slope. Dad and Uncle Nick who were at the rear corners were sprayed neatly with mud from the spinning rear wheels and both let out a stream of obscenities; Dad's I had heard before but Nicks were in his native Yugoslav Tongue and although we did not understand the words we knew they were far from polite.

Geordie Little faired much worse; he was in the middle at the back and his left hand had been holding the boot handle as he pushed; when the car's tyres fi-

168

nally gripped and Percy floored the accelerator wanting to make sure he climbed the bank and make the track without further problems. The only problem was that as Geordie Little tried to pull his left hand away, his leather watchstrap caught on the boot handle!

Accelerating the car up the hill, Percy was unaware that he was dragging Geordie along behind and that he was screaming blue murder. George and I raced after it shouting at Percy to stop but he did not, in fact oblivious to Mr Little's plight, he did not stop until he had driven the 100 or so yards to the other cars where he climbed out with a satisfied smile on his face.

Mrs Little, who had watched the whole thing, first with amusement then with horror as she saw her beloved husband dragged off behind the speeding car, ran screaming toward the rear of Percy's car expecting to find her husband dying in a ragged bloody heap. Marti who had been trying to dry herself with a large old towel handed to her by my Mam, also started to scream at the sight of her man apparently dragging Geordie Little to his certain death!

As his wife reached the back of the car, a shoeless Geordie stood up; his trousers torn and muddy and were down around his knees. Visibly shaken but with menace in his eyes, he ignored his wife's fussing and started towards Percy but immediately tripped over his trousers. This only added to his rage, jumping to his feet, he pulled his trousers up and ran at Percy who still had no idea that he had nearly dragged his friend to his death.

Geordie shouted, 'Ye frigging imbecile,' and took an almighty swing at Percy but luckily missed by a mile as Percy jumped back in fright. The two men began to wrestle madly, Geordie bent on ripping Percy's head off, while Percy just wanted to subdue the lunatic who had attacked him for no discernible reason.

Marti and Mrs Little were screaming hysterically, young Percy was wailing madly, the rest of us lads were laughing and cheering madly while Viv and Jennifer Lawson were screaming like banshees, all adding to the terrible commotion.

Chuckling to themselves, Dad and Uncle Nick walked quietly up before stopping to watch for a couple of seconds before dragging the two combatants apart.

Dad said, 'Reet come on Rocky Marciano and Joe Louis, that's enough of that.'

A while later, just about everyone was in his or her cars ready to go when Uncle Nick walked up to Mam's window and said, 'Here Etty, somevinck for dinner tonight,' and thrust a dead chicken through the window.

Mam grabbed the chicken without a word and stuffed it down by her feet - Now I knew whom I had seen walking toward the farm last night!

I decided to travel back with Alan Lawson in their car in an effort to distance myself from Jennifer who had jumped into the back of our car with Viv but at the last moment, Jennifer jumped out of our car, ran across, and climbed in next to me! I spent the drive home half-enjoying myself and half-worried at having her

169

lean on me –I hoped it would not lead to babies!
The roast chicken dinner that night was delicious!

16

Apples and Dungeons

The following Saturday morning, having recently acquired an old touring bike frame, I was in the garage trying to adjust the dodgy brakes on the homemade bike I had just finished building. I had managed to tighten the front brakes that now appeared to be working savagely but was struggling to get the rear brakes to tighten when the big rear garage doors swung open and Jack Moody who was straddling his bike outside shouted, 'Haway Syd we're gannin doon to the water-fall at Bothal te gan swimming.'

Cousin Alec and Frank were there on their bikes making revving up sounds as though they had 650cc Triumph motorbikes, not cobbled together pushbikes. I dropped the tools, pushed my bike out the garage, closing the big door behind me before mounting and pedalling furiously to catch them up as they raced off down the Fourth Row.

It was another glorious summer's day as we pedalled past the old Black-smiths at Cooper's Corner; all singing loudly and off key,

'Well I saw my Baby walkin',
With another man today,
Well I saw my Baby walkin',
With another man today.
When I asked "what's the matter?"
This is what I heard her say.'

Alec sang the first line of the chorus and the rest of us shouted the second:

'See you later you later Alligator,'
'AFTER WHILE CROCODILE,'
'See you later Alligator,'
'AFTER WHILE CROCODILE.'

Then all of us again;

'Can't you see you're in my way now?'
'Don't you know you cramp my style?'

Murdering Bill Haley's song with gusto, we pedalled on down the quiet country road toward Bothal.

Surrounded by woods thick with bluebells in spring, Bothal is a charming,

171

tiny village set by the river Wansbeck. The village consisted of an ancient, yellow sandstone church, a few detached and semi-detached sandstone houses, and its gem, the castle; an occupied, boys own castle built of the same yellow sandstone as the church.

Just before Bothal, the road from Ashington drops steeply down the winding and infamous 'Bothal Bank'. A sharp left-hander leads to a right-hand hairpin bend, followed by a second 90-degree left-hander where the road runs into Bothal. As we approached the steep bank we were roaring through Bill Haley's first hit,

'One two three o clock four o clock rock,
Five six seven o clock eight o clock rock,
Nine ten eleven o clock twelve o clock rock,
We're gonna rock around the clock tonight.'

Our young and enthusiastic voices echoed around the woods as we swooped around the first corner and raced steeply downhill,

'We'll have some fun
When the clock strikes one,
We're gonna rock around the clock tonight
We're gonna rock rock rock...'

Our voices tailed off as we concentrated on the steep hill, already travelling far too fast for safety but the exhilaration of the moment and the exuberance of youth cast aside our concerns as we hurtled toward the hairpin. I could hear rear brakes screeching in protest as they gripped the madly spinning hubs slowing the bikes before the bend. I squeezed mine – nothing; I had not finished tightening them in the garage and now they were useless.

My left hand began to tighten the front brake but I was worried that if I squeezed too hard I would catapult over the top!

I was already ahead of the others and I heard Jack shouting, 'Slow doon ye mad bugger,' as I squeezed and released the brake repeatedly causing the bike to wobble but I held it and leaning madly over like a TT racer I flew round the hairpin.

As I straightened up, I continued to feather the front brake as a shape sped past me; it was Frank, he was flying and he shouted, 'CHICKEN,' as he raced past. Releasing my front brake, I flew after him followed by the other two and we whooped and shouted, our voices echoing through the trees.

After applying a little rear brake, Frank just managed to get round the last bend but immediately released it for the straight into the village. About twenty yards ahead, there was a 'Sleeping-Policeman' type hump in the road, where it had been dug up for the burial of some utility or the other. Frank hit this at speed with an almighty thump!

172

His bike bounced into the air with Frank hanging onto it, when to our shock and horror his buckled front wheel, fell away from its forks! The bike came down hard, the front forks digging into the tarmac, catapulting Frank over the handle bars and hurling him onto the road a few yards ahead where he slid for several more yards, stripping skin from his hands, forearms, knees and worse the side of his face.

Pandemonium broke out behind him as we all desperately braked and swerved to avoid the same fate with varying degrees of success. Alec slammed on his front brake and slid off his seat onto the crossbar crushing his testicles, causing him to let out a long, low moan before falling onto his side with his bike still between his legs and lay writhing on the ground clutching his groin, moaning pitifully.

Jack had jammed on his rear brake and skidded to a perfectly controlled halt just before the hump; I had used my front brake a little but not enough and hit the hump hard but luckily not as hard as Frank. My bike bounced over and I landed safely, travelling another twenty or so yards before I slowed sufficiently to turn and race back to Frank.

He looked terrible, bloody rashes on most of the exposed skin on his body caused him to roll around in agony as Jack desperately tried to hold him down. Lying on the other side of the road clutching his battered manhood, Alec had too much pain of his own to worry about anyone else and continued to moan.

A car that had been coming the other way stopped alongside us and the concerned driver, who had seen the accident, leapt out and rushed across to take charge of the battered Frank.

Scooping him up, he placed him on the back seat of his car yelling at us, 'Gan and tell his parents that am taking him to Ashington Hospital,' and left us to stand and watch in bewilderment as he sped off.

Snapping out of our shock, Jack and I ran across to Alec who was now sitting up on the kerb holding his groin, rocking back and forward muttering, 'Frigging hell, frigging hell'

Looking at him and smiling, Jack said unsympathetically, 'Yor voice'll be even higher noo Alec lad.'

Alec stuck two fingers up at him and spat, 'Get stuffed.'

Feeling sorry for Alec, I nevertheless had to force myself not to laugh.

It was then that I heard a gentle voice from behind say, 'Come ower here lads, I've got the kettle on for a nice cup of sugary tea for ye, it's just what ye'll want for yor shock.'

We turned to see a tiny, grey-haired woman walking back toward one of the houses. I said to Jack, 'Ye tek Alec ower and Aa'll get Frank's bike.'

Jack walked after me and said, 'I'll get the wheel and ye get the frame, that fat bugger can help hessell.'

The woman who was smaller than I was, said, 'Wait in the garden boys,' before disappearing back into her house. We did as she told us and after leaning

173

our bikes on the outside of the garden wall, sat on a bench in the garden. Alec joined us, sitting down between Jack and me, still cradled his battered testicles and rocking back and forwards.

Jack asked Alec, 'Are ye still gannin swimming then?'

'Nur Am not, Am gannin hyem - after Aa've had some Tea,' he replied dejectedly.

'Good, then you can call in at Franks and tell his Mam what's happened,' then to me he said, 'Aa divvint fancy swimming noo Syd, shall we gan doon to the stepping stones and swing bridge for a bit?'

Before I could reply, the tiny woman reappeared with a tray, full with cups, saucers, teapot, and a small plate of biscuits.

'Here ye are then Bonny Lads,' she said as she placed the tray on the bench before standing smiling at us.

I asked, 'Can we leave wor friend's bike here Missus? The front wheels buckled and we cannit push it hyem so we'll have te get his faather to come and pick it up.'

She nodded, stroked my cheek, and replied, 'Aye pet, of course ye can.'

Looking at Alec who was still pale and shaken, she said, 'Where hev ye hort yorsell pet? Do ye want me to look at it for ye?'

Alec was mortified and gingerly stood up saying, 'Nur, it's aalreet, I'm gannin hyem noo,' and blushing madly he carefully mounted his bike and pedalled off toward home.

'Divvint forget to tell Frank's mother,' I shouted after him to which he waved in response.

Jack and I thanked the woman for her tea and biscuits and pedalled off to the track that led down through the woods, past the castle and onto the narrow suspension footbridge over the river. Standing in the middle, we jumped madly up and down and managed to create quite a bounce until; worried that the bridge would break up, I ran back to the bank, bouncing madly with the bridge as I did so.

Following me, Jack asked, 'Did ye see the apples hanging ower the castle waall when we went by?'

'Aye, tha were some big buggers worn't tha.'

'Yep, shall we gan and get some?'

Nodding, I answered, 'Haway then.'

We rode back to the wall surrounding the castle's orchard and although part of the castle it was only about six or seven foot high. Branches, heavily laden with bright green fruit hung over the wall where we propped our bikes and climbed precariously onto the frames. Reaching up, we attempted without success to grab the apples so we climbed on top of the wall, and from there scrambled into the branches of the tree where we sat like monkeys eating an apple each.

The sound of barking dogs grabbed our attention and we watched as two large Alsatians raced through the orchard from the direction of the main wall and castle. The dogs skidded to a halt below us and began barking even louder, prompting Jack to throw his half-eaten apple at the dogs and bark back at them. Knowing we could easily climb back onto the wall and drop to safety, the dogs did not intimidate us so we both barked back at the dogs that made them bark even more wildly.

What we had not seen were the two men coming up behind and when we did it was too late! The men reminded me of Abbot and Costello, one was skinny and serious faced and the other fat with a chubby, smiling face.

Skinny shouted, 'Right! Ye two little buggers get doon here noo and divvint think aboot getting back ower tha waall or we'll let the dogs oot after ye's.'

I looked at the two barking dogs and said, 'We're not coming doon we them two dogs there man, they'll eat us!'

Fatty fastened leashes to the dogs and said, 'If they divvint, Aa will, noo git doon here.'

We climbed down onto the lowest branches and swung down onto the ground as Fatty pulled hard on the leashes of the two dogs that were still barking madly, straining at their leashes to reach us.

Skinny grabbed us both by the collars and said, 'Haway then, it's the bloody dungeons for ye two!'

I was horrified, not only were we in danger of being a meal for a fat man and his two mad dogs, I imagined we were going to be locked up in some cold, dark dungeon where we would probably be suspended in chains by our ankles while rats nibbled at our heads!

My heart was racing as they led us through a massive oak door in the side of the castle and down stone steps into a long, flagstone-floored corridor. Despite the corridor having electric lights and not burning torches, this definitely looked like dungeons to me.

Skinny pushed us through a wooden door into a dark room lit only by a recessed window high up on the opposite wall and we stood in the centre of the musty smelling room, trying to see where the chains were when skinny switched on the light.

'Ye'll stay here till I get the Polis,' he growled and walked out locking the door behind him.

'Frigging hell Syd, Aa thought they were gannin to torture us,' Jack said half laughing.

'So did Aa man, I was sure them dogs were gannin to hev us,' I answered laughing nervously.

We looked around the room; it was about twelve foot by twenty with white washed walls and a concrete floor and although it had a few spiders' webs, it was not damp!

Walking over to a pile of empty beer crates stacked in one corner, we sat down on one to consider our predicament.

'That's me knackered if they fetch the Police,' Jack said, 'them buggers hev got in for me like.'

175

'Me Dad'll kill me if the Police tek us to the Police Station,' I added forlornly.

'Then we'll just hev to fugging escape,' Jack said, his cheeky permanent smile growing even larger. Looking up at the window, we saw that it was metalled framed with two fixed, multi-paned panels at each end with a small double-paned, opening panel in the centre; it had no bars and it did not appear to be locked!

Without a word we quickly stacked several crates on top of each other and stood back to look; the pile reached three-quarters up the wall to about three-foot below the window. The window was recessed by about two-feet with sloping walls leading to the inside wall and we could see that the window was recessed considerably more on the outside creating a small shelter of about two-foot high by two-foot deep and four-foot wide.

Jack said, 'Ye are the smaallest so ye gan forst and I'll push ye through and ye can help pull me through.'

'Right,' I said and climbed up onto the teetering boxes, reached forward and after opening the window and wiping away the cobwebs, I grasped the frame and pulled myself up into the gap. Half way through I found I had nothing for my feet to push against and nothing at the other side to grip.

I shouted back, 'Push me feet man Jack, Aa canna get through.'

Feeling his hands grab my feet, I began to push – until I heard the dogs! I could hear them barking and the barking was getting closer very quickly!

'Pull me back, pull me back,' I shouted, but Jack was still pushing, unaware of what was happening outside.

'This is it, Am gannin te be eaten by two bloody big Alsatians!' I thought.

I hated Alsatians after having seen Fly attacked by the one in the Fourth Row and in my vulnerable position I was sure they would rip me apart as the barking grew louder until the first dog raced into sight and tried to stop to get at me but momentum carried it on, its paws scrabbling for grip. The second dog barrelled into it and they both rolled over giving me enough time to get back in - but I couldn't, not with Jack pushing hard at the other side.

Wrapping my arms and hands around my face, I waited for the attack, and it came quickly – the first dog scrambled into the recess where it began licking my arms, hands, and head, shoving its wet nose into my face as it wagged its tail madly. The second dog joined in; I was in no danger of them ripping me apart, instead, I was now in great danger of them licking me to death!

The pushing on my feet stop and then I felt hands grasp my ankles to pull me back through so I shouted, 'Its alreet man, tha friendly, keep on pushing,' but the grip tightened and despite my struggles and protestations I was dragged back into the cellar leaving the two dogs barking happily at the window.

Jack was standing in the corner laughing madly while Fatty held onto him.

Skinny, who had pulled me back through the window said, 'Yor bloody lucky that Stan's got them dogs as soft as he is or ye would have been savaged.' Too traumatised to reply, I stood shaking, trying to wipe dog slaver from my head

176

and arms.

Skinny took me by the arm and said, 'Haway yor gannin noo,' and led Jack and me out of the cellar as Fatty followed behind.

'Are the Police here?' Jack asked as they frog-marched us back through the orchard toward a door in the wall.

Skinny waited for a moment before replying, 'There'll be nee polis teday but if ye bloody little wasters come here again there will be.'

Jack smiled and just as the men thrust us through the door, said, 'Ta mister, can we hev some apples te tek with us?'

The man took a half-hearted swipe at Jack and said, 'The only thing ye'll get is my bloody boot up yor arse, noo bugger off before Aa dee call the Polis.'

Cycling back home in high spirits, we managed another chorus of, 'See you later Alligator,' followed by a quick murdering of Guy Mitchell's, 'Singing the Blues,' before we arrived back at the Fifth Row where we called in at Frank's to find out how he was.

'Hello Mrs Thompson, I said when she opened the door to our knock, 'how's Frank?'

She looked at me puzzled and answered, 'Champion as far as Aa knaa but I thought he was with ye lads, swimming.'

Her expression quickly changed to anxiety as she realised that something must have happened to Frank and she gasped, 'Eeee divvint tell me he's had an accident swimming!'

'Nur he hasn't had an accident swimming....'

'Eeee, thank God for that, for a moment Aa thowt ye were gannin te tell me he was hurt or something.'

I gulped and said, 'I was Missus Thompson, he's had an accident on his bike and a man took him to hospital in his car.'

'Hospital!' she yelled before throwing a barrage of questions that Jack and I did our best to answer; when we could get a word in that is.

She finally calmed herself enough to say, 'Right Am off to the hospital, will one of ye lads gan and tell his Dad at the Winder what's happened?'

Jack nodded and said, 'Aa will, I live in the Sixth Row not far from the Winder but did Alec Lowry not come and tell ye, Missus, he said he was.'

She looked past us, her mind racing and said, 'No Pet Aa've seen nebody all day.'

Jack and I pedalled off, Jack to the Winder, (Frank's dad worked one of the huge winches that wound the cable pulling the cages up and down the mine shafts) and I to see Alec, to find out why he had not told Mrs Thompson about the accident.

Walking into Alec's house in the Third Row, I found him sitting at the kitchen table greedily eating homemade scones and saw his enormous mother, just visible, lying on the double bed in the sitting room, a cup of tea in one podgy hand and a woodbine in the other. The bed had become a permanent fixture in the sit-

177

ting room, now that she was too fat to get up and down the narrow stairs!

Alec's tiny Dad was peeling potatoes in the pantry, an apron tied around his waist to keep his waistcoat clean; it was the first time I had seen him without a jacket and I noticed that his shirt was a brilliant white and his tie knotted as immaculately as ever. The contrast between Mr and Mrs was amazing.

Looking at Alec with contempt, I spat, 'Why didn't ye gan and tell Frank's Mam aboot the accident?'

Alec looked at me sheepishly and replied through a mouthful of scone, 'Aa couldn't remember what number he lived at, and I was hungry.'

'Ye could hev asked somebody man,' I snarled, 'his Mam's just foond out.'

Alec shoved another lump of scone into his mouth and said defiantly, 'I didn't want te cos me knackers were hurting so Aa came hyem.'

Becoming angrier by the second, I said, 'Ye nowt but a useless fat git.'

Alec jumped up and shouted, 'Aa'll burst ye, ye skinny twat ye.'

'Nee swearing lads and if you are going to fight, take it outside please,' Uncle Joe said in his quiet manner.

'Right,' I said, anger making me brave but foolhardy; although Alec was a year younger than I was, he was as taller and a lot heavier, 'ootside noo,' I shouted.

Alec pushed his chair back and shouted, 'Aa'll bloody flatten ye,' and followed me out the door.

I stormed across back lane, through a hole in the wall between the coal houses and onto the rough track behind the Fourth Row. As I turned to face Alec, he lunged at me but seeing it coming I sidestepped him and grabbed him around the neck and twisted while locking my hands together. Using my weight around his neck, I forced him onto the ground and stretched my body and legs as far from him as I could in order to stop his flailing hands from hitting me.

We lay there for ages, my headlock squeezed as hard as I could while Alec wriggled like a huge slug as he tried to escape. Eventually, exhausted and tearful, he gave up wriggling, and just lay there.

With barely enough strength left to maintain my grip, I said, 'De ye give up?'

'Aye,' he gasped through the chokehold, 'Aa give up ye pig ye.' I released my grip and stood up brushing dirt off my jeans as Alec got onto his knees and hauled himself to his feet wiping snot and tears from his face.

Uncle Joe shouted from across the lane, 'Now that you've finished that, come and have a cup of tea.'

It was the last time Alec and I argued, we had established a pecking order and as a result, we became a lot closer. Later in life, when he became a teenager he was to loose most of his fat and become very tough!

Sporting some superb tarmac rashes, Frank came out of hospital the next day! His suffering was not in vain - his Dad bought him a new bike.

17

Butch Settles a Score

Our main holiday that year was a fortnight at Seahouses; a small fishing village on the Northumbrian coast that was in imminent danger of losing its old-world charm to penny arcades and fish and chip shops. It was still a thriving fishing port as well as an up and coming tourist destination in 1957 as boat-trips out to the wild Farne Islands to view the birds and seals were fast becoming a major attraction.

Dad hired a large static caravan on a site overlooking the sea and harbour that was just a quick stroll from the village. Only Dennis, Vivian and I holidayed with Mam and Dad; George had decided he would rather spend the time at home knocking around with his pals than holiday with us.

Earlier in the year, George had rather stupidly passed his 13+ and had faced the wrath of Mam and Dad for having the temerity to go against their wishes. It had come as a bit of a shock to them especially as they had not realised he was so bright, hiding as he did, his intelligence behind his rough and ready mannerisms.

Mam had told him emphatically, that he would not be going to Grammar School; they did not want to spend beer and bingo money on education! However, it did not end there as George found himself selected as one of the two top boys in Ashington Secondary schools and offered a place at Cheshire Camp School. Initially, Dad had said no but when he found out all expenses were included, he jumped at the chance of getting rid of his ever more hostile son for 12 months.

Although very enjoyable, the holiday passed uneventfully and we returned home to spend the rest of the school holidays gallivanting around the fields and streets with our friends.

Eric, now seventeen, thought he looked like Tony Curtis but although he undoubtedly had good looks, he was still skinny and looked more like a young Frank Sinatra. In an effort to convert his skinny limbs into muscular powerhouses, he had written to Charles Atlas and asked him to send him his course on 'Dynamic Tension' but after two sessions on the kitchen floor that provided much amusement for everyone at home, he gave up.

Not being shy and just a tad in love with himself, he had his fair share of the local lasses and boasted regularly of his latest conquests, some of whom, even I at twelve years old, had thought not the most beautiful of creatures.

His latest venture though was Skiffle. Although rock and roll was busy taking over the world, Britain in its own inimitable way, gave the world, skiffle. The likes of Lonny Donegan took Country Music, added a little bit of rock and roll, and produced the skiffle sound.

Eric played guitar not very well, tall John Little the tea Chest base, Gordon

Carter the washboard, and little Jimmy sang lead. For a few weeks of the summer of '57,' every evening after work at the pits, the four of them gathered in our scullery and hammered out the new skiffilized country songs. With the back door open, my friends and I stood in the yard listening to them thumping away at their instruments while they tried to memorize the words to the songs.

Slowly but surely they improved, albeit not very much while they mastered the words to 'It takes a worried man to sing a worried song', and 'Rock Island Line'. They were far from brilliant but were not bad and grew confident enough for Eric to book them a turn in the 'West End Workingmen's Club'.

The 'West End Club' had a grand if faded marble frontage and was part of a terrace of shops and clubs in High Market next to the 'Rows' or 'Ra's' as we called them. Their performance took place on a lovely summer's evening and as word had gotten around the 'Ra's' that a live group was on in the 'West End', the place was full of fag smoking, beer drinking miners of all ages waiting to be entertained.

Standing outside the open door to the club with Jack, Frank, Alec, and Tom Payne, I could smell beer and tobacco smoke and hear the noise of animated chatter from within. Eric and the other three had nervously gone in earlier and cleared a space in the bar for them to set up, not that it took a lot of setting up; space for the Tea Chest base and a little more for the other three to stand in.

Eventually, we heard a raised voice among the chatter and the place fell silent for a second or two before a slightly timid Jimmy sang; 'It takes a worried man to sing a worried song,' and then with all four of them thrashing their instruments, they all sang the same line and were away into the song:

'It takes a worried man to sing a worried song,
I'm worried now but I won't be worried long...'

It sounded good from where we were and when the second chorus came we burst into song, Alec with his 'Choir Boy' voice, leading.

Carried away with the music and singing, we did not realise the noise we were making until one of the men in the club came to the door and said, 'Shut up or bugger off.' We shut up and listened to the singing! When they finished there was a short pause before the place erupted in cheers and applause; I was impressed.

They sang 'Rock Island Line', and received another cheer and shouts of, 'More, more.' The only problem was that they only knew those two songs, so they sang them again....and again! After the fourth time, enough was, enough and they went to the bar for their wages, a pint of Newcastle Exhibition each, which they downed while basking in short-lived admiration. It was the only time I recall them performing in public.

Jim left the army after completing three years that included the Suez war.

180

In Cyprus, waiting for posting back to the UK for discharge, he found himself billeted with a group of National-Service soldiers awaiting demob, most of whom were Jocks. One of them took it upon himself to murder one of the other lads in the hut which led to a long SIB investigation that prevented the discharge/demob of all the occupants of the billet including Jim. After three months of delays, Dad wrote to his MP demanding a resolution of the problem and discharge of his son; amazingly, Jim was home within a fortnight!

Once home, he initially, worked as a driller with a team of hard men including 'Killer Ramshaw,' drilling to find coal for opencast mining. This lasted a few months before he became a bus driver, and then bored with that, he went back down the pit where the pay was better.

It was while he was working as a driller that he started dating Mary Knight, a very pretty girl from the Sixth Row, much to the chagrin of a girl who lived a few doors down the lane who had had Jim in her sights for some years!

To Mam and Dad's annoyance, Eric, like Jim before him, decided that working 'doon the pit' and home life was not for him and joined the army going into the REME (Royal Electrical and Mechanical Engineers). Mam and Dad's annoyance were due to the loss of a wage coming into the house, not the loss of a son!

It was while Eric was doing his basic training that Dad did one of his Saturday morning tricks; disappearing in his old Vauxhall, returning with a large Austin A75 shooting brake/estate car and, a passenger!

A bunch of the lads including me were playing street cricket on the corner by the scout hut when Dad pulled up outside the house. Frank saw him first and shouted to me as I was for waiting delivery of what turned out to be a Yorker from Alec, 'How Syd! Look ye Dad's got another new car.'

I turned to look just as Alec completed his run up and threw the ball across the street at me; it hit me on the side of the head knocking me back against the wall where I stood rubbing the sore spot.

'Ye mad bugger ye, could ye not see that Aa wasn't looking man?' I shouted at him.

Alec laughed and shouted, 'Nur Aa was in full pelt man, good job it's a tennis baall and not a cricket baall, Aa would have had ye heed off!'

Propping the bat against the chalked stumps on the wall, I walked across to examine the car with the rest of the lads, admiring its curvaceous front and wood trimmed rear. As we approached, I walked round to the passenger door, peered in the window and was startled when a brown shape leapt up at me from the passenger seat.

I jumped back in shock as Frank ran off a couple of steps and Alec shouted, 'Look at the size of that bloody thing man!'

Dad, who had gone into the house, returned with Mam to show her his latest acquisition but Mam ignored the car to look at the brown monster on the front seat that was slavering all over the window and asked, 'What in God's name is

181

that?'

'That's Butch,' Dad replied, opening the door to let out a huge, brindle dog that looked like a Staffordshire bull terrier on steroids. It was a perfect example of a big-jawed, powerful Staffordshire but the beast was the size of an Alsatian. Tail wagging madly and pulling at the leash Dad was hanging on too, he introduced himself to us, using his very wet nose to push us around in greeting; he was brilliant!

Butch soon established himself in the family pecking order, Dad, Butch then the rest of us!

Dad's chair by the sitting room fire was the seat we all tried to get into when Dad was occupying it but Butch decided, as he was Second in Command, the chair was rightfully his when Dad was not using it. Once there it was impossible to get him out. Even tipping the chair forward only resulted in a lot of warning snarling as he slid onto the floor, but he still beat us back into the chair when we put it down. If we were foolish enough to sit in the chair before him, he would simply climb up and lie all over you until you gave up and moved.

He loved children, loved to play, and was a big softy – with humans. However, it was a different matter with dogs; they would be okay just as long as they were wise enough to stay off his patch!

A couple of days after Butch took up residence, Dad handed me a shilling and said, 'Gan te Billy Scott's and get a tin of Lassie for Butch and tek him we ye.'

Walking to the back door, I said, 'Haway Butch,' and the big Brindle trotted obediently after me.

Short, rotund, and reminding me of Mr. Pickwick, Billy Scott owned the Post Office and General Dealers in High Market, an old-fashioned shop with the Post Office on the left of the shop and the counter for the groceries etc., on the right.

With Butch trotting alongside, I walked through the cuts - the narrow tarmac path that ran between the Rows and gardens to High Market and the shop. Stopping at the Zebra Crossing I ordered butch, 'Sit,' which he did, then after checking left and right I ordered, 'Haway,' and he followed me over the crossing and into the shop.

'Can Aa hev a tin of Lassie please?' I asked Mr Scott, placing the shilling on the counter. He nodded and placed a tin on the counter, opened the till and gave me change. Taking the tin, I held it in front of Butch and he gently wrapped his massive jaws around it and followed me out the shop and back home. Opening the tin, I scooped the smelly contents into his bowl and watched as he devoured the food before giving the bowl a severe licking, his tail banging on the plywood kitchen units in the scullery. Satisfied he had left no trace of the food he trotted out of the back door.

Two days later, I went to Scott's for a loaf of bread and handed over a shilling to Mr Scott who squinted at me from behind the glasses perched on the end of his nose.

'Who is going te pay for the tins of Lassie your dog's had?'

Not understanding, I looked at the short round man with his chubby dour face and asked, 'What tins of Lassie Mr Scott?'

'The four tins that that bloody big dogs had - them tins of Lassie!'

'But Aa hevn't been for any tins of lassie for a couple of days Mr Scott, Butch has been heving wor left owers.'

'Listen,' he said in a mildly aggravated voice, 'when your dog walks in here, puts his paws on my counter and barks, I give him a tin of lassie and owt else he wants!'

He continued, 'He walks out of here, stops at the crossing, sits doon then gets straight up and crosses regardless of any traffic, the beast has nearly caused a couple of accidents man!'

I imagined Butch wandering off with the tins of Lassie and wondered what he did with them, I hadn't seen him with them, nor had I seen any empty tins of the foul stuff lying round in the house or back yard.

'Aa hevn't enough money te pay for the Lassie Mr Scott but Aa'll tell me Dad when Aa get hyem,' I said walking toward the door.

'Aye and mek sure ye dee,' he said after me.

When I told my dad he just laughed and said, 'If that soft-shite is stupid enough te give tins of food te a dog, it's his problem not mine.'

Dad then gave me the job of trying to ensure Butch did not intimidate Mr Scott anymore by showing him how soft Butch was. I took Butch back to the shop and got Mr Scott to order Butch to 'sit' and 'leave' while pointing at the door, Butch got the message, but Mr Scott did not get the money for the four tins of Lassie!

Walking back home through the cuts, Butch strolling nonchalantly behind, occasionally sniffing at the markings of other dogs. He was a few yards behind when I reached the Fourth Row and stopped to look for traffic. I heard a snarl to my right and my stomach went hollow as I realised without looking that the big black Alsatian was out, the same one that had so savaged Fly, the same one I had kicked between its back legs! I turned to see it trotting menacingly toward me, its head lowered, teeth barred and tail down and I knew it was out for blood, my blood!

My first thought was to run but I knew I stood no chance of escaping the dark beast and raised my arms to protect myself as the dog lunged toward me...

At the last moment, I glimpsed the massive shape of Butch flying through the air just before he hit the Alsatian full on, as it realised too late, that Butch was there. Butch knocked the black dog across the road ending up with it below him as it scrambled to get back on its feet and protect itself but it was to no avail, Butch clamped his huge jaws around the back of its neck and shook the terrified beast as though it were a rag doll.

Rooted to the spot at the shock of the near attack and my rescue, I stared as Butch straddled the Alsatian pinning it to the ground with his weight and grip. The black dog's screams of terror and pain jolted me out of my inactivity and I ran forward and shouted at Butch to let go, but Butch was not prepared to let go.

The Alsatians owner had come out and was now screaming as loud as her dog as she hopped around in circles fearful for her pet but too terrified of the big brindle to intervene.

Luckily, Dad had been working in his garage a few yards from the cut and hearing the commotion, he came running to see what was happening.

Swiftly taking stock, he shouted, 'Butch, Butch here lad!' That was all it took, Butch relaxed his jaws and freed the Alsatian that immediately bolted for its home, closely followed by its screaming owner.

Butch shook himself and walked across to Dad to look up at him with what I was sure was a look that said, 'There'll be no more bother from him then!'

To confirm this Dad patted Butch on the head and turning back toward the garage he said to me, 'Ye winnit be bothered by that frigging thing again lad, noo tek the dog hyem.'

At the end of the school holidays, George, resplendent in his new uniform, set off for Cheshire Camp School, Viv and I went back to Bothal School, while Dennis continued at Wansbeck. I had a reasonable year in school, enjoying history and geography as well as art but much to my regret, I did not put any effort into maths and English. My effort and concentration or lack of it showed in my results, I stayed in the middle of the class coming top in History and Geography both of which I found exciting but was only adequate in maths and terrible in English.

On the completion of ten weeks basic training at Blandford Forum, Eric passed out as a REME soldier. Fresh from his Pass-Out Parade, wearing his best khaki battle dress uniform, highly bulled parade boots, full webbing and carrying all his kit in a kit bag and suitcase, he caught the train home on a foul autumn day for a week's leave prior to travelling down to Taunton for 'Trade Training'. After several changes of trains and a long and tedious journey, he arrived at Pegswood's tiny station just after midnight.

Pegswood is about three miles from High Market using the road through Bothal but a new straight road, was under construction that when complete, would shave a mile or more off the distance. There were no taxis at the station and Dad would be at work, not that he could have rung to ask to be collected as we did not have a phone and he doubted that Dad would have come for him anyway. Burdened with all his kit, Eric decided to follow the new road and set off from the tiny station in a torrential downpour

With his bulging kit bag over one shoulder and carrying his heavy suitcase in hand, he staggered off, leaning into the wind and rain and onto the new road. The going was okay for a hundred yards or so where workers had lain hard-core, but after that, his nightmare began. The work on the new road had barely begun and consisted of a wide and very muddy track stretching for a straight two miles to

Ashington. Eric marched on and was soon soaked to the skin; his battle dress sodden and heavy; his best boots caked in mud and his kitbag and suitcase becoming heavier by the second!

By the time he reached the turn off for Longhirst, he was exhausted and close to collapse but he needed to get out of the foul weather and staggered along, determined to reach home. He thought that once he reached the old road he might get a lift for the last mile and concentrated on that.

Thirty minutes later, he reached the old road and was at last out of the mud and onto solid ground. The rain had not let up and continued its onslaught, his feet were soaking from muddy puddles and rain running down his legs but he was past caring and plodded on, hoping a car would come by but at one thirty in the morning there was little chance of that. He had to force himself not to abandon his kit, as the weight was now almost unmanageable.

Eventually, he reached home in a state of utter exhaustion and despair, a despair made worse when he found the back door locked. Not wanting to scare everyone in the middle of the night and knowing Mam rarely locked the big sash kitchen window, he walked across the yard and gently slid it open. With his last ounce of strength, he lifted his right foot up and over the low windowsill, through the curtain and onto the kitchen table that stood at the other side.

'Sod the mud,' he thought wearily and grasped the window frame to pull himself through the gap. That was when he heard a noise on the other side of the curtain! He froze as he tried to figure out what it was and then he felt something grab his ankle - very tightly. The heavy webbing gaiters he was wearing protected his ankle from whatever it was that had grabbed him but the grip was vice like.

Thinking that one of us had grabbed him, he shouted, 'For fucks sake, let gan man, Am too bloody knackered to frig aboot!'

Hearing no response, he tried to pull his leg back but a very deep and menacing growl stopped him! Butch had been asleep on Dad's chair in the sitting room when Eric had tried the back door. Instantly awake, Butch had trotted to the door and waited. Not your typical guard dog, he did not bark to scare off would-be intruders; he wanted them to come inside where he could get at them, he never barked.

Now totally exhausted, desperate and slightly panic stricken, Eric realised that some powerful beast had his ankle in a grip he could not break and it was slowly dragging him into the window. Far too tired to put up much of a struggle, he began to scream for help!

The first thing I knew of Ric's plight was hearing Mam who was standing over Jim in the other bed saying, 'Haway Jim some buggers trying te brek in and Aa think Butch has got him!' I followed Mam and Jim downstairs, as Pat and Viv, who had come out of their room to see what the commotion was, followed me. Dennis stayed snug in the warm bed I had just left, content that we would sort the problem out whatever it was.

Jim and Mam went into the kitchen and switched the light on as I waited in the sitting room with Pat and Viv, just in case there was a mad man on the loose as the noise coming through the kitchen window sounded as though a maniac was screaming! I heard Jim starting to laugh and rubbing my eyes, saw Butch lying on the kitchen table with a very muddy boot protruding from his mighty jaws.

'Bloody Hell!' I shouted, 'He's eating somebody.'

'Divvint be sackless,' Mam said. 'He's just biting some bugger.'

Pat shouted, 'A hope he bites their leg off.'

'A bet Eric hopes he doesn't,' said Jim laughing.

Viv said, 'Eric's not here man.'

'Aye he is, that's his leg,' said Jim.

'Ee my God,' Mam cried, 'Get doon Butch, get doon lad,' as she realised one of her brood was in danger of losing their leg.

Jim pulled at Butch's collar who reluctantly let go of his prize and jumped on the floor where he belatedly began barking and wagging his tail as if to say, 'Didn't I do well?'

This just added to the pandemonium as Eric, with his leg released stuck his head through the window; bedraggled, soaking, weary and squinting in the bright light, he said, 'This is a fucking charming welcome home!'

'Welcome home lad,' said Jim.

Pat said, 'Eee look at the state of him.'

Viv added unnecessarily, 'He's aall wet.'

I joined in by saying, 'How de ye like Butch Eric?'

'Like him!' he spluttered, 'the frigging thing tried to eat me!'

Mam said, 'Open the door and let him in Jim and Aa'll put the kettle on for a cup of tea.' She had already lit a woodbine and was coughing on the foul smoke as she sucked it into her lungs.

Autumn dragged into a cold grey winter that made Ashington and the Rows bleaker and more miserable than ever so I spent as much time as I could over the 'Rec' exploring the fields and marshes beyond the slag heaps. I also took on my first paper round for Wilkinson's the newsagents in High Market, delivering the evening papers around the 'Rows'.

Christmas approached and the tired old paper decorations brought out and festooned once more around the sitting room with the odd battered paper ball or bell pinned onto pictures. Mam placed the imitation Christmas tree on the small table in front of the sitting room window and made it festive with a few tinsel streamers and cheap Christmas lights. Tawdry though they were, the decorations still brought much-needed cheer.

Eric was at Taunton, George at Cheshire, Jim spent most of his time in the Sixth Row with Mary and Pat was working at the Granary on the edge of town while Betty was living near Eton.

George was the first to re-join the family for Christmas and I listened enthralled to his tales of cross-country runs, dormitories, three meals a day and Cheshire. Eric was next but we did not see much of him as he had his mates to see and lasses to chase.

A few days before Christmas George asked me in a conspiratorial tone, 'De ye knaa where the Christmas presents are?'

'Nur, Aa divvint and Aa haven't seen any brought in either, Aa divvint think they've got any yet!'

Mam normally hid Christmas presents in the wardrobe in her and Dad's bedroom but we had both looked there and had not found any. Having searched the house we realised that it was nearly Christmas and there were no presents; we knew Mam's motto was 'Never do today what you can put off until tomorrow,' but this was cutting it fine.

After another sneaky but fruitless search George said, 'How Young'un, gan 'nd ask me, Mam, what we're getting for Christmas so we knaa if she's got owt.'

I already felt miserable as I already knew the answer and replied, 'Aa've already asked her and all she said was mebe and mebe not.'

Heading for the back door, George muttered, 'Frigging charming,' and punched the goose hanging on the back of the door before he went out.

Dad had obtained the goose from the farm next to Coneygarth Drift where he worked, no doubt in exchange for a bag or two of coal, or some firewood from the timber yard where the pit props were stacked. Although dead, the goose was quite intimidating as it rolled against the door when you opened or closed it, Dennis would certainly not go past it without an escort.

Having wondered where our Christmas presents were, I was surprised when on Christmas Eve, Mam grabbed me and thrust an envelope into my hand before ordering, 'Here gan doon to Bob Orwell's with this note.' I realised then that we had no Christmas presents.

Pulling on my battered mac, I set off into a dark and rainy Christmas Eve for Bob Orwell's house. Mam had told me to go to his house, as he obviously would not be at his shop, and gave me his address 'doon the Horst,' some two miles away. I walked along hunched against the wind and rain, excited at the thought of getting some Christmas presents but also a little apprehensive at the thought of having to carry a load of toys all the way back.

It was about six o'clock when I opened the back gate to the large yard of the terraced house where Mr Orwell lived. Christmas tree lights shone brightly through the well-lit window, bathing the yard in a welcoming glow that lifted my spirits despite being cold, wet, tired and nervous. I was beginning to feel a wee bit excited as I knocked on the door and stood back expectantly.

Mr Orwell opened the door and stood peering at me in the gloom; he was chewing and the smell of food wafting from inside his house compelled me to look beyond him where I could see his wife and kids sitting at a table eating; whatever it was it smelled delicious.

187

'Well what do ye want Lad?' he asked gruffly, annoyed at having been disturbed in the middle of dinner on Christmas Eve.

I thrust the envelope at him and spluttered, 'Me Mam told me to give ye this Mister Orwell.'

I stood back and wondered if he would finish his dinner before we went to his shop for presents. Mr Orwell ripped open the envelope and quickly read the letter, shaking his head as he did so, his face darkening in anger.

'This doesn't look good,' I thought to myself as he finished the letter stuffing it back into the envelope.

Just as he was about to speak his wife shouted from the table, 'Who's that at the door Bob, yor dinner's getting cowld, what dee they want?'

'Nebody?' he shouted back, then to me he said in a low voice, 'There is nee way am gannin te my shop at this time of day especially te night and even if I felt like it Aa wouldn't, not for yor Mam, am still waiting for her to pay for the last lot she got from me.'

In a slightly kinder tone, he said, 'Am sorry lad but not tonight, noo get yorsell off hyem,' and he closed the door on me.

Devastated, I turned around and headed for the back gate, the cold and wet suddenly making its presence felt and I shivered as I opened the gate and stepped out into the wind to head for home. It was an awful trudge back, especially through the brightly lit main street with the shops full of Christmas displays that did nothing to brighten my gloom.

When I finally got home and opened the back door the bump of the goose was gone, he was in the oven filling the house with the delicious smell of roasting, at last, something to lift my spirits. Hanging my wet Mac up and kicking my shoes off I walked through the kitchen where Uncle Alec's pipe smoke was fighting a losing battle with the roasting goose and into the sitting room where the family were sitting in front of a roaring fire watching television.

Dennis looked up and asked, 'Where's the toys Syd?'

'Aa didn't get any, Mister Orwell said we couldn't hev any until the last ones were paid for!'

Mam sneered at me, 'Can ye not de nowt right ye simple sod ye?' as though it was my fault.

I snapped back, 'There wouldn't be a problem if ye paid yor debts.'

Viv piped in, 'Does that mean there're nee toys for tomorrow Mam?'

With a smug smile, Mam replied, 'Not for him but Aa've a dolly for ye,'

'Aa divvint want a dolly Mam, Aa want some roller skates man!'

Ignoring her, Mam blew out a lung full of woodbine smoke and sat back with her lips tightly closed, wearing her mean faced look.

Dad, who had listened to the exchange, spat at Mam, 'What did ye de with the money Aa gave ye for the kids Etty?'

'Aa've had te spend it on other things.'

'Aye bloody Bingo and fucking sherry,' Dad snarled back.

Mam ignored him and drew in another lungful of tobacco smoke.

Then to our surprise, Dad said, 'Aa've got ye a remote-controlled helicopter but ye'll all hev te share it.'

'Who'll hev te share it?' asked George from the piano stool behind the sofa.

'Ye, Syd and Dennis,' Dad answered and got up and walked into the kitchen to make himself a cup of tea as Vivian and Butch made a dive for his chair, Butch won!

Later, lying in bed with George and Dennis, we discussed the remote-controlled helicopter with excited anticipation!

I speculated aloud, 'Aa wonder if the controller can be fastened te yor wrist like that lad in the comics?

George added, 'Aa wonder hoo far it can gan up and hoo far it can fly from the remote?'

'We'll hev te tek it ower the Rec te stop it flying inte things,' I said.

With the assurance born of being Mam's favourite, Dennis said, 'Am heving furst gan we it.'

Not wishing to wake anyone else so that I could have first play with the helicopter, at about five o'clock in the morning, I slipped quietly out of bed and sneaked downstairs. The glow of the low fire and Christmas tree lights bathed the sitting room in a warm glow but did not provide enough light to see properly so I switched on the main light and stood blinking trying to see where the helicopter was.

As my eyes adjusted to the brightness, I walked around the settee and saw our present; it was on the floor in front of the television and my jaw dropped with disappointment.

We had been expecting a remote-controlled, free-flying helicopter that could soar into the sky, instead, it was a cheap tin model tethered by rods and wires to a single up and down lever, connected to a small electric motor powered by the battery of a miners' lamp that Dad had obtained from work. It was crude and cheap and did not look as though it would last very long in our household. I spent 30 minutes flying the helicopter around in its tethered circle, landing it on a book I had placed strategically but I soon became bored and abandoned it to go back to bed where climbing in, I woke George.

'Hev ye being playing with the helicopter?' he demanded.

'Aye, I've had it oot in the back lane and it really gans fast and high, it's really brilliant,' I lied.

George pulled on his jeans and hurried downstairs as I lay there smiling and waiting for the inevitable. I could hear shuffling sounds downstairs, and then a very loud 'Frigging Shite!' as George discovered our new toy. He was back in bed in five minutes.

He whispered, 'What a load of rubbish.'

'Whey man it's better than nowt, at least me Dad got us summick!' I said.

189

George sneered, 'He was probably giving it, or won it, Aa canna see him gannin te the shops te buy us owt.'

Even though I found the goose very rich, Christmas dinner was delicious, the pudding and custard especially tasty and the day itself went off relatively peacefully for us in that there were no major punch ups or rows, not that you could say the same for New Year's Eve!

Geordies celebrate New Year's Eve just as hard as Jocks celebrate Hogmanay in Scotland, the Carr household participating fully in these celebrations!

That year, the day started with Mam busy in the scullery, she had Viv and I peel a small sack of potatoes as she prepared barley, carrots, lentils, and other pulses while a tray full of fatty mutton waited for her attention. Dad lit the fire under the potboiler in the corner of the scullery and poured in a bucket of water to boil the potatoes and carrots, while Mam chopped, then fried the mutton before throwing it, along with the other vegetables, pulses and copious amounts of salt and pepper into the pot. Then placed the lid on the pot, she left it to simmer for several hours.

She then set about scrubbing all the tabletops and worktops in the scullery before placing a dozen or more enamel mugs next to the pot. Next, she laid tumblers for drinks and plates for stottie cakes on another bench before finally, arranging a dozen bottles of her lethal homemade wine and other concoctions next to the tumblers. Finally, Dad stacked several crates of stout and brown ale in the corner and the house was ready for the onslaught.

Eric dressed and preened himself before going downtown 'on the pull,' with big John Little. Pat had gone off to the Red Row dance where she hoped to meet a nicer class of lad, one of the RAF lads from Acklington. Mam and Dad went off to the 'Fell Em Doon' Social Club at seven leaving George, Viv, Dennis and I in the house with a pot full of Scotch broth, bottles of Mam's various homemade brews and Dad's crates of ale!

Cousin Alec and Allan, and Jennifer Little joined us to help celebrate, although I think Alec came primarily for the broth.

The smell of the broth in the scullery was making our mouths water but we had been told to wait until everyone was back before having any. Alec was having great difficulty obeying this order and spent most of the time in the scullery smelling it and looking into the huge Pot. Inevitably, George made the first move.

'Bugger this!' he said, grabbing an enamel mug and dipping into the thick steaming broth to fill it to the brim. He put the mug on the bench, picked up a huge Stottie loaf and ripping a chunk off, he dipped it in the broth and blew on it before swallowing it.

Viv who had come into watch said, 'Am gannin te tell me Mam on ye and ye'll get inte trouble.'

'Piss off ye sackless cow,' George hissed and gingerly sipped the hot broth

190

before saying, 'By that's bloody champion!'

Alec and I dived for mugs and quickly filled them. I handed mine to Dennis who was standing wide-eyed and waif-like, licking his lips in anticipation. I quickly filled another for myself, grabbed a piece of Stottie and began to tuck into the delicious broth.

Viv reached for a mug as the rest of us said in mocking unison, 'Am telling.'

Allan and Jennifer filled a mug each and we all stood in the scullery slurping broth and making 'mmmm' noises.

I looked into the pot and said, 'Ye canna tell that any's been taking oot tha's that much of it man.'

'Is there any pop, George?' Alec asked through a mouthful of broth as he looked at the crates of beer.

George shook his head and said, 'Na but am gannin te hev a beer,' and took a bottle of Brown Ale from a crate, opening it with the bottle opener that was tied by a long piece of string to the top crate.

As George took a swig from the bottle, Viv began to say something but George stopped her with, 'Aa knaa, yor gannin te tell me Mam, whey piss off and tell her,' and he took another long swig that made him shudder at the unfamiliar taste.

He looked at the rest of us and said, 'Whey gan on get one they'll all be too drunk te notice when they come hyem man.'

Knowing he was right, I grabbed a bottle and opened it before taking a sip of the strong brown liquid. It tasted disgusting but I was not going to show it and took another sip before saying, 'By that's great.'

Alec said, 'Aa divvint like beer man.'

George said, 'Whey hev some of me Mam's homemade pop, it's champion,' then reaching for one of the bottles of her grey looking concoctions, he pulled the cork out and poured some into a tumbler.

Alec took a large gulp, screwed his face up and said, 'Bloody hell that's strong ginger ale,' but still took another large gulp.

Dennis who had been quietly slurping away at his broth asked, 'Can Aa hev some pop, George?'

'Whey aye man,' George said and poured a full tumbler for him.

Dennis took a huge gulp of the brew, wiped his lips, smiled, and said, 'That's nice.'

George and I looked at each other in amazement, both of us knowing how potent Mam's brews could be.

By the time, Uncle Alex returned from the 'White House' Social Club, we had all finished our mugs of broth but Dennis had slurped two and Alec three! Alec and Dennis had also finished off the bottle of homemade booze and George was on his second Brown Ale. I was still slowly sipping my way through the first bottle.

Uncle Alex creakily followed his normal routine, pouring himself a cup of cold tea; he creakily took his seat in front of the kitchen fire. After slurping his tea and wiping his moustache, he took out his pipe and in between spits into the back of the fire; he soon produced a foul-smelling fog of tobacco smoke.

Dennis, who was very happy at this stage, watched Uncle Alex closely for a while then asked, 'Can Aa hev a smoke of yor pipe Uncle Alex?'

Uncle Alex looked at him, chortled and said, 'Aye if ye want bonny lad,' and handed the foul implement to Dennis who grabbed it and flopped down on the small stool next to the fire, pushing the pipe into his mouth and sucking hard! We had all stopped talking and sat or stood staring, waiting for Dennis to choke but he didn't; he just calmly blew out a huge cloud of foul tobacco smoke and then grinned like a skinny version of the Cheshire Cat.

We should not have been surprised as at seven, after nagging her for ages, he had taken a cigarette from my Mam and much to everyone's amusement and had smoked the strong woodbine as if it were no stronger than a sugar cigarette.

He took a couple more puffs of the pipe before trying to spit into the fire but failed and just dribbled down his chin.

Uncle Alex reached over a bony hand and said, 'That's enough of that noo, Aa'll hev it back,' and rising stiffly from his chair, he shuffled off through the sitting room to his little back bedroom.

Looking decidedly green, Dennis said, 'Am thirsty, is there any more pop?'

Alec came out of the sitting room and said, 'Aye am thirsty te, Aa'll open another bottle of that pop,' and went off into the scullery returning a couple of minutes later with two full tumblers of Mam's wine. Handing one to Dennis he sat down on the floor next to him where the two of them sat sipping their drinks and giggling like schoolgirls.

At eleven o'clock, with Buddy Holly's voice belting, 'Rave On,' out of the radiogram, Viv, Jennifer, Alec and Allan were bopping in the kitchen while George and I watched Dennis, who was looking even greener, had curled up on Uncle Alex's chair in front of the kitchen fire.

A few minutes later the back door burst open and Mam staggered in laughing drunkenly, closely followed by Marti and Mrs Little who were giggling madly. Dad, Geordie Little, and Percy Page followed, filling the house with drunken chatter and the smell of beer and cigarette smoke.

The men took bottles of beer from the crates in the scullery, opened them, and walked into the sitting room to stand in front of the fire to warm themselves. Meanwhile, Mam had joined in the dancing, doing a hideous version of a Highland fling mixed with Bop while Marti and Mrs Little clapped and cheered.

Alec, who had slowly turned the same putrid green as Dennis, started to wretch and bolted for the back door, reaching it just in time to throw up all over his diminutive Dad who was helping his massive wife across the back yard. Still hanging onto his wife, Uncle Joe grabbed Alec as he fell through the door and vomited again. This time with even greater force and straight over his Dad's shoulder, narrowly missing his sister Maggie who had been following her parents.

'Eee my God whatever's wrang we wor Alec?' his huge mother gasped.

Uncle Joe staggering beneath the combined weight of his wife and plump son said quietly, 'He's been drinking by the look of him.'

After pushing his wife over the step and into the scullery he said, 'Ye two gan on in and I'll tek Alec home and clean myself up, I'll join ye later,' and he staggered off, half carrying his drunk eleven-year-old son.

Aunty Jen staggered into the kitchen and plonked herself down on the small cottage settee filling it completely.

Mam shouted into the sitting room, 'George come and get your Jen a glass of wine,' an order he completely ignored as he was in the middle of telling a dirty joke to Percy and Geordie, a joke that George and I were trying to eavesdrop despite the din from the kitchen.

The party continued to grow as Jim and Mary came in and stood in the kitchen watching the antics of Mam and her two friends who had taken over the tiny dance floor and were being cheered on by the kids to the sound of, 'That'll be the Day'.

Mary had lived a relatively sheltered life and you could see by the expression on her face that she was amazed at the women's antics but luckily for Jim, she was not a prude and after a long, 'Eeeeee,' she started to laugh and joined in the clapping while Jim went for some drinks.

Just before midnight, Eric and John Little arrived with two lasses they had met at the Arcade dance and took them into the sitting room to start bopping behind the sofa. Most of the adults were drinking as if their lives depended upon it whilst smoking just as hard and quaffing the occasional mug of broth. The house was full of smoke and the smell of beer and broth so I opened the back door to allow in some fresh air.

That was when I saw Mr Little.

He was propped up against the table in the scullery with a bottle of beer in one hand, a half full mug of broth in the other and a chunk of stottie cake sticking out of his mouth that was already full of broth. He was desperately trying to chew and swallow before he choked but bits of stottie and broth were dribbling down his chin. Almost gagging, he had to spit the half-masticated food into his mug, most of it splashing onto the floor. He managed to take a deep breath before snorting up the snot that had gathered in his nose and then raised his left hand to wipe away the tears, forgetting that he was holding a bottle of beer, pouring the contents down his shirt. The cold beer made him gasp and jerk involuntarily throwing half the contents of the mug over himself.

I watched this in amazement and wondered if he was going to end up disappearing into a pile of broth, beer, and vomit!

Grabbing a towel from the rail, I handed it to him and said, 'Here Mr Little ye better dry yorsell off.'

193

He raised his head slowly and tried to focus on me while trying to stop his head from waving around. Gathering his breath, he replied, 'Ne bother lad am champion.' He staggered off into the kitchen with bits of broth, stottie, and beer running down his front, while still holding his now almost empty bottle of beer and the half-full mug of broth.

A couple of minutes before midnight, Mam grabbed a protesting John Little and pushed him toward the back door saying, 'C'mon Bonny Lad ye can be wor Forst Foot,' a job John did not want as he had just started to kiss the lass he had brought with him.

He was forced outside and the door locked behind him while Mam ran around shouting, 'Shush, be quiet it's almost time,' making more noise than everyone else as she did so.

Someone stopped the record on the gramophone and switched the radio so that we would hear the chimes of Big Ben. Everyone stopped what they were doing and waited quietly, listening for the chimes, everyone that is except Mr Little who was leaning against his wife singing, 'If you were the only girl in the world.' She tried unsuccessfully to shut him up as well as trying to keep his soiled shirt and grubby hand off her new blouse.

The colliery siren or 'Hooter' sounded in the distance as the chimes of Big Ben boomed from the radiogram and everyone cheered and began shaking hands and kissing. Eric took full advantage of the celebration and had a good snog with both the lasses that he had brought. Viv and Allan Lawson had a kiss and Jennifer came to me and said, 'Ye can kiss me on the cheek if ye want Syd.'

Blushing madly, I quickly kissed her on the cheek, said, 'Happy New Year', and walked briskly away.

A loud banging on the back door reminded Mam of her First Foot and she shouted, 'Quiet while Aa let the Forst Foot in,' and walked quickly to the door.

Turning the key to the locked door, she pulled it back, peered out and said, 'Nur not ye man Joe, yor too small,' and pushed my Uncle Joe back from the door.

Having changed his shirt and jacket, Uncle Joe had decided to come back with Alec and timed it to arrive in time to be First Foot. He met John Lawson standing in the yard and asked if he was going to be the First Foot. John had said yes but that he would rather not and was glad for Joe to do it.

With a lump of coal in his hand, Uncle Joe staggered back saying, 'But Am yor Forst Foot Etty!'

Looking at him with disdain, Mam said, 'Nur yor not man, Aa want good luck for the year, John get yorsell here with a lump of coal for the fire, noo.'

Walking forward and taking the coal sheepishly from Uncle Joe, John was shocked as Mam grabbed him and planted a huge wet kiss on his lips shouting, 'Happy New Year,' and dragged him into the house.

Wiping his mouth, John made his way through the crowd to deposit the lump of coal on the fire before turning round to shout, 'Happy New Year everybody,' to which there was huge cheer before the party continued.

194

Dennis had been asleep on Uncle Alec's chair throughout all this but woken by the cheering; he sat staring like a zombie into the fire while gagging slowly on the wine and broth he had quaffed earlier.

More and more people were arriving, picking up drinks and a mug of broth from the scullery before joining the party, the house becoming more chaotic by the second as Dad walked into the scullery for another beer and found Marti sipping a mug of broth.

'C'mon Marti give is a New Year's Kiss,' he said as he wrapped his left arm around her shoulder, pulling her toward him, grabbing her backside with his right hand.

With a mug of broth in one hand and a glass of wine in the other, Marti was caught off guard and could not stop him kissing her but Mam, who unbeknown to Dad, had followed him into the scullery could. She took the cigarette from her lips and stubbed it forcibly on the back of Dad's neck! Dad's head shot forward, his forehead smacking Marti on the nose causing her to yelp in pain and shock as she dropped her wine but she just managed to hold onto the broth.

Grabbing his burnt neck, Dad span around to see what had happened and was confronted by Mam, her lips set in that tight mean look of hers, she snarled, 'Eee Am sorry Pet, did Aa spoil yor fun?'

Dad stepped past her and spat, 'Ye blidy swine ye,' and bumped into Percy who had come to investigate his wife's cry of pain.

Marti was clutching her nose, a small dribble of blood showing through her fingers.

'What on Earth is going on?' Percy asked as he rushed to comfort his wife.

'Eeeeee George hit me with his heed,' Marti cried as Percy put his arm protectively around her.

'What did you want to do that for George?' Percy asked, his normally placid face clouding over in anger.

'It was a bloody accident man; ask this bugga here what happened,' and snatching another bottle of beer, Dad stormed off into the sitting room.

'What sort of accident Etty?' Percy asked angrily. Mam ignored him and walked back into the kitchen leaving Percy consoling his wife in the scullery.

Feeling very indignant and self-righteous, Mam pushed her way through to the fireplace where she saw her bairn curled up on the chair looking decidedly unwell. She snatched Dennis up, clutching him to her bosom, and plonked herself down in the chair and started to rock back and forth, ranting as she did so:

'Eee what's the matter with ye Bonny Bairn, niver mind yor Mother's here te look efter ye, not like that fucking baldy headed bastard of a whoremonger the bloody waster that he is, Aa'll swing for the bugger one of these days....' and on and on.

None of which comforted Dennis who was struggling to free himself from her clutch - the rocking motion was the last thing he needed. The inevitable happened; pulling back his head, he let forth a stream of vomit all over Mam! She leapt to her feet, keeping Dennis and the vomit clutched to her as she made her way to the scullery to clean the mess up. The throng moved swiftly out of her way as she stormed through, just as Dennis let forth another stream of vomit, all of which she caught on her chest while not relaxing her grip for a moment.

This made me feel queasy and I decided to go to bed and made my way through the sitting room and door to the bottom of the stairs. In the semi-dark, I stepped on someones feet and heard a curse! Pushing the door to the sitting room back to let some light in, I saw Eric's bare bum in between a pair of legs!

'Bugger off Man,' he shouted over his shoulder and I retreated, back into the party, shocked and confused at what I had seen.

George was sitting on the piano stool drinking a cup of tea while doing his Little Richard impersonation on the piano with his other hand, singing, 'Lucille.'

'How, George, listen,' I said trying to get his attention.

'What man?' he said as he stopped singing but continued to hit one piano key with his left hand.

'Gan through there and tell me what's gannin on will ye?' I said wanting confirmation of what I had seen.

George looked at me as if I was mad but walked over to the door, opened it, and stared in for a few seconds before shouting, 'Gan on Eric yor dorty bugger,' and then closing the door; he walked back to the stool laughing madly.

'Was he shagging her?' I asked not sure if that was the right terminology.

Still laughing, George said, 'Aye Young'un, a right good shagging,' and he started singing 'Lucille' again, banging the piano keys with both hands.

A little while later the door opened and Eric put his head round and said, 'How Syd, get me that red coat from the chair lad.'

Picking up the coat from the pile on the chair, I asked, 'This one?' before handing it to Eric.

'Aye,' he said grabbing it and retreating behind the door. I heard the bolt on the door into the garden sliding back, the door open and then close as Eric and his lass disappeared into the night.

Wandering back through the kitchen to the scullery for another mug of broth, I found Alec who, despite having thrown up earlier, was helping himself to more. The two of us were discussing what I had seen at the bottom of the stairs when Mam came in after just having put Dennis to bed.

Filling a tumbler with her wine she said to me, 'It's time ye were in bed, haad away upstairs and mek sure the bairns aalreet,' and then wobbled back into the party.

Finishing my broth, I walked through the drunken crowd and made my way upstairs, I was ready for bed and despite the noise down stairs; I fell asleep almost instantly as the party continued on until the early hours of the morning

In the spring of 1958, Jim proposed to Mary and the two of them planned

196

their wedding for the summer. I'd tried the scouts for a bit but found them less than inspiring and left them after a couple of months, besides I had seen some army cadets and wanted to join them but was told I had to be fourteen.

My Thirteenth birthday came and was celebrated in the normal Carr fashion; when I woke up, I quickly dressed and ran downstairs hoping there might be a card or present for me, though not really expecting anything. As expected, there was neither and I walked to school feeling miserable.

Sitting at my desk after assembly, I lifted the lid to take out my maths book and found a folded piece of paper that I had not put there. Opening the paper, I saw someone had drawn a large red heart and some flowers with a multi-coloured message that read, 'Happy Birthday Sydney,' followed by a row of kisses, but no name.

Sitting next to me, Tom asked, 'What's that?'

I looked at him and asked, 'Did ye put this in me desk?'

'I haven't put owt in yor desk man, what is it?'

I showed him the card and after reading it, he said, 'One of the lasses must hev written this man.'

'Aye,' I said, 'but which one?'

We both looked around the class at the lasses trying to see if any of them were looking or giving any hints or clues that it might be them. If they did, we did not spot any and I never found out who put it there, but it made my day and that night I lay in bed trying unsuccessfully to figure out which one of the lasses had written it.

The older fourteen and fifteen-year-old lads and lasses often gathered in one of the old air raid shelters in the back lane for games of 'Dare, Truth, Will or Force', 'Postman's Knock' and other innocent games that involved kissing. Often invited to participate, I was the recipient of many kisses from the older lasses who preferred to kiss me rather than show they were interested in one of the older lads. I obviously did not mind them using me in this way, unaware of the politics of courtship; I enjoyed the kissing for what it was.

The summer holidays marked George's return from Camp School and his return to the attic bedroom that Dennis and I shared with Jim. George had excelled at accountancy at Cheshire and had been given a letter to hand to Mam and Dad with details of a course he should attend in order to enable him to pursue a career in accounting. The day after he arrived home, he dug the letter out of his small suitcase and rushed downstairs with it. It was a Sunday morning and Mam was at the kitchen table smoking and drinking a cup of tea while she read the Sunday Sun. Dad was sitting in front of the fire reading the News of the World while I was sitting on the cottage sofa in the kitchen reading 'The Broons' when George brought the letter in.

George handed the letter to Mam and said excitedly, 'Here Mam, read this

197

will ye, the Heed at school said Aa should dee this course and become a clerical accootant, he gave me extra lessons becos Aa was so good at it and he said Aa could have a good career at it.'

Mam took the letter and read slowly through it as she puffed one of her fags and sipped her tea. She finished the letter without saying a word, then stood up and walked into the sitting room.

She pushed the letter at Dad saying, 'Here read this; the School say that George should dee an accootants course and look for a job in an office.'

Dad took the letter and without reading it threw it into the fire and snarled, 'Aa knaa where he's gannin te work,' and went back to the newspaper.

Standing at the sitting room door, George turned away, hiding the tears in his eyes and muttered, 'The frigging bastard,' and stormed out the house.

I felt sorry for him as he had told me the night before of his hopes of having a good job outside of the NCB and how much he was looking forward to going on the course; instead, he did not even receive a word of praise for his efforts, Dad having already consigned him to the pits.

Jim and Mary's wedding took place on a hot summer's day at the tiny Methodist Chapel at the end of the Second Row. Mam had bought two light blue and very thick double-breasted suits on tick for Dennis and me. The suits were tight and uncomfortable and being at the age when I was just beginning to care about my appearance, I was horrified at the width of the trousers. Whereas the jacket was a snug fit, the trousers were very wide and flapped around our skinny legs threatening to trip us at each step. We were lucky there was no wind as I was sure they would have acted likes sails and carried us both away.

Mary looked beautiful and Jim beamed like a young Tyrone Power, they both looked very happy but were having to start their married life living in the Sixth Row with Mary's Nan and Aunt. The wedding itself went off perfectly and the reception in the Fell Em Doon passed without incident or none that I noticed, being too worried about hiding my legs from the lasses that were there!

Summer Holidays involved a very long drive down to Eton Wick to stay with Betty at her lodgings. Her Landlady was a Mrs Howard whom we all had to call 'Mam Howard'.

Peter, a Tall, dark, well-educated and well-spoken lad from Eton, was courting Betty. Mam called him, 'That Bloody Jap' because of his narrow eyes, which I thought must be a term of endearment as once when she was vexed she called him, 'A slant-eyed bastard'.

I spent a quite a lot of the time wandering around the area with a sketchpad trying to capture some of the wonderful sights, including Windsor Castle and Kings College. Betty was very happy and Mam and dad were in a good mood - most of the time, so overall, it was a good holiday.

The new term started and George began his training with the NBC while I, resplendent in his cast off and freshly pressed (by me) Cheshire School navy blue jacket, grey trousers, white shirt and tie, marched off to school feeling the bees knees. I managed to keep them in good order for the whole year and even received another anonymous note written in the same colourful hand saying, 'We think you are the smartest boy in the Form,' followed by two rows of kisses! Did I have two secret admirers? Could it be the glamorous blonde twins? I hoped so but never found out.

18

The Sorry Affair of the Army Cadets

Although I would not be fourteen until the following year, along with a lad from the First Row called Roger, I joined the Army Cadets in September. Tom was going to come but did not want to lie about his age fearing that might be treason!

The cadet hut was behind the Central Hall at the far end of town, about a mile and a half's walk but well worth the effort. The hut was not huge consisting of a couple of training rooms, an office, a store and a small area for making tea and coffee. I loved the training, especially drill with the huge Lee-Enfield rifles and looked forward to receiving our uniforms until I found out, that we had to provide our own boots!

Held on Thursday nights and Sunday mornings, the Cadets for me were the best part of the week and gave me something to look forward too during a particularly grey Autumn. Three weeks later, after First Parade on a Thursday night, the Cadet Sergeant issued me with my khaki battle dress uniform and reminded me that I had to provide my own boots before wearing it.

Mam had become a regular at the Bingo held in the Miner's Institute several times a week, Thursday being one of them. Arriving home before her, I waited for her return hoping she had had a good night and would be in a generous mood.

She came in just after ten and I poured her a cup of tea before asking with trepidation, 'Mam can ye get me a pair of black boots for me army cadet uniform?'

Practically ignoring me, she took the tea and lit a woodbine so I asked again, 'Can Aa get some black army boots for me army cadet uniform?'

She looked at me through a cloud of tobacco smoke said, 'Aye ye can get some if ye've got the money.'

I saw an opening and said hopefully, 'If ye buy them Aa'll pay ye back with money from me paper roond.'

She got up from the table to walk through to the sitting room and said over her shoulder, 'Aa hevn't got money to waste on bloody army boots, hev a look in the 'Dark Hole,' Aa think there's a pair in there,' and she sat down on the settee next to Dennis to watch television.

The 'Dark Hole' was the cupboard under the stairs in the corner of the sitting room that we used as a dump for cast off clothing and anything else that there might be a future use for, no matter how unlikely. Before entering, I paused to prepare myself for the task ahead; entering the Dark Hole was not a task you took lightly! I opened the door catching the chest-high pile of clothes and bric-a-brac that threatened to engulf me, pushing it back before I climbed in to spend a sweaty

201

twenty minutes borrowing through the contents, disappearing from view at one time as I tunnelled deeper and deeper.

Beginning to flag and on the point of giving up I eventually found one black boot and holding it up with triumph, I shouted, 'Foond one'

'Pipe doon ye sackless sod,' shouted Mam.

With renewed vigour, I dove back into the heap and soon uncovered the other boot that I clutched tightly to my chest as I fell out of the cupboard. With the boots placed to one side, I then spent a couple of minutes fighting the contents back inside so that I could shut the door but I had survived the Dark Hole and found a pair of boots!

With the door shut I examined the boots and found the uppers in excellent condition; they were not army boots but they were black and looked vaguely right and importantly, they were my size. It was when I turned them over to look at the soles that my joy disappeared. Although the heels were fine, protected as they were by small steel heel tips, the soles were a different matter. Worn through to the last flimsy layer of leather, the soles looked like ripples on a pond.

I looked at the boots with disappointment and asked, 'Mam can Aa get these repaired they've got big holes in the soles?'

'Aye,' she said, 'ye can use yor paper money te pay for them!'

A week later Jim showed me how to press the blouse jacket of my uniform to ensure, the six pleats in the back were the regulation length. He also showed me how to Blanco my belt and ankle gaiters, how to polish the buckles on the belt, and how to wear the beret with the badge over the left eye, with the red and white feather hackle of the Royal Northumberland Fusiliers standing proud. Suitably prepared, including my highly polished boots complete with thick pieces of cardboard inside to protect my feet, I marched off to the Cadets feeling as proud as a peacock.

I had taken the boots to the cobbler to ask how much it would cost to repair them. The ten bob he quoted was two weeks newspaper delivery wages so the repair would have to wait until I saved the money.

George finished his initial training at the pit and it was no surprise to us that he did not pass the interview for an apprenticeship. Dad ensured he would go underground when he was sixteen where he would earn two or three pounds more a week than apprentices were! Along with the other lads that did not get apprenticeships, he had to do various labouring jobs on the surface until he was sixteen; George however, because of his accountancy skills, went to work in the Colliery Offices, where he soon settled into office life.

During the school half term, most of the thirteen to fourteen-year-old lads and lasses in the area went 'Tettie Picking.' We all looked forward to it, two weeks hard-work picking potatoes for the local farmers for a pail of potatoes each

202

day and £5 at the end of the fortnight. Having just missed a slot at the friendlier Home Farm, Tom and I worked together at Coneygarth Farm, but still had a great time messing about with the lasses between turnovers. The money paid for the repair of my black boots, Mam claimed £2, which left me £1and 10 shillings for two weeks effort.

After rifle drill on a sunny Sunday morning in late October, the Senior, Cadet Corporal decided it would be a good day to march around the Hirst to try and attract some new recruits though I suspect his motive was more to provide him with the opportunity to show off to local lasses.

Twenty of us formed up in three ranks marched off down Woodhorn Road before wheeling right into Alexandra Road and down toward the Flower Park. I was in the front three as we marched along and swung my arms as high as I could and despite the glare of the sun, I held my head high. I felt as though all of the Hirst were watching us, admiring our superb marching skills, but in reality, we probably went unnoticed.

The Corporal halted us in front of the shelters by the bowling greens in the Flower Park and ordered, 'LEFT TURN - STAND AT EASE.' That was when we saw why he had chosen to stop there. A couple of girls were standing in the shelter, one of whom must have been his girlfriend as he went over to them and began chatting and showing off. One of the lads gave a loud wolf whistle and received a reprimanded for having done so.

As I looked around, I noticed another group of girls walking toward us - they were wearing skirts that were buoyed up by many petticoats and they all wor pastel coloured, cardigans fastened at the neck. They were also all wearing 'Bobby Socks' and some of them had ponytails giving them the appearance of American teenage girls I had seen at the cinema.

I stretched myself to my full five foot six and tried to look steely hard, not an easy task with a boyish face like mine.

The girls stopped a few yards away and were chatting and giggling while pointing at us. They looked as though they were about fifteen; a couple of years older than me and I noticed one girl standing aloof at one side. She was smaller than the others were and looked familiar and as I looked, I recognised those blue eyes and her shy smile. It was the girl I had seen at the fairground, and the Queen's drive past, the little girl from the beach at Newbiggin. I had thought of her often and had hoped to meet her, even if she did live in Newbiggin but here she was at Ashington Flower Park, I was thrilled.

Hoping she would recognise me, I smiled at her but she started to talk to one of the other girls just as the Corporal came back and ordered, 'SQUAD! SQUAD SHUN! RIGHT TURN, BY THE LEFT QUICK MARCH!'

Marching past the girls, I turned and smiled at Blue-Eyes – she smiled back and gave a shy little wave; my heart skipped, I had butterflies, she waved at me, she remembered me! I had not felt like this before, I felt euphoric; I wanted to run back and talk to her but knew I had to march back to the Cadet Hut.

I found it difficult to concentrate on the way back, the Corporal telling me a couple of times to, 'Swing yor Arms Carr.'

As soon as we fell out, I said to Roger, 'Am gannin back to the Floower Park for a walk roond, are ye coming?'

'What for?' he asked, 'we've just come from there man.'

I paused, before saying, 'Aa want te speak to one of them lasses we saw man and if we hurry Aa'll be able te catch her.'

Roger looked at me for a moment then said smiling madly, 'De ye fancy one of them lasses?'

'Aye,' I said, 'So haway man or we'll miss them.'

We set off at a fast pace but were too late, there was no sign of them when we got there and despite walking round the Park several times we did not see them again. Bitterly disappointed, I marched back home with Roger, not saying much as I was deep in thought, thinking of the girl with the blue eyes and the shy smile.

At the end of a Thursday drill night in November, the Cadet Sergeant Instructor gathered us together and issued us with raffle tickets, that he wanted us to sell for BLESMA – The British Limbless Ex-Servicemen's Association. He told us to sell the tickets for sixpence each and asked us to do our best to sell as many as possible.

Roger and I decided we were going to try to sell ours on Saturday morning and discussed where we would go; agreeing to stay out of each other's chosen area. After finishing my paper round, I donned my freshly pressed uniform and clutching the raffle tickets, I set off enthusiastically at nine o'clock on a bitterly cold, grey November morning, with a northeast wind blowing down the street added a biting wind chill.

I was going to try and sell my tickets in the 'Ra's' and marched around to First Row to begin at Number Two, Number One being offices. Steeling myself and feeling very nervous I knocked on the door.

'Hello Missus,' I began when the door opened, 'Would ye like to buy some raffle tickets for the British Limbless Ex-Servicemen's Association, they're a tanner each and the top prize is a pair of bikes?' Having rattled off my prepared speech, looking nervous, embarrassed and hopeful, I waited for her answer.

'No Aa wouldn't,' was her reply and she closed the door on me!

Disappointed and taken aback by her bluntness, I regrouped and marched to the next-door, knocked and when it opened, I gave my rehearsed speech again.

The man who opened the door smiled at me and said, 'Aa hope ye've got all your limbs son, hang on and Aa'll get a shilling for two of them.'

Delighted at having sold my first two tickets, I marched on more confidently, trying each door in each of the Rows as I went. Reception was mixed; some were rude, even hostile while others were kind and generous, and slowly but surely I sold the tickets.

It was bitterly cold and more than one housewife took pity on me shivering on their doorstep. By the time I reached the Third Row, my confidence was very high; playing the poor, wee boy-soldier, I found myself offered several cups of tea, biscuits and at one house, a slice of toast and jam, accepting them all gratefully.

The Rows seemed to go on forever as I plodded on, morning changing to afternoon until at three thirty, feeling very tired and cold, I reached the end of the Eleventh Row and stopped to take stock. I counted the money twice: I had five pounds seven shillings and sixpence. Despite being weary, I was chuffed, I had sold two hundred and fifteen tickets but I had started with a dozen books of twenty tickets each and still had twenty-five tickets left; I was determined to sell them all.

I walked over to Wansbeck Road, hoping I could sell my remaining tickets at the private houses where the people were slightly better off; I was right and sold my last ticket just before five o'clock. Feeling triumphant, I walked slowly home checking the money again; I had £6.

Walking into the kitchen, I was greeted by Mam hissing, 'Where the bloody hell hev ye been? The Bairn wanted ye te tek him te the pictures and he's had te sit in all bloody day.'

I flopped down on a chair at the kitchen table, smelling the mince and dumplings that the rest of the family had just had and said, 'Aa've been selling raffle tickets aall day for BLESMA.'

'What the bloody hell is that?' She sneered.

'It's the British Limbless Ex-Servicemen's Association; the cadets are selling raffle tickets te mek money for them"

'Whey, did ye sell any?' She asked.

Taking the ticket stubs and money out of my pockets, I said proudly, 'Aye, all of them, I made six pund.'

'Six pund!' she said her demeanour changing instantly, 'ye must be frozen, Aa'll just get yor dinner for ye Pet.'

She went into the pantry returning with a dinner plate and put the last couple of spoonful's of mash from the pan onto the plate and with her tongue sticking out in concentration, scraped the remnants of the mince and dumplings from the tray on the open oven door, onto the mash.

'There ye are Bonny Lad,' she said placing the scant meal in front of me, 'Get that doon yor, there're nee dumplings left but ye divvint like them anyway, and all the peas and cabbage have been eaten but the mince is lovely.' I stared at the congealed mince she had scraped onto the small pile of mash and taking a fork from another plate, ate the barely warm food.

'When dee ye hev te hand the money in?' she asked as she took a seat opposite me.

'On Thorsday,' I replied, placing the fork on top of the now empty plate.

'Aa'll get ye a cup of tea noo,' she said as she threw the dregs from a cup into the back of the fire, then wiping the rim with her piny, poured a cup of stewed tea for me.

205

'Yor might lose the money before Thorsday so ye best give it te me te look after till then, Aa'll keep it in me purse for ye cos if ye leave it lying aboot one of them buggers is sure to tek it,' she said smiling disconcertingly.

Like a fool, I handed over the pile of money I had spent all day collecting.

At five thirty on Thursday night, I finished pressing my uniform in the scullery and carrying it on a hanger I made my way through the house to go upstairs to change into it. I stopped in the kitchen where Mam was sitting with a cup of tea reading the Evening Chronicle while she waited for Dad to get up to for his dinner. Uncle Alec was in his normal position in front of the fire, Dennis and Viv were in the sitting room watching Children's' Television.

Looking at Mam who was trying to ignore me, I said, 'Give me my six punds back Mam please, cos Aa hev te hand it in tonight.'

Without looking up from the paper, she said, 'Ye'll hev te wait till Sunday cos Aa've got ne money at the minute.'

Horrified, I said, 'But Aa gave ye six punds in change, where is it?'

She looked at me spitefully and said, 'Aa've spent the bloody money so ye'll hev te wait until yor Dad's paid on Friday and ye can hev it for Sunday.'

I was mortified and felt totally betrayed, the money was not hers, and she had spent it!

My horror at her action and casual attitude turned to anger and I snarled, 'The money wasn't yours te spend man, that's like stealing, Aa hev te hand the money in tenight not Sunday so give me the bloody money back!'

'Are ye stupid,' she shouted, 'Aa hevn't got any bloody money til Friday, noo bugger off ye bloody simpleton ye.'

This was too much for me I just shook my head in disgust and spat, 'Yor frigging mental, ye bloody swine ye,' and dropping my uniform on the kitchen settee grabbed my jacket from behind the scullery door and stormed out, not wanting to be in the same house as her.

I walked through the cuts my mind in turmoil wondering what I was going to do, fearful that the Cadet Officer would call the Police who would charge us with fraud! I decided that I would have to take the money on Sunday and hoped that would be all right.

Roger, answered my knock on his door wearing his uniform and asked, 'Where's yor uniform, we'll be late if ye've got te gan hyem and get changed man.'

Trying not to show my anger or disappointment I lied, 'Aa canna gan te night Roger, Aa hev te gan te me Aunties with me Mam and Dad, can ye tell them Aa'll hand me money and stubs in on Sunday?'

Roger closed the door behind him and said, 'Aye Alright but it's supposed te be handed in tonight, Aa can tek it for ye tonight if ye want?'

Embarrassed, I said, 'Aa hevn't got it with me so Aa'll tek it on Sunday.'

Roger said, 'Aalreet,' and marched off to the Cadets.

I wandered off and found myself walking toward the Miner's Institute, where I usually spent a couple of nights a week playing snooker or table tennis with the lads. In the snooker hall, I found Cousin Alec who had shed a lot of his puppy fat but was still heavily built, playing on his own on one of the six tables.

I said 'Hiya,' and sat down on the long bench stretching the length of the wall and watched him finish his game.

'Come on then, 'best of three,' he said and we set the balls up for the first game.

'Aa thought ye went te the Cadets on a Thorsday?' he asked.

'Aye, but Aa thought Aa'd give it a miss tonight,' I answered and took my first shot.

I won the first game but Alec won the second two and as we took our cues back to the kiosk Alec said, 'Haway, Aa'll thrash ye at table tennis as weel.'

'Come on then, ye can try,' I replied as we made our way into the main entrance hall where twenty or more women were cueing up to buy drinks and snacks from the kiosk; they were from the large room upstairs where they played Bingo and came down to buy their refreshments during the interval.

As we walked past them, Alec stopped and said, 'Hello Aunt Etty,' to Mam who had turned her back on us as we approached.

She turned around, and with a look of tight-lipped defiance, answered, 'Hello Alec lad,' and then glared defiantly at me.

I stopped and stared at her for several seconds without saying a word, then shook my head and turned away in disgust.

Alec asked, 'Are ye not speaking te yor Mam?'

'She's not worth speaking te, haway am gannin te thrash ye at ping pong.'

Early on Sunday morning, I was in the kitchen polishing my boots when Mam came in, coughing her early morning smokers' cough.

She poured herself a cup of tea, sat down at the kitchen table and said, 'And before ye start Aa hevn't got any bloody money te give ye.'

My stomach turned over, I could feel anger rising but I kept calm and said, 'Aa divvint want *your* money, I want the Army Cadet money that yor looking after, the money you stole.'

'Are ye bloody simple or what, Aa hevn't got any money te give ye,' she spat back viscously.

I had half expected this further betrayal and said, 'No, but ye had money te gan te the Bingo on Thorsday and the Club last night didn't ye!'

She lit a cigarette and appeared to hide behind the foul smoke she blew across the table and I saw that once again, she had that mean tight, puckered-lipped look that said, 'Sod You,' and I knew I was wasting my time. Her misuse of the money I had worked so hard for meant I was unable to go back to the Cadets without telling them my Mam had stolen it.

Folding my uniform up, I tucked it underneath my arm and walked to the back door and spat, 'Mam yor a thief, a liar and ye divvint give a shit for anybody but yorsell,' and stormed out.

I am sure that she did not care one iota that she had caused me so much misery, I felt I just had to be away from her and walked round to Roger's house. Handing him my uniform, I told him that I would not be going back to the Cadets and although he did not mention it, I am sure he knew it had something to do with the raffle money.

I wandered around aimlessly until after eleven o'clock before walking back home to find Mam still at the kitchen table; I gave her a look of disgust before walking into the sitting room. Pat had joined Mam at the kitchen table and Uncle Alec was in his chair smoking his first pipe of the day. Dennis was lying on the floor in front of the sitting room fire playing with plastic soldiers, using Butch as an obstacle for them to fight over.

I sat down on the settee as Dad came downstairs and into the sitting room as he headed for the outside toilet. He stopped when he saw me and asked, 'Why aren't ye at the Cadets, ye not gannin te tell me it's too cowld for ye are ye?'

Fighting back tears of anger and frustration, I said, 'It's got nowt te dee with the cowld, I've finished we the Cadets.'

Puzzled, he asked, 'I thought ye liked them, what on earth hev ye finished for?'

'Ask the thief in there, she'll tell ye,' I replied.

Dad went to the door between the two rooms and said, 'Etty what's this bugger in here talking aboot leaving the Cadets for?'

'Aa divvint knaa what that soft shites talking aboot no div Aa,' she replied without looking at him.

Uncle Alex spat into the fire and said, 'I think ye dee Etty, tell George aboot the lad's raffle money.'

Looking even more puzzled and beginning to get angry, Dad asked, 'What bloody raffle money?'

I blurted out the story without pausing for breath, Dad listening intently.

When I finished he looked at Mam and asked, 'Is this right Etty?' Mam just blew out tobacco smoke and took a sip of sherry from the glass in her other hand and ignored the question.

Pat said, 'Eee ye haven't Mam?'

Dad turned to me and asked, 'Hoo much did ye say it waas?'

'Six punds,' I replied.

Taking out his wallet, he pulled out some money and held it toward me, saying, 'Here gan on and hand his in.'

I looked at the clock on the mantel and said, 'It's too late Dad, they finish at twelve and it's ten to noo, they'd be gone before Aa got there.'

Dad stuffed the money into his wallet and went into the kitchen saying to Mam 'Whey Aa hope yor bloody satisfied, ye bloody waster ye?'

Mam snapped back, 'Listen ye baldy headed bugger ye, if ye gave me mair money this wouldn't hev happened.'

Dad snarled, 'Aa just think I would, just so ye could spend it on fucking sherry and Bingo,' - the argument really kicked off.

Not wanting to listen to another one of their screaming matches, I said, 'Haway Butch,' and went out the door leaving the screaming and foul language behind. I walked over the Rec Bridge with Butch following, and into the recreation ground, to the rugby pitch where a match was in full swing but I did not pay much attention to it, I was just glad to be away from Mam.

19

Biking and Camping

Jim had had several jobs since leaving the army, including Bus Driver and Pitman but unable to settle and after many discussions with Mary, he re-enlisted and, this time, joined the REME.

Spring term at our drab school passed uneventfully and as the summer holidays approached, the kids in my class began to look forward to the Autumn Term that signalled our last school year. We also heard of plans to demolish the school and build a new one on the open ground opposite and were disappointed that we would not be there to see it happen!

I also noticed that Mam spent a lot of time at the kitchen table smoking the obligatory cigarette while sipping sherry and staring blankly out of the window. The sherry increased her mood swings leading me to spend as much time as possible out of doors, much of it riding my cobbled together bike.

Larry Payne, who lived a couple of doors down, and who was a year older than me, also enjoyed bike riding and on a Saturday afternoon asked, 'De ye fancy riding to Rothbury the morn Syd?'

I thought about it for a second or two before saying, 'It's a lang way te gan on wor bikes man, hoo lang will it tek?'

Larry smiled and said, 'If we leave early we'll be there and back before teatime, we'll hev all day te dee it.'

'Right,' I said confidently, 'What time are we starting?'

'Nine o'clock sharp and be there, Aa knaa what ye buggers are like for sleeping in on Sundays.'

Next morning at half past eight and while the rest of the family were still in bed, I climbed over Dennis and yawning madly, trotted downstairs. Butch looked up at me from my Dad's chair in front of the sitting room fire and thumped his tail a couple of times against the arm of the chair before jumping down and walking to the back door, waiting for me to let him out for his morning stroll.

Having let Butch out, I filled the kettle, plugged it in, emptied the cold tealeaves from the teapot into the rubbish pail, and scooped three teaspoons of fresh tealeaves into it.

Rummaging around the pantry for something to eat, I was not very successful and ended up having a slice of jam and bread, a handful of raisins and two cups of tea before I went to the scullery and scared my face with a splash of cold water. I went outside and across the street to the loo and had to use Mrs Lister's from next door, ours being blocked again!

Breakfast and ablutions complete, I walked back to the yard to get my bike and found Larry waiting.

He was wearing shorts and a Tee shirt and looked at me in my jeans, shirt and pullover and said, 'Aa knaa it's a bit early for ye te think Syd but hev ye not got any shorts te wear?'

'Shorts! What the bloody hell div Aa want te wear shorts for man, it took me lang enough te get lang pants?'

'Ye'll bloody roast in jeans and a pullower man,' he said mockingly.

'Right give is a second,' I said and I ran back into the house and upstairs to our attic room. I sorted through the pile of clothes on the chair next to our bed and dragged out my khaki shorts that I used for PT and quickly swapped them for my jeans before discarding my pullover and shirt for a tee shirt.

Closing the back door behind me, I took my bike from where it was leaning against the wall and pushed it out of the small backyard and into the street.

Larry looked at me and laughed, 'Maybe ye should hev kept yor jeans on, it looks as if they must hev been keeping ye up cos them legs are too thin to support owt.'

'Sod off,' I shouted and swinging my skinny leg over the saddle, I mounted and cycled down the lane after Larry.

Rothbury nestles in the beautiful Coquet valley about twenty-five miles from Ashington - depending on the route you choose, all of them include many hills, some steep and long; not ideal considering the condition of our bikes. Mine had no gears and only a front brake that meant going uphill was hard work and involved a lot of demounting and pushing, whereas going downhill could be scary as the front brake was ferocious and tended to try to lock up and throw you over the handlebars; I tried not to use it too much. I had however fitted an old set of racing handlebars to reduce drag! Larry's bike was only better in that it had a rear brake, making it safer for descents.

We pedalled on as the sun climbed above us and once past Pegswood we began to enjoy the fresh air on our faces and the warmth of the sun on our skinny limbs. As we cycled on we chatted and sang Buddy Holly songs or in my case murdered Buddy Holly songs, we were fresh and not the least bit tired but then we had not yet reached our first proper hill.

The hills started when we reached the A697 and we had to dismount to push our bikes up the first steep one causing us to sweat lightly in the hot morning sun. After whizzing down the other side and climbing another one I realised I was desperately thirsty and needed a drink.

'How - Larry!' I shouted at his back as we toiled up another hill, 'hev ye got any weter?'

He turned and shouted, 'Nur I hevn't but Aa could dee with a drink as weel.'

Reaching the top of the hill, we could see a small, grey stone cottage nestled by the side of the road a hundred yards or so further on.

'We'll get some water there,' Larry said and sped off down the hill with me in pursuit.

Standing outside the picturesque cottage, Larry said, 'Try te look tired, thirsty and hungry, we might get something to eat as weel,' he whispered conspiratorially.

I looked at him and whispered back, 'Aa divvint hev to try, Aa am knackered.'

Despite Larry's best efforts, all we got was a glass of water each. Still it quenched our thirsts and revived us as we pedalled on through Longhorsley towards Weldon Bridge and the turn off for Rothbury. The countryside was beautiful, the air full of the smell of gorse and ferns but the effort we had to put into climbing the hills stopped us from appreciating it. Reaching Weldon Bridge, we turned left into the Coquet Valley and the road levelled off somewhat enabling us to enjoy the ride again as we followed the river toward Rothbury.

Our lack of preparation was beginning to tell; thirsty again, I was now also very hungry, a jam sandwich and a few raisins were not going to sustain me through the day.

Not wishing to appear to be a moaner, I said, 'Are ye hungry Larry?'

He slowed down and pulled into the side of the road and said, 'Aye I am, we should hev brought a flask and sandwiches, we will the next time.'

'Next time, Next time!' I shouted and fell off my bike onto my back on the grass verge and said laughing, 'What bloody next time, Aa divvint think am gangin te survive this bloody time.'

Larry laughed and said, 'Haway man let's get gannin and Aa'll buy ye a tea and sandwich at Rothbury, it's only three miles noo.'

I leaped to my feet and climbing back onto my bike I said, 'Haway then, let's get gannin.'

Larry shouted, 'Hang on man, Aa was only kidding, Aa hevn't got any money, hev ye got owt?'

'Aye,' I said, 'A sore arse, sore legs and an empty frigging belly, that's what Aa've got; a right couple of sackless sods we are.'

Tired and thirsty we cycled another mile before we came to a large, stone-built house on the other side of the road. Larry stopped suddenly and said, 'Look at the apple trees in the garden.'

I slammed on my front brake to stop myself smashing into Larry and in doing so pitched forward over the handlebars and into the verge, a verge that was covered in waist high stinging nettles!

As I rolled into the nettles, I felt them stinging my unprotected arms and legs but worse, my face was also badly stung as I scrambled like the proverbial cat on a hot tin roof to get out of the nettle bed. Covered in stings that were turning a fiery red, I hopped about at the side of the road, desperately rubbing my arms and legs, trying to relieve the pain and itching. Through eyes that were rapidly closing with swelling, I saw Larry run up the road a few yards where he ripped vegetation from the verge.

He ran back clutching two handfuls of Dock leaves and began rubbing them on my arms, I grabbed some from him and rubbed them into my face and to my relief began to feel a small reduction in the pain and itching. I spent several minutes rubbing the dock leaves on my stings before I noticed Larry was sniggering.

I spat at him, 'Aa divvint think it's funny man.'

Trying unsuccessfully to control himself, he blurted, 'Nur yor right it's just that ye look like a bloody Jap with yor eyes like that man.'

Looking across at the house he said, 'Wait here and Aa'll gan ower te the hoose and see if Aa can get a drink and some apples, if ye come looking like that, ye might scare them.'

Continuing to rub the dock leaves on my arms and legs, I waited by the bikes as Larry walked over to the house. My eyelids were smarting and despite having, rubbed Dock leaves on them they felt very swollen.

Larry came back a couple of minutes later and said, 'Haway, the woman who lives here said the apples aren't ripe yet so she is making a pot of tea for us.' Leaving the bikes propped against the gate I followed Larry to the back of the house where we waited outside an open door.

After a couple of minutes a middle-aged woman came out holding a tray with tea and biscuits and placed them on an old table in the yard, saying, 'Here ye are lads; just leave the cups on the tray when yor finished.'

Not wanting her to think I was Japanese, I had kept my head down while she was there, so was not surprised when she said over her shoulder before disappearing back into the house, 'No need te be shy lad, get stuck in.'

Larry poured the tea and I added the milk and three sugars to each cup before we devoured shortbread biscuits while we waited for the tea to cool. The tea refreshed us and lifted my spirits despite the itching and burning.

We had just finished a second cup each when the woman came back with a pop bottle full of water and said, 'Here's some water te keep ye's gannin till ye get home.' We thanked her for the tea, biscuits, and water and made our way back to our bikes as she stared at my face, obviously thinking what a strange looking lad I was.

It was when we were pedalling again that I felt my lips and noticed for the first time that they had swollen as well, no wonder the woman had stared at me. I must have looked a picture, a swollen face, topped off with tousled hair, a grubby tee shirt that had seen better days and an old pair of khaki shorts with skinny legs dangling below!

A little while later, we rode triumphantly into Rothbury, tired and still very hungry but happy that we had done it. Just before the centre of the town, we turned left down to the bridge over the Coquet and sat on the riverbank resting and quenching our thirsts with water.

'All we hev te do noo is bike home!' said Larry

'Thanks for reminding me,' I replied and started to crawl back up the bank on hands and knees crying, 'An engine for my bike, my kingdom for an engine for

214

my bike.' That was when I saw them!

About six or seven teenage girls were sitting on and around a bench at the top of the bank, sharing a picnic. They stared at us with the scorn only teenage girls can mete out to younger boys. I was mortified; looking as I did but worse, there amongst the girls was the little blue-eyed girl.

I turned my face quickly away, not wanting her to recognise me, difficult as that might have been due to my swollen eyes and lips. Keeping my back toward them, I stood up and retreated to my bike.

Larry caught up with me and said, 'Aa knaa one of them lasses Syd, let's gan and see if we can cadge a couple of sandwiches off them.'

I replied, 'Nur I'm aalreet man, I think we should set off for hyem,' and picked up my bike while trying to appear nonchalant in my khaki shorts. Walking past the lasses with my head turned the other way, I headed back to the bridge, where I sneaked a look-back and to my dismay saw Larry chatting and laughing with the lasses. I pushed my bike onto the bridge, hid behind the wall, and waited.

Larry appeared pushing his bike with a couple of sandwiches in one hand and said, 'I asked the lasses for a sandwich and was telling them aboot ye falling inte the nettles and they were all having a laugh, except the little one, she said it was cruel and te give ye a sandwich.'

He handed me the sandwich as my mind raced, 'Had she recognised me and if she had what must she think of me, looking like this?'

Eating the sandwich without tasting it, I wondered about the blue-eyed girl when Larry said through a mouthful of sandwich, 'They wouldn't believe that we'd biked here, especially ye with them legs.'

Smiling, I replied, 'Bugger off man, they might be skinny but they get me aboot alright.'

Larry asked, 'De ye knaa that lass then?'

I thought for a bit before answering, 'Aa divvint knaa her as such, but Aa've seen her aboot a few times,'

He replied, 'She must gan te the Technical College cos that's where the lass Aa Knaa gans te,'

Still trying to work out how old she was as we climbed back on our bikes, I asked, 'They must be sixteen or seventeen then?'

'Aye, sixteen.'

I was crest fallen, sixteen, she looked the same age as me but if she was sixteen she wouldn't have anything to do with me - a skinny fourteen-year-old.

We filled the water bottle up at the drinking fountain in the main street and then headed for home, my mind filled with thoughts of the little blue-eyed girl and how, because of the age difference, I would never be able to go out with her.

It was three o'clock when two very weary lads pedalled up the Fifth Row and stopped outside Larry's house.

Easing myself off my bike I rubbed my backside and said, 'Aa divvint knaa which hurts the most; me arse or me legs.'

'Aye,' said Larry, 'we'll be stiff in the morning,' and wheeled his bike into the old air raid shelter opposite their house.

As I pushed my bike the few yards to our house, George, coming out of the yard asked in his brusque manner, 'Where hev ye been Young'un?'

'Rothbury,' I replied nonchalantly as I pushed past him.

'Aa divvint think see,' he said disbelievingly.

I was too tired to argue and walked wearily into the house in search of food.

Butch greeted me from my Dad's chair with a look that said, 'I'd get up and greet you but you might pinch the chair so, Hi.'

Dennis, who was on the sofa in the middle of the room watching television turned to stare at me when I went in and asked, 'What's rang we yor face?'

'Nowt, I got nettled a bit, where's me Mam?'

'In bed we Dad.'

'Hev they been to the club then?'

'Aye, after dinner.'

'Dinner,' I moaned, 'what time did ye have dinner?'

'Aboot two hours ago.'

In need of something to eat, I walked back into the kitchen and through to the pantry where I found a large bowl full of leftover vegetables ready for bubble and squeak. Picking up a fork from the tray, I dug into the cold vegetables and devoured half of them before I noticed the remnants of a leg of lamb. I quickly ate the one or two pieces of cut meat left on the plate and then gnawed at the bone, biting off the last bits of meat before eating more of the vegetables.

My hunger finally satisfied, I made myself a pot of tea and sat at the kitchen table drinking it when Dennis came through and asked, 'What ye deeing noo?'

I answered smiling, 'Waiting for a screaming Banshee te attack me when she finds oot Aa've eaten her supper.'

Looking puzzled, Dennis asked, 'What's a Banshee?'

'I'm not sure 'but yor Mam is a big bad bugger of a one.'

I waited for Mam to get up and hurl the inevitable tirade of abuse - I was not disappointed.

Lying in bed that night, the little blue-eyed girl filled my thoughts and I drifted off to sleep feeling despondent that I was too young for her!

Dad, driving his shiny two- tone and relatively new, Standard Ensign to the hire shop in Morpeth to collect a ridge tent and camp beds for the trip to Scotland he had planned, signalled the start of our summer holiday. Only Dennis, Vivian and I would be going with Mam and Dad; Jim and Eric were in the army, Betty was living down South and Pat and George considered themselves far too old to holiday with us.

The weeks before the holidays, I had been doing a morning paper round as well as a more lucrative evening job delivering groceries for the large grocery store near the Store Corner. The grocery delivery job was hard work, having to pedal the heavy delivery-bike that had a small front wheel to accommodate the heavy grocery basket above. A fully laden basket over the small front wheel made the bike tricky to handle and I had one or two mishaps but it was worth it, in addition to thirty bob pay, there were also tips from housewives in the big houses down at the bottom of Wansbeck Road.

Mam took five-bob of my earnings but I kept the rest including tips, which I had saved for the holidays. Hoping to walk up some hills in Scotland I had bought a water bottle with a carrying strap and a second-hand pair of clumpy walking boots, as well as some thick stockings. I did not want a repeat of the battered feet I had suffered when I climbed the hill in the Lake District wearing plimsolls! Naïve as ever, I thought that was all I required to climb Scottish mountains!

Because Dad always spent the first Saturday of his holiday readjusting his body clock from working fore-shift of 1 to 9 am, it was early Sunday morning before we set off on a slightly overcast morning, heading for Loch Lomond.

It was a long day, especially with Mam navigating, causing tempers in the front of the car to become more and more frayed, resulting in some very heated exchanges, especially in Glasgow:

'Which way?' asked Dad.

'Haad on, I'm not sure yet,' answered Mam.

'What the hell dee ye mean "Had on", Am in the middle of aall this fucking traffic, hoo the fucking hell can Aa haad on ye silly coo ye.'

'Divvint swear at me ye baldy heeded bugger, turn right back there!'

'Back there! Back bloody where ye stupid sod ye, can ye not read a pissing map man?'

'There're ower many bloody roads on here, hoo the hell am I supposed to tell which ones which, ye big moothed bugger ye?'

I sat in the back trying to ignore them while taking in the sights of Glasgow in all its dingy glory until Dad finally snapped and pulled up alongside the kerb shouting, 'Right, that's it get oot, get oot the fucking car noo.'

'What dee ye mean get oot the car?' asked Mam.

'Just get oot the bloody car noo before Aa throw ye oot.'

'Just ye bloody try Bonny Lad and Aa'll put a frigging cut in yor heed like a Navvies' bait tin.

This was too much for Dennis, he started to cry, 'Ye cannit leave me Mam here she's got to come we us.'

'He can if he wants,' I whispered but not quite quiet enough.

Mam shouted back, 'And ye can shut up ye bloody simpleton or Aa'll splatter ye an all.'

I looked out the window and spat back, 'Aa divvint think so.'

Dad continued, 'I've towld ye, get oot the car noo.'

Mam crossed her arms in defiance and pursing her lips stared straight ahead ignoring him. Seething, Dad climbed out the car slamming his door so hard behind him, it rattled my teeth.

Storming round to the other side of the car, he flung Mam's door open and yelled, 'Get oot noo and get inte the back of this fucking car before Aa swing for ye.'

It then dawned on Mam that Dad wasn't abandoning her in the centre of Glasgow; giving him a look that would scare the Devil himself, she climbed out the front seat while Dad opened the back door saying, 'Syd get inte the front and read that fucking map and get me oot of this fucking toon noo.'

Climbing into the front, I picked up the AA Book of the Road, and turning to the detailed City Maps at the back, I found Glasgow and tried desperately to orientate myself. The thought of Dad's wrath if I could not navigate him out of the city spurred me on.

'We'll probably end up back hyem with that bugger guiding us,' hissed Mam from the back as she cuddled Dennis for solace.

'Right,' I said trying to sound calm, and trying not to panic, 'Gan straight on and tek the third turn on the right.' Dad looked at me through narrowed quizzical eyes before putting the car in gear and driving off. A little while later, we were on the outskirts of Glasgow heading north for Loch Lomond and I was beginning to enjoy myself while Dad, at last, began to relax.

Sitting in front of the car navigating, having Dad following my directions - trusting my decisions, was exhilarating.

It was late afternoon when we arrived at the campsite between the main road and Loch, just north of the picturesque village of Luss. The campsite was right on the banks of the Loch with Ben Lomond standing massively on the far bank, it was picture perfect.

The place was busy with Glaswegians taking their annual holiday; two double-decker busloads had arrived shortly before us, the occupants busy erecting tents in a chaotic but jovial fashion. Under Dad's control, he and I had erected our tent within a few minutes while Mam made a brew on the primus stove and prepared a meal of tinned stewed steak, tinned potatoes, and tinned peas all thrown into one pot.

About 7 o'clock with the quarrel earlier in the day forgotten; Mam and Dad walked off down the road together to the Hotel for a drink, leaving me to look after the other two, I was not happy!

Bored with hanging around the tent, I said, 'Haway let's gan up the hill at the back, we'll be able to see right ower the Loch.

Dennis nodded in agreement but Vivian said, 'Am not gannin up any hills, am staying here and if ye leave me I'll tell me Mam.'

I growled at her, 'If ye staying here at the tent ye'll be champion but we're gannin up that hill just a bit so it's up to you.'

She did not answer and walked back inside the tent. Thinking she would stay there, I headed off with Dennis toward the road and crossed it before heading up the hill through the chest-high bracken.

We only climbed a couple of hundred yards or so before turning to admire the view; it was breath-taking, with the evening sun shining on the far bank and Ben Lomond and the smaller Ptarmigan standing proudly above the Loch.

A little later, we were exploring the bed of the stream that cascaded down the hillside when I found a small, almost new hand axe.

Dennis asked, 'Are ye gannin te keep it?'

'Aye of course I am, finder's keeper's man, somebody must have been up here chopping firewood for a camp fire.

Looking about, I saw that there were masses of dead wood lying in the gully and said, 'C'mon let's chop some wood and build a fire by the tent.'

We spent the best part of an hour scavenging wood, chopping it into smaller pieces before gathering up as much as we could, and staggering back to the campsite. When we got back to the tent I dropped the wood and went in to check on Vivian - she was not there.

Rushing out of the tent, I said to Dennis, 'Pigging Viv's buggered off so I'd better find her before me Mam and Dad get back.'

Dennis was on his knees piling our chopped wood up and said without looking up, 'It's aalreet, she's ower there we them lads,' and pointed over to the Lochside. Viv was at the water's edge flirting with two lads from the Glaswegian camp. Knowing where she was I forgot her and took over building a fire.

Just after ten, Dennis and I were sitting in front of the dying embers of our fire toasting bread, when Mam and Dad strolled back.

'Put that bloody fire oot noo or ye'll get us kicked off the site, there're nee fires allowed man,' snarled Dad as he approached.

We stood up and quickly stamped on the fire to put it out; a bit strange as the Glaswegians had two roaring campfires going and no one had told them to leave.

Mam looked into the tent and asked brusquely, 'Where's Viv?' I turned to point to the Lochside but when I looked, Vivian was not there.

I thought 'Bloody Hell, that's it, trouble again.'

Dennis said, 'She's ower there at that campfire.'

We all turned to look and saw Viv sitting amongst a large group of Glaswegians by one of the campfires; the lad next to her had his arm round her shoulders!

Mam went puce and growled, 'George gan and get that little bloody slut noo.'

Dad, who had just put the kettle on the primus and was busy lighting a cigarette answered, 'Ye want her, ye get her, Aa've had me fill of lasses in this bloody family.'

Mam was raging but just managed to control herself as she walked a few paces toward the fire and stopped to shout in a very strange, pseudo-posh accent, 'VIVIAN, VIVIAN, come her pet.'

219

Stupidly, Viv chose to ignore her even though those around her had turned to look at Mam.

Mam turned a deeper shade of purple and shouted a bit louder but in the same strange voice, 'VIVIAN, VIVIAN.' Viv still did not acknowledge Mam; she was enjoying herself with these two older lads and did not want to leave.

Mam boiled over, she stormed toward the fire and exploded in broad Geordie, 'HOW YE BLOODY BRAZEN BLOODY HUSSY YE, GET YOUR ARSE BACK HERE NOO OR A'LL BLOODY SWING FOR YE.'

I don't know who got the biggest shock; Viv or the people around the fire, suffice to say Viv scuttled back, trying to avoid Mam but was grabbed by the arm and frog marched back while the Glaswegians stared on for a few seconds before breaking into a rousing cheer, followed by much booing.

Fuming, Mam marched Vivian into the tent while giving her a non-stop telling off that would have made an RSM, blush.

Dad sat down on a stool next to the primus, chuckling to himself as he watched Mam's antics. He looked over at me and gave a conspiratorial wink before dragging contentedly on his fag. The night did not improve as the Glaswegians party got nosier and nosier and continued into the wee small hours preventing us from sleeping as Mam kept up an unnecessary running commentary that did not help.

'Listen te them buggers.'

'That's ridiculous when people are trying to sleep.'

'What the hell are they up te noo?'

'It's like bloody Sodom and Gomorrah oot there.'

'This your bloody fault for fetching us here.'

'Gan and tell them te keep the bloody noise doon.'

'Somebody should get the police te them.'

'They should be sent back te frigging Glasgow.'

'If they divvint stop shortly, Aa'll gan oot there and frigging well slaughter the lot of the Scotch buggers.'

'That's it, am not stopping in this bloody mad-hoose – we're leaving the morn!'

We did.

She had us up at six, making as much noise as possible as she made a pot of tea before packing blankets and camp beds into the car boot while we staggered around in a daze wondering what was going on. With Mam slamming doors at every opportunity, we had the tent collapsed and everything packed into the car, by eight o'clock. She had also kept up a constant flow of very loud orders throughout, all of which were unnecessary and ignored by us, as we were too tired to care.

She finally climbed into the front seat of the car, slamming the door behind her and yelled out of the open window, 'Haway then, let's get oot of this bloody hole of a place now before them sods start again.'

220

Dad walked to her side of the car, reopened the door, and said quietly, 'Get in the back - Aa divvint want a repeat of yesterday.'

Mam was about to say something but seeing the look on his face closed her mouth and slid off the front bench seat and climbed into the back. Dad looked at me and nodded at the seat; I climbed in and picked up the map without a saying a word.

Leaving the lovely but noisy campsite, we drove north through stunning scenery along the banks of Loch Lomond to the tiny hamlet of Tarbet. There we turned left onto the A83 and drove across to Arrochar and around the top of Loch Long before heading up to the top of Glen Croe where we stopped at a lay-by called, 'The Rest and Be Thankful'. Dad got the brew box out of the boot and we had a late breakfast of bacon butties washed down with strong, sweet tea while the sun climbed over the hills behind Loch long.

Mountains, moor and coast; all breath-taking, it was a fabulous drive to Fort William and included a ferry crossing of Loch Leven. Mam did some grocery shopping in Fort William before we drove into Glen Nevis and set up camp on a small site surrounded by trees just inside the Glen.

I was up early the next morning and made a pot of tea, pouring cups for Mam, Dad, and myself before eating two bowls of cornflakes with cold milk followed by two jam sandwiches. Pulling on my new, second-hand boots, I watched Dennis get up and pull his clothes on, yawning as he did so.

Mam demanded, 'What are ye deeing up so early?'

'Gannin up the hill,' I replied, filling my water bottle with orange squash and water.

'Whey divvint gan ower high we the bairn, Aa divvint want him worn oot.'

I was crestfallen and angry, I wanted to go on my own without the encumbrance of Dennis; he did not have any boots, which meant we would not be able to go very high.

'But I want to gan right up so Aa canna tek Dennis man,' I protested.

Mam snarled back 'Yor not leaving the bairn on his own so wait for him.'

I pleaded in vain, 'He can walk inte toon with Viv, Aa divvint want him we me teday, I'm always looking after him man but not teday.'

Stirring below her blanket, Viv said, 'Aa can tek him we me.'

Mam was adamant, 'He's gannin we ye so get on with it.'

Furious, I said, 'Aalreet but divvint blame me if he comes back crying and sore.'

'He better bloody not,' she warned.

I ordered Dennis to eat breakfast quickly and filled his water bottle before wrapping mars bars and jam sandwiches in the greaseproof paper from the bread.

Sitting up in his camp-bed, drinking his tea and coughing over his first fag of the day, Dad said, 'Ye can put yor sandwiches and drinks in the owld army rucksack the tools are in in the boot but mek sure ye leave the tools tidy.'

221

I was chuffed; a proper bag to carry my kit in, just like the ones I had seen climbers using in the hills.

Outside I said to Dennis, 'Look ye divvint want te come with me today cos I'm gannin right te the top and ye winnit like it, so ye might as weel stay here man.'

Dennis looked at me with his sad eyes and said, 'But Aa want te come.'

I argued with him briefly but gave up as time was moving on and I wanted to be off, and anyway I was sure he would turn back very quickly.

Twenty minutes later, we were crossing the bridge to Achintee House to start the climb to the top of Ben Nevis, the highest mountain in Britain. Mam and Dad had no idea that it was the 'Ben' I was going to walk up and I had no real idea how big it was or how long it would take. With my boots fastened, wearing jeans, and a tee shirt and with my jumper tucked under the flap of the rucksack, I worried that while Dennis wore jeans and a polo shirt, he had sandshoes on his feet, not the best footwear for climbing a mountain! The path was 'The Pony Track' also known now as the 'Tourist Track' and although it involves no scrambling, it is nevertheless a long, hard climb into what can be very hostile terrain in bad weather. We were lucky; it was a lovely early August morning and the weather was set to be good for the rest of the day.

The path initially climbed steeply and we were both panting heavily before it eased into a slightly gentler climb, stretching diagonally up the side of the mountain. After forty minutes of steady climbing, we sat down for a rest and a drink. The path was busy; we could see many small groups of figures stretched out ahead of us, and many others coming up behind. Sitting there, I tried to convince Dennis to turn back now before we went too far but he was not listening.

Two men stopped next to us and looked us over before one of them said, 'Aye and where dee ye two lads think ye are going?'

'Te the top mister,' Dennis answered naively.

'Really,' he answered. 'And do you know how high that is?'

I looked at him and said, 'Aye Aa dee, it's Ben Nevis, the highest moontain but he's not gannin right up, just me.'

The man shook his head and said, 'I think he'd better turn back now don't you and are ye sure ye now the way up?'

'Aa'll just follow the path to the top, then Aa'll come back doon again, ne bother.'

'Have ye got a map?' his companion asked.

'A map!' I replied, 'What dee I need a map for? I can see where am gannin and am sure I can find me way doon again.'

The two men looked at each other, shook their heads in disbelief, and walked on.

Dennis and I climbed on as the sun grew higher and hotter and we were soon sweating from our efforts. The path zig-zagged a couple of times before rounding the shoulder of the hill into a high valley that contained a small loch that we looked across to distant mountains. The path, however, continued to climb and as I followed it up with my eyes, I began to realise just how high the 'Ben' was.

Dennis was not interested, he was finished. He sat down exhausted and drained; he drank some more and shook his nearly empty bottle before saying, 'Ye'll hev te take me doon noo, Aa thought this was the top.'

'Listen,' I said angrily, 'I towld ye not te come and Aa towld ye Aa was gannin te the top, noo ye can either gan straight back doon yorsell or wait here for me, it's up te ye but Am gannin te the top.'

Dennis looked up the mountain and asked, 'Hoo lang will ye be?'

Looking up the mountain, I said, 'Aa divvint knaa but it looks as though there's still a lang way te gan.'

He thought for a moment then said, 'Aa'll wait here for a bit then probably walk back doon but ye'll be in trouble wiv Mam for leaving me.'

'Look, ye can see the path all the way doon and the campsite is just alang the road, ye'll be aalreet man.'

Handing him a Mars bar and jam sandwich, I left him sitting by the track as I turned and headed up the hill again, feeling guilty for leaving him there but sure he would not have a problem walking back down. I also felt angry that Mam had made me bring him and that he had insisted on coming. Then I thought 'Wait until she finds out that the hill is 'Ben Nevis', there'll be hell to play.'

I soon forgot my guilt and anger, the mountain, fresh air and stunning views lifted my spirits despite the steepness of the climb. The path now took huge zigzags that made the climb up the mountain a little easier but my thighs ached as I plodded on step after step, resting every now and then as I moved closer to the top over terrain that was now scree covered, looking rather like I imagined a lunar landscape.

Passed by walkers, going up and a few going down, I received some questioning looks and occasional word of encouragement until just before two o'clock; I finally made the summit, where despite my elation at having reached the top, I felt a little disappointment. I had been expecting a mountain peak but this was a broad flat plateau with some old ruins and a large cairn on the top. The view, however, was fantastic; I was on top of the world, all around me, mountains were stacked one after another as far as the eye could see.

I was amazed and turned around and around trying to take it all in when a voice from a group in the shelter of the ruins said, 'You'll take off if you keep spinning like that lad.'

I stopped and shyly sat down next to them before pulling my jumper on against the cool gentle breeze that floated across the plateau. Exhilarated, I chatted enthusiastically to people in the group as I ate my sandwiches and drank my over strong squash.

I must have been babbling with excitement as one of the men laughed at me and said, 'I take it you'll be climbing more hills then lad?'

I nodded enthusiastically and said, 'Whey, I'd better gan and get me

223

brother, he's waiting for me doon be the Loch,' and picking up my pack, I started the long descent.

It was a lot easier going down especially with my boots on, allowing me to admire the views even more, but the descent, like the climb, seemed never ending and the ache in my thighs increased with each step.

Eventually, as I crossed a gully with a stream, the Loch where I had left Dennis came into view enabling me to look for him. I could not see him so thought he must have got tired of waiting and walked down, as I must have been away for several hours. Hoping I was right and he had found his way back to the tent; I continued my descent and put the thoughts of the inevitable telling-off I would receive to the back of my mind.

Walking back into the camping field around six o'clock, I could see Mam standing outside the tent, arms crossed and her motor ticking over ominously.

'Aa well,' I thought, 'here goes.' I had had a lot of time to think as I walked down the mountain and had decided now was the time to challenge her!

She started when I was about twenty feet away:

'Ye bloody simpleton ye.'

'Ye bloody little waster ye, ye've nearly killed the bairn!'

'Aa'll swing for ye this time, so help me bloody God, Aa will.'

'Ye cannit even look efter the bairn withoot frigging it up.'

'Fancy trying te tek him up a bloody mountain ye sackless sod ye.'

On and on she went and I let it all wash over me until she paused for breath and I said, 'The bairn's eleven years owld and I told him te come back.'

'Come back! Come back!' she exploded, 'he was carried back! He's in there dying of heat stroke ye bloody simpleton.'

Now I was concerned and I walked toward the open flap of the tent to see how Dennis was, just as Mam lifted her hand to strike me. I stopped and glared at her and shook my head as if to say 'Don't you dare'. My stare was enough to stop her; she dropped her hand but continued her verbal barrage as I went into the tent.

Dennis was lying on a camp bed looking hot and tired with Dad sitting next to him, he had been sponging Dennis down.

'Is he aalreet Dad?'

'Aye he's aalreet, just a bit too much sun but he'll be aalreet the morn.'

'Aalreet,' Mam exploded, 'does he look al-bloody-reet, ye nearly killed him.'

'Etty, for God's sake shut bloody up,' shouted Dad, 'the bloody bairn's aalreet but you're not frigging helping gannin on like that.'

That started another argument that gave me the opportunity to ask Dennis what had happened.

Apparently, I had been gone about thirty minutes when four men had come across Dennis sitting forlornly at the side of the track, worried for his safety and well-being, they quizzed him as to why he was there. Dennis must have played up to them; telling them that I had left him there and he was too tired to walk down the mountain. The men carried him back to the tent and told my Mam they had rescued him from half way up Ben Nevis!

Dennis smiled at me and said, 'It was great being carried doon,' and I knew then that there wasn't much wrong with him.

The shouting between Mam and Dad subsided so I took a deep breath and walked up to Mam and said, 'Look, Aa knaa I hev to look after him, but Am nearly fifteen and sometimes, just sometimes, I'd like te dee things withoot him.'

Mam rounded on me and shouted, 'Ye'll bloody weel look after him and that's bloody well that.'

Dad stood up and said, 'Aye, Syd's right, he shouldn't hev to spend all his time looking after Dennis.'

Mam opened her mouth to speak but Dad beat her to it saying, 'Leave it alen Etty, that's a bloody nough.'

Later, sitting outside the tent eating a dinner of steak pies and peas, Dad asked me about the mountain and the climb, he was impressed that I had been all the way to the top and I began to realise how lucky I was that the weather had been kind to me, about the only bloody thing that was!

The next day and for several days after, my legs were stiff, very stiff!

The rest of the holiday passed without incident; Inverness where we saw the Highland games; Braemar where we camped in the Royal Showgrounds and I walked to the top of a couple of hills, and the beautiful Trossachs that include a boat trip on Loch Katrine. Overall, a great holiday that served to confirm my love of Scotland as well as being the last one I would spend with my parents.

20

Biking, Lasses and Apprenticeships

The Saturday after my holiday, Larry asked, 'De ye fancy a ride to Otter-burn Syd?'

I thought about it briefly, Otterburn is farther away than Rothbury and has more hills en-route but answered. 'Aye, when are we gannin?'

'Tomorrow and, this time, fetch something to eat and drink.'

That night, I fixed a tough plastic saddlebag I had acquired from Cousin Alec to the back of the seat on my bike and tried again without success to fix the rear brakes but failed when I realised that I needed a new brake cable and brake pads.

The next morning I filled a flask with tea, made some sandwiches and along with a bag of Smith's crisps and an apple, I put them in the saddlebag before wheeling my bike out to meet Larry who was waiting in the lane with a lad called Les.

I knew Les by sight; he was a keen Scout from the Scout Group across the road and I also knew that his family were better off than most, confirmed by the very smart racing bike complete with racing gears, water bottle holder and saddle-bag, that he sat astride. Larry and I were both very envious.

With Les leading, we set off on another hot August day, enjoying the rela-tively flat roads through Morpeth to Scots Gap and Cambo before we joined the A696 at Knowesgate where we stopped for a cuppa and sandwich. Refreshed we pedalled on along the main road with just a few cars for company as Les continued to set the pace on his superior bike.

After about another four miles we pedalled over the top of a hill overlook-ing a massive valley with a view of Otterburn Army Ranges in the far distance.

Larry said, 'Look at that view.'

The view was magnificent but I said, 'Niver mind the bloody view look at this bloody hill!'

Momentum had already started to take effect and we were rolling swiftly down the long hill that descended for at least a mile on a road that looked newly laid. Luckily, it was almost straight with only a couple of gentle curves. Les was still in front as our speed picked up while Larry used his rear brakes to keep his speed safe. I gingerly squeezed my savage front brake causing the front wheel to judder violently, not a good idea.

Deciding it would be safer not to use the front brakes and ride the descent flat out, I hoped to lose momentum when the road reached the bottom and climbed the hill in the distance. Our speed continued to increase and as Les began to use his rear brake to control his descent I shot past him beginning to enjoy the speed; it was exhilarating on the smooth wide surface of the road and I bent over the handlebars to reduce the wind drag.

The wind roared past my face and began to bring tears to my unprotected eyes as I whistled recklessly and at breakneck speed down the hill whooping with delight.

I then saw that I was gaining on a car that had overtaken us at the top of the hill! As I sped even faster, I grew ever closer to the car, an old and small Ford Prefect and realised I was going to have to overtake it or smash into the back of it! Squinting through half closed eyelids and baring my gritted teeth, I bore down on the unsuspecting car readying myself to overtake.

With only a few feet to go, I began to pull out to the middle of the road and spotted a car coming up the hill toward me!

Fear suddenly replaced exhilaration as I realised that the car would reach me just as I would have to pass the Ford! It was too late to stop; I had to go for it and began overtaking the Ford. As my speed was just a few miles an hour faster than the speed of the car, I clearly saw the surprised look on the faces of the elderly couple sitting in the back who were staring back at the squinting maniac with bared-teeth who was overtaking them on a bike! The driver turned to look and began to mouth something but I was too intent on the car racing toward us to pay any attention to him.

The car coming up the hill switched his headlights on and began tooting his horn as though I had not seen him! I was not going to make it!

There wasn't enough time or space to get past the Ford and I almost closed my eyes waiting for the inevitable crash when; at the last minute the Ford driver stepped on his brakes, as did the driver of the other car who also veered toward the side, allowing me to shoot through the gap with only inches to spare.

Letting out a long silent whistle of relief, I flew on down the hill leaving the two shocked drivers stopped opposite each other shaking their heads in disbelief just as Larry and Les shot past them!

My momentum and wild pedalling carried me a good distance up the other side of the valley before gravity and shaking legs forced me to stop and dismount. Standing holding my bike with legs like jelly, I watched as Larry and Les pulled up next to me.

'Yer bloody crackers man,' said Larry.

'Mental,' Les joined in, 'you were going far too fast, yor nearly got killed,' slightly jealous that I had beat him down the hill on my old wreck.

Larry said, 'Yor not ganging to hev te gan doon any more hills like that man Syd, Aa divvint want te hev te tell yor Mam that ye got smashed up.'

Having got my breath back I said, 'Ye divvint think Aa wanted te gan that fast dee ye? Me bloody rear brake doesn't work man - mind it was great.'

The Ford passed us horn blaring, and an irate driver waving his fist, but he did not stop.

We cycled the last couple of miles to Otterburn and sat by the old mill to eat our packed lunches before setting off for home, with me determined not to risk

228

death again by riding downhill out of control. I descended the hills very slowly from the start and by not allowing my momentum to pick up; I was able to use my front brake to descend safely.

Arriving home at teatime, worn out but happy, I rode past George who was playing cricket in the lane with some other lads.

He shouted mockingly, 'Where ye been Young'un, Rothbury again?'

'Nur,' I replied, 'Otterburn.'

'Bollocks,' he shouted, "ye couldn't bike te Morpeth 'n' back niver mind frigging Otterburn.'

I did not respond and smiled at him as I dismounted and wearily pushed my bike into the back yard.

The next week I took money from my paper round and bought a brake cable and brake pads for my bike.

Toward the end of the summer holidays, I met Fay; she was staying with her cousin Anne in the Sixth Row. A bunch of us that included Jack, Tom and Frank had been meeting up with Anne, Viv, Jennifer and a couple of other lasses for Postman's knock and other harmless petting games, often in Dad's garage but occasionally in one of our houses if our parents were out.

Having arranged to meet at Anne's, while her parents were at the 'Club' I arrived with Frank at seven o'clock to be met by a very pretty dark haired girl that welcomed us with a southern accent.

'Hi, come on in, I'm Fay and you must be Syd and Frank.

Blushing while trying to be cool, I spluttered, 'I'll be Syd if ye want me to be.' It made her smile and I realised we had made a connection that was pleasing and exciting.

Over the course of the evening, Fay and I engineered the games so that we ended up together and I thrilled at her sweet kisses behind the curtain at the front door. Playing Husbands and Wives, I showed my naivety - lying on the sofa with her holding her hand, it was Fay that made the first move, reaching over to cuddle and kiss leaving me a tad embarrassed in front of the others.

It was the start of a wonderful week spent in mixed company, especially with Fay and we often sneaked off to be together.

On a warm Saturday evening, we were all chatting on the front steps of the scout hut when Fay asked, 'Who's in your house tonight?'

Looking over at the open front door, I thought for a moment before replying, 'Nebody, the owlder ones have aall gone oot, Viv's here and Dennis is playing doon the lane.'

She stood up and taking my hand said, 'Come on then you can give me a cuddle on the settee.' I felt butterflies in my stomach and my mouth suddenly felt very dry as we ran into the house and into the sitting room where she fell onto the sofa dragging me down next to her. We lay there cuddling and kissing, my head swimming with delight when I felt her hand sliding down between us.

229

She pulled me close to her kissing my neck while her hand slid down until it gripped me through my jeans. I gasped with shock and excitement as she began stroking me. Feeling lightheaded and not sure what to do' I just clung on to her as she rubbed away. It was all over very quickly and she stood up giggling before kissing me quickly on the lips and running out the house, leaving me bedraggled, gasping, and not sure, what had just happened.

Too embarrassed to follow her out, after cleaning myself, I sat in front of a blank television screen, trying to rationalise her actions. I slowly came to the realisation that she had wanted me to make love to her and that I had missed the opportunity to have my first real sexual experience!

I resolved to put matters right the following day; I would take her off somewhere and take things to the next stage and this time I would be in control. Just thinking about it left me feeling lightheaded and I hardly slept that night, thinking in excited anticipation of what was to come.

The day dragged slowly bye as I waited impatiently until the afternoon before I thought it was the right time to go to and see Fay. About two o'clock, with my hair freshly Brylcreamed and combed I made my way up the Sixth Row trying hard to contain my excitement and look cool. I could see Anne and a couple of others bouncing tennis balls off the coalhouse wall as I approached but could not see Fay.

Leaning on the Netty wall I asked in what I thought was a nonchalant voice 'Where's Fay?'

Anne continued throwing tennis balls at the wall and said, 'She went home this morning!'

My jaw went slack and my mouth dropped open, I was devastated, 'Gone home!' I repeated unnecessarily before wandering off toward the allotments at the end of the lane, my mind in turmoil.

I swore at myself for having miss-read the situation and being so slow; on the other hand I did not feel upset that she had gone without saying goodbye, last night was obviously her way of saying goodbye and thinking about it; she couldn't have meant that much to me or I would have been really upset.

A voice shouting, 'How Syd, where ye gannin?' stopped me and I turned to see Tom sitting astride his bike in an opening in the outhouse walls that led into the top end of the Fifth Row.

Walking across to him, I answered, 'Neewhere, just oot for a walk like, what ye deeing up here?'

'Aa've just been te me sister's and I saw you in the allotments and wondered what ye were up to,' he replied as I sat on top of a bin and chatted, telling him about Fay but not the events of last night.

Two lasses came out of the house opposite and stood by the gate talking while obviously eyeing us up! A little while later the four of us were sitting on an old bench in the allotments chatting and laughing, I had already forgotten Fay!

One of the girls who called Mary who had neat, short, dark hair, suddenly leant against me and asked, 'Would ye like to be my boyfriend?'

'Aye,' I said without thinking; she was bonny, and I was without a girl-friend now!

The four of us hung round together for a couple of days and did a bit of petting which got me to thinking that maybe I was missing signals again and I re-solved not to miss out again. On the third day, I rode my bike the few hundred yards down the lane to meet her and found Tom already there talking to her and the other lass.

Having thought through what I was going to do, I left my bike against the coal house wall and said to Mary, 'De ye fancy gannin for a walk?'

She stood up taking my hand, asked, 'Where are we gannin?'

Beginning to feel nervous and excited at the prospects of making love to Mary, I croaked through a very dry mouth, 'Just inte the allotments.'

Knowing exactly where I was going to take her, within a couple of minutes we were leaning against the back of an allotment shed kissing. With mounting excitement, I put my left arm around her neck and held her tightly as we kissed, until carried away; I began to slide my right hand around to her breast.

Butterflies filled my stomach again and I was finding it hard to breathe as my hand reached underneath her cardigan close to her breast, until at the last mo-ment, she pushed me violently back and said, 'Ye can stop that now, I don't want any babies until I'm married,' and stormed off leaving me shocked, frustrated and looking a wee bit silly.

Feeling very confused, I walked back to where Tom was; I had been sure that she had wanted to make love!

Tom asked, 'What's the matter we Mary, she's just run inte the hoose?'

Picking my bike up I looked at Tom and his lass and shook my head and said, 'Buggered if Aa knaa, Aa'll niver understand bloody lasses,' and cycled off. Mary and I were finished, at least, I never went back to see her, although we did see each other a few times out and about.

The summer holidays ended and I returned to school, sitting next to Tom again for my last year. Our Form teacher was Mr Barron, a tall powerfully built man with a shiny baldhead and stern expression. He brooked no cheek and we gave him non for fear of him bringing the edge of his two-foot ruler crashing edge first down on our knuckles. I was not inspired and was not what you would call a regular attendee although I did manage to keep up with the rest of the class and often helped Tom with maths problems.

The last highlight of the year was tettie picking, this time Tom and I got onto Home Farm where we enjoyed an Indian summer working hard in the fields and chasing lasses in the barns at lunchtime.

Christmas Day was the quietest we had ever had; Betty was in Eton married to Peter, Jim married to Mary and back in the army, Pat was away, and Eric was on duty in the army, leaving Mam, Uncle Alec, George, Viv, Dennis and me. Dad had been on call for the pit and had disappeared to sort some problem or the other out at Coneygarth drift mine early in the morning.

As far as Christmas presents went, we were quite lucky that year. There was the normal selection of games and books as well as a clockwork train for Dennis and we had Christmas dinner to look forward too, a large Turkey from the Farm north of Coneygarth. The turkey was in exchange for timber, coal or some other commodity from the NCB stores.

Everything was going well, the table was set and Mam was just starting to mash the potatoes when George and I started arguing over a book I was reading.

'Ye've had plenty of time te read that man, give it te me noo,' George said grabbing the book and trying to pull it from my grip.

I shouted, 'Sod off,' and pulled back.

'Gis the book, or Aa'll bloody weel dad ye,' warned George.

'No man, am not finished it yet, ye can hev it later.'

Not satisfied George gave a mighty pull, ripping the hardback cover from the book, which he threw it to one side in disgust.

Furious, I shouted, 'Ye bloody stupid, big bull, look what ye've done man!'

Mam who was putting the food onto the table yelled, 'Ye two shut up and come in here and get yor dinner noo?'

Viv and Dennis were already at the table and Uncle Alex was levering himself from the cottage chair in front of the fire to join them.

George said, 'Divvint call me a bull ye twat ye,' and punched me hard on the arm. I reacted instantly and swatted him across the side of the head with the book knocking him off the arm of the settee where he had been perched. George leapt up and punched me square in the mouth and I tasted my own blood.

All hell broke loose; like a scene from a saloon bar brawl in a Wild West movie, we fought each other around and around the sitting room. Over the settee, crashing into chairs, rolling on the floor we fought; luckily, for me, George was not putting his full power behind his punches but they still stung.

The rest of the family had started to eat while Mam kept up her threats that if we did not join them immediately there would be hell to play. I threw a wild swinging right-hand punch that caught George on the nose bringing tears to his eyes. This was too much for him, the fun was over; pinning me to the floor he raised himself up and swung his right hand high in the air, readying himself to bring it crashing down on my unprotected face.

I looked up in horror at his rage-contorted face and waited for the blow to land but he suddenly disappeared to the left as the head of a broom smacked into the side of his head! Mam had had enough; picking up the broom from the scullery she had stormed into the sitting room, and swung at the first one of us she saw, luckily, for me it was George!

232

'Noo get up te the bloody table or Aa'll swing for the pair of ye,' she warned.

Rubbing the various bruises we had just collected, we obeyed and joined the others at the table. Half way through the silent meal that followed, the kitchen window began to shake, slowly and quietly at first before it gradually picked up speed and volume until it rattled violently and loudly for a minute or more. It did not interrupt our meal we had all heard it before. Dad had said that it was trams in the mine underneath the house. A story we accepted!

It was not until much later that I realised that was impossible and that along with many other strange goings on in the house, that we must have been haunted! After all, the house had at one time been the Pit Doctor's surgery, and several men had died in the back room currently occupied by Uncle Alec - no wonder it always felt cold in there!

The first term of 1960 started a new decade and marked my last term at school. Having determined that I was not going to follow my brothers and work down the pit, I had thought about other jobs in Ashington but there was not much choice outside of the NCB! I decided that I would try to get a vehicle mechanic's apprenticeship at one of the two big garages in Ashington, Gibson's in Highmarket or the Ford Garage near Stakeford Bridge. Knowing my dad knew the manager at Gibson's, I decided to ask him for his help and advice.

Several weeks before the end of term Dad was alone in the sitting room having a fag after dinner so I sat down on the sofa and said, 'Dad, am gannin to Gibson's to ask for an apprenticeship, dee ye think Aa'll get one?'

'What apprenticeship?'

'A motor mechanic, Aa've been told that they normally tek one on every year and thought ye might speak te the manager like.'

Dad sat forward and said, 'Aa divvint think ye'll have any luck there, ye'd be better off gannin te the NCB and getting one there.'

I thought about it for a moment before saying, 'Am gannin te try the garages forst and if Aa divvint get one Aa'll try the NCB but Aa divvint think they tek on motor mechanics.'

'Look, apprentices' wages are nowt,' he said, 'ye'd be better off working in the pit lad, so divvint bother with the garages.'

Having expected his help, I was bitterly disappointed but I was not going to give up and repeated, 'Aye but Aa'll try the garages forst!'

A little angrily he asked, 'Which garages are ye ganging te?'

'Gibson's and the Ford Garage and Aa might try H and H Motorbikes.'

Dad lit another cigarette and opened the Evening Chronicle signalling the end of the conversation!

About ten days, later, on a grey Saturday morning, after drinking a cup of tea and eating some toast, I washed at the scullery sink before putting on the suit Mam had bought on tick for me for Betty's wedding to Peter. Making sure my tie

233

was on straight and my shoes shiny I walked nervously to Highmarket and Gibson's Garage looking for a job.

Self-consciously, I walked into the large workshop, tucked away behind the car showroom and petrol pumps and found the place a hive of activity. I stopped to get my bearings when a man wearing a brown dustcoat came over.

Staring at me in a not to friendly manner, he asked, 'What can I dee for you, lad?'

Clearing a large frog from my throat, I answered, 'Aa've come te see if yor taking on any apprentices this year?'

The man smiled and said, 'We might be but ye'll hev te gan inte the office and speak te the Gaffer, he'll put ye right.'

He led me over to the office and once inside he said to the man behind a large desk, 'Lad here's looking for an apprenticeship.'

The man behind the desk looked at me and said, 'Right ye better sit doon then lad and we'll hev a chat.'

I sat on a chair in the corner as he fired questions at me about school and hobbies and all seemed to be going well until he suddenly went quiet and looked intently at me before saying, 'Yor not Geordie Carr's lad are ye son?'

'Aye I am sir,' I answered wondering if my dad had put in a good word for me after all.

'Aye whey I'm sorry lad but we've got no vacancies at the moment.' That was the end of it; it had seemed to be going so well!

On the way out I spoke to the Foreman and he expressed surprise that I had not been taken on! Disappointed, I caught the bus down to the far end of town where a similar sequence of events happened at the Ford garage, everything was going well until I gave my name, and then they just wanted rid of me!

Not wanting to give up I walked back into town and to H and H Motorcycles arriving just after eleven o'clock, walking around to the back of the building where I met one of my Brother George's mates, Dixie.

'How Syd lad what ye up te?'

'Looking for a job,' I answered hoping that he might give me some advice.

'The boss is upstairs, I'll show ye the way,' he said and led me through the small motorcycle repair shop.

At the top of the stairs, he said, 'Yore Owld Fella was here last week, he's not gannin back te a bike is he?'

'Not as far as I knaa,' I answered, and then the penny dropped.

Thanking Dixie, I leaned into the bosses office and said to him as he looked up, 'I was coming te ask for a job mister but being Geordie Carr's son Aa don't suppose there's much chance of that?' and turned and walked away without waiting for an answer.

I walked back home thinking of how Dad had ensured that all of his sons had ended up working underground in order for each of us to fetch a few more quid home than we would as apprentices and I felt angry, very angry, realising that

I had always been destined to work in the pits!

Part 3

Working Lad

21

Screens to Office

Just after my fifteenth birthday in the spring of 1960, having left school with no qualifications and with self-obsessed parents whose chief concern for their offspring was that they bring in as much money as possible; it was inevitable that I began training with the NCB. I hoped that unlike my brothers, I would gain an apprenticeship; unfortunately, like them, the odds were unfairly stacked against me in the form of my Father!

It was a bright, fresh spring morning when with very mixed emotions I walked the 400 yards to the NCB Training Centre housed in the wooden huts at the end of the Eleventh Row. I joined about twenty-five other lads awaiting induction, some of whom I knew from school and a few others I'd seen or met around town but there were others whom I'd not seen before.

All lads joining the NCB underwent eight weeks training and assessment; rather like military training but without the bull, although the instructors and teachers did impose discipline as tough as any Drill Sergeant could! The training consisted of two or three days a week underground, where subjects such as; how the pits worked, safe working practices, winch-operations, working with ponies and load handling were taught.

The other two days of the week, we spent at the mining college and First-Aid Training Centre. First-Aid training was a requirement for everyone working in the mines and we were required to pass a St Johns Ambulance test.

The first time we went underground, I like the others felt a mix of excitement and trepidation as we donned the issue navy blue overalls, pit helmets, thick socks and steel toe-capped, hobnailed boots. We collected miners lamps with their heavy, rechargeable batteries that we strapped around our waists with thick belts made from old conveyor belts and headed for 'the Cage' at the pithead. The Cage was the fast lift to the underground levels.

Issued with a little wooden tally, we were crammed about a dozen at a time into the Cage, all having to stoop in five foot three of headroom and all facing forward; rather like sardines in a tin. The cage operator then pressed a metal, electric-bell clapper, signalling the winch operator to release the winch. I felt the floor of the cage drop and my stomach tried to escape through my mouth as we hurtled downward for what seemed forever but after several seconds, we felt the cage slow before coming to a jerky halt at the pit bottom. It had been an exhilarating ride but one that I would soon become bored with.

Stepping out of the cage, we entered a world of never ending tunnels, some filled with chaotic noise and machinery and others quiet and foreboding. We were 'doon the pit'.

It was during training that I found out just how well I sang! We were underground and having spent the morning working with winches and tubs, our group of twelve were crammed into the 'Bait Cabin', a small, wood-lined space off the main working area. This was where we sat and ate our bait (packed lunches); it was about ten foot long by about four foot wide with wooden benches running down both sides

After devouring our various sandwiches and snacks, we talked about lasses, rock and roll, and motorbikes. A couple of the lads were talented singers and often started a singsong of the latest hits. Sitting next to me, a good-looking lad called Eric began singing the Everly Brother's latest hit.

'Don't want your love, anymore.
Don't want your kisses, that's for sure.'

His voice filled the little cabin and Howard, another good singer, joined him:

'I die each time, I hear this sound
Here he comes, that's Kathy's clown.'

They harmonised well and carried away with the moment, I along with a few others joined in the second chorus:
'Don't want your love, anymore.
Don't want your kisses, that's for sure.'

As we sang on, one by one the other lads stopped singing and instead, stared at me in disbelief.

I sang on with gusto before Eric eventually gave up and turning to me said, 'For fuck's sake Syd gan back to drawing cos ye canna fucking sing man, ye soond like a cat that's just had its knackers crushed,'

I stopped singing, as the rest of the lads began laughing and cheering. I couldn't understand it! I thought I sounded great!

A couple of days after starting work; I had broached the thorny subject of pocket money with Mam, who as normal was sitting with a glass of sherry and a woodbine at the kitchen table.

'Hoo much pocket money am Aa getting Mam?

'Ten bob,' replied Mam, as she sipped her sherry.

'TEN BOB!' I exploded, 'I got more than that delivering bloody groceries man.'

'Aye did you noo, that's bloody funny cos ye towld me ye only got five shillings!'

'Aye whey I knew ye would tek more if I towld ye hoo much I got man, and ten bob's not enough.'

'It's gannin te hev te be enough cos that's all yor getting but ye can open a savings account and hev the pit put a pund a week inte it.'

After a moment's thought, I said, 'That's okay becos me and Tom want te save up te get motorbikes but I expect to get a pund pocket money when am sixteen like wor Geordie and the rest of them.'

After a long drag, she blew foul smoke across the table and said, 'Aye as like as not,' and took another sip of the sherry signalling an end to the discussion.

That weekend the two of us walked to Station Road to the Trustees Saving Bank and opened an account; Mam had to open the account, as I was under twenty-one!

Outside of work, I continued to meet Tom twice or thrice a week to go downtown chasing girls, meeting with mixed success. I told him what it was like underground and what we did at the mining college; he took it all in, as he was due to start work there after the summer break when he hoped to get an apprenticeship as a fitter.

He asked me how tough the tests were and I explained that I had found them straightforward, most being basic. At school, when I was there, I had generally been able to assimilate studies a little faster than Tom and had often helped him with maths so he worried that if I struggled, he would not be able to cope.

On the Monday after opening my bank account, Tom and I were walking to the Regal to see the latest horror movie, Vincent Price in 'House on the Haunted Hill'. I told him about my savings account and he said he would have his Dad open one for him so we could both save to buy motorbikes when we were seventeen.

Sitting in the cinema with about two dozen others waiting for the film to begin, Tom and I chatted excitedly about BSAs, Royal Enfields, Triumphs, and Nortons and imagined ourselves astride our bikes with full panniers roaring off to tour Britain just like the bunch of lads I had seen camping at Ingelton a few years earlier. We decided on BSA C15s.

We stopped chatting when the film started, and soon became gripped by the horror of ghosts and skeletons scaring guests in Vincent Price's Guest House. It was during a scene where a skeleton advanced down a corridor toward a terrified woman that we all got a shock and a laugh.

As the skeleton disappeared off the right of the screen, a full size, imitation skeleton suddenly swung out from behind the curtain and began to fly across the auditorium! Unprepared for it, there were a few screams of horror and delight from the few lasses in the stalls and howls of laughter from the lads. The skeleton finished its journey to the back of the stalls and the film continued.

Along with most of the lads of our age in Ashington, we went back on Friday night, and we all waited for the skeleton! There was a huge cheer when it appeared and swung out over the stalls where it met a barrage of missiles intense enough to have brought down the whole of the German Luftwaffe. The lads had filled their pockets with marbles, stones, empty tin cans, the odd catapult, and even one or two air pistols, all of which were unleashed on the unsuspecting skeleton!

Despite the best efforts of the usherettes to try to stop the barrage, the skeleton soon began to disintegrate as more and more marbles, tins and other missiles slammed into it. Eventually, amid noisy cheering and stamping of feet that took the poor usherettes five minutes to quell, a battered, bodiless skull swung to a halt at the back of the auditorium!

Tom and I spent most Saturday afternoons in and around 'Dawson's', a newly opened and much-Americanised coffee bar. We would spend a couple of hours trying to make a bottle of Coca-Cola last as long as possible while listening to the jukebox and eyeing up the lasses; many of them wearing scarves to cover the rollers in their hair in preparation for the Saturday night dance.

Wearing denim jeans with the bottoms turned up the regulation four-inches, shirt collar up with the points folded back and an imitation suede jerkin (I could not afford the leather jerkin worn by most lads) and with my hair slicked back, I hunched over my Coke listening to Roy Orbison singing, 'Only the Lonely' and tried to look moody. Not an easy task when you are a baby-faced, fifteen-year-old.

I often saw the same group of attractive girls, all of whom were just over five-foot tall and exchanged looks with them. One, in particular, was very pretty and we always gave each other long looks but I did not have the courage to ask her out. She reminded me a little of the blue-eyed girl I still dreamed off, but she was more Audrey Hepburn while Blue-eyes was more Elizabeth Taylor. I would continue to see these girls around town but it would be some time before I asked one of them out.

I had been going out with a girl called Jean from 'Chinky Toon' a council estate at the far end of Ashington and had indulged in some really heavy smooching in the cinema, during which I had first touched the magic three inches of bare flesh at the top of her stockings. I was hoping to take it to the next stage but during a mid-morning break at Mining College, while myself and the other trainees were admiring a Triumph Tiger Cub, a tall blonde haired seventeen-year-old lad from the Hirst said, 'I see yor gannin oot with Jean Syd.'

Surprised at the question, I hesitated before answering, 'Aye, for aboot a fortnight like, why?'

'Aa've had her doon at Sheepwash, she's a right lovely shag, hev you had her yet?'

Shocked and embarrassed, I had naively thought that I was going to be her first but that didn't bother me, what did was this big lummox boasting about his exploits with her, which he continued to do in graphic detail.

'Nur I hevn't, not yet,' I replied sheepishly.

'Whey man gan on and get in there, she loves it,' he smirked.

The bell sounded before I could respond and I went back into the technical drawing lesson, my mind in turmoil. He had ruined any romantic thoughts I had of Jean, not that I was in love with her but I had enjoyed being with her. Worse, I was so shallow that I did not want to go out with a girl who I thought had a 'reputation' and much to my shame I stopped going out with her the following night.

The interviews for apprenticeships took place near the end of training and in preparation for mine I put on a shirt and tie, pressed my trousers, polished my shoes and pulled on my best - actually my only jacket, an old-fashioned checked one; I looked like a nerd! When I arrived, at the training centre, all the lads were wearing smart Italian or the Ashington version of Italian style suits, only one other lad was dressed similar to me, wearing a tweed jacket and he **was** a nerd!

We stood outside, nervously waiting to be called in, some smoking, some chewing finger nails but one or two supremely confident that they would be successful. During training, we had been put into syndicates based upon tests and I was number 3 of the top syndicate so was expected to get an apprenticeship without any problems.

The night before, I had been most surprised when Dad sat down next to me for a chat!

'What apprenticeship are you applying for?'

Startled by his unexpected interest I said, 'I had thought aboot underground surveyor but am not sure they are taking any on this year so; electrician,' I answered.

He shot back, 'Aa thought ye wanted te be a motor mechanic?'

'Aye Aa did before Aa went te the NCB.'

He thought for a second then said, 'Put in for motor mechanic and ye'll work in the garages at the top of the road and besides ye'll always hev a trade if ye leave the pits.'

The following morning sitting nervously in front of the three-man panel, I was surprised when the man in the centre said, 'I see you've applied for a motor mechanics' apprenticeship?'

I had not changed my application from electrician so I was a wee bit perplexed as to how it had been changed and spluttered, 'Yes but electrician as a second choice.'

The man looked at me sympathetically and said, 'Whey we're not taking on any motor mechanics this year as we don't require any for a few years yet.'

Shocked I asked, 'What aboot electricians?'

241

'Aye we're taking on lads for electricians but as it's yor second choice the lads who had it as their first choice will get places first and they've all been allocated.'

Later that night, talking to George about the interview he mocked, 'What did ye expect, none of us got frigging apprenticeships cos of them rotten bastards wanting us doon the pit just so they can get a few quid more man!'

I felt betrayed but not surprised that Mam and Dad could be so short sighted. George, who was nursing a broken collarbone from an accident in the mine continued, 'Aa've had enough of the twats, am joining up as soon as am owld enough.'

After induction training, the lads who had been successful at interview began their apprenticeships while the rest of us waited to be allocated jobs on the surface where we would work until we were sixteen and old enough to work underground.

The 'Screens' was the workplace we all dreaded! Older lads who had worked there had told us of this dreadful place, they made it sound like Hell on Earth. It was where men and lads picked stone from amongst coal carried along on steel conveyor belts. Women had once done the job, but those considered not mentally aware enough to work underground as well as some with minor physical handicaps and a few young lads not old enough to work underground now did the work.

The large building was steel framed with single-skin brick walls, standing on steel stilts spanning four railway lines that were constantly full of wagons cueing to be filled with coal or stone. Inside coal poured onto the four steel conveyor belts that clanked constantly along to the hoppers where the stone-free coal fell into the waiting wagons below. Men and lads stood alongside the conveyors picking pieces of stone from amongst the coal, dropping them into metal chutes next to them.

The chutes had heavy steel grids on the top, which meant larger stones, of which there were many, had to be broken up with sledgehammers before they would fall through. It was hard relentless work, hard on the back and harder on the hands and fingers, hot in summer and freezing in winter.

On a hot early summer's morning, Jack Moody and I climbed the steep steps to the screens, both of us consigned to work there along with four other lads. If it had not been for Jack's irrepressible good humour, I would have been miserable but as it was, we laughed and joked as we climbed the steps.

I took on an imagined hump and limp and shouted after him, 'Wait for me, Esmeralda.'

Jack stopped at the top of the stairs, turned and shouted in a mock female voice, 'Stay away you beast, I must enter and join my friends.'

He disappeared through the door and I ran up bumping into his back as he stood taking in the scene. The noise was deafening as the four steel-conveyors clanked away, the strong smell of industrial disinfectant from the toilets by the door added to our sensory overload as we slowly walked along the gangway that ran over the top of the belts.

A man waved us down to one of the belts and handed us a sledgehammer each, pointing to the chutes where we were to work and then left us to work. I walked to my allocated spot, pulling on a pair of industrial gloves before I started.

A huge bald headed man who appeared to have no neck, turned to look at me showing a tiny face hidden in his huge head. He laughed at me, displaying a few stumps of teeth; terrified I stood transfixed as he made a masturbating motion with his massive hands and shouted, 'Fugg off, Fugg off!' I appeared to be in bedlam!

Turning quickly, I started to pick stones from the metal conveyor, throwing them down the chute; smashing the larger ones with the sledgehammer. As I worked away, I became aware of singing and turned around to see Jack, who was working behind me singing at the top of his voice,

> 'Hooh! aah! hooh! aah!
> Hooh! aah! Hooh! aah!
> I hear something saying
> Hooh! ah! Hooh! ah!
> Hooh! ah! Hooh! ah!'

As he gathered his breath for the next line, he turned and grinned at me and we both shouted:

> 'Well don't you know
> That's the sound of the men
> Working on the chain ga-ang
> That's the sound of the men
> Working on the chain gang'

More of the lads and some of the men had joined in and we were all screaming;

> 'All day long they're singing
> Hooh! aah! Hooh aah!'

Even big Mr Baldy next to me was smiling and banging his hammer on his chute in time to ours.

We sang on until the charge hand came in and blew his whistle to stop us and shouted, 'The singing's aalreet but stop the hammering and get on we picking fucking stones.' We went back to singing and picking – thank god for Jack!

A week later just before the end of the shift, the charge-hand called me outside and said, 'Reet lad, yor finished on the screens; ye have to report to the 'Sickness, Accident and Compensation Office' - to Mr Craig; ye'll be starting work there the morn.'

I was surprised and elated at being able to get away from the screens. It was normal for one of the colliery offices to call for a lad to act as the office-boy and having the best academic results of the non-apprenticed lads, I found myself lucky enough to be escaping the screens and remembered that George had worked in the offices a couple of years earlier.

Walking back along the upper gangway of the screens, I looked at the men and boys toiling away and headed down the flight of stairs to where Jack was singing loudly as he worked.

'JACK,' I shouted over the noise of the conveyors and his singing.

He turned smiling and shouted back, 'Aye what's the matter?'

'Am off te work in the offices noo,' I shouted.

'Bloody lucky bugger,' he shouted back his smile dropping, allowing his face to register his real feelings for the dreadful place.

I turned and started to climb the stairs back to the gangway as Jack shouted after me, 'Quasimodo, come back, divvint leave me here.'

Turning, I hunched my shoulder and shouted back, 'Goodbye Esmeralda, I must away,' and hobbled with a mock limp to the door while Jack shouted after me.

It was the last time I saw Jack; a week later, he joined the army as a boy soldier and left the screens and Pit Rows behind him for good.

A few minutes later, I was standing nervously outside the colliery offices waiting for Mr Craig who I had just asked to see. A distinguished looking man with greying hair and glasses opened the door.

'You must be Sydney Carr then?'

'Aye Mr Craig, I was told te report to you ready to start work here tomorrow.'

He looked me up and down before smiling and saying, 'Right be here at eight thirty sharp and I hope you've a suit or jacket and tie as you cannot work here in your work clothes lad.'

Wearing the charcoal coloured suit that George had worn when he worked in the colliery offices, at exactly eight thirty the following morning, I reported to Mr Craig. The office had two large desks pushed together in the middle and another desk in one corner next to a number of filing cabinets where the typist worked. In the corner opposite the typist, there was a large shelf below a small window with a hatch; this was where I was to work.

An older man, who was working opposite Mr Craig, introduced himself as Joe; he was portly, grey-haired and had a grey complexion. Suffering from piles, he sat on a rubber cushion that he tried continually but unsuccessfully to make himself comfortable upon!

My job was to sit at the desk in front of the hatch where men would turn up to hand in sick notes that I took from them, entering details from the notes in a large register before passing them on for further processing. I also dealt with Accident Reports, the details from these I had to enter into another register before handing them onto Joe for processing. The most important day was Friday when I issued 'sick-pay' cheques to entitled miners. It was not a very demanding job but as time passed I was given more responsibility and worked there until I was sixteen and old enough to go underground.

Tom finished school at the end of the summer term and signed on at the NCB ready to begin his training after the summer holiday. Mam and Dad took Viv and Dennis camping again but I decided I would rather not spend another holiday with them and stayed at home with Pat, George, and Uncle Alex.

Tom and I spent the time hanging around Ashington and days out on our bikes talking about girls, motorbikes, and holidays. Near the end of the holidays, I was dating a tall, bonny-girl called Doreen while Tom was trying to date her friend. On the last Saturday afternoon of the holidays we had been to Crisps Coffee Bar with the girls and were walking them back to Doreen's house behind the Miner's Institute off Milburn Road when she said she wanted to go into the record shop to hear a new recording of Elvis singing 'It's Now or Never'.

Doreen and her friend went into one of the record booths to listen to the song while Tom and I talked about the BSA C15. Listening to Tom, I looked over his shoulder and saw the little blue-eyed girl and a friend come out of a booth and walk toward the counter. Talking excitedly about the record they had just been listening too; she looked over and our eyes met.

She was wearing her dark hair brushed back, showing her lovely face and beautiful eyes, I was lost.

She stopped and we stared at each other and I again had butterflies as a stupid grin spread over my face while she smiled sweetly back. It seemed an age, during which I could hear Tom talking but I was not taking in what he was saying; I was in the same room as Blue-Eyes and she was walking toward me. Feeling my heart beating madly, as Elvis sang, 'It's now or never,' I pushed myself off the counter I was leaning on and started forward to speak to her.

A hand grabbed my arm stopping me in my tracks; it was Doreen, she put her arm through mine and said, 'It's smashing but I've got the original at home so Am not going to buy it,' and pulled me toward the door.

Unsure what to do, I almost pulled away from her and stopped to turn to speak but found myself speechless, I did not want to hurt Doreen, she was a lovely girl and did not deserve me messing her about.

'What?' she said and I hesitated, turning to look at Blue-Eyes who had lost her smile and was walking back to her friend.

Devastated but totally unable to act, I instead, said to Doreen, 'Nothing, haway let's go.' Being so close to Blue-Eyes without talking to her was unbearable and I almost frog-marched Doreen the couple of hundred yards to her house, quickly kissed her saying, 'Aa'll see ye tonight,' and walked off quickly with a bewildered Tom hurrying to keep up with me.

'What's the hurry Syd?' he asked, striding along to keep up with my brisk pace.

'Aa just want to see somebody at the record shop but we'll hev to hurry man.'

She was not there and I swore as I headed back into town to look for her.

'Who are ye looking for man?' Tom asked for the third time.

I stopped and said, 'Did ye see the little lass in there earlier?'

'Aye she was a smasher,' he answered, 'I thought ye were gannin te taalk te her there for a minute like.'

'Aye, whey I've fancied her for ages but never had the chance te talk te her so I want te noo man.'

'What aboot Doreen?'

'I just want te talk te the lass man,' I lied not very convincingly to which he shook his head and laughed.

'Aye, Aa bet ye dee.'

We turned right at the Grand Hotel and headed toward the Hirst while I looked frantically for the two girls, my heart still pounding, and my mouth dry with excitement.

Tom said, 'Look,' and pointed to a bus that had just pulled out of the Bus Station, turning toward the Hirst. The two girls were on board, Blue-Eyes on the inside seat; I ran after it waving frantically but she did not see me and I stopped my chase feeling absolutely gutted, would I never get to talk to her?

After the holidays, Tom completed his training at the NCB and as predicted, became an apprentice fitter while I continued in the colliery offices. I took on more responsibilities and quite enjoyed the routine of the work but missed the company of younger people.

At ten thirty on a Friday morning in late September, I was sitting at the hatch issuing sickness pay-slips to sick and injured miners. I was also enjoying a cup of tea after the early morning rush when there was an aggressive rap at the hatch window. Placing my cup carefully on the sloping desk, I opened the window and let in the usual blast of air that had whistled down the outer corridor, only this time, the stench of stale beer and BO accompanied the air!

I said to the unkempt and slightly chubby man in his late thirties glowering at me through the hatch, 'Good morning, name please.'

He pushed his outstretched hand through the hatch and growled, 'Armstrong.'

Opening the large cardboard folder to look for his pay slip and hoping to deal with him quickly, I found the only slip for 'Armstrong', and asked, 'Tally number please?' - I required the number to verify the slip was his.

'512,' he growled back.

The tally number on the slip was different, 'Just a minute please, 'I said and searched the A's again but could not find his so began a quick search through the folder. Joe who placed the slips in the folder had occasionally put them in the wrong place.

Mr Armstrong was becoming very agitated and spat, 'Come on ye bloody little waster ye, give me frigging pay slip noo.'

I searched again, before looking up into his angry face, a face that had turned very red; and said, 'Am sorry Mr Armstrong but I divvint seem to hev one for ye.'

'What!' he exploded, 'listen, give me fucking cheque noo or Aa'll drag ye from yor fucking perch and put me boot up yor useless arse.'

The stench of beer and bad breath coming through the hatch and Mr Armstrong's abuse was too much, I spat back, 'Just had yor frigging horses ye nasty git ye and Aa'll check with Joe.'

Big mistake; Armstrong's hand shot forward and grabbing me by my collar and tie; he dragged me toward the small hatch shouting obscenities as he tightened his grip making it hard for me to breath.

Mr Craig who had been listening to the increasing volatile exchange came up behind me and grabbed my shoulders to stop me disappearing through the hatch, and squawked, 'Now then, we'll have none of this now.'

However, Mr Armstrong was having a lot of this, he was determined to pull me through the hatch and cause me grievous bodily harm. I managed to brace myself on the desk to stop myself from going through the hatch, which luckily for me, was not large enough for him to get his other arm in but he was slowly choking me!

Releasing my right hand, I grasped the window and swung it against his arm but that only made him madder and he raged on. Beginning to fear for my life and gasping for air with my vision starting to blur, I saw my plastic biro on the desk and grabbing it like a knife, I frantically stabbed at Armstrong's forearm until it disintegrated in bloody splinters.

The drastic action achieved my aim, he let go yelling, 'Ye fucking little waster ye, ye've bloody stabbed me, noo I'm gannin te fucking kill ye!'

Slamming the window shut, I pushed the bolt home before falling back off my chair, sucking in huge gulps of air as Mr Craig grabbed me to stop me from falling onto the floor.

Armstrong, now completely out of control was leaping up and down outside the hatch and shouted, 'Right! Bloody-fucking-right! Am coming roond there and Aa'll swing for the fucking lot of ye useless twats,' and turning he ran back down the corridor.

247

The typist was on the telephone calmly explaining the situation to some-one; Joe was doing a nervous jig and Mr Craig spluttered, 'My God, Syd you've got blood all over the payslips.'

I was aghast, did he not realise that a madman was on his way to butcher us all!

Shouting, 'Niver mind blood on the pay slips man, we'll all be covered in blood if that loony gets in here,' I rushed to the large , main door, slamming it shut and turning the key to lock it before I slid home a large bolt to make doubly sure it was secure.

I was just in time as Armstrong crashed into the door from the other side and after trying the handle, he began to batter the door with fists and boots.

'Open this fucking door,' he screamed repeatedly.

As strong as the door was it began to look as though the madman would batter it down so I looked at Mr Craig and asked, 'What are we going to do?' the battering of the door increasing as I spoke.

The typist said, 'I've told security but they said they couldn't deal with him and they are going to phone the police.'

'The Police?' old Joe muttered dancing even more, 'the Police? My-o-my.'

Mr Craig looked lost and I thought, 'I have to get Armstrong away from that door and the office.'

Thinking on my feet, I said, 'Okay, Aa'll lure him away from the door un-til the police come,' and jumping onto the big desk by the window, I undid the latch and heaved the big sash window up a couple of feet. Scrambling out through the window, I ran round the corner to where Mr Armstrong was hurling himself against the door - still shouting abuse as he did so, spit, and snot streaming down his face.

'How!' I shouted at him but he was lost in his rage and ignored me. 'How ye bloody lunatic,' I shouted as loud as I could; this time, he heard me.

He stopped and looked at me through drunken rage-contorted eyes for a few seconds before he realised I was no longer inside the office, 'Right ye little twat ye, Aa've got ye noo,' and he propelled himself toward me.

This was what I had been hoping for; believing that I could easily outrun this outraged bull of a man, and the chase began!

Expecting his rush, I was already standing in a racing start and sprinted off with Armstrong in pursuit. He was wasting a lot of energy screaming and waving his arms and his potbelly was not conducive to sprinting or cross-country running, so I easily kept myself ten or so yards in front of him, taunting him as I ran off around the square in front of the offices.

'Come on ye fat knacker ye, ye'll hev te dee better than that,' I yelled at him, managing to keep his rage and efforts stoked.

My plan was to keep him busy until the police arrived but I was not sure how long that would take so I ran off past the pay-offices and into the Eleventh

Row with Armstrong running after me. I don't know what the men queuing at the pay office thought of us running past, but it was not of sufficient interest for them to leave their places in the queue!

I ran down the Eleventh Row, slowing to allow Armstrong to keep up as he was beginning to look rather blown, I also threw back a couple more taunts to ensure he kept up the chase. At the end of the Row, with a very bedraggled Armstrong puffing behind, I turned back into the road that led back to the offices and as I approached the office square, I saw a small crowd had gathered outside next to a blue and white Morris Minor Police car where a large Bobby was talking to Mr Craig.

'Thank God,' I thought, although I had enjoyed the chase, enough was enough and I wanted rid of the lunatic behind me.

I jogged up to Mr Craig and the Policeman who both looked past me at the puffing and sweating Armstrong who no longer had the breath to shout, that was until he reached us, then he started again.

Leaning forward with his hands on his knees and between large gulps of air, he yelled at the Policeman, 'That little bastard stabbed me,' and pushing his bloody forearm forward he continued, 'Gan on arrest the little twat or Aa'll swing for him.'

The Policeman pulled a pair of handcuffs from under his tunic and I thought, 'Bloody charming now am gannin te get locked up!'

He walked behind Armstrong and pulling the drunkard's arms behind him, deftly handcuffed him.

This did not go down very well with Armstrong who began ranting at the Policeman, accusing him of all sorts of brutality and miscarriages of justice but the Bobby was having none of it and forced him into the back of the tiny police car before coming back to where I was standing with Mr Craig.

'Okay,' he said 'Aa'll be wanting statements from ye both if yor to press charges?'

'Well it was young Syd here that he assaulted but I see that ye'll want a one from me as well,' said Mr Craig.

I asked the Policeman, 'Does that mean it's up to me te press charges like?'

The Policeman looked down at me and said, 'Aye, that's right son.'

'Whey, in that case, I divvint want te press charges,' I said.

The three of us then had a long drawn out conversation on what had happened and what we should do about it.

Finally, the Policeman said, 'Aa'll tek him te the Station and give him a warning and send him on his way but as he's a bit of a regular with us am sure we'll keep in touch with him!' He walked back to his car but as he was doing so, Joe came shuffling over and stopped the Policeman to hand him a long pay slip.

'Can ye give him this, it's what he came for before he lost his temper, said Joe.

249

Taking the payslip, the Policeman gave Joe a quizzical look but turned and climbed into the car.

Armstrong shouted through the door of the police car, 'Watch yor back lad cos Aa'll hev me lads fettle ye!'

Mr Craig, whose jaw had dropped when he saw Joe hand over the pay slip asked, 'Where was the pay slip, no, don't tell me it was in the folder all the time?'

'No, it was with a couple of others that I must have forgotten to put in,' Joe said blushing with embarrassment as we walked back to the office.

I was not bothered about Joe's mistake, I was far more concerned with how many sons Mr Armstrong had, and how big and hard they might be! I'm still waiting to find out!

True to his word, a few weeks later George caught the bus to Newcastle where he 'Joined Up,' leaving a few days later to become the third 'Craftsmen Carr, following Jim and Eric into the Royal Electrical and Mechanical Engineers (REME).

Not long after George joined up, Tom and I went to the Welfare Dance for the first time. It was a revelation; just about every lad and lass in Ashington between the ages of fifteen and eighteen were there on Wednesday and Saturday nights, bopping and jiving, flirting and courting, fighting and feuding; it was the place to be.

It was brilliant, on Wednesday nights, we wore casual clothes, but on Saturdays, as was the norm, the lads wore suits to impress the lasses who would have spent all afternoon with their hair in curlers, ensuring they looked immaculate for the dance.

Mam had actually bought me a new dark-blue, pinstripe Italian suit on tick, and I wore it with regulation winkle pickers, a tie and a matching, false three-pointed handkerchief in the breast pocket; I felt the bee's knees. I must have looked ok as I had several girlfriends over the next few months, none of whom lasted long as my heart still yearned for Little Blue-Eyes.

One of the girls I took out was Jennifer Little; I had eventually realised that she had a crush on me and flattered, I took her to the cinema but it did not work out. When I kissed her, I felt as though I was kissing an old friend, which of course she was, but that was all it was for me and not wanting to lead her on, I did not ask her out again.

Just before my sixteenth birthday Mr Craig came over to my desk, 'Sydney, you're due to start work underground next week but I want to offer you a permanent position in this office with a view to you eventually taking over from Joe when he retires in a few years' time, now what do you think of that?

Surprised by this unexpected offer, I gulped nervously and looked around the office, my eyes stopping at Joe who was sitting half-grimacing and half-smiling on his rubber cushion.

I had a horrifying vision of myself, sitting there as a forlorn old man and quickly blurted, 'No thanks Mr Craig, I divvint think it's for me.' Over the next week, both Mr Craig and Joe tried to persuade me to stay but I was having none of it.

On the day of my sixteenth birthday, wearing an old pair of jeans, tee shirt, old battle dress jacket, pit boots, and helmet I went underground at Ashington Colliery to work on the winches with one of Eric's old school friends. That lasted a short week that he filled with tall tales of his exploits with lasses, adding enormously to my very limited knowledge of sex. At the end of the week, the Deputy told me that I had to catch the Monday Fore-shift bus to Coneygarth, the drift mine where my Dad was the Fore-Overman.

22

Coneygarth

Just before midnight on the following Sunday, after two hours sleep, I staggered downstairs to get ready to go to work; Dad was already up preparing his bait and filling his flask before driving off to the pit. Butch looked up from Dad's chair, thumped his tail against the arm a couple of times to say hello and settled back down. Dad never spoke to me that night or any of the other nights that we got ready to go to work; nor did he offer me a lift, leaving me to walk the few hundred yards to the pit baths to change into my pit clothes before catching the bus the mile or so to Coneygarth.

I had hoped to be given a job working with pit ponies, taking timber props and other material to the coal faces but was disappointed when at one o'clock a deputy took me to one side and said, 'Ah, young Carr, the fourth lad of Geordies te work here, Aa'll be taking you to the loader-end where ye'll be working.'

Mightily disappointed I followed him to the cave-like entrance to the Drift where a huge conveyor raced coal from the depths of the mine, spewing it into the waiting coal wagons above. We descended the concrete steps alongside the belt for a quarter of a mile to the bottom of the drift where another conveyor fed coal onto the main belt.

'This is the main trunk belt,' the Deputy shouted at me over the noise of the coal pouring through a metal chute and onto the main conveyor.

Following him through a wooden air control door, he led me along another wide, eleven-foot high tunnel with the trunk belt on the right and tram rails on the left, following it deeper into the mine. After a few hundred yards, I could see a light from someone's lamp in the distance and as we approached, I could hear the noise of another large conveyor feeding coal onto the trunk belt.

As we approached the junction, a man in his late fifties rose creakily from a wooden bench next to the huge metal electric switch box that controlled the conveyor.

'Aye then is this the lad that's got the Fore-shift?' he asked as we approached.

'Aye, this is Geordie's lad Syd, show him the ropes then, Am off in-bye,' the Deputy replied before he climbed warily over the trunk belt and disappeared down the other tunnel.

'Whey lad they've given ye a reet bloody miserable job here noo,' said the older man as he limped toward the switch box.

He pointed to a shovel and a couple of very large crowbars that were propped next to the box before saying, 'Use these to mek sure there are nee blockages on the loader end and shovel up the spillages te keep the place tidy noo.'

'Righto,' I replied, trying to sound positive, realising I was to spend eight hours on my own in the bowels of the earth watching coal pour from one belt onto another!

'Noo,' he said pointing to a large red button on the switch box, 'pay attention becos, this is the emergency stop button; bang this and all the belts in the pit stop which means every bugger stops work!'

He glared at me before warning, 'Whatever ye dee, pray ye divvint hev to use it as every bugger will be efter yor blood for stopping them working and yor owld fella will bloody lynch ye. Got that?'

I asked nervously, 'Aye, right, I've got it - but what if there *is* an emergency?'

He looked back at me half smiling and answered, 'It better be a bloody big emergency for ye te stop the frigging belts lad, noo hev ye got owt te read cos it's a bloody lang shift doon here on yor aan?'

Thinking of spending eight hours here on my own, I swallowed a lump that had just formed in my throat!

'Nur, I didn't bring owt, Aa didn't knaa I'd be deeing this man, and dee ye mean that I winnit see anybody else aall shift?

He reached into his bait bag, pulled out a battered Western paperback, and handed it to me before turning to leave.

'If ye see any bugger doon here they'll be skiving or it might just be 'Owld Harry'.'

Fearing the worst, I asked, 'Who's Owld Harry?'

'Owld Harry is the ghost of the last Fore-shift Operator, he disappeared, and has niver been seen again,' he chuckled and limped off toward the drift bottom leaving me to take in my surroundings and check round for any signs of 'Owld Harry'!

After mooching around for a few minutes, I sat down on the wooden bench wondering what sort of emergency there would have to be to stop the belts and prayed there would be none. The noise of the powerful electric motor running the feeder belt and the coal thundering over the chute hid all other sounds, including the creaking of girders and old timbers but did nothing to mask the misery of the job. I looked up and down the main tunnel and down the feeder tunnel the few yards that my lamp illuminated, wondering where they went too and who worked there.

This first shift was the worst; I thought it would never end; I was almost too scared to read at first, taking ages to relax enough to sit and open the book. When I eventually began to read, I looked up after almost every line to make sure the coal was flowing freely and that Owld Harry was not creeping up on me! I only had to free a couple of minor snags and clear away spillage three times during

254

the whole shift, for the rest of the time, I sat trying to read or wandered up and down a few paces trying to hurry time along.

Eventually, the sight of miners' pit lamps coming along the feeder belt as they finished their shifts and rode the conveyor belts out of the pit came as a huge relief, signalling as it did the end of my stint for the day. Just before they reached the loader end, the men jumped off the belt and made their way past it before jumping onto the trunk belt to continue their way out.

A little while later the day shift operator relieved me, another old man with a limp who grunted, 'Aye' and sat down on the bench where he pulled out a book and started to read ignoring me completely as he did so. I happily jumped on the belt and sped out of the pit, glad to be leaving the miserable spot where I had just wasted eight hours of my life.

The first week dragged on as I tried without much success, to settle into the routine of sleeping through the day and working through the early hours. I felt too tired to go out during the evening, which was unfortunate as I was courting a girl from Newbiggin called Ann who wanted to see me most nights. I only saw her twice during that first week but promised to make it up to her the following week when I would be working Day Shift.

Leaving the pit just after nine o'clock at the end of my shift on Friday morning, I was, therefore, bloody angry when the charge hand informed me that I would be staying on Fore-shift for another three weeks - until the regular operator returned to work!

I wanted to confront my dad and tell him what I thought but decided not to mention it, not wanting to give him the satisfaction of knowing that he had brassed me off. It was no surprise that in the early hours as we got ready to go to work, the atmosphere was decidedly icy. It also caused problems with Ann, who was unhappy at not seeing me as much as she wanted.

The Charge-hand told me that I would start Timber Leading, at the end of the three weeks so I had that to look forward too. Sixteen to nineteen-year-old lads worked at Timber-Leading, using ponies to pull trams or tubs filled with wooden props and other material to the coalfaces. You worked either on your own or with one other lad and were mainly unsupervised and left to get the work done.

At about three thirty in the morning on the Wednesday of the second week I was hunched up on the bench reading the 'Wooden Horse,' a thrilling paperback about POWs escaping from Nazi Germany during the war. I had stopped worrying about Owld Harry and had become accustomed to the loneliness of the shift. I also knew instantly from the change in noises when there was a blockage on the loader end, so I felt fairly, relaxed.

A sixth sense made me look up and I saw a light coming down the feeder tunnel toward me.

Wondering who could be riding the belt out at this time of the morning, I put my book down, and stood up stretching the stiffness from my limbs, watching the light move quickly toward me.

255

'I'll ask him where he's gannin,' I thought to myself as he approached the point where the miners normally jumped off the belt before the loader end; I was looking forward to a quick chat to relieve my boredom with whoever it was - except he didn't jump off!

One or two of the more daredevil lads said they always went over the loader ends but I had never seen anyone do it and was shocked to see whoever it was, ride straight over.

I was not greatly concerned until he hit the main belt and his helmet came off and began bouncing along behind him, flashing light, wildly around the tunnel as the trunk belt sped him away. I stood motionless for what seemed like ages but must have just been a couple of seconds, wondering what I had just seen, then realised there was something seriously wrong with the man on the belt.

Without thinking, I turned, banged my fist on the emergency stop button and then raced toward the dangling lamp in the now eerie silence, broken only by my thudding boots as I covered the fifty yards to the motionless man on the belt.

As I reached the man, the telephone at the loader end behind me began to ring impatiently and I knew it would be Dad up above in the offices wanting to know why the belt had stopped.

I shouted, 'How Jacky what the hell's up?'

My question went unanswered as I stopped running and looked at the man stretched out before me.

Suspended by cables hanging from the girders above; the conveyor was about chest high and I saw that the man was huge, he must have been well over six foot and overweight and very still.

The telephone continued to scream for attention as I tentatively shook his arm, whispering, 'How Jacky, Jacky,' but there was no reply and I knew with dread that he was dead. A shiver ran down my spine as I stood there in shocked disbelief until the noise of the telephone grabbed my attention again.

Running back to the jangling telephone, I snatched it off the hook, and was about to speak when the voice on the other end screamed, 'WHAT THE FUCKING HELL ARE YE DEEING DOON THERE? GET THAT FRIGGING BELT STARTED NOO, YE BLOODY SACKLESS TWAT YE.'

Taking a deep breath, I blurted, 'There's a deed body on the belt Faather.'

He screamed back, 'A DEED BODY! WHEY GET THE FUCKING THING OF THE BELT AND GET IT STARTED NOO, DE YE UNDERSTAND?'

Shouting back 'AYE,' I slammed the metal phone back onto its cradle, before jogging reluctantly back down to the body. It never crossed my mind to question my Dad's orders as I ran back to the dead man, wondering how I was going to get him off the conveyor.

Shivering with revulsion I grabbed his coat and heaved, expecting him to slide off the belt, I was shocked when he did not budge. Sixteen stone of dead weight was not going to be easy to shift. Grabbing his coat on the side farthest

256

away from me, I heaved and managed to move him almost onto his side but as soon as I tried to adjust my grip, he slid back.

Climbing onto the belt, I spent five nightmarish minutes, heaving, pulling, shoving, and tugging, until finally, swimming in sweat, with my back against a girder and using my feet, I pushed the dead man the last few inches off the belt. He fell the four-foot landing with a dull thud as I fell on my hands and knees panting for breath, looking down at his crumpled body lying in a heap, below me.

The telephone began to shout at me again, so I wearily jumped off the belt making sure I did not land on the corpse and hurried back to the telephone.

'WHEY, HEV YE GOT HIM OFF?' shouted Dad down the earpiece.

Panting heavily, I gasped, 'Yes, he's off.'

'Well start the fucking belt then,' and I heard him slam his handset down on its receiver.

Grasping the 'On' lever, I lifted it up until it clicked into position and the noise of machinery and coal flowing over the chute began again.

Swallowing a large lump that had formed in my throat, I walked slowly back to the dead man with the intention of straightening him up and for the first time shone my lamp on his face. It gave me a little shock when I recognised him as a deputy I had seen each shift travelling on the pit bus to and from work.

I began stretching him out laying his arms by his side and realised I was talking to him as I did so; 'Aa'll just mek ye look a bit more comfortable before people come, am sorry for heving pushed ye of the belt but yer a big bugger aren't ye.'

It was fifteen long minutes before several lamps came bobbing up the roadway from the direction of the pit bottom and as I watched them approach, I could hear my Dad's voice hurling orders wrapped in foul language.

Someone was pushing a Flat Horny - a six-foot long wooden platform fixed on top of two sets of tub wheels that would normally be used to carrying girders. They lifted the body onto the Horny and disappeared back toward the pit bottom without anyone speaking to me.

I stood in dumbfound silence for several minutes trying to take stock of what had happened before I retreated back to the bench and poured myself a cup of tea from my flask

Half an hour later, Dad and another man came back and quizzed me unsympathetically as to what had happened. The next day I was timber leading! I found out much later that the dead man had had a heart attack just off the coalface; he must have known he was unwell and presumably was on his way out to seek help.

Given that, we had a fair amount of autonomy; timber leading was by far the most exciting job for young lads in the colliery. At the start of each shift, the coalface Deputies gave us lists of pit props, girders, chocks and other items re-

257

quired by their men at the coalface and it was left to us to deliver the equipment to them using trams or tubs pulled by pit-ponies.

Our shift at Coneygarth normally started with the half dozen of us gathering in the boiler room behind the offices where we chatted about conquests, motorbikes, and football while having a first cup of tea and sandwich from our bait. The air was thick with cigarette smoke, foul-language and banter and I enjoyed every minute of it.

Tall and gangly and looking like a young Jimmy Nail, the oldest lad was nicknamed 'Nipper' due to his habit of smoking his cigarettes down to a tiny little 'nip-end' that he pinched between his finger and thumb as he drew the last of the smoke from his fag before it burnt his fingers. Nipper, along with a couple of the other older lads had shown me the ropes in their rough and ready way and had tried several of the old sweat tricks on me, including telling me to go for 'a long stand' and other nonsensical items. Luckily, having three older brothers who had been through it all before me, I was wise to most of their tricks.

After half an hour in the boiler room, we would then wander over to the timber yard and load wooden-pit-props by flinging them in relay chains from the massive stacks into our individual trams. Once loaded, we pushed them to the pit-head and left them there for lowering to the bottom of the drift by winch whilst we walked down the drift to the stables to collect our ponies.

Having fitted harnesses to our ponies, we made our way to the drift bottom where our loaded trams waited, hitched our ponies onto them, and then drove them to our various coalfaces to unload. It was steady physical work and time generally flew by; if we finished early, we rode our ponies to one of our rest places where we would sit and chat before taking the ponies back to the stables.

Nipper never joined us as he worked the 'Low Fives,' a coalface beset with problems due to subsidence and a place the other lad's spoke of with fear! 7-foot, heavy-girders supported the roadways that led to the coalfaces, which in the case of the Low Fives, had sunk alarmingly, leaving sections of the roadway only two foot high!

I had not seen the subsidence at the Low Fives but the other lads spoke in awe of the increased workload it meant for Nipper. They were all in dread of the day he would leave to start Face-Work Training as it meant one of them would have to take over his job and that time was Friday of next week!

Back at home, Betty had come up from Eton-Wick with her new husband Peter and I was thrilled to see her looking so happy. Peter, being tall, dark-haired, very intelligent and well educated fitted into the Carr household well! Mam still called him 'That big ugly bloody Jap' behind his back, quite a compliment from her!

Eric, now stationed at Barnard Castle, had started to call himself 'Ric' and courting a local girl called Sandy, suddenly announced he they were to be married in a couple of weeks.

258

I could not work out why the rush until I heard my Mam say to Mrs Little, 'Aye that buggers niver been able to keep his flies shut; and she wants a white wedding ye knaa!'

Ric brought slim, blonde and bonny Sandy home to meet the family; I thought she was very posh because she did not speak with a Geordie accent! She settled in straight away and became one of us overnight.

I was still dating one of our Vivian's friends, Ann the girl from Newbiggin. As tall as I was, she was very pretty and quiet spoken. On Wednesday evening, I met her off the bus opposite the new social club at the top of Alexander Road and after greeting her with a kiss, we walked down to the Welfare for the weekly dance. The dance was busy as always with about a hundred youths dancing to the live group who were on stage belting out a Buddy Holly number while groups of lads circled the floor, eyeing up the lasses dancing together or others sitting on chairs around the walls of the hall.

Chatting to Cousin Alec who had had a few pints at the Grand Hotel before coming to the dance, I grinned as I realised that the beer had put him in a happy and gregarious mood, especially when he placed his arm around my shoulder and said, 'Yor me favourite cousin Syd lad.' I eventually managed to escape him by taking Ann onto the dance floor.

Toward the end of the night, we were having a last dance before I walked her back to the bus stop when I saw Little Blue-Eyes! She was about ten yards away dancing with a lad, laughing and joking with him and two other couples. She looked gorgeous, her blue eyes sparkling with fun and her cute smile enchanting those around her.

I must have been staring as Ann suddenly pulled my arm hard and petulantly demanded, 'Why are ye staring at that lass?'

Caught off guard I stammered, 'Was Aa.... it's because I thought Aa knew her that's all, dee you know her like?'

Ann looked at me with suspicion and said, 'She used to live at Newbiggin but I think she lives around here somewhere now, she went to the Technical College but I think she works as a secretary or something in the offices at the Welwyn.'

Trying to appear uninterested I ventured, 'Ur I see, dee ye knaa her name then?'

'No I don't and it's time we were leaving,' she said petulantly and dragged me toward the cloakroom.

We set off for the bus in frosty silence but she soon melted and gave me several passionate kisses at the bus stop before the bus arrived. We arranged to meet on Friday to go to the pictures and I waved her goodbye before anxiously looking at my watch. It was a quarter past ten and the last dance was not until half past; if I hurried, I might just....

Walking briskly the few hundred yards back to the welfare, I felt guilty but excited, hoping I would be in time to ask Blue-Eyes for a dance but when I walked up to the entrance I could see that I was too late, groups of lads and lasses were standing outside chatting and saying goodnight, the dance was over.

I slowed as I approached, and looked desperately among the groups of lasses hoping to see her and was concentrating so hard that I almost bumped into her. She had been standing behind a group of taller lasses and as I walked around them, I found myself looking straight into her smiling face. My throat was suddenly dry and butterflies were hurtling round my stomach again as I tried to think of something cool to say as she gave me an expectant look waiting for me to speak.

I opened my mouth just as a firm hand grabbed my shoulder and Cousin Alec's voice boomed out, 'Where's your lass Syd?'

'I've just finished with her because I want to ask this lovely lass to let me walk her home,' at least that is what I wished I'd said but instead, still looking into those deep blue eyes and blushing madly I spluttered, 'On the bus gannin hyem,' realising as I said it, that I'd just blown an opportunity again. The smile faded from her pretty face and she turned back to her friends who had also been waiting for me to speak.

'Haway then Aa'll walk doon hyem with ye,' Alec said as he put his arm around my shoulder pushing me back toward the gate.

'Shit! Bloody shit! Bloody frigging shit!' I spat as we walked away.

'What the hell's the matter with ye?' he asked.

'Not a frigging lot like, Aa've only been trying to meet that lass for bloody ages and ye went and blew it for me ye big berk ye.'

Still grinning, Alec looked at me and said, 'But yor courting man and hoo was I supposed to knaa ye were after someone else?'

He was right of course and feeling very guilty, I said, 'Aye yor right, I just wanted to meet the lass man,'

He laughed, 'Aye, noo why do Aa not believe ye.'

The next night, Tom and I ventured into the 'Portland' our local pub. Ashington had over twenty Working Men's Clubs but only three public houses, the Portland being the most youth orientated of the three in that it had a jukebox in the lounge and often had local, fledgling groups performing, or trying to perform some of the latest hits.

It was warm and sunny early evening when Tom and I picked up the courage to try to buy our first pint!

'Ye gan in first and I'll follow,' said Tom.

'Aalreet but ye ask for the beer, right?

Tom went pale and stuttered, 'Nur, Aa'll gan in forst and ye order the beer.

I knew it was pointless arguing, there was no way Tom was going to ask for the beer even though he looked older than I did, so I said, 'Howay then let's gan in.'

A very nervous and shifty looking Tom led the way through the swing doors and into the cool of the large entrance hall that contained a bar serving the lounge at the far end. The hall bar backed onto the main bar where the regulars gathered, and not wishing to confront or upset any of them and not having the courage to explore any of the other rooms, I walked up to the bar in the hall. Trying to look nonchalant, I failed miserably, especially when my foot slipped off the polished brass fender causing my casually placed elbow to slip of the top.

The tall and very pretty barmaid gave us a suspicious look before asking, 'What do you want lads?'

I tried to speak but found my mouth had suddenly gone very dry so I coughed embarrassingly and blurted too loudly, 'Two pints of Best please.'

Looking through narrowed eyes, she said; 'Nee need to shout, am not deaf,' and then she asked the obvious, 'Are ye two owld enough te be in here?'

Tom blushed scarlet and wilted but drawing myself up to my full five foot eight and trying to sound offended replied, 'Aye man of course we are.'

She started to pull the pints and half smiling said, 'Ye knaa Syd, I always thought ye were in wor Brenda's class at school but ye couldn't hev been could ye, cos that would mean ye would only be sixteen and I couldn't serve ye noo could I.'

I blushed and smiled back before saying, 'Ye must be mistaking me for my brother, I'm eighteen.'

Handing over the two beers, she said, 'Aye I must, that'll be one and ten pence please.'

Handing over the money, I picked up the glass of luke-warm beer and took a sip and immediately felt as though I had just committed a grievous sin and that at any second a couple of policemen would burst in and arrest us. However, after a few sips and gulps. we began to relax and enjoy the beer and the thrill of being at the bar.

The beer obviously did wonders for Tom; when he finished his pint he thumped the glass on the bar and said in an overly loud voice to the barmaid, who was serving someone in the main bar, 'Another two of them Pet.'

She made him wait until she was good and ready before walking round to him and staring at him in an not too pleasant manner, said, 'Am not yor Pet and these'll be ye last two teday, got that?'

Tom gulped hard and squeaked, 'Aye, sorry.'

We drank the beer and left the pub feeling strangely elated as if we had come of age and we could now go where the men were, even though we had not dared enter the main bar and, Tom was looking a tad green.

On Friday of the following week, just after one o clock in the morning, I was back in fore-shift loading the trams in the timber yard with the other lads when the Charge-Hand walked up to us and shouted, 'Right lads come ower here a minute.'

261

Stopping what we were doing, we slowly gathered round him, waiting for him to speak, Nipper sucking the last dregs of smoke from his fag end before flicking it nonchalantly across the tramlines.

The Charge-Hand glared at him and muttered, 'Ye knaa yor not supposed to smoke here man.'

Nipper gave him a lop-sided grin and said, 'Really, what a bugger eh?'

The Charge-Hand looked at us nervously and said, 'Ye knaa that Nipper here is starting his coal-face training on Monday and has te gan te book in later teday, so this is his last shift here, so he will hev to show his replacement the ropes on the Low-Fives teday.'

We waited as he paused to look around us, while we all turned to look at Jimmy, a small but well-built, good-looking blonde-haired lad who, as the next oldest, was waiting to hear the inevitable.

'Ok,' said the Charge-Hand, 'Carr, when ye've finished taking your load inte the TU gan ower te the Low-Fives and Nipper here'll show ye hoo te gan on, reet?'

I was shocked; none of us had for a moment thought it would be me.

I was speechless but Nipper wasn't, 'Ye've got te be joking man, he'll niver manage, he's too bloody young and skinny man! It should be Jimmy here he's the next owldest!'

Shaking his head, the Charge-Hand replied, 'Aa've towld ye what's happening, noo get on with it,' and walked quickly away preventing any further discussion.

Nipper rounded on Jimmy, 'Whey ye didn't hev owt te say did ye? Eh?'

Jimmy answered just as loud, 'Whey man nee bugger's gannin te volunteer te tek ower the Low-Fives, are they?'

Feeling pretty well pissed off, I butted in, 'It's alreet lads, Aa'll dee it - it's me frigging faather making sure he does me nee favours.'

'Nee bloody favours!' shouted Nipper, 'he's trying to fucking knacker ye man!'

There was nothing more to say and we finished loading the trams before pushing them to the drift head ready for winching down.

When we finished, Nipper came over, placed his big hand on my bony shoulder and said, 'Aa'll see ye later Syd lad, yor gannin te hev te build some bloody meat on ye or ye'll not last lang, and mek sure ye bring yor kneepads.'

Having only one load to take in, by three o'clock I was ready to go to the Low Fives and with some trepidation, made my way there.

The pony I had that morning was Neil, a cantankerous, ginger and, black and white piebald that loved to bite or kick anyone that let his guard down. He also had an annoying habit off running back to the stables if you failed to hitch him up or tie his reins to a girder. This resulted in a twenty-minute walk to the stables to get him back!

262

Having been bitten once, and narrowly missed being kicked several times, as well as having had to chase him twice when he tried to run off; I wasn't in the best of moods when I shouted, 'Baaa,' to stop him at the entrance to the tunnel or 'Barrier' that led to the 'Low-Five' coalface.

Dismounting from the limber, I tied Neil's reins tightly to a girder whilst avoiding his sly attempt to nip me. Fastening on my kneepads, I warily walked down the 'Barrier,' full of apprehension, not sure what I would find.

The first twenty or so yards were fine, the girders were solid seven footers that had not sunk or twisted and provided well over 6 feet of height. The supports for all the tunnels or roadways were two curved steel girders that when connected by fishplates made an arch. The girders came in various thicknesses and lengths from six to fifteen feet.

It was normal practice to use Seven-foot heavies where there was a danger of subsidence and as I continued along, I noticed that despite the use of these girders, the height was beginning to decrease rapidly and I soon had to stoop to stop from banging my head. Water dripped from the roof, leaving an inch or so of grey slime underfoot that splashed up from my heavy pit boots as they thudded into the ground as I stooped lower and lower, the further I went in.

Eventually, I came to a tram with a dozen Dowty props lying inside. Used where normal timber props were not strong enough, these heavy, steel hydraulic-props, could be pumped up from two to four feet, and were buggers to manhandle. There was just sufficient height to reach over the sides of the four-foot high tram to pull them out.

Squeezing past the six-foot long and three-foot wide tram, I shuffled on another fifty or so yards to where a diminutive pony stood patiently in front of a coffin tram. Coffin trams were the same height and length of a normal tram but were half the width, which meant they could go further into the arch of the girders before the sides stuck. Trigger, the pony was barely ten hands but unlike Neil, he was quiet and well trained.

Patting him on the neck, I squeezed past the coffin tram that contained a few more Dowtys and found Nipper sitting on two wooden planks balanced on some wooden chocks, providing a dry seat amongst the stink and slime.

'Aalreet Syd lad' he said, 'welcome to the shite-hole of the universe!'

As I sat down next to him, I said, 'It's a lovely place ye've got yorsell here,'

'Aye, Nowt but the best doon here lad, tek five and we'll tek that lot in,' he said pointing to a flat-horny with six Dowtys strapped to it.

Four tram wheels with a wooden platform on top, a 'flat-horny' was low enough to use where the girders had sunk too low for a tram, and even tiny Trigger.

Nipper put his thumb over his left nostril and snorted dust and snot out of the right one then wiping his hand he rose into a low crouch and said, 'Haway then lad let's get on we it.'

263

I followed him as he pushed the flat horny along the tramlines until the ever-decreasing height forced us onto our hands and knees and I tried to crawl crab-like in an effort to keep my knees and lower legs out of the slime but it was impossible.

Nipper stopped when the top girders were almost touching the Dowtys strapped on the horny.

'Reet Syd, this is where it starts te get really shity!'

I did not think it could get much worse but it did; there was only about two foot of headroom and it looked as though it was even lower further on!

Having crawled to the front of the horny, Nipper grabbed a Dowty and slid it off and onto a five-foot by three-foot piece of heavy-duty conveyor belt lying on the rails, a foot, or so in front of the horny.

'Come on then, pull a couple more onto here,' he said, pointing at the piece of belt.

Once we had three Dowtys on the belt, Nipper scrambled in front of them and picked up a length of rope and canvas strap attached to the front corners of the belt. That was when I realised it was a makeshift sled; slipping the strap over his head and under his arms, he began to crawl along the tramlines pulling the belt with the three heavy Dowtys on, behind him.

I could see the effort it took as he pushed his boots against the sleepers to gain purchase while grabbing the sleepers in front to pull himself along through the slime. I crawled crab-like behind him wondering how far we had to drag the loads this way in this nightmarish place.

After about twenty yards, the height began to increase very quickly and Nipper stopped in front of another flat horny.

'We load these three, onte the horny, then ye can gan back for the other three.'

I nodded as he continued, 'Then we push this lot along to the tram further on, cross load and gan back for the next six until we have the full load in the tram, reet?'

'Aye,' I said as I looked down the roadway and asked, 'Hoo far is the tram like?'

Nipper spat and answered, 'Just twenty or thirty yards, then ye've got te push the tram another twenty or so te the coal face reet?'

'Aye right,' I answered feeling my stomach churn as I thought of the relentless and back breaking effort involved.

Ninety minutes later, soaked in slime and sweat, I sat exhausted on the bench next to Nipper who had taken his flask out of his ex-army gas mask bag, the type we all used to carry our bait and flasks. After taking a large mouthful he passed it to me saying, 'So, that's it Young'un, ye just keep at it till yor loads in.'

I leant back against the crude timber backrest that Nipper had made and wearily asked, 'Hoo many loads dee ye get a day?'

264

'Normally a couple but it's been a bugger this last week, heving te take in aall these Dowtys, there canna be many more te gan in though, then it's back te the normal replacement stuff.'

He then dropped a bombshell: 'Divvint forget that ye'll be in tonight for another shift, the Deputy asked me te dee the shift te finish getting the Dowtys in so ye'll hev te dee it noo.'

I was shocked, 'Ye've got te be joking man, am gannin te me brother's wedding at Barnard Castle tomorrow,' I spluttered, hoping he was joking - he wasn't.

'Whey ye'll be home by half past nine in the morning and ye'll get time and a half pay lad, some of the other lads are working as weel like.' I myself worked most Saturday morning shifts for the extra pay but that was not in the Low-Fives.

Standing in a shower cubicle in the pit baths later that morning, I let the hot water wash away the filthy slime and coal dust from my weary body and winced as it burnt the reddened and scrapped skin on my shoulders where the makeshift sled harness had chafed me. Clean and feeling a bit refreshed I walked home hardly noticing the bright morning sunshine; I wanted my bed.

Climbing out of bed at six in the evening, I stumbled downstairs and picked at congealed liver, onions, and mash before leaving to meet Ann for a night at the flicks. I met her off the bus next to the Wallaw Cinema where I paid for two seats in the corner of the stalls and despite being a tad tired, we still engaged in some very enjoyable heavy petting. Nonetheless, I was home by ten thirty and went to bed before been woken by Mam at twelve to get ready for the last shift of the week. After staggering downstairs, I as normal filled my flask and made my sandwiches while Dad made his without a word exchanged between us.

I wanted to say, 'Thanks for putting me in that shite hole ye miserable owld git ye,' but not wanting to give him the pleasure of hearing me complain, I left for work without saying a word.

Sitting in the boiler room having a cup of tea with the lads before we start-ed, I rotated my shoulders to ease the stiffness from yesterday's toil.

'Ye alreet Syd lad?' Jimmy asked.

'Aye, just me shoulders ora bit sore from the frigging sled harness that's all.'

Looking quickly away, he took a long drag from his cigarette before blow-ing it out slowly but said no more.

Thirty minutes later the nightmare had begun again; I was cross loading the first load of Dowtys from the tram to the coffin tram bashing knuckles and scrapping elbows as I pulled and heaved them over the side, through the small gap below the girders.

After an hour of non-stop effort and feeling pleased with my progress at having got the first half load in - I sat wearily down on the bench and devoured a

265

jam sandwich and cup of tea. Wet through, I soon began to chill so I scrambled back to the tram and started the process over again.

In an effort to stop the sled strap from rubbing my neck and shoulders raw, I took a Hessian sack from the bench and wrapped it around the strap, trying to provide some padding; it helped a little.

The twenty-yard sled pull became twenty yards of pain, each one worse than the one before but I continued to toil, refusing to let it beat me while trying to ignore the pain caused by the strap and the bumps and scrapes from man-handling the steel props in such a confined space.

Eventually, I finished the first load, hooked Trigger onto the empty tram, and rode the limber to the end of the roadway where I lifted his limber pin from the hole in the tram. The little pony immediately turned round and stepped to one side of the tramline to allow me to push the tram past him and into the main tunnel. Trigger then backed up to the waiting full tram until his limber touched it and stopped, waiting for me to come and hook him up.

The next hour was a blur of heaving, dragging, pushing, grunting, and cursing as I struggled to get the load in. Then harnessed to the sled, I got to the point when I felt I could not pull anymore and I collapsed into the slime gasping for air while cursing everything and everyone.

'Why the hell am I deeing this for six pund a week?' I thought.

I lay there for what seemed like ages but it must have just been a couple of minutes, enough time to gather my thoughts and a recover a bit before slipping out of the harness and crawling back to where Trigger stood patiently in front of the tram. I took off his protective head guard and the bit from his mouth, placed his nosebag over his head and patted his neck fondly. I left him munching as I walked back to the bench to eat my sandwiches and a bag of crisps.

Feeling a little refreshed I resigned myself to finish the last half load as quickly as possible and get out of this miserable hole and restarted the punishing routine.

Twice I almost gave up but after pausing for a minute or two each time, I toiled on until eventually, completely exhausted; I stood by Trigger thankful to be finished and glad to be leaving.

Hooking Trigger's limber into the front of the tram, I clambered inside, too weary to ride the limber, I lay full stretch in the tram, knowing Trigger would pull it to the Drift bottom.

'Hadup,' I shouted and the little pony leant into his harness and started forward. Lying on my back absolutely exhausted, I watched the girders pass by overhead as we made our way out of the barrier tunnel until we reached the junction with the main tunnel and Trigger stopped!

Annoyed at him having stopped, I shouted, 'Come on Lad, Hadup,' but he did not move, just snorted and scraped the stony ground with a hoof. I pulled myself up and peered forward, pointing the lamp on my helmet at Trigger and just past him where I could see a dark shape blocking his way and wondered what mischievous sod had pushed a tram there to block our way out.

Climbing stiffly out I walked forward to push the tram, into the main tunnel but when I reached it, I saw to my horror that it wasn't an empty tram, it was full of Dowty props!

I looked at them in dread, 'Two loads, just two loads, that's all, not frigging three,' I said out loud trying to convince myself this load was not for me or, was there ready for Monday's shift.

I found the Deputy's docket fastened to the tram and felt sick as I read it – 'Last load for today and the last of the Dowty Props.'

Holding back tears of frustration and exhaustion I considered saying, 'Stuff it,' and leaving the load but something – pride perhaps, or not wanting to be ridiculed for not coping; I'm not sure which, but it made me lean into the tram and push it back into the main tunnel so that I could move the empty one out the way.

I began the exhausting routine again; cross loading, pushing, heaving and dragging - trying to concentrate on each little part of the task, trying not to think of the overall effort required, but within an hour, I was beaten. I lay in the slime with the harness around my neck unable to find the strength to drag the load another inch, the pain in my now, red-raw shoulders almost unbearable.

Feeling pretty miserable and almost in despair; I did not want to give up and told myself without conviction, 'Just rest here for a couple of minutes, and then ye'll be able to get this one te the end,' trying not to think about the other twelve props that still had to be dragged through. Beyond caring, I was cold, wet, and shivering; I felt as if I was slowly sinking beneath the slime and I could do nothing about it.

'I just needed a little rest - then I'll start again,' I said to myself!

I don't know how long I had lain there before the sound of boots on stones and flashing lights stirred me from my half sleep of exhaustion and I heard Jimmy's voice, 'Yor not heving a frigging kip there are ye Syd lad?'

Raising my head wearily, I looked back and saw three lights coming up behind me, Jimmy was in the front with Peter and another lad scrambling along behind.

Answering Jimmy's question I said, 'Aye I am, I'm fucking knackered man, what are ye three deeing here?'

Jimmy lifted the harness from my shoulders and said half mockingly, 'We knew a skinny little git like ye would need a hand, move ower lad.'

I did not argue and rolled to one side as Jimmy took the weight of the sled and crawled forward.

Peter started to push the horny back to the coffin tram, and asked, 'Is this yor forst or second load?'

I shouted after him, 'Me third,' it stopped him in his tracks.

He turned and repeated, 'Third!' then paused before pushing again and shouting over his shoulder, 'Not bad for a skinny little git.'

The three of them finished taking the load in no time at all and we gathered round the now empty third tram.

'Ye've had a frigging hard Saturday shift Syd lad,' said Jimmy, 'we normally skive on Saturdays man, ye'll hev us oot on strike if ye gan on like this,' and wrapped his arm around my shoulder in a mock-strangle hold. It was all I could do to stop myself crying out in pain as he squeezed my skinned and bruised shoulders.

Peter shouted, 'Haway then let's see whose forst back te the stables,' and the three of them jumped onto the backs of their waiting ponies and rode off at full gallop toward the drift bottom. They had been like the cavalry in the films I had watched at the Regal, coming to the rescue just in the nick of time. If they had not come, I am sure I would have still been lying in the cold slime of the sled drag!

Hitching the quiet and dependable Trigger onto the front empty tram that had the other two hooked on behind, I sat on the limber and said, 'Hadup lad.' The little pony leaned willingly into his load and took the empty trams and me away from the Low Fives.

It was a warm, sunny, summer morning when a little later, I wearily walked out of the drift and clambered onto the colliery double-decker bus bound for the Pit Baths.

Sitting behind Jimmy I was leaning back enjoying the feel of the sun through the window and had just about drifted off when he turned around and asked, 'How Syd, what coalfaces is yor Dad gannin te look efter at Ashington?'

Surprised by his question and not fully understanding it I sat up and asked, 'What dee ye mean, Ashington? He's still working here.'

'Not from Monday,' said Jimmy, 'He's starting at Ashington, isn't he Peter.'

Sitting opposite, Peter turned and said, 'Aye that's reet, had yor not hord?'

Too tired to care I answered, 'Nur Aa hevn't, why would he be gannin te work at Ashington when he's the Four-Owerman here man?'

Jimmy looked at me, laughed and said, 'De ye Knaa nowt lad, they're gannin te close Coneygarth doon in the next few weeks man, we'll aall hev te gan te Ashington then!'

I was surprised; Dad had not mentioned it to me, but then again he hardly spoke to me so it wasn't that surprising that I found out from someone else. As I sat half asleep, I wondered when I would move to Ashington and hoped it would be soon, I did not care where I would work as long as it was not the Low-Fives!

After a long hot shower in the baths, I walked the few hundred yards home longing to go to bed but as I approached our house, I could see a large coach parked outside and a gaggle of family and friends in their suits, best dresses and costumes standing next to it talking and laughing.

Leaning against the yard railings, Cousin Alec stepped forward as I approached and said, 'Yor muther's gannin spare Syd, we were supposed to have left ages ago!'

I nodded and walked into the cool of the kitchen where Mam was standing in a blue crimplene suit, her engine running at full throttle:

'What bloody time dee ye call this?'

'Ye've got every bugger hanging roond like spare bloody parts.'

'Whey divvint just stand there get yorsell changed ye bloody waster ye.'

Far too tired, hungry, and sore to care, I ignored her and stood at the kitchen table where from amongst the clutter, I took two slices of bread and smothered them in butter and jam before taking huge bites as I looked for a clean cup to pour myself a cup of tea.

Mam's rant continued:

'Ye hevn't got time for that, Aa'll not tell ye again, get bloody ready!'

'Viv gan and get yor Dad to come and mek this frigging waster get ready.'

'Aa'll bloody swing for ye one of these days, ye bloody waster ye.'

'Divvint stand there with that brazen look on yor face cos Aa'll bloody murder ye!'

I finished my sandwich and washed it down with a cup of cold tea and said quietly, 'Thanks for me breakfast Mother and if ye canna wait any longer then gan cos am too tired to give a bugger.'

Dennis, who had been standing quietly watching Mam rant, said, "Aa've put yor shirt and tie on the bed and yor suits hanging up behind the attic door Syd.'

'Ta lad,' I replied and walked past him and Butch, who had been standing wagging his tail madly obviously enjoying the commotion and went upstairs to change into my new suit.

Once on the coach and having told Cousin Alec to, 'Shut up!' I slept all the way to Barnard Castle and then twice fell asleep in the Church but saw that Sandy looked beautiful and Ric handsome in his flash way before I nodded off again during the reception dinner and then slept on the coach all the way back. When we arrived back, Alec told me that everyone had had a great time; the coach only had to stop four times for the men to have a pee break at the side of the road.

Unfortunately, I didn't see Ann at all that weekend, effectively ending our going out together and although she came to see me a couple of times, I'd decided she was far too nice a girl to string along as I was unable and unwilling to get Little Blue-Eyes out of my mind!

The following week, back at work, the loads reduced to one or two a day and were mainly wooden chocks, and although it was still a hellish place, I learnt to pace myself and settled into the tough, muddy, routine.

On Thursday, just before I went underground, the Deputy stopped me and said 'Reet young Carr, there's only one load teday and it's Dowty props but it is

269

yor last load, they're closing the Low-Fives doon next Monday cos it's nee longer viable.'

Cheesed off at the thought of another load of Dowtys but glad to hear the terrible place was closing, I thought for a second and then asked, 'Whey if the place is closing, why dee the still want Dowty props?'

The Deputy looked at me with some sympathy, 'Whey Aa knaa they're hard work getting in but the face will keep on producing coal until it finishes, so they're still needed.'

I started to turn to go down the drift when he stopped me, saying, 'Hang on a minute, ye might not want te knaa, but the salvage teams start on Monday and after they've got the cutter and conveyor oot they'll be taking oot all them Dowtys ye've just teking in!'

'Bloody marvellous,' I said, feeling like saying a lot more but I bit my tongue.

'On the good side, ye start timber-leading at Ashington Training-Unit on Monday, reet?'

'Aye, champion, but what shift?'

'Back-shift lad, hev ye not heard the rules hev changed? Ye can only work back-shift until yor eighteen noo.'

'That's great,' I replied, feeling delighted that I would not be working in the early hours of the morning again; back-shift was the day shift of eight till four.

The Deputy finished by saying, 'Mek sure ye see me at the end of yor shift the morn reet?'

'Aye,' I answered and left to tackle the Dowtys, feeling a lot better after his news but wondering why he wanted to see me tomorrow. I found out when I caught up with him as he walked to the bus at the end of Fridays shift.

Digging into his pocket, he pulled out a grubby envelope that he handed over to me and said, 'Here this is from the men on the face for keeping the Dowtys coming.'

I took the envelope from him and climbed onto the bus where I ripped it open, to find six pound notes and two half-crowns! It was more than a week's wage! It was normal for the coalface workers to give their timber-leaders a few bob each out of their holiday pay at summer and Christmas; that is if they had done a good job, but I had not expected anything and was surprised and delighted. It amounted to about five shillings from each of them and was a very generous gesture.

On the way to the pit baths, I thought about the money and decided it I would put it away and use it to buy a helmet, goggles, and gauntlets that I would need when I bought a motorbike next March.

23

Mam Shows Her True Colours

Working at the huge Ashington Colliery was a massive change to working at tiny Coneygarth Drift. There were numerous different levels and areas of coa faces, Dad having been put in charge of the 'Ls' while I thankfully, was sent to work with a lad called Bob at the Training-Unit in another part of the pit.

Everything seemed to be on a much larger scale, especially the stables. Whereas Coneygarth Stables consisted of one row of twelve stalls, Ashington had four rows, each with about twenty stalls; all immaculately clean, whitewashed and brightly lit - the stable hands took pride in their job!

Bob was hardworking and conscientious but lacked a sense of humour, taking life and work very seriously. However, he did take time and effort to show me the work routine and methods he used and I learnt a lot from him.

The Training Unit was where 19-year-old lads learnt how to work at the coalface and was a fully functioning coal-producing unit. We also had to keep the area neat and tidy with everything in its place, as it was the part of the colliery used to show visitors around. I soon settled into working permanent day shift and enjoyed a great working relationship with Bob.

Outside of work, nothing much changed; Tom and I continued to go to the Welfare dance twice a week, enjoying varying degrees of success with girls and although I kept on searching for Little Blue-Eyes, I was always left disappointed as she remained as elusive as ever and I still had not found out where she lived.

After dinner, on a cold wet, miserable winters night, I was sitting in front of a roaring fire watching television when Mam said, 'Yor not gannin te work the morn, yor gannin te see Sandy in hospital we me.'

'Which hospital and why is she in?' I asked.

Taking a sip from the cup of tea she was holding, she answered, 'She's at Durham, and she's just had a bairn.'

I had forgotten the reason for Eric's hasty marriage and did not relish the thought of going to visit Sandy in a hospital.

'Why do Aa hev te gan with ye?'

'Because am not travelling all the bloody way on me an, so get yor suit on tomorrow, yor coming we me.' I knew Mam did not want me for my company but she needed someone to make sure she caught the correct buses and find the hospital for her.

271

The following morning at twelve o'clock, we caught a bus from Ashington and changed buses twice before we scurried through the rain into the hospital just after three.

Sitting in the maternity ward watching Mam and Sandy fussing over baby Craig, I felt embarrassed and disconnected. I had looked at the baby and made the normal comments but found the whole visit uncomfortable. We had been there for twenty or so minutes when the Ward Sister came up to the bed and took a long look at me before leaning over Mam, whispering something in her ear.

Mam erupted and spat out in one breath, 'Whey ye stupid bugger ye he's not the bloody faather - the baby's faather's in the bloody army; that's his faather's brother wor Syd, he's too bloody young te be any bugger's faather and yore a brazen bugger for saying that he was; as if this canny lass would be deeing it with a young lad like that whey man Aa've niver hord the bloody like!'

The hapless Sister stood in opened mouth shock; obviously wishing the harridan in front of her would shut up, while regretting that she had spoken to her in the first place. The Sister did the wisest thing possible; turning on her heels, she walked swiftly away leaving Mam fuming, Sandy giggling and me burning with embarrassment, not at Mam's outburst, I was used to those, I was embarrassed at someone thinking that I had done 'it' with Sandy!

I was happy to leave the hospital and happier still to get home after the dreary return journey; however, my happiness was short lived as Mam told Dad of the Maternity Sister mistaking me for the father, then repeated the story several times to Aunties and neighbours who came in to find out about the new bairn. Her storytelling becoming more and more lurid with each telling, until it bore no resemblance to what had happened; 'I gave the Sister a piece of mind' to 'I wiped the bloody floor with her and chased her oot of the ward.' I was horrified but not surprised at Mam's exaggerations.

Early the following year a tough looking lad called Colin came to work with Bob and me; the Training-Unit had expanded into three shifts and as we were only allowed to work day shift we had been hard pressed to keep up with the demand for props, girders and other supplies. Colin looked like a young Klaus Kinsky and was strong and a hard worker but did not always use safe or sensible solutions to work tasks, tending to charge at a problem without putting any thought into it; nevertheless we all got on well together and enjoyed the challenges that we were given.

In March, Tom and, I became excited as the time to buy our motorbikes drew close; we had even been to H&H Motorcycles to discuss delivery, colours, and HP terms. I had calculated that by the time I reached my seventeenth birthday, I would have saved over £100, more than half the overall cost of the BSA I hoped to buy. I had used the money the men on the Low Fives had given me to buy a crash helmet and goggles and hidden them in Dad's garage and tried them on almost daily, looking forward to when I would have the motorbike to go with them.

Just before my birthday, I was at work, sitting on a makeshift bench with Bob and Colin eating lunch when Bob said, 'De ye fancy joining the TA?'

His question came as no surprise; Colin and I both knew Bob had been in the TA for some time as he often talked about the training weekends and where they went.

'Aa would like te,' I answered 'but am not owld enough, ye've got te be seventeen and a half, hevn't ye?'

'Aye, but just lie aboot yor age, I did when I joined and they niver checkup.' he replied smiling. 'If ye join tonight, ye'll be able te gan te Alnwick this weekend, we're doing annual rifle classification, and ye get paid as weel,'

'Right, Aa'll hev a go at that so Aa'll join tonight if yor gannin in.'

'Aye, me an all,' Colin said through a mouthful of spam sandwich.

That night I became Fusilier Carr S of 'B' Company, 7th Battalion the Royal Northumberland Fusiliers; Bob was right, they did not ask for proof of age but did ask me to repeat my false date of birth twice. Looking older than I did, Colin had no such problems.

A sergeant briefed us on the forthcoming weekend and as I had been in the Army cadets and had handled the Lee Enfield .303 rifle, he told me I could classify. Colin had to stay behind and do some basic rifle training. They also issued us with denim, fatigue dress jacket and trousers to wear, as it would be a couple of weeks before we would receive our battle-dress uniforms.

As we were leaving, the platoon Sergeant warned, 'Mek sure ye bring some wellies, it will be wet and cowld on the moors this weekend.

Memories of a beating had stopped me from owning a pair of wellies for a long time and I certainly did not intend to obtain any, so resigned myself to having cold and wet feet; I was not to be disappointed!

Early on Saturday morning, carrying a holdall with washing and shaving kit and a few other bits and pieces, I climbed onto the back of a three tonner and joined the rest of my section for the 14-mile trip to Alnwick Drill Hall. I knew most of the other lads already, including Colin's cousin Dave who lived in the Sixth Row, all of them keen to give Colin and I stick for being dressed like a couple of convicts in our Denim Fatigues.

It was a bright, sunny day with a bitterly cold Northeast wind howling across the moors when we jumped off the back of the trucks at the entrance to the ranges. It was not the place to be wearing flimsy leather 'Winkle Pickers,' the ground was sodden with patches of slushy snow and I soon felt cold and wet. However, the excitement of the day and the camaraderie pushed the discomfort to the back of my mind as I looked forward to the shoot.

Eventually it was the turn of our section to zero our weapons and we lay down on sodden ground sheets at the 100-yard firing point waiting to for the

273

Range Officer to brief us. Lying with Colin on my right and Bob on my left, we bet each other on who between us would do best.

'TWO WARMERS INTO THE BANK, IN YOUR OWN TIME CARRY ON,' yelled the Range Officer and I worked the bolt pushing the first round into the breach, took aim at the sand bank down at the butts and squeezed the trigger. The thump of the rifle butt into my shoulder took me by surprise; I had pulled the rifle tight into my shoulder and expected a big kick as I fired but had not expected the recoil to be so strong, it gave a hefty kick but it just added to the excitement of the day.

After firing both rounds, the NCOs issued us with another five rounds to fire at large white targets with small black squares in the centre. The idea was to try to obtain a neat grouping on the black square, the strike of each shot indicated with a pointer by the lads working in the butts.

I remembered all my training, taking aim at the target, I exhaled and gently squeezed the trigger; the pointer came up and indicated a spot just up and to the left of centre.

I looked across at Colin as he shouted, 'What the fuck does that mean?' pointing to the round disc that was been waved across the front of his target.

'Quiet,' shouted the range Officer as an NCO knelt down next to Colin and said, 'It means ye missed the target completely; hoo the hell can ye miss something that big?' he chided.

'Me sights must be knacked,' Colin spat.

'It's not the sights that are Knacked,' the NCO said before giving him some guidance.

After the first five rounds, we adjusted our sights and issued another five rounds to prove the adjustment and to improve our grouping.

'Well done Carr,' The Platoon sergeant said as we stood on the butts looking at our targets.

'That's a good five-inch grouping.'

'Jammy bugger,' Colin shouted as the Platoon Sergeant walked to his target.

'Whey ye hit the target, it's just a pity ye tried te spread them aboot se much lad,' the Sergeant said as he searched for Colin's strike marks.

Bob who had done even better than I, shouted, 'Pints on ye Colin!'

Colin shouted back, 'Bog off, the bets for the morn morning when we fire the classification not this poxy zeroing.'

Despite enjoying the firing, we spent a great deal of time waiting and I was glad to be out of the cold and wet when we eventually arrived back at the Drill Hall to put up camp beds for later that night.

We had a good night out in Alnwick and another lad and I ended up canoodling with two lasses behind one of the pubs.

'Will I see you again?' the bonny dark haired lass I was with asked as I walked her home.

274

'If ye come te Ashington ye will,' I said expecting that to be the end of it as I was not keen enough to travel to Alnwick.

'Okay, 'Aa'll get the three o clock bus tomorrow if ye meet me at the bus station?'

I suddenly felt a lot more interested, if she was willing to travel to Ashington, she must be keen.

I said 'Aye, that'll be great; I'll meet you at the bus station then,' looking forward to the next day already.

The next morning, after washing and shaving in hot water in the ablutions of the Drill Hall, the highlight of the weekend came, for me anyway; a full fried breakfast and a huge dollop of porridge! It was the largest breakfast I had ever had and I devoured it greedily along with two pieces of toast and a fresh mug of tea to wash it all down.

Bob who had been quizzing me unsuccessfully as to my success with the lass last night asked, 'De ye want me te see if there're any seconds Syd?'

'Yes please,' I answered drooling at the thought of more sausages and bacon.

'Am only joking ye greedy bugger, ye'd think ye've niver been fed man.'

I looked at him smiling and answered, 'Aa've niver had a breakfast like this before and if it's like this every time we gan away then am signing up for life!'

Sunday morning on the ranges was just as cold and even wetter than the day before as we were hit with several squalls of sleet that left us soaked but not miserable. Our turn for classification came and out of the section, both Bob and I qualified as 'Marksmen'. Colin managed to get 'Second Class Shot' and consequently took a lot of ribbing but still blamed his sights for his poor performance and, refused to honour the bet we had made, not that we had expected him too anyway!

I was still damp when I got home at two o clock and after a cup of tea and a couple of hastily made sandwiches, I sat down in front of the fire in the sitting room to thaw out. Mam, Dad, and Dennis had gone to Aunt Aggies leaving Butch alone in the house. He climbed on the sofa next to me and rested his head on my lap as the two of us, warmed by the coal fire, drifted off to sleep.

Butch suddenly jumping up when the back door opened woke me with a start; it was Mam, Dad, and Dennis returning.

Dennis came into the sitting room and asked, 'What was it like Syd?'

I was just about to answer but I saw the time on the mantle clock; it was after three o clock, I was supposed to be at the bus station meeting the lass from Alnwick!

Rushing into the scullery, I grabbed my toothbrush, frantically scrubbed my teeth over the Sunday dinner pots and pans, grabbed my jacket, and raced out the back door. I practically ran the mile to the bus station and was almost there when I saw heading toward me, a red 'United' bus with 'Alnwick' showing on the front. I stopped as it went past and on board, I could see the lass from the night before buying a ticket from the conductor - I never saw her again!

Tom joined the TA the following week and we both attended Thursday parades and enjoyed weekends away at places such as Otterburn, Worksop, and Holy Island.

We even went on Tuesday evenings and took up Judo classes, taught by a lad that lived in our old house in Pont Street, but that only lasted a few weeks before he was unable to continue due to other commitments; however the few moves we mastered came in handy later on in life.

On the Saturday morning before my Seventeenth Birthday, Tom was on the sofa in my sitting room trying without much success to stop Butch from climbing onto his lap while I searched for my savings book. I wanted to have it brought up to date to confirm exactly how much money I would have to spend on a motorbike the following weekend.

Unable to find it in the sideboard drawer where I thought it was, I turned to Mam, who was at her normal place on the chair at the kitchen table, fag in one hand, and a glass of sherry in the other.

'De ye knaa where me bank book is Mam?'

She sat upright and fixed me with one of her tight-lipped stares.

'What dee ye want that for?'

'I want te get it marked up so Aa knaa how much Aa have in'

She spat back, 'Hoo the buggery should Aa Knaa where it is,' and took another drag of her Woodbine.

I continued to search until Tom, who now had Butch on his lap with the dog's huge head resting on his shoulder, said, 'Ye might not need yor book to find oot how much yor have in, just ask one of the assistants and they should tell ye, but ye will need it next week to draw oot yor money.'

'Aye that sounds all right,' I said 'haway then let's gan doon the street and find oot.'

On the way to the bank, Tom told me that he would not have enough money saved until after the summer holidays and that our plans for a motorbike camping trip would have to wait.

I said, 'That's alright, ye can learn to ride on my motorbike, and we can always gan doon to Creswell camping on our push bikes.'

A little while later, standing in the queue at the bank, I waited nervously for my turn while Tom was telling me about a girl he fancied.

'She's a right smasher but she's always with another lass, hoo aboot ye taking her mate oot so I can ask her oot.'

Not concentrating, I said, 'Aye only if she is nice looking - and she wants te gan oot we me of course.'

When my turn came I walked to the counter where a young Bank Clerk stood smiling behind it and clearing my throat, asked, 'Aa'd like te knaa how much I have in my savings account but I cannit find my savings book?'

Still smiling the man answered, 'Not to worry, I'll just take some details and I'll find out for you.' He picked up a pen and took down the answers to several questions before disappearing to the back of the bank.

He reappeared carrying several sheets of paper that he looked at quickly before saying, 'Right Mr Carr, you currently have two pounds and seven shillings and sixpence in your account - OK.'

'How much?' I exploded.

'Two pounds, seven shillings and sixpence,' he repeated slowly as if I was a half-wit.

'But there should be well ower a hundred pund in there man, Aa've been putting in a pound a week for two years and Aa hevn't drawn out oot!' I said, feeling my stomach churn.

'Yes that's correct,' the Bank Clerk answered in a matter of fact voice, 'but your mother has been drawing it out at least once a month!'

I felt myself blushing madly as a blind rage began to creep over me, I realised too late what a huge mistake it was to have my mother as my adult account holder.

I needlessly asked, 'So she's been drawing oot my money as fast as I've been putting it in then?'

The Clerk looked at me sympathetically and answered, 'Yes, that's about the size of it.'

'Right,' I growled angrily, 'I want my account closed now and I want what's left of my money now.'

He cleared his throat and said, 'I'm sorry lad but you can't draw out the money without your bank book and your mother's authority and ye'll also need her to close your account.'

I'd had enough; fighting back tears of rage and frustration I stormed out of the bank and headed home ready to commit murder while Tom walked briskly one step behind me knowing now was not the best time for conversation!

My emotions were a mix of despair and anger as I marched home but by the time I opened the back door, I had already realised the futility of venting my anger on the hard-faced woman that was my mother. She was in the sitting room watching television with Dennis, Vivian, and Butch. Dad was at the little betting shop he and one of his cronies ran and would not be home before teatime. Butch battered Dad's chair with his tail again as I walked in and Dennis stared at my red face as Mam crossed her arms in defiance, ready for anything I was about to say.

'Mother, you are a bloody thieving, deceitful swine, and hate does not begin to sum up what I feel for you right now'

She looked at me with cold eyes and spat back, 'Aye well bugger off oot my sight ye simple sod because Aa divvint bloody care.'

Looking perplexed, Dennis asked, 'What's the matter, Syd?'

'What's the matter? Yor bloody Mother has stolen my savings for my motorbike to buy bloody fags and sherry and play bloody bingo that's what's the bloody mattered,' I said angrily and stormed out the house not wanting to be near her.

There was another massive argument between my mother and father that evening when Vivian told Dad at the tea table, 'Wore Syd's not getting a motorbike cos me Mam's spent his money.'

I was not there but Dennis said the argument was very loud and lasted for ages and ages!

I stopped the savings deduction from my wages the following week and began taking two pounds for pocket money. Tom, the mate that he was, never mentioned motorbikes again, I did give him my helmet and goggles as I knew I would never need them.

24

Fighting and TA Camp

The following weekend, George was home on leave and suggested we go to the dance at Bedlington Station on Friday night. Never having been before and with nothing else planned, I agreed to go with him and a couple of hours later we jumped on the train at Ashington Station for the three-mile journey, walking into the dance hall at eight o clock.

The Hall was not as big as the Welfare, I think it may have been a TA Drill Hall but it was full of teenagers dancing and chatting while a band played on stage. Although it was busy and lively, it did not have the same atmosphere as the Welfare and felt rather dismal and depressing.

This was not our home ground and I felt vulnerable as we walked around the dance floor eyeing up the girls. George got his eye on a brassy looking, dark haired girl and was soon jiving with her; it was the first time I had seen him dance, it was interesting!

Wandering over to the drinks kiosk, I bought a Coca-Cola and turning to watch the dancers, I bumped into a pretty girl in a tight red sweater and even tighter black slacks.

'Sorry,' I muttered shaking dribbled coke from my hand as I looked at her now smiling face.

'That's OK,' she said as she squeezed past me to join the queue for drinks.

As George was obviously well in with the Brunette, finishing my drink, I began another tour of the dance floor and found the girl in the red sweater. She smiled at me so I stopped and waited until the band finished their number and when they started playing Chubby Chequer's, 'Let's Twist again', I walked over and asked her to dance.

We had several dances with little chats in between and I thought it was going well enough to ask, 'Can I walk ye home?'

She smiled and said, 'Am sorry but am with me boyfriend.'

Disappointed, I said cheerio and wandered off to look for George; finding him standing talking to the Brunette.

I turned to walk away when he stopped me, 'Look Young'un Am gannin ootside with this lass for a bit so Aa'll see ye at the Station at half-past ten right?'

Nodding, I said, 'OK' and looking at the time I saw that it was already ten o clock and after having another coke I set off for the station.

Strolling onto the platform, I turned to look back and saw two lads about twenty yards behind me walking toward the station. Not thinking anything of it, I turned around and wandered up to the timetable to look for the times of the Ashington Train.

'How I want a word with ye!' came from behind. I turned to see the two lads facing me, one standing excitedly just behind the one who had spoken. The lad in front was about my age and size; blonde haired and wearing a 'Teddy Boy' drape jacket. He looked nervous and as he continuously clenched and unclenched his fists, I realised he had come spoiling for a fight.

'Ye were dancing with my lass and Am gannin te have ye!' he spat at me.

Aware that there was two of them and the one behind was obviously encouraging the blonde lad to have a go, I shifted my left foot forward waiting for him to swing at me.

Hoping to defuse the situation, I said, 'Hoo the hell was Aa te knaa it was yor lass and anyway as soon as she towld me Aa left man.'

That was not good enough for Blondie, he was here to defend his manhood in front of his mate and with him to back him up; he was going to sort me out.

'We've had enough of ye Ashington lot coming ower here, trying to take wor lasses,' he said as he worked himself up to attack.

I began to think that he was going to be all talk and no action when a voice behind me boomed, 'Stick the heed on the twat Young'un!'

It was George, and without thinking, I obeyed, smacking Blondie on the bridge of his nose with a head-butt. It was not that hard as far as head-butts go, I was never any good at heading footballs! However, it was hard enough for him to step back and blink his eyes - enough time for me to grab his shoulder and hip and execute a good Hane-Goshi hip throw.

Blondie landed flat on his back and I followed through, straddling him, pinning both his arms down with my knees, and pushed his head back with my left hand while clenching my right fist ready to strike.

George who was holding the other lad by the throat said, 'Go on Syd, batter the twat.'

I raised my clenched fist but this time, I did not obey him; I could not bring myself to punch the undefended, shocked face below me, I climbed off him and waited to see what he was going to do.

He scrambled to his feet and the pair of them began backing away, Blondie shouting, 'Ye better not come back here or we'll fucking have ye, ye bastards,' but they left and George and I stepped into the two-carriage train that had pulled in behind us.

On the way home, George, who played football for the REME Corps Team, told me that he had been head-hunted by a Talent Scout for Southampton FC and had spent a week with them but they had found a problem with his knee that they said could be a serious problem for a professional footballer. He said he was 'frigging disappointed,' but they had paid him well for the week; not that that was any sort of compensation for a brilliant footballer who had just found out that he could not pursue his dream.

I never went back to Bedlington Station again, not because of Blondie but because I much preferred the Welfare.

Late on a Friday evening in early summer, Sister Pat and her fiancé John came to stay prior to their marriage later in the year. John, a good-looking blonde electrician from Ipswich, reminded me of a young Des O'Connor.

The following morning the sun was shining and despite on-going tense relations with Mam, I was in a great mood. Tom came just after lunch ready for our normal Saturday afternoon walk downtown and I introduced him to John.

I asked John, 'Hev ye ever tried Newcastle Exhibition? It's the best pint ye can get.'

His face broke into a big smile and he answered in his gentle Suffolk drawl, 'No but I'd like to give it a go if you boys fancy a pint?'

The three of us were soon walking briskly to the sandstone, square built, 'Portland Hotel' and walked out of the bright sunshine into the cool gloom of the public bar that greeted us with the smell of beer and cigarettes.

When I had heard John was coming to stay I had said to Tom, 'We'll tek him to the Portland and get him drunk on Newcastle Ex.' - Oh the rashness of youth!

In his early twenties and great company, John stepped up and bought the first round!

After holding up his pint and examining it, he took a long swallow of the cool, clear beer, wiped his mouth, and said, 'Yor right lads this is a great pint.'

Tom and I took long swigs, enjoying the freshness of the beer then realised that John was taking the last mouthful of his pint and hurriedly drank ours to catch up.

'Same again John?' I asked.

He smiled his charming smile and said, 'Yes please.'

We had a great time drinking and chatting, the beer helping the conversation flow easily. The problem was trying to keep up with John! After six pints in just less than two hours, I was wondering why I was having difficulty focusing on the two Johns that I was talking too and Tom could not understand why his elbow kept slipping off the bar. Despite that, I felt great, if a tad queasy!

'De ye want anuder fugga beer Jim – George – Ric - I mean John?' I asked not understanding why my voice was not saying what I wanted it to.

John looked at Tom and me and said, 'No thanks Syd I've had enough for this afternoon but we can come out tonight and have a few more, ay?'

'Right, great!' I answered; convinced that Tom and I had just out drunk this soft Southerner and looked forward to more of the same later.

The walk home was entertaining; we appeared to be in the grip of a series of earthquakes that made it almost impossible to walk in a straight line and what was worse, on several occasions, I was for no apparent reason attacked by walls and fences. John must have been very drunk because he was holding Tom's and my arms very tightly to stop himself from falling over; at least, I think that is why he was holding onto us.

Back at the Fifth Row John steered us into the sitting room and dropped us both onto the sofa where Tom and I sat grinning like idiots wondering why we were sitting in a madly spinning Waltzer!

'Eeeh, whatever's wrong with those two?' I heard Pat ask John.

'Nothing,' he answered smiling, apparently stone cold sober, 'they must have had a bad pint.'

'What?' I spluttered, 'Bad Pint! Necasssle Brewerieries divvint mek bad beer man, it must be ye, Aa think ye've got holla legs, or yer a bloody fish, a thorsty blidy fish.'

Noticing that Tom had fallen asleep on my shoulder, I pushed him off and said, 'Gerroff me ye drunken bugger ye,' and almost immediately felt my own eyes beginning to close.

I could feel John pulling me up from the sofa saying, 'Come on Syd I'll help you to bed so ye can get a couple of hours sleep before we go out tonight.'

Struggling to open my eyes, I woke up feeling as though my tongue had swollen to twice its normal size and my mouth was so dry I was having difficulty swallowing, in addition to which, I must have banged my head very hard as it was very, very painful. I sat up realising that it was beginning to get dark outside and heard Tom snoring from the other bed in the corner. I staggered downstairs into the sitting-room and found Dennis and Butch watching Tele.

'What time is it?' I asked, making my way to the scullery for a drink of water.

Dennis was laughing and said, 'It's half past ten and John said to tell ye when ye get up that he'll see ye for a pint in the 'Fell Em Doon'.'

I groaned and said, 'Aa just want a cup of tea!'

It was a hard way to discover John's, legendary ability to enjoy drinking large quantities of beer without suffering any adverse effects!

Shortly afterwards, John started work as an electrician at the newly opened Area Workshops that had been built on the old material storage area on the other side of the 'Rec' bridge. As we both finished work at roughly the same time we began having our main meal together and I quickly saw that Mam always gave John a larger portion than me, or a better and different meal altogether. It was another indication of how she would ingratiate herself with others at the expense of her own. John obviously noticed it as well and commented so to me but I just accepted it as the way she was and got on with my life.

About the same time, I began to suffer from stomach cramps and pains that slowly became worse. I was unable to keep food down and became sick with a fever. Having an outside loo on the other side of the back-lane was not a pleasant experience when forced to visit it almost constantly. I was unable to go to work or travel to the doctors so Mam eventually and reluctantly walked to the telephone box and arranged for him to visit.

282

I cannot remember what his diagnosis was as I was frankly beyond caring but remember having pencilling injections in my buttocks followed by a regime of pills. I had also lost some weight, leaving me feeling weak and exhausted but a few days later when Tom called to see how I was, I felt well enough to agree to go to the Arcade dance with him on Saturday night. He was keen to see if the girl he was chasing after was going to be there and did not want to go alone.

On Saturday night after a couple of pints at the Portland Hotel, we walked up to the Arcade Dancehall above the Co-op; a rather grand building clad in marble with an elegant staircase leading up to the upper floors. There was a separate set of steps leading up to the large, brightly lit dance hall. I felt bloody awful, and the beer had not helped, but wearing our best suits, we circled the dance floor looking for the girl and quickly found her dancing with her friend.

'Come on,' said Tom, 'Let's ask them to dance.'

Not feeling at all like dancing I reluctantly agreed and we were soon dancing to Dion singing, 'The Wanderer'. June, the girl I was dancing with was a very attractive, brassy blonde with a superb figure, not my normal type but as Tom was obviously smitten with her friend Margaret I backed him up by flirting with June.

After a couple of dances, I said to her, 'Tom's teking Margaret home can I tek you?'

She smiled and said, 'Aa would like you to but am courting and he'll be coming here later, but Aa'll finish with him if ye want to take me out next week.'

It was beginning to sound familiar, me always chatting up unavailable girls.

Not really caring and feeling pretty rough, I said in a rather brusque manner, 'No, if yor gannin out with someone else I'm off,' and turned to leave when she grabbed my arm.

'If we leave now ye can walk me home and I'll finish with him tomorrow,' obviously, she was very keen.

Tom who had been listening nodded his head for me to say yes and said, 'Haway let's gan.'

I found myself walking her home and despite feeling bloody awful, enjoyed the feel of her body pressed next to mine when we canoodled outside her back door. After arranging to meet her on Wednesday at the Welfare Dance so that she would have time to finish with her boyfriend, I met up with Tom for the long walk home.

By the time I got home, I was exhausted; the next morning I was unable to get out of bed, and received no sympathy for having made myself ill again. By Wednesday, I was still not back at work but the medication was beginning to take effect and I felt well enough to meet Tom and catch the bus to the Welfare.

On the bus, Tom said, 'Aa've foond oot who June's boyfriend is and he's got a bit of a reputation.'

Looking out of the bus window I said, 'That's all Aa bloody need, De ye think he'll be at the dance?'

283

'Margaret said he'll probably come looking for ye and that he's always fighting!'

'Bloody charming!' I thought to myself; 'I only took this girl out to keep Tom company and now it looks as if I'm going to be in a fight when I still feel as weak as a kitten,' but I didn't complain to Tom as he'd stood by me many times in the past.

We met up with girls in the dance and were having a reasonably good time when late on in the evening, her ex, came marching up to where we sitting at the back of the hall. Seeing from his demeanour that he meant business, I stood up as he approached. Slightly taller and heavier set than me, he walked in an aggressive manner with his head slightly down. He was wearing a leather jacket, which, I found out later, he had borrowed for the fight!

'Ootside,' was all he said before marching off to the main entrance. I followed him, feeling not in the least bit aggressive toward the lad, after all in his shoes, I would be blood angry; I had acted like a jerk and deserved his wrath.

I was just behind him when we reached the two swing doors at the entrance that he pushed open with both hands before immediately letting go of them, resulting in doors swinging back at me. I instinctively put up my hands to catch them as he turned in a well thought out manoeuvre and swung a crashing right hook into my unprotected face!

Survival kicked in and I ran at him grabbing him around the neck in a two handed choke hold before making the mistake of letting go with my right to punch him two or three times ineffectively in the face. In my weakened state he was easily able to shrug off my one armed hold and wrestled me to the ground pinning both arms with his knees as I had done with the lad at Bedlington Station but unlike me, he did not hesitate in punching and began raining swinging left and rights into my unprotected face.

Desperately, I tried without success to heave him off my chest and arms and then began to swing my legs and feet up to kick the back of his head, managing a couple of times but the punches kept coming. Joe the bouncer hauling the lad off me eventually saved me from further punishment.

'That's enough,' he said throwing the lad to one side before lifting me to my feet.

The lad stormed away without a look-back and I stood shaking my head to clear my vision.

Joe asked, 'Are ye alright young Carr?'

'Aye,' I said and in truth, I was, I had not felt any pain during the beating and still didn't feel any, although I could feel both eyes rapidly swelling.

Joe walked back into the hall and it was then that I noticed several lads close by who had watched the fight.

One of them, a big meaty lad of about five foot ten, who I knew was called Trevor stepped forward and said to Tom, 'Come on then Payne, noo that he's been fettled Am gannin to hev ye!'

Surprised by this unprovoked challenge and looking shocked, Tom reluctantly put his fists up to defend himself but it was all a bit one-sided, Tom dodging wildly swinging blows from the overweight Trevor but not throwing any in return. Inevitably, one or two blows did land and badly rocked Tom causing him to drop to his knees.

I shouted, 'That's enough Trevor, leave it,' but he was not listening; seeing Tom down he moved forward to finish him with a kick.

Without thinking, I ran forward and jumped onto his back, wrapping my right arm around his chubby neck and pulling while at the same time I stamped down hard on the back of his left knee making his left leg buckle.

As he toppled to his left side, I slipped my hip under his and using his weight and momentum, threw him onto his belly. The wind knocked out of him, he looked up in shock as I swung my right foot back as if to kick him in the head but I didn't and instead shouted, 'I frigging said that's enough, noo leave it.'

Trevor slowly heaved himself up and I waited, expecting him to have a go at me but after looking at Tom, he turned and walked back into the dance floor muttering under his breath.

After Tom regained his composure he went inside and brought the two girls out; I could see from June's face that she was disappointed that I had lost the fight and she did not seem to care that I had taken a beating, as she never asked how I was. 'This relationship was going to be short-lived,' I said to myself.

The following day at work when I called to see the Deputy for the list of the next loads, he saw my face and said with some concern, 'Bloody hell lad what the buggery has happened?'

I had forgotten that both my eyes had swollen, providing me with a matching set of slits and answered half-joking, 'The gallowa (pony) kicked me.'

The Deputy immediately sent me to the Medical Centre on the surface while he took details of 'the accident' from Colin, who managed to provide him with a convincing story. The Nurse at the Medical Centre had a quick look and sent me to Ashington Hospital!

After listening to my story and examining my face, the Doctor smiled and said, 'Yes they must be very dangerous, those two-fisted ponies you work with!' I was back at work the following day.

I was still having problems forming any sort of lasting relationship with the girls I dated; no matter how hard I tried, I could not get Little Blue-Eyes out of my mind. At night I did not dream of the girl I was dating; it was always Little Blue-Eyes! When Tom and I left on Saturday morning for the annual fortnight TA Camp at Thetford, Tom was upset at leaving his girlfriend, whereas I was not in the least bit upset at leaving June for a fortnight.

In fact, on the first night there I caught the recreational transport to Norwich with the rest of the lads from the Section, all of us hoping to chat up one of the local lasses while Tom stayed in camp to write to Margaret. I had some success with the local girls and dated a girl from Norwich for the first week and a girl from Swaffham for the second.

I had looked forward eagerly to attending the camp and was not disappointed, enjoying the complete military experience. Thetford Training Area resembled a country park, the tented camp, in particular, was in a beautiful setting and was massive as it accommodated not only our battalion - 7th Battalion, but also the 6th Battalion from the Newcastle area.

Putting the two battalions together, sharing facilities, especially a huge NAAFI tent, was not a sensible idea as there was a great deal of bitter rivalries between the two units. Luckily, on nights off, the majority of the TA soldiers left camp, preventing any on-camp aggravation but it was a different matter in the local towns and villages where several fights occurred when soldiers from the two battalions bumped into each other.

The training itself was well organised and great fun; starting at section level training, it progressed through platoon training and onto company training before the final battalion exercise.

A Seven-a-Side inter-battalion football competition was held during the middle weekend, all teams hell bent on beating their opponents and I mean beating in both senses of the word. Our Section lasted three matches before we limped off the pitch after a very physical game in which we lost four goals to two. I played in goals and suffered several very physical attacks when diving for the ball in the goalmouth; no prisoners were taken! The competition only served to aggravate the growing vicious rivalry between the two Battalions.

Much to our surprise and delight, our section won the Inter-Battalion Assault Course Competition! During the course of the fortnight, each section paraded at the assault course at a given time where the Physical Training Staff met them and demonstrated how to tackle the various obstacles. After a practice run through, each section then carried out a timed run that was brilliant fun. Our Section consisted of fit young pit lads and knowing we had set a fast time, we were chuffed when we heard we had won the trophy. We never saw the trophy; apparently, it would have our section number engraved on it and then be displayed in Battalion Headquarters.

On the two-day final exercise, our Company spent the first afternoon digging a defensive position on 'Frog Hill,' a small wooded hill, used countless times before by other units before us. Despite the chalky ground, the digging was easy; the best places for slit trenches having been dug over many times in the past. Trenches dug and ready to defend ourselves we waited for the enemy. Our Section position was on the north side of the wood, affording a great view over open ground that extended for a mile or more in front of us.

Just after 'Stand To' at last light we were told to get our heads down, which meant wrapping our waterproof capes around our shoulders, and trying to sleep whilst sitting in the bottom of our trenches.

I was just starting to nod off when the Platoon Sergeant sent me to the 'Bren Gun' trench to go on watch with the Section, Second-in-Command; a small and very neat Lance Corporal called John.

John said, 'Right Syd Ye gan on stag on the gun until midnight then Aa'll tek ower and ye can get yor heed doon.'

Leaning against the trench wall, I lifted the butt of the Bren into my shoulder and slowly moved the barrel through its arc, half-expecting to see the enemy from the 6th Battalion charging our position; I felt a tad tense.

After thirty minutes of staring into the dark, I was having difficulty staying awake and my eyes were beginning to play tricks; I kept on seeing bushes move and had to concentrate and stare at them to steady my vision. After an hour of rubbing my eyes to stay awake, I saw what appeared to be a line of bushes moving slowly from left to right, a hundred yards in front of me!

Staring hard at the bushes, I watched as they began to take on human shape before they turned toward me! Now I was awake; I was still not convinced that I was seeing the enemy, as they had not set off any of the trip flares that the Platoon Sergeant set up there before last light. Just in case it was the enemy, I pulled the stock of the Bren light machine gun into my shoulder, slipped the safety catch to Automatic, and held my breath as the crouching figures slowly, very slowly inched toward me.

I was sure that soldiers in the other trenches must have seen them and someone would challenge them but no one did. I did not want to wake the sleeping John up in case I was wrong and continued to watch. Eventually, the first figure was no more than ten or twelve yards away and looked enormous to me from my hole in the ground, and what's more, he was coming straight at me.

'Mike Mike?' I challenged with the first part of the password in a not too loud voice, hoping it sounded firm.

The figures froze in uncertainty but did not answer and I felt my finger squeeze the trigger of the Bren blasting four wooden blanks at the outlines in front - shattering the quiet of the night.

The first figure let out what sounded like a shriek of pain as they turned and bolted for the night, hurried along by another burst from my Bren. They might have avoided the trip flares coming in but going out they ran straight into them, the night sky lit up I saw them follow their training and dive for cover.

The rest of the company had woken up and there was sporadic fire from the trenches to the right and left of me. I fired another three round burst before John grabbed my shoulder.

'Steady on man we've only got one magazine of blank ammunition,' he said.

287

As the flare burnt itself out, the section fired one or two more rounds at the last position we had seen the enemy but soon all was quiet again and a few minutes later John took over the Bren. As I settled down in the back of the trench to try to grab a couple of hours sleep, two shadowy figures approached from the rear.

'Who was manning the Bren?' a whispered voice demanded. It was the CSM with the Platoon Sergeant.

Without thinking, I answered, 'Me Sir.'

'Who the fucks me lad?' the CSM snarled.

'Carr Sir.' I said nervously, wondering if I was going to receive a roasting for firing the Bren.

'Bloody well done Carr, I'm glad to see some bugger is awake in this shagging Company,' he whispered and slinked away into the dark followed by the Sergeant.

John whispered, 'Ye'll be after my bloody stripe noo, it's not often that owld bugger praises anyone.' I settled down feeling very chuffed with myself and imagined myself as Lance Corporal Carr, I quite liked the idea!

Before I could nod off the Platoon Sergeant came back and whispered into the trench, 'Carr are ye awake?'

'Aye Sarge,'

'Right yor gannin oot on a fighting patrol; get yor kit sorted oot and report to Company HQ.'

'What's a fighting patrol, Sarge?' I asked.

The Sergeant growled, 'God bloody help us - ye knaa that lot ye fired at?'

'Yes Sarge.'

'Whey they were a fighting patrol from the enemy, got that?'

'Aye Sarge,' I answered excited at the thought of sneaking around the countryside before attacking some unsuspecting enemy to take them all prisoner.

Chuckling, John said, 'That's your reward for being alert; wandering roond the woods all night and nee sleep!'

I didn't care; I was excited and asked, 'What kit do I need?'

John turned from staring into the night and said, 'Change into your plimsolls, put on your cap comforter and take your rifle, leave everything else here.'

Changing into my plimsolls I asked, 'Do I not need my webbing?'

'No,' John answered, 'ye've got to move light and fast and mek nee noise.'

He then showed me how to fold my cap comforter to make a commando style, cloth hat before saying, 'Noo, Audie Murphy bugger off, and win the frigging war!'

At Company HQ, I met up with other lads taken from the rest of the company to make up the patrol, before the young officer who was to lead us, briefed us on our mission – 'to take a prisoner'.

A huge Corporal checked to make sure we had nothing on us that would rattle or make any noise, then issued us with ten rounds of blank ammunition each, the most I had seen as we generally only ever got two.

A few minutes later, we moved off in single file, everyone alert and tense with weapons at the ready. Progress was slow as we kept going to ground while the Officer stopped to check his map and listen for noises. We were very much alert with our eyes wide open as we tried to detect any signs of movement, or enemy positions.

After an hour, the tension in my body eased as I began to feel the effects of having had no sleep. I was only seventeen and like any other young teenager, I needed, at least, eight hours a night! Just when I was beginning to feel a wee bit bored we went to ground once more and the whispered word came back that the enemy position was fifty yards to our front, we were about to go in!

I was alert again; adrenalin pumping as we moved forward, crouching as low as we could go, our fingers on triggers and thumbs on safety catches. I could make out the edge of a wood to our front as we sunk onto bellies to crawl the last twenty yards into the enemy position. As we crawled across the damp grass I was expecting a challenge to come from the wood but none came and I mentally prepared myself for some hard fighting as I was sure no-one in 6th Battalion was going to surrender easily, if at all. Nerves screaming, we reached the woods and paused, searching desperately as we tried to locate a trench.

'Buggeration!' whispered the Officer in an almost polite manner, 'this must be the wrong wood, there's no one here!'

It was a huge anti-climax and I could feel tension drain from me as we scanned the empty wood.

The Officer checked his map again and consulted with the Corporal before we formed up into single-file again and moved off toward another wood.

Three woods later, I had lost interest; I was weary, very tired and fed up of crawling into empty woods! We had been out for several hours and it was beginning to get light. I was now having great difficulty staying awake and in between woods, walked with my rifle across my shoulder with my head resting on my rifle; it was the first time I realised that you could sleep while walking, even if it was just a couple of steps until you tripped over something.

Half an hour later we were marching very quickly back to our Company Position as we needed to get back before first light when the Company would be 'Stood To'.

We failed; we approached Frog Hill through patchy ground mist just as the sun was rising over the woods to the east, and to make matters worse, the Officer blundered into a trip flare!

All hell broke loose; at 'Stand to Positions' the Company were all awake in their trenches, weapons at the ready in case there was a first light attack, and as far as they were concerned, we were it! Two Bren Guns rattled off several bursts'

289

rifle fire crackled from the trenches along the front of the wood facing us and a flare gun shot a red flare unnecessarily into the morning sky.

Instinctively diving for cover, I lay there listening to fire orders been shouted within the wood and turned to look into the face of the lad next to me and we both burst out laughing.

Through giggles, he said, 'The useless bugger couldn't even get us back without getting us all frigging killed.'

'Quiet!' the Corporal yelled as he stood up and walked toward the position waving his rifle above his head.

The gunfire subsided as the soldiers in the company recognised him and he then turned and shouted, 'Come on you lot, follow me.'

He looked thoroughly fed up and ignored our young officer who followed sheepishly along at the back into the Company position where we took a lot of ribbing as we walked through our trenches and back to HQ for debriefing.

When we got there the CSM sent us straight back to our sections whilst the Company Commander, who looked as though he had just eaten something disgusting, said to our young Officer, 'Jonathon, come here, a few words if I may.'

Back at the trench, I pulled my boots back on and thought, 'I'll get some shut eye,' just as the Platoon Sergeant and CQMS came round with rations for breakfast.

The Sergeant ordered, 'Get yorselves sorted oot and eat, we're moving oot at eight o'clock!'

Feeling knackered, I wearily splashed water on my face for my ablutions and then lit a hexamine block in a little disposable cooker, placing a mess tin full of water on to boil for tea. John cooked a tin of beans and sausages that we ate with two slices of bread each for breakfast.

He had to nudge me awake a few times while we waited for our breakfast to cook, 'Come on Audie bloody Murphy, any bugger would think ye've been awake all night!'

A couple of hours later we were in a new position trying to dig shallow trenches in very hard, flint laden soil. The scorching mid-summer sun added to my lethargy as I waited my turn to use the pick. The Platoon Sergeant had moved me into the Bren Gun Team of our Section with John and another lad and like everyone else in the Company; we were struggling to make headway through the concrete-like ground.

The Officers and NCOs were excited and agitated, as our trenches had to be completed in time to receive a final attack from two companies of the 6th Battalion and at ou present rate of digging we would be lucky if we managed to dig out shell scrapes! I had handed back eight of the ten rounds of ammunition issued for the fighting patrol leaving me two rounds of blank for my rifle but we had a full magazine of twenty-eight rounds for the Bren.

Eventually, ordered to stop digging and take cover in readiness for the attack, I flopped down next to John who was manning the Bren and I immediately began to feel the effects of the hot sun on my back through my thick khaki battle dress. That and lack of sleep was too much for me; I was having great difficulty staying awake as officers and NCOs shouted orders to prepare us for the attack.

Through half closed eyes, I saw the enemy emerge from a large wood in the distance and begin to advance toward us; their officers using wooden football rattles to simulate sub-machine-gun fire. Ordered to hold our fire as they approached, we lay in the hot sun squinting at the advancing figures, at least a hundred of them to our immediate front moving steadily forward, waiting for their order to charge the last fifty yards to our position.

Slipping the safety catch off my rifle, I waited for the order to fire; the sun was even hotter and I was very tired and struggled to stay awake and failed!

John shaking me and saying, 'Some bloody Audie Murphy ye are,' startled me and half-awake, I sat upright and looked forward expecting to see the enemy but there was no sign of them.

'Where are they?' I asked wondering what had happened.

'Turn roond and look.' John said pointing to the rear where the two companies who had charged through our position were now advancing on the reserve company location; I had slept through all the action!

We returned to camp an hour or so later and packed our personal kit and company stores ready for the journey home the following morning. As it was the last night in Norfolk, the two Battalion RSMs had confined everyone to camp, which, considering the animosity between the two units was probably not a sensible decision.

Our Section had decided to keep away from potential trouble by staying in one of our two tents playing cards but by eight o clock we were all thoroughly bored and when Dave said, 'Any bugger fancy a pint in the NAAFI?' we all muttered in agreement and headed for the large marquee that contained the NAAFI bar.

We found the huge tent packed with men from both battalions, all drinking, some talking, some singing but quite a few glaring at each other. Despite the noise, the tension was obvious, so we found a part of the very long bar where we could see lads from our company drinking and squeezed in feeling less vulnerable and ordered beers.

After a couple of beers each, we noticed an increase in tension and began looking nervously around, concerned that if a fight kicked off it would be a big one. A large powerfully built NCO from one of our other platoons was gathering men and lads around him and said to us, 'Keep close lads and when it starts we'll rush the bastards!'

Tom started to visibly shake and Dave said, 'Fuck him lads, come on let's get the fuck oot of here noo.'

There was no argument; we pushed our way out of the tent and stood outside sucking in the fresh night air after the stench of beer, cigarette smoke, and sweaty bodies in the marquee.

As our eyes became accustomed to the dark, we could see a group of about a dozen men a few yards in front of us. They had formed a circle and appeared to be goading someone. Curious, we walked over and saw that the men forming the circle were from the other Battalion; Byker lads, and they were taunting a Blackman from the Morpeth Company of our battalion. They were yelling racist terms, most of which I had never heard before but the Blackman was standing his ground and by his stance, he was ready to defend himself.

One of the Byker lads ran at him from behind swinging his fist in the air but some sixth sense warned the Blackman and turning, he caught the swinging blow with his arms and using the Byker lads own momentum, threw him to the ground. Another lad lunged forward with a kick that the Blackman blocked with his own foot before another tried to rush him.

He was holding his own and had begun trading blows with the Byker lads but it was obvious that if they all rushed him he would go down.

Dave shouted, 'Come on,' and thinking he meant we were going to pile in and help the Blackman, I started forward, only to be yanked back by Joe who shouted, 'Haway ye daft twat dee ye want te get killed?'

I turned and saw the rest of the section walking quickly away from the fight and tried to knock Joe's hand off my shoulder and turn back to the fight but as I did, the battle erupted! Twenty or more lads led by the big NCO, some clutching huge tent pegs, came pouring out of the marquee and swarmed over the Byker lads, punching and kicking them to the ground.

I stood open mouthed as more and more men from both Battalions poured out and into the fracas, the fight spreading like wildfire. I felt Joe's hand grip me tighter and pull me away from the mayhem: I did not resist. We turned and ran off to catch up with the others and as we reached them, we saw that fights were breaking out all around us.

The eight of us kept close, as we made our way back to our tents, fending off two wild-eyed rampaging lads who ran at us screaming obscenities.

We knocked them both to the ground and kept on moving, Tom asking, 'Wor they theirs or ours?' We didn't know and were not concerned; our only thought was to get away from the bedlam around us.

Sitting on the beds in our tent listening to the battle that raged a couple of hundred yards away was intimidating, screams of pain and anger, shouts and moans, and the noise of wood breaking and canvas ripping filled the night. There was no question of Dave and his three tent mates going back to their tent, the eight of us spent the night in ours with tent pegs at the ready. By two o clock, the noise had all but ended, only the odd shouted obscenity punctuating the night.

At six-thirty, after some fitful sleep, we made our way to the ablution huts through a scene of devastation; ripped and torn tents, tables, chairs, bottles and tent pegs littered the camp. Standing next to a couple of ambulances, a gaggle of exhausted Warrant Officers and SNCOs who had spent most of the night trying to stop fights were discussing what to do next, a few of them bearing battle scars that testified to the fury of the fighting.

An hour or so later as we were making our way to the fleet of double-decker buses lined up to carry us to the railway station for the journey north, we passed the two RSMs standing surveying the scene, both knew that they could not hold back TA soldiers to clear up the devastation and both looked very angry. Passing them, I heard the 6th Battalion RSM said to ours, 'Trust this to bloody happen on my last two weeks in the frigging army!'

25

Time to Go

I had thoroughly enjoyed the two weeks with the TA, especially the camaraderie within our Section and so felt a bit down on return to Ashington. Tom
went rushing off to see Margaret whereas I did not intend to see June again; having
felt it was all over between us before I left, I had no great desire to restart our relationship, besides I think she already had her eyes on another lad.

After a week hanging around with Tom and a group of other teenagers, I
returned to work at the colliery and found that Bob had moved to another job leaving me running the job at the TU. Colin and I worked well together but the workload was just too much for the two of us leaving us both knackered at the end of
each shift.

On the third day back at work, we had to take a replacement coal cutter into the coalface, a job that required the two largest and strongest ponies in the pit as
the cutter was very heavy and the route included a long incline. The tram with the
cutter on board waited for collection at the end of a winch at a bank-bottom, a
hundred yards down a utility tunnel.

Hitching big Spot and powerful Sam to the tram, we walked them round to
the roadway that led to the coalface several hundred yards away. Spot at twelve
hands three was the biggest pony in the pit but he could be a bit lazy, while Sam, a
fraction smaller, was very powerful and always keen to work but could be difficult
to control. Aware of this we had taken a third pony from the stables; Tom was
only ten hands two but what he lacked in size he made up for in effort and man-
ners.

We hitched Sam directly to the tram with Spot hitched to him and Tom at
the very front. This meant that when ordered, Tom would be off; Spot would follow him and Sam who was contained at the back, would be under control.

We set off with me riding the limber, Colin riding the bumpers at the back
of the tram, ready to run forward and throw a metal spike called the dreg into one
of the wheels to provide a brake should we need to slow the load down or stop it
running backwards if the ponies stalled. With Spot and Sam leaning into the collars, their powerful legs pushing hard we were soon moving forward at a good
pace.

Using his metal and leather-head-protector, Tom pushed open the several
wooden air doors on the route, Colin leaning out to swing them shut once we
passed through.

When we reached the main incline, I dismounted and ran alongside Spot
urging him on in an effort to make sure he kept pulling, knowing that Tom and

Sam would need no such encouragement. Colin ran alongside the tram ready to use the dreg as a brake, should the ponies lose momentum.

Half way up the incline, there were two more air doors, the first of which Tom knocked open and we passed through with me screaming at Spot and Sam whose hooves were scrabbling for grip on the stony ground as they fought to haul the load up the bank. Tom reached the second air door, knocked it open and met a dozen or more lamps shining in his eyes, accompanied by a cacophony of screaming voices!

Spooked by the lights and screaming, he balked and slipped to the left causing Spot to bump into him and balk, leaving Sam with the full weight of the load.

I ran forward screaming obscenities at the people holding the lamps and grabbing Tom's reins I pulled him back between the lines urging him on, hoping that Spot would follow.

'GET OOT THE FUCKING WAY YE STUPID BASTARDS, TURN YOUR LAMPS AWAY' I yelled at the top of my voice as the group had not moved from the tramlines or stopped their screaming. Colin was poised to throw the dreg into the rear wheels as I fought to get the ponies moving again but it was too late; despite my best efforts, Spot was still trying to move backwards and Sam was unable to hold the weight of the load.

'Dreg,' I screamed back to Colin who had already seen the danger and thrown the dreg into the rear wheels successfully braking them but the weight of the load was too much. With the rear wheels locked, the tram slowly began to slide backwards! Tom had gone down on his knees and Spot was panicking as Sam desperately tried to stop the trams backward movement. Colin was heaving at the tram and I had grasped Spot's reins and was trying frantically to calm him and get him to use his size and weight to stop the tram but we were fighting a losing battle.

Sam was soon exhausted and was unable to fight the weight of the tram any longer and I was been thrown around while hanging onto Spot's headgear in an effort to calm him while poor Tom, who had totally lost his footing was been dragged back on his knees. Even after Colin had thrown another dreg into the front wheels, the momentum of the tram increased as it slid to the bottom of the bank dragging the three ponies, Colin, and me with it.

When the tram eventually came to a halt a few yards passed the bottom of the incline, Tom scrambled back to his feet and I finally managed to calm Spot, providing us with the opportunity to take stock. Sam was blowing hard with a lathered sweat covering his shoulders; Spot was unmarked and still relatively fresh while Tom stood panting heavily but was calm despite having bloodied both his front legs.

I had to restrain Colin who had started to scream obscenities at the group of people walking down the bank toward us as he advanced toward them, ready to carry out bodily harm to whoever it was that had endangered our lives and those of

296

our ponies. Feeling like joining him, I resisted the temptation knowing we had to look after the ponies first but that did not stop me from adding a few obscenities myself.

The group descended the bank, coming reluctantly closer and I suddenly realised that they were school kids aged about thirteen or fourteen and that most of them were girls of whom some were crying! I calmed myself while still trying to control Colin who still wanted to, 'Smash their fucking heeds in!'

The group stopped and a burly figure came forward - their guide, and he was non-too-pleased with our language.

'That's enough of that, am gannin to report the pair of ye.'

'Bollocks,' I interrupted, 'we nearly lost wor bloody ponies because of ye sackless buggers and if ye are in frigging charge, why the bloody hell did ye not have them under control and in single frigging file?'

He leaned forward and threatened, 'Aa divvint hev te tek your lip ye cheeky sod ye, noo bugger off oot me way or Aa'll daad ye.'

Colin pushed forward and spat, 'Aye go on then, just try and we'll knacker ye.'

We exchanged a few more insults before he left, shepherding his shocked group with him, warning us that we had not heard the last of this! Colin and I calmed the ponies, rested, and fed them before we made another and, this time, successful attempt to deliver the cutter.

An hour or so later, the deputy came panting up to us as we were loading some girders onto a flat horny prior to delivering them to the 'Mothergate.'

'What the hell hev ye two been up too? Nur divvint answer, the Owerman wants te see ye both noo, so get up te the winch heed he's waiting there,' he blurt-ed, obviously angry at having to leave the coal face to speak to us.

As he turned to leave, I said, 'But we've got te get these girders in yet and two mair loads of props man!'

The Deputy shouted back over his shoulder as he walked away, 'Aa'll ge ye each two hoors owertime te get it finished noo get on we ye.'

'Fucking champion,' shouted Colin, 'We nearly get fucking killed by some sackless twats, and we are gannin te get fucking fired, fucking champion,' and we headed off to find out whether or not we still had jobs.

As we walked up to the Cabin by the main winch, the Overman waved us in and after telling us to calm down; he asked us what had happened. Colin started with a rush but the Overman stopped him and asked me to tell the story.

He listened intently before he stood up and said, 'Aye, right ye are lads, get back to work and Aa'll have a word and mek sure ye niver get put in danger like that again and Aa nah it's pointless but try and watch yer swearing when tha's visitas doon there.' That was it, matter closed or so we thought until the following morning the big man from the day before came and, very reluctantly, apologised!

The following day, a sixteen-year-old, skinny lad of about five foot five arrived with the Deputy!

'This is young Terry, he's here to work with you two so mek sure ye look after him and show him the ropes, reet?'

'Aye, great,' I replied while Colin looked him over suspiciously and muttered, 'He looks like a right useless sod te me.'

Terry was keen but as Colin had suspected, not very able mainly due to a lack of experience that I'm sure he would soon rectify; that was if Colin would allow. Colin still rushed into jobs without much thought and was adapt at bulldozing through tasks, the problem was that he expected everyone else to do the same - he expected Terry to be as able as him. This was clearly impossible as Terry was much smaller and had not yet learnt all the different techniques required for manhandling different materials.

This led to frustration and anger on Colin's behalf, and fear and intimidation for Terry, whilst I tried to ensure that I left Terry alone with Colin as little as possible. After a week, it came to a head; Terry, who had been helping Colin move some girders into the Mothergate, came up to me crying or as good as crying.

'What the hell's the matter with ye?' I demanded.

Through half sobs, Terry said, 'Aa cannit tek anymore, I'm fed up of Colin bashing me aroond, he's always picking on me; he only thumps me when ye are not there, can ye tell him to stop or am leaving?'

Unaware that Colin was thumping the lad, I was a tad annoyed; it was the last thing we needed, as we had to go flat out to keep up with the workload. In addition to which, I did not want a confrontation with Colin as despite our differences we got on very well and were a good working team but we needed a third lad and Colin needed to be talked too!

'Colin what the fuck hev ye done to Terry, yor supposed te be showing him hoo te work, not knock him aboot man,' I said when I caught up with Colin in the Mothergate.

'Whey man he's a useless sod, he nearly had me fingers off when we were stacking the fucking girders so I thumped the twat.'

I knew this had to be resolved quickly and said, 'Whey that's not good enough man, he's still trying to learn and he is trying, so if ye cannit work with him he'll have to stay with me all the time.'

Colin was not happy and said, 'That's not bloody right man; we've got to share the workload!'

'Yor right, just so lang as ye keep yor hands off of him and yor temper under control, OK?

'Aye bollocks,' he spat back but the message got through and although he didn't ease off on Terry, he did not hit him anymore.

The following Saturday I was with Tom listening to an Adam Faith record in a booth in the record shop when I saw two lasses walk into the shop giggling.

For a moment, I thought one of them was Little Blue-Eyes as she was about the same height and was certainly very bonny.

A short while later I was talking to her next to an empty booth and we were getting along well; she was telling me that she was going to college when her friend interrupted, saying, 'Titch we'll miss the bus if we don't leave straight away!'

Titch said, 'Am sorry but Aa'll hev to go.'

Taking a deep breath, I asked hopefully, 'Whey can I tek ye te the pictures or dance tonight?'

Smiling, she said, 'Yes, meet me off the bus at five past seven and we can go to the Wallaw.'

I was chuffed, she was not Blue-Eyes but she was very pretty and easy to talk too and I thought that something might develop.

It was not to be, later in the cinema, she asked, 'Where do you work?'

'Ashington Colliery,' I replied wondering why she asked.

'Are you an apprentice then?'

'No, I'm a timber leader,'

'Oh, so you are just a pit lad then?'

'Yes, that's right,' I answered defensively wondering where this was going.

'You don't look like one, I'm sorry Syd, but I don't want to get attached to a pit lad'

Gobsmacked, I spluttered, 'What dee ye mean?'

'Well, I won't be seeing you again I'm sorry.'

'But I thought ye liked me?'

'I do but you haven't got any prospects and I don't go out with pit lads.'

Hurt and upset, I said, 'Aye weel hev a nice life,' and got up to go.

She grabbed my arm and said, 'We can still watch the picture together, and ye can still walk me to the bus stop.'

I took her hand and gently removed it from my arm and said, 'Aa don't think so,' and left.

Walking through the streets toward the Welfare Dance, I felt pretty miserable, thinking about what Titch had said, 'no prospects' and angrily thanked my Father for his success in preventing me or my brothers from having apprenticeships.

At the dance, I met Viv who was with a group of her friends and ended up taking a girl called Dot home, arranging another date with her before I kissed her goodnight.

At the end of the shift on the following Monday, Colin and I were pushing the trams and tubs that we had emptied, round to the bottom of the bank ready to be reloaded. I was pushing three tubs to join the remainder while Colin waited ready to hook them on.

299

With my back against the rear tub, I pushed hard with my legs to move the tubs to where Colin waited, shouting, 'Come On, Come On.'

Holding the steel coupler of the tub he was standing next too, he leant forward ready to drop it onto the hook on the front of the three tubs I was pushing.

'Come On for fucks sake,' he urged wanting to finish, 'Come On, Come On – Right – STOP- ARGH- FOR FUCKS SAKE!' he screamed and jumped back grasping his right hand with his left.

'What the hell's the matter?' I asked as I ran up to him.

'Ye've just nipped me fucking finger off,' he said thrusting his hand at me. The skin was missing from the top knuckle joint of his middle finger leaving a stub of bone exposed!

Colin was tough, and despite the pain he said, 'What dee ye think?'

'What do I think?' I answered, 'Aa think we should get ye te the deputy for a bandage and te bank for the Medical Centre, divvint ye?'

'Aye, but first help me look for the top of me finger they might be able te stick it back on!'

Grubbing around in the muck and stones, I found the finger end, complete with its nail but it was pretty much squashed and I did not hold much hope of it being reattached but did not tell Colin that.

Placing the sticky stump into his bait tin, the two of us walked off to find the deputy, Colin saying, 'Aa thought that useless twat Terry would hev me fingers off, not ye Syd!'

I left Colin with the deputy and went back to meet Terry to take the ponies back to the stables and told him what had happened.

He was shocked but I could see a smile of relief when I said, 'I divvint think we'll be seeing Colin for a good few days.' In fact, it was the last time I saw Colin for several years; the following day a lad called Gordon came to work with us.

I had started dating Dot regularly and although we enjoyed each other's company and enjoyed some heavy petting sessions, it was a light and enjoyable affair, not a serious relationship and we both knew it.

On a warm sunny Sunday afternoon, a week or so later in early September, Tom and I had wandered into Ashington Cricket Club and were lounging on the grass watching the match with not too much interest, when Tom said, 'Isn't that the lass ye fancy ower there?'

Looking over toward the front of the clubhouse where Tom was pointing, I saw her; she was sitting alone on the grass watching the game!

My stomach immediately filled with butterflies and my brain began racing – 'Now was my chance to ask her out; I hope she went out with pit lads'! Then there was Dot but that wasn't serious, and if I didn't seize the opportunity it might be ages before I saw Little Blue-Eyes again; I had to act now!'

Standing up I brushed bits of grass from my denim jeans and straightening my shirt I said to Tom, 'Right, here goes, I'm gannin to ask her oot.'

'Good luck,' Tom said as I turned and walked nervously toward her.

I could see that she was wearing her hair piled high as was the fashion and that she was wearing dark slacks and a blouse with a red cardigan draped over her shoulders, she looked lovely. I was about fifteen yards away when a blonde-haired lad in cricket gear appeared out of the clubhouse and walked up to her. My pace slowed as I watched him sit down next to her before he put his arm round her shoulder.

I stopped and watched as the two of them smiled at each other and began chatting animatedly. My stomach turned as I realised they were a couple!

Devastated and miserable, I stood there not knowing what to do when I heard Tom, who had come up behind me, say, 'Looks as though yor too late, again!'

We turned and walked away, I felt absolutely gutted and said to Tom, 'I should have realised that a lass like that would have a boyfriend, what a pillock I am.'

Tom said, 'Whey ye've still got Dot, man!'

'That's not the same, Dot and me aren't serious and ye knaa hoo much I fancy that lass,' I said feeling miserable.

After a moment's thought, I said to Tom, 'Am not getting at ye but yor aalreet, ye've got an apprenticeship, ye've got a motorbike and yor courting the lass ye want, I've got frig all.' 'My life's like a Waltzer - flying roond in circles withoot getting anywhere and filled with lots of meaningless ups and doons, Aa need te get off and sort me life oot.'

Having said it, I realised that I was seventeen and a half and as Titch had rightly said, I had no prospects work wise, and now, it looked as if I had no chance of going out with the girl I wanted, I had just seen her with a boyfriend - the blonde haired, cricket playing swine.

The following day Terry, Gordon, and I were sitting having our lunch when a lad called Toddy from another part of the pit road up on his pony. He was in my section in the TA and we had gone through NCB training together and got on well.

He jumped off the pony and stood smiling in front of us; a gregarious lad he said, 'Am gannin te the toon temorra te join up Syd, are ye coming?'

'Join what?' I asked wondering what he was talking about.

'The army man, what dee ye think?'

'The army?' I repeated unnecessarily. 'Why are ye asking me?'

'Whey I felt sure ye'd want te join like yor brothers man.

'Aye whey ye thought wrang man,' I said laughing but a picture of Little Blues-Eyes with the blonde haired lad came into my head and Titch's biting statement, 'You haven't got any prospects.'

301

'Are ye sure?' Toddy asked.

I stood up and said, 'What bus are we catching?'

Part 4

Khaki Clad

26

Basic

At eight o'clock on a sunny September morning, having donned my suit, white shirt and a blue tie, I finished a cup of tea while listening to Billy Fury singing 'Last night was made for love' from the loudspeaker of the ageing Rediffusion radiogram in our kitchen.

When the song ended, I picked up my holdall and taking the last sip of barely warm tea, I patted Butch on the head and said to Dennis, 'See ye.'

Through a mouthful of cornflakes, he spluttered, 'Aye,' and I turned and left the Fifth Row to join up, the Fourth Lad to leave our house in the hope of a better life. Mam had not bothered to get out of bed to see me off, not that I had expected her too, and Dad; well, he had not spoken to me for a few days so I was more than happy to be on my way.

Sitting on the bus to Newcastle my thoughts once again went back to my decision to join up. I had spent most of my last night at home wondering if I had done the right thing but I was also very excited at leaving home. There was no patriotic need urging me to join, Great Britain was not involved in any major conflict, the main threat to our country in 1962 was Russia and the Warsaw Pact, - we were in the middle of the cold war. Any reasons I had for joining were purely personal and selfish.

Having thoroughly enjoyed the excitement and camaraderie in the Army Cadets and TA, especially the weekends away from the drab colliery Rows, I had also realised that joining up was almost an inevitability. In addition, having three older brothers who used the Army as a means of escaping home and the pits and who, when on leave told me tales of exotic places and adventures, meant joining up must have always been in the back of my mind.

No one at home was surprised when I said I was leaving; Dad had taken the news with silent anger and I had not told my Mam, as I did not want any aggravation and frankly, her opinion was of little concern to me now.

Dennis only said, 'Aa'll be on me an in the bedroom noo!'

National Service recruitment had ended eighteen months earlier and the last of forcibly recruited soldiers were leaving the services, resulting in the Army having to recruit hard and successfully to fill the gaps left by them. The fact that I was to become part of a completely volunteer Army escaped me at the time; I was just looking forward to having a better and more exciting life.

304

Apart from making a decision as to which regiment or corps I would join, the recruiting process had been straightforward. I initially asked to join the REME as my brothers before me had done but when I was told I would have to wait until the new year before I could join recruit training with the REME, I opted for the Royal Artillery (RA). The only reason for choosing the RA was simply that it was Toddy's choice and, I could start as soon as I reached seventeen and a half, which was two weeks later!

I also expressed a wish to become an Army Commando as opposed to a Royal Marine Commando but the Royal Artillery Recruiting Sergeant informed me that I could only apply to join one of the Royal Artillery Commando Regiments after I had completed two years' service in the RA.

Having chosen to join the RA to be with Toddy and other lads I was a bit miffed when they left a week before me, as they were already old enough.

Because our relationship was not serious, neither Dot or I were overly upset at my leaving, but on the night before I left she asked me to meet her at her house instead of in town.

I had spent most of the last day sorting out the meagre essentials I required to take with me. I was going to wear my latest navy blue, pinstripe 'Teddy Boy' style suit complete with Beetle-Crusher' shoes to travel in; still considered the height of sartorial elegance in Ashington but probably not elsewhere.

My 'Italian' suit, washing and shaving kit, a pair of jeans, a couple of shirts and some underwear made up the rest of my travel kit but I then spent ages looking for something to put it all in. Forced into having a last foray into the 'Dark Hole' beneath the stairs, I emerged with a battered old holdall that I stuffed my kit into before racing off to meet Dot.

Arriving an hour late and expecting to take her to the pictures I was surprised when instead she coyly invited me into her sitting room where her kid brother was watching television.

Smiling at me, she said, 'Me Mam and Dad are at the Bingo and Lenny is going to his friend's house, aren't you Lenny?'

Dragging the reluctant Lenny from the sofa, she pushed him toward the door but Lenny was apparently not too keen on the idea and moaned, 'Oh dee Aa hev te man?' Dot pushed him out the door, switched off the television and put a record on the Dansette.

Brian Hyland started to sing, 'Sealed with a kiss,' as she sat next to me on their large sofa, and then to my surprise, she lay back and whispered, 'We've got the house to ourselves now!'

It was lost on me – my mind was full of the journey tomorrow, and the army and all though we engaged in some hot canoodling; in my innocence and like an idiot, I missed the signals that she was offering herself to me that night. Wanting to be fresh for the following day and after promising to write, I left a disappointed Dot at ten o'clock.

305

The next morning, the 26th September, as arranged by the recruiters, I joined three other lads who I had not met before at Newcastle Railway Station and caught the train to Oswestry and 17 Training Regiment Royal Artillery.

Park Hall Camp, Oswestry, was a huge barracks that consisted mainly of black-creosote painted, wooden huts accommodating 17 Training Regiment Royal Artillery and an Infantry Junior Soldiers Regiment. The accommodation consisted of numerous groups of seven huts; three huts either side of a central ablution and latrine block all connected by wooden passageways. Each hut had beds for twenty recruits with a small NCO's bunkroom by the door.

Having been processed and issued with what was to me, a vast amount of clothing and equipment; I was busy making my bed as was the lad who had been assigned the bedspace next to me.

He was a six-foot-four-inch, gangly Scot who looked across and asked, 'Where ye from?

'Ashington, near Newcastle, ye'll be from Scotland then?' I said looking up at him.

'Aye that's reet, I'm Jock Broon.'

The two of us continued chatting as other lads came in and took up the remaining bed spaces until a middle aged, slightly portly, but immaculate Sergeant came in and shouted, 'STAND UP!'

We all stood up; those of us with some military training, standing to attention as a young, good-looking Lieutenant entered the room.

'Relax everyone and continue what you are doing,' he said in a very posh voice, before wandering around the room to talk to his new recruits - this was our Troop Commander.

Reaching the space between Jock's and my bed, he paused as Jock and I stood to attention.

He looked us both over with almost disdain and ventured, 'Judging by your dress, I take it you are both Northerners, am I right?'

Jock answered first, 'Scotland Sir.'

'Northumberland Sir,' I said.

The Sergeant butted in, 'Another bloody Geordie, Jocks with their heads kicked in!'

The Lieutenant gave the Sergeant a scathing look and almost whispered, 'Northumberland is God's own country Sergeant; it is also my home county.'

The Sergeant's face reddened and he gave me a warning glare as I smiled at the Troop Commander's remark.

The Troop Commander asked my name before continuing, 'Well Carr, do you think you are going to enjoy Basic Training?'

I thought for a second and answered, 'Whey it's the forst time Aa've had a bed on me own Sir, and Aa've just been given all this kit, as well as some jewellery so, am sure am ganging to like it!'

306

'Jewellery?' the Troop Commander asked.

'Yes Sir,' I answered and reaching into my locker, lifted out the knife, fork and spoon I had been issued with and held them up and with a smile and said, 'Aa've niver had jewellery like this before Sir.'

He smiled and turned away as the Sergeant leaned into my face and said, 'A comedian aye Carr, let's see if yor still laughing in a week's time?'

I was; the Sergeant who was called Daily turned out to be rather decent and jolly and a bit of a father figure but unfortunately, he was replaced halfway through training by a miserable looking, mean faced, newly promoted Sergeant called Fraser, who, for some reason took an instant dislike to my boyish face!

I thoroughly enjoyed basic training and in common with most of the other lads there, I never felt the least bit homesick, although I did lie in bed at night thinking of a little blue-eyed girl before sleep quietly stole her away.

I also made several good mates, some of whom I would serve with for several years. One of these was a muscular cockney called Dick who had had the cartilage in his nose removed, leaving him with a squashed and soft nose.

'My old Dad had it taken out so it wouldn't get broken when I boxed,' he told me, 'only trouble is I never wanted to box and joined up to get away from him!'

'Join the club!' I retorted.

With every minute of the day taken up with drill, weapons training, physical training or one of the many other subjects we had to master; training flew by and it was soon time for our first evening pass that allowed us to go into town. Up until then, having been confined to barracks, our evenings had been spent bulling our boots and preparing our kit for the following day's activities, although we did usually manage to spend an hour in the NAAFI canteen sipping a pint while trying to understand what our new found mates were saying in their strange accents!

The NAAFI was a huge wooden building, serving teas, pies, cakes and the like during the day, then at night it operated as a bar with music blaring constantly from the jukebox. Telstar was the favourite during the day but at night the favourites for love sick soldiers were, 'Send me the pillow you dream on so darling I can dream on it too' and 'It might as well rain until September' but the most played was, 'I'll send you all my love every day in a letter sealed with a kiss.'

As a way of protest, I always played Neil Sedaka's, 'Breaking up is hard to do,' warning those around me, 'Divvint expect yor lasses to wait for ye while we're gallivanting roond here lads.' Little did I realise I would be an early casualty of love lost!

Before the Troop Sergeant issued us passes to leave barracks and spend an evening in 'town,' we had to parade by our beds wearing the civvies we intended to wear downtown. This parade was for the Troop Commander who had to ensure that our civvies were presentable. I had my freshly pressed 'Teddy Boy' suit on

307

and waited nervously as the Troop Commander and Sergeant inspected the lads nearest the door; he refused one of them permission for a pass as he was wearing a scruffy jacket and did not have a tie.

I came rigidly to attention as the Troop Commander approached but it was Sergeant Fraser who reached me first, spitting, 'There'll be no bloody Teddy Boys going out tonight Carr so you can forget it!'

Crestfallen, I was just about to turn away but the young Troop Commander said, 'Just a moment Sergeant Fraser, let me see the criteria for walking out dress.'

Sergeant Fraser handed him the millboard with the details clipped to it and stood back with a self-satisfied smirk on his face.

'Let me see,' the Troop Commander said. 'Well pressed suit or smart jacket and trousers – check.'

'But Sir it's a bloody Teddy boy suit Sir,' Sergeant Fraser exploded.

'It is a suit and it is clean and well pressed is it not?'

'Yes Sir,' a tight-lipped Sergeant Fraser replied.

'Has he a clean shirt and tie Sergeant Fraser?'

'Well it's a clean shirt but he's wearing a pencil tie Sir!' Sergeant Fraser answered smirking.

'Is it a tie Sergeant?'

'Yes, Sir.'

'Good, next – let me see, highly polished shoes?'

Sergeant Fraser had just about given up and answered, 'Yes Sir but they are Beetle-Crushers Sir.'

The Troop Commander who was half smiling said, 'Good, he meets the dress requirements, give him his pass Sergeant.'

He then turned to me and asked, 'Are you enjoying it here in Oswestry Carr?'

'Aye Sir, it's brilliant, Aa have a bed of me own and am woken up every morning and teking to a nice big warm cookhouse where I have a big breakfast and then gan back again for dinner and tea; and, what's more, I get paid for it as well, it's great here Sir.' I said trying to look serious.

The Officer smiled and walked on as Sergeant Fraser reluctantly thrust the pass into my hand and warned, 'You'd better not be late back tonight Carr!'

I made sure I wasn't but I was to find out later that Sergeant Fraser was not about to forget that I had unintentionally embarrassed him in front of the Troop Commander.

Oswestry itself turned out to be a bit of a disappointment, the town suffered weekly invasions of hundreds of young recruits trying to chat up the local girls whilst getting hopelessly drunk on a few pints of beer each. We had far more success at the Friday night Garrison dance when it was our Troop's turn to attend.

A great many of the Infantry Boy-Soldiers attended the dance but as they had to wear uniform and paid a pittance, they had very little success with the throngs of local lasses who bussed into the dance. I chatted up one of the lasses who, after a snogging session outside, I promised to see again but of course never did.

Having realised what I'd missed on my last night at home, I exchanged a few letters with Dot and had tried to make them sound a bit passionate but obviously failed as not unexpectedly, I received a Dear John letter a couple of weeks after I left. I pinned it to the notice board to join several others already posted by other lads whose lasses had sought pastures new.

Although I enjoyed it immensely, Basic Training passed without any real highlights until the final three-day exercise at Sennybridge Training Centre in South Wales. Dressed in green combat kit and wearing our '1937' pattern webbing we travelled there in the back of 3-tonners, singing songs and joking. We discovered it was the 25th birthday of a lad named Brian, the oldest, more mature and worldlier wise recruit in the troop, the one we looked to for advice. During the journey to Sennybridge, we decided to have an impromptu birthday party for him at the local pub that night.

On arrival, Sergeant Fraser marched us to our accommodation and he was obviously in a bad mood, 'LEFT, LEFT, LEFT RIGHT LEFT, PICK IT UP YOU BLOODY BUNCH OF GIRL GUIDES YOU – SWING THOSE BLOODY ARMS SHOULDER HIGH – CARR GET THEM UP!' he screamed as we marched along trying our best to meet his demands.

It was to no avail; he continued to berate us then screamed, 'CARR I WON'T TELL YOU AGAIN – SWING THOSE ARMS SHOULDER BLOODY HIGH!'

I was swinging my arms as high as I could but he was after blood.

'That's it Carr you idle tosser, you are on cookhouse fatigues tonight lad!'

Moaning inwardly, I kept swinging my arms as high as I could in case he had some other fatigue he wanted to heap on me.

We spent that afternoon on the brilliant, Battle Assault Course, similar too but larger than the one my TA section had done so well on at Thetford. A large and very well built Physical Training Instructor – PTI, briefed us on how to tackle the various obstacles, with demonstrations provided by another equally large PTI.

After the briefing, the PTIs divided us into groups of six before chasing each group individually around the course; some of us had little difficulty scaling the obstacles but some of the others struggled. My experience at Thetford gave me an advantage and I managed to find time to urge my group on, leading it all the way round. After all the groups had finished, the PTIs called six of us out and announced that they were going to challenge us to set the fastest time possible and, try to beat the time of a 'Trained Soldier.'

The PTI called the 'Trained Soldier' forward and we saw that it was our driver.

Turning back to us, he said, 'I've just grabbed the nearest trained soldier who I will send over the course to show you lot how it should be done.' Grinning madly, he continued, 'Then you six, miserable, untrained, unqualified, undisciplined, undernourished and overpaid recruits will try your pathetic best to get as close as possible to his time.'

Dropping his belt and beret on a bench, The 'Trained Soldier' walked to the start of the course and took up a racing start, stance.

The PTI blew his whistle and the very fit looking 'Trained Soldier' sprinted to the first obstacle, a six foot wall which he just about leapt in a single bound and we watched in awe as he flowed swiftly over the remaining obstacles until he reached the last one, a huge wall about ten foot high. Without pausing, he ran full tilt at the wall, leaping at the last moment so that his right foot hit the wall and using his momentum; he pushed up his outstretched hands, grasped the parapet, hauled himself up, rolled over the top, and dropped to the other side. Sprinting to the finish, he bent over with hands on knees sucking in great gulps of air - very impressive!

Standing next to me, Brian whispered, 'He's a ringer, Syd.'

'A what?' I queried.

'A bloody ringer, he's a PTI, not a driver; I've seen him in the Gym back at camp.'

'Bloody cheats,' I whispered back.

Brian laughed and said, 'It's to be expected but we can match his time we've both been over assault courses before, let's show the buggers how it's done.'

'Right ye are,' I replied feeling none too confident.

Looking down at his stopwatch the PTI yelled, 'Two minutes and forty-seven seconds, let's see how close the fastest six recruits can do.

Lining the six of us up in single file, he ordered us to drop our webbing and berets on the ground next to us. Brian was third to go, the first two having done quite well but not as fast as the Trained Soldier had. He did brilliantly, until the big wall, where, although he used the same technique to leap up and grasp the top, he struggled to pull himself over and lost valuable time, finishing in just over three minutes.

I was next to go, and leant forward waiting for the whistle, adrenalin pumping madly as I listened to the lads shouting and screaming encouragement.

The Trained Soldier or PTI, or whatever he was, was muscular and heavier than I was, whereas I, after eighteen months hard graft in the pits, carried no fat, and was very fit. Having already set the fastest time in the troop for the 100-yard dash, I was eager to go. Without my webbing, I felt light and free, ready to sprint.

The whistle blew and I raced off, flying over the six-foot wall and on; it was a blur of ropes, walls, catwalks, ramps and ditches; my lungs bursting but I didn't feel tired, the adrenalin and cheering driving me on. Seeing the final wall, without hesitating; I used my last reserves of energy, and sprinted at it, clearing it as fast as the trained soldier had. Racing on, I threw myself across the finish and collapsed onto my knees totally spent.

310

The lads were cheering wildly waiting for the PTI to announce my time but before he did he shouted, 'Come on lad on your feet you have to be ready to fight after the assault course and you can't do that on your bloody knees, come on get up!' I pushed myself up panting furiously; sweat pouring off me despite the cold.

'Not bad lad,' he almost whispered as the cheering subsided, the lads in the troop waiting to hear my time.

'Two minutes,' pause, 'Forty,' a longer pause, 'nine Seconds.' There were gasps of disappointment accompanied by some cheers from the lads as they real-ised how close I had come to reaching the same time.'

While the last two lads tried unsuccessfully to match the fastest time Brian said, 'I made that two, forty-two Syd, but I haven't got a stop-watch, at least not one calibrated like there's!' I was too knackered to care!

We all enjoyed the afternoon immensely, especially me, having managed to set the second fastest time! Sergeant Fraser had just congratulated the two lads who had come second and third but ignored me.

Brian said, 'I don't know what you've done to upset that miserable bugger but it was obvious that he was going to put you on fatigues no matter how high you swung your arms this morning and he should have taken you off them when you set the fastest time on the assault course,' he said.

I looked at him quizzically and said, 'Aa didn't set the fastest time, I was second.'

'You were first Syd, they just changed the time, and don't worry about to-night, I'll make sure you come out with the rest of us.'

I wondered what he meant but just said, 'Nur it doesn't matter man, it's no big deal; I'll just dee the fatigues and get them ower with.'

Brian said, 'You haven't seen Troop Orders yet Syd, he's put you on Guard Duty tomorrow night!'

'The bloody swine,' I spat. 'Just because the TC let me gan doon toon in me drape jacket!'

The loss of face that he believed he had suffered in front of the lads must have been eating at Sergeant Fraser and he was determined to make me suffer for it but thankfully, I was wise enough to know not to fight it. I had passed all the training tests with flying colours and training would soon be over so I felt I could take his bile for another few days.

Just after half past five, I reported to the young Lance Corporal (L.Cpl) chef in charge of the after dinner clean up in the kitchen. He led me to a huge stainless steel sink where two other lads, were scrubbing away at pots and pans taken from a mountain of others stacked on the adjacent stainless steel tables.

'Right Carr get your jacket off and get stuck into that lot with them,' he said before he went back to wiping down surfaces.

I was soon scrubbing pots from the seemingly, never decreasing pile on the table, enjoying the banter with the other two. It was depressing work but hardly life threatening and I resigned myself to bashing on until we finished the pots when Brian walked into the kitchen.

'Who's in charge?' he asked.

Busy putting cleaned utensils away, the young L.Cpl., answered, 'I am, why?'

A large smile spreading across his face, Brian walked up to the L.Cpl. who must have been five years his junior and said, 'Hi Corporal, I know you and the lads are working very hard but did you know that it is Carr's eighteenth birthday today?'

Leaning forward, he whispered conspiratorially, 'He doesn't know It, but me and the rest of the lads in the Troop have organised a party for him, we've even got a birthday cake for him – so I was wondering if you could please, possibly let him off now so we can catch the transport at six?'

The young NCO initially stood his ground and said, 'Sorry there's no chance, they've only just started the pan wash and…'

Brian butted in and began another long pleading speech and slowly but surely wore the L.Cpl. down until he said, 'OK go on then take him but the other two will have to work longer!'

Grabbing my arm, Brian winked and said, 'Come on Syd we've a birthday party to attend.' I felt guilty at leaving the other two lads in the pan wash but was delighted to be joining the rest of my mates for a night downtown.

Judging from the looks on the rest of the lads' faces at Roll Call the following morning, they had obviously had as good a night out as I had, most of us were suffering from excellent hangovers!

It had snowed heavily during the night and occasional flurries of snow still blew across the square as Sgt Fraser briefed us on the helicopter training that was organised for that morning.

Having finished briefing, he walked slowly up to where I was standing in the front rank and asked, 'Enjoy your birthday party last night Carr?'

Caught off guard, I spluttered, 'Pardon Sarge?'

'Your birthday Party last night, you know the one you skived off fatigues to go to, did you enjoy it?' he hissed.

'Yes thanks very much Sarge, it was brilliant.' I answered as my brain slowly began to function again.

'Did you now, so that would have been a practice for your real birthday in March then, would it?'

He obviously had me so I replied, 'Yes Sarge.'

'Right ye bloody toe-rag you, you're on cookhouse fatigues tonight and this time, there'll be no skiving off – Right?'

I hesitated before replying and just as he started to turn away, I said, 'There's just one problem with that Sarge.'

'There's a problem is there Carr, and what might that be?' he snarled.

'You've already put me on guard duty tonight so Aa won't be able to do the fatigues will I?'

His face turned bright red and he screamed, 'Don't get bloody clever with me Carr; I'll have your bloody guts for garters lad!'

I was not sure what other punishments he would think up for me, and stupidly, replied, 'Thanks very much Sergeant, I hope they fit!'

This brought titters of suppressed laughter from many of the other lads and another screaming rage from Sgt Fraser that I let wash over me knowing that he would have to finish quickly as the Troop Commander had appeared and was standing by our transport looking at his watch.

I don't know why but that was the end of the hostilities; I did my Guard Duty that night but received no more fatigue duties, probably because we had almost finished our basic training and there was no time to fit any in, our time being taken up with preparations for our Pass-Out Parade. In addition, Sgt Fraser became almost friendly toward me, which I found very disconcerting! However, I did learn that it was much easier to toe-the-line and vowed never to be a smart arse again!

Back at Sennybridge, an hour after First Parade, the Troop was in a field at the foot of the Brecon Beacons listening to an RAF NCO brief us on the drills for entering and exiting the Whirlwind helicopter parked a few yards behind him.

We were all excited to be carrying out helicopter training and listened intently, especially when we realised that 'exiting the helicopter' was to be carried out 30 foot above the top of Pen-y-Fan and involved climbing 30 foot down a rope dangling from the side of the aircraft while wearing full battle order, including steel helmets and rifles!

Once on the ground, we would then have to trek from the top of the mountain back down to the field we were standing in. Divided into sections of eight with an NCO in charge of each section, we waited our turn for the flight to the top.

My Section was the first to go and once we received the thumbs up from the RAF Loadmaster, we quickly climbed aboard, fastened our seat belts, and waited for take-off. Sitting between Dick and Jock Brown, directly opposite the large open door, we watched as the Loadmaster talked into his throat mike as the helicopter lifted off. Lanky Jock fidgeted with his webbing nervously, while Dick looked like a pit bull terrier waiting to savage someone or something.

The smell of burnt aviation fuel blasting through the open door added to the excitement as the engine laboured to lift the helicopter on its circular journey up the thousand or so metres to the top of the mountain. Once there, it hovered over the flat snow covered summit as the Loadmaster hung perilously out of the door surveying the ground below, talking constantly to the pilot through his throat mike.

Obviously satisfied with what he saw, he released the rope that dangled from the hoist above the door before turning to look at our white, wide-eyed faces. After a final check outside, he gave the sign to unbuckle that we all quickly did and then pointing to Dick sitting next to me, gave him the thumbs up and pointed to the rope dangling a foot or so from the door.

Dick stood quickly up, adjusted the sling of his rifle that held it across his back and stepped enthusiastically toward the door, his metal studded ammunition boots scrabbling to grip the much worn anti-slip surface of the floor and unfortunately for him, failing!

His right foot shot from under him, quickly followed by his left; his forward momentum propelling him horizontally toward the opening as the Loadmaster tried frantically to grab him but missed - Dick disappeared out of the of the helicopter!

The noise of the engine and rotor blades drowned the many gasps of, 'Bloody Hell!' 'Shit!' and the like as we all stared at the empty void while the Loadmaster leant even farther out of the aircraft talking into his microphone.

I was staring at the empty door where Dick had disappeared when I felt Jock tugging my arm and as I looked up at him, I shouted, 'What?'

'There's noo way am going oot there!' he shouted back.

The helicopter flew around in a steeply banked circle and we could see through the open door the shape of a spread-eagled man in the snow. The snow must have been deep as there was no sign of Dick just a man-shaped hole.

The helicopter hovered again and the Loadmaster called our NCO to the door to shout instructions into his ear. He then looked the NCO in the face and gave him thumbs up sign to which a not too happy looking NCO gave a return thumbs up before leaning out to grab the rope, swing out and climb down to where Dick had disappeared.

The helicopter flew us back to the field where we dismounted to allow a team of NCOs to climb aboard and fly back up to the top of the mountain to rescue poor Dick. We later found out that he suffered, only mild concussion, although he was unconscious for some time!

Much to our dismay, his slip ended helicopter training for the day; the RAF deciding conditions were too dangerous for flying! Dick suffered a lot of ribbing from the lads when he re-joined us back at Oswestry a few days later!

At the end of Training on an overcast and drab day in early December, we paraded in best Service Dress along with two other troops for our Pass-Out-Parade.

Prior to marching onto the square we watched a few families take their seats next to the saluting Dias, all of us hoping to see our own Mothers, Fathers or siblings but in truth there were very few there and I certainly had not expected to see any of mine but still looked; just in case! There was none.

After the parade I said my farewells to the many pals I had made during training and made arrangements to meet Jock Pattinson and Jock Brown on the Edinburgh to London train when it stopped at Newcastle after Christmas leave. Along with many others, we were to report to 14 Regiment Royal Artillery, stationed at Horseshoe Barracks, Shoeburyness, just east of Southend.

Recently returned from Hong Kong, the Regiment was down to cadre-strength as the last National Servicemen left on completion of their service. To fill the huge manning shortfall, the Cadre had carried out basic training for two recruit troops at Horseshoe Barracks with about a hundred more of us posted in from Oswestry. The result was a Regiment with a very young average age.

After the Pass-Out-Parade, I caught the train home from the tiny halt at Gobowen and staggering under the weight of a full kit bag and crammed suitcase changed at Manchester then Newcastle, finally arriving at Ashington just in time to catch the last bus down to Highmarket.

Opening the back door, I thankfully dropped my kit on the scullery floor as Butch trotted out of the sitting room with his tail wagging to greet me. Mam, Dad, Vivian and Dennis were watching television in front of a glowing fire and grunted or nodded greetings, I was back home but felt no real joy at being there.

Having spent some time away, I now saw our house in the Fifth Row for what it was; a grim, end of terrace colliery house with one cold-water tap and a toilet on the other side of the back street. The toilet as always was not a pleasant place to be, especially in winter.

Having arranged to meet Tom on the day after I arrived back, a Saturday, we met just after lunch and walked into town, I wore my new Service Dress, hoping to impress as many girls and old friends as possible! I was not disappointed as just about all of our peers were out and about town.

Walking up Station Road, a group of lasses approached us and I saw Dot was with them. Having recognised me as we slowed to let them pass, she stepped in front of me to say, 'Hello Syd I was wondering...'

I do not know what she was wondering but I did not let her finish.

'Hello Dot,' I said in reply, as I walked around her and straight on leaving her staring at my back.

Tom asked, 'Aren't ye gannin te talk te her, Aa thought ye were gannin oot with her?'

'She sent me a 'Dear John' letter, not that we were serious, so why the hell should I talk to her, bugger her man.'

We met and talked to quite a few of our friends and acquaintances and were talking to a group of lads outside Woolworths when I felt a tug on my arm, it was Titch; the lass that did not go out with pit lads!

'I was told that you had joined up but I didn't believe it,' she said smiling.

I smiled back and said, 'Unless this uniform's issued to Pit Lads then it must be true.'

315

She pulled me to one side and said, 'You look really smart in your uniform, I just wanted to say that I hope you know that I didn't mean to upset you when we were at the pictures?'

'Ye did but that's forgotten now,' I lied.

She smiled again and said, 'Will I see you at the Welfare tonight then?'

'You will, Tom and I, are both going so I'll probably see you there.'

She said cheerio and walked off with her friends.

Changed into my suit, that evening I had a couple of pints at the Portland with Tom and Cousin Alec before we caught the bus to Alexandria Road and walked into a packed Dance Hall just after nine.

The band on the stage belted out a fair representation of Cliff Richard's, 'Do you want to dance?' as we did the normal walk around to suss out the talent of which there was plenty.

Half way round I met Titch, who had seen us approach and waited for me to reach her.

'Hello again,' she said obviously waiting for me to ask her to dance.

'Hello,' I said and continued with the other two without looking back to see her reaction.

Alec said, 'Aa think yor in there Syd.'

'Aa thought I was once before and was bloody disappointed man, so I don't really like her, but I will ask her for a dance later.'

I did and we were jiving on a very crowded dance floor, the band making conversation impossible until the end of their version of Dion's 'The Wanderer.'

When the band changed the tempo, the crowd on the floor thinned allowing us to go into a smooch and she asked about my training, where I was posted to and seemed genuinely interested so I brought her up to date and told her that I was going to train to be a signaller in my new Regiment. She told me that she had left college and was looking for a job in Newcastle but had not managed to find one just yet

After the dance I escorted her off the floor and said, 'Aa better go and see where Tom and Alec are.'

'I'll save that last dance for you if you're going to walk me home?' she said.

Putting my hands on her shoulders and smiling, I said, 'I'm very sorry Pet but I don't go out with jobless lasses,' and turned and walked away.

I almost regretted doing so but thought if she could not accept me for who I was and not my position in life, then she obviously did not care that much for me, besides, she didn't have blue eyes!

I re-joined Tom and Alec for another walk round the dance, hoping that I might see Little Blue-Eyes but she was not there, leaving me feeling a wee bit forlorn. I ended up dancing with an old girlfriend who I walked her home and dated for the rest of my leave.

27

Shoeburyness

My Leave passed all too quickly and a couple of days after another loud and boozy New Year's Eve party at home, I packed my belongings ready for the journey to my new Regiment on the following day, a Sunday. I had to catch the first train from Ashington that left before the buses began and concerned about having to walk a mile carrying all my kit, I was up early, allowing myself plenty of time to reach the train station.

As I expected, no one got up to see me off; even Butch remained in Dad's chair, just thumping it with his tail a couple of times as I patted him on the way to the door. I had to wear Service Dress for the journey, hardly warm enough for the bitterly cold wind and snow flurries racing down the long back lanes as I left the warmth of the house.

The effort of carrying my heavy suitcase and bulging kit back soon warmed me but the handles were biting into my hand. I tried carrying the kit bag on my shoulder but by the time I reached the store corner, barely a third of the distance, I was beginning to worry that I was not going to make the station or my train.

Staggering on with my head down to avoid the wind-blown snow, I was startled by the sound of a horn and turned to see a milk float pulling up alongside, the driver waving me across.

'Where are ye gannin Lad?' he shouted through the wind.

'The train station,' I shouted back hopefully.

'Hoy yor kit on the back and Aa'll run ye doon there, it's oot me way but Aa'll soon hev ye there,' he said as I thankfully threw my suitcase and kit bag on the back of the float.

'Is there nebody at home that could hev given ye a hand?' he asked as he drove off.

Smiling at him, I replied, 'Aye me Faather is at home and he's got a car but he couldn't be bothered to get oot of bed!'

He shook his head, and muttered, 'Bloody families!'

A few minutes later, I thanked him profusely when he dropped me off and I walked into the station twenty minutes before the train was due.

The rest of the journey south passed without problem; I met up with the two Jocks, on the Edinburgh to Kings Cross train that was so crowded, we had to stand for the whole journey; chatting as we watched the snow deepening the further south, we travelled!

Horseshoe Barracks was a fine, mid-nineteenth century barracks standing on the edge of the marshes of the Thames Estuary; the Barracks billeted 14 Regiment and a Proof and Experimental Establishment who test-fired shells into the marshes. The soldiers of the latter wore white trousers and black reefer jackets and had very little to do with soldiers in our Regiment, believing themselves to be a cut above all other squaddies.

Carrying our suitcases and kit bags, the three of us staggered the two hundred yards from the station to the entrance of the barracks where the guard on the gate directed us to the Headquarters building for processing and allocation to a Gun Battery.

A short while later, we were waiting outside the Regimental Office when a tall, bespectacled figure, immaculate in Service Dress and with an air of absolute authority, strode down the corridor toward us.

Recognising the large 'Coat of Arms' badges on his lower sleeves, I whispered out of the corner of my mouth to the other two, 'RSM!'

We came to attention when he stopped in front of us, scrutinising us with a look of mock disdain.

'What have we got here then, the Long and the Tall and the Short? No, it's three more civvy rejects, here to join the rest of the bloody young virgins that some buffoon has allowed to join Her Majesties finest Regiment of Artillery – Names,' he demanded.

'Gunner Broon Sir,' spluttered big Jock.

'Broon,' the RSM responded, 'I follow your family in the Sunday Post, how's Paw, Ma and your brother Joe?'

Lanky Jock was unsure as how to respond to the RSM's wit and ventured, 'There fine Sir and still in Glebe Street.'

The RSM showed no sign of amusement and growled, 'You have your belt on the wrong way around, you great long streak of Scotch mist – get it sorted.'

Looking down at Jock Pattinson, he demanded, 'Name?'

'GUNNER PATTINSON SIR,' Jock thundered back far too loudly.

'Another bloody Haggis basher,' the RSM spat, 'get your bloody epaulette tucked under your collar, you scruffy soldier.'

Desperately hoping that there was nothing wrong with my turnout, I waited until the RSM stepped in front of me and glared down at me menacingly before I snapped in a non-too confident voice, 'Gunner Carr Sir.'

'And are you a Jock as well Carr?'

'No Sir, I'm a Geordie Sir.'

'A Jock with his head kicked in or so I'm reliably informed,' he mused sarcastically. 'Well, I suppose being a Geordie Regiment we have got to have the likes of you here,' he spat as he turned away.

'Sir.' I acknowledged, relieved that he had not found fault with my uniform but as he walked away he shouted over his shoulder, 'CARR IF YOU DON'T GET YOUR CHIN STRAP THE RIGHT WAY AROUND IN THE NEXT FIVE SECONDS YOU WILL BE SPENDING THE NEXT FIVE NIGHTS ON GUARD DUTY!'

I changed it in four seconds!

The three of us joined 1st Medium Battery (The Blazers) Royal Artillery, one of the three gun batteries in the Regiment. 1st Battery was equipped with 5.5-inch medium field guns while the other two batteries; 5 Niagara Field Battery and 13 Martinique Field Battery, were both equipped with the 25 pounder, a lighter and smaller field gun. Both types of guns were robust, reliable and of World War II vintage.

As the three of us were to become signallers, we found ourselves billeted in the same room along with five other lads, four of whom had arrived earlier. One of them was muscular Dick; he had totally recovered from his hasty exit from the helicopter.

The fifth lad, a chirpy Scouser about the same height as me, introduced himself as 'Scouse Bolt'. Having been in the Army for two years spent with the Regiment in Hong Kong, he was an 'old-sweat' to us. He told us he was there to help us settle into the Battery and a great job he did.

Our room was on the ground floor of one of eight accommodation blocks grouped like a horseshoe around the parade ground – hence the name of the barracks. There were eight beds, each with a steel locker and bedside cabinet, spaced evenly around the room with a coal-fired stove sitting in the centre.

Later, after Troop Commanders interviews, Scouse showed us around camp before taking us to the cookhouse for dinner after which, walking back to the billet he said, 'Okay, Syd lad, I'll take you to the NAAFI later and you can buy me a pint and meet Ray, he tells cracking jokes like.'

'Only if you buy me a pint back?' I replied.

Scouse smiled and said, 'That's a problem cos I'm skint!'

We did go to the NAAFI and had a few pints – on me and listened to Lance Bombardier (Bombardiers are Corporals in the Royal Artillery) Ray Sewell tell stories in the fashion of Dave Allen.

Ray looked very neat and had the freshly scrubbed appearance common to soldiers that had served from the age of fifteen to seventeen and a half in the Royal Artillery Junior Leaders Regiment; he had been a boy Battery Sergeant Major and expected to do well in the regulars. My friendship with Ray would develop later, and was to last a lifetime. I listened enthralled as Ray and Scouse told story after story of their time in Hong Kong, interspersed with Ray's jokes, it was a grand evening.

Our first week was spent listening to familiarisation briefings and lectures as well as meeting the Officers and SNCOs who would command us. We also found out that the Regiment was to move to Dortmund in Germany at the end of May!

We also met our Signals Sergeant, a 23-year-old, blonde, blue-eyed rugby player called Redding, nicknamed Baron Von Redding for obvious reason, he was a firm but fair SNCO whom all the new lads admired.

The following week the Regiment went into a period of Individual Training during which all of the new soldiers, at least, two hundred, underwent initial trade training. I joined twenty-five other lads for a six week Standard Three Signals Course, learning all the skills required to man and operate the Regiment's radios as well as cable laying and the maintenance of field telephones.

At the same time, we were getting to know the lads in the Battery and were finding our way around Southend, which, despite it being winter, was a brilliant place to spend our spare time. We took the fifteen-minute train ride there as often as we could afford it and enjoyed some memorable nights out!

I had become mates with a Geordie Clerk in Headquarters Battery called Rob and it was on the third weekend of my Signal Course that he and I donned our suits and headed into Southend to go to the dance at the Kursaal. After two or three pints in the Criterion Pub listening to a massive woman playing the organ and making fun of everyone with her non-stop banter, we headed off to the dance.

A cold wind hurried us along the seafront to the entrance of the Kursaal below the dome that served as a local landmark. Inside, the brilliant dance floor was heaving with teenagers doing various forms of bop, jive and twist to the group that played loudly on the ornately surrounded stage while above, on the huge balcony that travelled all the way around the ballroom, more teenagers stood drinking and chatting whilst watching the dancers below.

Rob and I walked around the dance floor to suss out the talent before heading upstairs for a drink, noticing that there were a few lads from the Regiment scattered around the dance hall and nodded to one or two of them as we walked up to the balcony

Leaning nonchalantly, I hoped, against the rail of the balcony, I was sipping my pint when Rob said, 'Aa think yor in there Syd!'

'Where?' I answered looking around, my eyes stopping on a pretty blonde who was smiling coyly at me over a glass of coke she was stirring with a straw.

'She's been eyeing you up since we came up here,' Rob said.

I had not really noticed her until then but as I looked at her, she held my stare, giving me the almost certain feeling that she wanted to meet.

Seeing that she was with a couple of other lasses, I said to Rob, 'Haway, let's gan and see if they'll dance with us.'

Still Trying to look cool and not spill my beer I walked toward her with my eyes holding hers and in doing so managed to bump into the back of a lad who had stepped back from the balcony.

I had not spilt any beer and muttered, 'Sorry,' to the lad as I advanced toward the Blonde.

The lad said something back but I ignored him in order to say to the Blonde in my smoothest Geordie, 'Helloah Bonnie Lass, dee ye fancy a dance?'

She took her time to answer, first giving me a very unnerving once over before saying, 'I'd love too, but I'm here with my boyfriend and I don't think he'd like that but perhaps another time?'

I feigned a grimace and said, 'Story of my bloody life Pet, where's your boyfriend?'

The smile had gone from her face as she answered, 'He's the one you bumped into and he doesn't seem very happy, I think you best leave.'

Turning, I noticed that Rob was still over by the balcony and he looked decidedly worried as the lad I had bumped into stood glaring at me; worse, he had four equally angry looking lads with him. Realising the danger I was in I put my pint on a table and moved toward the wall, away from the railings, facing them all the way; I did not want to turn my back to them, having learned the hard way the perils of having your back to an antagonist!

The five of them advanced menacingly toward me, stopping a foot or so in front of me before the Blonde's boyfriend spat, 'First you barge into me then you try to chat up my bloody girlfriend, who the fuck do you think you are mate?'

I gulped and tried humour, 'Well obviously not yor mate, mate; Am sorry but how was I supposed te knaa that she had a boyfriend?'

The lad spat back, 'A fucking Northern Teddy Boy and, I bet he's a fucking soldier!'

Seeing that he was getting ready to lash out, I had instinctively brought my hands up ready to defend myself, 'Don't go down whatever happens, or they'll kick the shit out of you,' I thought to myself.

A hand suddenly appeared between the lads and grasped the left shoulder of the girl's boyfriend and another hand appeared and grasped the right shoulder of the lad to his left!

The hands parted the two startled lads and a smiling face pushed through, 'Are ye heving a spot of bother Marra?' the face said.

I recognised him as one of the new drivers in our Battery who I had not gotten to know yet; he was six foot tall with boyish good looks, very similar to a young, white Cassius Clay. His name was Allan Storey and he was very welcome.

'Ye could say that,' I answered just as Allan tilted his head back.

In a blur of super-fast movement, he swept his head right then left smacking first into the nose of the boyfriend who dropped like a stone, then onto the cheekbone of the other lad who staggered back from the force of the blow. Allan followed that up with a crunching right hook into one of the other lads on my right sending him flying.

Without thinking, I swung a right into the lad on my left as I threw myself forward swinging madly.

All hell broke loose as Allan and I lashed out at the lads, the speed of our assault taking them completely by surprise. But more local lads were joining in and it was soon clear that we would not win this alone, I started to feel kicks and punches raining in as I fought to stay on my feet while Allan battered anyone stupid enough to step within his range.

Rob who had watched dumbfounded from a distance finally rushed forward to help, and was joined by another lad from HQ Battery called Frank who was only five foot three and the white, double of Sammy Davis Junior! What he lacked in height he made up for in ferocity, weighing in with feet and fists.

Allan shouted, 'Stay together,' as he kicked the legs from under a lad who had rushed at him but even he could see that despite being joined by Jock Pattinson, we were too heavily outnumbered to last much longer. Grabbing a lad by the scruff of the neck and the seat of his pants, Allan pushed him face forward over the balcony so that the lad was two-thirds the way over, his arms swinging madly as he imagined himself hurling to the floor below.

Allan screamed at the advancing locals, 'Stay back or Aa'll throw this bastard ower!'

Everyone stopped and looked at him dangling the screaming lad over the edge before he shouted at us, 'The stairs, Aa cannit hold this bastard,' and he let go!

As the lad pitched forward, two of his mates grabbed his legs, just in time to stop him from plummeting to the dance floor below where the dancing had stopped as the dancers watched the mayhem above.

Without hesitation, we obeyed Allan's order and ran to the stairs, barging aside anyone foolish enough to get in the way. The five of us crashed down the stairs, through the entrance and onto the street, pursued by what seemed like a hoard of screaming demons.

Allan again shouted, 'Stay together, back te back,' which we had already instinctively begun to do as we were surrounded by fifteen or more baying locals, many of whom had blood-streaked faces.

There was a short standoff before one of them ran at us, receiving punches from Rob and Jock that sent him reeling.

Another lad ran at Allan and tried a flying kick but Allan just grabbed his foot and using the lads own momentum, swung him 180 degrees, and sent him crashing to the pavement. That slowed them and they began moving around us like a pack of hungry wolves, hurling abuse and threats but none of them tried rushing us again.

Keeping closed up and back to back, we started to move across the pavement and over a side road to continue back down the seafront, away from the Kursaal. The local lads made a couple more of half-hearted runs at us, both of which we drove back easily before they stopped following us and instead, stood shouting threats and warnings, including, 'Stay away from the Kursaal or you'll die!'

We took that threat very seriously and did not go back for a whole week, in force!

Adrenaline pumping, we broke formation and looked at each to compare bumps and bruises; shouting and laughing with a mix of excitement and relief that we had fought our way out and we had given better than we had taken.

'Whey Aa divvint knaa aboot ye lot but Aa could morder a frigging pint Allan?' said as we strode down the sea front.

'What about that club opposite the Station, it's always open late?' I said.

Everyone agreed and we picked up the pace as we headed for a beer. The club was in a cellar below a shop in a terraced row opposite the Railway Station, a regular for lads waiting to catch the last train to Shoeburyness. Still in a highly agitated and excited state, we poured down the stairs and noisily made our way to the bar laughing at Rob whose nose was not as straight as it had been that morning.

Allan shoved his way through a small group to get to the bar and shouted, 'Five pints of bitter mate.'

One of the lads in the group he had pushed through, a tall spiteful looking lad with a large pointed nose and lank blonde hair grabbed his arm, turned to look at us, we recognised him as a soldier in 13 Battery.

The lad glared at Allan, grabbed his arm and warned, 'You want to be careful who you push fella or you'll get into serious trouble.'

Allan smiled back at the lad and said in a quiet but menacing voice, 'Not as much trouble as ye'll be in if ye divvint tek your fucking hand of me arm!'

The lad released his grip and snarled, 'Be careful I've just been on a Para course!'

I could not for the life of me understand what he thought that statement would achieve but Allan picked up on it immediately and said scornfully, 'Whey you must hev failed the fucka or ye wouldn't be here noo would ye, ye fucking wanker.'

Furious, the Lad demanded, 'Outside now.'

Allan turned round, picked up one of the pints the barman had pulled, held it up and looked at it closely before taking a long slow drink, consuming half the beer before placing the glass carefully back on the bar and looking at the lad contemptuously, he let out a long loud belch.

'Haway then, let's be having ye!' he said to the lad.

Before he left, he said to the barman, 'I'll be back for me beer, and pay for it in a minute,' as he moved to the door.

The 13 Battery lad began to follow Allan and I saw that two of his mates were going with him so I stepped forward to join Allan but he held up his hand and said, 'Nah it's alright Syd Aa can handle these three tossers on me own.' Nonetheless, the four of us followed them up the stairs and onto the street.

It reminded me of the showdown scene from High Noon, Allan walked into the middle of the road and turned as the three, 13 Battery lads also walked into the road and stopped about ten yards away, turning to face him. I could see by the looks on their faces that they were none too sure of themselves.

Allan undid the large buckle on his leather belt and pulled it free from the loops on his jeans before wrapping it around his right hand, leaving twelve inches of leather, free with the big metal buckle dangling at the end.

'Come on then one at a time or aall three together, let's be having ye,' he shouted.

The sight of the belt and the confidence exuded by Allan was too much for the three of them, they retreated to the station, hurling threats in an effort to save face but when he made a short charge toward them, they turned and fled.

I hoped that would be the end of hostilities for the night and as we descended the stairs back into the Club, I said to Allan, 'Try not te upset anybody else man and let's just finish wor drinks.'

He put his arm around my shoulder and said, 'Me, not upset anyone, ye've got a nerve, look at the bother ye started at the dance!' He was right of course and I vowed to be far more careful when it came to chatting up lasses!

We finished our beer and had another, probably one more than my five-pint limit, so I suggested we went for a coffee and share a taxi back to camp. The late opening coffee shop on the sea front was rather like someone's front room and was full of students talking pretentious rubbish while trying their hardest to portray themselves as Bohemian. They were obviously not happy to have five rowdy soldiers invade their space.

The coffee was foul and left a bitter taste in my mouth and I could see by the looks on the faces of the other four that they were none too impressed either. Little Frank spoke for all of us when he said in a loud voice, 'By this coffee tastes like shite and this place is like a shitehoose, lets bugger off!'

The following morning - Sunday, I was lying in bed with my head about to explode and my throat so sore and dry, I could not swallow. I listened to someone moving around the room and desperately wanted to them to stop, as the sounds they were making seemed to sound like thunder to me. I gingerly slid the sheet from my face and saw Scouse sitting on his bed smoking a fag and drinking tea that he had brought back from breakfast in the cookhouse.

I tried to ask for a slurp but my throat was so dry I could only croak but it was enough for Scouse to look over and ask, 'Want a cup of tea Syd La?' as he held the mug up.

'Yeh,' was all I could manage to croak.

Smiling cheekily, he said, 'Then get out of bed and go to breakfast.'

I groaned and pulled the sheet back over my face only to have it whipped back by Scouse who pushed the mug toward me saying, 'Here, you look as though you need this more than me.'

I tried to sit up but the pain in my head was so intense I had to lie back for a few seconds before I slowly and gingerly eased myself onto my elbow and reached for the mug.

'How much did you have to drink last night?' asked Scouse without sympathy?

Gathering my thoughts, I took a sip of still hot and very sweet tea before saying, 'Just five or six pints Aa think, Aa canna understand why my heads so bad.'

'You can't handle it mate, you should lay off it,' he joshed.

I tried to remember how many pints I had drunk but thinking was painful and I lay back to try and ease the pain in my head when from the opposite corner of the room, a low, slow, groan came from below Jock Pattinson's blankets.

Scouse walked over to Jock's bed and pulling the blankets from his head said, 'Another one who can't handle his booze!'

Jock groaned, 'Fuck Off,' and pulled the blanket back over his face.

It was about then, I felt an itch on the back of my right hand and slowly lifting it in front of my face, to my horror I saw the tattoo of a swallow! Memories of the night before came flooding back, the dance, the fight, Allan's confrontation with the 13 Battery lads and the coffee bar. Then I remembered the tiny tattoo parlour and the five of us taking turns to have ourselves defaced.

As the latter part of last night came into focus, I held up my left arm and saw a 'skull, and crossbones' on my forearm!

'Shit,' I muttered and asked, 'How's your arm Jock?'

'What?' he groaned back from under his sheets.

'Yor tattoo how is it?'

'What tattoo - oh that one - all right I think but just leave me alone will ye?'

Neither Jock nor I got out of bed that morning, both of us feeling terrible and both wondering why we had such diabolical hangovers.

One of the other lads in the room, Ryan, a large spotty Londoner, gave us both aspirins from his stock of medications but they had little effect and we suffered on. By late afternoon, it was clear to Scouse that we had more than a hangover so he and Dick brought us sausage sandwiches and mugs of tea back from the cookhouse that we accepted gratefully.

The next morning, feeling no better, we dragged ourselves out of bed at half past six, washed, shaved and put on our khaki battle dress uniforms, packed washing and shaving kit, pyjamas, and plimsolls into our small packs and reported sick.

'Tonsillitis,' the MO said to me across his desk after he finished looking down my throat.

'Tonsillitis,' he repeated as he scribbled notes on my medical documents before ushering me out the door.

'Tonsillitis,' I croaked to Jock as I walked past him in the waiting room.

A little while later, Jock, and I were standing shivering with the rest of the trainee signallers on parade on the wind-swept square as Sergeant Redding called out our names.

Jock whispered, 'Tonsillitis,' to me while nodding his head.

'Did he give you owt?' I asked.

'Nur just said Tonsillitis,' Jock whispered.

Sergeant Redding shouted, 'QUIET you pair of gossiping girl guides.'

Just as he finished calling the roll, a small, dapper Medical Lance Bombardier came running up to him.

'Excuse me Sergeant,' he blurted, 'are Carr and Pattinson here?'

Sergeant Redding looked down at the NCO and asked, 'Yes they are, why what have they been up too?'

The Medic looked flustered and said in a high-pitched voice, 'Oh my God Sergeant they've got tonsillitis, there supposed to be bedded down in the Medical Centre!'

Sergeant Redding said sarcastically, 'It's not the end of the bloody world Bombardier.'

The Medic shook his head exasperatedly and said, 'No but they're spreading it about and we can't have that can we Sergeant?'

'No we can't Bombardier,' replied Sergeant Redding, mimicking the NCO's voice, and then shouted, 'Carr, Pattinson get your germ infested bodies to the sick bay, now – COME ON DOUBLE AWAY.'

Jock and I began to jog painfully toward the Medical Centre but the Medic caught us up and spluttered, 'Please stopping running lads, you're both poorly, please just walk slowly; I am sorry but the MO should have told you to report to me.'

A few minutes later, we were in the Medical Centre, clad in our army stripped pyjamas, our heads still pounding as the NCO ushered into beds in a small austere ward that had three beds on each side of the room with a table in the centre.

The Medic waited until we were both in bed before saying, 'Don't get too comfy cos I have to give you both penicillin injections!'

It was then that I noticed a figure lying on his side in the bed at the other side of Jock. He had a face like a wizened grey monkey and looked sadly back at me.

I ventured quietly, 'Hi Mate, what you in for?'

He replied in a pathetic voice, 'The grapes of doom!'

'The grapes of doom! what's that?'

'Piles, bloody piles mate that's what they are.'

I was not sure what piles were but judging from the look of him, I was sure that I did not want them. A Bombardier in HQ Battery, the little monkey appeared to be very old and in a great deal of discomfort.

The first of the penicillin injections into my buttocks was not too bad; lying face down on the table in the centre of the room the Medic had slapped my arse a couple times saying, 'Relax now,' before sticking the needle in. However, we had three injections a day, each one being more painful than the last as our buttocks refused to relax no matter how many times he slapped them.

Painful as they were it was nothing compared to what happened to the little old Bombardier. Twice a day, three medics hauled him onto the table in the middle of the room and performed all sorts of torture on the poor man's rectum as he screamed and groaned in agony. I did not know and did not want to find out what they were doing to him but whatever it was; it left him sobbing in his bed!

327

Sgt Redding came to the Medical Centre at lunchtime on the first day to find out how long we were to remain 'bedded-down.'

After speaking to the medics, he came into the ward and said, 'Right you two it looks as if you'll be off the course for the rest of the week so I've brought some pamphlets and hand-outs for you to study, I expect you to learn these by heart in the next couple of days.'

Not feeling at all like doing any studying, I grimaced but we both grunted, 'Right Sarge.'

We did read and digest the pamphlets, practiced our phonetic alphabet and voice procedures on each other to the extent that by the third day, the little NCO had had enough of our chatter, and threw a flip-flop at us.

'Bugger Off or die!' he threatened.

We retreated to a small storeroom, where, sitting on boxes, we continued to practice. It was worth it as three weeks later I finished the course achieving top marks throughout all the tests. As a reward, Sergeant Redding told me I was to join him in the Battery Commanders Party, not the Battery Command Post Crew that I wanted to join.

We spent the next two weeks cleaning and painting vehicles, guns, and equipment in preparation for the Annual Administrative Inspection, carried out by a visiting General.

Having drawn a few caricatures of the lads in the Billet, word reached the MT Sergeant that I was a bit of an artist and he grabbed me and gave me a small paintbrush and a pot of white paint.

Perplexed, I asked, 'What's these for Sarge?'

'Get down to the garages and start painting the numbers '14' onto the Royal Artillery red and blue squares on the front and back of our vehicles,' was all he said and I suddenly found myself nominated as a temporary, acting, unpaid and much abused, Battery sign-writer. The job only lasted a week before I was back cleaning the underneath of trucks again!

Two weeks after a successful parade and inspection, the Regiment drove in convoy to Tilshead Training Camp on Salisbury Plain to commence two weeks training. This was essential as the majority of the soldiers in the Regiment had no experience of the guns firing or the way in which the Regiment deployed for exercise let alone operations. We learned how to put into practice the lessons taught on our various trade courses and slowly but surely, built up crews and teams able to operate our equipment competently.

The two weeks passed without major incident, apart from celebrating my 18th birthday with a few of the lads in the camp NAAFI, providing me with a very superior hangover the following day.

The highlight of the two weeks for me was sending over the radio the Fire Orders for the Regiments first Regimental Fire Mission without cocking it up, earning a grunt of, 'OK, not bad,' from Sergeant Redding.

The weather had been kind to us on Salisbury Plain but it changed for the worse as the Regiment made the long, two-day drive up to Otterburn Ranges, in my home county of Northumberland.

Unlike our two weeks at Salisbury where we had spent every night in the brick and wood huts of the training camp, at Otterburn, we spent the majority of the two weeks living off our vehicles on the ranges and it was cold, very cold. Strong winds drove sleet and snow across the Cheviot Hills, turning our exposed flesh white and saturating our combat suits as our useless old pattern ponchos proved incapable of keeping us dry.

I was one of the two Signallers in the Battery Commander's Party that consisted off an Austin Champ (an over engineered British Jeep) that the Battery Commander (BC) travelled in with his driver, a tiny Irishman, while myself and the other signaller, nicknamed Smokey, sat in the back operating the radios. Sergeant Redding followed in an Austin one-ton radio vehicle, with his driver, a huge Scotsman called Jock Low.

On the second to last night, the weather was particularly wild, wind driven snow adding to that already lying on the hills. Conditions on the Gun Position were especially grim, forcing the gun crews to scurry into their crew tents after each Fire Mission. The BC was concerned that the cold would adversely affect the performance of his soldiers so much so, that instead of spending the night with the Forward Observation Parties, he decided to deploy us near the Battery Gun Position so that he could visit the gun crews to see how they were coping.

Having helped to erect the lean-to frame and shelter on the back of the Austin, Smokey and I struggled in the wind and snow to put up our little two-man bivouac tent. Sergeant Redding and Jock Low slept in the lean-to on camp beds with Arctic sleeping bags they had obtained on their travels while Smoky and I had to make do with lying on our next to useless ponchos with two blankets each to wrap ourselves in. Comfortable and warm was not an expression I'd use to describe a night in a tiny bivouac tent on Otterburn Ranges in winter!

At eleven pm, I climbed into the rear of the Austin, to start a three-hour stint operating the radios that would finish at 2 am when Smokey would replace me. It was bitterly cold sitting in the back of the Austin as my eyes adjusted to the dim glow of the little 24-volt lamp powered by the same batteries as the radio, but at least, I was out of the wind!

My stag started at the same time as the BC, along with the Battery Captain (BK) began their round of visiting the six gun-crews, two Battery Command Posts and ammunition vehicles and crews. They took with them two very large bottles of cold-weather, issue rum, giving each man a generous tot as they chatted, officer to soldier, under the various shelters erected by the crews.

329

Just after midnight, the two of them climbed into the back of the Austin and sat discussing the day's events while Sergeant Redding sat next to me, waiting for the BC to go off to bed so that he could go to his own.

The BC, who reminded me of an absent-minded professor, handed me a sheet of paper with a number of hand-written messages on it and said, 'Here's a series of Sitreps I want you to send to the Regimental and Battery Command Posts at thirty-minute intervals throughout the night.'

Glancing quickly at the messages, I answered, 'Right Sir,' but was distracted when the BK placed a three-quarter full, bottle of Rum on the signals table!

'Here you go Carr, take a good tot of rum, it'll help keep the cold at bay and have another wee nip before you go off stag,' he said, smiling.

I thanked the BK as he and the BC left to bed down for the night.

Sergeant Redding took the top of the bottle of rum and took a long, slow slug, screwed up his face and said, 'Blah that's bloody awful but it sure does give you a glow.'

Putting the cork back in the bottle he said, 'Right young Carr, make sure you keep an eye on the battery power and if it starts to drop get the vehicle engine started and leave it on tick over, got that?'

'Aye Sarge,' I responded as he rose and lifted the flap at the back of the truck, before jumping down and dropping the flap behind him. I could hear him taking his boots off and climbing into his huge Arctic sleeping bag – 'Lucky Sod,' I thought to myself.

Sitting in the gloom of the tiny light, I was freezing; my feet, in particular, felt like blocks of ice as I pulled the cork out of the rum bottle and sniffed the contents apprehensively. The smell was sweet, strong, and surprisingly pleasant. Lifting the bottle to my lips, I poured a large mouthful down my throat, feeling its warm glow spread through me until the rum bit back; I almost choked on it and fought to keep it down as I screwed my face up. This was cheap and very strong rum!

I remember sending the first two messages on the BC's sheet and receiving acknowledgements from the Command Posts. I also remember around one o'clock taking another longer slug of rum – just to keep warm, and I think I remember taking another slug. What I definitely remember, is waking up shivering wildly, my head thumping madly, so bad I could hardly open my eyes and when I did I thought I had gone blind; I could just see a faint glow from the almost dead 24 volt light bulb.

'Bloody hell,' I muttered as I realised I had allowed the batteries to run low, so low the radios were not working and worse I could not remember if I had sent the rest of the messages as ordered. Not that I cared too much, I felt far too ill and cold to care, I just wanted to find a warm bed to curl up in and die.

330

Hauling myself unsteadily to my feet, I staggered to the rear of the truck and wrestled with flap for a few seconds before I fell headlong off the back, straight onto the sleeping Sergeant Redding!

'What the fucking hells going on?' he spat as he struggled to sit up and undo the zip of his sleeping back.

I was still lying half across him when he broke free and threw me from him, straight onto Jock Low who, awakened by the commotion, was also trying to open his sleeping bag.

I slithered off Jock and under the canvas of the lean-to as the Sarge and Jock hurled boots, belts and anything else that could get their hands on at me. I vaguely remember crawling on my hands and knees in the snow, as I looked for my tent but not much more.

Apparently, I did find the tent and woke Smokey up muttering, 'Start the bloody, frigging engine up,' before I fell into a deep sleep.

Smoky unwrapped himself from his blankets and taking pity on me, he threw them and mine on top of me before looking at the time on his watch – it was 4.30 am, I was an hour and a half late!

At nine o'clock my still booted feet were grabbed by Sergeant Redding, who dragged me out of the bivouac and hoisted me to my feet, holding me by the shoulder as I screwed my eyes up against the glare of the snow, wondering where the hell I was.

'How's your head you drunken sod you, I hope it's giving you bloody hell lad?'

'It is Sarge,' I winced as the pain in my head increased violently.

'Look at this,' he snarled, pointing at the snow as I tried desperately to comprehend why he was pointing at the snow.

'What Sarge?

'This, your bloody trail in the snow.'

I looked again and could see a wide trail in the snow, meandering from my bivouac tent back to the lean-to; it took a very winding route and I realised I must have spent some time crawling around in the dark looking for my bed.

'Sorry Sarge,' I spluttered not sure if I was about to be jailed or hung.

'Sorry,' said Sergeant Redding laughing, 'Sorry, you better be bloody sorry, I'm going to put this one down to experience but you ever, and I mean ever, let me down again lad, and you're for it; now get yourself sorted out.'

Despite my pounding head and nausea in my stomach, I felt relieved the Sarge had seen the funny side of my first and only brush with rum and, importantly, was not going to charge me.

I tried to gather my thoughts, as I needed to find hot water for a wash and shave and wandered over to the Austin.

Jock Low who had been standing by a small petrol cooker by the side of the vehicle watching Sergeant Redding chastise me, shouted, 'Here Syd, a cup of tea and a bacon burger sandwich.'

331

The tea burned my gullet as it went down but it was heaven sent and I even managed to eat the sandwich without throwing up.

A while later, washed and shaved and feeling a tad better, I helped Jock pack up the lean-to and prepare the Austin to move as Sergeant Redding had said he had to deliver some equipment to the Regimental Command Post. The BC had left earlier to join the Observation Parties with Smokey as the signaller, Sergeant Redding having told the BC he needed me to help him.

When we were ready to go, I asked Jock, 'What kit are we taking to the RCP Jock?'

Jock looked at me as though I was stupid, 'There's no kit, we're going to the café down on the main road for coffee and a proper breakfast!'

Sitting by the tailboard in the back of the Austin with the flap rolled up so I could take advantage of the view, I sucked in as much fresh air as I could as we drove down a steep hill toward the main road. We seemed to be going rather fast as things in the back were beginning to move and rattle loudly.

Releasing my grip on the tailboard, I reached forward to grab a torch that had bounced onto the floor of the truck when we started to fly! Half way down the hill and traveling quite fast, the truck hit a cattle ramp that some idiot had built horizontally on a steep hill, the result of which, it acted like a take off ramp. The truck took off, and I felt myself floating in the air until the wheels crashed back down, causing me to smash the side of my head against the tailboard.

Lying semi-conscious, on the floor of the truck with my back resting on the tailboard, I could feel Jock wrestling with the controls as he brought the Austin to a screeching halt. I then heard him and Sergeant Redding jump out of the cab and run round to the back of the truck.

'Where the fuck is he?' Jock shouted.

'Quick drop the tailboard and see where he is,' I heard the Sarge say.

They dropped the tailboard and I dropped out, straight onto the tarmac banging my forehead as I did so.

'Oh for fuck's sake, we've killed him!' Jock spluttered, as I lay there motionless, blood seeping from a cut on my forehead and more appeared to be trickling from my left ear.

'He's not dead, not yet anyway,' Sergeant Redding said, 'come on lift him back in, and we'll take him to the MO.'

They drove me to MO in Otterburn Camp; half carrying me into see him. The MO looked at the small cut on my forehead then checked my ears and spent a lot of time looking into my eyes before holding several fingers up.

'How many?' and other questions I answered as coherently as possible, considering the circumstances.

Eventually, he said to Sergeant Redding, 'Probably mild concussion, the blood in his ear is from his forehead, not his ear and that cut just needs a plaster, take him to the hangers, and put him to bed and I'll check on him later.'

Because the weather was so atrocious, the CO wanted to give everybody the chance to dry off and the drivers to have a good night's sleep before the long drive back to Essex and had instructed the Quartermaster to arrange some accommodation for the Regiment's last night at Otterburn. Because the camps were full of other units, the Quartermaster took over two huge, newly built garages and filled them with beds that he and his staff must have spent ages erecting and making up.

Despite the fact that I had messed up pretty badly the night before, I spent the last day of my first exercise warm and cosy in bed, while the rest of the Regiment shivered out in the freezing cold. Just after dark at about six pm, the regiment drove into camp and the lads all piled into the garages. Apart from a mild headache, I was fine the next morning and enjoyed the long drive back to Shoeburyness.

A couple of weeks later the Regiment was fully committed to the preparations for the move to Dortmund; cleaning and checking all the guns, vehicles, equipment and barracks ready for handover to the incoming unit. The days were hectic but as spring came, we enjoyed our nights in Southend, becoming regulars at the bowling alley on the pier as well as one or two local hostelries where there were plenty of girls to chase. I enjoyed a fair amount of success but did not start any real relationships, I still found it difficult to maintain any interest longer than one or two dates; I was still in love with a dream.

It was about this time that the Mods in Southend began to influence the way I dressed, my Teddy-Boy jacket and drainpipes were ditched in favour of polo shirts, pullovers, and barrel bottom jeans, although my slick backed, hair remained.

At the beginning of April, the CO gave most of the Regiment a long weekend break, so Rob and I, along with a gaggle of Jocks and other Geordies, caught the 4.15 train from Kings Cross to Edinburgh and headed for the bar. Much to the amusement of the others, the barman refused to serve me, he did not believe I was eighteen; it was not the first time, nor would it be the last that I had to use my identity card to prove my age.

We spent the journey chatting and drinking in the bar until myself and the other Geordies slid off the train at Newcastle. Rob and I walked up to the bus station at the Haymarket and onto the bus to Ashington, arranging for Rob to come over the next morning for a drink with Tom and me at the 'Fell Em Doon' Club before I waved him cheerio when he got off the bus at Bedlington.

Just after noon on the following day, the three of us walked into the large bar of the 'Fell Em Doon' and sat down at a table by the window. I offered to buy the first round and walking up to the bar I bumped into my Dad and Percy Page.

'What are ye having?' Dad asked half smiling.

'Three pints of Exhibition,' I replied mildly shocked at my Dad's generosity but more shocked when he said that he and Percy would join us!

Dad was obviously in good spirits, after I introduced him to Rob he told us a couple of amusing stories of his time in the Home Guard. He then went onto to recall his youth with his two pals; Bob and Curly, including the time that they carried pails of water to the sand dunes at Duridge Bay and sell the water for a penny a cup to the people who had gone to watch cars racing on the beach.

I was gobsmacked; this was the most I had heard my Dad talk, being more used to his usual monosyllabic grunts and along with the others, I was enjoying his very polished story telling. I bought another round of drinks and as I placed the last two pints in front of Dad and Percy, Dad began another story.

'De ye knaa hoo Curly got his name lads?' he asked with his sardonic smile.

The three of us said in unison, 'No,' as Dad leant forward conspiratorially.

'The poor lad had a curved spine and a bit of a hump so he was always called Curly by his mates, even after he got married, his Missus even called him Curly.'

I thought that was a bit sad, and that Dad had finished but he sat back took a long drink from his glass, wiped his mouth with the back of his hand and started again.

'Unfortunately, not lang after he got married and heving just moved into a farm cottage, he got pneumonia and quickly up and died!'

He took another sip of beer and I noticed that Percy was smiling at this rather sad piece of information but Dad continued.

'Whey man, Bob and me were devastated by the news – wor best mate had passed away and we hadn't even been to see him when he was in his sick bed - we were mortified.'

There was another pause as he took another sip before continuing.

'Whey me and Bob decided we would gan aroond and pay wor respects to Missus Curly and see our owld mate before the lid was screwed doon on his coffin, so off we went te the Club at Reed Ra and had a pint or two before we went ower to see him.' 'Standing in the bar, Bob said to me, "Ye knaa Geordie, Curly was one of the best, nur he *was* the best mate ye could hev, he would dee owt for ye; by lad he was a champion fella and am really gannin te miss him."'

'Whey I agreed with him and we had another pint as we talked aboot wor great mate Curly and hoo wonderful he waas.'

Dad leant forward again and whispered, 'Ye knaa I said Curly had a curved back and a bit of a hunch?'

We nodded and Dad went on, 'Whey the undertaker had a spot of bother getting him te fit in the coffin, because of his curl like; so they ended up heving te put wires across his thighs and across chest, fastened te either side of the coffin in order te keep him doon.'

I was incredulous but before I could challenge Dad, he went on.

334

'After four or five pints Bob and me heads ower to the cottage where straightening wor ties, we took off wor caps and knocked on the widow's door; "Hello Missus Curly," I says, "we've come te see wor mate for the last time lass."'

'Mrs Curly ushered us in and thanked us for coming and Bob said to her, "Eee Missus, he was a great lad, we had some smashing times together and we'll miss him, he really was one of the nicest, kindest men I've known." She thanked Bob and towld us te gan into the front parlour where Curly was laid oot.'

I looked at Tom and Bob who appeared to be totally enthralled at Dad's storytelling and then looked at Percy who still had a knowing smile on his face as Dad continued.

'Whey the two of us walked quietly into the parlour with wor caps in hand and stood by the coffin looking doon at wor owld friend.' He paused for another slurp, with a twinkle just beginning to appear in his eyes. 'Whey Bob started again – saying what a great lad he was and how kind and good he was, when there was an almighty "TWANG" as the wire across Curly's chest snapped, and up he sits in his coffin, his right arm swinging forward, his hand landing on Bob's showlder!'

'Bob screamed in terror and swiping Curly's hand off his showlder he shouted, "Get yor frigging hand of me ye humpty backed little bastard ye." and raced oot the hoose nearly knocking Missus Curly Doon!' Dad finished.

I nearly choked on the mouthful of beer I had just swallowed as both Bob and Percy burst out laughing followed by Dad and me but Tom looked at us as though we were heathens.

'Did they strap him back doon Mr Carr?' he asked solemnly.

Dad looked at him through tear filled eyes then taking a deep breath to control his mirth answered, 'Aye, of course they did Bonny Lad,' and winked slyly at Bob and me.

Finishing our pints, we left Dad and Percy and headed off, stopping at 'Cuthbertson's' for a bag of chips each before going into Ashington town centre that was bustling with Saturday shoppers and others out just to see who was about on a lovely spring day. We called in at 'Dawson's' coffee shop and played 'Please Please Me,' by a group called 'The Beatles' who were taking the pop world by storm before we discussed the new Geordie group, 'The Animals'. The atmosphere in the coffee bar was not what it had been a year or so earlier. It was all but empty, prompting us to finish our coffee and continue into town to look for something more interesting.

As we walked past the 'Buffalo' Cinema Tom grabbed my arm.

'Look Syd, there's that lass ye fancy.'

He pointed across the road where three girls were walking in the same direction but slightly ahead of us.

Bob asked, 'Which one is she then?'

Tom answered for me, 'The little one in the middle.'

Bob smiled, 'She's a cracker Syd, have you not asked her out?'

335

I shook my head and almost disconsolately answered, 'I've nearly asked her out a few times but never really had the chance, and anyway she's got a lad.'

Bob looked at me quizzically. 'I didn't think that would stop you from trying, knowing you like?'

'It has and if I did get the chance I wouldn't want te spoil me chances by rushing in too quick, so I think I've had it there.'

I knew that I wanted so much to say, 'Sod it' and run across the road, grab her and tell her how lovely she was and that I wanted to be with her; but I didn't and like a fool I let her walk away again.

The three of us patrolled the town for another hour or so before heading back to Tom's, where Tom played his guitar and sang a couple of Adam Faith songs while we ate ham sandwiches. Tom's singing was as good as ever and I urged him, as I had several times in the past, to join a group and get up and perform on stage but he was still reluctant to do so due to his shyness.

Rob and I enjoyed the rest of the weekend, especially Saturday night at the Welfare Dance where we met up briefly with Tom and his girlfriend, she was the same girl he had been courting last summer and they seem to be very happy and I envied him that.

Tuesday soon came and we caught the train back to camp meeting up with some more of the lads, one or two who had obviously had more than a couple of drinks but we managed to get them back into barracks without any problems.

Having spent all my cash on the long-weekend, I could not afford to go to Southend until payday and rather than spend the lovely spring evenings moping around the billet, Rob and I wandered onto the foreshore just outside the camp gates. There were a few locals about, walking dogs or just out enjoying the warm spring evening after a particularly cold winter.

Quickly bored we were heading back toward camp when we saw a group of girls chatting on a bench, they had obviously noticed us as there was a bit of pointing and giggling going on as we approached them.

'Hi ye,' I ventured as we walked by.

'Hi ye,' one of them replied smiling, 'are you from the camp?'

That was enough for us to stop and have a chat with girls, one of whom was definitely giving me 'the eye'.

She stood up pushing her way past one of the other girls and asked, 'What's your name, I'm Dora?'

She was about my height - five foot eight with had short dark hair, and was very pretty with a lovely figure.

Before I could answer, Rob said laughing, 'His nickname's Buzz, cos he's always buzzing around.'

Rob had only called me that a couple of times but I went along with it.

'Yep, I'm Buzz.' After six months in the army, I was beginning to shed some of my very strong Geordie accent and although I would use less and less Geordie words, I would always retain my Geordie lilt.

Dora obviously saw that I found her attractive and very sexy and took full advantage, leaning close to me to talk so that her breasts brushed against my arm. I didn't need any more indication that she was making a play for me and we soon wandered off together to continue our wooing. Before long, we were lying in a sandy nook engaged in some hot kissing and fondling.

She said that she was from Great Wakering, a small village about a mile north of where we were and with that in mind, I thought that we could have a torrid two or three weeks before the Regiment moved to Germany.

Her friends interrupted our passion when they approached, stopping at a discreet distance before shouting, 'It's time to go!'

Walking to the bus stop with her, I arranged to meet her just outside her village the following evening; thinking, if the weather is as it is tonight, we can continue where we left off without interruption.

Walking back to the billet, I asked Rob how he had made out.

'Nah, no luck there,' he said, 'but I thought I was going to have to throw a bucket of water on you two!'

'I'm in there; I'm seeing her tomorrow so no buckets of water please.'

I met her just after six thirty and we wandered off, hand in hand down a quiet country lane with only one thing in mind! I could feel the tension in her grip as I looked for a suitable spot to canoodle. When we stopped to kiss, she pressed herself invitingly against me and I took the hint, I guided her off the road and onto a grassy bank behind some trees where we lay down to continue our kissing.

She eased her back as I fumbled to undo her bra before sliding my hand around to caress her firm breasts. My passion was at boiling point as I slid my hand up her smooth, nylon-clad leg until I reached the top of her stockings, stopping to feel the silky, smooth softness of her inner thigh, between stockings and panties. Breathing heavily with our lips locked together, I slid my hand further expecting to find silk panties – but instead felt thick, very thick and very big knickers!

Confused at what I was feeling, a dreadful realisation hit me; I knew what these were! I eased myself up and lifting her skirt slightly, I looked down and saw she was wearing navy blue school knickers!

'Bloody hell,' I muttered as passion subsided, 'how old are you?'

Still lying on her back she tried to pull me back down as she said in a husky voice, 'Fifteen; well in a couple of months I'll be fifteen, but that doesn't matter does it?'

As desperate as I was to continue to make love as any red bloodied youth would, I still had morals and sitting up I said, 'It does bloody matter, you're far too young, but bloody hell I thought ye were seventeen man, come on I'm taking you home.'

337

I don't know who was more disappointed, her or me, but despite her pleas, I took her back to her village.

I said, 'Look in five years' time, three or four years difference won't matter but not now, it's not right and it's against the bloody law!

Kissing her on the cheek, I said, 'Go on before I do something I shouldn't.'

'Goodbye Buzz,' she said as I left.

I walked back to camp with very mixed emotions but glad she had worn the school knickers; it was the last time I was called Buzz but I did find out a few years later that Dora married another Geordie soldier that she called Buzz!

On May the 20th, our last night in England, I again wandered onto the foreshore where I met another girl, a student who lived in one of the big houses near camp – she was not wearing school knickers! It was a very pleasant way to say goodbye to Shoeburyness…

28

The British Army of the Rhine

It was with some excitement, that the following morning, about fifty of us from the Blazers, along with a hundred or so more from the rest of the Regiment, loaded our suitcases and kitbags onto coaches and climbed aboard for the journey to Gatwick airport to catch the Air Trooping flight to Düsseldorf. As this was to be the first time abroad for most of us in the Regiment, the coach was full of speculative chatter and banter on what we would discover in Germany, the words fraulein and beer, mentioned most frequently.

We were all looking forward to the flight as very few of us had flown before, including the old-sweats that had travelled to and from Hong Kong by troop ship, as a result, there was a bit of a scrabble to get a window seat when we boarded the BEA, Vickers Viscount.

I managed to slide into one just before Scouse Bolt, who then sat down next to me muttering, 'Bloody Geordie sprinter, I should have known you'd be first in, just like the dinner and NAAFI queues, you're always first there too.'

Smiling at him, I said, 'If it's worth going for, you've got to go for it Scouse Lad.'

Laughing, he replied, 'Bollocks.'

The journey on coaches from Düsseldorf to Dortmund showed us how strange Germany was; as well as driving on the wrong side of the road, the cars, and trucks were different. Mercedes, Opels, Audis, NSUs, huge trucks with trailers, and coaches with glass roofs filled roads lined with strange traffic signs and advertisement boards but what struck me most, were the buildings. Despite it being a sunny day, it was dull. Here in the industrial Ruhr, all the buildings appeared drab, either grey or dull cream and were mainly square, featureless and almost monolithic but all of this just added to the excitement of being in a foreign country.

We joined Route 1, the old main road through the Ruhr that was now mainly dual carriageway/autobahn, with tramlines in the centre where the road cut through towns.

It was during the first stretch of Autobahn that we began to learn German; Scouse shouted, 'The dirty sods look at that sign, AusFARHT, bloody Ausfarht, does that mean you have to let your farts out there?'

Sitting behind us, Ray said pompously, 'Cretin, it means exit.'

'Nah, Bollocks,' Scouse shouted, 'it's a farting place, that's what it says.' Ray tried to reply but the lads drowned him out with a thunderous assault of imitation farts.

I shouted at Scouse, 'I hope none of those farts is real or we are in the shite!'

Scouse nodded as the coach passed Westfalen Park where we saw the very tall and very slender space-age tower with a revolving restaurant on top.

Entering Dortmund, Route 1 took us from the North East side to the North West side, where West Riding Barracks stood on the corner of the junction with a minor road called the Nussbaumweg. As we turned into the Nussbaumweg, we could see the barrack's wall on our left and the large grey barrack blocks beyond. To our right, and looking totally out of place, was a black and white, half-timbered 'Westfalen' farmhouse that we later found out was the YMCA amenities building – 'The Stonk Club', Stonk being the military term for an artillery barrage.

The coaches turned off the road into a sweeping half-moon shaped cobbled entranceway, through the main gate, past the guardroom, and up a drive to the imposing Regimental Headquarters building where we turned right to our Battery Block. Built in the 1930s, to accommodate Hitler's ever-expanding army; this barracks had also been the Air Defence Headquarters for the Ruhr and had a huge underground complex that had been sealed off some years earlier.

Our block and the other accommodation blocks were 'L' shaped, rendered grey and consisted of huge cellars housing stores; ground floors containing offices and more stores; first floors for accommodation; second floors with German dormer style windows that were mainly empty and finally large attics at the very top.

The BSM greeted us outside our Battery Block with various warnings and briefings before handing us over to NCOs from the advance party who showed us to our rooms. I found myself jostling for a bed in a room with six lads from the Battery Command Post and managed to grab a corner bed.

Turning, I said to the rest of the lads, 'Welcome to Deutschland and the British Army of the Rhine.'

One of them shouted, 'Sieg fucking Heil!'

That night, a couple of the NCOs from the advance party took a group of us into Dortmund for our first taste of Germany, our first stop being a Chinese Restaurant!

Later, with bellies full of food and German beer, we followed them into an area known as 'Little Soho' that proved to be too expensive, so they took us across a newly levelled bomb site that was awaiting redevelopment, and into a small bar where we met Wolfgang, the bar owner. He was a large, loud, moustachioed and jovial German who welcomed British Squaddies, just as long as they behaved themselves; the bar became a regular for many of the lads from the Battery.

The Chinese food and German beer did not agree with everyone as I found out when I went to the 'Toilette' and found Jock Pattinson being violently sick in one of the cubicles.

I Joined Dick at the urinals, just as Jock threw up again.

Dick said drunkenly, 'Fugging Jock can't take his fogging beer!'

The sound of vomit splattering around the toilet bowl came from the cubicle as Jock vomited yet again; this proved too much for Dick, he retched before

341

turning to run to one of the cubicles but didn't make it, throwing up violently. His vomit plastered the door of the cubicle but worse, he had been in the middle of emptying his bladder and his pride and joy was waggling around, spraying the area with urine!

Unaccustomed to German beer, more and more of the lads became stupidly drunk and I and a couple of others left vowing never to get as drunk as that – difficult in Germany in the early sixties.

The Regiment soon settled into its new barracks and with some excitement, we began preparing our equipment for our first six-week long, annual practice camp on the Soltau and Munsterlager Training Areas that lay two-hundred miles to the northeast.

In camp, I worked in the Signals Stores located in the cellars at the end of the Battery Block, accessed by a steep cobbled ramp. There, Sgt Redding kept us busy mounting radios into vehicles, testing communication harnesses, charging batteries and preparing radios for mounting into vehicles.

On the Monday morning of our third week in Germany, I was in the stores winding telephone cable from packs onto metal reels when the BK, Captain Piper wandered in and up to Sgt Redding who was at his desk writing loading lists.

A slightly podgy, scholarly looking officer, Capt Piper was, in addition to being the BK, also the Regimental Catering Officer!

'Sergeant Redding can I speak to Gunner Carr?' he asked standing in front of the desk.

Sgt Redding pointed to me and said, 'There he is Sir; Carr come here.'

Placing the reel of cable on the floor, I saluted Captain Piper and said, 'Yes Sir?'

Clearing his throat, he asked, 'I'm led to believe that you are something of an artist Carr, is that correct?'

'Yes, I suppose so Sir, a bit of a one,' I replied, wondering where this conversation was going.

'That's good,' he said, and then turning to Sgt Redding, asked, 'I have a little job for Carr, is it all right to take him for a while?'

'Yes, certainly Sir,' said Sergeant Redding, trying hard to conceal his annoyance at losing one of his workers.

I followed Captain Piper up out of the Signals Stores and toward the huge building that housed the Cookhouse, Dining Room, NAAFI and Junior NCOs Mess.

Curious as to where we were going and what the 'little job' was, I asked, 'What's the job, Sir?'

'All will be revealed shortly,' he replied in a non-committal voice.

Climbing the wide stairs into the entrance hall of the building, I followed him into the huge Dining Room, which was strictly 'Out of Bounds' outside of mealtimes. The room was about fifteen foot high, very wide, with six large windows on each side. The wall between the windows was about five-feet wide and painted battleship grey from the floor to a dado at about three feet high, the remainder a drab cream.

Weaving between the dining tables and chairs, Captain Piper stopped in the centre of the room, next to a dining table that had a large book on it.

He said, 'Ok Carr this is the job,' he said as he gestured with a sweeping motion, the whole room.

'What, you want me to paint the Dining Room?' I asked incredulously.

'No, I want you to paint murals on the walls.'

He picked the book up from the table and opening it, he held it out to me, saying, 'Murals of figures in German National Dress,'

I was gobsmacked; I had never painted a mural before let alone ten of them.

'And how big do you want these murals, Sir?' I asked, trying to take in the size of the task.

'Oh about seven foot I would think, I'll let you decide which costumes to paint from this book and you can crack on, right?'

I wondered if he had taken leave of his senses and asked, 'What about paint and paint brushes and ladders and other things Sir?'

He smiled at me as though I was a little backward and turning on his heel, said, 'See the BQMS (Battery Quartermaster Sergeant), he will I am sure, provide you with everything you need,' and walked out leaving me to take stock of 'the little job'.

Gathering my thoughts, I headed toward the BQMS Stores, making a mental list of the things I would need while not looking forward to asking the grizzly Staff Sergeant BQMS for them.

A little later, standing behind the counter that closed off the corridor of the cellar, I shouted nervously, 'Hello,' and waited, wondering what reception I would receive.

I had to wait several minutes before the Bombardier Storekeeper came out of one of the rooms further up the corridor.

'Right Syd, what can I do for you?' he asked as he approached the counter.

'Hiya Bom,' I answered, 'I need cans of emulsion paint of each of the primary colours, a can of white and black, a three-inch, a two-inch and a one-inch paintbrush and...'

'Whoa, just a bloody minute, what the bloody hell do you want all this for and what makes you think we've got it - and if we have, that we'll give it to you?'

Expecting this sort of reaction, I had resigned myself to a prolonged engagement and answered, 'The BK has told me to paint murals in the Dining Room and to get all the kit I need from the BQMS, so here I am Bom.'

'The BK! Murals?' he muttered, 'We don't know anything about that, hang on, and I'll get the BQMS.'

343

He disappeared up the corridor and into the BQMS's office where I could hear he was obviously briefing him on my outrageous request as I heard the BQMS's raised voice say, 'WHAT!' several times.

Trying to remain calm, I waited for the inevitable bollocking and it was not long in coming. Thin and gaunt with skin like leather, the BQMS stormed out of his office with his large, black mongrel dog and the Bombardier trotting behind. On seeing me, the dog sped past the BQMS and reaching the counter first, it jumped up placing its front paws on the counter, looking for all the world that it was waiting for me to speak.

'Can I have some paint and paint brushes please?' I asked the dog – it began barking madly.

'SHUT THE FUCK UP DOG,' the BQMS yelled at his dog before saying to me, 'Speak to me you fucking maggot, not the fucking dog,' and began a superb bollocking, occasionally interrupting it by screaming 'SHUT UP,' at his incessantly barking dog;

'Where the fuck, 'SHUT THE FUCK UP,' (to the dog) do you think you are lad, a fucking paint shop? This is the fucking BQMS Stores, 'QUIET' (to his dog) we store fucking things, we don't fucking issue them, 'GET FUCKING DOWN AND SHUT UP' (again to his dog), then it would be a fucking Issues, wouldn't it you bloody maggot? 'FOR FUCK SAKE DOG, SHUT UP, or in your fucking case a 'Give Away fucking Shop' wouldn't it?' he ranted while the dog continued to ignore him, barking even louder.

'Sorry 'Q', do you want me to be quiet or answer?' I asked feigning an innocent look.

'NOT FUCKING YOU, MY FUCKING DOG,' he shouted back as he swiped the dog's paws from the bench. The dog obviously, either did not like this or thought it was a game and to make matters much worse, it grabbed the BQMS's trousers by the ankle and began snarling and worrying them.

The BQMS hopped on one leg and screamed at his dog, 'FUCKING LET GO YOU BLOODY, FUCKING MONGREL AND STOP FUCKING BARKING OR I'LL FUCKING CASTRATE YOU.'

The dog obviously understood this as it let go and started barking and growling at the BQMS. I noticed his Bombardier had made a tactical withdrawal to a room further down the corridor and felt like retreating myself as I was finding it very difficult to stop myself from laughing.

The BQMS finally chased the barking dog back down to his office, kicked it inside and closed the door behind him before turning back toward me, his face bright red with anger.

As he approached me the dog began barking loudly from inside his office, he screamed, 'FOR FUCKS SAKE, SHUT FUCKING UP!'

'I'm sorry Q,' I said quietly, 'I haven't said anything.'

'Not fucking you smartarse, the fucking dog, now where was I?'

'Giving me a bollocking Q,' I replied cheekily.

344

The BQMS, accompanied by his dog barking in the background, began ranting at me again and then suddenly fell silent as Captain Piper entered the stores and walked up to stand next to me.

He said loudly so that he could be heard above the sound of barking, 'Ah BQ, I see Carr is already here to collect paint; there's not a problem is there?'

The BQMS glared madly at him before saying, 'No fucking problem here Sir, everything is fucking, hunky, fucking dory,' and then shouted, 'FUCKING SHUT UP!'

Captain Piper was aghast and spluttered, 'I beg your pardon BQMS?'

'Not fucking you Sir, my fucking dog – SHUT FUCKING UP!' but the dog ignored him and continued to bark.

Captain Piper was obviously not sure how to handle the now mildly deranged BQMS, and turning on his heels he said, 'OK BQMS, please see that he gets everything he needs,' and beat a hasty retreat up and out of the stores.

'I'll see he gets every fucking thing he needs,' snarled the BQMS, 'like my fucking boot up his fucking arse!'

'BOMBARDIER!' he screamed, and to his dog, 'SHUT FUCKING UP!'

The dog did not shut up but the Bombardier came running out of his hiding place and asked the BQMS timidly, 'Yes Q?'

Much to my relief the BQMS had had enough and snarled, 'Bom give this fucking maggot want he wants and make sure he signs for everything on a fucking ten, thirty-three.'

The Bombardier took me into the paint store where we spent ages sorting paint, paintbrushes, and chalks into a pile, which he noted onto the AFG1033 Issues Form, eventually making me sign it.

Keen to get rid of me, he said, 'Right Syd, get this stuff out of here before he changes his mind.'

Happy to oblige, after three or four trips back and forth, I had taken all the paint and other items I had managed to coax out of the Bombardier to the dining room. I also collected a number of empty tins from the cookhouse to mix the paints in but now looking up at the walls, the size of 'the little job' hit me. Never having painted a mural before, I did not know anything about using grids for ensuring dimensions were correct, or that you could use an overhead projector to throw the image onto a wall and trace around it.

Looking through the book that Captain Piper had left, I chose the first picture, a woman in a Bavarian costume of some sort. Clearing a space by a wall, I slid two tables together and placing a chair on top of these, I climbed onto it with the book in one hand and a piece of blue chalk in the other and carefully drew a matchstick figure of the woman; climbing down several times in order to step back to see if I had the proportions right.

Happy with the proportions, I then fleshed the figure out before drawing the costume in detail, spending some time on the face, hair, and hands - not wanting anything to spoil the drawing. By the time, I was ready to start painting it was lunchtime, and lads who were queuing up for lunch began heckling.

'Her tits aren't big enough Syd!'

'Put her in a bikini.'

'Nur draw her naked,' and other, not so subtle suggestions.

A Lance Bombardier stepped forward and shouted, 'She looks like Irma from the Strasse!' (The Lenin Strasse was the brothel street in Dortmund and generally referred to as 'The Strasse').

He knew he had made a mistake as soon as he had shouted it and sure enough, the lads turned and began heckling him.

'Who is Irma?'

'How do you know what she looks like?'

'You dirty bugger, how often do you see her?' and on and on, the remarks becoming more and more crude, until the Catering Corps Sergeant behind the hotplate shut them up, bringing order back to the Dining Room.

After lunch, the cheery-faced Warrant Officer, Master Chef, accompanied by one of his Corporals, came out to watch me tentatively apply the first brushstrokes of paint.

He stood watching quietly for a few minutes then said, 'I like the look of what you are doing son, come and tell me when you finished the first one.'

He turned to his Corporal, 'Make sure he gets a brew when he wants one, and a bacon butty in the morning won't go amiss,' he said before wandering back into the kitchen whistling Colonel Bogey.

Shortly after, I was perched on the chair, painting detail onto the face when I heard Sergeant Redding's voice behind me.

'Some bloody little job this looks like Carr?' he snapped.

I carefully turned on the chair and replied, 'Yor right there Sarge, it took me by surprise as well.'

'And how long do you think this is going to take, because presumably, you've got to paint all the walls?'

'I have Sarge, and I'm not sure, maybe two or three weeks.'

He said, 'We're going on practice camp in three weeks so you better get a bloody move on lad,' and turned and left me to it.

I finished the first mural just before NAAFI break the next morning and asked the Master Chef if he would like to come and see it.

'That's excellent, you're bloody wasted in the army,' he said and as he walked off, added, 'Bash on son, I can't wait to see the rest of them.'

I soon got into the swing of it and developed a system of my own, enabling me to complete the other figures in a few hours each.

It was during this period that the lads established routines for our off duty time; some spent most evenings in the Battery Bar endeavouring successively to reach a reasonable level of drunkenness by consuming as much Amstel Beer as possible; some went downtown trying unsuccessfully to chat up local girls and others hung around the Stonk Club. Rob and I however, discovered that in the local Married Quarters there were a handful of eligible teenage daughters!

One of them called Shirley had exchanged looks with me several times at the Cinema in the nearby Suffolk Barracks but the opportunity to talk to her did not occur until she started work in the gift shop of the Stonk Club. A red head with striking looks and a superb figure, she had already cold-shouldered several lads who had tried to chat her up.

Feeling as if I knew her, I walked confidently up to the counter, smiled and said, 'Hi, I was wondering if I could take you to the pictures sometime?'

She smiled back and said, 'How about Friday night - do you know what's on?'

Gobsmacked by her acceptance, I managed to stop my smile from becoming gormless and answered, 'Nur I haven't a clue what's on but does that matter?'

'No, not really,' she said smiling back.

During that first date, I found out she had a friend who we arranged to blind date Rob, luckily, they hit it off and we spent many double dates together. I was to date Shirley for several months until she moved with her family to Aden. We enjoyed those months together, especially babysitting when we could canoodle in the comfort of someone's house; neither of us took the relationship too seriously, although we did enjoy ourselves very much.

I also enjoyed painting the murals and took pleasure in the favourable comments hidden within the lads' heckling and the fact that I set my own pace. The chefs keeping me topped up with tea and sarnies also helped! Captain Piper visited every day and became more and more excited as I finished each mural until after two and a half weeks, whilst I was putting the finishing touches on the last figure, he rushed in with the Master Chef and excitedly announced that the CO (Commanding Officer) was coming to see the murals.

Climbing down from the table I had been standing on, I wiped my hands on a cleaning cloth as the Master Chef directed a couple of fatigue men to straighten up the tables and chairs. They had just finished and the Master Chef was telling me how the paintings brightened up the dining room when the RSM flung open the door to the entrance hall and marched in.

'GENTLEMEN!' he shouted.

We sprang to attention as the CO, a large imposing man, strode into the centre of the room accompanied by his Adjutant. After returning Captain Piper's salute, the CO, with the Adjutant and RSM following, walked slowly around the room studying each mural briefly, as Captain Piper walked alongside explaining what each figure represented.

The Master Chef and I remained where we were and he nudged me and winked, nodding with his head at Captain Piper as if to say 'creep.'

347

The CO looked at each painting with a satisfied smile on his face whilst almost ignoring Piper's dialogue before he came up to where I was standing and looked down at me.

'Carr is it?'

'Yes Sir,' I replied waiting for comment but he turned to the Master Chef.

'What do you think of them Master Chef?'

I immediately thought, 'He doesn't like them and he wants a second opinion.'

'I think they are terrific and I think that young Carr is wasted in the army, Sir.'

The CO smiled and said, 'Steady on Master Chef, I think they are excellent and they do brighten the place enormously and he undoubtedly has talent but let us not say he is wasted in the army, I'm sure he has a bright future with us.'

I was beginning to think that he thought I was too unimportant to talk too directly but I was wrong as he then spent, at least, fifteen minutes discussing the murals with me and appeared surprised that they had been my first. He also asked detailed questions as to how I had painted them and what sort of paints I had used.

A little while later, having returned the leftover paint and paint brushes to a madly barking black dog and a grizzly BQMS I walked passed our wheeled, armoured vehicles that had signallers crawling all over them, fitting radios and batteries, before I wandered down the cobbled ramp into the Signals Stores.

Sgt Redding looked up briefly from his desk and said, 'Don't just stand there give Smokey a hand to load the BC's Champ.'

That night, sitting on a bench in the park-like cemetery with Shirley, she seemed impressed when I told her about the murals but she was also a little sad that I was leaving the next day for a six-week practice camp. She was very receptive to my advances that night and she almost took my mind of a certain blue-eyed girl, almost but not quite.

29

Practice Camp

Early next morning the Regiment formed up into six, large convoys and set off on a slow, daylong drive to the Training Area North of Hannover. Normally, The Battery Commanders would drive up independently of the convoys but as this was the Regiments first move in Germany, the CO had rightly decreed that the Battery Commanders had to lead their Battery Convoys.

The journey passed without incident and at five pm, our Battery Convoy halted on a wide and deeply rutted, sandy track in the middle of a pine forest in the Soltau Training Area. The advance party had erected tents, in what seemed an almost haphazard way but had been necessary to take advantage of the available space between the trees. After lining the vehicles and guns up, NCOs took us to the tents that we would sleep in for the next three weeks, I found myself allocated to a single panel marquee with about twenty other lads from my Troop.

The camp consisted of two marquees for the soldiers, ridge tents for the officers and SNCOs and a large, three-panel marquee for the cookhouse and dining room that also doubled as a bar at night. Next to that stood a single panel marquee for the Officers and SNCOs bar and dining tent and another single panel marquee divided into stores, offices and an area for the guard to sleep in. There was a rudimentary ablutions area and finally, a communal toilet - a large trench with a perching log! Not the Ritz but considering the lovely summer weather, it was comfortable enough.

The first three weeks of training was 'Dry', which meant training without live ammunition for our big guns and was designed to improve our low-level tactics with much of the time, spent learning the art of camouflaging and concealing our guns, vehicles and equipment. For the first two weeks, we only deployed twice at night, the rest of our nights, we spent in camp and soon became very bored, as there was little to do other than sit in the Bar tent or wander the woods searching for wild boars!

Disturbingly, a large, rough looking Geordie called Washington had spent some time fashioning wicked looking spears with heads made from empty food tins. He disappeared into the forest several times with his homemade weapons, hoping to kill a boar – luckily, for them and him he did not find any!

I was also bored with my job on the Battery Commanders Crew; although we moved around a lot and we had two radios to operate, we sent very few messages, spending most of the time recording what others transmitted. I wanted to move to the Command Post Crews where all the action was but Sgt Redding kept saying I was lucky to be on the BC's Crew so hadn't thought it right to ask.

We did have a couple of film nights in the Bar, both films I had seen before but we were promised a night in Hamburg, so, at least, we had something to look forward to. We had heard many stories of the nightlife in Hamburg, some of them almost impossible to believe! The problem was that on the second Saturday when that trip came, we had to wear our Service Dress uniform, not what you wanted to wear for a night on the town!

Just after lunch, dressed in Service Dress and full of excited anticipation we climbed aboard 3-tonners ready for our assault on the unsuspecting Hamburg. Despite the journey in the back of the truck taking well over an hour, our spirits were kept up by the 'old sweats' relating tales of the Reeperbahn, but we were all glad to jump down from the trucks and take stock of our surroundings when we finally arrived at around three o'clock.

Finding ourselves next to the City Fairground, I wandered into it with Ray, Scouse Bolt and two others while most of the others headed for the Reeperbahn, hoping to find excitement; not very likely this early in the day.

Walking around the Fair, Scouse said, 'We should go to the Star Club, that's open 24 hours a day.'

I asked, 'What's the Star Club?'

Scouse looked amazed and said, 'I thought you were a Beatles fan, Syd?'

He explained that it was where the Beatles had played for a number of months before they hit the big time and that he thought English groups played there 24 hours a day, in fact, The Beatles could even be there tonight!

The five of us made our way to the Reeperbahn and found the Star Club where we spent the afternoon and evening watching and dancing to live music, drinking beer and eating the occasional bratwurst with a portion of pomme-frites. There were plenty of girls there, all of whom were more than happy to dance, but that was as far as their fraternisation went.

We had decided earlier that we had no intentions of going to a strip joint or other dive to pay a fortune for a drink, only to end up frustrated at the end of it, so we were more than happy to watch the groups do their gigs. The performances were non-stop, each group playing for an hour or so before handing over to the next. It was like a who's who of Scouse groups; The Swinging Blue Jeans; The Rebel Rousers; The Searchers; The Undertakers and another group whose name escapes me.

Some of the guys from the groups joined us between gigs and we ended up with around twenty at our table next to the stage; all in all, we had a great time without seeing anything else of the Reeperbahn. We left just after eleven in order to catch the truck that was due to leave at eleven thirty but, needless to say, drunken stragglers delayed our departure, so it was well after midnight before the truck left for the long drive back to camp.

On the way back, we listened to tales of strippers and live sex shows and were shocked to hear that several lads had been duped into paying small fortunes when they had bought drinks for hostesses; we were glad that we had gone to the Star Club.

351

The following day Paddy, the BC's driver left for demob and Jim Padding-ton, a hard case who resembled Jack Palance, replaced him. A good welterweight boxer with a reputation as a brawler, he had a chirpy and slightly abrasive manner but beneath his hard exterior, he was a decent bloke and I got on well with him.

On the third week, we packed up the camp and moved to another forest site on The Munsterlager Artillery Ranges where we re-erected the tents. There was a little more space at this campsite, it even had a sports field complete with a set of goal posts. However, despite firing live ammunition from the guns, the rou-tine was still boring and we still spent most nights in camp.

Lads in the other two batteries were obviously just as bored as we were; one of them illegally borrowed an Austin Champ jeep and drove it back to Dort-mund overnight to see his girlfriend. Running out of fuel on the way back, he missed First Parade, and found himself posted AWOL. Another two had taken a Champ for a night on the town in Soltau that was short lived, the Regiment alerted the RMPs who arrested them within an hour!

As a result of these misdemeanours our Battery Sergeant Major (BSM), took steps to ensure no one in our Battery would misuse, borrow, or steal one of our Champs. He had two rows of barbed wire erected to form a square large enough to contain all eight of the vehicles. The enclosure had a small entrance at the end next to the track that he had closed off with a removable barrier. As the Champs did not require keys to start them, his main security measure was to have the steering wheels removed and placed in the Guard Tent overnight!

He then paraded us on the sports field and briefed us on the steps he had taken that included an additional six-man guard each night whose sole responsibil-ity was, to provide two men to guard the Champs throughout the night.

Finally, rising to his full five foot five he warned, 'There will be no misuse of vehicles in the Blazers.'

This sounded like a challenge, and meant the main topic of conversation in the Bar Tent that night was the BSM's security measures. Sitting under a haze of cigarette smoke in the semi-gloom of dusk inside the marquee that smelled of stale food and beer, lads suggested various ideas on how to take a Champ from the barbed wire compound but most of them had little chance of success or required bulldozers to succeed, not really an option.

As the discussion went on, the REME NCO started the huge trailer mount-ed generator, sparking into life the row of bare bulbs hanging from a thick wire that stretched across the tent.

Blinking under the sudden glare, Scouse took a long pull from his bottle of Amstel beer, looked across at me, and said, 'You've not said much Syd, any ide-as?'

'There's nowt to say, if I wanted to take one I would, it wouldn't be diffi-cult would it?' This brought hoots of laughter and a fair amount of derision, which I chose to ignore.

Instead, I said to Scouse, 'You've been AWOL before and you can drive, you and me could take one – no bother.'

Scouse took another swallow of beer and said, 'Yes of course we could - how?'

'Easy,' I said, 'you distract the Guard Commander while I slide under the back of the tent and grab a steering wheel, then it's just a matter of crawling through the woods, waiting for the prowler guard to be on the opposite side of the compound, crawl in and wait for the right moment to fit the steering wheel.'

'Hold on a minute,' Scouse interrupted, 'how are you going to cut your way through the wire?'

'I wouldn't cut it, I'd wriggle underneath; the silly sods that erected it overstretched it, so it wouldn't be too difficult.

'And the Prowler Guard?'

'We'd both lie under the Champ until they are around the back of the compound, I would run forward and throw the barrier to one side while you jump in the champ and drive through – easy.'

Scouse sat silently for a moment thinking through what I said and was about to speak but was interrupted by another lad, Yorky Jones, who said determinedly, 'Count me in!'

Scouse said, 'Hang on, we are just talking – aren't we?'

'Yes,' I said, 'just talking,' but the three of us continued talking in Scouse's bivvy tent after the bar closed and what had been just a suggestion became a plan! There was no talk of the consequences of taking a Champ and going AWOL, just the method of achieving it.

I decided that two, not three would have a better chance of crawling into the compound so we agreed that Yorky would take a large pack with some tins of rations, and our washing and shaving kit and wait for us on the range road about half a mile from camp.

Just after midnight and with everyone in the Battery in bed except the three of us and the Guard, holding a bottle of beer each, pretending to be inebriated and whistling drunkenly, Scouse and I wandered toward the entrance flap of the tent housing the guard.

The marquee that housed the stores and offices also had an area separated from the rest of the marquee by a tent inner wall, providing a space for use as a guardroom. The Guard Commander, a very Latin looking Bombardier and one of the guards were sitting behind the six-foot table just inside the flap and looked up smiling as we staggered into view.

Scouse held his right thumb up in his favourite gesture and accompanied it with his favourite saying, 'Swinging, Nick mate.'

'All right Scouse, shouldn't you be in bed?' the Bombardier queried,

Scouse nodded and slurred, 'Just come for a goodnight chat mate,' and began to waffle on about the exercise.

353

Leaning on Scouse's shoulder, I pretended to be interested in his waffle while I looked around the tent confirming that the steering wheels were lying on top of another six-foot table at the back and that three of the four off-duty Guard were trying to sleep behind another four-foot high flap.

Satisfied I could sneak under the rear flap I said, 'Am off to me pit, Goodnight,' and turned and slouched away as Scouse waffled on.

Walking quickly around to the rear of the Guard tent, I stood quietly in the shadows, watching and listening for any sound of movement. Apart from the drone of Scouse's waffle and snoring from one of the SNCOs tent, there was silence. Happy that there was no one about, I knelt down next to the wall of the tent and as quietly as possible, I undid two of the rope-ties from one of the large wooden pegs that held the wall taught.

Lying down on the pine-needle covered, sandy ground; I gently lifted the bottom of the tent wall and peered inside. I could see the backs of the Bombardier and the guard, and Scouse still sitting on the table now talking about the Star Club. Two bulbs lit the area where they were but the rear of the tent was in deep shadow, providing me with, I hoped, enough cover to take a steering wheel without anyone seeing me. I wriggled under the tent wall directly under the six-foot table that the steering wheels were on and waited, catching my breath and watching.

Scouse must have seen me as he raised his voice and began singing a 'Searcher's' number to hide my movement; 'Needles and Pins – a,' he sang loudly and off key.

'They were bloody great and …,' on and on, he waffled.

I was just about to reach up for a steering wheel when one of the sleeping off-duty guard suddenly stood up from where he had been lying a few feet to my right!

I thought, 'That's it he is going to see me,' but he just yawned, scratched and tugged at his groin, farted loudly and squinted at the brightness of the bulbs.

'I'm off for a slash, that noisy Scouse git is stopping me from kipping,' he complained, then walked out past Scouse and away from the tent to relieve himself.

The Bombardier stood up and leant across the table, 'That's enough Scouse, bugger off to bed - NOW!'

As Scouse stepped back half shouting, 'OK, OK keep your hair on, I know when I'm not wanted, I'll bugger off,' I reached up, grabbed a steering wheel and quickly wriggled back under the tent, slipping the rope ties back over the pegs.

Quietly, standing up, I looked around just as Scouse came round the side of the tent, holding his thumb up as if to ask OK?

Holding the steering wheel up, I whispered, 'Have you got the adjustable spanner?' Scouse nodded affirmatively showing me the spanner and the two of us walked quietly through the tents toward the Champ compound, stopping every few yards to make sure there was no one about. Crouching low as we got closer to the compound, we stopped again when we were about twenty yards away and silently lay down to take stock.

Only a half-moon provided light from the darkness of the night but it was bright enough as there was not a cloud in the sky, just thousands of stars twinkling silently. We stared at the compound, confirming that the Champs were still parked in the normal order of two rows of three, with a third row of two at the back, with space between vehicles to enable anyone of them to be driven out past the others.

Luckily, for us, because of the hot summer weather none of the Champs had their side doors fitted, just the canopies stretched from the windscreen to the rear of the small 4 x 4s.

'We'll take the middle one in the second row, that'll give us most cover to put the steering wheel on,' I whispered and Scouse nodded.

The two prowler guards were slowly walking around the barbed wire whispering to each other, occasionally using the pick-handles they carried to hit for six, pinecones that they tossed in the air.

Waiting until they had walked past us and around the back of the wire, we crawled quickly forward and through the wire, taking it in turns to hold it up for the other to wriggle through. Scouse's trousers snagged for a second or two before we wriggled clear and crawled between the vehicles to the middle Champ where we lay panting in the deep shadows watching the Guard.

The Guard had not seen us and while I kept a look-out, Scouse took the steering wheel and half sitting inside the Champ, he quickly secured the steering wheel with the spanner, and then slumped down next to me smiling nervously - so far so good.

Raising myself onto all fours, I watched the Guard who had now stopped by the wooden barrier pole for a fag. The barrier consisted of a twelve-foot pole wrapped in a single strand of barbed wire and secured by chains and padlocks to two wooden tripods. I hoped I would be able to lift one of the tripods with the pole in place and just swing the whole thing around, if not we would be caught by the guard.

Scouse's eyes were wide with excitement when I nudged him after confirming the guard had continued their round to the rear of the compound. He nodded as I leapt up and sprinted the twenty or so yards to the barrier and grabbed the pole. Grunting under the weight of the pole and tripod, I heard Scouse start the engine of the Champ and was surprised at how light the tripod felt, probably due to the adrenaline feeding my muscles. I quickly ran it around in a semi-circle and threw it to the ground as a madly revving Champ came racing toward me with Scouse grinning madly behind the wheel.

He barely slowed down as he steered through the gap, forcing me to fling myself onto the front seat, grabbing frantically at the windscreen and seat back to prevent myself from falling out as we sped away with the sounds of the Guard screaming at us in the distance, we had done it!

355

Driving unnecessarily fast and over revving before each gear change, Scouse raced the Champ down the sandy track and onto the tarmac covered range road before he switched the lights on and slowed as we looked for Yorky. He was standing waving at the side of the road and jumped into the back as Scouse slowed almost to a stop before accelerating away.

He looked wild-eyed and a little bit frightened, so I said, 'Whey that was the most fun I've had all camp - you can slow down Scouse, by the time they get organised it will be too late, so they won't send anyone after us.' Scouse nodded and I saw him physically relax as he slowed the Champ down.

Once onto the main road I asked, 'Is the Tank full?'

Scouse looked down at the fuel gauge and shouted, 'Yep,' over the roar of the engine and wind noise.

'Have you got the map?' shouted Scouse.

Unfastening the map pocket on the thigh of my combat trousers, I pulled out a dog-eared, Shell map of Europe, and waved it at Scouse as we sped onto the almost deserted Autobahn racing off into the night. Our plan was to drive to Amsterdam, buy some postcards and drive back and give ourselves up as we had no plans to remain absent, having done this for the sheer hell of it!

A few hours later as the sky lightened, Scouse was having difficulty staying awake, so he drove into a Rastplatz where we parked in a quiet spot and tried with varying degrees of success to snatch some sleep.

By nine o'clock as the sun rose higher, the increase in temperature stirred us from our attempted sleep. The three of us emptied our bladders discussing our next move; 'Breakfast?' said Scouse.

'Wash, shave, and breakfast,' I added.

'Bloody hell we're AWOL and you still want to wash and shave!' said Yorky.

'We're still soldiers,' I warned as we searched behind the rear seats of the Champ for the little petrol cooker they all carried.

Scouse had walked to the front of the Champ to look at the small metal sign fastened to the grill and seeing the letter 'M' painted on it, he said, 'Mike, it's the bloody Mike truck; Redding's truck, there's bound to be a good brew kit behind the seat!'

There was; coffee, tea, sugar, and cans of evaporated milk, all in an old metal ammunition box next to the petrol cooker. We were soon drinking cups of hot sweet coffee as we waited for the kettle to boil for hot water to wash and shave.

'Sergeant Redding is going to love us taking his vehicle,' said Scouse. 'He'll already be drawing up a kit list we will supposedly have lost to make up his deficiencies,'

I was not exactly sure that I understood him correctly and asked in confirmation. 'Do you mean he'll claim that we have lost kit from his Champ that's not even here?'

'Got it in one,' Scouse answered. 'Any kit that he is deficient from his stores, he will claim was aboard this Champ and we lost them when we took it.'

'What sort of stores,' asked Yorky.

Scouse smiled and answered, 'The normal losses – aerials, handsets, headsets, you know that sort of thing, I bet he had loads in here.'

'But there isn't any,' Yorky said.

'That's right,' Scouse continued, 'we all take them off at night to stop them being nicked but I bet Redding says they were lots of them on board!'

After washing, shaving, and devouring a breakfast of tinned beans and sausages, we rolled our shirtsleeves up to the regulation length, put on our berets and climbed aboard the Champ ready for Amsterdam but that was when one of the Champs great shortcomings came into play.

Scouse switched the ignition on and cursed.

'We've only got half a tank of fuel left!'

The Champs only did ten miles to the gallon and we knew that even with a full jerry can on the back, we did not have enough fuel to get to Antwerp and back, and we certainly could not afford to fill the vehicle up.

'What do you reckon?' Scouse asked, looking tiredly at me.

'Back to camp, I reckon.'

That is exactly what we did; Scouse drove to the next junction and we took the Ausfarht, crossed over and back onto the Autobahn and headed back to Munsterlager Ranges. We talked very little on the drive back, each of us wondering what price we would have to pay for our little jaunt!

It was a scorcher of an afternoon, the air full of the smell of pines as Scouse, slowly and with some trepidation, drove along the sandy track leading to the camp. He drove past the lined up, trucks and guns, stopping opposite the football field where a game of inter-troop football was in full swing.

One of the spectators recognised us and shouted, 'They're back!' that was enough to stop the game, as both footballers and spectators came running over shouting and cheering.

The three of us sat in the Champ as the lads swarmed round, bombarding us with questions and quips, one of them shouting in a mock German accent, 'Velcome back to Stalag Luft Drei, for you the var is over!'

Our Troop Sergeant Major (TSM) who had been refereeing the match shouted, 'QUIET! Get back to the pitch you lot and you three, get out, and wait there.'

The TSM looked us up and down, shook his head and walked off to the Officer's and SNCO's Mess tent.

A tight-lipped, Sgt Redding was the first to come over.

'You bloody cheeky bloody sod's, stealing my bloody Champ, how much kit have you lost?' he said climbing into the Champ to look around.

Scouse looked at me with a knowing smile, 'Told you, I bet he's already got a list of deficiencies made out!'

I turned and said to Sgt Redding, 'We didn't steal it Sarge, we just borrowed it, and there were no radio ancillaries on board when we took it.'

He climbed out the vehicle, leant close to me and said, 'It's for me to decide what was or was not on board Carr and you are a frigging idiot - I was recommending you for promotion but you can forget that now!'

He turned and walked back to the Mess Tent, leaving me wondering if our little jaunt had been worth it.

The BSM was next and he did what BSMs do best – gave us a very good bollocking! He was obviously angry at our having defeated his security measures but surprisingly, he was I believe, quite impressed that we had done so.

Events moved very swiftly; within half an hour, a charge sheet was prepared and the BSM marched us in front of the Battery Commander. The charges were; misuse of MOD property, thirteen hours absence without leave and loss of MOD property.

The Battery Commander listened to the BSM's evidence before looking at the three of us and asked, 'Have any of you anything to say?'

'No Sir,' we replied in unison.

He found us guilty as charged and remanded us for Commanding Officer's orders, as he did not have sufficient powers to punish us appropriately.

A little while later, along with two escorts, we climbed aboard a three tonner for the short drive to Regimental Headquarters to be marched in front of the CO.

'This means nick,' said Scouse dejectedly, 'otherwise the BC would have dealt with us.'

I sat in silence wondering how much detention the CO would give us and if we would stay on at camp or, be sent back to the Guardroom at Dortmund.

'RIGHT, MY HAPPY BLOODY LITTLE WANDERERS,' the RSM bellowed as we pulled up outside the RHQ marquee, 'OFF THAT BLOODY WAGON, QUICK AS YOU LIKE – COME ON GET A MOVE ON!'

After ripping into us with a quick preliminary roasting, the RSM lined us up outside the Marquee, confirmed our names, ranks and numbers, and marched us into the CO. The CO listened as the Adjutant read out the charges and then to the BSM as he gave his evidence. The CO digested the evidence before looking up at us saying, 'Why?'

Scouse half shrugged his shoulders and muttered, 'I don't know Sir?'

'SPEAK UP AND STAND BLOODY STILL!' screamed the RSM

'I don't know Sir,' said Scouse almost shouting.

'STOP SHOUTING,' shouted the RSM.

The CO looked at me and asked, 'Well?'

358

'Boredom Sir,' I gulped, in what I hoped was a clear and not too loud voice,

'Boredom!' the CO repeated. 'We can't have our soldiers bored, can we RSM?'

'No Sir,' replied the RSM menacingly.

Leaning on his desk, the CO placed his fingertips together and said in a measured tone, 'I find all three guilty do you accept my award or do you elect to go for trial by Courts Martial?'

'Your Award Sir,' the three of us replied crisply.

He studied our conduct sheets for a few moments before placing them carefully back on his desk.

'Carr and Jones you both have clean conduct sheets but you Bolt, I see you have been absent before – in Hong Kong?'

'Yes Sir,' replied Scouse.

The CO then spoke very quickly.

'Bolt as you were obviously the ring leader - on charges one and two, I award you seven days detention and, ten pounds stoppages of pay on charge three.'

He paused, 'Carr and Jones, on Charges one and two, I award forfeit of one week's pay, and on charge three, ten pounds stoppages of pay, March them out please RSM.'

I tried to speak, to protest that it was unfair that it was not Scouse's idea but the RSM bellowed, 'SIR, ORDERS LEFT TURN, QUICK MARCH, LEFT RIGHT LEFT RIGHT!' and chased us out of the marquee where he kept us doubling to attention while he spoke to the BSM.

The Provost Sgt took a dejected Scouse away for his punishment as Yorky and I returned to camp with the BSM. Although I was chuffed that the CO had not awarded me detention, I felt guilty that Scouse had taken the brunt of the punishment but found out later that he bore no resentment and we continued to be good mates.

Sgt Redding was waiting for us when we climbed down from the Bedford, and after he spoke with the BSM he said, 'Come here Carr.'

Marching quickly over, I stood to attention in front of him, and said, 'Yes Sarge?'

'Right you bloody idiot, you're off the BC's party, report to Sgt Cage tomorrow morning, you'll spend the rest of the camp on his gun crew and, believe me, he will run you ragged - you won't have the chance to get bloody bored.'

I was half-expecting something of the sort and knew that the tough ex-commando, Sgt Frank Cage would run me ragged, but I was more concerned about my signalling career.

'Does that mean I'm on the guns permanently Sarge?'

'No you bloody clown it doesn't, just for the remainder of this exercise, I'm putting you on the Command Post Crew when we get back!'

I was delighted but tried not to show it, I had wanted to join the Command Post, and here was Sgt Redding moving me onto it as punishment!

Trying to look disappointed I said, 'Thanks Sarge.'

There was a disturbing incident that night - just after midnight, a terrifying howl of pain woke the camp!

On guard duty, Geordie Washington saw a large black shape snuffling around the stores tent and believing it to be a wild boar, crept up to it and lifting above his head, the metal-ended pick-handle carried by the guard, he brought it crashing down onto the back of the BQMS black mongrel!

The dog let out a terrifying howl of pain and collapsed into a whining broken-backed heap, dying painfully a few minutes later.

It took four SNCOs to stop the BQMS from attacking Washington, and although he faced no charges for the act, most of us believed he knew it was the BQMS's dog and immediately ostracised him.

The 5.5-inch medium guns that the Battery was equipped with had entered into service in 1941 and were reliable and robust but weighing just less than six tons and with each shell weighing 82lbs; they required a lot of physical effort to bring them into action and fire. A full gun crew was ten but due to manpower shortages, the average size of a gun crew in the Battery was seven, it meant the lads worked hard.

Mentally and physically tough, square-jawed and bald, Sgt Cage was a five-foot-eight no-nonsense SNCO; he ran me ragged for the last four days of Practice Camp, the CO's final exercise.

The Battery moved at least twice a day, firing both by day and night and I thoroughly enjoyed it, even though Sgt Cage found ways of keeping me busy during lulls in activity.

'Carr, go and refill the jerry can.'

'No I don't like the taste of that water, take it back, and refill it.'

'Take that shell over to 'B' Sub and swap it for one of theirs.'

'That shell looks bored; take it for a walk around the gun position.'

'Clean the cooker.'

'Make a brew.'

'Get the grub on,' and on and on.

I did not mind, knowing it was part of my punishment, I knew that it was not personal with Sgt Cage; he was just following instructions.

I just got on with it saying 'Right Sarge,' every time he gave me a ridiculous or unnecessary task.

My mate Dick of helicopter fame was part of the crew and was given the task of showing me how to prepare and handle the ammunition as part of the duties of an Ammunition Handler, the job Sgt Page assigned me too, the one requiring the least amount of training.

360

On the third day of the exercise, another hot dry summer's day, we had just moved to a sandy, undulating gun position where the Battery's six guns were deployed about fifty yards apart amongst a scattering of scrub, pine trees and silver birches. Sweating heavily from the exertions of getting the gun into action and erecting the huge camouflage net, we fired three rounds onto a pre-recorded target before resting at the rear of the gun.

As the rest of the crew crashed out or lit cigarettes, I automatically started to set up the cooker to make a brew when Sgt Cage said, 'Leave that Carr,' then to Dick, he said, 'Bell you get the brew on.'

As Dick took over brew making, Sgt Cage took me back to the gun and said, 'Okay lad I'm going to show you how to lay the gun (set the sights for firing).' I was gobsmacked but delighted and quickly grasped the sequences involved until another Fire Mission interrupted the training.

That was the end of being chased around by Sgt Cage; I was now part of his gun crew and enjoyed it, but at every opportunity I visited the Command Post to talk to Jock Pattinson and the other signallers, looking forward to taking my place inside.

At the end of the exercise, the Battery formed up into two convoys ready for the long overnight drive back to Dortmund. The towing vehicles for the guns were massive Leyland six wheelers with huge cabs containing three rows of seats for the ten-man crews. The seats were narrow and uncomfortable, especially for long journeys so Dick, I and another lad climbed into the cargo bay at the rear of our truck and bedded down on top of the camouflage net for the overnight drive.

We slept well until woken by the sound of horns and looking out we saw the sun was already high in the sky and we were driving through what looked like the residential area of a city! Our driver was having difficulty negotiating the huge truck and gun through some of the narrow streets, causing delays and much annoyance to early morning commuters.

Unsure as to where we were, Dick climbed onto the tailboard to look forward.

He shouted, 'Fucking Hell! you'll never guess where we are?'

The truck had turned slowly into another narrow street and wondering why we were there and not on the autobahn, I shouted back, 'Where the fuck are we then?'

Dick jumped back in laughing. 'The fucking Leninstrasse – the brothel street, surely old Jack Cage is not after a shag at this time in the morning?

It transpired that the convoy had disintegrated due to breakdowns and early morning fog, so not being sure of the route, Sgt Cage had followed signs to Dortmund and then become lost on the southern outskirts.

His Bombardier spotted the Leninstrasse, 'Go down there, I know my way back to camp from there,' he said. Sgt Cage did not ask any questions, he was just grateful that his Bombardier was a regular visitor to the 'Strasse' and could navigate him back to camp!

I spent another two days working with the gun crew, cleaning and maintaining the truck and gun before Sgt Cage called me to one side and said, 'The kit's ready for BC's inspection so you can return to the Signals Stores unless you want to stay on my crew and I'll be glad to have you?'

I thought about it for a split second and said, 'Thanks Sarge but I'm a signaller and I want to join the Command Post,' and marched off to report to Sgt Redding in the Stores where the rest of the signallers took the opportunity to take the Mickey for several minutes:

'Carr's here Sarge, got any more deficiencies?'

'Yor in the wrong stores Syd, there's no gun kit down here!'

'Lock up yor Champs!'

I said, 'There's no need, I won't be going AWOL again!'

30

A Disastrous Night Out

Shirley was strangely impressed when I told her about being AWOL, asking me to relate the complete silly saga in detail but it seemed to gain me some sort of kudos with her, maybe she liked naughty lads! We continued our relationship for another month before she left with her family for Aden and although we exchanged a couple of letters, I felt no great sorrow at her leaving but did miss our nights of passion.

The rest of the summer passed quickly, the Regiment as part of the Brigade we supported, drove down to a training area in the South of France. It took four days just to get there but it was my first exercise working in the Command Post and I soon established myself as the number one signaller.

I already knew the rest of the crew very well as I lived in the same room as them, Jock Pattinson the other signaller; two Technical assistants; Larry Pain, a large well-spoken Yorkshire man, and Chris Bryson, a cheerful well-educated Cockney-Jew. A tall lanky West Country lad called John Church was our driver and Ray Sewell the NCO. Finally, the Command Post Officer was the Troop Sergeant Major, an autocratic, red-haired Warrant Officer with no sense of humour and someone who would not accept second best at anything. It was an excellent team.

A month after the three-week exercise in France and with newly issued Landrovers replacing the Champs, we took part in our first Divisional Exercise. Two Divisions battled it out through towns, villages and across the farmland of Northern Germany, doing copious amounts of damage as we fought each other with blank ammunition and other pyrotechnics. Well compensated for any damages done to their property, the Germans grudgingly accepted that it was part of the price they had to pay to have NATO troops on their soil, providing as they did, the deterrent that stopped the Soviets from marching in.

That week as I prepared to go on leave, I finally changed my hairstyle from my fifties slick backed wave, to a flopped forward semi – Beatles style cut. I visited the NAAFI and bought a new black Reefer Jacket for the cold end of October weather as well as two hundred cigarettes and a bottle of whisky for Mam and Dad.

On arrival at the Fifth Row and after handing over the cigarettes and whisky I had the now normal fall out with Mam who demanded half my leave pay but only got a few quid as I already sent her a weekly allowance that I believed should have been sufficient.

As Tom was still courting, I only saw him a few times and consequently spent most of my leave hanging round with a lad from North Seaton, a mining hamlet on the southern edge of Ashington. It was there at the Saturday night dance that I met Jill Jones. She was a very pretty, diminutive dark haired girl that I had seen a number of times before, part of a group of girls, all of about the same height.

We hit it off and started dating, although I still went to the Welfare on my own on Wednesdays, hoping unsuccessfully, to see a certain little blue-eyed girl as no matter who I was with, they were going to have to play second fiddle as I could not stop thinking about her. Jill was very accommodating but was also quiet and never really put an opinion forward but I enjoyed being with her and I think she took our relationship quite seriously, writing to me when I returned to camp.

It was our Battery Day on November the 22nd - we celebrated by walking down to the Army Cinema to watch a spy film, followed by an Inter-Troop football and rugby competition, neither of which I took part in, as I had no talent for either. I was however in the Battery athletics team and had competed successfully in the summer in the 100 and 200-yard sprint as well as the pole vault - winning small trophies for all three.

The BSM organised a Battery Dinner in the Regimental Dining Room with the new CO and RSM as guests of honour. With everyone wearing Service Dress, we sat at three long tables that ran down from a top table where the Officers sat. A few of the Officers and SNCOs had not seen my murals and commented on how good they looked, which of course gave my mates an excuse to rib me.

We were each given two cans of Carlsberg and with most of us having had a couple of drinks in the Battery Bar before dinner, the atmosphere was very jovial and the food excellent.

After desert, coffee came round and as some of the lads lit cigarettes; Scouse nudged me and said, 'Look,' and he pointed to the top table.

The Adjutant, accompanied by the Orderly Officer, had walked into the back of the room and the two of them approached the CO. The Adjutant crouched down beside the CO and appeared to be brief him on some matter. The CO nodded gravely before asking questions that the Orderly Officer answered before he and the Adjutant left. Just about everybody in the room had seen them; leading to a great deal of speculation as to what had happened as it must be important to warrant interruption of our Battery Dinner.

A few minutes later the CO stood up and in a very solemn tone announced, 'Gentlemen I have just been informed that the President of the United States of America - John F Kennedy - was assassinated at Dallas, Texas; today at twelve-thirty their time.'

He paused briefly before adding, 'That is all the information I have at the present time.'

Our imaginations went into overdrive; there were all sorts of wild speculation, most of us believing that the Russians were responsible for the assassination because of the Cuban missile crisis last year. This led to a great deal of talk of getting our gear ready for the inevitable war that was bound to kick off over night.

We did not go to war the next morning, just back down to the Signals Stores to continue our speculations.

The following Friday, Jim Paddington, the BC's new driver asked if I fancied going downtown for a few drinks and as I was at a loose end, I agreed. After a beer in the Battery Bar, we headed off to the Stonk Club for steak and chips in order to fortify ourselves for our night in Dortmund.

Jim, a good welterweight boxer, looked tough, a bit like a five foot ten Jack Palance. He also had a reputation as a bit of a scrapper as well as being a bit pushy, but I stood up to him and we got along very well. He had been a Lance Bombardier but lost the stripe for some minor misdemeanour, he was also someone you could rely upon in a tight situation and was also, a very good soldier.

Eating our steak and chips in the crowded café, someone fed the jukebox and Jim Reeves began singing in his mournful, dreary voice, 'I hear the sound of distant drums far away far away.'

'I wish the miserable bugger would sing a lot farer away!' I muttered.

'There're some boring farts in here tonight,' said Jim loudly through his last mouthful of steak and chips, providing me with a glimpse of what was to come.

Having finished my meal I stood up and said, 'Come on let's get out of here before we die from despair at having to listen to any more of him!'

Onc downtown, we had a couple of beers at Wolfgang's before heading into 'Little Soho' where we visited a couple more bars, having a small beer in each.

'Let's go down the Leninstrasse and see who can get the biggest discount?' said Jim as he finished his beer.

'As long as ye don't expect me to actually pay for one,' I said, having no desire to pay for the services of a prostitute but still curious as to what the women looked like.

Jim laughed and said, 'Don't worry there's no way I would waste my hard earned pay on one of them, we'll just have a laugh.'

It was my first and last time in the 'Strasse and I was taken by surprise when I saw the women or should I say girls who were in various stages of undress in the windows; they were not the worn out women I had imagined, most of them were attractive young women. I found myself far too embarrassed to be able to ask them how much let alone barter a price; Jim, on the other hand, had no such reservations.

'Wie Viel, Was Kostet?' he asked a blonde girl who had been quietly reading in one of the windows a few feet above our head.

She looked down at Jim with disdain and said in English, 'Twenty-five,' and went back to her book.

'Zu Viel, to bloody much,' said Jim laughing, 'how about twelve marks?'

The blonde ignored him completely so we walked down to the next window and Jim tried again with a sultry looking brunette who was wearing a tawdry red negligee; he actually got her to agree to twenty marks.

Jim looked at up her and said laughing, 'Thanks but I'm not that desperate,' and walked away.

I thought he had gone far enough and said, 'C'mon Jim I've had enough of this, let's go back to little Soho for a beer,' and turned and headed back down the Strasse, Jim following on, laughing wildly.

It was then that I saw three young men walking purposely toward us; they stopped a few feet in front of Jim, a few yards to my left.

One of them stepped forward and said something in German to which Jim replied, 'Sorry me old fruit, Ich nicht sprechen Kraut!'

The German leant back slightly, telegraphing the swinging right he threw at Jim, but Jim had seen it coming and ducked below it, only to have the German grab the bottom of Jim's jacket and pull it up and over his head in order to trap him. The German was obviously no mug and used to fighting but so was Jim, he simply held his arms out straight in front of him resulting in the German pulling the jacket completely and unintentionally free.

Left holding Jim's jacket, the German looked confused long enough for Jim to spring up and land four or five very fast punches that floored the German.

Having watched this in motionless, stunned amazement, I realised that the other two might wade in and without thinking moved swiftly to Jim's side but I need not have bothered. The other two Germans picked up their downed friend who was trying to stop the flow of blood from his split lip and dragged him down the street throwing some German profanity at Jim as they left.

Jim picked his jacket up from the street and as he pushed the sleeves back through the armholes he looked at me and with his cheeky grin still intact, he said, 'Why the fuck did they start that?'

I thought for a moment and wondered if they were part of the prostitutes' protection or maybe they just did not like Jim's wild laugh or, his taunting of the women, 'It must be your good looks mate!' I said.

He laughed and threw his arm around my shoulder and said, 'I need a beer,' and we headed out of the Strasse.

On the edge of Little Soho we found a bar that neither of us had been in before and walked in through an outer hall and through a large heavily carved door into the low lit bar, furnished in what can best be described as Manhattan Chic. Jim and I were both impressed at how smart the room was and quietly walked up to the end of the bar and waited for the huge, leather waist-coated barman to take our order.

'Zwei Beir Bitte,' I said as he approached.

German beer is always served very cold, with just the right amount of froth but takes a long time to serve as the bar person has to pump through a little at time, wait for the froth to settle before pumping a little bit more and so on. It can take up to five minutes to serve two small beers.

While we waited, we discussed the attack on Jim in the Strasse, wondering if the prostitutes had complained to someone about his behaviour even though it was not that bad as I am sure they must have seen worse. The barman finished pumping our beers and carried them along to us as Jim started to demonstrate the punches he had thrown! He placed the two cold beers on the bar just behind Jim as Jim swung his right arm back to show me his right hook, unfortunately, he connected with the two beers, sending them flying; soaking the barman as they spun across the top of the bar and crashed to the floor.

I do not know who was the more surprised, Jim or the barman but I certainly know who was the unhappiest! Jim tried to apologise but the huge barman exploded, screaming at us in German.

His rage was completely disproportionate to the accident as he screamed, 'Raus, get out Englanders, Raus, Raus!'

He threw his bar towel at Jim and I seeing that Jim wanted to retaliate, I just managed to grab his arm as he reached for a barstool.

Pushing him toward the door, I said, 'Come on it's not worth it and we haven't paid for the beer anyway.'

As I pushed Jim through the huge door, I could see the fat barman lifting the flap of the bar to chase after us so I slammed the big wooden door shut and as I did so, I saw that the keys were in the door, a large bunch of them. I turned the key locking the door and then took them out of the lock and threw them into the corner of the hallway.

'Whey I don't think we'll be going back there again,' I said laughing.

'Only to burn the fucking place down,' Jim threatened without meaning it.

Intending to get some frites before heading for the tram, we made our way around the edge of Little Soho until we came to a junction blocked by a green and white German police car with blue lights flashing. It was not an unusual sight in this part of town and not for one moment believing it involved us, we walked toward it as two policemen climbed out, showing a great deal of interest in Jim and me.

With his right hand on his holster, one of the Policemen stepped into the road in front of us and said in a matter of fact voice, 'In the car please.'

One thing you learned quickly in Germany was to obey the police and do not, whatever you do, upset them. I looked at Jim, concerned that he might kick off but he did not and we both climbed quietly into the back of the police car wondering what was going on.

The Police said nothing during the five-minute drive to the Police Station, that added to our confusion as to why they had, seemingly arrested us.

They continued to be silent until we were inside when one of them held out his hand and said, 'Keys Please.'

The penny dropped.

368

'If you mean the keys to the bar, I threw them into the corner of the hall-way.'

He must not have fully understood what I had said and with a quizzical look asked, 'Again please?'

I started to repeat myself but the other Policeman had obviously under-stood and interrupted me, explaining to the other in German what I had said.

The first Policeman left the room as the remaining one ushered us to sit down.

'Why did you take the keys?'

Jumping in before Jim could speak, I explained what had happened and that I had locked the door only because I thought we were about to be assaulted.

The Policeman nodded and said in perfect English, 'We will see; the own-er of the nightclub believes you have stolen the keys in order to return to break in later.' We were both shocked at this revelation and protested telling him we had not kept the keys.

We sat in silence for a few minutes more before the first Policeman came back and said much to our relief, 'The keys have been found.'

Jim stood up and asked, 'Can we go now?'

To our dismay, the English speaking Policeman said, 'No you must wait here as we have to hand you over to your Military Police, I am sorry but that is the procedure we must follow; would you like coffee?'

We both said yes and as the two Police Officers left, Jim said to me, 'Bloody MPs that means fucking trouble.'

'We haven't done anything wrong and the Germans seem happy so there shouldn't be a problem man,' I replied.

The English speaker brought in two coffees and handed them to us. 'We will not be taking this matter any further, however, I would advise you to stay away from that nightclub, I do not think you would be welcome there,' he said and smiled and left the room closing the door behind him.

Ten minutes later the door swung open and two immaculate Military Po-licemen stepped inside. Wearing expertly pressed khaki-battledress uniform, white shoulder straps fastened to white belts with gleaming brasses, white pistol holsters, white ankle gaiters and khaki peaked caps with the red cover; they looked the pride of the Royal Military Police. The first of the two, a wiry, mean looking Corporal of about five foot nine, stood with his hands on his hips, studying us for a moment as his partner a much taller, fresh-faced Lance Corporal walked past him to stand quietly behind me.

The Corporal took off his cap and holding it by the peak he stepped over to where Jim was sitting and spat, 'I won't have any trouble from you.' Then raising his cap, he brought the rear of the headband crashing down on Jim's unprotected nose, splitting it across the bridge, splattering blood across Jim's face!

There must have been a metal strip concealed in the back of the headband for it to cause so much damage but the blow had the opposite effect to that the Corporal probably expected.

Having hit Jim he stepped back, looking down at him with an arrogant and contemptuous sneer that he quickly replaced with shock as Jim sprang from his chair and launched a barrage of punches, flooring the Corporal. The swiftness of Jim's response took everyone by surprise and as Jim pinned the Corporal to the floor daring him to move, the Lance Corporal began to move forward and I found myself stepping in front.

'Your mate started it, let it go,' I said.

Unsure as to what to do and obviously intimidated, the Lance Corporal stayed where he was as Jim let go of the Corporal and rose to his feet, wiping the blood from his nose with the back of his hand.

The Corporal struggled to his feet and holding up his hand, said, 'Sit down and let's start again.'

'Just as long as you don't try anything stupid again,' Jim said as he sat warily down.

It was then that I noticed that the two German Policemen were standing in the doorway grinning as they discussed what they had just seen; they shook their heads as if to say, 'Crazy Englanders,' and walked away.

The Corporal, whose eyes were now both puffy and red said, 'Right, what have you been up to?'

Jumping in again, I explained what had happened, that it was not our fault and that the German Police would confirm what I said.

The Corporal listened to my story and then said to the other MP, 'Wait here while I speak to the 'Locals,'' and walked out leaving a very nervous young MP watching us. By the time, the Corporal returned we were chatting to the younger one, even sharing a joke with him.

'Right lads, sorry about that I got the wrong end of the stick from the Germans, they've confirmed what you said and that they won't be bringing any charges so we'll run you back to camp and we'll just forget about our little misunderstanding, OK,' said the Corporal.

Very relieved, I nodded and Jim said, 'Yep, no problem.'

They drove us back to camp in their open-topped Champ, chatting freely on the way, the Corporal even recommended a couple of trouble free bars to us and confirmed that he would drop us off at the guardroom and that would be the end of it. Swinging the Champ off the Nussbaumweg and up to the Barrack's gate, he waited while the soldier on guard duty swung it open, before driving up to the front of the guardroom where he stopped the vehicle at the foot of the stairs to the entrance.

Thinking that was the end of it, Jim and I climbed out and went up the stairs into the Guardroom to book in, but the mean faced Corporal followed us and as we signed in, he said to the Guard Commander, 'Fetch the Duty Sergeant, now!'

370

The Bombardier Guard Commander picked up the phone and called the Sergeants Mess and after a brief pause said into the handset, 'You're needed by the RMP in the Guardroom Sarge.' Placing the phone back on the receiver, he said to the MP, 'He'll be here in two minutes.'

Jim and I looked at each other shaking our heads in disbelief; Jim saying to the Corporal, 'I thought you said...' but the Corporal stopped him.

'Quiet and stand to attention the pair of you.'

Jim glared at him but kept quiet as the two of us grudgingly stood to attention and waited for the Duty Sergeant.

When he arrived, I was relieved when I recognised him, it was the young and well-liked Signals Sergeant, Sergeant Delaware from 13 Battery; not one of the miserable or cantankerous older Sergeants that still served in the Regiment. A wry smile crept across his face when he saw the MP Corporals battered face and Jim's swollen nose.

'What's the problem then Corporal?' he asked?'

'These two have been arrested for causing a fracas in the Berliner Nightclub and you are to put them under close arrest pending an RMP investigation,' the Corporal answered.

Jim and I were both horrified and began to protest but Sergeant Delaware stopped us.

Looking at the Corporal, he said, 'Sergeant!'

The Corporal looked confused and said, 'Sorry?'

Sergeant Delaware pushed his face close to the Corporal's and said, 'You will address me as Sergeant, got that Corporal?'

The Corporals face coloured and he muttered, 'Yes Sergeant.'

The Corporal then told Sergeant Delaware that we had caused a disturbance in the Nightclub and stolen the door keys before the German Police arrested us and that he wanted us held in close arrest pending an interview by the RMP – there was no mention of the fight in the police station.

Sergeant Delaware listened carefully before saying. 'There's always two sides to a story Corporal and I'll listen to theirs in a minute and then I'll decide if they should be held in Close Arrest but as they don't appear to be drunk or abusive I shall probably send them to their beds.'

The Corporal appeared not to like having his instructions ignored and began to speak but Sergeant Delaware stopped him. 'That's enough Corporal, you can go, I will deal with these two tonight,' and turning his back on the fuming Corporal he ushered Jim and me into the rear of the guardroom.

'Right you two what really happened, how did you get the swollen nose and how did the MP come by his black eyes?' he asked.

We explained exactly what had happened, both of us confirming what the other was saying or adding to it as we expressed how the Corporal had not provided the full story.

When we finished he said, 'OK, I'll brief your BSM in the morning and I'm sure the RMPs will send for you for an interview but in the meantime bugger off to bed and report to your BSM first thing, okay!'

We said, 'Okay Sarge, thanks,' and buggered off to bed.

The BSM was quite sympathetic as he listened to our story in the morning but told us that the matter rested with the RMP and what action they would take. It did not take long, a couple of hours later the BSM sent for us and told us to report to the RMP Station in Suffolk Barracks for an interview.

The interviews were a farce, no mention of the MP attacking Jim and when I tried to broach the subject, the MP told me that it was not part of his investigation. In addition, even though the German Police had confirmed that the owner of the Berliner had found his keys, the MPs said that we had stolen them and worse, they wrote statements that neither Jim nor I were happy with and then they coerced us into signing them.

A few days later, the MP report came through, and the BSM summoned us to his office.

'The RMP have charged you under section 69 of the Army Act 1955 - conduct prejudice to the good order of military discipline that on the night in question in the Berliner Night Club you failed to act in a manner expected of a British soldier; in other words nothing bloody specific,' said the BSM.

'Sir, what about the attack on Gunner Paddington,' I asked, trying to hide my annoyance.

He shook his head. 'There's no mention of that and frankly, I'm not surprised, and if you brought it up, it would be their word against yours; what I suggest is that as this is a very minor charge, you accept the BC's award and leave it at that.'

We did and based on the evidence put in front of him, the new BC awarded us seven days restriction of privileges each, which was no big deal. Confined to camp, we had to parade at the guardroom in best dress twice during the evening as well as carrying out some extra fatigues. I was dating the daughter of one of our Sergeants at the time and she was more upset than I was, I soon forgot the incident.

31

A Bad Choice

The tail end of the year came quickly and as this was the Regiment's first year in Germany, very few of us were allowed leave, resulting in a couple of hundred soldiers moping around camp over the festive season; some got very drunk during the stand-down period but most did very little.

The lads in our room consisted of Technical Assistants, Surveyors, and Signallers, and supposedly having a little bit more intelligence than that required to get drunk, we pooled our resources and bought Christmas goodies, decorations, drinks, a Christmas cake and fruit and nuts. Along with music provided by the British Forces Broadcasting Company (BFBS) on the radio, we had a reasonable time, including, when just on the right side of tipsy, we attended Midnight Mass, sitting behind the BC and his family! He was impressed.

The lads in the Battery had a request for the RMPs played on BFBS-'Catch me if you can.' A little while later they sent one back – 'I'll get you in the end'!

In January and February, I completed a Standard II signals course, passing it with ease, then along with Jock Pattinson and several others from the Regiment, I attended the local Army Education Centre for the Army Certificate of Education Class 2 Course, that I also passed without a problem.

March saw us again camped out for two weeks in freezing weather but this time on Munsterlager Ranges where the Regiment carried out Calibration Firing, a very slow and tedious procedure of firing single rounds from each gun in order to calibrate their accuracy.

In April, I managed to save enough money to at last buy myself a smart three buttoned, black, leather jacket that had button down pockets and a half belt at the back. I had wanted a one for a long time but had been unable to afford one until now.

I also had three weeks leave in April and continued to date Jill as well as going to the dances searching for little Blue-Eyes but did not see her and returned to Germany knowing I should forget her but also knowing that I never would. I also spent as much time as possible out of our house and thus avoided too much conflict with Mam.

In late July we once again drove north for six weeks practice camp, spending the first three weeks camped in the woods while we carried out training without live ammunition. The training went well apart from our Troop Sergeant Major having a vindictive rant at Chris Bryson, one of the Technical Assistants in the Command Post. Chris had been a little slow in producing gun-firing data during a very tense Fireplan and the Sergeant Major who was the Command Post Officer smacked him on the back of the head with a ruler shouting at him to hurry up.

Taken by surprise, Chris instinctively swore. 'You Twat,' which made the Sergeant Major go ballistic. Not only did he take Chris outside where he gave him a tremendous bollocking, but he also, and much to our annoyance, put all of the crew on guard duty that night. That was not the end of it; the Sergeant Major continued to vent his bile on us for the slightest mistake.

Great competition existed between all the Battery Command Posts, especially in being first to report ready for firing that was heavily dependent upon the speed the Technical Assistants could compute the firing data required from the information provided by the Observation Parties. There was also a great deal of kudos achieved from by being the first to report ready and our Sergeant Major wanted that kudos.

Our crew was slick and the gun crews fast, we reported ready first, more often than not but that was not good enough for the Sergeant Major; if we were not first every time, one of us would bear the brunt of his frustration. The atmosphere in the Command Post had become almost unbearable and only lifted when the other Command Post Officer, a young Subaltern took over for a few hours at a time.

For the live firing phase of camp, we moved into Trauen, a huge German Army tented camp. The accommodation consisted of large metal framed, double-skinned tents warmed by smelly oil fired stoves that left everything smelling of diesel. The dining room, cookhouse, canteen, medical centre, and other buildings were in wooden structures with only the German Administrative Headquarters, housed in a large, grey-rendered brick building. There were also two huge tarmac squares where guns and vehicles parked; it was a miserable place that reminding me of prisoner of war camps I had seen in films.

Nevertheless, it was preferable to camping in woods, especially as the camp had showers, proper toilets, and a canteen selling beer and bockwursts but on the downside, it was miles from anywhere, prompting one of the lads in one of the other Batteries to take a Landrover and drive to Celle. German Police arrested him and brought him back to the Regiment to face charges the following morning.

The inevitable happened - when in camp, all vehicle work tickets and keys had to be handed into the Battery Office and orders for the Gate Guard amended to include the close scrutiny of any work ticket before allowing individual vehicles to leave.

As a reward for the training going well, the new CO had decreed that the whole Regiment, apart from duty personnel, were to be offered a trip to Hamburg on the Saturday of the second weekend at Trauen. For this reward, the CO expected everyone to work even harder for his three-day exercise that marked the end of Practice Camp.

On the Friday before the Hamburg trip, the Battery deployed on a gun position about nine miles from Trauen and were firing in support of each of the three Battery Commander's Fireplans. The first two had gone well, especially our own Battery Commander's that had been a particularly complicated one in which our Battery fired most of the Fire Missions used to record targets in readiness for the coordinated Firing of the Regiment.

Everything was going well until the final Fireplan; the Sergeant Major misread data produced from Chris and began sending it to the Guns.

Chris spotted the error immediately and said, 'Stop Sir, that's incorrect.'

The Sergeant Major exploded and blamed Chris for not writing clearly but I could read it easily and was not as close as the Sergeant Major. Not that that mattered to him, as far as he was concerned it was Chris's fault and he screamed at him for thirty or forty seconds.

When I interrupted his rant with, 'Call Sign 3 has reported ready, Sir,' he banged his fist down on the Command Post table and screamed at us all for preventing him from being first to report 'Ready'.

The end of the Fireplan signalled the end of the days training. After receiving orders to move back to camp the Gun Position Officer screamed, 'Prepare to Move,' - the order to pack everything away, dismantle camouflage and the Command Post Shelter, take down the two 27-foot elevated masts for the radio aerials and pack up the trailer, all, hopefully before any of the guns were hitched up ready to move. We achieved it and we were soon sitting in our six-wheeled Saracen armoured command vehicle, waiting for the guns to line up behind us when the Sergeant Major called Chris out from the back of the vehicle.

We could see him giving Chris another dressing down that finished when he pointed in the direction of Trauen and then we saw Chris turn and head off in that direction on foot. Ordered to walk back to Trauen, Chris arrived three hours later, thirty minutes after the evening meal finished but I had booked him a late meal and joined him along with Larry Pain and John Church as he devoured it hungrily.

Chris muttered through a mouthful of mashed potatoes, 'I swear I'll murder that frigging swine, one of these days!'

Larry said, 'It might have to be sooner than you think because we are all on guard again tomorrow night!'

Chris slammed his knife and fork down and spat, 'The Bastard, it's not fair on you lot is it?'

I shook my head, 'No it's not but that's not all Chris, we are all on cookhouse fatigues tomorrow and Guard again on Sunday so frigging Hamburg is off.'

John said, 'Come on let's go to the canteen for a beer and discuss what we can do about it.'

I had already complained to Sergeant Redding but all he had said was that we should just get on with it and try to keep a low profile until the Sergeant Major left on promotion in a few months' time.

Sitting in the large and austere canteen, the cold beer did not lighten our mood as we sat proposing various methods of disposing of the Troop Sergeant Major, most of which involved some sort of physical violence and were completely nonsensical.

Larry said, 'The best way to hurt the bastard is to stop him from getting any praise for having the best Command Post.'

Chris added, 'Yeh great idea, but we'd only end up on duty and fatigues until he leaves.'

'Unless we are not here,' I added.

There was silence for a moment as they digested the statement before lanky John said in his Somerset lilt, 'That's it, let's fuck off, and leave him to the CO's exercise without us.'

The beer was beginning to cloud our judgement as Larry became very animated, 'You mean go AWOL, I'm up for that, I've had enough of the Ginger headed bastard.'

Chris looked at me and said, 'OK if we are going how are we going to do it?'

'Same as I did last year, we'll take a Landrover but, this time, we'll take it to England.'

The other three nodded enthusiastically and we began to plot how we could get a Landrover past the latest security procedures.

John was the only one of us with a driving licence so the part of driving a vehicle through the main gate and past the guard was going to have to be down to him. The tricky part of getting the work ticket and keys from the Battery Office tent and past the Battery Duty Clerk and the Battery Orderly NCO (BONCO) needed resolving.

I said, 'The BONCO is sat over there and doesn't look to be in a hurry to get back, I'll wander into the Battery Office and chat to young Clive the Clerk and tell him I'll give him a break. While he's away I'll sort out a work ticket and keys – OK.'

Everyone agreed, we also agreed that John would have the best chance of getting the vehicle out on his own and that the rest of us would take our large packs and climb over the ten-foot-high, security fence and wait for him –simple!

A little while later, I wandered nonchalantly into the tent that served as the Battery Office and saw Clive, the young Battery Clerk sitting behind a six-foot table reading a book. He spoke with an officer's accent, looked somewhat like a caricature of a chinless young officer, and was slightly pompous but was a genuinely nice bloke if somewhat green.

'Hi Clive, how's it going?' I asked as he looked up.

'Oh hello Syd, All's well here just a tad quiet.'

'I was just wondering if the TSM has confirmed that the CP Crew is on extra duty tomorrow and Sunday.' I asked already knowing the answer.

Clive looked apologetic and answered, 'Yes I'm afraid he has.'

I said, 'The bloody swine he's really got it in for us,' and chatted for a few more minutes before saying, 'Look, I'm not going anywhere, why don't you pop over to the canteen for a coffee and a bockwurst?'

He was delighted and hurried off promising to be back in ten minutes.

As soon as he left, I went over to the table where the vehicle work tickets and keys were lying and sorting through them, pulled out the canvas folder containing the work ticket and keys for a cargo Landrover. Taking out the work ticket I wrote under the details section, 'Return to Dortmund – collection of stores,' and under authorisation I signed the Battery Commanders name, then confirming the keys were inside, I closed the folder and shoved it inside my combat jacket.

Clive returned a little later thanking me for sitting in for him.

'No bother, I'm off for a beer then bed,' I said and left him thinking to myself, 'sorry but you'll be in bother tomorrow morning.'

Despite his outward bravado, John was becoming increasingly nervous about driving the vehicle through the main gate but we convinced him it would not be a problem as he had the signed work ticket to verify his journey and the sooner he did it the better.

We packed a few clothes along with washing and shaving kit, some rations, and hexamine cookers into our large packs, then changed into civvies; I pulled on a pair of jeans, a casual shirt, and my leather jacket.

It was just after eleven pm when John, Chris, and I sneaked up to a part of the perimeter fence behind the Medical Centre that was in deep shadow. After making sure the coast was clear, we started climbing. Chris and I had no problem climbing to the top of the chain link fence where we draped a double folded blanket over the top of the three strands of barbed wire before easing ourselves carefully over and down the other side. Larry, on the other hand, took ages to haul his large, slightly plump body up and was on the top trying not to snag his pride and joy on the barbed wire when the lights of a vehicle came toward us from the direction of the main gate.

I said, 'Fuck if this is not John we are right in the shit!'

Larry finally dropped to the ground just as the vehicle, with its headlights on full, slowed and pulled up a few feet from us. The three of us stood rooted to the spot squinting into the lights, trying desperately to see who was in the Landover, worried that it may be the Duty Truck.

The headlights switched off and the vehicle moved forward slowly stopping next to us and we saw John lean across from the driving seat to open the passenger door and say, 'England anyone?'

Chris beat me to the front seat, so Larry and I climbed into the back as John engaged gear and we left Trauen and a miserable, ginger-headed, Sergeant Major behind.

Our plan was to drive the Landrover to Ostend, leave it at a police station, and catch the morning Mail Ferry to England. It sounded simple enough and we put aside money for the ferry tickets, leaving us enough cash for food to hopefully, last until we arrived in London tomorrow, at which time Chris promised to borrow some money for us from his mother.

Mindful of the fuel problems I had with the Champ last year, we decided to drive to Dortmund first and agreed that Jim should go into our barracks and fill up, giving us enough fuel to get us to the Channel, hopefully.

The autobahn drive to Dortmund was uneventful, we even managed to get a couple of hours sleep in a Rastplatz before John, dropped Chris, Larry and me off at the Stonk Club at nine in the morning, before he drove off into barracks to fill up.

He returned half an hour later with a huge smile spread across his hawk-like face and in answer to our barrage of questions about what had happened, said, 'I was filling up no problem when the Battery Captain and his driver pulls up alongside me.'

'Bugger,' said Chris.

John continued with a self-satisfied smile, 'He asked me what I was doing back here and I just said I was here to pick up signals kit that Sergeant Redding had left behind.'

I quickly asked, 'Did he swallow that?'

'Course he did, he asked me when I was going back to Trauen and I said tonight, so he says have a safe journey back and I'll see you tomorrow, so I answers 'Right O' Sir, and having filled up drove off – easy.'

We all laughed at his narrow escape and then walked into the Stonk Club for breakfast.

Having decided that we would cross into Belgium at Aachen and take the Motorway to Ostend via Brussels, we set off, in no real hurry being too late to catch the mail-boat today, we had plenty of time to drive to Ostend and catch it tomorrow.

All went well until we arrived in Aachen; thinking it would be too risky to cross the border at the Autobahn crossing point, we drove to a small crossing on a busy single-carriage road in the western suburbs and joined a queue of vehicles waiting to cross; we were all very nervous.

We watched as the German Customs Officer stopped each car and quickly checked the occupants and in a couple of cases, checked passports.

John asked Chris, 'Are you sure we just need our ID Cards to cross?'

Chris, held his head back and looking down his nose in his peculiar fashion, said, 'Yeh, I'm certain, that's all I needed when I crossed last year.'

I kept my eyes on the German Policeman standing a few yards behind the Customs Officer, he was huge and stared at us intently but I said nothing, not wanting to panic John.

When it was our turn, the Customs Officer waved us forward and then held up his hand to stop us so that the cab window was next to him.

John pushed our ID Cards into his hand saying, 'Guten Tag,' but the Officer ignored him and briefly studied the ID Cards before looking in at us and handing them back.

John hurriedly put the vehicle into gear but the Customs Officer stopped him from driving off by thrusting his open hand into the cab demanding, 'NATO Travel Order!'

'NATO Travel Order?' John repeated not having a clue what one was and nor did the rest of us.

The Customs Officer obviously did and he said to John as if he was a dim child 'Ja, you must have a NATO Travel Order to cross the Border in a military vehicle.'

Having the gift of the gab, John could normally blag his way through most problems but the German Policeman was now starting to show even more interest, and started to walk toward us, I nudged John and nodded my head at the Policeman.

He took the hint and said, 'Of course the NATO Bloody Travel Order, how stupid of us, we thought we only needed one if we were going to cross the Channel – OK no problem we'll drive back and get one.'

He swung the Landrover across the road and onto the return carriageway but before, he could drive off, the Policeman stepped in front of us forcing John to stop.

Walking slowly around to the passenger window, he scrutinised us carefully before asking, 'Where were you going?'

Smiling nervously and without thinking, I said in an unnecessarily loud voice, 'Vogelsang.'

The Policeman nodded his head and said, 'Ach so, yes the Training area?'

'Yes,' I answered and to my surprise and relief, he stepped back and waved us on.

'Vogelsang, where the hell's Vogelsang,' John asked as he drove off.

'Fucked if I know, I just know it's a Belgium Army Training Area that the Brits use - according to Sergeant Redding anyway!'

John drove for a few hundred yards before pulling up at a bus stop and asked, 'What now?'

We discussed the problem and all agreed that we should leave the vehicle and hitchhike to Ostend, after all, we should still be able to get there for tomorrow morning, or so we thought. Rather than just abandoning the vehicle, I suggested leaving it at a German Police station with the keys in but that we should take the rotor arm off to prevent anyone from stealing it – there were some dodgy people about!

We did not have to drive far, there was a Police Station near the crossing and we parked the Landrover up in a parking bay directly in front of the entrance and as Chris lifted the bonnet to take out the rotor arm, John changed into civvies in the back and I scribbled a note saying;

Please return to 14 Regiment Royal Artillery, Camp Ten, Rhurschnellweg, Dortmund.

Picking up our large packs, we left the Landrover and walked off toward the border. We found out later that German Police did indeed contact the Regiment, who sent a REME Sergeant and driver to collect the vehicle.

A few minutes later, trying to look nonchalant, the four of us approached the border but we need not have bothered as we walked across without anyone stopping us or indeed paying us any attention at all – we were in Belgium. We changed what few Deutsch Marks we had left for Belgian Francs in a small Bureau de Change and after consulting the map, decided to stay on the road we were on, the N3, which would take us to Brussels and then we intended to follow the N9 to Ostend. We also discussed trying the motorway but decided against it for the time being.

Just after 3 pm, we set off in good spirits and as we walked along, we took it in turns to wag our thumbs at passing drivers but had no success. We walked on chatting, almost without a care in the world, none of us at this stage worried about the lack of lifts. However, by six-o-clock, feeling a little dispirited, we stopped at an Imbiss to buy frites and burgers that we washed down with a shared coke. The food did wonders and we marched on for another four hours before we began to look for somewhere to spend the night.

Having expected to be in Ostend by nightfall and with no money to spend on accommodation we were prepared to sleep almost anywhere as we were all very tired, especially John who had had little sleep the night before.

Approaching a small town, I noticed a caravan sales park and thinking aloud I said, 'We could sleep in the awning of one of those caravans.'

John and Chris both thought it was a great idea but Larry was dubious and said, 'We're sure to get caught if we try to get into one of the awnings, it's far too risky, I think we should try somewhere else?'

I said, 'Hang on here and I'll walk past and have a recce of what's actually there,' and slowly walked past the Sales Park.

About a dozen large caravans with awnings attached sat on an open area that was bounded on three sides by fencing with only a low single chain fence on the side open to the road. Shale tracks ran amongst the caravans with flower tubs and manufacturer's signs that divided the area into plots. A small sales kiosk at the front displayed an opening time of 9 am and that was it, apart from the large house a few yards further on.

I walked back to the others and said, 'There're no lights on, no security and not a soul about, it'll be a doddle just to walk into the park from this side and get into one of the awnings for a kip.'

'Right, come on let's go, I need a kip,' said Chris.

The four of us walked quickly into the park and up to a large awning near the back where Chris reached down and slowly pulled the zip of the canvas door up. It made a sound like fabric ripping and we felt sure that it would set off alarms or have someone come running from the house to investigate but nothing happened and we slid into the awning closing the zip slowly behind us.

Chris took his large pack from his shoulder and began to take his poncho from inside it when John said, 'I wonder if the caravan is locked?' It was not!

Inside there was a double dinette at each end of the caravan and not believing our luck, we quickly settled onto a settee each.

We'll have to be out and away by seven,' I said.

After a whispered discussion on what we were going to do the next day, we were soon asleep.

I was in heaven; the smiling, little blue-eyed girl nestled her head on my shoulder and clung tightly to me as we danced slowly on an empty dance floor - until Larry shook me awake.

'Come on it's light, we'll have to get going before someone comes,' he said.

Sitting up I rubbed my eyes, looked at my watch and saw that it was only half past five, and said, 'Bloody hell Larry man it's a bit frigging early.'

Five minutes later with the collar of my leather jacket turned up and walking briskly to keep warm, we entered the small town that had not yet fully woken. A little later the smell of freshly baked bread, directed us to a small bakery where we bought two large French loafs and two bottles of milk that we devoured as we left the town, walking slowly toward Brussels.

Lift wise, the day was a total waste of time and after a discussion, we realised that as long as we stayed together there was little chance of anyone stopping to pick us up. We agreed to stay together for the last couple of hours of the day but that we would split up tomorrow and meet up at the first roundabout in Ostend.

Later, our search for somewhere to sleep led us to three World War Two vintage, ex-US Army ambulances parked in between some houses in a small village. Chris and I climbed into the back of one of the unlocked ambulances while John and Larry climbed into another. The ambulances were in great condition, complete with stretchers that made excellent beds for the night, however, I don't think any of us slept too well as the stupidity of what we were doing was slowly beginning to dawn on us.

We rose early again but, this time, did not hurry off, having found a water tap against a low brick wall at the rear of the ambulances, we decided to was and have a hot drink. Using our hexamine cookers' we heated water in our mess tins for a wash and shave followed by a drink of hot Oxo made from the pack I had in my rucksack.

By the time, we packed up and set off, the little village was busy and we attracted many curious stares from the locals but no one approached us as we strolled out along the main road.

Half a mile outside of the town the road we split up; John and Larry stopped where they were and began thumbing madly as Chris and I walked on to find a suitable spot to start hitching ourselves. The sun was already very hot when we stopped just past a road junction a mile further on and took up position to begin. Standing as close to the road as was safe, I held my thumb up as the first vehicle, a lorry approached. It did not stop but John and Larry waved from the cab as the lorry sped past!

'Our turn next,' Chris said hopefully and sure enough, within a few minutes a Peugeot saloon pulled up and the driver beckoned us to get in.

A smartly dressed middle-aged man; he spoke very good English and asked, 'Where are you walking too?'

Sitting in the front, I answered, 'Ostend.'

'Oostende,' he corrected before saying, 'I will be able to save you much walking, I can drop you off at the far side of Bruxelles at the A10 motorway, this will take you direct to Oostende, good ay?'

'Excellent,' I replied and looked back at Chris who nodded, beaming a satisfied smile.

'And why are you hitch-hiking through Belgium?'

'We're in the British Army and we are on a leadership course, we've been given an initiative test to complete and have to get to London and send a postcard of Buckingham Palace back to camp. Then we have to report to a barracks at Woolwich,' I said, hoping it sounded plausible. We had agreed on this for our cover story as such initiative tests were commonplace at the time.

Our Belgium Driver became very interested and asked several very searching questions that Chris and I answered the best we could but I do not think he was convinced. He drove into Brussels, pointing out the striking Atomium and even shared some sandwiches with us before he dropped us off on the slip road to the A10 at midday.

Within minutes, a small Citroen van stopped and took us half way to Ostend, dropping us off on a slip road leading up to a minor road that crossed the motorway into a small hamlet.

Chris said, 'I'm bloody starving; let's see if we can find a café.'

Just off the bridge, there was what appeared to be a café, although it was hard to tell through the net curtains hanging inside the two large shop front windows.

Tentatively, I opened the door, looked inside, and saw that it did appear to be a café, albeit an empty one. We walked in and sat at one of the half-dozen or so, plastic tablecloth covered tables and looked around for a menu without success.

Knowing that I just had a few Francs, I asked Chris, 'How much have you got left?'

383

'Not much, just a few Francs,' he answered as a plump woman in a black dress with white apron finally came out and asked us something in French.

Not understanding a word she said, I plonked my few francs on the table and pointing to my mouth said, 'Food please!'

She shook her head and rattled off in French again but when she realised that we could not understand her, she went back through the door she had entered and came back a minute later with a basket of eggs and some bread and said, 'Only this.'

We cottoned on and Chris placed his francs on the table and said, 'Only this.'

The women shuffled the francs with her finger, counting swiftly before snatching most of it up, and saying, 'Oui,' before disappearing into the back again.

A few minutes later she served us four fried eggs each, a small loaf of bread and two cups of very strong and very sweet coffee; it was nectar but hardly filling and after almost licking the plates, we left to seek another lift. Approaching the bridge over the motorway, we saw that a small truck had parked underneath and two men had climbed down from the cab and were, in true continental style, relieving themselves against the bridge in full view of the traffic.

'Come on Chris,' I said as we ran toward them, 'we'll get a lift with them.'

Puffing slightly, I ran up to the men who were zipping themselves up and asked, 'Lift to Ostend Please?'

'Non,' The men replied.

'Lift please?' I repeated.

'Non, it is not possible,' one of the men said.

'Come on fellas, give us a lift please?' begged Chris.

'Non, we cannot,' one of the men said.

'Please, a lift, please, just to Ostend,' I pleaded.

'Non,' the man repeated, shaking his head as he made to climb into the cab.

'Just to Oostende,' I pleaded again and stepped closer to him.

The other man walked towards the rear of the truck and began unfastening the tarpaulin flap that closed off the rear and said, 'Look, I show you why lift is not possible.'

I walked to the rear to look in, expecting it to be full of goods - it was; it was full of strawberries!

'See,' he said, 'you cannot travel with the fruit, you will eat them.'

It did not deter us and we continued to beg, promising not to eat any strawberries.

The men weakened under our constant pleading until eventually one of them said, 'OK, but please do not eat fruit,'

We agreed and climbed into the rear of the truck in the space between the tailboard and the strawberries as the men rolled up and fastened the tarpaulin before climbing back into the cab and driving off.

384

Our agreement not to eat the strawberries lasted for about thirty seconds before we were greedily snatching handfuls of the delicious ripe fruit, devouring them hungrily. Quickly stuffed and feeling guilty, we slowed our onslaught down to one or two every few minutes, just to keep ourselves topped up as the truck sped on toward Ostend.

'There not going to be very happy with us when the see how many we've eaten!' Chris said as we approached the coast.

'Yor right,' I said looking at our stained fingers and mouths, 'We best leap out the first chance we get.' Chris nodded in agreement.

We did not have to wait long, half an hour later we felt the lorry slowing, and saw that the other vehicles around us were also slowing as they came to the end of the motorway.

When the truck slowed to almost a standstill to negotiate a roundabout, the first roundabout at Ostend, I picked up a basket of strawberries and Chris and I leapt out.

The unsuspecting driver drove on as we walked around the outside of the roundabout, holding our bellies while laughing and saying, 'No more strawberries please,' and up to John and Larry who were sitting waiting at the far side.

'Have you two been having a snog?' John asked as we approached.

I replied, 'Yep but not with each other, with a truckload of strawberries and now I feel sick as a dog.'

Larry shouted, 'You sods, you might have brought us some!'

Bringing the basket of strawberries from behind my back, I said, 'Divvint be cheeky or you won't get any of these.'

Larry snatched the strawberries out of my hand, he and John quickly gulping them down as Chris and I watched in amusement.

Wiping his mouth with the back of his hand John said, 'We're only a few minutes from the docks and the boat leaves at nine in the morning so we'll have to spend the night here.'

'Any ideas where?' asked Chris.

Larry pointed to a building site a few hundred yards away, 'We've already had a look over there and found a house that is nearly finished and thought we could spend the night there.'

We waited until nine o'clock before venturing onto the building site and climbed through the space for a window in one of the houses before making our way upstairs. Apart from the money for the mail boat, we were penniless and hungry but I still had half a dozen Oxo cubes with which I made a strong drink, sharing it with the others. The concrete floor was hard but we all managed to sleep and still had enough discipline to have a wash and shave in the morning before we set off to catch the boat.

We were there early, concerned that we may have trouble going through customs with just our ID cards but in the event, we had no problem and were soon at sea, sitting on an outside bench watching Ostend slowly disappear as our stomachs growled angrily.

Always affable and with a great gift of the gab, John had stuck up a conversation with a middle aged couple and was explaining in great detail that we were on an initiative test and were becoming pretty hungry as we were only given ten German Marks to get to London. They obviously took pity on him and us as twenty minutes into the crossing, they handed us each a ham and mustard sandwich that we pretended was unnecessary before eating them gratefully.

Delighted with his success, John tried the same story with another man but failed to get any sandwiches, instead the man gave him enough money to buy us each a cup of tea, which we drank as the ship entered Dover harbour. Seeing the other passengers gathering at the railings as they waited for the passenger ramp, we joined them pushing our way forward to watch the crew dock the boat.

An elderly lady struggling with two large suitcases tugged at John's sleeve and asked if he could help her off the boat with them - which he of course, did while we waited for him on the dockside where he handed over the cases to a porter before joining us.

'That was okay, she gave me half a crown for my troubles,' he said.

Taking his cue, the four of us forced our way back up the ramp against the flow of people coming down and began to offer to carry their bags but had to give it up when angry porters told us in no uncertain terms to, 'Sling our hooks.'

The half-crown was enough to buy us another cup of tea and Kit-Kat each at the café on the docks, as we discussed our next move, deciding that we would again split up, hitchhike along the A2 to London, and meet in the waiting room at Waterloo Station. Chris said he would then go home and borrow a few quid for us from his mum to last us until we made it to our own homes.

Chris and I quickly hitched a lift to Lewisham but had to walk the rest of the way before we met up with the other two in the railway station at seven-o-clock. As arranged, Chris left for home promising to be back within the hour.

Sitting in the almost empty waiting room, the three of us discussed our next move; Larry and I agreeing to set off up the A1 tomorrow and try to get home, which for Larry was Leeds and then we would give ourselves up to the local police the following day.

John dropped a minor bombshell, 'I'm going to hand myself in tonight,' he said almost nonchalantly.

I said, 'But Aa thought we'd all agreed to get home before we handed ourselves in?

He smiled and said, 'I wouldn't be welcomed home if they knew I was AWOL and I don't think my parents will believe the initiative test story - but don't worry I won't tell anyone where the rest of you are.'

Chris returned with five pounds and listened quietly as John told him that he was going to hand himself into our main depot at Woolwich Barracks.

386

'I'm going to wait two days to give Syd and Larry the chance to at least make it home but I understand you wanting to pack it in,' he said.

Two British Rail Policemen, who had already wandered around the waiting room a couple of times, came back in and slowly walked past us before they left, which was enough for us to move on before they became suspicious.

Chris gave John enough money for the tube to Woolwich and asked Larry and me what we were going to do.

'The Union Jack Club tonight, now that you've given us some cash, and tomorrow the tube up the Northern Line and hitchhike home,' I replied as Larry nodded in agreement.

Chris and John wished us luck and headed into the underground as Larry and I headed for a night of relative luxury in the Union Jack Club, just a stone's throw from the station.

We only had to show our ID Cards to book an incredibly cheap room and breakfast in the ageing but well maintained Edwardian building. I then spent ages soaking in one of the bathrooms before we went downstairs for a substantial and very cheap dinner in the comfortable dining room. Having checked the price of the tube tickets to High Barnett, we reckoned that we had enough money left to buy us a beer each and still have a bob each for the journey tomorrow.

Not knowing when we would eat again, we pigged out at breakfast, eating everything we could, including many slices of toast before we caught the tube to the end of the Northern Line. It then took us half an hour to walk from the tube station to a roundabout on the A1 where we put our thumbs out for a lift, only waiting a few minutes before a large lorry pulled up next to us.

John opened the cab door and the driver shouted, 'Where ye gannin lads?'

Recognising the accent, I shouted past John, 'Newcastle for me and Leeds for him.'

The driver smiled and said, 'Yor in luck, am gannin te Newcastle and I can drop the big lad of at the Leeds roondaboot."

At 9 pm, I was walking up the A1, past the Town Moor in North Newcastle, my thumb working overtime as I tried to hitch a lift to escape the rain that was falling steadily and complete the last fifteen miles home. I had just about resigned myself to a long walk when a dark saloon car pulled up alongside.

The driver leant over to open the passenger door, asked, 'Hoo far ye gannin lad?'

'Ashington,

'Get in then, am gannin te Amble so I can drop ye off nee bother.'

We chatted for the thirty-minute drive to Ashington and I told the driver that I was on a long weekend leave from Woolwich before he took great delight in telling me all about Amble. I did not tell him that my Grandparents and several aunts and uncles lived there and I knew the place well!

387

He dropped me off in High Market and a couple of minutes later, I walked into the scullery of our house in the Fifth Row where Butch met me wagging his tail so hard his whole body was twisting. I knelt down, patted him, and then went through the brightly lit kitchen and into the sitting room where Mam, Dad, and Dennis were watching television in front of a low fire.

All three were smoking and the staleness of the air forced me to stop in the doorway as Mam turned and said, 'Bugger my eyes, what are ye deeing here?'

'Am on three days leave, I've just completed an initiative test to travel across Europe to London,' I said to a sceptical looking Dad. I embellished my story a little and went back into the kitchen to make myself a cup of tea and jam sandwich while they continued to watch television, only Butch showed any interest in my being there.

The next day I walked round to the Post Office and drew out the few pounds I had in my account and wandered downtown to buy some socks, underwear, a pair of jeans and a couple of polo shirts. I then walked back to the pit baths where I took a long hot shower and changed into my new clothes.

I met Jill that night and told her what I had been up to and although it worried her, it also quite excited her leading to a night of passion but I still felt as if this was just a temporary affair and I think she sensed that.

I had been home for six or seven days when I received a telegram from Larry asking me to telephone him at home, which I did from the public call box in High Market.

'I think we've proved our point and I'm going to hand myself in tomorrow,' Larry said over the phone.

'Yeh, I agree, I think we need to get back and face the music but I'll have to wait until the day after tomorrow as I need to tell my girlfriend what's happening. I can't see her until tomorrow night, so if the local police give me a travel warrant I'll see you in Woolwich in a couple of days.'

We chatted about what we had been up to before saying, 'See you at Woolwich.'

The next morning after I had washed and shaved at the cold-water tap in the scullery, I was sitting at the kitchen table having a cup of tea when Dad came in from work.

'Isn't it aboot bloody time ye went back lad?' he knew by then that I was AWOL.

'Aye, I'll go doon te the Police Station later this morning,' I replied.

I still felt that I should see Jill tonight and explain to her that I was going back and that I was bound to be in big trouble, so I decided to stick to my plan to see her and hand myself in tomorrow. A few minutes later, I walked downtown and had a cup of coffee at Dawson's Café before walking back home, expecting Dad to be tucked up in bed but to my surprise, he was sitting at the kitchen table under a haze of thick cigarette smoke.

'What happened with the Polis?' he asked nonchalantly.'

'They told me to go back tomorrow morning and they'll give me a travel warrant,' I lied.

'He took another long drag from his cigarette and blowing it out slowly, said, 'I see; there's a mate of yours te see you in the sitting room.'

Pushing open the sitting room door, I stepped through and came face to face with a very large, young Policeman who had been listening behind the door. He put his hand on my shoulder and smiling said, 'Go on get yor kit together, ye'll be coming doon te the station with me.'

Dad had somehow guessed I would not hand myself in and had gone down to the Police Station and brought the young Bobby back with him!

He drove me and the Policeman to the Police Station, dropping us off without saying a word, leaving me to walk in alone as the Policeman walked off down toward Station Road.

Inside the hall of the Edwardian red-bricked building, I tapped on the window of a small hatch and waited a minute or so before it opened and a middle aged, grey haired Police Sergeant stared through at me.

'Yes, what can I do for you lad?'

'I'm Gunner Carr and I'm AWOL and am handing myself in Sergeant,' I said nervously.

'Aye, so you are young Carr, yor Father said ye would be gracing us with your presence, hang on.'

Opening the door, he led me through to a large desk where he took my details, including my unit and where our Regimental Depot was.

That over, he led me through to the cells and ushered me into one, 'Wait in there and I'll see you get a cup of tea and something to eat, I'll have te lock ye in, I canna hev a desperate criminal like ye wandering roond the Station noo can I?'

'No Sergeant,' I agreed and sat down on the wooden bed wondering how long I would be locked up here and what punishment I would be given when I got back to the Regiment – at least the Sergeant had recorded me as surrendering to the Police.

True to his word, the Sergeant sent through a cup of tea and an hour or so later, a large meal of steak pie, mash, and peas smothered in gravy that I thoroughly enjoyed, the best meal I'd had for a while.

An hour later, the Sergeant opened the cell door, 'I'm going off duty now young Carr and I'll give you a lift roond te your lass's so ye can say goodbye then I'll run ye te Newcastle Station. I have a travel warrant for ye to Kings Cross and I'm going to put ye on the slow overnight train Right?'

I replied, 'Right, thanks Sergeant,'

He gave me five minutes to say goodbye to an upset Jill before he tooted the horn of the Panda car urging me to get back in. On the way to Newcastle, he gave me a pep talk, a father to son pep talk, something I had never had before. I enjoyed listening to him telling me to sort myself out and decide what I wanted to do with my life and whatever it was, as long as it was legal, to go for it and put some effort into doing it. He was right off course and I knew it, I just had to figure out what it was that I wanted; there was also the little matter of a price to pay for absconding.

32

Retribution

It was a beautiful summer's morning when I climbed off the train at Kings Cross Railway Station and made my way through the morning rush to the underground where I caught a tube to Woolwich. I did not feel the least bit apprehensive, more relieved and when I reached the huge, sprawling; yellow-bricked Garrison built at the beginning of the last century, I happily reported to the main guardroom.

The Bombardier on duty gave me a scathing look and yelled, 'Stand to bloody attention you miserable specimen you.'

I thought I was standing to attention but braced myself even more, expecting a real bollocking but instead, he said, 'Report to the Detention Centre Carr.'

'Where's that Bombardier?' I asked.

'WHERE'S THAT, WHERE IS FUCKING THAT, you dumb shit, you'll find out where it is and what it's all about, so you fucking will my son, now fuck off before you annoy me.'

I smiled, said, 'Thanks very much Bombardier,' and hurried out the door as a tin ashtray bounced off the wall behind me.

The sentry on the gate gave me directions to the Detention Centre and I made my way across a couple of roads and into another part of the barracks wondering what awaited me. I had never heard of the Detention Centre before and later found out that its sole purpose now, was to hold in detention soldiers who had been AWOL and were waiting to return to their units. This was to prove slightly controversial in the case of myself and the other three, we had all handed ourselves in and technically need not have been held under close arrest!

A high brick wall led to the Victorian built Detention Centre that looked as though it must have been a guardroom earlier in its life. A set of three or four steps led up to a huge wooden door flanked on either side by large windows complete with metal bars. I grabbed an old-fashioned bell pull to the right of the door, gave it a tug, and waited.

An immaculately turned-out, wiry, hard-faced Lance Bombardier, Regimental Policeman – RP, opened the door and glared down at me.

'Carr is it?'

'Yes Bombardier,' I replied.

'Welcome to Hell Lad!' said the RP and ushered me into the hallway of the Detention Centre.

A door to the left of the hall led into a room that I noticed had a couple of white Formica, topped tables, both with four stacking chairs pushed into them. A door to the right led into the RPs' office containing a large desk opposite of which and under the window were a couple of armchairs. Two metal cupboards stood against the wall behind the desk and on the main wall hung a huge board divided into columns and rows, each with a heading in white paint with large letters along the top spelling the words 'Soldiers Under Close Arrest'.

I just managed to read the first name on the top of the list and saw it was Church! I was surprised that John was still here as he had given himself up a week earlier but my thoughts were short lived.

A huge, blonde-haired Sergeant, standing behind the desk, said, 'Drop yor large pack there,' then looking at the Lance Bombardier, he said, 'Three-Star get him across to the QM's for some kit and make sure he's sweating by the time he gets back.'

I was already beginning to feel warm in my leather jacket but before I could take it off 'Three-Star' shouted, 'Outside at the double; come on move your idle self!'

Once outside he shouted, 'You do everything at the double here Carr.'

'BY THE LEFT DOUBLE MARCH,' he screamed as I doubled off twenty or more yards with him marching behind screaming, LEFT RIGHT LEFT, GET THOSE BLOODY KNEES UP.'

'DOUBLE MARK TIME,' he yelled to keep me doubling on the spot until he caught me up, before shouting, 'FOR-WARD.' We moved caterpillar-like to the Quartermaster Stores in a manner that was to become second nature to me.

The QM's Storeman issued me with a towel, a set of fatigue dress denims, two Khaki shirts, three pairs of grey woollen socks, two pairs of large green underpants, and a pair of the new rubber soled boots. He then made me sign a form to deduct the costs from my wages – should I get any in the future!

Three-Star ordered, 'Hold your arms out,' and as he piled my new kit into my arms ready for the march back, I saw how he got his nickname; he had a small, blue star tattooed on each ear lobe with a third one just above his nose!

He doubled me back to the Detention Centre, screaming at me all the way. I had expected exactly this sort of treatment and just got on with it, even when I dropped a boot that sent him slightly berserk as he kicked it across the road, screaming at me to pick it up. I had to stop myself from smiling as his screams reached another level when I dropped the boot for the second time; he achieved his aim though as I was sweating heavily when he chased me back inside the Centre.

The RP Sergeant said, 'Get that bloody jacket off and leave it with your large pack.' I gladly took my leather jacket off and placed it carefully on top of my pack, only for Three-Star to snatch it up and pull it on.

'What do you think Sarge, it's a great fit, can I keep it?'

The Sergeant grinned and said, 'No you bloody can't, that would be thieving, and you don't want to be a thief like this toe-rag do you?'

His statement shocked me, as Three-Star took off my Jacket I said indignantly, 'I'm not a thief Sarge!'

'Yes you bloody well are, you stole a bloody Landrover didn't you?'

'No Sarge, we just borrowed it,' I said, naively believing that was the case.

393

'BORROWED IT!' he bellowed, 'BORROWED IT! - Did you take it back? No you bloody didn't so you bloody well stole it; you're a bloody thief lad,' he paused and added, 'and a bloody deserter!'

Now I was worried, it was bad enough having to face possible charges of theft, but desertion as well! That would mean a Courts Martial, months in the Military Corrective Training Centre at Colchester and then probably a discharge – 'services no longer required,' I was horrified.

'But we didn't desert Sarge, we only went AWOL and we have all handed ourselves in so it cannit be desertion can it?'

The Sergeant looked at me with just a trace of sympathy and said, 'Well your Adjutant says it's desertion and theft of a vehicle lad and that's that.'

'Shit!' I cursed.

'That's exactly it lad, 'shit' you are up to your neck in it and it ain't going to get better anytime soon.'

He was right, and now for the first time, I realised with some foreboding, the extent of the trouble we had created for ourselves.

The Sergeant told Three-Star to take me through to the cells and have me change into uniform and then he turned back to the large board to finish chalking up my details.

Three-Star opened the door at the end of the hall and doubled me through into the Cell Block dominated by a wide corridor with the most highly polished floor I had ever seen. Immediately to the right of the door, an opening led to the ablutions and latrines while to the left, a flight of stairs led up to an overflow room. Beyond these, on each side of the corridor, were four or five cells and at the very end, a door that led out to an exercise yard.

Three-Star doubled me into the first cell.

'Get changed into uniform and make up a bed box, I'll collect your civvies shortly.'

Looking around, I studied the cell; it was ten foot by six foot with cream-painted brick walls, a red-painted floor, and a barred window high up on the back wall. The metal-framed bed had a green mattress with a pile of bedding on it; next to this was a green wooden soldier's box. It was a standard army cell with a bell push with the wiring in metal piping and a close fitting ceiling light with the switch outside the door - depressing.

I changed into fatigue dress and began folding my blankets and sheets to make the regulation army bed block when I thought I heard a voice in the distance saying my name! I stopped folding blankets to listen but not hearing anything, I started again only to stop almost immediately, sure, that I could hear someone calling my name.

I listened harder and heard it again from near the cell door, 'Syd, Syd, Syd.'

It was very faint and I could not work out where it was coming from so I walked up to the door to see if it was someone in the hall but when I stood next to

394

the door the voice seemed to be coming from the bell push! I put my ear close to it and heard my name again and the voice sounded familiar!

Feeling slightly foolish, I put my mouth close to the bell push and said, 'Is that you Scouse?' and put my ear back to the bell push.

'Yeah, it's me, Chris, how are you la?' came back through the metal tubing.

Although Chris spoke with a mixture of Scouse and Cockney and nick-named Scouse by the lads in the Battery, he did not like it and kept telling everyone, 'Call me Chris.'

It was slow and quite difficult to have a conversation through the bell push tubing but it was enough for Chris to tell me that in addition to the four of us, there were another two lads in the Block.

Before he could tell me more, Three-Star slammed the door open and grinning, said, 'I see you've discovered the Cell Inter-com?'

Before I could answer, he said, 'Outside your cell now, stand to attention here,' and he pointed to a spot just in front of the cell door where I took up position and watched out the corner of my eyes as he opened the other cell doors shouting at the occupants to, 'FALL-IN.'

Chris was first out, giving me a wink as he took up position, as Larry emerged from another cell looking very morose, then two lads I did not know joined us and finally, directly opposite me, John came out smiling madly.

'I'll wipe that frigging smile off your face Church lad.' Three-Star shouted up at John, who was a good six inches taller than he was.

Three-Star then walked down the corridor, opened the door to the exercise yard, and screamed, 'OUTSIDE, FALL-IN TWO RANKS MOVE – FUCKING MOVE, COME ON FASTER YOU MISERABLE CRIPPLES.'

'Soldiers under Close Arrest' are soldiers who are awaiting trial and, therefore, are exempt from any punishments or fatigues, unless they volunteer. However, exercise twice a day is mandatory.

This was my first session and it was a revelation! Three-Star was good at it, very good, he gave us close order drill – drill done in short sharp steps at twice the normal speed. He used every inch of the exercise yard until our shin and thigh muscles screamed with the awkwardness of the fast short sharp steps. When he was satisfied he had us sweating hard enough, he stopped the drill and started us on a punishing exercise routine of squats, star jumps, press ups, sit ups, stride jumps and more until we were all struggling, especially Larry.

Unbelievably, he then gave us a smoke break, handing their own cigarettes from the contraband box to the two strangers, while the rest of us, all non-smokers, chatted trying to catch up on what we had been up to over the past week.

I said, 'Do you know that the Adjutant is going to charge us with theft and desertion?'

The other three were as shocked as I had been and began to mutter angrily but Three-Star yelled, 'Right, FALL-IN,' and began the exercise routine all over again.

During the second smoke break John told me about meals and our cleaning jobs, warning me that I would be on 'the corridor' but before I could ask what that entailed, we had another and an even harder session with Three-Star working us so hard, sweat poured off us by the bucket load.

Satisfied that he had beasted us enough, he opened the door to the cell block and ordered us to 'Fall-In' in front of our cells and started to lock us in one by one.

When he came to me, I asked, 'Do we get a shower now Bom?'

He leant close to my face and spat, 'What do you think this is, fucking Butlin's Holiday fucking camp – you'll get a shower when we tell you to, not when you fucking want, now get into your fucking cell, you fucking moron.'

Locked back in my cell I finished making my bed block and sat down on top of the wooden box staring at the wall, my mind racing as I thought of the consequences if charged with theft and desertion. It could mean discharge, not what I wanted; although I had not exactly covered myself in glory since joining up, I still enjoyed the army and had never once thought of throwing in the towel and returning to Civvy Street.

After half an hour, I realised that there was going to be some long boring hours spent alone in my cell and began to think of ways to pass the time. I started by counting the bricks in the end wall, not being the least upset when I lost count and had to start again – several times. Lunchtime came and quickly showed that meal times were the best time in the Detention Centre as the RPs left us alone in the dining room to eat our meals.

John and one of the other lads were dining room orderlies and had been double-marched to the cookhouse to collect our lunch meals, placing them on the tables in front of us on their return.

It was great to chat freely and discuss events. I was confused as to why we were held under close arrest and not open arrest as we had all surrendered and asked the other two lads, both Jocks, if they had been AWOL.

'Nah we'd both done a proper runner,' one of them answered, 'I'd been gone six months before the coppers got me and Jamie here had been away even longer.'

Jamie nodded and through a mouthful of Welsh rarebit said, 'Aye, I had no intentions of going back but the bastards caught me in ma local pub!'

'That proves my point,' I said, we should be under open arrest in barracks awaiting flights, not in here, the Regiment must have told them to keep us under close arrest which means they must be trying to charge us with desertion!'

They all agreed but we knew there was nothing we could do about it and would just have to take events as they came.

After our evening meal and showers, Larry acquainted me with our 'cleaning job'; I found myself on my hands and knees, 'bulling' the corridor floor with yellow dusters, boot polish, and spit. As it was impossible to bull the whole floor in one session, we first gave the whole floor a light dust and polish with dry dusters, and then got down to the serious business of bulling a section to the same standard as our best boots, i.e. immaculate. It was slow work, hard on the knees and back but hardly life threatening, just bloody tedious. We polished and bulled for three hours before being locked up for the night.

While Larry and I polished the floor, Chris and one of the Jocks cleaned the ablutions and John and the other Jock, holding the two top posts of Dining Room Orderlies, cleaned the tables and washed and dried the dishes and cutlery, handing the latter into the RPs Office to prevent them from being used for 'other purposes'.

I quickly settled into the routine of the Detention Centre and through diligence and hard work on the floor, and much to Larry's annoyance, found myself promoted to shithouse and ablutions cleaner, the Jock having to go back to polishing floors. I enjoyed the exercise sessions and slowly found out that Three-Star's bark was far worse than his bite.

On the third day, supervised by Three Star, Chris and I were cleaning the overflow room on the first floor. The room contained five double bunks, five stacking chairs and I noticed that unlike our cells, the light was a damaged, old-fashioned hanging pendant. The light fitting was hanging loose with about a foot of metal conduit pulled away from the ceiling.

Curious, I asked Three-Star, 'What happened to that Bom?'

He smirked wickedly and replied, 'We're waiting for the electrician to change it for a close fitting one because we had a Wally in here a couple of weeks ago who decided to try and hang himself from it!'

'Bloody hell,' I said, 'what happened, did he choke?'

Three-Star leant nonchalantly against one of the beds, pushed back his peaked cap and said, 'Not fucking quite, I heard him screaming so came rushing up here and found him dangling like a fish, kicking and moaning. So I says to the stupid twat, if you want to hang yerself I'll help you and jumped up and grabbed his legs to help choke the fucker but the whole bloody light fitting came away and we crashed to the floor, so I gave him a good kicking.'

Chris and I looked at each other and raised our eyebrows not wanting to believe him but wondering if he really did swing on a hanging man's legs; whatever the truth, he looked as though he was quite capable of doing so!

The long spells alone in our cells with nothing to read or do was beginning to get everyone down, especially poor John who had been there for over ten days, he moaned constantly about it at meal times. I resolved to try to keep active while in my cell and began by very carefully, and very slowly, unpicking one of my grey

397

wool army socks. Once I had deconstructed the sock I then found several different ways to wrap it into little balls, or twist it into string, eventually, I took up weaving with it – exciting stuff – not, but it kept me occupied.

By the fifth day, my superb cleaning standards saw me elevated to the dizzy heights of number two 'Dining Room Orderly!' Collecting meals meant a rare trip outside even though it was just to the cookhouse a couple of hundred yards away. Cleaning the dining room was an easy task as was washing the dishes; I was, however, after the top spot – drying dishes!

It didn't take long as the next morning John was picked up for having a scruffy bedding box and sent back to polishing the corridor floor with the result that everyone moved up one place and, importantly, I became the 'big fish' – 'number one'! I had made it to the top spot and I was delighted, boasting of my success to the others continuously throughout the day.

That night I was enjoying drying the dishes that, the also newly promoted Chris, was washing, chatting away as we worked. Chris handed me the last plate and instead of taking it with the tea towel, I grabbed it with my bare hand, grasping it too firmly, unintentionally squeezing the plate out of my hand. I watched it bounce off the wall and onto the floor, smashing loudly into dozens of pieces!

Shocked, I quickly knelt to pick up the bits and hide the evidence of this dreadful crime but I was too late; the noise travelled to the Office and the large blonde-haired Sergeant came in to investigate and found me trying to conceal the evidence behind my back.

He stood with hands on hips looking down at me for a few moments before saying, 'Corridor floor Carr, tell them all to shuffle up one.'

I stood up and said, 'Thanks Sarge,' and joined John in the Corridor; my first promotion run was over.

The following morning Three Star double-marched John, Chris, Larry, and me to the QM's stores where we were issued with new Service Dress uniforms complete with, shirts, ties and forage caps, the cost of which would, of course, be deducted from our wages! This could only mean one thing; we were about to be 'Returned To Unit' and we exchanged whispers before John asked Three-Star, 'Are we going back to our Regiment then Bombardier?'

He gave us a mock sad face and answered, 'Yes, I'll be losing my little playthings won't I? You're going back under escort the day after tomorrow.' The four of us were relieved that at last we would be going back but we all wondered what we would be charged with and if we were to face a Courts Martial.

Later that afternoon, with the sun was shining through the open dining room window as we ate our tea meal; we discussed our 'Return to Unit'. Chris wondered who the escort would be and we all speculated that it could be Regimental Policemen from our Regiment or worse still Military Policeman! Regimental Policemen were soldiers like Three-Star, who were taken from their normal jobs for a spell of duty as Unit Policemen responsible for running unit guardrooms, looking after soldiers under sentence and arrest, staffing the main gate during working hours and any other task the Unit's RSM might give them. Military Police, on the other hand, were professional Police with far-ranging powers over soldiers and generally feared as they were, in the main, right bastards.

Distracted by the brightness of the sun I got up and pulled the curtain across to provide some shade but as I did so, I looked closely for the first time at the bars on the other side of the window.

Turning to the others I said, 'I reckon Aa could squeeze through these bars, they're pretty wide.'

The other three and the two Jocks looked across and made various derogatory comments but John got up to have a look.

'I'm too long to get through, Larry's too fat so maybe you or Chris could squeeze through but why would you want to, you're not going AWOL again are you?' asked John.

'Not likely but ye know, I think Aa'll just give it ago; Chris watch the door for me,' and with Chris keeping watch, I climbed up onto the window ledge and tried my head first; it went through easily. Pulling it back, I squeezed myself sideways through the bars, struggling briefly to get my rib cage through but with a little tug, I found myself balanced on the window ledge outside the Detention Centre and jumped down to the ground below.

I looked back up at the window and saw the others, grinning and cheering silently and I bowed as though I was Harry Houdini.

Larry whispered through the open window, 'Come on get back in before you get caught,'

I shook my head and said, "Na, I've got a point to prove,' and walked up the steps to the main door and gave the bell pull, a firm tug, hearing the bell ring in the office as I stepped back and waited. The door unlocked and I watched as the big RP Sergeant swung it open and step forward, glaring down at me.

'Well, come on get bloody inside,' he said, which I did and turned to see him look outside for an escort. Not seeing one he stepped outside for a better look and still not seeing one he turned back to me, his face beginning to cloud over as the penny dropped, 'How the bloody hell did you get outside Lad?'

'Through the dining room window Sarge,' I answered solemnly.

'Bollocks, how did you bloody well get bloody outside?' he demanded again.

'Though the dining room window Sarge - the bars are far too wide and I thought I'd show you that we are not deserters as we could escape anytime we are in there.'

Luckily for me he had a sense of humour, as struggling to stop himself from smiling, he shouted, 'Get to your bloody cell, you're back on polishing the bloody corridor floor lad,'

I said, 'Thanks Sarge,' and returned to my cell not mentioning the fact that he must have forgotten that I was already floor cleaning. The next morning, civvy workers attached heavy-duty wire mesh to the bars!

On the morning of our 'Return to Unit', wearing Service Dress and anxious to be on our way, the four of us waited in the dining room for our escort and transport to arrive. Eventually, the Sergeant called us into the office and was briefing us on the journey when Three-Star came in and announced the transport was outside.

'What about the escort?' the Sergeant asked.

'They're already on board and they look a right mean bunch of bastards Sarge!' he replied.

The Sergeant grinned and said, 'Right you four, get your cases and get out of my Guardroom now, go on bloody well bugger off and don't bloody come back - you won't be welcome.'

We hurried outside to where a 3-ton Bedford truck sat with its engine running, the tailboard down ready for us to climb into the back but the four of us stopped in our tracks when we saw our escort! Two fresh-faced, frightened young soldiers, straight out of basic training, sat on the bench seat peering nervously down at us!

John was first to speak, 'You've got to be kidding haven't you,' he said to Three-Star, 'these virgins aren't here to escort us are they?'

'More like us escort them!' said Chris grinning at the two lads.

'We only need a couple of kids to look after you four Tossers now get on board,' said Three-Star, grinning madly.

We climbed on board and sat opposite the two lads, staring at them intently without saying a word, which unnerved them even more.

One of them, a chubby-faced lad, who despite wearing Service Dress, looked dishevelled, spluttered, 'Listen, listen, listen, please, we didn't volunteer for this escort, we were ordered to, so please, please, listen, will you not give us a hard time as we'll get into trouble.'

The way he repeatedly said 'listen' before he spoke, led me to believe that, he was not used to people listening to him, so he obviously thought it was necessary to shout to get anyone's attention.

As the Bedford pulled away I said, 'We won't give you a hard time, we'll be off as soon as the Bedford stops at the first set of traffic lights.'

The lad's face turned bright red and seemed to swell up as he shouted, 'No, listen, listen, listen, no please, we've signed for you, no please don't,' he begged as his partner just looked on silently, too scared to speak.

Chris said, 'If you've signed for us you're going to be in trouble if you lose us.'

This started the lad off again. Worse, he looked as though he was about to have a heart attack, when a little later the Bedford stopped at a set of traffic lights and the four of us, without saying a word got up and started to climb over the tail board!

'NO, LISTEN, LISTEN,' he screamed, 'Please don't, don't, no please,' he begged until we sat down and he realised we were just joking.

'You Bastards,' he cursed.

John stood up pretending to look very angry and snarled, 'What did you call us?'

This set the poor lad was off again, 'No, no. listen, listen, I didn't mean it honest, no please.'

Realising that the lad was genuinely panic-stricken, we stopped teasing him and I asked' 'What's your name?'

'Scouse - Scouse Williams, listen, we're joining 1st Battery,' he answered.

'Another lamb for the Blazers,' said Larry.

'No, listen, listen; I'm joining 1st Battery in 14 Regiment, not the Blazers,' he said confidently.

The four of us erupted into howls of derision, worrying the lad even more until I said, 'Look Scouse lad, The Blazers are 1st Battery; 1st Battery is the Blazers, ye need to learn that quickly or you'll find yourself in real trouble when we get there.'

On the journey to Gatwick We told the two lads about the Battery and the Regiment but after that, we became pretty well silent for the remainder of the trip, wondering what would happen we got there.

'You're under close arrest,' the large, Irish RP Sergeant said to us when we climbed off the army bus outside the guardroom late in the afternoon.

'GET INSIDE NOW, COME ON MOVE YOURSELVES!' he shouted chasing us into the corridor of the guardroom.

He quickly dispelled any thoughts we had of going back to the Battery lines and open arrest when a few minutes later we were marched up to RHQ where the Assistant Adjutant, a very tall and angry, Lieutenant ex-Ranker, formally remanded us under close arrest.

On our third day of close arrest, Sergeant Bolden the TARA Sgt that Larry and Chris worked for was the Regimental Duty Sergeant of the day. A debonair, handsome, affable, and very popular young Sgt, I urged Chris to ask him if he knew what was going on. Later, after he had completed his rounds with the Orderly Officer, we got the opportunity to speak to him in the Guardroom.

What he told us was unsettling.

'The Ack Adj is standing in for the Adjutant and is trying to have you court-martialled for desertion and theft, he's still collecting statements at the minute.'

Chris spoke for us all when he said, 'But we didn't desert did we, we just went AWOL, we all handed ourselves in so it can't be desertion can it?'

401

Sgt Bolden thought for a moment and said, 'Well if that's the case you shouldn't be under close arrest either, I'll speak to the BSM in the morning and see what I can find out.'

Released to open arrest the following day, we reported to the Battery where we received the expected bollockings from the Sergeant Majors and heckling from the lads. We had already given statements at Woolwich but had to give them again while we waited to go on Battery Commanders Orders.

A few days later, late in the afternoon, we were standing outside the BSM's office waiting for him to brief us.

He came out and stood in front of us looking at us each in turn before he said, 'Listen carefully; you will be on Battery Commanders Orders tomorrow at oh nine hundred hours, dress will be No 2 Service Dress and best boots, got that?'

We all answered, 'Yes Sir.'

The dress for Battery Commanders Orders was normally working dress so that meant we must be going straight onto Commanding Officers Orders!

The next morning the BSM marched us in front of the Battery Commander where we waited with some trepidation to hear what the charges were.

The Battery Commander read aloud each of our number, rank, and names and then said, 'All four of you are charged with absence without leave.'

We suppressed sighs of relief as he continued, reading the date and time we went AWOL and the different dates and times we handed ourselves in before he read out the charge for theft of the Landrover.

He asked if we understood the charges and after we had replied, 'Yes Sir,' he said, 'I do not have sufficient powers to deal with these charges, you are remanded for the Commanding Officer, March them out BSM please!'

Outside the BC's office, the BSM said, 'Some advice - the Assistant Adjutant wanted to have you court-martialled for desertion but Army Legal said no because a charge of desertion would not stand, and that you had been held too long under close arrest without being charged.'

He went on, 'Do not repeat what I've said or I'll have your bloody guts for garters. I suggest you take whatever punishment the CO hands out, and without question, understood?'

'Yes Sir,' we all said.

The RP Sgt and two RPs marched us to RHQ and CO's Orders that were a bit of blur, ending up with him asking, 'Do you accept my award or do you wish to elect for trial by Courts Martial?'

We each responded in turn, 'Your Award Sir.'

The CO then gave us a superb CO's telling off, finally saying, 'I sentence all four of you to twenty-eight days detention – March them out RSM.'

Outside the CO's office, the new, intelligent looking RSM, immaculate in his uniform, stood in front of us, quietly studying us.

'You may have noticed that I do not do a lot of unnecessary shouting - but you should in no way interpret that as an indication of me being in any way, easy going. You are about to enter my guardroom as Soldiers under Sentence and believe me, you are going to be mightily glad when your twenty- eight days are up as I am going to have you run ragged and you will swear, 'never again' when you leave my little holiday camp.' He was true to his word!

His routine for us began in earnest the next day.

Reveille at 6 am., wash, shave, make up our bed blocks and lay out all our military clothing and equipment on our beds in accordance with a diagram, with no room for the slightest deviation.

Double to the cookhouse for breakfast and double back before the normal breakfast time.

Clean the guardroom, cells, toilets, ablutions, guard's rest room, and outside area.

Parade outside the guardroom at 9 am, wearing 'Battle-Order' webbing that we had scrubbed almost white and polished the brasses until they gleamed, ready for the RSM's inspection that we always failed. We wore battle order webbing and steel helmets every time we left the guardroom.

The RSM then inspected our kit layout in our cells, throwing most of it on the floor for us to do again.

After the RSM's inspection, it was four or more times around the assault course to ensure, that as well as being knackered, our webbing was suitably filthy, requiring scrubbing and polishing again that night.

Work in the regimental garden or piggery or any other fatigue that the RSM could dream up.

Lunch at 12, followed by at least thirty minutes, close-order drill on the Regimental Square, timed so that the soldiers returning to their Batteries after lunch would see us being beasted.

More fatigues, mainly in the piggery until tea at four, then back to clean the guardroom again ready for handover to that night's guard.

Two hours to clean webbing, polish brasses, refold all the clothing the RSM had thrown around in the morning, showers, and lights out at ten.

The upside of having a busy routine was time passed quickly, we were glad of that.

The Commanding Officer was also busy, he had the other cells filled, one of them by Allan Storey who had rescued me at the dance in Southend and another by loud-mouthed Geordie Washington who had killed the BQMS's dog at camp.

Geordie Washington tried to become the 'Big Man' in the cells but we just ignored him, not wanting to get into any trouble with the RPs or RSM. All of us that is, except Allan, who hated Washington and it was therefore, inevitable that there would be trouble between the two.

403

It came on the third night they were in the guardroom; Chris, Allan, and I were in the exercise yard scrubbing our webbing on two six-foot collapsible tables when Washington strode in and demanded, 'Move your fucking webbing so I can get mine on there!'

Chris and I both said, 'Bollocks!' prompting Washington to grab an ammunition pouch and fling it into the corner of the yard before plonking his own webbing down on the table.

The trouble was that it was Allan's pouch! He was not pleased; placing the scrubbing brush slowly on the table, he turned to face Washington.

'Goodnight,' he said, then floored Washington with a brutal right that left him sitting dazed in the corner with blood trickling from a busted lip.

The next morning, the RP Sergeant was inspecting us prior to the RSM's inspection when he noticed Washington's swollen and split lip! He looked at it carefully then walked along the line to where Allan was standing and looked him closely in the eyes.

'It looks as if Washington has bumped into a cell door, Storey?'

Hiding a smile, Allan replied, 'It does Sarge.'

The RP Sergeant stepped back a few feet so that he could see us all and said, 'Dangerous buggers them cell doors - Washington lad, you need to keep your mouth shut and concentrate on where you're walking as we wouldn't want you to go and bump into another door now would we?'

We received his message loud and clear, especially Washington.

We had one other problem during our spell in the guardroom, the RSM's eyes; they were ever so slightly crossed! This was not normally a problem but it could be confusing during morning inspections, borne out by events on the fifth morning. As per his routine, he was inspecting us in front of the Guardroom on a very sunny morning, the sun shining brightly in our eyes.

Having inspected Chris and me, the RSM stepped in front of Larry and said, 'Your bloody shirt pocket is undone you scruffy unkempt excuse for a soldier, get it fastened now.'

Larry did not move and I could see out of the corner of my eye that the RSM was slowly turning bright red as Larry ignored his order.

'Are you deaf or bloody stupid?' he growled but still Larry ignored him.

I thought, 'My God, he's dicing with death, what the hell is he playing at?'

The RSM pushed his face forward so that his nose was practically touching Larry and screamed, 'FASTEN YOUR BLOODY POCKET YOU INSUBORDINATE APE,' spraying Larry with spittle as he shouted.

Larry responded in a surprised, slightly offended and ever so refined way, 'Oh I am sorry Sir; I thought you were looking at Gunner Church and talking to him!'

The RSM went ballistic and ordered the RP Sergeant to chase us round the assault course until we dropped - he happily obliged.

At lunchtime, suffering from the effects of the assault course punishment, we discussed the problem and resolved not to make the same mistake again. Keen not to misinterpret the direction of the RSM's gaze, the following morning, we all responded to everything he said, causing him to go off on another one. It took us four assault course punishments to get to grips with which direction he was looking!

On our tenth day in the guardroom, much to our delight and the annoyance of the others, Chris and I had our routine changed; one of our Battery officers signed us out every afternoon for athletics training in readiness for the Inter Battery Athletics meeting scheduled to take place three weeks later. Both sprinters, I was also competing in the pole vault, so we trained hard and were delighted to be away from the guardroom for a couple of hours each day.

Due to the seriousness of our misdemeanours, the CO did not grant the customary two days remission from our sentence, we served the full twenty-eight days before we were marched to the RSM's Office in service dress and best boots ready for release. We carried our forage caps as Soldiers under Sentence do not wear headgear, although we had worn steel helmets as a punishment throughout our time in the guardroom.

The RSM came out of his office and inspected us thoroughly before saying, 'Hats on.'

After we had carefully pulled our forage caps on, he continued, 'I do not want to see any of you in my guardroom again, if I do it means it wasn't tough enough and I will have to make it even tougher!'

He then inspected Chris and me again and said, 'Carr, Bryson you are both going to be on the Quarter Guard for the visit of the GOC in ten days, the Guard Sergeant will contact you with details of drill practice and uniform inspections.'

This was a bit of a shock to Chris and I but understandable as our uniforms and boots were immaculate, in addition, we were both five foot eight and looked good in our uniforms, unlike lanky John and podgy Larry.

I received another shock when he said, 'Carr you are going in front the Commanding Officer - stand fast; you other three, FALL OUT.'

As the other three marched away to freedom, I wondered what trouble I was in now and frantically tried to think if there was anything else I had done that I should not have but my mind was a blank.

The RSM ordered me to wait outside the CO's office and disappeared inside leaving me to continue to worry as to why I had been summoned by the CO; perhaps extra punishment as I had been AWOL the longest and had also been AWOL the year before.

A few minutes later, the RSM came out of the office and said, 'Right Carr the Commanding Officer will speak to you now.'

I automatically took my hat off but he stopped me.

'Keep your hat on lad, you're not on orders and make sure you salute when you march in.'

He marched me in, halting me in front of the CO's huge desk and as I threw up the smartest salute I could, the RSM reported, 'Gunner Carr Sir.'

The CO sat back in his chair studying me closely before leaning forward to speak.

'Here it comes,' I thought to myself.

'Carr, I have before me my Battery Commanders' recommendations for promotion that they submitted a few weeks ago, just before you absented yourself without leave in fact, and you appear on the list for 1st Battery!'

He paused to allow me time to digest this piece of information; I needed it as I thought of another wasted opportunity through my stupidity but could only say, 'Sir.'

The CO crossed his fingers pushing his thumbs together and went on.

'I can see that you are surprised, it may also surprise you to know that I had agreed to that recommendation - but that was before your latest misdemeanour, I obviously withdrew my agreement; however your Battery Commander sticks by his recommendation and believes that you will make a first class NCO.'

I was both surprised and shocked that the BC would still recommend me and was beginning to think I was about to be promoted.

The CO continued, 'He speaks very highly of you as does your Battery Sergeant Major and I myself am aware that you are a very good signaller. However, be that as it may, I cannot possibly promote someone who has just completed a sojourn in the Guardroom as I am sure you will see that it would appear to the soldiers in the Regiment that you were being rewarded for your misdemeanour - do you agree?'

'Yes Sir,' was all I could say, wondering why he bothered explaining this to me, after all, he was the CO and could have left it to the BSM to tell me, or not even bother at all.

'You have wasted two years of excellent service, however, what I am prepared to do, is to promote you within the year; if and I mean if, you soldier in the manner that you are capable of and demonstrate that you are a soldier worthy of the confidence your Battery Commander has in you, do you agree?'

'Yes Sir, thank you Sir,' I quickly answered.

'I will also endorse your Signals Sergeant's recommendation that you attend a Junior Signals Instructors course as soon as you are promoted; now it is up to you to prove to all concerned that you are worthy of their recommendations - March him out RSM please.'

I saluted smartly and the RSM marched me out.

Outside, he said, 'You'd better not let your Officers and SNCOs down Carr because if you come in front of the CO again, you will be out thrown out of Her Majesty's Army lad, and that's a promise now get back to your Battery.'

I decided not to tell anyone of the recommendation for promotion, telling the other three that the CO gave me another bollocking and put me on a three-month warning, which they accepted.

406

The next day the new Troop Sergeant Major, a Welshman with a sense of humour as well as being a very fair disciplinarian, summoned me to his office.

After I came to attention in front of him, he said, 'So you're the famous escape artist are you?'

'Yes Sir, I'm sorry about that Sir and I would like to say that sort of thing is all behind me Sir.'

He gave me a stern look. 'Lovely bit of bullshit Carr, make sure you do behave yourself but that's not why you're here, I'm catching up on Troop admin and I see you have only had half of your leave entitlement this year, that's official leave I'm talking about, right?'

'That's right Sir,' I answered.

He looked down at a large chart on his desk and said, 'Fill in a leave application now for three weeks in January; I am not going to let you have Christmas, okay?'

Leave had not crossed my mind but I did as directed, glad to be back to some sort of normality.

At the Inter- Battery Athletics Meeting, I won three small silver cups to add to the two I had won last year and earned myself a place in the Regimental Team that took part in the Divisional Competition where we did not fair very well.

The week of the Athletics also marked my completion of two years' service, reminding me of my application to try for selection for the Royal Artillery Commando Regiments.

Wondering why I had not heard anything, I asked the Troop Sergeant Major if he knew anything about it and he said he would look into it. He sent for me a few days later and informed me that the Commandos had rejected me as I had too many entries on my conduct sheet and that the charge of stealing the Landrover was sufficient in itself for them to turn me down! I wasn't too upset as I was enjoying myself in the Blazers at the time and never questioned the truth of what I was told, although I did later consider whether or not I had been rejected or if the Battery Commander had not been prepared to let me go.

407

33

The Only Way Is Up

January is a miserable time of the year; Christmas festivities long past and the fun of New Year parties fast becoming memories as people returned to work and boring routines. Ashington appeared to be more miserable than ever as I arrived on leave facing the prospect of no one to hang around with as all my old mates were at work during the day and most of them courting long-term girlfriends at night.

I did not have my normal saved up leave money, having had to pay for the additional uniforms issued to me at Woolwich that resulted in reduced wages for three months. Nonetheless, I had managed to take home duty-free cigarettes and brandy as expected of me by Mam.

She again asked me for money to pay for my food, not that I thought for a moment that any money I gave her would be used to buy food, so I refused as I still sent her a weekly allowance, plus I only had twenty-five quid to last me three weeks. This led to another slanging match when she once again demonstrated just how poisonous her language could be.

In order to spend as little time as possible in the house, I took to going for a walk around town in the morning and in the afternoon, going over the footbridge to the Rec for a work out in the gym. This had the added bonus of allowing me to have a daily hot shower and use of an indoor toilet, neither of which was available at home!

Rather than eat at home, that is of course if my mother had made me anything to eat in the first place, I started to eat at the pit canteen but that quickly began to eat into my leave money.

Early in the morning after a week at home, I was preparing to go for a walk when I discovered that there were twenty pounds missing from my wallet! Only one person would have taken it. Walking down stairs, I saw her sitting at the kitchen table smoking one of the cigarettes I had brought her and judging from the set, defiant look on her face, she was expecting a showdown.

'Have you taken money from my wallet?' I asked in a tight voice as I fought to keep my anger under control.

She sneered at me and said, 'Yes I bloody well have, it's only what you should have given me anyway,' and turned away, taking another long pull at her fag.

I knew there was no way she was going to give me the money back and spat, 'I suppose it will buy you a few more bottles of sherry and brandy and a couple of nights at the Bingo,' and walked out of the house wishing there was somewhere else I could go.

That night I was watching television with Dennis who was telling me about attending Technical College; like the rest of us he had left school without any qualifications and as he knew he would not be able to join the army due to his poor hearing, he had enrolled at College to study for a couple of GCEs. He had also become a very talented artist and said he was going to go down to Ipswich to stay at Pat's and try to enroll in the local Art College.

Dad, after his 'Fore' shift and sleeping from ten in the morning came downstairs for his dinner at six o clock, and sat at the kitchen table as Mam served his dinner before she sat down opposite him, lighting a cigarette.

When he was half way through his dinner, I went into the kitchen to make a cup of tea and as I plugged in the kettle he asked, 'I hevn't seen you heving dinner since you got back?'

'Nur you hevn't,' I said, 'If I've got to pay for my food I'd rather eat at the pit canteen.'

Putting his knife and fork down, he said, 'What the bloody hell are you saying?'

I told him about Mam demanding money for food and me going to the canteen.

Mam got up and walked into the scullery as Dad exploded, saying to her retreating back, 'Nee bugger is gannin to eat in the canteen and nee bugger has te pay for food in this fucking hoose but me.'

I retreated to the sitting room as the two of them exchanged pleasantries in their normal fashion.

Vivian, who had been upstairs preening herself ready for a night out came into the sitting room as the argument subsided.

'What was all that aboot?'

Dennis stroked Butch who was lying at his feet and said, 'Me Dads just telling Mam hoo lovely his dinner was.'

'Aye and pigs fly,' said Vivian.

A little later Dad joined me in the sitting room as Dennis pulled on his jacket and went out to see his mates.

'It's Friday night are ye not gannin oot?' Dad asked.

'I hevn't got any money so I'll be staying in,' I answered, sipping my cup of tea.

'Aa thought ye'd hev plenty of money for your leave, what's happened to it?'

'Ask me Mam,' I answered.

'What the bloody hell has she done noo?'

'She took twenty quid out of my wallet for food and that just leaves me a quid to last the rest of my leave.'

Dad stood up, opened his wallet that he had fished out of the back pocket of his trousers, took out four, five-pound notes and handed them to me saying brusquely, 'Here.'

I initially refused but when he dropped them on my lap, I gratefully picked them up knowing he could afford it.

He wasn't finished though; after he had a wash and shave he came back in and said, 'Are you seeing your lass tonight?'

I had not seen Jill since I was AWOL, 'No not tonight.'

'Right you are then, get your coat on and we'll gan te the Fell Em Doon for a couple of pints.'

I stood up and grabbed my coat as Mam, who had heard my Dad's invitation from her seat at the kitchen table said, 'Hang on, and I'll brush me hair and get me coat.'

Dad walked past her and said, 'Yor not invited,' and we walked out leaving her fuming behind us.

Standing at the busy bar of the Fell Em Doon, Dad ordered two pints and said, 'Ye hevn't towld me what happened when ye got back te camp?'

As we supped the beer, I told him about Woolwich, CO's orders and detention and then as we started on our second pint, my Dad's two cronies, Mr Page and Mr Little, joined us.

'Is that it then?' Dad asked as I ordered more beer.

'Nur not everything,' and I told him about the interview I had with the CO and of possible promotion but by then he had lost interest.

I finished my beer, left them at the bar and walked to the Portland where I met up with Tom and Cousin Alec for a couple more beers.

Alec had heard that Jill and I had split up and asked if I was going out with anyone else.

'Nur, but there is one lass I've fancied for a long time but I hevn't seen her for ages and I expect she's still courting or engaged or bloody married by noo.'

Alec said, 'If yor mean that little dark haired one yor kept wanting to chat up, I hevn't seen her at the Welfare or anywhere else for that matter.'

That didn't make me feel any better and I felt as though she was gone for good.

Tom told me that he was finally trying to put a group together and I wished him luck with that as we reminisced over the times we had sung Buddy Holly songs in his front room - well he sang while I accompanied him badly.

I did date a bonny blonde Mod who turned out to be a police Sergeants daughter - it did not last!

On my last night of leave, I was at The Portland where I started to chat to a girl who I knew vaguely and whom I had heard had a bit of a reputation. Marjorie was not really my type, she had a rather sharp looking face, but thinking that I might get lucky, I walked her home and enjoyed a bit of heavy petting on her sofa. That was as far as it went and I left after we agreed to write to each other.

410

A couple of weeks after leave, about thirty of the younger members of the Battery along with fifteen from HQ Battery, were given the privilege of going skiing for a few days at the small village of Usseln, about 140 kilometres south-east of Dortmund, near the ski resort of Winterberg.

Before we left, the BSM informed us that on arrival at Usseln, the BQMS would issue us with all we would need to ski and that a Professional Ski-Instructor would teach us but we had to take our army boots as we would be skiing in them – the last bit of information did not bode well.

Excited at the prospects of whizzing down ski runs, we were a tad disappointed when we arrived and found that there wasn't any in the immediate vicinity, although there was a ski jump just outside the village – not that we were allowed anywhere near it, which was probably just as well!

Our accommodation consisted of a number of three-tier bunk beds crammed into the village sports hall with an area cordoned off for dining that doubled up as a bar in the evenings.

After claiming a bed each, we dumped our bags on them and excitedly lined up ready for the issue of our ski kit. Our excitement was dampened a wee bit when we saw the kit; white, winter-warfare combat suits that apparently only came in size extra-extra-large! Skis, made from what looked like floorboards with bindings made from rhinoceros hide, and ski poles that were stout lengths of bamboo with a wooden hoop attached to the bottom by more rhino hide!

My vision of whizzing down slopes in ski-sartorial elegance completely disappeared when our ski instructor greeted us.

He was a Norwegian Army Captain who did not need a horned-helmet to show he was a Viking! Tall, handsome, athletically built and wearing a very smart Norwegian Army ski-suit, complete with what looked like ridiculously narrow skis when compared to ours; he stood surveying the rabble in front of him.

We did look more than a little ridiculous. We all had to roll up the very long sleeves of our winter warfare jackets but our hands still disappeared up inside them, and the trousers were so long that they hung in folds around our ankles. Our khaki army knitted gloves became soaked as soon as we touched the snow and were useless, as were our poor quality army boots, which, sodden from wet snow, scrunched up when we fastened the skis to them.

The Ski Instructor introduced himself and said in excellent English, 'We will not be downhill skiing we will be cross-country skiing or langlauf skiing as they call it here in Germany.'

Cross-country skiing sounded like hard work and it was; once he had confirmed that we had all strapped on our skis, albeit that most of us had fallen over, and then without any sort of instruction as to how to move forward, the Norwegian shouted, 'Okay, single file follow me!'

Off he went, followed by a long line of white-suited clowns, who fell, bumped, slid and cursed, but managed to laugh and follow him, slowly picking up enough skill to stay upright as he skied off into the woods surrounding the village.

Initially, I was behind Scouse Williams, the lad who had been our escort for the journey to camp from Woolwich.

He fell over every few yards shouting, 'Listen, listen, listen, no please help me up, no listen please, don't pass me,' but we did pass him, leaving him floundering like a beached seal.

After about an hour of skiing along a very undulating and narrow path through the woods, much of the time spent in picking ourselves up, we arrived battered and bruised but in extraordinarily high spirits at a very large clearing that fell away sharply to our right. It looked as though, beneath the snow, it was a very large sloping field, confirmed by what looked like a barbed wire fence at the bottom, some one or two hundred yards away.

'Form a long line along the top of the hill,' our instructor ordered.

We tried to comply, except gravity intervened and the vast majority of us slid down the hill either sideways or on our backs. It took a good thirty minutes before he finally got us in a long line, balanced precariously on our skis facing downhill.

He shouted, 'You must learn how to snowplough when going downhill - I will demonstrate by skiing to the bottom and when I raise my arm in the air, you will all snowplough as I show you, to the bottom.'

Choosing to ignore the many derogatory remarks made by us, he turned and snow-ploughed beautifully down the hill, demonstrating sublime control as he zigzagged downwards before stopping with a flourish at the bottom.

He looked up at us revving up our skis at the top of the hill, and then raised his hand in the air; the result was stupendously hilarious.

We all pushed off together; some fell over immediately, taking out those on either side of them, others' skis slid ahead of their bodies, resulting in them windmilling their arms as they tried to remain upright before inevitably crashing. Some managed to ski in a straight line looking remarkably good despite being totally out of control, while some skied a little way, fell over, picked themselves up, skied a bit further before falling over again, and so on.

No-one snow-ploughed but somehow we all managed to reach the bottom, some of us rather faster than we wanted to; I managed to stay upright and found it far too exhilarating to want to spoil it by snow ploughing. The trouble was stopping; I had no idea how to execute any sort of stop that did not involve falling down. As the barbed wire fence at the bottom of the hill raced toward me, I threw myself onto my side and slid into it without doing too much damage to the fence or myself.

Eventually, we were all at the bottom, making up one of the several piles of laughing and cursing soldiers before we slowly struggled to our feet and brushed off the snow, all that is apart from one lad who had selfishly managed to break his leg and another lad who had dislocated his shoulder!

The ski lesson for the day was halted due to their injuries and the need for first aid and ambulances but the rest of us, including one or two walking wounded had to ski back to the sports hall, the Norwegian Instructor managing to add a couple of enjoyable extra miles to the trip.

The first day set the pattern for the rest of our stay there; none of us became what you would call competent skiers, apart from, and much to everyone's surprise, Scouse Williams! We did, however, all have a great time trying to ski, as well as some rowdy evenings that involved a great deal of singing of bawdy songs.

On the third day, an Officer and Cameraman from the Public Relations Branch came to take some 'Local-Boy' pictures and I found myself selected!

The PR Officer told me to get into my ski kit but when he saw the state of the winter warfare clothing, he muttered, 'No, no that won't do, get into civvies, and see if you can find a nice ski jumper to wear.'

Not having a nice ski jumper myself, I went on the scrounge, managing to borrow a rather flash Scandinavian style jumper that although slightly long on me, it could have graced the best Ski slopes in Europe, or so I thought. The PR Officer thought so too and several photos of me posing at the top of the bank that surrounded the village sports field were taken and eventually sent back to the local papers in the North East under the heading, 'Geordie Soldier enjoys skiing holiday in Germany.'

I had exchanged a couple light-hearted letters with Marjorie but it came as no surprise, nor did it cause me any upset, when she wrote and said she was going out with another lad. I had only walked her home and to be honest, I did not really fancy her other than someone to possibly have sex with, not a very good basis for a relationship.

A week or so later back at camp, I was in the NAAFI bar with Rob who told me that his girlfriend of eighteen months had moved back to England with her family on posting and asked if I had heard anything of her friend Shirley. I told him that we exchanged a couple of letters but as we were unlikely to meet up again, I had stopped writing to her.

He knew there was only one girl for me, 'Little Blue-Eyes' and asked if I had seen her on my last leave. It hurt me just telling him that I had not seen her for a while and despite believing that she was courting another lad, I could not stop thinking of her.

We discussed the Commandos and their reasons for rejecting me before he said he was thinking of having a go at Para selection and asked me if I fancied giv-

413

ing it a shot. Having no reason not to and as I was fairly fit after training every day on leave, I said that I was up for it and we agreed to start training together.

Rob wanted to go for a run every morning at 6 am, a time I was not too keen on, especially when we could train in the evenings but as he was eager, I agreed to get up and run with him. The trouble was he had to wake me each morning as I lacked a wee bit of motivation and that annoyed him. It annoyed him even more when he realised I was quite a bit fitter than him. At my insistence, we changed to running and training in the evening and were able to put much more effort into it, although Rob was still quite slow on the runs. This resulted in me finishing ages before him, as I needed to push myself if I was to improve my own fitness.

After three weeks, we put forward our requests to try for selection into the Royal Artillery Parachute Regiment but were told that another two lads in our Regiment also who wanted to try, therefore we would first have to undergo a fitness test by our PTI's to see if we had any sort of chance of getting through selection.

Three days later, on a frosty March morning, Rob and I, along with Roger, a tall thin lad from the Blazers, reported to the Gym ready for the test, the fourth lad had decided he no longer wanted to try.

Three PTIs waited for us, one of them a tough looking and very fit NCO, greeted us at the door with, 'My God why does England tremble? 'Get fell in single file and listen in, I'm going to give you a workout like you've never had before. I'll judge if any of you has what it takes to pass Para selection, so I'm now offering you the chance to bugger off to your Batteries before the pain begins - well are you still up for it?'

'Yes Bombardier,' we replied.

'Okay twice around the camp circuit as fast as you can go, GO ON GET GOING,' he screamed.

The camp circuit was just over a mile, the three of us chased by one of the PTIs set of at a fast pace but Rob was soon struggling to keep up and I slowed and encouraged him to speed it up.

The PTI shouted, 'It's every man for himself, don't wait for anyone, push it out.'

I sped up and ran past Roger, keeping up a fast pace, until with lungs bursting and legs running out of steam, I ran up to the Gym to be greeted by the NCO who said, 'One-minute recovery then the real work begins.'

After a minute, the third PTI chased me into the gym and started me on circuits of nonstop exercises; sit-ups, press-ups, heaves to the chin, star jumps, squat thrusts, dips on the parallel bars and more and more.

Starting the second circuit of the exercises, I saw that Roger was having real trouble trying to do heaves to the bar, as Rob began his first sit-ups. After twenty minutes of torture, I had a two-minute rest and watched the struggles of the other two as they tried to complete their circuits.

The PTI chased me around two more circuits before the NCO blew a whistle and despite the fact that the other two had not completed three circuits, he ordered us to the foot of the ropes, dangling from the ceiling way above us.

'Your last chance to show what you've got - climb up, touch the top and then a controlled descent – GO,' he shouted.

Reaching up as high as I could I grabbed the rope and lifted my feet as far as I was able, crossing them over the rope as we had been taught, then pushed up with my legs, followed by my arms reaching high again. I climbed quickly to touch the top and using my feet on the rope to control my descent, I swiftly clambered down.

Roger was stuck half way up and just did not have anything left to give after the circuits while Rob just made it to the top.

The NCO shouted at Roger, 'That's it for you lad, get back to your Battery!'

He almost fell off the rope before staggering dejectedly out of the gym.

The NCO looked at me and said, 'What the bloody hell are you standing still for? Get back up that rope.'

I climbed again, my thighs burning with effort, and my arms aching but I quickly made it up and down again as Rob started his second climb. Rob struggled but completed the second climb but did not have any energy or strength left to start a third time and the PTIs sent him back to his Battery.

On the fifth climb, I ran out of steam a few feet from the top and clung to the rope, trying to use my feet to take my weight before I tried again.

The PTIs were actually screaming encouragement as I pushed myself up and touched the top, before sliding down a little too quickly while the NCO shouted, 'CONTROL IT, CONTROL IT.'

Standing at the bottom of the rope, legs shaking, hands still grasping the rope, I thought, 'That's it surely that's enough for them.'

I was wrong, the NCO said quietly, 'Well why have you stopped? Get up again.' I almost gave up but a picture of me, dragging Dowty props, through cold wet slime came to me and I remembered that you can always give a little more than you think you can and reaching up, I began the climb again.

The skin on my hands was fiery red as I struggled to grip the rope tight, and my legs trembled as I pushed slowly up and up but I made the top and clung to the rope, sucking in air before I climbed back down.

'You've stopped again,' warned the NCO as I clung to the rope for support.

I heeded the warning, reached up, and started again. Using the last ounces of strength I had, I forced my pain-wracked limbs to haul me back up the rope again, struggling to find the strength in my legs and ankles to grip the rope between my feet in order to lever myself up.

415

The PTIs had stopped shouting encouragement and watched silently as I slowly, slowly made my way to the top where I struggled to let go with one hand to touch the rafter.

My hands burned from the rope as I controlled my descent. At the bottom, I slid off the rope and onto my backside, my hands falling palms up onto the floor.

The PTI NCO almost whispered, 'You've stopped again!'

It took everything I had left to pull myself up from the floor and reach up to grab the rope but I managed and stood gasping for air while trying to shut out the aches before I again heaved myself up, clamping my feet onto the rope. I managed one more reach and pull, before shaking with effort, I girded myself for another pull, but the PTI stopped me.

'Enough come down lad.'

Dropping the five foot I had just climbed, I just managed to stop myself from falling onto my knees before I straightened myself up and stood to attention.

The PTI NCO came up to me and said, 'Okay, to finish off, twice around the camp circuit – GO.'

Leaning wearily toward the door of the gym, I started to shuffle forward but he stopped me again.

'Hold it there; I just wanted to see if you would try. Okay Carr, you are the only one of the three we will recommend, well done off you go lad.'

I did my best to jog out of the gym and made my way back to the Battery Lines, and found that despite my exhaustion, I felt elated and noticed that as I shuffled on through the crisp frost that still lay bright and white on the ground, energy was slowly coming back to my weary limbs. The elation I felt would be short lived!

After I had showered and donned my fatigue uniform, I reported to the Battery Sergeant Major, keen to tell him that I had passed the PTI's assessment.

I waited outside his office until he shouted, 'Come in Carr,' and I marched smartly in and stood to attention in front of his desk.

The BSM looked at me with a half-smile and said, 'Well done Carr, the PTI Bombardier has phoned to say that you are the only one of the three that he considers would have any chance of getting through 'P' Company.'

'Thanks Sir,' I said and was about to ask when I would be going but the BSM stopped me.

'The BC has said that while he accepts he cannot stop you from attempting 'P' Company, he cannot afford to lose you from the Command Post at the beginning of this year's training period, so, he will not let you try until the latter part of the year!'

Confused I asked, 'I'm ready now Sir, is there no chance of going in the next few weeks?'

The BSM's smile disappeared, 'I've told you what the BC has ordered now take that onboard and consider your future carefully lad. If you stay, there's the possibility of promotion but if, and it's a big if, if you get into the Paras, you will be starting from scratch as well as letting the BC down after he supported Sergeant Redding's recommendation that you are promoted. Now fall out and get back to work.'

With very mixed emotions, I reported back to Sergeant Redding, not at all sure of what I was going to do or wanted to do, not even sure if I wanted to stay in the army. I did not have much time to ponder as the lads in the Signals Stores asked how I had done and how the other two had faired.

When I told Sergeant Redding what the BSM had said, he just grinned and said, 'Maybe it's for the best Carr lad.'

I decided that I needed to go on leave and think through my options before I made a decision. I applied for three weeks leave at the beginning of the new leave year, commencing on the 1st April and was surprised and relieved when the TSM approved it.

In bitterly cold but sunny weather, the Regiment carried out technical firing at Munsterlager Ranges for the last two weeks of March. Slow and boring, the exercise seemed never ending but it did eventually finish and we packed up our tented camp ready for the journey back to Dortmund.

On return to Dortmund, I had two days to sort out my exercise clothing and equipment, buy duty frees and clean and press all my civvies, before I went on leave.

Rob asked me if I fancied going down to Horde for a drink at the Corner house before I went home and having no other plans, I agreed. After having a couple of pints in the NAAFI, we walked the mile toward the steel town, past a scrap yard that contained a madly barking dog, before walking down a short bank into the nearest German pub to camp – The Corner House. Although used by tough steel workers the pub was also popular with lads in the Regiment thanks to its closeness to camp; that night was no exception as about ten or twelve lads were already at the bar when we walked in.

We joined a couple of lads from HQ Battery who were sitting at the end of the corner bar and ordered a couple of beers as Rob let it drop that after his disappointment at not passing the fitness test, he was going to leave the army at the end of his three years.

'What about you?' He asked as I took a sip of ice-cold beer.

'Whey I signed on for nine years to get the better pay rate but am not sure if I'm going to stay in - seeing that the Commandos don't want me and I cannit try for the Paras until the end of the year when I'm pretty sure the BC will find another reason for not letting me go.'

The other group of lads from the Regiment were from 13 Battery and had obviously had a wee bit to drink as they burst into song, preventing us from becoming too maudlin. A Lance Bombardier named Gerry who I knew to be intelligent, well educated, and just a tad eccentric led their singing. He was in fine

417

voice, singing the verses to, 'An Engineers Wife,' with the rest joining in the raucous chorus,

Ah hum titty bum, titty bum,
Ah hum titty bum, titty bum.

We joined in and spent the rest of the night singing rude, crude army songs, drinking beer and schnapps and becoming drunker by the song.

Much later, the Landlord had obviously had enough of our loud off-key singing and shouted, 'Enough please gentlemen, now please to go home, no more beer. I have closed the bar.'

We voiced our objections to this but as it was well after midnight, we knew he was serious and we reluctantly left.

Rob and I, along with the two lads from HQ Battery left first, the crew from 13 Battery still singing loudly following a few yards behind us. As we walked up the bank we approached the corrugated fence of the scrap yard on the other side of the road from behind which, the savage barking of what must be a very large and angry dog greeted us.

The dog did not appreciate Gerry and the other lads singing, its barking became louder and more intense, and I could hear it jumping at the six-foot high fence in a vain effort to get over and devour us.

It was then that Gerry stopped and said with a slight slur, 'I'm going to get that dog!'

Considering the noise from behind the fence, it was a stupid statement to make, so we waited to see what he was going to do.

The 13 Battery lads who had been laughing at Gerry, stopped laughing when they realised he was serious and suggested that it was a pretty mad thing to contemplate but Gerry said, 'Bollocks, I'm having it,' and jumped up grabbing the top of the corrugated iron.

The dog went insane as Gerry pulled himself to the top, doing a perfect roll over and into the snarling, snapping jaws of the enraged beast below. We were horrified, having believed he was only kidding and would not actually drop into the scrap yard, but he had and the noises coming from inside were terrible to listen too. The sounds coming from the dog were truly frightening as it attacked Gerry and the sounds he made were equally frightening, but slowly his voice became more dominant than the mad dogs barking, and then eerily, it went quiet!

'The fucking things eaten him!' gasped Rob as we all stared in horrified silence at the fence.

The sound of scuffling and grunting came from the other side, and shortly after and much to our amazement, the ears of a dog became visible, poking over the top. As we watched with open mouths and accompanied by more grunting from within the scrap yard, the ears moved upwards until the dogs mad eyes came into view followed closely by its huge slavering mouth. It was a huge Alsatian and more and more of it was coming into view as Gerry struggled to push it up and over the fence!

Eventually most of the dog was in view, teetering on the brink of falling back into the scrap yard but a final thrust from Gerry below, pushed it over the top and it fell with a thump at our feet. The sight of the beast sent us scampering away, lest it attacked us but it did not, it remained crouched where it had fallen, snarling and snapping with its tail pulled down between its legs; this was a seriously mad dog.

We continued to watch as Gerry climbed the fence and dropped down beside the dog, where he stood panting heavily, wiping blood from his hands, and trying in vain to straighten his ripped and ragged sleeves.

To our utter disbelief, he grabbed the snarling beast by the collar and started to drag the reluctant dog toward camp! It initially struggled and tried to shake itself free. When it failed, it tried digging its paws in but Gerry was having none of it and dragged the dog on and although it snarled fiercely, it did not attempt to bite him.

Eventually, the Alsatian stopped struggling and snarling and walked half crouched alongside Gerry but if any of the other lads approached, it immediately snapped at them. Gerry had his dog and he kept it, but he was the only one who could control it, and woe betides anyone foolish enough to get too close to it. In typical Gerry fashion, he named the dog 'Dfor', D for Dog!

I had a bit of a hangover when I caught the early morning flight the next day but plenty of fluids on the journey home cured that, and I felt fine if a little depressed when I walked into our house, just after six o clock on the evening of Wednesday the 31st March 1965.

On the journey back to Ashington I had been thinking over the events of the last few months and it left me feeling low. I had again missed promotion due to my own stupidity, I had also scuppered my chances of joining the Commandos and it looked as though I was unlikely to be able to try for Para selection anytime soon. Added to that I was in love with a dream, a little blue-eyed girl, and that dream seemed to spoil any long-term relationships I had with other girls.

I felt as though I was at a crossroads, unsure as to which way to turn; whether to leave the Army and look for work back home or knuckle down and regain my right to promotion and make the Army a long term career. Lacking a point of focus in my life, I could not make my up mind as to what to do for the best.

After issuing the duty frees and having a bite to eat I stepped into the sitting room to drink the tea I had just poured myself and joined Dennis and Vivian who were watching television.

Dennis asked, 'Are you going across to see Cousin Alec cos he said to let him know when you got home?'

419

I was about to say, 'Yes,' but Vivian butted in and said, 'He gans to the institute on Wednesdays, so he winnit be in and dee ye knaa that there's a Disco on at the Portland on Wednesdays? It's supposed to be really good.'

I digested this and decided I would go to the Portland and check out the new Disco, then walk the couple of hundred yards to the Miners' Institute to see Cousin Alec. Finishing my tea, I put the kettle on to boil some water for a wash and shave and a little while later, wearing my favourite black leather jacket, a new dark blue shirt and a pair of new, dark hipster trousers, I walked into the bar of the Portland. Ordering a pint, I looked around to see if there was anyone there I knew; there was not.

Disappointed, I asked the barmaid, the girl from the Fifth Row that I had gone out with when I was fourteen, where the Disco was.

She smiled and said, 'It's upstairs and there's a bar upstairs an all, it's a pity I'm working as we could have had a dance.'

'Aye that would be nice,' I said, taking my pint and wandering back into the entrance hall and up the stairs to check out the disco and immediately bumped into Marjorie coming down the stairs holding the hand of a tall dark haired lad.

She stopped and said, 'Hello, when did you get back?'

'A couple of hours ago,' I told her and continued on up feeling not the least bit jealous of her being with another lad, just a tad jealous of the fact that they looked happy together, something that seemed to elude me.

I found the bar on the large landing at the top of the stairs and saw Disco lights flashing out of the darkened room beyond where the DJ was playing 'Baby Love' by the Supremes.

Finishing my pint, I bought another before walking into the Disco, a largish room with seats arranged in cubicles down the wall to the left while the Disco set up, complete with ultraviolet lights, was against the wall to the right of the door. There were a few lads and lasses sitting in the seats, with a dozen or so, mainly girls, dancing.

Roy Orbison had replaced the Supremes on the turntable and was singing 'Pretty Woman' as I adjusted my eyes to the darkness, before walking around to see if I knew anyone.

Noticing three girls dancing on the far side of the small dance floor, my attention immediately focused on one in particular who had her back to me. She was smaller than the other two, her hair brushed up high from her neck, a cloth hairband dividing her fringe from the rest of her hair. She was wearing a dark shift dress with a slashed neck, very much in the Mary Quant style and I could feel my heart race and a breathlessness come over me as I was sure it was Little Blue-Eyes!

I put my beer on an empty table and continued to walk slowly around to where they were dancing and as I drew close, she turned and I saw that it was the pretty blue-eyed girl that I dreamed of except - she was no longer pretty, she was beautiful.

420

My mind was in turmoil as I watched, trying desperately to think what to do. I determined not to waste this chance to meet her and when she leaned forward to one of the girls she was dancing with and asked, 'What colour is my hair band in this light?'

I stepped forward and said, 'Blue,' aloud, and to myself, 'Blue like your beautiful eyes.'

She gave me a fleeting look and stifling a smile, she turned her back on me as she continued to dance but I was not going to let her get away this time and stepped back to wait.

Roy Orbison finished singing and as the dancers waited, the DJ started to play, 'Tired of Waiting for You,' by the Kinks.

I knew it was now or never, and walked up to her, 'Do you want to dance?' I asked, smiling nervously.

She returned my smile and nodded and I followed her onto the floor grinning like a Cheshire cat as my stomach did somersaults. The music was too loud to speak while we danced and I could not take my eyes off her, she looked like a very young and demure Elizabeth Taylor, thrilling me with an occasional lovely little smile.

When the Kinks finished and the Moody Blues began to sing, 'Go Now,' I stepped forward placing my hands on her waist as she put hers on my shoulders and we moved close to dance slowly around the room.

I did not want the music to stop but it did, and not wanting to let her go, I asked her if she wanted a drink.

She nodded, 'Yes,' and I steered her to the table where I had left my beer and went to the bar for the coke she had asked for.

Back at the table, conversation came easily, she said, 'I've seen you before haven't I?'

Nodding, I replied, 'Yes, I've seen you around a lot but this is the only time I've seen you here.'

She smiled and said, 'That's because it's the only time I've been here, I only came because three of my friends from work asked me to come.'

'I must thank them for bringing you,' I said as I realised how lucky I was to be home on leave for this night.

We sat and chatted, I told her that I was in the army and had just got home on leave, she told me her name was Elizabeth and she worked in the offices of an Electrical Components Factory at Bedlington.

I was besotted and just wanted to take her in my arms but tried not rush it, scared I might say or do something that might ruin things but still found myself asking far too early, 'Can I walk you home later?'

She looked down at her drink, shook her head slightly, and said, 'No.'

Cursing myself for trying to rush things, I determined not to take 'no' for an answer and asked her to dance. She agreed, and we had three or four more dances before we returned to the table, this time, I held her hand and she seemed happy for me to do so. Back at the table, we talked for a while before I again asked if I could walk her home but she gave me the same little shake of the head.

I was beginning to wonder what was wrong, she seemed to like me and we certainly seemed to be hitting it off, I could not contemplate letting her go again, and asked if she wanted another drink to which she agreed.

Back at the table, I said smiling, 'You are going to let me walk you home, aren't you?'

She smiled and said, 'No, I'm sorry, you can't.'

Not prepared to lose her I said, 'But why not?'

Looking down at her drink, she answered quietly, 'Because I'm meeting my sisters at the bus station and I will be walking home with them.'

'That's not a rejection of me,' I thought and quickly said, 'Great, I'll walk to the bus station with you, you don't want to be walking through town on your own late at night do you?'

Looking closely at me, she replied, 'It won't be late because I'm meeting them at half past ten,' and paused before saying, 'but you can walk me to the bus station.'

Feeling like jumping up and cheering, I instead, grinned and said, 'Great.'

The walk through town to the bus station was magical, we talked non-stop and as we crossed over the road at the Grand Corner and I said, 'You could tell your sisters that I'm walking you home,' but she did not answer; instead, she took hold of my hand, releasing more butterflies in my stomach.

Her two sisters seemed surprised but happy enough when she told them that she was walking home with me, especially when I said that we would walk behind them to make sure they got home safely, which we did.

Later, we had our first kiss on the step of the door that led into the back-yard of her house where we chatted and kissed for an hour before she said she had to go in.

Before I let her go, I asked if I could see her tomorrow but she said she wasn't sure if she should but much to my joy, she did agree and I arranged to meet her at the bus stop near the Portland the following night.

The following morning, unable to sit still, I went for a long run ending up in the gym in the 'Rec' for a light workout, followed by a long hot shower. Later I shaved and put on my navy blue Italian suit before walking down to the bus stop praying that she would be on the bus until as it approached, to my delight and relief, I saw that she was in the doorway waiting for it to stop.

We spent the evening in the snug of the Portland telling each other about ourselves, I felt happier than I had ever been and probably talked far too much. I asked her if she remembered all the times, we had seen each other over the years and she smiled and said, 'Yes, I think the first time was on the beach at Newbiggin when I lived there.'

422

I was thrilled, I never for a moment thought she would remember the moment that she stole my heart, but she did. I told her about my antics in the army, that I had reached a point where I needed to decide what I was going to do with my life and that I was going to decide on this leave whether to stay in the army.

She asked me if I enjoyed being in the army and when I nodded she said, 'Well it seems to me that, that's your answer!'

A little while later my happiness evaporated when she said, 'I'm sorry but I have to tell you that I'm courting, and I have been courting the same lad for four years!'

My mouth went dry as I realised she was talking about the lad I had seen her with at the cricket ground just before I had joined up - she was still going out with him! Now I knew why she was so reluctant to let me walk her home last night. My mind raced as I tried to imagine not seeing her again or her being with someone else.

I was having difficulty accepting the situation, I had been in this position before with other girls, and it always ended badly but here and now she seemed to enjoy my company and her kisses last night seemed to confirm that, I resolved to try to win her, this was one fight I was not prepared to lose.

As we sat looking at each other, I asked her where this left us but she looked as confused as I felt and said so.

I said, 'Four years is a long time, how serious is it?'

She thought for a while and said, 'We haven't committed to anything, yet, we've just been seeing each other one or two nights a week.'

Just after ten pm, we left the Portland and wandered arm in arm down to the park where we sat on a bench and continued to talk before I took her in my arms and kissed her and felt her respond. A little later, we continued to talk as we walked the mile or more back to her house and I felt we were growing closer by the minute but she was obviously upset, not wanting to hurt anyone.

Outside her house, she told me that she needed time to think things over and I was sensible enough not to pressure her too much but did tell her how much I thought of her. I told her that I would be at the Welfare Dance at ten o clock on Saturday night and if she were there, I would know that she had decided she wanted to be with me. She agreed to that and I kissed her tenderly before she said goodnight when we realised it was after one o clock.

Friday was a nightmare, Saturday even worse as I wondered and worried what she was going to do, the thought of her not being at the dance was almost too much to bear, I longed just to hold her again. I could not believe that she would break off with a lad she had been dating for four years to go out with me, a soldier with an uncertain future and felt sick at heart and sick in the stomach, convinced that there was no way she would choose me.

The hours dragged by before I met up with Cousin Alec and we made our way down to the Grand Hotel for a couple of pints before going to the dance. I had seen Alec the night before and had told him about her, and how I was hoping, she would be at the dance.

'Aboot bloody time ye took her oot,' he said.

Standing at the bar of the 'Grand' waiting for the two beers I had ordered, a shadow fell over me and a deep voice from behind me said, 'How, Syd!'

Not sure, who it was, I turned slowly, wary that someone might be threatening me and found a very tall, well-built, blonde-haired lad looking down at me.

I instantly thought, 'This must be Elizabeth's boyfriend here to have it out with me,' but he smiled at me and said, 'Are ye aalreet?'

He obviously knew me but I did not recognise him and said, 'Aye I'm great, who are you?'

'It's me Terry man.'

The penny dropped, it was the little blonde-haired lad who had worked with Colin and me at Ashington Colliery, except he was not little anymore.

I said, 'Bloody hell Terry lad, Aa bet Colin doesn't kick sand in your face anymore?'

The three of us stood talking for an hour about times down the pit while we supped our beer but my mind was elsewhere and I wanted to be going. Just after nine o clock, I hurried Alec out of the bar and we walked down to the Welfare, my stomach tying itself in knots. On the way there he said, 'Wait until you see who's playing tonight!'

Walking into the Welfare, I had never seen the place so full; it appeared to be bursting at the seams, probably because the rival dance at the Arcade had closed but whatever the reason there was hardly room to move. I could only see a few yards ahead as we squeezed through the throng in the doorway, through the hall and on into the dance hall.

The group was performing Buddy Holly's 'Everyday' the singer sounding very familiar and as Alec nudged me and pointed I realised it was Tom! He sounded very good and I was delighted for him but my mind was elsewhere.

Over the noise of the music and the chatter of people, I said, 'I'm going to walk round and see if I can see her.' Alec nodded and followed me as I squeezed my way through the throngs of youths standing around the dance floor.

My stomach continued to churn as I made my way slowly around, straining to see if she was either on the dance floor or amongst the crush on the sides but I could not see her and began to think the worse; there was no way she would give up a boyfriend of four years for me.

By the time I had completed a circle of the floor, I was desperate.

'Did you see her?' asked Alec.

'No,' I answered dejectedly, 'have you?'

He shook his head and I said, 'I'm going around again.'

Alec nodded and shouted, 'Right.'

424

I started again, squeezing through the crowd but by the time I reached the stage, I still had not seen her and looked up at Tom who had just started to sing 'Oh Boy' and saw that he was staring at me, smiling as he sang. I gave him the thumbs up and he pointed to the opposite corner of the stage and held his hand up indicating little!

I knew instantly what he meant and squeezed through the crowd in front of the stage and then I saw her; she had seen me coming and was waiting for me to reach her. She looked stunning, an unsure little smile on her face that changed to a beam as she saw that I had seen her and was pushing my way through the packed bodies to get to her. An incredible feeling of joy and happiness came over me, all I could see was her lovely face; the noise, everything and everyone around her disappeared into an unfocused silent picture as I walked up to her.

She was with one of her sisters whom I barely noticed as I took my Little Blue-Eye's hand, leant forward, and said to her, 'Hi, you look gorgeous, do you want to dance?'

She nodded and I guided her through the crowd and onto the dance floor and took her in my arms as Tom sang 'True Love ways'.

Holding her close to me, and feeling her holding me tight, I was the happiest I had ever been; I knew that from here, the only way was up!

Epilogue

Elizabeth and I met every night for the rest of my leave and every night of every leave after that. We married two years later and after another two years, my lovely wife gave birth in Malaysia to our beautiful daughter Samantha. She herself is married and we are the proud Grandparents of two wonderful teenagers.

Three months after meeting Elizabeth, I received my first promotion and within seven years, I was a Sergeant Major. By the time I was thirty-four, with the help and support of my beautiful wife, I had risen to the rank of Regimental Sergeant Major. Commissioned in 1982, I retired in 1999 with the rank of Lieutenant Colonel, the highest rank than can be achieved by an officer commissioned from the ranks.

Elizabeth and I are still very happily married and I am still very much in love with my little blue-eyed girl.

Geordie Words used in this book

Aa	I
Aaful	awful
Aalreet	alright
Aa've	I have
Alen	alone
Arooned	around
Baal	ball
Bairn	Baby or small child
Bait	food carried to work
Blackclock	cockroach
Boond	bound
Cannit	cannot
Clarty	muddy
Cowld	cold
Daad	strike
Dee	do
Div	do
Divvint	do not
Droon	drown
Forst	first
Fund	found
Gan	go
Gannin	going
Gis	give me
Grund	ground
Gully	large knife
Haad	holdway
Haway	come on

Hurd	heard
He'ssell	himself
Hev	have
Hevn't	have not
Hoo	how
Hord	heard
Hyem	home
Ivvor	ever
Knaa	know
Mair	more
Marra	friend or workmate
Mek	make
Mesell	myself
Nee	no
Nen	none
Nettie	lavatory
Nivvor	never
Nur	no
Nowt	nothing
Ower	over
Owld	old
Owt	anything
Plodgin	paddling
Reet	right
Roond	round
Sackless	dozy
Shows	the fair
Sowldgers	soldiers
Summick	something
Tecking	taking
Tha	they're

Tetties	potatoes
Thowt	thought
Towld	told
Whey	well
Willicks	winkles
Winnit	will not
Wiv	with
Wor	our
Worsells	ourselves
Ye	you
Yor	your
Yorsell	yourself

Printed in Great Britain
by Amazon